CORPORATE COMPLIANCE
ANSWER BOOK
2011–12

VOLUME 2

PLi
PRACTISING LAW INSTITUTE

This work is designed to provide practical and useful information on the subject matter covered. However, it is sold with the understanding that neither the publisher nor the author is engaged in rendering legal, accounting or other professional services. If legal advice or other expert assistance is required, the services of a competent professional should be sought.

QUESTIONS ABOUT THIS BOOK?

If you have questions about replacement pages, billing or shipments, or would like information on our other products, please contact our **customer service department** at (800) 260-4PLI.

For library-related queries, **law librarians** may call toll-free (877) 900-5291 or email: libraryrelations@pli.edu.

For any other questions or suggestions about this book, contact PLI's **editorial department** at: editorial@pli.edu.

For general information about Practising Law Institute, please visit **www.pli.edu**.

Copyright © 2011 by Practising Law Institute. All rights reserved. Printed in the United States of America. No part of this publication may be reproduced, stored in a retrieval system, or transmitted in any form by any means, electronic, mechanical, photocopying, recording, or otherwise, without the prior written permission of Practising Law Institute.

ISBN: 978-1-4024-1383-4
LOC: 2010924112

CORPORATE COMPLIANCE ANSWER BOOK 2011–12

VOLUME 2

HOLLAND & KNIGHT LLP

Edited by
Christopher A. Myers
&
Kwamina Thomas Williford

Practising Law Institute
New York City

#32646

PLI'S COMPLETE LIBRARY OF TREATISE TITLES

ART LAW
All About Rights for Visual Artists
All About Tax Tips for Collectors
Art Law: The Guide for Collectors, Investors, Dealers & Artists

BANKING & COMMERCIAL LAW
Asset-Based Lending: A Practical Guide to Secured Financing
Bankruptcy Deskbook
Consumer Financial Services Answer Book 2011
Documenting Secured Transactions: Effective Drafting and Litigation
Equipment Leasing–Leveraged Leasing
Hillman on Commercial Loan Documentation
Personal Bankruptcy Answer Book
Structured Finance: A Guide to the Principles of Asset Securitization

BUSINESS, CORPORATE & SECURITIES LAW
Accountants' Liability
Antitrust Law Answer Book 2011–12
Broker-Dealer Regulation
Business Liability Insurance Answer Book 2011–12
Conducting Due Diligence in a Securities Offering
Consumer Product Safety Regulation: Impacts of the 2008 Amendments
Corporate Compliance Answer Book 2011–12
Corporate Legal Departments
Corporate Whistleblowing in the Sarbanes-Oxley/Dodd-Frank Era
Covered Bonds Handbook
Deskbook on Internal Investigations, Corporate Compliance and White Collar Issues
Directors' and Officers' Liability
Doing Business Under the Foreign Corrupt Practices Act
Exempt and Hybrid Securities Offerings
Financial Product Fundamentals: Law, Business, Compliance
Hedge Fund Regulation
Initial Public Offerings: A Practical Guide to Going Public
International Corporate Practice: A Practitioner's Guide to Global Success
Investment Adviser Regulation: A Step-by-Step Guide to Compliance and the Law
Insider Trading Law and Compliance Answer Book 2011–12
Labor Management Law Answer Book 2011–12
Legal Opinions in Business Transactions
Mergers, Acquisitions and Tender Offers: Law and Strategies
Mutual Fund Regulation
Outsourcing: A Practical Guide to Law and Business
PLI's Guide to the SEC's Executive Compensation and Related Party Transaction Disclosure Rules
PLI's Guide to Securities Offering Reforms
PLI's Guide to the Sarbanes-Oxley Act for Business Professionals

Pocket MBA 1: Everything an Attorney Needs to Know About Finance
Pocket MBA 2: Everything an Attorney Needs to Know About Finance
Pocket MBA 3: Everything an Attorney Needs to Know About Finance
A Practical Guide to the Red Flag Rules: Identifying and Addressing Identity Theft Risks
Private Equity Funds: Formation and Operation
Pro Bono Service by In-House Counsel: Strategies and Perspectives
Proskauer on Privacy: A Guide to Privacy and Data Security Law in the Information Age
Public Company Deskbook: Sarbanes-Oxley and Federal Governance Requirements
Securities Investigations: Internal, Civil and Criminal
The Securities Law of Public Finance
Securities Litigation: A Practitioner's Guide
Soderquist on Corporate Law and Practice
Soderquist on the Securities Laws
Sovereign Wealth Funds: A Legal, Tax and Economic Perspective
Terminating Derivative Transactions: Risk Mitigation and Close-Out Netting
Variable Annuities and Variable Life Insurance Regulation

COMMUNICATIONS LAW

Advertising and Commercial Speech: A First Amendment Guide
Sack on Defamation: Libel, Slander, and Related Problems

EMPLOYMENT LAW

Employment Law Yearbook 2011
Corporate Whistleblowing in the Sarbanes-Oxley/Dodd-Frank Era

ESTATE PLANNING AND ELDER LAW

Blattmachr on Income Taxation of Estates and Trusts
Estate Planning & Chapter 14: Understanding the Special Valuation Rules
International Tax & Estate Planning: A Practical Guide for Multinational Investors
Manning on Estate Planning
New York Elder Law
Stocker and Rikoon on Drawing Wills and Trusts

HEALTH LAW

Medical Devices Law and Regulation Answer Book 2011-12

IMMIGRATION LAW

Immigration Fundamentals: A Guide to Law and Practice

INSURANCE LAW

Insurance Regulation Answer Book 2011
Reinsurance Law

INTELLECTUAL PROPERTY LAW

2011 Federal Circuit Yearbook: Patent Law Developments in the Federal Circuit
Copyright Law: A Practitioner's Guide
Faber on Mechanics of Patent Claim Drafting
How to Write a Patent Application
Intellectual Property Law Answer Book 2011–12

Kane on Trademark Law: A Practitioner's Guide
Likelihood of Confusion in Trademark Law
Patent Law: A Practitioner's Guide
Patent Licensing: Strategy, Negotiation, Forms
Patent Litigation
Pharmaceutical and Biotech Patent Law
A Practical Guide to Life Science Companies: Commercializing and Protecting Innovation
Substantial Similarity in Copyright Law
Trade Secrets: A Practitioner's Guide

LITIGATION

American Arbitration: Principles and Practice
Electronic Discovery Deskbook
Evidence in Negligence Cases
Federal Bail and Detention Handbook 2011
How to Handle an Appeal
Medical Malpractice: Discovery and Trial
Product Liability Litigation: Current Law, Strategies and Best Practices
Sinclair on Federal Civil Practice
Trial Handbook

REAL ESTATE LAW

Commercial Ground Leases
Friedman on Contracts and Conveyances of Real Property
Friedman on Leases
Holtzschue on Real Estate Contracts and Closings:
    A Step-by-Step Guide to Buying and Selling Real Estate
Mortgage Finance Regulation Answer Book 2011–12

TAX LAW

The Circular 230 Deskbook: Related Penalties, Reportable Transactions, Working Forms
Internal Revenue Service: Practice and Procedure Deskbook
Langer on Practical International Tax Planning

GENERAL PRACTICE PAPERBACKS

Drafting for Corporate Finance: What Law School Doesn't Teach You
Thinking Like a Writer: A Lawyer's Guide to Effective Writing & Editing
Working with Contracts: What Law School Doesn't Teach You

Order now at www.pli.edu/pubs
Or call (800) 260-4754 Mon.–Fri., 9 a.m.–6 p.m.

Practising Law Institute
810 Seventh Avenue
New York, NY 10019

When ordering, please use Priority Code NWS9-8TRWT.

Table of Chapters

VOLUME 1

Chapter 1	The Business Case for Compliance Programs
Chapter 2	Implementation of Effective Compliance and Ethics Programs and the Federal Sentencing Guidelines
Chapter 3	Assessing and Managing an Ethical Culture
Chapter 4	Risk Assessments and Gap Analyses
Chapter 5	Records Management
Chapter 6	Internal Investigations
Chapter 7	Electronic Discovery
Chapter 8	Voluntary Disclosure of Wrongdoing
Chapter 9	Witness Preparation
Chapter 10	Settling with the Government
Chapter 11	The False Claims Act
Chapter 12	Conflicts of Interest
Chapter 13	Privacy and Security of Personal Information
Chapter 14	Procuring Computing Resources: IP Licensing, Outsourcing, and Cloud Computing
Chapter 15	Government Contractors
Chapter 16	International Investigations
Chapter 17	The Foreign Corrupt Practices Act
Chapter 18	Export Controls
Chapter 19	Corporate Political Activity

VOLUME 2

Chapter 20	Healthcare Organizations and Providers
Chapter 21	Medicare Part D
Chapter 22	Managed Care Organizations
Chapter 23	Pharmaceutical and Medical Device Manufacturers
Chapter 24	HIPAA Security and Privacy
Chapter 25	Ethical Conduct in Banking and Finance
Chapter 26	Anti-Money Laundering
Chapter 27	The Troubled Asset Relief Program
Chapter 28	Sarbanes-Oxley Act of 2002
Chapter 29	The Law and Accounting: The Convergence of Sarbanes-Oxley, COSO, the Federal Sentencing Guidelines, and *Caremark* Duties
Chapter 30	SEC Investigations of Public Companies
Chapter 31	Executive Compensation
Chapter 32	Institutions of Higher Education
Chapter 33	Environmental Law
Chapter 34	Labor and Employment Law
Chapter 35	Consumer Product Safety Act

Table of Contents

VOLUME 1

About the Editors vii
About the Contributors ix
Acknowledgments xxvii
Table of Chapters xxix
Table of Contents xxxi
Introduction ci

Chapter 1   The Business Case for Compliance Programs 1
              Christopher A. Myers & Michael Manthei

Q 1.1   What is a compliance program? 2
    Q 1.1.1   What does the Sentencing Guidelines' definition mean by "due diligence"? 3
    Q 1.1.2   Should the primary focus of a compliance program be on criminal conduct? 4
Q 1.2   What makes a compliance program "effective"? 4
Q 1.3   How does a compliance program help prevent unethical or illegal conduct from occurring? 6
    Q 1.3.1   How can a program change a corporate culture? 6
Q 1.4   Why does my organization need a compliance and ethics program? 7
    Q 1.4.1   Can't we just start a compliance program after we get hit with a government investigation? 8
    Q 1.4.2   What happens if we don't have a compliance program, learn of a government investigation, and *still* don't implement a program? 8
Q 1.5   Does the law require businesses to have compliance and ethics programs? 9
    Q 1.5.1   Are there state law requirements related to compliance and ethics programs? 9
    Q 1.5.2   Do some agencies require (rather than recommend) compliance programs? 11
    Q 1.5.3   What have the courts said about compliance programs? 12

Q 1.6	Can our business afford a program?		13
Q 1.7	What are the potential costs of an investigation?		13
	Q 1.7.1	Why not just pay the fine and move on?	15
	Q 1.7.2	Shouldn't compliance programs be viewed as cost centers?	15
Q 1.8	What other benefits does an effective compliance program provide?		16
	Q 1.8.1	What is the proof that there is a link between corporate governance and corporate performance?	18
	Q 1.8.2	What if I have a program and wrongdoing still occurs?	20
Q 1.9	How do I tell if my company already has a compliance program?		21
	Q 1.9.1	If we do not already have a functioning compliance program in place, how do we start from "zero" to build one?	21
	Q 1.9.2	What happens as my business grows and changes over time?	24

Chapter 2   **Implementation of Effective Compliance and Ethics Programs and the Federal Sentencing Guidelines** 29
Steven D. Gordon

Q 2.1	What are the Federal Sentencing Guidelines?		30
Q 2.2	How do the Sentencing Guidelines relate to an effective compliance program?		31
	Q 2.2.1	Why should my company care about the Sentencing Guidelines if it conducts business honestly and is unlikely ever to face criminal prosecution?	31
Q 2.3	What policies and procedures should my company implement to meet the Sentencing Guidelines' requirements?		32
	Q 2.3.1	What are the elements of an effective compliance program that will satisfy the Sentencing Guidelines?	32
	Q 2.3.2	What specific steps must our company take to create an effective compliance program?	32
	Q 2.3.3	Is there a standard compliance program that most companies can use?	34
Q 2.4	Are industry practice and standards considered in assessing the effectiveness of a compliance program?		34
	Q 2.4.1	Does the company size matter?	35
	Q 2.4.2	What are the differences between compliance programs for large companies and small companies?	35
Q 2.5	When it comes to putting a compliance program together, where do we start?		35

Table of Contents

Q 2.5.1	What are the most common risk areas that we may need to address in our compliance program?	36
Q 2.6	Is a code of conduct a required part of a compliance program?	41
Q 2.6.1	What are the legal requirements for a code of conduct?	42
Q 2.6.2	What are the elements of a good code of conduct?	42
Q 2.6.3	How many codes of conduct should a company have?	44
Q 2.7	How do we administer and enforce a compliance program?	44
Q 2.7.1	Who should administer the compliance program?	46
Q 2.7.2	Which senior executive(s) should be placed in charge of the compliance program?	46
Q 2.7.3	What role does top management have in administering a compliance program?	47
Q 2.7.4	What is meant by a "culture" of compliance?	49
Q 2.7.5	How can we demonstrate a culture of ethics and compliance?	49
Q 2.7.6	What are reasonable efforts to exclude bad actors?	49
Q 2.8	What is required in the way of training and communication?	50
Q 2.8.1	Who within our organization needs to be trained?	51
Q 2.8.2	Do we need to educate every employee about every policy?	51
Q 2.8.3	We hold a training session for new employees. Is a thorough, one-time training session on our code and policies enough?	51
Q 2.9	How can my company maintain the compliance program's effectiveness?	52
Q 2.9.1	What should an audit of the program be examining?	52
Q 2.9.2	What is internal auditing?	53
Q 2.9.3	Why should an organization have internal auditing?	53
Q 2.9.4	What is internal auditing's role in preventing, detecting, and investigating fraud?	54
Q 2.9.5	What is the appropriate relationship between the internal audit activity and the audit committee of the board of directors?	54
Q 2.10	What type of reporting system does my company need to have?	54
Q 2.10.1	What is a non-retaliation policy?	55
Q 2.11	How can my company effectively enforce the compliance program?	56
Q 2.11.1	Despite our best efforts to promote a culture of honesty and integrity, some criminal or unethical conduct has occurred. How should the company respond?	56

Chapter 3	**Assessing and Managing an Ethical Culture** 61	
	David Gebler	

Q 3.1 If a company has a compliance program and employees know they must act in accordance with those standards, why does misconduct still occur?................................63
Q 3.2 Why should compliance officers focus on culture? 64
Q 3.3 How do we know if our implementation of the elements of the Federal Sentencing Guidelines is sufficient? 65
    Q 3.3.1 What do regulators and prosecutors think about culture?.. 66
    Q 3.3.2 How can an organization evaluate behavior as part of its compliance program? 67
Q 3.4 What are the elements of an ethical culture/a culture of compliance?..68
Q 3.5 How do individual and organizational goals help create an ethical cultural framework?..70
    Q 3.5.1 How are goals rewarded? 71
    Q 3.5.2 How are business goals and ethics linked?........... 71
    Q 3.5.3 Can challenges to business goals be safely raised?............ 72
Q 3.6 What is organizational tone, and what is its role in supporting a culture of ethics and compliance? 73
    Q 3.6.1 What is the role of top management and organizational leaders in setting the appropriate tone? 73
    Q 3.6.2 What is the role of middle management in setting the appropriate tone?.. 73
    Q 3.6.3 What is the role of regular employees in setting the appropriate tone?.. 74
    Q 3.6.4 Is the organizational tone always set from the top down?.. 74
Q 3.7 What values are important to an ethical culture framework?......74
    Q 3.7.1 What is the role of collective/shared values in an ethical culture framework?.................................... 75
Q 3.8 How do the elements of the ethical culture framework work together? 77
    Q 3.8.1 How do you align goals and values?...................... 77
    Q 3.8.2 ... goals and behaviors?... 78
    Q 3.8.3 ... behaviors and values?....................................... 78
Q 3.9 What are the barriers to an ethical culture?.................................78
    Q 3.9.1 What risks factors exist, and how should they be addressed?... 79
Q 3.10 How do we know if our culture creates ethics and compliance risks? 83

	Q 3.10.1	Can't we use our existing employee survey data to assess our compliance risk?	84
	Q 3.10.2	What is the goal of a culture risk assessment?	84
	Q 3.10.3	What information are we looking for in a culture risk assessment?	85
Q 3.11		How do we reduce risks to an ethical culture?	86
	Q 3.11.1	What are our top ethics issues?	86
	Q 3.11.2	What are the risk factors?	86
	Q 3.11.3	Why are these risk factors permitted to flourish?	89
	Q 3.11.4	What's needed to address the root cause problem?	90
	Q 3.11.5	How can we link the solution back to the ethics issues?	91
Q 3.12		What is the easiest first step in addressing culture issues?	92

Chapter 4   Risk Assessments and Gap Analyses 97
Jennifer Dure

Q 4.1		What are the goals of a risk assessment?	98
	Q 4.1.1	Why should our company perform a "risk assessment"?	98
	Q 4.1.2	What is senior management's role in a risk assessment?	99
	Q 4.1.3	Who should perform the risk assessment?	99
Q 4.2		What risk areas should my company be assessing in the first place?	99
	Q 4.2.1	What do we do once we have identified the company's potential risk areas?	100
Q 4.3		What are the different methods we should use to gather the data?	100
	Q 4.3.1	What documents should we review as part of the risk assessment?	101
	Q 4.3.2	How much data is enough? When can we stop gathering data and start using it?	101
Q 4.4		What do we do with the data we have gathered?	102
	Q 4.4.1	What is a compliance matrix?	102
	Q 4.4.2	Is a matrix the only way to catalog the risk assessment information?	104
	Q 4.4.3	Once we identify the various risks facing the organization, how can we prioritize the organizational response to those risk areas?	104
	Q 4.4.4	Once the risk areas have been prioritized, what do we do with this information?	105
Q 4.5		What is the purpose of a compliance "gap analysis," and how does it differ from a risk assessment?	105
	Q 4.5.1	How do we perform a gap analysis?	105

Chapter 5	**Records Management** 109	
	Ieuan G. Mahony	
Q 5.1	What are the benefits of a records management program? 110	
Q 5.1.1	What are the constituent parts of a records management program?	111
Q 5.1.2	Our organization already has a records "destruction" program; do we still need a records "management" program?	112
Q 5.1.3	When it comes to designing a records management program, where should we begin?	114
Q 5.1.4	What role should senior management play?	114
Q 5.2	What is meant by a "record" in "records management"? 115	
Q 5.2.1	Does our records management program need to apply to all of our records?	116
Q 5.3	Should our records management program cover electronic information? 116	
Q 5.3.1	What is metadata and how is it relevant to a records management policy?	117
Q 5.3.2	How can ESI be used to support a records management program?	118
Q 5.3.3	For management purposes, should all records be treated the same?	120
Q 5.3.4	How should we handle duplicate records?	120
Q 5.4	What do we do once we have determined the lifecycle for each record type? 121	
Q 5.4.1	What specific goals should an effective records management policy accomplish?	121
Q 5.5	What should a retention schedule look like? 125	
Q 5.5.1	How should we determine retention periods for a particular category of records?	127
Q 5.5.2	Should we retain metadata?	127
Q 5.5.3	Does the statute of limitations play a role in setting retention periods?	129
Q 5.5.4	When a retention period expires for a record, is the record destroyed?	129
Q 5.6	What if we make mistakes here and there in following our records management policy? 130	
Q 5.6.1	Should we have a training program?	130
Q 5.6.2	Should we consider sanctions for noncompliance?	130
Q 5.7	How is our organization's Disaster Recovery Plan different from a records management program? 131	
Q 5.7.1	Can't we just rely on our Disaster Recovery Plan's backup system for records management?	131

Q 5.8		How do ESI rules affect policy?	132
	Q 5.8.1	How can we be best prepared to respond to requests for ESI?	133
	Q 5.8.2	How should concerns about litigation inform our retention of records?	136
	Q 5.8.3	What if requested records have already been destroyed in accordance with our retention schedule?	136
Q 5.9		What is a litigation hold?	137
	Q 5.9.1	How do we put a litigation hold in place?	138
	Q 5.9.2	How long should a litigation hold last?	138

Chapter 6 Internal Investigations 143
Gregory Baldwin

Q 6.1		What triggers an internal investigation?	145
	Q 6.1.1	What kinds of allegations trigger an investigation?	146
	Q 6.1.2	Are all allegations of wrongdoing subject to investigation?	146
Q 6.2		What determines the type of internal investigation to conduct?	147
	Q 6.2.1	How is the decision about the appropriate type of internal investigation made?	147
Q 6.3		How should low-risk allegations of misconduct be investigated?	148
	Q 6.3.1	How should high-risk allegations of misconduct be investigated?	149
	Q 6.3.2	How do internal allegations affect the investigation?	150
	Q 6.3.3	How do external allegations from government authorities affect the investigation?	150
	Q 6.3.4	When subject to a government investigation, how does a company determine the scope of the government's inquiry and its own investigative response?	150
	Q 6.3.5	What does the issuance of a search warrant tell us about the government's intentions?	151
	Q 6.3.6	What does the service of a grand jury subpoena or CID say about the intended scope of the government's investigation?	151
	Q 6.3.7	What information can a government agent or attorney provide?	152
	Q 6.3.8	How do allegations from external nongovernment sources affect the type of investigation to be pursued?	153
Q 6.4		What steps does the company need to take once a decision to investigate is reached?	154

Q 6.4.1	How does the company determine the logistical needs of and methods to be used in an investigation?	154
Q 6.5	When should a company initiate an investigation?	155
Q 6.5.1	Is it beneficial to commence an investigation immediately?	156
Q 6.6	What kinds of inquiries will be involved in an investigation?	156
Q 6.6.1	What factors should the company consider in determining the scope of an investigation?	157
Q 6.6.2	When should the scope of the investigation be determined?	158
Q 6.7	Who should be in charge of an internal investigation?	159
Q 6.7.1	How does legal counsel maintain the confidentiality of the investigation?	159
Q 6.7.2	Who is in charge of the investigation—inside counsel or outside counsel?	160
Q 6.8	How are an investigation's staffing needs determined?	161
Q 6.8.1	What circumstances warrant the services of professional investigators?	162
Q 6.8.2	Is the work of a professional investigator protected?	162
Q 6.8.3	What circumstances warrant the services of forensic experts?	162
Q 6.8.4	Is the work of a forensic expert protected?	163
Q 6.9	How are the facts in an investigation determined?	163
Q 6.10	How should a company approach its documents and e-data at the initiation of an investigation?	164
Q 6.10.1	How does an investigation affect a company's routine document destruction policies?	164
Q 6.10.2	Is e-data subject to the same ban on destruction?	165
Q 6.10.3	Is the e-data preservation directive confined to the on-site locations?	165
Q 6.10.4	How can documents/data be classified as relevant?	166
Q 6.10.5	Where can we look for guidance in identifying relevant documents/data in external allegations of criminal misconduct?	166
Q 6.10.6	What steps should the company take to collect relevant documents for review by counsel?	167
Q 6.10.7	What is a "litigation hold"?	168
Q 6.10.8	When should a litigation hold be imposed?	168
Q 6.10.9	What are the responsibilities of the "records custodian"?	169
Q 6.11	Who must be interviewed?	169
Q 6.11.1	When should interviews take place?	170
Q 6.11.2	Who should conduct the interviews?	170
Q 6.11.3	Who do the interviewers represent?	171

Table of Contents

Q 6.11.4	What should the interviewers tell persons who are interviewed?	171
Q 6.11.5	How are Upjohn warnings given to a witness?	171
Q 6.11.6	What should be included in the Upjohn warnings?	172
Q 6.11.7	Is there a standard form for Upjohn warnings?	173
Q 6.11.8	Is a witness allowed to have separate counsel?	174
Q 6.11.9	What happens if the witness refuses to cooperate?	174
Q 6.11.10	Is the interview privileged?	174
Q 6.11.11	Is the witness covered by the privilege?	175
Q 6.11.12	Can the confidentiality of the information disclosed during an interview be waived?	175
Q 6.12	Should notice be given to the entire company that an internal investigation is underway?	176
Q 6.12.1	Should the notice identify the investigated employees or group of employees?	176
Q 6.12.2	How should the notice be circulated?	177
Q 6.12.3	Should a notice include a statement in defense of the company?	177
Q 6.12.4	What information should be included in the notice?	177
Q 6.12.5	What information should be included in a notice if the company is under a criminal investigation?	178
Q 6.12.6	What are an employee's rights if he is approached by law enforcement agents for an interview?	178
Q 6.12.7	Should the company obtain and pay for legal representation for officers, directors, or employees who may be interviewed by law enforcement agents?	179
Q 6.12.8	If the company obtains counsel for officers, directors, or employees, should it enter into a joint defense agreement with that counsel?	179
Q 6.12.9	What if an officer, director, or employee is named as a subject or target of a criminal investigation?	180
Q 6.12.10	What other information should be contained in the notice to employees?	180
Q 6.13	Should internal investigations be kept confidential?	182
Q 6.13.1	How are internal investigations protected?	183
Q 6.14	When does the attorney-client privilege attach?	183
Q 6.14.1	Does the privilege apply to communications with former employees?	184
Q 6.14.2	Does the privilege apply to communications with third parties?	184
Q 6.14.3	Is the attorney-client privilege absolute?	185
Q 6.14.4	Does the crime-fraud exception apply to all disclosures of criminal activity?	185

Q 6.14.5	May a disclosing witness prevent a company from disclosing their admission of past criminal conduct?	185
Q 6.15	What is protected under the work-product doctrine?	186
Q 6.15.1	How does the scope of the work-product doctrine compare to that of the attorney-client privilege?	186
Q 6.15.2	Must a company release its entire work product upon a third party's showing of substantial need and undue hardship?	186
Q 6.16	Can the attorney-client privilege and work-product protection be waived?	187
Q 6.16.1	What motivates companies to waive their privileges?	187
Q 6.16.2	What is required under a voluntary disclosure?	188
Q 6.16.3	What is the scope of a waiver of the attorney-client privilege or work-product protection?	188
Q 6.17	What guidelines do federal prosecutors follow when seeking a waiver of the attorney-client privilege and the attorney work-product protection?	188
Q 6.17.1	What is the Holder Memorandum?	189
Q 6.17.2	What is the Thompson Memorandum?	189
Q 6.17.3	What is the McNulty Memorandum?	190
Q 6.17.4	What is the Filip Memorandum?	191
Q 6.17.5	What is the current policy?	192

Chapter 7   Electronic Discovery 199
Sonya Strnad

Q 7.1	Why is electronic data so significant?	200
Q 7.2	What is e-discovery?	201
Q 7.2.1	In what context does e-discovery usually occur?	202
Q 7.3	What can our company do now so that we are in a better position if we are ever sued?	202
Q 7.4	What data should be preserved?	203
Q 7.4.1	How is ESI preserved?	204
Q 7.4.2	How do we prevent data from being unintentionally deleted or altered?	204
Q 7.5	When is the duty to preserve or issue a "litigation hold" triggered?	205
Q 7.5.1	In what format should a litigation hold be issued?	205
Q 7.5.2	Who should receive the litigation hold notice?	206
Q 7.5.3	How do we determine who the "key players" are?	206
Q 7.5.4	What should the litigation hold cover?	207
Q 7.5.5	What are in-house counsel's or upper management's obligations with respect to implementing and maintaining a litigation hold?	208

	Q 7.5.6	What are outside counsel's obligations?	208
Q 7.6		What can happen if I fail to take reasonable steps to preserve data?	209
	Q 7.6.1	What is spoliation?	209
	Q 7.6.2	What are some of the hazards to be aware of in trying to implement a litigation hold?	210
	Q 7.6.3	What kinds of sanctions can result from a failure to preserve data?	210
	Q 7.6.4	When can we lift the litigation hold?	210
Q 7.7		How soon after preservation will we need to start collecting documents?	213
	Q 7.7.1	How should we begin collecting the internal documents that our litigation counsel will need?	214
	Q 7.7.2	Is keyword searching an effective way to collect ESI?	214
	Q 7.7.3	What is "imaging"?	215
Q 7.8		What is an e-discovery vendor?	215
	Q 7.8.1	When should I consider hiring one?	215
	Q 7.8.2	Are there any special concerns with regard to using an e-discovery vendor for data collection?	216
	Q 7.8.3	Do I have to collect data from backup tapes?	216
Q 7.9		What are some of the document collection hazards I should be aware of?	217
	Q 7.9.1	What can happen if data that the other side wants in the litigation was destroyed?	218
	Q 7.9.2	Are there special considerations for collecting data outside the United States?	218
Q 7.10		In what format should my data be produced?	219
	Q 7.10.1	What are my options regarding data production format?	219
Q 7.11		How much does it all cost?	220

Chapter 8 Voluntary Disclosure of Wrongdoing 225
Michael Manthei

Q 8.1		What is a voluntary disclosure of wrongdoing?	226
	Q 8.1.1	Why would a corporation disclose wrongdoing rather than simply fix the problem?	226
	Q 8.1.2	Does voluntary disclosure of wrongdoing preclude criminal prosecution?	227
Q 8.2		What are the basic elements of a voluntary disclosure?	228
	Q 8.2.1	What information should be included in the initial disclosure?	228
Q 8.3		What happens after the initial disclosure?	229

Q 8.3.1	What should an internal investigation cover?	229
Q 8.3.2	What information should be reported regarding the scope of the activity?	230
Q 8.3.3	What information should be reported regarding the discovery and response to the problem?	230
Q 8.3.4	How does the company assess the financial impact of the disclosed activities?	231
Q 8.3.5	What happens after the company submits its disclosure and self-assessment reports?	232
Q 8.4	How does voluntary disclosure affect the attorney-client and work-product privileges?	233
Q 8.5	When are requests for privileged information permitted?	233
Q 8.5.1	What is the Holder Memorandum?	234
Q 8.5.2	What is the Thompson Memorandum?	234
Q 8.5.3	What is the McNulty Memorandum?	235
Q 8.5.4	What is the Filip Memorandum?	235
Q 8.5.5	What is the current policy?	236
Q 8.6	What happens if I change my mind after disclosure?	237
Q 8.7	How are voluntary disclosures finally resolved?	237

Chapter 9 Witness Preparation 241
Daniel I. Small

Q 9.1	Why is witness preparation important?	242
Q 9.1.1	Is witness preparation unethical?	243
Q 9.1.2	Isn't witness preparation expensive?	244
Q 9.2	What can a company do in advance?	244
Q 9.3	Why do our own employees need counsel for an internal investigation?	245
Q 9.4	Is it more efficient for in-house counsel to represent company employees?	246
Q 9.4.1	Don't the Upjohn warnings protect company counsel?	247
Q 9.5	What is the process for obtaining outside counsel for witnesses in an internal investigation?	248
Q 9.6	What is the difference between witness preparation and witness coaching?	248
Q 9.7	What is "real" witness preparation?	249
Q 9.7.1	How can effective witness preparation help "level the playing field"?	250
Q 9.8	What are the ten most important rules for witnesses?	251

Chapter 10 Settling with the Government 255
Jennifer A. Short

Q 10.1	What role does compliance play in settling with the government?	256
Q 10.2	What kinds of compliance provisions can settlement agreements impose?	257
Q 10.2.1	How does the government ensure ongoing compliance monitoring?	258
Q 10.2.2	Who selects the monitor and who pays for it?	258
Q 10.3	How are settlements affected by parallel proceedings?	259
Q 10.3.1	What is a global resolution?	259
Q 10.4	How do settlements with an administrative agency differ from those with an enforcement agency?	260
Q 10.4.1	What compliance-related provisions might an administrative agency seek to include in a settlement agreement?	260
Q 10.4.2	What are some common types of settlement agreements?	261
Q 10.4.3	What is a corporate integrity agreement?	261
Q 10.4.4	What compliance-related provisions can a CIA mandate?	262
Q 10.4.5	What is a certification of compliance agreement?	263
Q 10.4.6	What is an administrative compliance agreement?	263
Q 10.4.7	What does an administrative compliance agreement specifically require?	264
Q 10.5	How are settlements with the SEC different from those with other administrative agencies?	265
Q 10.5.1	What are the mechanisms for settling with the SEC?	265
Q 10.5.2	What kinds of sanctions may be imposed?	265
Q 10.6	Can a civil settlement agreement include compliance and reporting provisions?	266
Q 10.6.1	What happens when an agency joins a civil settlement agreement?	267
Q 10.6.2	Will an administrative agency always join in a civil settlement agreement?	268
Q 10.7	Do plea agreements contain compliance and reporting provisions?	268
Q 10.7.1	What is a deferred prosecution agreement?	269
Q 10.7.2	What are the advantages of a deferred prosecution agreement?	269
Q 10.7.3	What are the drawbacks of a deferred prosecution agreement?	269

Chapter 11   The False Claims Act 273
            Jennifer A. Short

Q 11.1   What kinds of actions are typically brought under the
           False Claims Act? 275
Q 11.2   What specifically does the FCA prohibit? 276
   Q 11.2.1   What is a "claim" for purposes of the FCA? 277
   Q 11.2.2   When is a claim "false"? 277
Q 11.3   What does it mean to present
           a false claim "knowingly"? 278
Q 11.4   What are the penalties for violating the FCA? 279
Q 11.5   What conduct most commonly leads to FCA liability? 280
Q 11.6   What is a "whistleblower" or "relator"? 284
Q 11.7   Who can be a whistleblower? 284
Q 11.8   How much can the whistleblower make? 285
Q 11.9   What is the procedure for filing a qui tam action? 286
   Q 11.9.1   How long does the complaint remain under seal? 286
   Q 11.9.2   How and when does the government become involved
               in the prosecution of a qui tam action? 286
   Q 11.9.3   How does a defendant learn that an FCA action
               is pending? 287
Q 11.10   What happens after the defendant learns that an FCA case
           has been filed? 288
Q 11.11   Our company has just received a subpoena that indicates
           the government is investigating a potential FCA violation;
           what should we do? 288
   Q 11.11.1   The government refuses to narrow the scope of its
               broad requests; what can we do? 288
   Q 11.11.2   The government has narrowed the scope of its
               requests; what do we do? 289
   Q 11.11.3   What use can the government make of our documents
               once produced? 290
Q 11.12   Why should we conduct an internal investigation? 290
   Q 11.12.1   Would we ever choose to disclose our findings to the
               government attorneys? 291
Q 11.13   Who should be interviewed during an internal
           investigation? 291
   Q 11.13.1   What should we do if, during the course of our
               investigation, we discover that an employee has
               engaged in illegal or unethical conduct? 292
Q 11.14   What kind of information can we get from the government,
           and how should we go about getting it? 292
Q 11.15   When is it in our interest to share information with the
           government? 293

Q 11.16	What happens once the complaint is unsealed?	294
Q 11.17	How are damages and penalties calculated under the FCA?	294
Q 11.17.1	How should we approach damages in the context of settlement?	295
Q 11.18	Is the process of negotiating a settlement in an FCA case different from that in any other litigation?	295
Q 11.19	What should we do if we learn that the whistleblower is a current employee of our company?	296
Q 11.19.1	What should we do if we learn that the whistleblower works for one of our contracting partners?	296
Q 11.20	What are the most common defenses to an FCA claim?	297
Q 11.21	What is the statute of limitations for an FCA violation?	299
Q 11.22	Can a compliance program prevent FCA claims?	300
Q 11.23	Does the lack of a compliance program pose an FCA risk?	301
Q 11.24	What is the Deficit Reduction Act of 2005 and how does it affect the FCA and compliance programs?	301
Q 11.25	Do states have false claims act statutes?	302

Chapter 12 Conflicts of Interest 311
Kwamina Thomas Williford

Q 12.1	What is a conflict of interest?	312
Q 12.1.1	What concerns do conflicts of interest raise?	313
Q 12.2	How do conflicts of interest arise?	313
Q 12.2.1	Why should my business be concerned if an individual employee has a conflict of interest?	314
Q 12.3	What concerns arise if an employee has an interest in a competitor's business?	314
Q 12.3.1	What can a company do to avoid conflicts of interest related to an ownership interest in a competitor company?	314
Q 12.3.2	What concerns arise if an employee works for a competitor while also working for you?	315
Q 12.3.3	What can a company do to avoid such conflicts of interest related to employment in a competitor company?	315
Q 12.4	Can conflicts arise if an employee has a relationship with a non-competitor company?	315
Q 12.4.1	What can a company do to avoid conflicts of interest related to vendors or customers?	316
Q 12.5	If my employees have access to confidential or business-sensitive information, what kinds of policies should I have in place?	316

Q 12.6		How can I reduce the risk that an employee may divert corporate opportunities to his personal benefit?	317
Q 12.7		What conflict-of-interest issues are raised by doing business with the government?	317
	Q 12.7.1	If my business's work involves interaction with government officials, what kinds of policies should I have in place?	318
	Q 12.7.2	If my business contracts with the government, what kinds of policies should I have in place?	318
	Q 12.7.3	What other industries create special concerns regarding conflicts of interest?	319
Q 12.8		Am I required to have a conflicts of interest policy?	319
	Q 12.8.1	What should be included within a conflicts of interest policy?	320
Q 12.9		What should be done if a potential conflict of interest arises?	321

Chapter 13   Privacy and Security of Personal Information 327
Ieuan G. Mahony, Maximillian Bodoin & Peter I. Sanborn

Q 13.1		What are the particular concerns that drive privacy law?	329
	Q 13.1.1	What is the legal definition of "personal information"?	332
	Q 13.1.2	What steps should our organization take to ensure compliance with data protection laws?	334
Q 13.2		Should we implement a privacy policy?	337
	Q 13.2.1	Where should our organization place its privacy policy?	337
	Q 13.2.2	What principles should inform our privacy policy?	337
	Q 13.2.3	What types of choices should data subjects be allowed?	339
	Q 13.2.4	How should my organization administer its privacy policy?	339
	Q 13.2.5	What happens if we modify the privacy policy?	339
	Q 13.2.6	Should our organization display any third-party seals of approval?	339
Q 13.3		What privacy rules apply to our organization's employees?	340
	Q 13.3.1	What criminal sanctions does the ECPA provide for?	340
	Q 13.3.2	Are we allowed to monitor our employees' email?	340
	Q 13.3.3	Do we need a written email policy?	340
Q 13.4		What is identity theft?	341
	Q 13.4.1	Is my organization required to detect or prevent identity theft?	342
	Q 13.4.2	What should our identity theft prevention program include?	342

	Q 13.4.3	We are not subject to the Red Flags Rule, but we provide services to entities that are. Do we need an Identity Theft Prevention Program?...................	344
Q 13.5		What security protections should we have in place?...............	344
Q 13.6		What should our privacy and security program look like?	347

Chapter 14 Procuring Computing Resources: IP Licensing, Outsourcing, and Cloud Computing.......... 351
Ieuan G. Mahony

Q 14.1		What are "computing resources"?...	353
Q 14.2		What alternatives are generally available to my organization for procuring computing resources?	353
	Q 14.2.1	What is the "in-house model" for obtaining computing resources?	354
	Q 14.2.2	What is the "outsourcing model" for obtaining computing resources?...	354
	Q 14.2.3	How does "cloud computing" relate to my organization's computing resources?	355
Q 14.3		What are the key considerations when comparing the options for obtaining computing resources?	356
Q 14.4		In these transactions, what vendor intellectual property rights, if any, should my organization be concerned with?......	357
Q 14.5		Should my organization be concerned about its own intellectual property rights?	358
	Q 14.5.1	My organization engages a range of other vendors in connection with its computing resources. Do we need to address system access by these third parties?	360
	Q 14.5.2	A vendor proposes to develop software for my organization using an "agile development" methodology. What does this mean for us?.......................	360
Q 14.6		Are there any special considerations our organization should be aware of when integrating the new computing resource within our existing systems?	362
	Q 14.6.1	What are "rights in interfaces"?...	362
	Q 14.6.2	What is open-source software?	363
	Q 14.6.3	What open-source software considerations may affect our system?	363
	Q 14.6.4	What concerns are raised by legacy data?........................	364
Q 14.7		What factors affect maintenance of our computing resource assets and monitoring of performance?	365
	Q 14.7.1	What role do SLAs and SLOs play in maintaining computing resources?...	365

Q 14.7.2	How can we use audit requirements to enhance maintenance of our system?	366
Q 14.7.3	Can company policies enhance system maintenance?	367
Q 14.8	How do computing resources relate to our compliance obligations?	367
Q 14.8.1	Can an organization procuring computing resources be held responsible for actions of a service provider?	368
Q 14.8.2	How do we address conflicting regulatory requirements for cross-border operations?	368
Q 14.9	What compliance risks are raised by storing data with a third party?	369
Q 14.9.1	What data security protections should be in place?	370
Q 14.10	How do we disengage from a licensor or service provider?	371
Q 14.11	How can an organization seeking to terminate its relationship with a vendor reduce the threat of vendor lock-in?	371
Q 14.11.1	How do we get unconditional access to portable data?	371
Q 14.11.2	What is transition assistance?	372
Q 14.11.3	What are escrow agreements?	373

Chapter 15 Government Contractors 377
*David S. Black, Thomas Brownell,
Oliya S. Zamaray & Allison Feierabend*

Q 15.1	What are the benefits to contractors of developing, implementing, and maintaining a compliance program?	379
Q 15.2	Generally speaking, what should a government contractor's compliance program aim to do?	380
Q 15.3	Does the Federal Acquisition Regulation (FAR) include provisions requiring compliance programs?	381
Q 15.3.1	Who is subject to these new rules?	382
Q 15.3.2	How must contractors fulfill the code of conduct requirement?	383
Q 15.3.3	What is required in an internal controls system and training program?	383
Q 15.3.4	Who should participate in a training program?	384
Q 15.3.5	What is required for an internal reporting system and hotline poster?	385
Q 15.3.6	What are the mandatory disclosure requirements?	385
Q 15.3.7	What is the timeframe for disclosure?	386
Q 15.3.8	How is disclosure made?	387
Q 15.3.9	To whom is disclosure made?	387
Q 15.3.10	What must be disclosed?	387
Q 15.3.11	What is "knowing" failure to disclose?	387

Table of Contents

Q 15.3.12	What is required for "full cooperation"?	387
Q 15.3.13	What are the implications of suspension and debarment for knowing failure to make mandatory disclosures?	388
Q 15.3.14	What constitutes failure to report "significant overpayments"?	389
Q 15.4	Are contractors required to flow-down the clauses into subcontracts?	389
Q 15.5	Will a contractor's compliance program be considered in performance evaluations?	389
Q 15.6	What does a government contractor risk by not having a compliance program?	390
Q 15.6.1	Can a contractor be found liable for the acts of its employees?	390
Q 15.6.2	What types of liability might government contractors incur?	391
Q 15.7	What criminal and civil penalties may government contractors face?	391
Q 15.7.1	What makes a case criminal rather than civil?	392
Q 15.7.2	How are criminal fines determined?	392
Q 15.7.3	How can contractors be held liable under the False Claims Act?	392
Q 15.7.4	What constitutes a false statements violation?	393
Q 15.7.5	What constitutes criminal mail fraud violations?	393
Q 15.7.6	What constitutes wire fraud violations?	394
Q 15.7.7	What constitutes a major fraud violation?	394
Q 15.7.8	How can the conspiracy statute affect government contractors?	395
Q 15.7.9	How can the Racketeering Influenced Corrupt Organizations Act affect government contractors?	395
Q 15.7.10	What behaviors can subject a government contractor to obstruction of justice liability?	396
Q 15.7.11	What is required to avoid liability under the Truth in Negotiations Act?	396
Q 15.7.12	What are "cost or pricing data"?	396
Q 15.7.13	What are the requirements for providing cost or pricing data to the government?	397
Q 15.7.14	How might a contractor incur liability?	397
Q 15.7.15	What civil remedies can the government seek for such violations?	398
Q 15.7.16	What are the civil penalties for violations of the Program Fraud Civil Remedies Act?	398
Q 15.7.17	What are the civil penalties for violations of the Foreign Assistance Act?	398

Q 15.7.18	What other civil penalties might government contractors be subject to?	399
Q 15.8	What administrative penalties may government contractors face?	399
Q 15.8.1	What are the implications of suspension?	399
Q 15.8.2	What are the implications of debarment?	399
Q 15.8.3	What kinds of contractor acts can result in suspension and/or debarment?	399
Q 15.8.4	What penalties are available under the Program Fraud Civil Remedies Act?	400
Q 15.9	What other contractual clauses might trigger penalties in government contracts?	401
Q 15.10	What compliance issues may arise when preparing bids on government contracts?	402
Q 15.10.1	What kinds of certifications might contractors be required to make?	402
Q 15.10.2	When is a contractor eligible to bid on a government contract?	403
Q 15.10.3	What makes a contractor "responsible"?	404
Q 15.10.4	What are "organizational conflicts of interest"?	405
Q 15.10.5	Under what circumstances might an OCI arise?	405
Q 15.10.6	What can a government contractor do to identify OCIs?	406
Q 15.10.7	How can the impact of organizational conflicts of interest be mitigated?	408
Q 15.10.8	What recent changes and developments in the field of OCIs should contractors keep track of over the coming year?	409
Q 15.10.9	What are a federal contractor's compliance responsibilities regarding accounting for costs?	411
Q 15.10.10	How must a contractor comply with the FAR's "cost principles"?	411
Q 15.10.11	How must a contractor comply with the FAR's Cost Accounting Standards?	411
Q 15.10.12	What are the compliance requirements of the Truth in Negotiations Act for government contractors?	413
Q 15.10.13	What requirements regarding anticompetitive behavior must a contractor comply with?	414
Q 15.11	What potential improper business practice violations occur during contract performance?	415
Q 15.11.1	What are the statutes/regulations dealing with disclosure of procurement information with which a government contractor must comply?	416
Q 15.11.2	What compliance issues does gift-giving raise?	417

Q 15.11.3	What is the difference between a bribe and a gratuity?	417
Q 15.11.4	What are acceptable gifts?	418
Q 15.11.5	What are the penalties for illegal giving of "things of value"?	418
Q 15.11.6	What are a federal contractor's compliance obligations regarding kickbacks?	419
Q 15.11.7	What is a contingent fee?	419
Q 15.11.8	What compliance considerations regarding contingent fees should a federal contractor be aware of?	420
Q 15.11.9	What compliance issues should contractors engaging in foreign business activities be aware of?	420
Q 15.11.10	Are there any kinds of payments to officials that are permitted?	421
Q 15.11.11	What are the penalties for violations?	421
Q 15.11.12	What kinds of relationships may create personal conflicts of interest?	422
Q 15.11.13	What are the restrictions on current government employees seeking employment from government contractors?	422
Q 15.11.14	What are the restrictions on former government employees currently working for government contractors?	423
Q 15.11.15	What are the restrictions on government employees who previously worked for government contractors?	426
Q 15.11.16	What can a contractor considering hiring a government employee do to avoid liability?	427
Q 15.11.17	Under what circumstances might an organizational conflict of interest arise *after* the procurement of a government contract?	428
Q 15.11.18	What kinds of lobbying activities are restricted?	428
Q 15.11.19	What kinds of lobbying requirements must federal contractors comply with?	429
Q 15.12	What are a contractor's ethical obligations in relation to subcontractors?	429
Q 15.13	What wage-and-hour statutes and regulations should a compliance program account for?	430
Q 15.13.1	What are a government contractor's obligations regarding compliance with the Davis-Bacon Act?	430
Q 15.13.2	... with the Service Contract Act?	431
Q 15.13.3	... with the Walsh-Healey Public Contracts Act?	432
Q 15.13.4	... with the Copeland Act?	432
Q 15.13.5	... with the Contract Work Hours and Safety Standards Act?	433

Q 15.13.6	... with Equal Employment Opportunity requirements?	433
Q 15.13.7	... with the Drug-Free Workplace Act?	434
Q 15.14	Are government contractors subject to any special employment verification requirements?	434
Q 15.15	What is E-Verify?	435
Q 15.15.1	Are there E-Verify exemptions?	435
Q 15.15.2	Must a contractor verify its entire workforce?	435
Q 15.15.3	When must a contractor enroll and use E-Verify?	436
Q 15.16	What proprietary intellectual property concerns should a compliance program account for?	436
Q 15.16.1	What technical data and computer software rights should a government contractor be concerned with?	437
Q 15.16.2	What copyright protections should a government contractor be concerned with?	440
Q 15.16.3	What rights in patented inventions should a government contractor be concerned with?	440
Q 15.17	What are a government contractor's obligations regarding the products/components and services it uses?	441
Q 15.17.1	What domestic and foreign preference statutes and regulations should a compliance program account for?	442
Q 15.17.2	What are a government contractor's obligations regarding compliance with the Buy American Act?	442
Q 15.17.3	Are there any exemptions to the Buy American Act?	443
Q 15.17.4	What remedies may be sought for violations of the Buy American Act?	445
Q 15.17.5	What are a government contractor's obligations regarding compliance with the Trade Agreements Act?	445
Q 15.17.6	... with the Berry Amendment?	446
Q 15.17.7	... with the Fly American Act?	447
Q 15.17.8	... with the Arms Export Control Act?	447
Q 15.17.9	What are the Arms Export Control Act's licensing requirements?	448
Q 15.17.10	What are the penalties for violations of the Arms Export Control Act?	449
Q 15.17.11	What are a government contractor's obligations regarding compliance with the Foreign Military Sales Program?	449
Q 15.18	What compliance obligations exist regarding tracking expenditures under government contracts?	450
Q 15.19	What particular types of government contracts raise special compliance issues?	451

Table of Contents

Q 15.19.1	What special issues should a small business compliance plan address?	451
Q 15.19.2	What issues may arise on GSA contracts?	452
Q 15.20	How does the Sarbanes-Oxley Act affect government contractors?	453
Q 15.20.1	What advantages do government contractors have in dealing with Sarbanes-Oxley?	453
Q 15.20.2	What obligations do officers of government contractors have under Sarbanes-Oxley?	454
Q 15.20.3	What obligations do program managers and product line executives have?	454
Q 15.20.4	What are in-house lawyers' obligations?	454
Q 15.21	What compliance issues may arise under the Freedom of Information Act?	455

Chapter 16   International Investigations 469
Steven D. Gordon

Q 16.1	What is an international investigation?	470
Q 16.2	What are some of the special issues raised by international investigations?	471
Q 16.3	What kinds of considerations are raised by special issues related to document collection and review?	471
Q 16.4	What special issues exist relating to witness interviews?	472
Q 16.4.1	Can telephone interviews be used?	473
Q 16.5	Does the attorney-client privilege apply in an international investigation?	473
Q 16.6	When do U.S. courts have jurisdiction over a company's foreign activities?	474
Q 16.6.1	Do U.S. laws apply to conduct outside the United States?	474
Q 16.7	Does international travel in international investigations raise any special issues?	475
Q 16.8	What are some of the major practice areas where international investigations typically occur?	476
Q 16.8.1	How frequent and significant are government investigations of suspected international cartels?	476
Q 16.8.2	Does the government face special problems in investigating and prosecuting international cartels?	477
Q 16.8.3	Why has the government been so successful in prosecuting international cartels?	477
Q 16.8.4	What are investigation "triggers" in the area of noncartel anticompetitive and unfair business practices?	478

Q 16.8.5	What laws address bribery in an international context?	478
Q 16.8.6	Who is subject to the Foreign Corrupt Practices Act?	479
Q 16.8.7	Is there an international consensus on anti-bribery regulation?	479
Q 16.8.8	Why do export controls trigger international investigations?	479
Q 16.8.9	Is there a particular industry significantly affected by U.S. export controls?	479
Q 16.8.10	What sorts of issues commonly arise in international investigations of export control issues?	480
Q 16.8.11	What failures in corporate governance trigger an investigation?	480
Q 16.8.12	Are there external triggers for a corporate governance investigation?	481
Q 16.8.13	What industries are vulnerable to international intellectual property rights infringement?	481
Q 16.8.14	What legal actions are available to a party whose IP rights are being infringed abroad?	481
Q 16.9	What preliminary considerations are necessary prior to carrying out an international investigation?	482
Q 16.9.1	Who will conduct the investigation?	483

Chapter 17 The Foreign Corrupt Practices Act 487
Don Zarin

Q 17.1	What do the foreign payments provisions of the FCPA prohibit?	488
Q 17.2	Who is subject to prosecution under the FCPA?	489
Q 17.2.1	Which "issuers" are subject to the FCPA?	490
Q 17.2.2	What is a "domestic concern"?	490
Q 17.2.3	What other jurisdictional requirements are there for potential liability under the FCPA?	491
Q 17.3	What is the scope of the requirement that a payment be made "corruptly"?	492
Q 17.4	What is the scope of "foreign official"?	492
Q 17.5	What is the meaning of "anything of value"?	493
Q 17.6	How can U.S. companies be held liable for illicit payments made indirectly through intermediary third parties, such as agents or consultants?	494
Q 17.7	What is the "knowledge" standard under the FCPA?	494
Q 17.8	What is the standard for "authorization" of illicit payments made by a third party?	495

Table of Contents

Q 17.9 Is the FCPA limited to payments designed to influence a foreign official's acts or decisions? 496
Q 17.10 What is the business purpose test under the FCPA? What is its scope? 497
Appendix 17A Foreign Payments Provisions Under the FCPA 503

Chapter 18 Export Controls 557
Antonia I. Tzinova, Ronald A. Oleynik & Jonathan M. Epstein

Q 18.1 Generally speaking, what do U.S. export laws and regulations aim to achieve? 558
    Q 18.1.1 How do export controls seek to achieve those objectives? 559
    Q 18.1.2 Which U.S. agencies regulate exports from the United States? 559
Q 18.2 How are defense exports regulated? 559
Q 18.3 What is the scope of the ITAR? 560
    Q 18.3.1 What is a defense article? 560
    Q 18.3.2 What is technical data? 560
    Q 18.3.3 What are defense services? 561
    Q 18.3.4 What is "look through" treatment under the ITAR? 561
    Q 18.3.5 What does the USML cover? 561
    Q 18.3.6 How can an exporter determine that an item is ITAR-controlled? 561
Q 18.4 What constitutes an export under the ITAR? 563
    Q 18.4.1 What are re-exports and retransfers? 563
    Q 18.4.2 How can a company obtain DDTC authorization to export? 564
    Q 18.4.3 Are there exemptions to ITAR licensing? 564
    Q 18.4.4 Who is a broker? 565
    Q 18.4.5 What is brokering? 565
Q 18.5 How are commercial goods and technology exports regulated? 566
    Q 18.5.1 What is the scope of the EAR? 567
    Q 18.5.2 What categories of items and technology require a license to export under the EAR? 567
    Q 18.5.3 What are the CCL categories? 568
    Q 18.5.4 What constitutes an export or re-export? 569
    Q 18.5.5 How does an exporter determine if it needs a license to export dual-use goods and technology? 569
    Q 18.5.6 How can a license be obtained? 570

CORPORATE COMPLIANCE ANSWER BOOK 2011–12

Q 18.6 What activities are prohibited by U.S. economic sanctions programs? 571
    Q 18.6.1 Are there exceptions to the prohibition on exportation to embargoed countries? 571
    Q 18.6.2 What are terrorist and other barred entity lists? 571
    Q 18.6.3 Who administers economic sanctions programs? 573
    Q 18.6.4 Who is a "U.S. person"? 573
    Q 18.6.5 What are the jurisdictional limits of OFAC embargo programs? 573
Q 18.7 What are the penalties for violation of the controls on defense exports? 574
    Q 18.7.1 What are the penalties for violation of the controls on dual-use item exports? 574
    Q 18.7.2 What are the penalties for exporting to an embargoed country? 575
    Q 18.7.3 Who is subject to penalties for export violations? 576
    Q 18.7.4 How are penalties determined? 576
    Q 18.7.5 What factors do the DDTC, BIS, and OFAC take into account in assessing penalties? 576
Q 18.8 What are the industry best practices related to export compliance? 579
    Q 18.8.1 What is the role of management? 580
    Q 18.8.2 What are the roles of those groups recognized as "compliance personnel"? 580
    Q 18.8.3 How important is an export compliance program manual? 580
    Q 18.8.4 What role should training play? 581
    Q 18.8.5 What are a company's record-keeping obligations? 581
    Q 18.8.6 What is the importance of internal audits? 584
    Q 18.8.7 How should suspected violations be reported? 584
    Q 18.8.8 Why does a company need clear disciplinary procedures? 584
Q 18.9 What are the first steps a company should take when drafting a compliance program? 585
    Q 18.9.1 Isn't there a one-size-fits-all program we can adopt? 585
    Q 18.9.2 What are the pitfalls to avoid in designing an export compliance program? 586
    Q 18.9.3 What key questions should be posed when designing an export compliance program? 586

Table of Contents

Chapter 19 Corporate Political Activity 593
Christopher DeLacy

Q 19.1	May a corporation contribute to a candidate directly out of its treasury?..	595
Q 19.2	How may corporations participate in the federal political process?	595
Q 19.3	May a corporation expend any resources in relation to a federal election?	596
Q 19.4	What is a PAC?	596
Q 19.4.1	Are there restrictions on who can participate in a PAC/SSF?..	596
Q 19.4.2	Are there limits and restrictions on how a corporation can support an SSF?..	597
Q 19.4.3	What kinds of restrictions are there on solicitation of contributions to SSFs?...	597
Q 19.4.4	Who makes up the "restricted class"?	598
Q 19.5	How does a corporation form a PAC?	598
Q 19.5.1	What are the disclosure requirements for a PAC?	599
Q 19.5.2	What are contribution limits for PACs?	599
Q 19.5.3	How can a corporation ensure PAC compliance?	600
Q 19.6	What is express advocacy?	600
Q 19.7	What is issue advocacy?..	601
Q 19.8	What is an electioneering communication?	601
Q 19.9	What is an independent expenditure?	601
Q 19.10	What is coordination?	601
Q 19.11	What may a corporation communicate about a federal candidate to its employees?	601
Q 19.11.1	What may a corporation communicate about a federal candidate outside its restricted class?	602
Q 19.11.2	How is express advocacy regulated?	603
Q 19.11.3	Is issue advocacy regulated?...	604
Q 19.11.4	How are electioneering communications regulated?.........	605
Q 19.11.5	Is coordination permitted?..	605
Q 19.11.6	What disclosure requirements apply to corporate communications?..	605
Q 19.12	How much can individual employees contribute to federal candidates?	606
Q 19.12.1	What other limitations and conditions exist for contributions from individuals?	606
Q 19.13	What is "bundling"?	607
Q 19.13.1	May corporate employees "bundle" contributions to federal candidates?...	607

Q 19.14	May corporate employees engage in political activity related to a federal election while at work?	607
Q 19.15	May corporate resources or facilities be used in conjunction with a federal election?	608
Q 19.15.1	May a corporation invite a federal candidate to its facility?	608
Q 19.15.2	May a corporation allow a federal candidate to fly on its private aircraft?	609
Q 19.16	What is the Lobbying Disclosure Act of 1995?	610
Q 19.16.1	Who must register under the Lobbying Disclosure Act of 1995?	610
Q 19.16.2	What are the penalties for violating the LDA?	610
Q 19.16.3	What is a "lobbying contact"?	610
Q 19.16.4	What is not a "lobbying contact"?	611
Q 19.16.5	What are "lobbying activities"?	611
Q 19.16.6	Who is a "lobbyist"?	611
Q 19.16.7	Who is a "covered official"?	611
Q 19.17	What is the process for registering under the LDA?	612
Q 19.17.1	What are the contents of the LDA registration?	613
Q 19.17.2	What are the contents of the LDA quarterly reports?	613
Q 19.17.3	What are the contents of the LDA semi-annual report and certification?	614
Q 19.17.4	What is the filing schedule under the LDA?	615
Q 19.17.5	What if my corporation only lobbied the executive branch?	615
Q 19.17.6	Does an in-house lobbyist for a foreign corporation also need to register under the Foreign Agents Registration Act?	616
Q 19.18	Has anyone ever been prosecuted for an LDA violation?	616
Q 19.19	Will my LDA reports be audited by GAO?	616
Q 19.20	What should an LDA compliance program include?	617
Q 19.21	Who is subject to the House and Senate gift and travel rules?	618
Q 19.21.1	Do other government entities have their own rules?	618
Q 19.21.2	Are House and Senate rules the same?	619
Q 19.21.3	How can a corporation obtain information about House and Senate rules?	619
Q 19.22	What House and Senate rules should a corporation be aware of?	619
Q 19.23	What is the gift rule?	619
Q 19.23.1	What is a "gift"?	619
Q 19.23.2	What gifts are acceptable?	620
Q 19.23.3	What are some relevant exceptions to the gift rule?	620
Q 19.23.4	May a lobbyist provide a gift?	620

Table of Contents

Q 19.23.5	What is the "personal friendship" exception?	621
Q 19.23.6	What is the "widely attended event" exception to the gift rule?	621
Q 19.23.7	What is the "charitable event" exception?	622
Q 19.23.8	What is the "commemorative item" exception to the gift rule?	622
Q 19.23.9	What is the "food or drink of a nominal value" exception to the gift rule?	623
Q 19.24	What are the rules for travel?	623
Q 19.24.1	What is "officially connected" travel?	623
Q 19.24.2	What are "necessary expenses"?	624
Q 19.24.3	Who may pay for officially connected travel?	624
Q 19.24.4	What are the new rules for "One-Day Event Trips"?	624
Q 19.25	What are the House and Senate rules for travel on private aircraft?	625
Q 19.26	What do corporations need to know about state and local laws and regulations?	626
Q 19.27	What are pay-to-play laws?	626
Q 19.27.1	Does the federal government have pay-to-play laws?	627
Q 19.27.2	Which states have pay-to-play laws?	627
Q 19.27.3	Which localities have pay-to-play laws?	627
Q 19.27.4	Do any other entities have pay-to-play laws?	628
Q 19.28	How does pay-to-play disclosure work?	628
Q 19.29	What should a pay-to-play compliance program include?	629

VOLUME 2

Table of Chapters vii
Table of Contents ix

Chapter 20 Healthcare Organizations and Providers 639
Lisa Sterneck Katz, Reetu Dua & Jonathan E. Anderman

Q 20.1	Why do healthcare organizations need compliance and ethics programs?	642
Q 20.1.1	Are there financial incentives for having an effective compliance program?	642
Q 20.1.2	Is having an effective compliance program a guarantee that we won't be investigated?	643

Q 20.1.3	How can I anticipate federal government enforcement actions?	643
Q 20.2	How do I begin to create a compliance and ethics program?	644
Q 20.2.1	What industries does the OIG guidance cover?	644
Q 20.2.2	What kind of resources/guidance does the OIG offer that might be of value?	645
Q 20.2.3	Is the OIG guidance mandatory?	645
Q 20.3	What makes a compliance program effective?	646
Q 20.3.1	What specific things does an effective compliance program need?	646
Q 20.3.2	What is the OIG's role in investigations of healthcare organizations and providers?	648
Q 20.3.3	What are Corporate Integrity Agreements and Certification of Compliance Agreements?	649
Q 20.3.4	What new enforcement initiatives have come out of the current administration and the Congress?	650
Q 20.3.5	What additional enforcement provisions were included in healthcare reform legislation?	651
Q 20.4	In what areas might healthcare violations/investigations typically occur?	652
Q 20.5	What are the government sources of payment for healthcare services?	652
Q 20.5.1	What is Medicare?	652
Q 20.5.2	What is Medicaid?	653
Q 20.5.3	What are employee benefit programs?	653
Q 20.6	Which statutes and regulations govern the areas of healthcare typically subject to government investigation and enforcement?	654
Q 20.7	What is the False Claims Act?	654
Q 20.7.1	What constitutes a violation of the FCA?	655
Q 20.7.2	What are some risk areas under the FCA particular to healthcare entities?	655
Q 20.8	What is the federal anti-kickback statute?	657
Q 20.8.1	What does the federal anti-kickback statute mean by "remuneration"?	657
Q 20.8.2	How is "knowing and willfully" defined?	657
Q 20.8.3	What if there are other good purposes for the arrangement?	658
Q 20.8.4	What are the penalties for violating the AKS?	658
Q 20.8.5	Are there exceptions to the AKS?	659
Q 20.8.6	What are AKS safe harbors?	659
Q 20.8.7	How does a business arrangement qualify for safe-harbor protection?	660

Table of Contents

Q 20.8.8 What is an OIG advisory opinion? 661
Q 20.9 What are the Stark rules and regulations? 661
    Q 20.9.1 Can a party self-disclose actual or potential Stark violations? 663
Q 20.10 What is HIPAA? 664
Q 20.11 What is EMTALA? 665
    Q 20.11.1 What are EMTALA's key requirements? 665
    Q 20.11.2 How is EMTALA enforced and what are the penalties for an EMTALA violation? 666
Q 20.12 What is the Deficit Reduction Act? 666
    Q 20.12.1 Who may be affected by the DRA? 666
    Q 20.12.2 What types of companies does the DRA apply to? 667
    Q 20.12.3 What does the DRA require? 667
    Q 20.12.4 Do the policies required by the DRA have to be on paper? 668
    Q 20.12.5 What if my company does not have a document called an "employee handbook"? Do we need to create one? 668
    Q 20.12.6 What are the penalties for noncompliance with the DRA? 668
Q 20.13 What is the HITECH Act? 669
    Q 20.13.1 What are the rules and requirements of the HITECH Act? 669

Chapter 21   **Medicare Part D** 675
Jeffrey W. Mittleman, Elizabeth Sanghavi & Jonathan E. Anderman

Q 21.1 What is Medicare Part D? 677
    Q 21.1.1 Is Medicare Part D mandatory? 677
    Q 21.1.2 What benefits are provided under Part D? 678
Q 21.2 Why does my company need a compliance program for Medicare Part D? 678
Q 21.3 What is MIPPA and how does it impact Part D? 678
Q 21.4 Generally, what kinds of risks does a Medicare D compliance program aim to mitigate? 679
Q 21.5 How are pharmacies and manufacturers at risk of violating the AKS? 679
Q 21.6 What is a patient assistance program? 680
    Q 21.6.1 What are the AKS implications associated with a manufacturer-affiliated PAP? 680
    Q 21.6.2 What is TrOOP? 680

Q 21.6.3	What are the AKS implications for PAPs affiliated with independent charities?	681
Q 21.7	What are the AKS implications for PAPs operating outside of Part D?	681
Q 21.7.1	Do PAPs run any risk of violating the AKS by offering services to uninsured patients?	682
Q 21.8	How are waiver of coinsurance and deductible amounts regulated by the AKS?	682
Q 21.9	How can pharmacies offer free or discounted drugs without violating the AKS?	683
Q 21.10	How should pharmacies handle manufacturer rebates or other price concessions?	683
Q 21.11	What is co-branding?	684
Q 21.12	How does patient steering pose a risk?	685
Q 21.13	What is the electronic prescribing safe harbor?	685
Q 21.14	What is the electronic health records safe harbor?	686
Q 21.15	What is the waiver or reduction of cost-sharing exception to the AKS?	687
Q 21.16	What are the elements of an effective Medicare Part D compliance program?	687
Q 21.16.1	What should our written policies and procedures say?	688
Q 21.16.2	What requirements must be met to have an effective compliance officer and compliance committee?	689
Q 21.16.3	What do we need to do for training and education?	689
Q 21.16.4	How can we develop effective lines of communication between individuals involved with compliance?	690
Q 21.16.5	How do we enforce our compliance standards?	690
Q 21.16.6	How do we effectively monitor and audit our program?	690
Q 21.16.7	What should our fraud and abuse plan look like?	690
Q 21.16.8	Is self-reporting mandatory?	691
Q 21.17	Can compliance duties under a Part D contract be delegated?	691
Q 21.18	Can CMS audit plans?	691
Q 21.19	Has OIG audited plans?	691

Chapter 22 Managed Care Organizations 697
Jeffrey W. Mittleman & Jonathan E. Anderman

Q 22.1	What are the areas of focus in monitoring MCOs for fraud and abuse?	698
Q 22.2	Do MCOs need to be concerned with fraud and abuse areas that do not involve under-utilization?	700

Q 22.3	What have states done to enforce regulations for MCOs?	700
Q 22.4	Why does our MCO need to adopt a compliance program?	701
Q 22.5	Can our MCO implement the same compliance program as an FFS plan?	701
Q 22.6	What are the CMS requirements for a compliance program?	701
Q 22.6.1	What is required of a compliance plan's written policies, procedures, and standards?	702
Q 22.6.2	What are the functions of the compliance officer and committee?	703
Q 22.6.3	What kind of training should our MCO have?	704
Q 22.6.4	What is meant by "effective lines of communication"?	704
Q 22.6.5	What are the required procedures for internal monitoring and auditing?	705
Q 22.6.6	How should standards be enforced through disciplinary guidelines?	705
Q 22.6.7	What procedures for corrective action should an MCO implement?	705
Q 22.6.8	What specific requirements are there for MA-PD plan compliance programs?	706
Q 22.7	What are the consequences of failing to comply with CMS's mandates?	706
Q 22.8	Why should MCOs be concerned about the False Claims Act?	706
Q 22.9	Who, in a managed care context, can liability be imposed on?	707
Q 22.9.1	What is required for liability under the FCA?	707
Q 22.9.2	What penalties does the FCA provide for?	707
Q 22.10	What other statutes might pose liability issues for MCOs?	707
Q 22.11	How are MA MCOs vulnerable to false claims liability?	708
Q 22.12	What liability issues can an MCO face related to Physician Incentive Plans?	708
Q 22.13	What are CMS's prompt payment requirements?	709
Q 22.13.1	What is a "clean" claim?	709
Q 22.13.2	What are potential consequences of failure to make prompt payments?	709
Q 22.14	When does denial or unavailability of care by an MCO constitute fraud and abuse?	710
Q 22.14.1	What are potential consequences for denial of care?	710
Q 22.15	What are Medicare MCOs required to do in their marketing practices?	710

Chapter 23	**Pharmaceutical and Medical Device Manufacturers** 715	
	Michael Manthei, William F. Gould, Patrick O'Brien & Jenna Phipps Bigornia	
Q 23.1	What are the major risk areas in the pharmaceutical and medical device industry?..718	
Q 23.2	What is labeling? 718	
Q 23.2.1	What must a prescription drug label include?.................	719
Q 23.2.2	What must an over-the-counter drug label include?.........	719
Q 23.2.3	What must a medical device label include?	720
Q 23.2.4	What happens if labeling does not comply with FDA requirements?...	720
Q 23.2.5	What are the potential consequences of noncompliance with label requirements?...	720
Q 23.3	Generally speaking, how important is advertising/labeling compliance? 721	
Q 23.4	What is "advertising"? 721	
Q 23.4.1	What are prescription drug advertisements required to include?...	722
Q 23.4.2	What is the "brief summary" of side effects, contraindications, and effectiveness?..............................	722
Q 23.4.3	Must a broadcast advertisement contain the "brief summary" of side effects, contraindications, and effectiveness?	723
Q 23.4.4	What does the FDA consider true, balanced, and not-misleading advertising?..	723
Q 23.4.5	Are there exceptions to these advertising requirements?...	724
Q 23.4.6	Does the FDA pre-approve advertising?............................	730
Q 23.4.7	Is pre-approval of advertising ever mandatory?	730
Q 23.4.8	Must advertisements be filed with the FDA?	731
Q 23.4.9	What happens if drug/device advertising does not comply with FDA requirements?	731
Q 23.4.10	What are the possible consequences of a misbranding violation?	732
Q 23.5	What is meant by "off-label"? 733	
Q 23.5.1	Is it illegal for a physician to prescribe a drug "off-label"?	733
Q 23.5.2	Is advertising or promotion of off-label uses permitted?...	733
Q 23.5.3	How might off-label promotion constitute misbranding?...	734

Q 23.5.4	How might off-label promotion constitute the introduction of an unapproved new drug?	735
Q 23.5.5	How does FDA determine the "intended use" of a regulated product?	735
Q 23.6	What laws and other guidance apply to the sale and marketing of pharmaceuticals and medical devices?	736
Q 23.6.1	How do the states regulate sales and marketing practices?	737
Q 23.7	What is the federal anti-kickback statute?	738
Q 23.7.1	What are some of the key risk areas implicating the AKS?	738
Q 23.7.2	What are the primary AKS considerations with regard to discounts?	739
Q 23.7.3	... product support services?	739
Q 23.7.4	... educational grants?	739
Q 23.7.5	... research or other charitable organizations?	740
Q 23.7.6	... equipment lease and storage agreements?	741
Q 23.7.7	... price reporting?	741
Q 23.7.8	... consultant training, education, and sales meetings?	742
Q 23.7.9	... gifts?	742
Q 23.7.10	... "switching arrangements"?	742
Q 23.7.11	... consulting arrangements?	743
Q 23.8	What is the federal False Claims Act?	744
Q 23.8.1	How does the marketing of drugs and devices implicate the False Claims Act?	744
Q 23.9	What is the Prescription Drug Marketing Act of 1987?	744
Q 23.9.1	Is it still permissible to provide free samples?	745
Q 23.10	What are the major compliance risks arising from the conduct of biomedical research?	745
Q 23.11	What rules and regulations govern conflicts of interest in clinical trials?	745
Q 23.12	What are the Public Health Service Rules?	747
Q 23.12.1	To whom do the PHS Rules apply?	747
Q 23.12.2	What do the PHS Rules require?	747
Q 23.12.3	What is a "significant financial interest" under the PHS Rules?	748
Q 23.12.4	What types of remuneration do not constitute a significant financial interest?	748
Q 23.12.5	Who is considered an "investigator" to whom the significant financial interest disclosure and other requirements apply under the PHS Rules?	749
Q 23.12.6	What are the responsibilities of the designated institutional official?	749

Q 23.12.7	What is a "conflict of interest" for purposes of the PHS Rules?	749
Q 23.12.8	What mechanisms are available to "manage" conflicts of interest as required by the PHS Rules?	750
Q 23.12.9	What are the consequences for failing to comply with the PHS Rules?	750
Q 23.12.10	Beyond suspension of funding or imposition of additional corrective action, what other consequences might there be for a failure to comply with the PHS Rules?	751
Q 23.13	What are the National Science Foundation requirements?	752
Q 23.13.1	To whom do the NSF requirements apply?	752
Q 23.14	What are the National Institutes of Health Guidelines?	752
Q 23.14.1	What are the main "considerations" for sponsored research agreements?	753
Q 23.15	What is the Bayh-Dole Act?	753
Q 23.15.1	What are the considerations for nonprofit grantees?	754
Q 23.15.2	What considerations require "heightened scrutiny"?	755
Q 23.16	What are the FDA Financial Disclosure Requirements?	756
Q 23.16.1	What is a "disclosable" financial arrangement?	756
Q 23.16.2	What are the obligations of the investigator?	757
Q 23.16.3	What factors will the FDA consider in assessing the potential of a disclosable financial interest to bias a study?	757
Q 23.16.4	What actions may the FDA take if it believes that the integrity of the research data may have been compromised by an investigator's financial interest?	757
Q 23.17	What rules govern the protection of human subjects?	758
Q 23.17.1	What is the Common Rule?	758
Q 23.17.2	What are the FDA regulations concerning human-subject research?	759
Q 23.17.3	What are the HHS regulations concerning human-subject research?	760
Q 23.17.4	What is the ICH Guidance?	760
Q 23.17.5	What is the World Medical Association Declaration of Helsinki?	761
Q 23.18	What are the general requirements for informed consent?	762
Q 23.18.1	Are there exceptions to the informed consent requirements?	763
Q 23.18.2	What are the "emergency exceptions" to the FDA's informed consent regulations?	763
Q 23.18.3	What are the exceptions to the Common Rule's informed consent regulations?	765
Q 23.18.4	What are the membership requirements for IRBs?	766

Table of Contents

Q 23.18.5 What are the operational requirements for IRBs?............ 767
Q 23.18.6 What are the criteria for IRB approval of research?......... 768
Q 23.18.7 What is "expedited review"?... 768
Q 23.18.8 What is "minimal risk"?.. 769
Q 23.18.9 What is an "assurance of compliance" with the
Common Rule?.. 769
Q 23.19 Is it appropriate to charge for investigational drugs?............... 770
    Q 23.19.1 What is a "treatment IND"?... 770
    Q 23.19.2 Is it appropriate to charge for the study drug under
a treatment IND?... 770
Q 23.20 Will Medicare pay for the healthcare services given to
Medicare beneficiaries participating in clinical trials?............. 771
    Q 23.20.1 What does Medicare consider "routine costs"?................. 771
    Q 23.20.2 What is a "qualifying" clinical trial?..................................... 772
    Q 23.20.3 What types of clinical trials are deemed to automatically
qualify for reimbursement of routine costs?...................... 773
    Q 23.20.4 Does Medicare cover the costs of treating complications
arising from the study?... 774

Chapter 24   HIPAA Security and Privacy 781
Shannon Hartsfield Salimone

Q 24.1 Who must comply with HIPAA?... 783
    Q 24.1.1 What is meant by "health plan"?... 783
    Q 24.1.2 Are employers considered covered entities?..................... 783
    Q 24.1.3 What is a business associate?.. 783
    Q 24.1.4 Does HIPAA apply to business associates?....................... 784
Q 24.2 What is the Privacy Rule?.. 785
    Q 24.2.1 What is PHI?... 785
    Q 24.2.2 How are use and disclosure of PHI restricted by
the Privacy Rule?... 786
Q 24.3 What is the Security Rule?... 786
    Q 24.3.1 What is considered ePHI?.. 786
    Q 24.3.2 What are covered entities required to do under the
Security Rule?.. 786
Q 24.4 As a covered entity or a business associate, where do we
begin when approaching compliance measures?....................... 787
    Q 24.4.1 What does a risk analysis involve?...................................... 787
    Q 24.4.2 Who is responsible for these compliance tasks?............... 788
Q 24.5 What are some of the key documents that a covered entity
or business associate needs?... 788
Q 24.6 As a covered entity, we implemented a compliance program
when the Rules became effective back in 2003,
so we're all set; right?.. 789

Q 24.7	Do we need to be concerned about state law?	789
Q 24.8	As a covered entity, how should we handle subpoenas?	790
Q 24.9	What should happen if there is an improper disclosure?	790

Chapter 25   Ethical Conduct in Banking and Finance 799
Timothy N. Bergan & Michael Weissman

Q 25.1	Why does my institution need a compliance and ethics program?	800
Q 25.1.1	What are the consequences of ethics breaches?	801
Q 25.2	What is compliance risk?	801
Q 25.2.1	What are the consequences of noncompliance?	801
Q 25.2.2	What's the difference between informal and formal sanctions?	803
Q 25.3	What is the best structure for a compliance and ethics program?	803
Q 25.3.1	What specific policies should banks adopt?	804
Q 25.4	What are some of the important federal regulations to consider?	805
Q 25.4.1	What agencies regulate banks?	805
Q 25.4.2	Do we need a separate policy to cover each regulation?	806
Q 25.4.3	Should policies for state laws and regulations also be included?	808
Q 25.5	How do nonbanking activities and affiliates fit into a compliance program?	809
Q 25.5.1	What kinds of special compliance considerations do affiliates raise?	809
Q 25.6	Aren't audits and examinations enough?	811
Q 25.6.1	How often should independent testing be done?	811
Q 25.6.2	What is the current emphasis in bank compliance?	812
Q 25.6.3	How can an institution keep up-to-date on changes to so many laws and regulations?	812
Q 25.6.4	Who should keep track of all the legal, legislative, and regulatory developments?	813
Q 25.6.5	How can employees be motivated to embrace compliance?	813

Chapter 26   Anti-Money Laundering 819
Gregory Baldwin

Q 26.1	What are the goals of money laundering?	821
Q 26.1.1	How does money laundering work?	821

Table of Contents

	Q 26.1.2	What is placement?	822
	Q 26.1.3	What is layering?	822
	Q 26.1.4	What is integration?	822
	Q 26.1.5	What forms aside from cash can funds for laundering take?	823
Q 26.2		What are the federal anti-money laundering statutes?	823
	Q 26.2.1	To whom do these AML laws apply?	824
Q 26.3		What does the MLCA provide?	825
	Q 26.3.1	What does "some form of unlawful activity" mean under the MLCA?	825
	Q 26.3.2	What constitutes "knowledge" under the MLCA?	826
	Q 26.3.3	What is a "specified unlawful activity" for purposes of the MLCA?	826
	Q 26.3.4	What are "financial transactions"?	827
	Q 26.3.5	What are "monetary instruments"?	827
	Q 26.3.6	What are "financial institutions"?	827
Q 26.4		What does section 1956 of the MLCA prohibit?	828
	Q 26.4.1	What is "transaction money laundering"?	828
	Q 26.4.2	What is "transportation money laundering"?	828
	Q 26.4.3	What are the prohibitions related to "sting" operations?	829
	Q 26.4.4	What are the MLCA penalties for violation of section 1956?	829
	Q 26.4.5	What extraterritorial jurisdiction does section 1956 of the MLCA have?	830
Q 26.5		What does section 1957 of the MLCA provide?	831
	Q 26.5.1	What is a "monetary transaction"?	831
	Q 26.5.2	What is "criminally derived property"?	832
	Q 26.5.3	Does the government have extraterritorial jurisdiction to prosecute violations of section 1957 of the MLCA?	832
	Q 26.5.4	What are the penalties for violations of section 1957 of the MLCA?	832
Q 26.6		What is the Bank Secrecy Act?	832
	Q 26.6.1	To whom does the BSA apply?	833
	Q 26.6.2	What is the definition of "financial institutions" for purposes of the BSA?	833
Q 26.7		Which financial institutions must implement AML compliance programs, and which are exempted?	834
	Q 26.7.1	What are the general regulatory requirements for subject financial institutions?	835
	Q 26.7.2	What are the BSA's requirements for anti-money laundering programs?	836
	Q 26.7.3	What is a "risk-based" anti-money laundering program?	836

Q 26.8	What are the BSA's requirements regarding CIPs?	836
Q 26.9	What is a "suspicious transaction"?	837
Q 26.9.1	Who must report suspicious transactions?	838
Q 26.9.2	Doesn't reporting a suspicious transaction expose me and/or my company to legal risk?	839
Q 26.9.3	What are the filing requirements for reports of suspicious transactions?	839
Q 26.10	What is "information sharing"?	839
Q 26.10.1	What is section 314(a) mandatory information sharing?	840
Q 26.10.2	Who is subject to section 314(a) mandatory information sharing?	840
Q 26.10.3	What must a financial institution do upon receipt of a section 314(a) mandatory information sharing request?	840
Q 26.10.4	Should a positive response to a section 314(a) mandatory information sharing request include records?	841
Q 26.10.5	Are section 314(a) mandatory information sharing requests and responses confidential?	842
Q 26.10.6	Should a section 314(a) mandatory information sharing request trigger the filing of a suspicious activity report if there is a positive match?	842
Q 26.10.7	What is section 314(b) voluntary information sharing?	842
Q 26.10.8	What information may be shared among financial institutions under section 314(b) voluntary information sharing?	843
Q 26.10.9	Who may share information under section 314(b)?	843
Q 26.10.10	How does one participate in section 314(b) voluntary information sharing?	843
Q 26.10.11	Who may information be shared with?	843
Q 26.10.12	Is information shared under 314(b) confidential?	844
Q 26.10.13	Should a section 314(b) voluntary information sharing request trigger the filing of a SAR?	844
Q 26.10.14	May a financial institution that shares information under section 314(b) be sued civilly by the subject of the information?	844
Q 26.11	Why does the government require large cash transactions to be reported?	844
Q 26.11.1	What forms are used to report large cash transactions?	845
Q 26.11.2	What are the requirements for filing a Currency Transaction Report (CTR)?	845

Table of Contents

Q 26.11.3	What are the requirements for filing an IRS Form 8300?	846
Q 26.11.4	What constitutes "currency" for purposes of Form 8300?	847
Q 26.11.5	What is a reportable transaction?	847
Q 26.11.6	When are transactions considered "related"?	847
Q 26.11.7	How are multiple-payment transactions handled?	848
Q 26.12	What records must be made and kept under the BSA?	850
Q 26.13	What is "bulk cash smuggling"?	851
Q 26.13.1	What are the filing requirements for FinCEN Form 105?	851
Q 26.13.2	What are the consequences of bulk cash smuggling?	851
Q 26.13.3	For purposes of bulk cash smuggling, what are "currency" and "monetary instruments"?	852
Q 26.13.4	Are there any exceptions to this reporting requirement?	852
Q 26.14	What is structuring?	853
Q 26.14.1	What are the penalties for structuring violations?	853
Q 26.15	Who are the "specially designated persons" that federal AML statutes prohibit transactions with?	853
Q 26.15.1	Who is considered a "United States person"?	854
Q 26.16	What kinds of transactions with SDNs are prohibited?	854
Q 26.16.1	What are the consequences of conducting business with an SDN?	855
Q 26.17	What are the AML requirements for Money Services Businesses?	855
Q 26.18	What are the AML requirements for foreign Money Services Businesses?	856
Q 26.19	Why should my company care about having an anti-money laundering compliance program?	857
Q 26.19.1	Our institution is currently exempted from anti-money laundering compliance program requirements. How can we keep track of changing regulations should our status change?	858
Q 26.19.2	What are the elements of an effective anti-money laundering compliance program?	858
Q 26.19.3	What are the key considerations in appointing a compliance officer?	859
Q 26.19.4	What are the key considerations when approaching employee training?	860
Q 26.19.5	What are the key considerations regarding independent audits?	861
Q 26.19.6	How can we confirm a customer's identity?	862

Q 26.19.7	What if verifying a customer's identity is not possible?	862
Q 26.19.8	What are the actual steps a company must take to create an effective anti-money laundering compliance program?	862
Q 26.19.9	What is the relationship between a compliance program under the U.S. Sentencing Guidelines and an anti-money laundering compliance program?	864
Q 26.19.10	Is there a standard anti-money laundering compliance program that my company can effectively use?	865
Q 26.19.11	How do we go about designing an anti-money laundering compliance program?	865
Q 26.19.12	What are the basic considerations for the ongoing administration and enforcement of an anti-money laundering compliance program?	867
Q 26.19.13	Who should administer the anti-money laundering compliance program?	869
Q 26.19.14	What role does top management have in administering the program?	869

Chapter 27 The Troubled Asset Relief Program 879
Thomas Morante & Michelle T. Hess

Q 27.1	What is TARP?	881
Q 27.2	What are the TARP programs?	881
Q 27.2.1	What is the Capital Purchase Program?	881
Q 27.2.2	... Capital Assistance Program?	882
Q 27.2.3	... Systemically Significant Failing Institutions Program/AIG Investment Program?	882
Q 27.2.4	... Targeted Investment Program?	883
Q 27.2.5	... Asset Guarantee Program?	883
Q 27.2.6	... Term Asset-Backed Securities Loan Facility?	883
Q 27.2.7	... Public-Private Investment Program?	884
Q 27.2.8	... Unlocking Credit for Small Businesses/Small Business Administration Loan Support Initiative?	884
Q 27.2.9	... Automotive Industry Financing Program?	884
Q 27.2.10	... Auto Supplier Support Program?	885
Q 27.2.11	... Auto Warranty Commitment Program?	885
Q 27.2.12	... Making Home Affordable Program?	885
Q 27.3	Who oversees the EESA and, as a result, monitors TARP funding?	885
Q 27.3.1	What are the oversight and enforcement responsibilities of the Financial Stability Oversight Board?	886
Q 27.3.2	... Office of the Special Investigator General TARP?	886

Table of Contents

Q 27.3.3 ... the Congressional Oversight Panel?............................... 887
Q 27.3.4 ... the Government Accountability Office?.......................... 887
Q 27.4 What legal, compliance, and enforcement risks does a company face by participating in TARP? 887
Q 27.5 What is the best way for my organization to manage the risks associated with participating in TARP? 889

Chapter 28 Sarbanes-Oxley Act of 2002 895
Richard T. Williams & Jerome W. Hoffman

Q 28.1 To whom does SOX apply?.. 897
Q 28.2 Which companies are "issuers"? 898
Q 28.3 Generally, what does SOX require? 898
Q 28.4 What should a company put in its code of ethics?..................... 898
    Q 28.4.1 What does a company do with its code of ethics once it is adopted by the board? 899
Q 28.5 How does SOX affect boards of directors? 899
    Q 28.5.1 Do boards have to act in a manner different from the way they did before SOX?....................................... 900
Q 28.6 What does an audit committee do?... 900
    Q 28.6.1 How does SOX affect the make-up of the audit committee? 900
    Q 28.6.2 What if no one in the company is an independent financial expert?... 901
    Q 28.6.3 Does SOX change the audit committee's responsibilities?... 901
Q 28.7 What are the new requirements for officers and directors?..... 902
Q 28.8 What are the SEC's penalties for officers and directors if they violate SOX? 902
    Q 28.8.1 Do officers and directors face any penalties beyond those imposed by the SEC? 902
    Q 28.8.2 Have the SEC and law enforcement actually used these new powers?... 903
Q 28.9 Are violations of SOX by officers and directors generally covered by liability insurance?... 903
    Q 28.9.1 Other than insurers, who else is concerned with the effect SOX could have on officers and directors?............. 903
Q 28.10 How does SOX protect whistleblowers?..................................... 904
    Q 28.10.1 What does a whistleblower employee need to show to prove that the company is taking retaliatory action against him or her?... 904
    Q 28.10.2 What procedures should be in place to help stave off successful legal action by whistleblowers?...................... 904

Q 28.10.3	What should the company do once a complaint is filed?	905
Q 28.10.4	What happens if the whistleblower wins the case?	906
Q 28.10.5	Are there any repercussions beyond what is owed to the whistleblower?	906
Q 28.10.6	Do states have similar protections for whistleblowers?	906
Q 28.11	The landscape has changed for public companies, but what about for accounting firms?	906
Q 28.12	Has SOX affected the relationship between the companies and auditors?	907
Q 28.12.1	What about "one-stop shopping" for financial and accounting services?	907
Q 28.13	What is the relationship between the audit committees and the auditors?	908
Q 28.13.1	Can a company keep using audit partners with whom it has an established relationship?	908
Q 28.14	What are new procedures that auditors must follow?	908
Q 28.15	What powers does the PCAOB have over the auditors?	910
Q 28.15.1	What can the PCAOB do if it uncovers a violation?	910
Q 28.15.2	How have the new PCAOB rules changed audits?	910
Q 28.16	What effect does SOX have on foreign auditors?	911
Q 28.16.1	What if a U.S. accounting firm relies in part upon a foreign accounting firm?	911
Q 28.17	How does SOX affect lawyers for issuers?	911
Q 28.17.1	What responsibilities does the SEC impose upon lawyers under SOX?	912
Q 28.17.2	Which lawyers are affected by SOX?	912
Q 28.17.3	Are there any limitations on the applicability of the SEC rules on attorney conduct?	913
Q 28.18	What is "up-the-ladder" reporting?	913
Q 28.18.1	Do the requirements depend on whether the attorney is in a supervisory position?	913
Q 28.18.2	What if an attorney has reason to believe that reporting to the CEO or CLO would be futile?	914
Q 28.18.3	How do these requirements apply to outside counsel?	914
Q 28.19	Who is a "supervisory attorney"?	914
Q 28.20	Who is a "subordinate attorney"?	914
Q 28.20.1	As long as there is an attorney above you on the chain, are you a subordinate attorney?	915
Q 28.20.2	Are the definitions of supervisory and subordinate attorney static?	915
Q 28.21	What do SOX and the SEC require of a lawyer?	915
Q 28.21.1	How does this affect the attorney-client relationship?	916

Q 28.21.2	What sanctions are there for violations by an attorney of the SEC rules under SOX?.................................	916
Q 28.22	What does "becoming aware of credible evidence" actually mean?...	916
Q 28.22.1	How should companies define "credible evidence"?........	917
Q 28.23	What constitutes a "material violation"?.....................	917
Q 28.24	At what stage must a future possible violation be reported?	918
Q 28.25	What is a qualified legal compliance committee (QLCC)?........	918
Q 28.25.1	How is a QLCC established?..................................	918
Q 28.25.2	How does the QLCC operate?................................	919
Q 28.26	What steps must a CLO take when presented with a report of evidence of material violation?	919
Q 28.26.1	What kind of paper trail should the inquiry have?...........	920
Q 28.26.2	What would be considered an "appropriate response"?......................................	920
Q 28.26.3	How does a reporting attorney determine whether the response was appropriate?...............................	920
Q 28.26.4	What does a reporting attorney do after the company has responded?...	921
Q 28.26.5	In the absence of an appropriate response to a report of a material violation, what should a conscientious counsel do?	921
Q 28.26.6	What options do lawyers currently have when a SOX violation may be occurring?.............................	921
Q 28.27	Does SOX also apply to foreign lawyers?	921
Q 28.28	How do the SEC rules compare with American Bar Association and state rules?.......................................	922
Q 28.28.1	What is the difference between the SEC and ABA and state rules?..	922
Q 28.28.2	What is the relationship between the SEC and state rules?..	923
Q 28.29	How should law firms and lawyers adjust to the new standards?...	923
Q 28.29.1	What should the training entail?.............................	923
Q 28.30	Has the SEC punished lawyers for misconduct?................	924
Q 28.30.1	How has the SEC punished lawyers?........................	924
Q 28.31	How do the new SEC rules affect insurance for lawyers?.........	924
Q 28.32	What should the role of the general counsel be in the new environment?...	925
Q 28.32.1	How have the SEC rules changed the relations among general counsel, directors, and management?	925
Q 28.32.2	How does the new environment affect the CEO vis à vis the general counsel?..	926

Q 28.32.3	How has SOX changed the role of the general counsel?	926
Q 28.32.4	What new tasks does the general counsel have under SOX?	926
Q 28.32.5	How do the new SOX requirements interact with the need to protect privileged communications?	927
Q 28.32.6	What organizational steps and tools are out there to assist the general counsel?	928
Q 28.32.7	How does a general counsel determine the best interests of the corporation?	929
Q 28.33	What factors are relevant to the SEC in the course of an investigation?	930
Q 28.33.1	Has the SEC indicated the areas of greatest concern?	932
Q 28.33.2	What are the biggest obstacles to cooperation?	932
Q 28.34	What are SOX's certification requirements?	933
Q 28.34.1	What must the SOX 906 certificate contain?	933
Q 28.34.2	What is the test for liability under the financial certificate requirements?	934
Q 28.34.3	What else must the CEO and CFO do under SOX section 302?	934
Q 28.34.4	What must the CEO and CFO actually certify under SOX section 302?	934
Q 28.34.5	Does the CEO have to sign the company's federal tax returns?	935
Q 28.34.6	What should the CEO and CFO do prior to certifying a report under SOX?	936
Q 28.35	What is non-GAAP reporting?	937
Q 28.35.1	How must a company report a non-GAAP financial measure?	937
Q 28.36	What enforcement action can the SEC take upon discovery of false certifications?	938
Q 28.37	What internal controls does SOX require?	938
Q 28.37.1	What is the scope of internal controls over financial reporting?	939
Q 28.37.2	What are the elements and scope of internal controls?	940
Q 28.37.3	Is there a specified process for designing, monitoring, or testing internal controls?	940
Q 28.37.4	What can be expected from internal controls?	940
Q 28.37.5	What is a "reasonable assurance"?	940
Q 28.37.6	Whose responsibility is it to design and develop internal controls?	941
Q 28.37.7	How do auditors advise on internal controls without violating the stringent requirements of auditor independence?	941

Table of Contents

Q 28.37.8	What are the processes for developing internal controls for financial reporting?	941
Q 28.38	What areas of financial reporting appear to be most vulnerable to manipulation?	942
Q 28.38.1	What aspects of revenue recognition should be considered in particular?	942
Q 28.38.2	What aspects of expense accounting should be considered in particular?	943
Q 28.38.3	What aspects of asset valuations should be considered in particular?	944
Q 28.38.4	What aspects of contingent liability valuations should particularly be considered?	944
Q 28.38.5	What aspects of special purpose entities should particularly be considered?	944
Q 28.38.6	How should companies document internal controls?	945
Q 28.38.7	What else is management required to do beyond developing, documenting, putting into operation, and using internal controls?	945
Q 28.38.8	What should management use to assess their internal controls?	946
Q 28.39	What are the auditing standards?	946
Q 28.39.1	What should testing encompass?	947
Q 28.39.2	What other inquiries should be made?	947
Q 28.40	What should management do if it finds problems with the internal controls?	948
Q 28.40.1	What is a "control deficiency"?	948
Q 28.40.2	What is a "significant deficiency"?	948
Q 28.40.3	What is a "material weakness"?	949
Q 28.40.4	What factors should be considered in categorizing a shortcoming?	949
Q 28.40.5	What kinds of deficiencies are least likely to be considered significant?	950
Q 28.40.6	What kinds of deficiencies are likely to be considered material?	951
Q 28.40.7	What should accompany the disclosure of material weaknesses?	951
Q 28.41	What is the PCAOB's auditing standard?	951
Q 28.41.1	How important is documentation to an audit?	952
Q 28.42	What is the proper standard for documentation?	952
Q 28.42.1	What are the relevant subjects for which management's records should be retained?	953
Q 28.43	What should a company do to sustain SOX compliance?	953
Q 28.43.1	What specific expectations does the SEC have regarding companies' ongoing compliance efforts?	954

Q 28.43.2	What approach should a company take to achieve "optimization"?	955
Q 28.43.3	What is the advantage of a top-down approach?	955
Q 28.43.4	What can a company use to augment the top-down approach?	955
Q 28.43.5	What kinds of risk analysis should be used?	956
Q 28.44	What are disclosure controls?	956
Q 28.44.1	What are the certification requirements related to disclosure controls?	956
Q 28.44.2	What exactly must the CEO and CFO certify about the disclosure controls?	957
Q 28.44.3	What is the purpose of disclosure controls?	957
Q 28.44.4	Is the procedure for disclosure important?	958
Q 28.44.5	What should the disclosure contain?	958
Q 28.44.6	How should a company handle disclosure?	958
Q 28.44.7	What should the disclosure controls consist of?	959
Q 28.44.8	How should a company sustain and enhance disclosure controls and enterprise risk management?	959
Q 28.45	How has SOX enhanced the powers of the SEC?	960
Q 28.45.1	How much has the SEC grown under SOX?	960
Q 28.45.2	How has the increased budget affected enforcement?	961
Q 28.45.3	Has the SEC expanded into any new areas?	961
Q 28.46	Are there any express private rights of action under SOX?	962
Q 28.46.1	Did SOX enhance any existing private rights of action?	963
Q 28.46.2	Does SOX have any effect on private 10b-5 litigation?	963
Q 28.46.3	Does SOX create a private right under which investors can file claims against the issuer's attorneys?	964
Q 28.47	What are the SOX penalty provisions that apply to also-private companies?	964
Q 28.48	What are the SOX record retention requirements that apply to all companies and persons?	965
Q 28.49	What are SOX's requirements for ERISA and notice of pension-fund blackout periods?	965
Q 28.50	Does SOX apply to almost-public companies?	965
Q 28.50.1	How does SOX affect almost-public companies?	966
Q 28.51	Does SOX cover non-public banks?	966
Q 28.52	Does SOX affect non-public insurance companies?	966
Q 28.53	What problems has SOX caused for international companies?	967
Q 28.53.1	Has the EU responded to SOX with a law of its own?	967
Q 28.53.2	How has the EU coped with SOX?	968

Table of Contents

Q 28.53.3 Is there any hope for a convergence of EU and SEC standards? 968
Q 28.54 How are non-profit governmental organizations treated under SOX? 969
Q 28.55 Does SOX apply to colleges and universities? 969

Chapter 29 The Law and Accounting: The Convergence of Sarbanes-Oxley, COSO, the Federal Sentencing Guidelines, and *Caremark* Duties 975
James D. Wing

Q 29.1 Is the Sarbanes-Oxley Act of 2002 (SOX) primarily aimed at improving corporate governance and legal compliance? 976
    Q 29.1.1 How did SOX try to accomplish its goal? 976
    Q 29.1.2 What prompted Congress to act? 977
    Q 29.1.3 What was the precise mechanism Congress used? 977
Q 29.2 What is COSO? 978
    Q 29.2.1 Does the COSO report relate only to details of financial reporting and concepts of accounting? 978
    Q 29.2.2 Have there been any subsequent developments since the first COSO report? 979
    Q 29.2.3 Is COSO II mandated by law? 980
    Q 29.2.4 What does COSO II's integrated framework recommend? 980
    Q 29.2.5 What are the specific components of COSO II? 980
    Q 29.2.6 What other principles guide risk management? 981
Q 29.3 Are these principles exclusively applicable to public companies, or do they have broader implications? 981
    Q 29.3.1 Isn't there a massive political reaction against this, particularly given the huge cost to companies for instituting these programs? 982
Q 29.4 Has the financial collapse of 2007–2008 interrupted recent developments in audits and compliance? 983

Chapter 30 SEC Investigations of Public Companies 985
Mitchell E. Herr

Q 30.1 What does the SEC investigate? 987
    Q 30.1.1 What individuals are subject to investigation? 987
    Q 30.1.2 Who at the SEC is responsible for conducting investigations? 988
    Q 30.1.3 What triggers an SEC investigation? 989

Q 30.1.4	What is the difference between a "preliminary" investigation and a "formal" investigation?	990
Q 30.1.5	Are all SEC investigations private?	991
Q 30.2	What are a company's obligations to its SEC defense counsel?	991
Q 30.3	What role does cooperation play in SEC enforcement investigations?	992
Q 30.4	What are the potential benefits of cooperation with the SEC?	993
Q 30.5	What are the potential benefits to an individual of cooperation with the SEC?	994
Q 30.5.1	What is a proffer agreement?	995
Q 30.5.2	... a cooperation agreement?	995
Q 30.5.3	... a deferred prosecution agreement?	996
Q 30.5.4	... a non-prosecution agreement?	996
Q 30.5.5	... an immunity request?	996
Q 30.6	Does the SEC coordinate investigations with other law enforcement authorities?	999
Q 30.6.1	Do parallel civil and criminal investigations present additional risks?	1000
Q 30.6.2	Must the government disclose that there are parallel civil and criminal investigations?	1001
Q 30.6.3	Will both the criminal and civil proceedings proceed simultaneously?	1002
Q 30.7	Can we rely on directors' and officers' policies to cover the costs of responding to an SEC investigation?	1003
Q 30.7.1	What kinds of expenses related to an enforcement action might not be covered by a D&O policy?	1004
Q 30.7.2	What other D&O policy issues/considerations are raised by SEC investigations?	1004
Q 30.7.3	How can we mitigate the risks of rescission of our D&O policy?	1005
Q 30.8	How is an SEC investigation conducted?	1005
Q 30.8.1	Has the SEC disclosed how it conducts its investigations?	1006
Q 30.9	What are a company's obligations regarding documents?	1007
Q 30.9.1	Are there special considerations for preserving electronic documents?	1007
Q 30.9.2	What are the consequences of inadequate document preservation?	1008
Q 30.9.3	What can our company do to make sure that it meets its preservation obligations?	1008
Q 30.9.4	Should we preserve everything or only those documents we think the SEC will want produced?	1009

Table of Contents

Q 30.10	What can we expect from the document request process?	1010
Q 30.11	Can we negotiate with the SEC about our document production?	1012
Q 30.12	What are the advantages of hiring an outside e-discovery vendor?	1012
Q 30.13	Why is the question of selective disclosure of information in SEC investigations important?	1013
Q 30.14	Can privileged information be selectively disclosed to the SEC?	1013
Q 30.14.1	What is the outlook for selective disclosure?	1014
Q 30.14.2	Should we consider disclosing privileged information?	1015
Q 30.15	From whom is sworn testimony likely to be requested?	1015
Q 30.15.1	Should witnesses speak informally with SEC enforcement staff?	1016
Q 30.16	How should we respond after a request for sworn witness testimony has been made?	1017
Q 30.17	What can we expect from an SEC witness examination?	1017
Q 30.18	What rights do witnesses have?	1017
Q 30.18.1	Can a witness refuse to testify?	1018
Q 30.18.2	What are some important considerations in deciding whether or not to refuse to testify?	1018
Q 30.18.3	What is a witness's counsel permitted to do during an examination?	1018
Q 30.19	What other important considerations should we keep in mind when anticipating a witness examination?	1019
Q 30.20	Should the same counsel represent the company and its employees?	1019
Q 30.20.1	What are the advantages of using the same counsel?	1019
Q 30.20.2	Are there any limitations or provisions to using the same counsel?	1020
Q 30.21	What if an employee decides to retain separate personal counsel?	1020
Q 30.22	What are the opportunities for informal advocacy during the investigation?	1021
Q 30.23	What is a Wells Notice?	1022
Q 30.24	What is a Wells Submission?	1022
Q 30.24.1	Should a Wells Submission automatically follow a Wells Notice?	1023
Q 30.25	What kind of charges can the SEC bring?	1023
Q 30.26	What remedies can the SEC obtain against a company?	1024
Q 30.26.1	How large are civil monetary penalties?	1024

Q 30.26.2	What factors does the SEC consider in deciding on whether or not to assess a penalty on a company?	1027
Q 30.26.3	Does the SEC ever seek other remedies?	1029
Q 30.27	What remedies can the SEC seek against directors and officers?	1029
Q 30.27.1	What monetary penalties can the SEC seek against directors and officers?	1029
Q 30.27.2	What other kinds of relief can the SEC seek against directors and officers?	1030
Q 30.28	How does the SEC approach settlements?	1031

Chapter 31   Executive Compensation 1043
Robert J. Friedman, Richard J. Hindlian, David G. O'Leary & Meredith L. O'Leary

Q 31.1	How do employers generally provide and document executive compensation arrangements?	1045
Q 31.2	What types of compensation are usually provided by an employment agreement?	1045
Q 31.2.1	What types of compensation are generally provided by a "plan"?	1045
Q 31.2.2	What types of compensation arrangements are not considered "plans"?	1046
Q 31.2.3	What is severance pay?	1047
Q 31.2.4	What is a change-in-control agreement or plan?	1047
Q 31.3	What are the general rules that apply to taxation of executive compensation?	1048
Q 31.3.1	What are gross-up covenants?	1049
Q 31.3.2	What is an incentive stock option (ISO)?	1050
Q 31.3.3	What is the AMT?	1051
Q 31.3.4	How should an executive prepare for the AMT?	1051
Q 31.4	What is the general rule for the taxation of non-qualified deferred compensation?	1052
Q 31.4.1	Does a rabbi trust affect the treatment of a deferred compensation plan under the Code or ERISA?	1052
Q 31.4.2	How does Code section 83, concerning transfers of property as compensation for services, affect executive compensation?	1052
Q 31.4.3	How does Code section 422, concerning ISOs, affect executive compensation?	1053
Q 31.4.4	What are the general tax rules for non-qualified stock options?	1054

Table of Contents

Q 31.4.5	Are there adverse tax consequences from mispriced stock options?	1054
Q 31.5	What is deferred compensation?	1055
Q 31.6	What are the general attributes of a non-qualified deferred compensation plan?	1056
Q 31.6.1	What types of non-qualified deferred compensation plans are there?	1056
Q 31.6.2	How does an excess plan work?	1056
Q 31.6.3	Are there any requirements with respect to SERP?	1057
Q 31.6.4	What is a select group of management and highly compensated employees?	1057
Q 31.6.5	May a deferred compensation plan be funded?	1058
Q 31.6.6	What is split-dollar insurance?	1059
Q 31.6.7	How is split-dollar insurance taxed?	1059
Q 31.7	What rules does Code section 409A impose?	1059
Q 31.7.1	What is a non-qualified deferred compensation plan for purposes of Code section 409A?	1060
Q 31.7.2	What is a deferral of compensation?	1060
Q 31.7.3	What is a "service provider"?	1061
Q 31.7.4	What is a "service recipient"?	1061
Q 31.7.5	Which non-qualified deferred compensation plans are subject to Code section 409A?	1061
Q 31.8	What types of plans and arrangements are generally exempt from the requirements of Code section 409A?	1062
Q 31.8.1	What are short-term deferrals?	1062
Q 31.8.2	What are statutory stock options and employee stock purchase plans?	1063
Q 31.8.3	What non-statutory stock options are exempt from the section 409A requirements?	1063
Q 31.8.4	What kinds of stock appreciation rights are exempt from the section 409A requirements?	1063
Q 31.8.5	What are restricted property and stock plans covered by Code section 83?	1064
Q 31.8.6	What are qualified employer plans?	1064
Q 31.8.7	What are welfare benefit plans and arrangements?	1064
Q 31.8.8	What kinds of foreign plans are exempt from the section 409A requirements?	1065
Q 31.8.9	What kinds of severance payments are exempt from section 409A requirements?	1065
Q 31.8.10	What happens if the service provider uses the accrual method of accounting?	1065
Q 31.8.11	What if the service provider is actively engaged in the trade or business of providing substantial services?	1065

Q 31.8.12	Why is fair market value of stock important and how is it determined?	1066
Q 31.8.13	If a deferred compensation plan or arrangement is not exempt from section 409A, what restrictions are necessary to prevent immediate taxation to the service provider?	1067
Q 31.8.14	What constitutes a "substantial risk of forfeiture"?	1067
Q 31.8.15	If there is no substantial risk of forfeiture, what requirements must be satisfied?	1067
Q 31.8.16	Does section 409A restrict the time and form of payments of deferred compensation?	1068
Q 31.9	What are permitted "distributable events" under Code section 409A?	1068
Q 31.9.1	When has an employee separated from service?	1068
Q 31.9.2	When is a service recipient considered disabled?	1069
Q 31.9.3	What are the requirements for specified-time or fixed-schedule payments?	1069
Q 31.9.4	What constitutes a change in control?	1069
Q 31.9.5	How is an "unforeseeable emergency" defined?	1069
Q 31.10	When can deferred compensation be paid?	1070
Q 31.10.1	When must payments to key employees of a public company be delayed?	1070
Q 31.10.2	Under what conditions may a plan permit the acceleration of the time or schedule of any payments under the plan?	1071
Q 31.10.3	Under what circumstances can payments be delayed?	1071
Q 31.10.4	Does section 409A provide rules affecting initial and subsequent deferral elections?	1072
Q 31.10.5	When must an initial deferral election be made?	1072
Q 31.10.6	What are the special rules for an initial deferral election related to performance-based compensation?	1072
Q 31.10.7	What is the effect of changes to an existing election?	1072
Q 31.10.8	What effects does Code section 409A have on the use of rabbi trusts?	1073
Q 31.11	What are the penalties for failure to comply with Code section 409A?	1073
Q 31.11.1	What are the reporting requirements?	1074
Q 31.11.2	What is the effective date of Code section 409A?	1074
Q 31.11.3	What is a "material modification" of a plan?	1075
Q 31.11.4	What relief from section 409A violations can be sought under the IRS "Voluntary Compliance Program"?	1075
Q 31.12	Are there any special rules that apply to offshore non-qualified deferred compensation plans?	1076

Table of Contents

Q 31.12.1	What is a "nonqualified deferred compensation plan" under section 457?...	1076
Q 31.12.2	What is a "nonqualified entity?".......................................	1076
Q 31.12.3	What is a substantial risk of forfeiture?..........................	1077
Q 31.12.4	What rules does section 457A impose?.........................	1077
Q 31.12.5	Are there any exceptions to the requirements of section 457A?..	1078
Q 31.13	What are golden parachute payments?........................	1078
Q 31.13.1	What types of payments are considered parachute payments?..	1078
Q 31.13.2	What types of payments are exempt?.............................	1079
Q 31.13.3	What are "excess parachute payments"?.......................	1079
Q 31.13.4	What is an executive's "base amount"?..........................	1079
Q 31.13.5	Which executives are "disqualified individuals"?...........	1080
Q 31.13.6	What are "payments in the nature of compensation"?..	1080
Q 31.13.7	What payments are considered "contingent on a change in ownership or control"?....................................	1080
Q 31.13.8	Is there a minimum "threshold" for change-in-control payments to be considered excess parachute payments?...	1081
Q 31.13.9	How are excess parachute payments taxed?.................	1081
Q 31.14	What are the advantages of equity-based compensation?	1081
Q 31.14.1	What are the different types of equity compensation plans?...	1082
Q 31.14.2	Do equity awards have to be issued pursuant to a plan?..	1082
Q 31.14.3	What are the main differences between granting an ISO and a non-qualified stock option?....................................	1082
Q 31.14.4	What are the rules with respect to ISOs?.......................	1083
Q 31.14.5	What are the rules with respect to non-qualified options?...	1083
Q 31.14.6	What is a grant of restricted stock?................................	1083
Q 31.14.7	What is a stock appreciation right (SAR) and how do SARs work?...	1083
Q 31.14.8	What is phantom stock?..	1084
Q 31.14.9	Can a company reissue stock options if the price goes down?...	1084
Q 31.14.10	What are the concerns about backdated stock options?..	1085
Q 31.15	What are the general rules about accounting for options?...	1086
Q 31.15.1	How are SARs and phantom stock accounted for?........	1087

Q 31.16		What kinds of obligations and limits do the securities laws place upon companies and executives? 1087
	Q 31.16.1	How do the SEC's 2006 Proxy Disclosure Rules affect the company's disclosure obligations with respect to executive compensation? 1088
	Q 31.16.2	Are there special rules for small business issuers? 1088
	Q 31.16.3	Are there other classes of companies that are subject to special disclosure rules? 1089
	Q 31.16.4	What is the Compensation Discussion and Analysis? 1089
	Q 31.16.5	What period does the CDA cover? 1091
	Q 31.16.6	Which executives are covered by the Proxy Disclosure Rules? 1091
	Q 31.16.7	What if compensation policies differ among the NEOs? 1091
	Q 31.16.8	What if performance targets/goals contain sensitive information? 1092
	Q 31.16.9	What are the "tabular disclosures" that must accompany the CDA? 1092
	Q 31.16.10	Are narratives required with respect to the tabular disclosures? 1092
	Q 31.16.11	What is a perquisite or personal benefit? 1093
	Q 31.16.12	Must perquisites and personal benefits be disclosed? 1093
	Q 31.16.13	What disclosures are required for grants of stock options and stock appreciation rights? 1093
	Q 31.16.14	What disclosures are required for director compensation? 1095
	Q 31.16.15	Are there other SEC-required disclosure rules that relate to executives and directors? 1095
	Q 31.16.16	What are the disclosure requirements regarding related-party transactions? 1095
	Q 31.16.17	What are the disclosure requirements regarding other corporate governance matters? 1096
	Q 31.16.18	Are company disclosures required to include a Compensation Committee Report? 1097
	Q 31.16.19	Do the CEO and CFO certifications apply to the CDA and the CCR? 1097
Q 31.17		For purposes of registration requirements under the Securities Act of 1933, what is a "security"? 1097
	Q 31.17.1	Is an interest in a non-qualified deferred compensation plan treated as a "security" under federal securities law? 1098

Table of Contents

Q 31.17.2	When might a participant's interest in a NQDC plan be treated as a "security" under federal securities law?	1098
Q 31.17.3	Does the Securities Act of 1933 require registration of sales of stock in connection with employee stock plans?	1099
Q 31.17.4	Does the Securities Exchange Act of 1934 require registration of sales of stock in connection with employee stock plans?	1099
Q 31.18	Are there any exemptions from the registration requirements of the Securities Act of 1933 that apply to interests in a NQDC plan or the stock sold to a participant in connection with an employee stock plan?	1100
Q 31.18.1	What form should be used to register interests in NQDC plans and the stock sold pursuant to employee stock plans?	1101
Q 31.18.2	If a NQDC plan or employee stock plan is registered, what disclosures must be made to plan participants?	1101
Q 31.18.3	If a NQDC plan or employee stock plan is not registered, are there any disclosure requirements?	1101
Q 31.18.4	Do the anti-fraud provisions of federal securities law apply to disclosures in connection with NQDC plans and employee stock plans?	1102
Q 31.18.5	Are there other disclosures to the SEC required in connection with NQDC plans and employee stock plans?	1102
Q 31.18.6	What plans must be approved by shareholders pursuant to stock exchange requirements?	1102
Q 31.18.7	What plans are exempt from the shareholder approval requirements of the stock markets?	1103
Q 31.18.8	What is the profit recovery rule of section 16(b) of the Securities Exchange Act of 1934?	1103
Q 31.18.9	Who are "insiders" under section 16(b)?	1104
Q 31.18.10	What happens if a person becomes an insider within six months of a stock purchase or sale transaction?	1104
Q 31.18.11	What filings are required by an insider under section 16(a) of the 1934 Act?	1104
Q 31.18.12	What transactions are exempt under Rule 16(b)-3 from the profit recovery rule of section 16(b)?	1105

CORPORATE COMPLIANCE ANSWER BOOK 2011–12

Q 31.18.13	Under what circumstances and conditions can a plan participant resell public company securities purchased or otherwise received through an employee benefit plan?	1105
Q 31.18.14	Who is an affiliate for purposes of resales?	1106
Q 31.18.15	What are the conditions that must be met under Rule 144?	1106
Q 31.18.16	Does Sarbanes-Oxley prohibit trading by executives of a company stock during pension blackout periods?	1107
Q 31.18.17	Does Regulation BTR provide any exemptions to the trading prohibition?	1107
Q 31.18.18	Is there a notice requirement relating to the trading prohibition?	1108
Q 31.18.19	What remedies apply to a violation of the trading prohibition?	1108
Q 31.18.20	Does Sarbanes-Oxley impose any other restrictions impacting executive compensation?	1108

Chapter 32   Institutions of Higher Education 1113
Kwamina Thomas Williford, Paul Lannon & Nathan Adams

Q 32.1	Is it necessary for an institution to have a compliance program?	1115
Q 32.1.1	What should a compliance program for a higher education institution entail?	1116
Q 32.1.2	Who should be involved in the implementation of a compliance program at institutions of higher education?	1116
Q 32.2	What are the greatest areas of risk for institutions?	1118
Q 32.3	May academic institutions take race and gender into account when making admissions decisions?	1119
Q 32.3.1	When do institutions have a compelling interest to consider race in admissions?	1120
Q 32.3.2	When is an institution's implementation of a race-conscious admissions policy narrowly tailored?	1121
Q 32.3.3	In what circumstances may the consideration of gender in admissions be constitutional?	1122
Q 32.4	What are the consequences of a noncompliant admissions policy?	1122
Q 32.5	What obligations regarding disability should an institution be aware of?	1123
Q 32.5.1	How should institutions respond to the ADAAA?	1125

Table of Contents

Q 32.6	What are the eligibility requirements for an institution to participate in federal student aid (FSA) programs?	1126
Q 32.7	What are the requirements for an academic program to be eligible for FSA?	1127
Q 32.8	What requirements must an institution comply with in order to participate in FSA programs?	1128
Q 32.8.1	What limitations are there on the compensation of student recruiters?	1129
Q 32.8.2	What types of compensation plans are permitted for student recruiters under Title IV?	1129
Q 32.8.3	What requirements and limitations are there on institutions providing students with a list of preferred lenders?	1131
Q 32.8.4	What are an institution's obligations regarding a code of conduct?	1132
Q 32.8.5	What are an institution's disclosure and notification obligations regarding student loan information?	1133
Q 32.8.6	What obligations does an institution have regarding financial counseling for students?	1134
Q 32.8.7	What requirements and limitations are there on the activities of private lenders?	1135
Q 32.8.8	What are the penalties for violating Title IV student aid regulations?	1135
Q 32.9	What liability does an institution have for violence on campus?	1136
Q 32.9.1	What are the requirements of the Clery Act?	1137
Q 32.9.2	What are the repercussions for failing to comply with the Clery Act?	1138
Q 32.9.3	What are some best practices for preventing and responding to campus violence?	1139
Q 32.9.4	What is the role of legal counsel in improving campus security?	1141
Q 32.10	What is FERPA?	1141
Q 32.10.1	What are the privacy rights students have under FERPA?	1142
Q 32.10.2	Who enforces FERPA?	1142
Q 32.10.3	Can a student bring a lawsuit against an institution for FERPA violations?	1142
Q 32.10.4	What is the process for FERPA investigations by the FPCO?	1143
Q 32.11	What are the consequences of a FERPA violation?	1143
Q 32.12	How does an institution determine what constitutes "education records" covered by FERPA?	1144

CORPORATE COMPLIANCE ANSWER BOOK 2011–12

Q 32.12.1	What information is excluded from the definition of "education records"?	1144
Q 32.13	When must an institution allow a student to view his or her education records?	1146
Q 32.13.1	Are there any limits on a student's rights to access to his or her education records?	1146
Q 32.13.2	Can students amend their education records after inspecting them?	1147
Q 32.14	When is student consent not required for disclosure?	1147
Q 32.14.1	What is disclosable "directory information"?	1148
Q 32.14.2	When can parents view education records without the student's consent?	1149
Q 32.14.3	Does FERPA allow a student's former high school to send records to a university or college?	1149
Q 32.14.4	What types of outside institutions can access student education records?	1149
Q 32.14.5	Can college and university officials share information in the education record with each other?	1151
Q 32.14.6	What if there is a court order or subpoena for information in a student's education record?	1151
Q 32.14.7	What happens to protected records when there is a legal action between the student and the educational institution?	1152
Q 32.14.8	What is the health or safety emergency exception?	1152
Q 32.14.9	To whom may institutions disclose information in case of health or safety emergency?	1153
Q 32.15	When does FERPA allow outsourcing of information in student education records?	1154
Q 32.15.1	What steps must be taken to comply with FERPA when student education records are outsourced?	1155
Q 32.16	What guidance does the DOE provide for protecting access to student records within an institution?	1155
Q 32.17	What records does FERPA require an institution to keep after it discloses information in a student education record?	1156
Q 32.17.1	What should the institution include in its annual FERPA notice?	1157
Q 32.18	How are student health/medical records protected by institutions?	1158
Q 32.18.1	How does FERPA interact with HIPAA?	1158
Q 32.18.2	When are student records protected under HIPAA?	1159
Q 32.19	What does the Copyright Act protect?	1159
Q 32.19.1	How is a copyright created?	1160
Q 32.19.2	What benefits does a copyright holder enjoy?	1161
Q 32.20	Who owns the copyright in faculty-produced work?	1161

Table of Contents

Q 32.20.1	Are there any exceptions to the work-for-hire doctrine?	1162
Q 32.20.2	Can a faculty member use copyrighted materials without permission from the copyright owner?	1164
Q 32.21	What is "fair use," and does it apply to institutions of higher education?	1165
Q 32.22	Should an institution implement a copyright policy?	1166
Q 32.23	What exposure does an institution face if found liable for copyright infringement?	1167
Q 32.23.1	Can an institution be liable for copyright infringement based on the acts of its students or faculty?	1168
Q 32.23.2	Can an institution limit its exposure from students who use the institution's computer network to commit copyright infringement?	1169
Q 32.23.3	Does the DMCA address copyright infringement by faculty and graduate students?	1171
Q 32.24	Why should U.S. institutions of higher education be concerned with export controls?	1172
Q 32.24.1	What is an "export"?	1173
Q 32.24.2	What do export controls concerns related to the defense and high-technology sectors have to do with institutions of higher education?	1173
Q 32.24.3	Who is a "foreign student" for purposes of export controls?	1174
Q 32.24.4	Can an institution's treatment of foreign students differ from that of U.S. students?	1174
Q 32.25	What institution activities may fall under the export controls?	1175
Q 32.26	Is all information taught at universities subject to export controls?	1175
Q 32.26.1	What information qualifies as "publicly available" and thus not subject to export controls?	1175
Q 32.26.2	How is educational information subject to export controls?	1176
Q 32.27	Are the results of fundamental research subject to export controls?	1177
Q 32.27.1	How does an institution apply the fundamental research exception in practice?	1178
Q 32.27.2	What are the limitations on publication or dissemination of the research results?	1178
Q 32.27.3	What are some pitfalls to avoid in negotiating research grants or funding?	1179
Q 32.28	Can a U.S. university professor teach abroad?	1180
Q 32.29	Are there limitations on setting up a foreign campus?	1180

Q 32.30	How can an institution set up successful screening and compliance procedures?	1180
Q 32.31	What specific requirements pertaining to research sponsored by a federal grant or contract should institutions be aware of?	1182
Q 32.31.1	What are an institution's obligations regarding time and effort reporting?	1183
Q 32.31.2	... summer salary calculations and reporting?	1183
Q 32.31.3	... cost transfers?	1184
Q 32.31.4	... cost sharing?	1184
Q 32.31.5	... human-subject research?	1185
Q 32.31.6	... receiving American Recovery and Reinvestment Act funding?	1186
Q 32.31.7	... patentable inventions created with federal money?	1187
Q 32.32	How does False Claims Act liability affect institutions?	1188
Q 32.32.1	How does improper medical billing expose institutions to False Claims Act liability?	1189
Q 32.32.2	How do certification requirements regarding adherence to federal and state laws expose institutions to False Claims Act liability?	1190
Q 32.32.3	How has federally sponsored research exposed institutions to False Claims Act liability?	1192
Q 32.32.4	Are public institutions immune from claims under the False Claims Act?	1194
Q 32.33	How can an institution limit its exposure to False Claims Act liability?	1195

Chapter 33   Environmental Law 1217
Bonni F. Kaufman & Stacy Watson May

Q 33.1	How are environmental issues regulated in the United States?	1221
Q 33.2	What are the major federal environmental laws with general application to business operations that we need to be aware of and comply with?	1221
Q 33.3	What is the Resource Conservation and Recovery Act?	1222
Q 33.3.1	What is "hazardous waste"?	1222
Q 33.3.2	How does a generator properly manage and dispose of hazardous waste?	1223
Q 33.3.3	What are the reporting requirements for hazardous waste generators?	1223
Q 33.3.4	What are the allowances for hazardous waste storage?	1224

Table of Contents

Q 33.3.5	How are underground storage tanks (USTs) for hazardous waste regulated?	1224
Q 33.3.6	What am I required to do if I release hazardous waste?	1225
Q 33.3.7	Is used oil subject to RCRA regulation?	1226
Q 33.3.8	Is lead-based paint subject to RCRA regulation?	1226
Q 33.3.9	What are the penalties for RCRA violations?	1226
Q 33.4	What does CERCLA provide?	1227
Q 33.4.1	What are CERCLA's hazardous substance release reporting requirements?	1227
Q 33.4.2	How does CERCLA govern clean-up of property containing hazardous substances?	1228
Q 33.4.3	Who is subject to CERCLA liability for release of a hazardous substance?	1228
Q 33.4.4	Is anyone exempted from liability?	1229
Q 33.5	What is the Superfund Recycling Equity Act?	1229
Q 33.5.1	What is "recyclable material"?	1229
Q 33.5.2	What does the SREA consider "recycling"?	1229
Q 33.5.3	What are some defenses to CERCLA liability?	1230
Q 33.6	What is the EPCRA?	1231
Q 33.6.1	How does the EPCRA regulate hazardous chemicals?	1231
Q 33.6.2	What are the penalties for noncompliance with EPCRA?	1232
Q 33.7	What is the intent of the Clear Air Act?	1233
Q 33.7.1	What kinds of air pollutants does the CAA aim to clean up?	1233
Q 33.7.2	How does the CAA regulate criteria pollutants?	1233
Q 33.7.3	What are some of the ways the CAA regulates HAPs?	1234
Q 33.7.4	How does the CAA regulate greenhouse gas emissions?	1234
Q 33.7.5	What kinds of CAA reporting/compliance requirements should businesses be aware of?	1235
Q 33.7.6	What constitutes a violation of the CAA?	1237
Q 33.7.7	What are the penalties for CAA violations?	1237
Q 33.8	What is the aim of the Clean Water Act?	1237
Q 33.8.1	What kinds of pollutants are regulated by the CWA?	1237
Q 33.8.2	How does the CWA protect the nation's waters?	1238
Q 33.8.3	What are point source discharges?	1238
Q 33.8.4	What are nonpoint sources?	1238
Q 33.8.5	What is an NPDES permit required for?	1238

CORPORATE COMPLIANCE ANSWER BOOK 2011–12

Q 33.8.6	What are the requirements for a discharging facility to be issued an NPDES permit?	1238
Q 33.8.7	Which kinds of storm water discharges require an NPDES permit?	1239
Q 33.8.8	What kind of permits are required for municipal sewage treatment plants?	1240
Q 33.8.9	What other permits are required by the CWA?	1241
Q 33.8.10	What regulations should facilities dealing with oil be aware of?	1241
Q 33.8.11	What does the SPCC consider "oil"?	1241
Q 33.8.12	What must an SPCC plan include?	1242
Q 33.8.13	What other requirements do the SPCC regulations impose?	1243
Q 33.8.14	What are the penalties for CWA violations?	1243
Q 33.9	What is the intent of the Toxic Substances Control Act?	1244
Q 33.9.1	What substances does the TSCA address?	1244
Q 33.9.2	Are all substances not on the inventory of existing chemicals banned?	1245
Q 33.9.3	What reporting requirements does TSCA impose?	1245
Q 33.10	How is asbestos regulated?	1245
Q 33.11	How is lead-based paint regulated?	1246
Q 33.12	How are PCBs regulated?	1247
Q 33.12.1	What uses of PCB-containing materials/equipment are permitted?	1247
Q 33.12.2	What are some of the requirements for permitted uses of PCBs?	1247
Q 33.13	What are the penalties for violations of the TSCA?	1249
Q 33.14	What other federal regulations should businesses be aware of when considering environmental issues and compliance?	1249
Q 33.14.1	What are covered facilities required to do under CFATS?	1249
Q 33.14.2	How does DHS enforce these standards?	1250
Q 33.15	What other compliance obligations related to environmental issues should businesses be aware of?	1250
Q 33.15.1	What are Contingent Remediation Liabilities?	1250
Q 33.15.2	What kinds of environmental legal proceedings must be disclosed?	1251
Q 33.15.3	What are "Description of Business" disclosures?	1252
Q 33.15.4	What are MD&A disclosures?	1252
Q 33.15.5	What are "Conditional Asset Retirement Obligations" disclosures?	1252
Q 33.16	What does the SEC require companies to report with respect to the impact of climate change?	1253

Table of Contents

Chapter 34　Labor and Employment Law 1257
　　　　　　Mark E. Baker

Q 34.1　　What are an employer's obligations regarding documentation of an employee's legal authorization to work in the United States? 1260
　Q 34.1.1　What are the Form I-9 filing requirements? 1260
　Q 34.1.2　What are the consequences of failure to file? 1260
　Q 34.1.3　What federal laws/regulations governing employment background checks must an employer comply with? 1261
　Q 34.1.4　What does the FCRA require? 1261
Q 34.2　　What federal laws govern employment discrimination? 1262
Q 34.3　　What types of discrimination are prohibited? 1262
Q 34.4　　How does Title VII protect against discrimination? 1262
　Q 34.4.1　What is "disparate impact" discrimination? 1263
　Q 34.4.2　What is "association" discrimination? 1263
　Q 34.4.3　How must an employer protect an employee's rights regarding religion? 1264
　Q 34.4.4　What are the rules regarding a pregnant employee? 1264
　Q 34.4.5　What are indications of discrimination based on national origin? 1265
　Q 34.4.6　Can an employer insist that English be spoken in the workplace? 1265
Q 34.5　　What are an employer's compliance obligations regarding discrimination based on age? 1266
Q 34.6　　How is a disability protected in the workplace? 1266
　Q 34.6.1　What is the ADA's definition of "disability"? 1266
　Q 34.6.2　What qualifies a person to be protected under the ADA? 1267
　Q 34.6.3　How does ADA protection extend to an employee's family? 1267
　Q 34.6.4　How must an employer assist a disabled individual? 1267
　Q 34.6.5　What kind of standards can employers maintain for disabled employees? 1268
　Q 34.6.6　What compliance issues arise during the hiring process when disabled applicants are involved? 1268
　Q 34.6.7　What are the ADA's confidentiality requirements? 1269
Q 34.7　　What are the rules governing pay differences between men and women? 1269
　Q 34.7.1　What kinds of pay differences are allowed? 1269
Q 34.8　　What types of employment-related actions are subject to the discrimination prohibitions? 1270

CORPORATE COMPLIANCE ANSWER BOOK 2011–12

Q 34.9	What affirmative accommodation obligations are imposed by employment discrimination laws?	1270
Q 34.10	What written statements and policies should be adopted to help assure nondiscrimination compliance?	1271
Q 34.11	What notice requirements are imposed by employment discrimination laws?	1271
Q 34.12	What compliance issues are triggered by discrimination claims or other assertions of employee rights?	1272
Q 34.13	What types of harassment are prohibited?	1272
Q 34.13.1	What kinds of conduct constitute harassment?	1273
Q 34.13.2	What policies should be adopted to address harassment concerns?	1274
Q 34.13.3	Are there particular notice requirements that must be met to address harassment concerns?	1274
Q 34.13.4	What compliance concerns does the threat of retaliation raise?	1275
Q 34.14	What minimum wage and overtime requirements apply generally to employees?	1275
Q 34.14.1	Which employees and employers are subject to the minimum wage and overtime requirements?	1276
Q 34.14.2	Who is exempt from the minimum wage and overtime requirements?	1277
Q 34.14.3	What are the rules for application of the "white-collar" exemptions?	1277
Q 34.14.4	How must exempt employees be paid to ensure that they are paid on a "salary basis," as required for their exempt status?	1278
Q 34.14.5	Who qualifies for the "computer-related professionals" exemption?	1279
Q 34.14.6	Can "compensatory time" be provided in lieu of overtime pay?	1280
Q 34.14.7	What are compensable hours of work?	1280
Q 34.14.8	What policies should be adopted to assure compliance with wage/hour laws?	1281
Q 34.14.9	What notice requirements are imposed by wage/hour laws?	1281
Q 34.14.10	What other requirements should be considered?	1281
Q 34.15	What types of benefit programs are subject to federal regulation?	1282
Q 34.15.1	What does ERISA generally require?	1282
Q 34.15.2	What are the reporting requirements associated with employee benefit plans?	1283
Q 34.16	What are the HIPAA requirements?	1283

Table of Contents

Q 34.17	What are an employer's obligations regarding family and medical leave?	1283
Q 34.17.1	Who qualifies for FMLA leave?	1284
Q 34.17.2	When is FMLA leave available?	1284
Q 34.17.3	What qualifies as a "serious medical condition" under the FMLA?	1285
Q 34.17.4	Must a "serious medical condition" also qualify as a "disability" under the ADA?	1285
Q 34.17.5	Is a leave for the birth or adoption of a child only permitted for the mother?	1285
Q 34.17.6	How does an employee request FMLA leave?	1286
Q 34.17.7	Are there restrictions on how FMLA leave time may be taken?	1286
Q 34.17.8	What notice and medical documentation are required for FMLA leave?	1286
Q 34.17.9	What are the requirements pertaining to pay during FMLA leave?	1287
Q 34.17.10	What are the requirements pertaining to benefits during FMLA leave?	1287
Q 34.17.11	What are an employer's obligations to an employee returning from FMLA leave?	1287
Q 34.17.12	What leave rights does an employee caring for a sick or injured service member have?	1288
Q 34.18	What FMLA policies should employers adopt?	1288
Q 34.19	What statute governs military leave?	1289
Q 34.19.1	What notice requirements does the USERRA impose?	1289
Q 34.19.2	How must pay and benefits be handled for employees on military leave?	1289
Q 34.19.3	What requirements apply to reinstatement of employees returning from military leave?	1290
Q 34.20	What statute governs employees' medical insurance?	1290
Q 34.20.1	What are "qualifying events" under COBRA?	1291
Q 34.20.2	What are the notice requirements under COBRA?	1291
Q 34.21	What are the notice requirements for plant closings and layoffs?	1291
Q 34.21.1	What events trigger WARN requirements?	1291
Q 34.21.2	What notices must be given if a WARN trigger event occurs?	1292
Q 34.21.3	When must the notices be given?	1292
Q 34.22	When may polygraphs be used for employment-related purposes?	1292
Q 34.22.1	What limitations apply to the use of polygraphs?	1293
Q 34.23	What employee activity is protected under unionization?	1293

Q 34.23.1	What legal obligations apply when employees try to join or form a union?	1294
Q 34.23.2	What are the compliance implications of employees unionizing?	1294
Q 34.23.3	What are the compliance implications of a collective bargaining agreement?	1294
Q 34.24	What laws govern employment issues with government contractors?	1295
Q 34.24.1	How must employers comply with requirements regarding identifying under-utilization of women or minorities?	1295
Q 34.24.2	What types of prevailing wage requirements might apply?	1296

Chapter 35   Consumer Product Safety Act 1299
Charles E. Joern, Jr.

Q 35.1	How are consumer products regulated in the United States?	1301
Q 35.2	What is a "consumer product" for regulatory purposes?	1301
Q 35.3	What businesses are covered by consumer product safety laws?	1302
Q 35.4	What consumer product safety laws does the Commission enforce?	1302
Q 35.5	How important is consumer product safety law compliance?	1302
Q 35.6	What constitutes a violation under the CPSA?	1303
Q 35.7	What requirements must a business meet to comply with the CPSA?	1304
Q 35.7.1	What does it mean for a business to "comply"?	1304
Q 35.7.2	What are a business's specific testing and certification obligations?	1304
Q 35.7.3	What are a business's reporting obligations?	1304
Q 35.8	Does the Commission certify that products comply with applicable product safety standards?	1305
Q 35.9	How does a business know what product safety standards apply to its product?	1305
Q 35.9.1	How do we determine if our product is a "consumer product" under the jurisdiction of the Commission?	1305
Q 35.9.2	Once we determine that our product is a consumer product, how do we decide what specific standards apply?	1306

Table of Contents

Q 35.9.3	What sources of information can we use to determine what regulations apply to our product?	1306
Q 35.10	What is an "unregulated" product?	1307
Q 35.11	What are voluntary standards?	1307
Q 35.12	Is the Commission's treatment of children's products different from its treatment of non-children's products?	1308
Q 35.13	What testing and certification requirements apply to our product?	1309
Q 35.13.1	Are all businesses required to issue certifications?	1309
Q 35.13.2	What is a "reasonable testing program" as required for a General Conformity Certification?	1310
Q 35.14	Currently, do all consumer products have to be tested and certified?	1311
Q 35.14.1	The stay is applicable to what products?	1311
Q 35.14.2	May a company rely on testing of component parts in order to fulfill compliance requirements?	1312
Q 35.15	What reporting requirements should a business be aware of?	1312
Q 35.15.1	What type of information can trigger a report?	1313
Q 35.16	What is a "substantial product hazard"?	1313
Q 35.17	What should we do if we are uncertain if there is an actual product safety problem with a product?	1314
Q 35.18	How soon must a company report a problem?	1314
Q 35.19	What should a firm do to ensure compliance with CPSA reporting obligations?	1315
Q 35.19.1	If a lawsuit is filed against my company, do I have to file a report with the Commission?	1315
Q 35.19.2	If I report a suspected problem, will my business have to recall the product?	1315
Q 35.20	When does a company have to recall a product?	1315
Q 35.20.1	Under what circumstances does the Commission decide that a recall is not necessary at all?	1316
Q 35.21	What is a fast-track recall?	1316
Q 35.22	What information must be included in recall notices?	1316
Q 35.23	Is there a database of consumer product safety complaints?	1317
Q 35.23.1	Does the database affect businesses?	1317
Q 35.23.2	Is a company notified of reports concerning its products?	1317
Q 35.23.3	Can a company submit anything to the database?	1318
Q 35.24	What aspects of the CPSA are expected to change?	1318

Index 1325

20

Healthcare Organizations and Providers

*Lisa Sterneck Katz, Reetu Dua & Jonathan E. Anderman**

Healthcare organizations are strongly encouraged, if not required in many cases, to have an effective corporate compliance and ethics program.[1] Operating in one of the most heavily regulated and scrutinized industries, healthcare organizations have a significant risk of violating one of the many laws or regulations that pertain to the delivery and payment of healthcare items and services.

Combating healthcare fraud and abuse has been and continues to be a top priority of the federal government, and over the past few years state governments have also become increasingly sophisticated in detecting wrongdoing and improper behavior in healthcare organizations. This enforcement initiative essentially began in 1993 under then-Attorney General Janet Reno. It was enhanced by passage of the Health

---

* The authors would like to acknowledge Christopher A. Myers, Suzanne M. Foster, and Kwamina Thomas Williford for their contributions to this chapter.

Insurance Portability and Accountability Act of 1996, which gave the Department of Health and Human Services' Office of Inspector General (OIG) and the U.S. Department of Justice (DOJ) investigational funding and authority to increase penalties for healthcare fraud and abuse.[2]

Today, the consequences of a healthcare institution committing fraud or abuse are severe, but the potential liability and penalties can be mitigated by having in place an effective compliance and ethics program. This chapter provides guidance on corporate compliance and ethics programs in healthcare organizations, key legal risk areas, and a brief overview of some of the pertinent statutes and regulations.

Healthcare Compliance and Ethics Programs 642
    The Basics 642
    Creating an Effective Program... 644
    OIG Guidance... 644
Investigations of Healthcare Industry Violations 648
    The Role of the OIG.. 648
    Corporate Integrity Agreements and Certification of
        Compliance Agreements.. 649
    Increasing Enforcement Initiatives 650
Key Legal Risk Areas for Healthcare Organizations............ 652
    Understanding the Reimbursement Framework 652
    Medicare... 652
    Medicaid... 653
    Employee Benefit Programs... 653
Pertinent Statutes and Regulations 654
    False Claims Act 654
    Anti-Kickback Statute 657
    The "Stark Law" 661
    HIPAA... 664
    EMTALA 665
    Deficit Reduction Act 666
    HITECH Act 669

Healthcare Organizations and Providers

Acronyms, initialisms, and abbreviations used in this chapter:

AKS	anti-kickback statute
ARRA	American Recovery and Reinvestment Act
CCA	Certification of Compliance Agreement
CIA	Corporate Integrity Agreement
CMS	Centers for Medicare and Medicaid Services
COBRA	Consolidated Omnibus Budget Reconciliation Act
DFRR	Disclosure of Financial Relationships Report
DHS	designated health services
DRA	Deficit Reduction Act
DRG	diagnosis-related group
EHR	electronic health records
EMTALA	Emergency Medical Treatment and Active Labor Act
FCA	False Claims Act
FERA	Fraud Enforcement and Recovery Act
HIPAA	Health Insurance Portability and Accountability Act
HITECH	Health Information Technology for Economic and Clinical Health (Act)
JCAHO	Joint Commission on the Accreditation of Healthcare Organizations
MA	Medicare Advantage
MA-PDP	Medicare Advantage Drug Plan
OIG	Office of Inspector General
ONC	Office of the National Coordinator of Health Information Technology
PDP	prescription drug plan
PPACA	Patient Protection and Affordable Care Act

Healthcare Compliance and Ethics Programs

The Basics

Q 20.1 Why do healthcare organizations need compliance and ethics programs?

Increasingly, the government is enacting laws and regulations that require healthcare organizations to have a compliance and ethics program.[3] Companies with effective compliance programs conduct timely audits and continuously monitor policies and behavior to ensure legal requirements are satisfied. Even where not mandated, however, a compliance and ethics program is a best practice and is expected by enforcement authorities. Compliance programs have even become a matter of interest to investors, insurers, business associates, and patients.

Q 20.1.1 Are there financial incentives for having an effective compliance program?

When standards for appropriate employee conduct are established, a company not only may prevent fraud and abuse, but also may ultimately experience fewer costly investigations and lawsuits. An effective compliance and ethics program can serve as a mitigating factor when determining sanctions, fines, and penalties in the unfortunate event that something goes wrong in your organization.

Under the Federal Sentencing Guidelines, a company that has violated the law may have an opportunity for reduced fines and other sanctions if the organization has in place an effective program to detect, prevent, and report misconduct and illegal activity.[4]

The government is not alone in its battle against fraud and abuse. By creating incentives for whistleblowers, including a generous reward when the government collects at least $100 as a result of the reporting, the government has established a system in which healthcare organizations' own employees are motivated to detect and report fraud, abuse, and waste.[5] This should create incentives on the part of healthcare organizations to understand the potential risk areas within their organization and then address them openly and transparently.

Q 20.1.2 Is having an effective compliance program a guarantee that we won't be investigated?

Even ethical healthcare companies can find themselves the subject of government investigations, either at the initiative of the government or as the result of allegations made by a whistleblower. These types of investigations can be costly.

> **CASE STUDY:** *In re Columbia/HCA Healthcare Corp. Qui Tam Litigation*[6]
>
> Thirty individual cases were consolidated and brought against the Columbia/HCA hospital company alleging cost report fraud, physician kickbacks, and other wrongdoing. The hospital settled a portion of the claims for $745 million in August 2001 and the remainder for $620 million in 2003. Over the past several years, there have been many multi-million-dollar settlements and sanctions against healthcare organizations. In most cases, these companies were not "bad companies"—they were simply examples of how "good companies" can run afoul of often-complicated laws and regulations.

Q 20.1.3 How can I anticipate federal government enforcement actions?

The best way to anticipate federal government enforcement actions is to become familiar with the OIG publications that discuss areas of concern to the federal government's monitoring of healthcare organizations and enforcement of fraud and abuse regulations.[7] (These publications are discussed below.) In addition, it is important to keep track of government enforcement actions in relevant segments of the industry. Such action against one company is often a precursor to similar actions against other organizations in the same industry segment.

Creating an Effective Program

Q 20.2 How do I begin to create a compliance and ethics program?

The OIG has published compliance program guidance materials that provide many segments of the healthcare industry a road map indicating especially risky areas likely to be heavily scrutinized by the government and emphasizing areas that should be closely monitored.[8] While the OIG compliance guidance is not legally binding, healthcare organizations would be prudent to follow it to reduce potential liability and sanctions. For industry segments not specifically covered, the OIG guidance also provides general advice on the development and implantation of effective compliance programs.

For more detailed information on the basic elements of a compliance program, please refer to chapter 2, "Implementation of Effective Compliance and Ethics Programs and the Federal Sentencing Guidelines."

OIG Guidance

Q 20.2.1 What industries does the OIG guidance cover?

- Hospitals
- Pharmaceutical manufacturers
- Ambulance industry
- Individual and small group physician practices
- Nursing facilities
- Medicare Advantage organizations
- Hospices
- Durable medical equipment, prosthetics, orthotics, and supply industry
- Third-party medical billing companies
- Home health agencies
- Clinical laboratories
- Recipients of certain government research grants

Q 20.2.2 What kind of resources/guidance does the OIG offer that might be of value?

The OIG publishes various guidance materials to advise and educate the healthcare industry of potential areas of fraud and abuse that the OIG is targeting or monitoring. The publications include, among others:

- special fraud alerts;
- special advisory bulletins;
- compliance guidance;
- advisory opinions;
- lists of recent enforcement actions; and
- annual work plans.

The OIG's annual work plan, usually issued every October, is a must-have publication. It sets forth in detail the areas that the OIG will be focusing on in the upcoming year. The work plan addresses areas of concern for hospitals, nursing homes, physician practices, home health agencies, and other healthcare providers, as well as pharmaceutical and device companies.

Guidance materials can be found on the OIG's website,[9] and anyone responsible for overseeing a healthcare organization's compliance program should frequently visit that site.

Q 20.2.3 Is the OIG guidance mandatory?

The guidance is not mandatory in and of itself. But the guidance offered by the OIG can serve as a blueprint for healthcare providers concerned with identifying the risk areas that are paramount in the eyes of the OIG. In addition, the OIG guidance expects that healthcare companies will tailor their compliance programs to their particular circumstances, resources and size and, in fact, frequently suggests practical and cost-effective compliance solutions for smaller healthcare practices (*e.g.*, in its guidance for individual and small group physician practices, the OIG suggests that smaller practices could share one compliance officer, given certain circumstances).[10]

Q 20.3 What makes a compliance program effective?

An effective compliance program is one that monitors and addresses the risks of the particular healthcare organization. It promotes a culture of compliance and ethics among its workforce. It is operational, as opposed to merely a collection of documents in a binder. One of the best illustrations of an effective compliance program is when employees are asked whether the company has such a program and they respond, "Yes!"

The Federal Sentencing Guidelines state that two fundamental components of an effective compliance program are:

- due diligence to prevent and detect inappropriate conduct; and
- an organizational culture that encourages ethical conduct and a commitment to compliance with the law.[11]

Q 20.3.1 What specific things does an effective compliance program need?

The Sentencing Guidelines provide clear references for the general components of an effective compliance and ethics program. The U.S. Sentencing Commission regularly makes adjustments to its guidance. (For a more detailed discussion of this guidance and the recent changes to it, refer to chapter 2, "Implementation of Effective Compliance and Ethics Programs and the Federal Sentencing Guidelines.") The OIG compliance guidance for specific healthcare industry segments is not as regularly updated; however, the OIG guidance does identify particular compliance risk areas that should be addressed in each industry sub-group. Therefore, both resources should be consulted regularly for the most current guidance.

The OIG guidance typically includes seven basic elements of an effective compliance program:

1. *Establishing written standards of conduct, policies, and procedures.* Every organization should have written standards that clearly state its commitment to compliance with all applicable federal and state statutory, regulatory, and other legal requirements related to a comprehensive program to detect, prevent, and control fraud, abuse, and waste. To help

foster a culture of compliance within an organization, senior management should communicate a strong and explicit commitment to ethical corporate behavior. The written standards should be updated as necessary to incorporate any changes in applicable laws and regulations, and should be made available to the medical staff, contractors, business associates, and other entities that perform work on the organization's behalf. All representatives should receive the written standards at the time of hire, when they are updated, and annually thereafter. The written standards should include a commitment to comply with:
   a. *Code of conduct and ethics.* A company's Code should be easily comprehensible, approved, and adopted by the organization's governing body, and reviewed periodically and validated by senior management.
   b. *Policies and procedures.* The policies and procedures should help reduce the prospect of fraudulent, wasteful, and abusive activity by identifying and responding to day-to-day risks. They should be readily available to employees and need to be reviewed and revised as changes in the law or practices occur, but at least on a regular basis.
2. *Designation of a compliance officer and compliance committee.* A high-ranking member of management should be appointed as compliance officer and given the appropriate resources necessary to manage the compliance function. The compliance officer is sometimes supported by a compliance committee that includes individuals with a variety of backgrounds and roles within the organization and reflects the size of the organization and the organization's resources.
3. *Training and education of leaders and employees.* Compliance training and education should be given to all employees at least annually and more often to individuals in higher-risk roles such as billing and human resources. The content of the training should be tailored to the individuals receiving the training. All new employees should receive training on compliance-related topics, the Code of Conduct, applicable policies and procedures, and reporting options. The board of directors (or equivalent) should also be trained, be

involved in the oversight of the program, and ensure that it receives appropriate resources.

4. *Effective lines of communication between compliance staff and personnel.* The compliance officer must have effective lines of communication with the organization's senior management team, employees, contractors, agents, directors, and members of the compliance committee. The compliance officer should also have a system in place to receive, record, and respond to compliance questions or reports of potential noncompliance while maintaining confidentiality, allowing anonymity if desired (*e.g.*, through telephone hotlines or mail drops), and ensuring non-retaliation against callers.
5. *Enforcement of standards through well-publicized disciplinary guidelines.* Consistent and appropriate sanctions should be enforced for noncompliant actions, with flexibility for aggravating or mitigating circumstances.
6. *Monitoring and auditing the compliance program.* Organizations should have their own work plan or auditing plan that identifies potential areas of risk for the organization and defines ways in which they will audit or monitor for violations in those identified areas.
7. *Methods of corrective action and response to violations.*[12] The organization should have a process for proper response to violations and a method for developing corrective action plans.

As with any program, healthcare industry programs should be based on the results of regularly conducted risk assessments.

Investigations of Healthcare Industry Violations

The Role of the OIG

Q 20.3.2   What is the OIG's role in investigations of healthcare organizations and providers?

The Office of Inspector General of the Department of Health and Human Services is often heavily involved in investigations of healthcare industry organizations. Its agents frequently work with DOJ lawyers and investigators in both civil and criminal investigations involving healthcare fraud and abuse statutes. The DOJ will investigate and negotiate any settlement of potential or actual litigation under the civil False Claims Act or any criminal statutes. The OIG has separate authority to impose civil monetary penalties for fraud and abuse violations. It also has authority to order suspension or exclusion from participation in federal healthcare programs of healthcare industry organizations found to be in violation of healthcare industry regulatory requirements. Frequently, as part of the settlement of an investigation, the OIG will require implementation of specific compliance program activities in the form of Corporate Integrity Agreements and Certification of Compliance Agreements.

Corporate Integrity Agreements and Certification of Compliance Agreements

Q 20.3.3 What are Corporate Integrity Agreements and Certification of Compliance Agreements?

When the OIG brings, or threatens to bring, an enforcement action, the resolution often includes one of these agreements. A provider or entity consents to these obligations as part of an administrative settlement with the government. In return, the OIG agrees not to seek an exclusion of that healthcare provider or entity from participation in Medicare, Medicaid, and other federal healthcare programs.[13]

The typical term of a Corporate Integrity Agreement (CIA) is five years. The more comprehensive CIAs include requirements to:

(1) hire a compliance officer/appoint a compliance committee;
(2) develop written standards and policies;
(3) implement a comprehensive employee training program;
(4) review claims submitted to federal healthcare programs;
(5) establish a confidential disclosure program;
(6) restrict employment of ineligible persons; and
(7) submit a variety of reports to the OIG.

While many CIAs have common elements, each agreement addresses the specific facts of the conduct at issue and is tailored to the existing capabilities of the provider. The integrity agreements often attempt to accommodate and recognize many of the elements of pre-existing voluntary compliance programs.

More and more frequently, CIAs include a requirement that the organization retain (and pay) a corporate monitor. Corporate monitors are frequently lawyers or audit firms with experience as federal prosecutors or in providing audit/consulting services in the industry. They oversee and report to the OIG (and often the DOJ) on the organization's compliance with the CIA. As might be expected, corporate monitors can be very expensive. Sometimes, the OIG will agree to eliminate the monitor requirement from a CIA if the organization's existing compliance program is sufficiently robust, particularly if the CIA resulted from a voluntary disclosure by the organization.

The Certification of Compliance Agreement (CCA) is an alternative to a CIA and is thought of as less daunting (and usually less expensive for the company) than a CIA. The relevant considerations for whether an entity may be permitted to enter into a CCA instead of a comprehensive CIA include those set forth in the November 20, 2001 Open Letter to Health Care Providers. The terms of a CCA include a requirement that the entity maintain its existing compliance program, as described in a declaration that is attached to the CCA. In addition, the entity is required to agree to certain compliance obligations that mirror those found in a comprehensive CIA, including reporting overpayments, reportable events, and ongoing investigations and legal proceedings to the OIG, and providing annual reports regarding the entity's compliance activities to the OIG during the term of the CCA.

Increasing Enforcement Initiatives

Q 20.3.4 What new enforcement initiatives have come out of the current administration and the Congress?

The current administration and Congress have made it clear that they are committed to increasing enforcement activities through monetary support, joint initiatives, and increased statutory and regulatory oversight. Various initiatives, projects, and legislation exemplify this commitment. A small sample includes:

- joint enforcement activities between enforcement agencies
- formation of the HEAT Strike Force[14]

- passage of the Fraud Enforcement and Recovery Act of 2009[15] and the American Recovery and Reinvestment Act of 2009[16]
- record-high settlements with healthcare entities
- increased funding for fraud enforcement activities

Q 20.3.5 What additional enforcement provisions were included in healthcare reform legislation?

Although the Patient Protection and Affordable Care Act, as amended by the Health Care Education Reconciliation Act (collectively the Healthcare Reform Law),[17] has been enacted into law, many of its precise requirements are still uncertain due to extensive impending supplemental regulations and questions regarding if and when specific provisions would be enforced. However, even with these uncertainties, the legislation clearly includes significant compliance, anti-fraud, and enforcement measures. Members of the healthcare industry would be wise to begin thinking of and implementing systems that will allow them to anticipate and address this next wave of enforcement efforts.

Summarized below are just some of the major anti-fraud, waste, and abuse measures that have been included in Healthcare Reform Law:

- mandatory compliance programs for some healthcare entities;
- increased fraud and abuse funding;
- Stark changes;
- lower intent standards for violations of AKS and AKS violations serving as explicit basis for FCA suits;
- mandatory return of overpayments;
- ban on new physician-owned hospitals;
- increased integrity data access and sharing;
- enhanced penalties;
- enhanced government auditing;
- greater transparency in physician-industry relationships;
- new federal healthcare fraud provisions;
- greater coordination between enforcement agencies; and
- uniform reporting.

Key Legal Risk Areas for Healthcare Organizations

Q 20.4 In what areas might healthcare violations/investigations typically occur?

Often, statutory or regulatory violations are dependent upon the payment source involved in the alleged violation. Basically there are three categories of payers:

- government-sponsored programs,
- private or commercial insurance companies, or
- the patients themselves directly.

A basic understanding of how healthcare services and items are reimbursed is critical for compliance officers and general counsels of healthcare organizations.

Understanding the Reimbursement Framework

Q 20.5 What are the government sources of payment for healthcare services?

Medicare, Medicaid, and Employee Benefit Programs.

Medicare

Q 20.5.1 What is Medicare?

Medicare has four parts.[18] Part A deals with hospitals. It generally covers expenses associated with inpatient hospitalization. Part A is funded through payroll taxes.

Part B is a voluntary and supplementary component of Medicare. It covers payments for physician services and other outpatient diagnostic and therapeutic services not covered under Part A, as well as certain drugs, durable medical equipment, and other supplies. Part B is funded by monthly premiums charged to beneficiaries.

Medicare Part C consists of several types of managed care plans and is relatively new. As part of the Balanced Budget Act of 1997, Medicare + Choice (Medicare Part C) was an alternative to Parts A and B. Those who were enrolled in both parts can now select a "Coordinated Care Plan" through which they receive an array of services and benefits, including prescription drugs. These are now called Medicare Advantage Plans (MA Plans).

Medicare Part D was enacted even more recently than Part C, and it deals with prescription drug coverage. Enacted in 2003, Medicare Part D builds upon managed-care principles. Beneficiaries can now receive outpatient prescription drug benefits through one of two alternatives: stand-alone prescription drug plans (PDPs) or Medicare Advantage Prescription Drug Plans (MA-PDPs). For either option, enrollees select from among many options dealing with various levels of benefits and premium payment requirements. Part D contains subsidies for low-income, dual-eligible populations who have previously received benefits from the Medicaid program.

Medicaid

Q 20.5.2 What is Medicaid?

Medicaid is another important government healthcare payor.[19] Medicaid eligibility is based on an individual's financial need. There are different types of coverage for low-income families with children or long-term care. It is a federal and state government-funded program. Each state has its own Medicaid program with its own rules for payment and participation. The states file their plans with CMS with a list of covered items.

Employee Benefit Programs

Q 20.5.3 What are employee benefit programs?

There are also several federal employee health benefit programs.[20] Depending on the type of healthcare entity with which one works, military health benefit programs (10 U.S.C. § 16201) and veteran's health benefit programs (38 U.S.C. § 1705) may be relevant and require you to seek additional guidance on their specific program requirements.

Pertinent Statutes and Regulations

Q 20.6 Which statutes and regulations govern the areas of healthcare typically subject to government investigation and enforcement?

Although not all can be discussed here, the relevant healthcare statutes and regulations that typically apply to almost every healthcare organization include:

- the False Claims Act
- the anti-kickback statute
- the Physician Self Referral Act (or "Stark" statute)
- the Health Insurance Portability and Accountability Act and regulations (HIPAA)
- the Emergency Medical Treatment and Active Labor Act (EMTALA)
- the Deficit Reduction Act (DRA)
- the Health Information Technology for Economic and Clinical Health (HITECH) Act
- the Patient Protection and Affordable Care Act (PPACA), as amended by the Health Care Education Reconciliation Act (HCERA) (collectively the Healthcare Reform Law)

These must be understood and considered when developing and overseeing a compliance program.

False Claims Act[21]

Q 20.7 What is the False Claims Act?

The False Claims Act (FCA)[22] prohibits any person from knowingly presenting, making, or using, or causing to be presented, made, or used, a false or fraudulent claim for payment by the U.S. government. The FCA also prohibits the making of a false record or statement to get a false or fraudulent claim paid. In addition, FERA recently amended the FCA to prohibit knowingly or improperly avoiding an obligation to pay (that is, retaining an overpayment) and to eliminate the requirement that a claim be presented to a governmental official. The government has used the FCA as the legal basis to bring a wide variety of healthcare enforcement cases and, as a result, has recovered enormous amounts of money.

In addition to the federal FCA, many states have passed state-specific versions of the FCA. Several of these state laws were passed in response to the DRA and its associated requirements.[23] Subsequently, states have increased enforcement activities and are now more frequently using these state antifraud laws as a basis for enforcement actions at the state level. (For a more detailed discussion of the specifics of the False Claims Act, see chapter 11, The False Claims Act.)

Q 20.7.1   What constitutes a violation of the FCA?

An organization or person can be liable under the FCA by violating one of its provisions "knowingly." In the context of the FCA, this means that the organization or person, with respect to claims or to information submitted in support of claims:

(1)   has actual knowledge of the falsity of the claim or information;
(2)   acts in deliberate ignorance of the truth or falsity of the claim or information; or
(3)   acts in reckless disregard of the truth or falsity of the claim or information.[24]

No proof of specific intent to defraud is required. However, innocent mistakes and negligence are not offenses under the Act. "Something beyond mere negligence, but falling short of specific intent, must be shown for liability to attach."[25] But the FERA changes have altered the content, liability, and interpretation of various provisions of the FCA, and it is not entirely clear how these will affect future enforcement actions.

Q 20.7.2   What are some risk areas under the FCA particular to healthcare entities?

The following inventory of risk areas that commonly give rise to scrutiny under the FCA, while by no means exhaustive, demonstrates the breadth of the False Claims Act:

• Upcoding, which occurs when a healthcare provider bills the government for a procedure that pays more than the

service actually performed would cost if coded properly. This is one area where healthcare organizations can easily put in place procedures (*i.e.*, audits and reviews) to ensure that upcoding is not occurring.
- Submitting claims for medically unnecessary services or services that do not meet quality of care standards.
- Failure to follow the "same-day rule," which means all outpatient services provided to a patient on the same day at the same hospital should be included on same claim.
- Violating Medicare's post-acute-care transfer policy in order to receive full DRG payment.
- Submitting claims for incorrectly designated "provider-based" entities.
- Retention of overpayments and other payments later discovered to have been in error (the extent of these risks is uncertain).
- For Medicare Advantage organizations, there are significant enforcement risks for failure to monitor carefully and ensure the accuracy of the "risk scoring" process by which physician diagnosis codes are converted into increased or decreased payment rates depending on how "sick" the beneficiary population is.
- Business relationships between healthcare providers and manufacturers of healthcare products.
- Transactions between healthcare-related entities.

Any organization that bills the government for services or items should have as part of its compliance program an auditing and monitoring component that includes having a sample of the organization's claims reviewed by a certified coder.

Along with complying with payment and coding rules, billing for services that lack the appropriate quality of care have been viewed as false claims by the government. Therefore, healthcare organizations should develop their own quality of care protocols in addition to compliance with JCAHO or state accreditation standards.[26]

Anti-Kickback Statute

Q 20.8 What is the federal anti-kickback statute?

The federal anti-kickback statute (AKS) prohibits any individual or entity from knowingly and willfully soliciting or receiving, or offering or paying any form of remuneration, either directly or indirectly, in cash or in kind, to induce the referral or recommendation for a referral of business covered by a federal healthcare program.[27] Specifically, it states:

> Whoever *knowingly and willfully* offers or pays [or solicits or receives] any remuneration (including any kickback, bribe, or rebate) directly or indirectly, overtly or covertly, in cash or in kind to (or from) any person to induce such person to refer an individual to a person for the furnishing or arranging for the furnishing of any item or service for which payment may be made in whole or in part under a federal health care program, or to purchase, lease, order, or arrange for or recommend purchasing, leasing, or ordering any good, facility, service, or item for which payment may be made in whole or in part under a Federal health care program, shall be guilty of a felony.[28]

Q 20.8.1 What does the federal anti-kickback statute mean by "remuneration"?

Remuneration is defined broadly in the statute to include the transfer of anything of value, including any kickback, bribe, or rebate, in cash or in kind, overtly or covertly.[29] It has come to mean virtually anything that can be viewed as "of value" to the person to whom it has been offered or given. In addition to money, it can include things as broadly disparate as meals, entertainment, travel, lodging, free personal or business services, performance of tasks that are normally done by the intended recipient of the kickback, and many other things limited only by the imaginations of the giver and receiver.

Q 20.8.2 How is "knowing and willfully" defined?

Only "knowing and willful" violations trigger liability under the statute.[30] The majority of the courts that have looked at this issue have applied a general criminal intent standard.[31] In other words, it is not necessary that the defendant have the specific intent to violate the AKS. Rather, he or she needs only to have intended to engage in the prohibited conduct with the general knowledge that it was unlawful.[32]

> **CASE STUDY:** *Bryan v. United States*[33]
>
> The Supreme Court has not interpreted the words "knowingly and willfully" in the context of the anti-kickback statute. Interpreting the same words as used in another criminal statute, the Supreme Court in *Bryan v. United States* concluded that an individual acts willfully when he or she acts with knowledge that his or her conduct is unlawful.[34] The Court held that as "a general matter, when used in the criminal context, a 'willful' act is one undertaken for a 'bad purpose.'"[35]

Q 20.8.3 What if there are other good purposes for the arrangement?

This is often the case. However, the OIG has adopted the "one purpose" standard as the test in its advisory opinions.[36] Under this test, if any one purpose of a transaction is to induce Medicare or Medicaid referrals, the position of the OIG is that the AKS is violated.[37] Similarly, in its 1999 "General Comments" to the 1999 Final Safe Harbor Regulations, the OIG states: "Payment practices that do not fully comply with a safe harbor may still be lawful if *no purpose* of the payment practice is to induce referrals of Federal health care program business."[38]

DOJ also uses the "one purpose" concept in analyzing potential AKS violations, relying on the Third Circuit decision in *United States v. Greber*,[39] that the AKS is violated "if one purpose of the payment was to induce future referrals...."

Q 20.8.4 What are the penalties for violating the AKS?

A violation of the AKS is a felony punishable by a maximum fine of $25,000 and imprisonment of up to five years. The OIG may also initiate administrative proceedings to exclude violators from participation in federal and state healthcare programs.[40] This means that the healthcare entity or provider is no longer eligible to bill a federal healthcare program, which can be detrimental, or even catastrophic, to almost every healthcare provider. In addition, the OIG may seek administrative civil monetary penalties of up to $50,000 per violation and damages up to triple the amount of the illegal remuneration.[41]

In addition to the penalties and sanctions listed above, a violation of the AKS is often viewed as triggering a violation of the False Claims Act. This occurs when a claim is submitted to a federal program for reimbursement but the claim is the result of a transaction that is in violation of the AKS. As a result, the claim is not appropriate and becomes a "false claim."[42] A violation of the False Claims Act potentially subjects the party to criminal and civil penalties, civil fines and treble damages, in addition to any sanctions imposed under the AKS or under the exclusion and civil penalty provisions of the OIG.

Q 20.8.5 Are there exceptions to the AKS?

The AKS includes three statutory exceptions:

- payments to bona fide employees;
- certain discounts; and
- specific practices related to group purchasing organizations.[43]

The statute further authorizes the Secretary of the Department of Health and Human Services to promulgate safe harbor regulations permitting certain types of specified payment practices.

Q 20.8.6 What are AKS safe harbors?

The safe harbor regulations specify arrangements that *will not* be subject to prosecution, civil penalties, or exclusion from the Medicare or Medicaid programs, even though they might present technical violations of the AKS. The safe harbor regulations *do not* expand the scope of the statute. Rather they carve out certain types of transactions that the OIG considers to present no more than a minimal risk of fraud and abuse and, therefore, that it will not subject to prosecution or civil remedies.[44] In addition to the current safe harbors, the OIG is now soliciting comment on additional potential safe harbors.

Q 20.8.7   How does a business arrangement qualify for safe-harbor protection?

For a business arrangement to enjoy the protection of a safe harbor, the arrangement must comply with every condition of the safe harbor. The failure to meet a safe-harbor requirement does not mean that an arrangement necessarily is illegal.[45] Rather, enforcement authorities look to a number of factors to determine whether there is an improper link between a particular payment and referrals of federal healthcare program business. The precise factors vary, depending on the circumstances and the type of arrangement. Generally, however, enforcement authorities look to whether the payments are fair market value for items or services that the recipient truly needs and that actually are delivered or rendered in a quantity and in a fashion that would be commercially reasonable in the absence of any referrals between the parties.

In order to be sure that an arrangement falling outside of a safe harbor would not be subject to AKS enforcement, entities may seek an advisory opinion from the OIG.[46]

The requirements of the safe harbors are often difficult to meet. For this reason and because of the broad reach of the statutory language, many arrangements fall into a gray area. The OIG has acknowledged as much:

> [T]he arrangement may violate the statute in a less serious manner, although not be in compliance with a safe harbor provision. Here there is no way to predict the degree of risk. Rather, the degree of the risk depends on an evaluation of the many factors which are part of the decision-making process regarding case selection for investigation and prosecution. Certainly, in many (but not necessarily all) instances, prosecutorial discretion would be exercised not to pursue cases where the participants appear to have acted in a genuine good-faith attempt to comply with the terms of a safe harbor, but for reasons beyond their control are not in compliance with the terms of that safe harbor. In other instances, there may not even be applicable safe harbor, but the arrangement may appear innocuous. But in other instances, we will want to take appropriate action.

> We do not believe the Medicare and Medicaid programs would be properly served if we assured protection in all instances of "substantial compliance," "technical violations," or "de minimis payments."[47]

To add to the confusion, it also is conceivable that an arrangement could facially comply with a safe harbor and yet not be exempt from prosecution. This could occur if the OIG determined that the arrangement is a mere "sham." For example, a consulting agreement could be structured to comply with the personal services safe harbor.[48] However, if the consultant in fact performs no services (or services valued at substantially less than the contract payments), the arrangement may violate the AKS even though it complies technically with the safe harbor.

Q 20.8.8 What is an OIG advisory opinion?

In addition to creating the opportunity for safe harbors, Congress also created a vehicle to obtain an advisory opinion from the OIG regarding the application of the AKS to a specific set of facts. Instructions for obtaining an advisory opinion from OIG are available at the OIG website.[49] Generally speaking, a requestor must comply with numerous technical requirements, pay at least $250, provide a detailed description of the facts and issues presented, and provide a signed certification attesting to the veracity of the facts set forth and the intent of the requestor.[50]

An advisory opinion expressing that the OIG would not impose sanctions in connection with a proposed transaction may be used to stop any future attempt to impose AKS liability. It must be noted, however, that advisory opinions are not binding on any party other than the requestor. Nonetheless, they may be viewed as substantial sources of guidance to other actors in the industry.

The "Stark Law"

Q 20.9 What are the Stark rules and regulations?

The Physician Self-Referral Act, known as the "Stark law" (42 U.S.C. § 1395nn), prohibits a physician from referring Medicare or Medicaid patients for certain health-related services, which are defined as designated health services (DHS), to an entity with which the physician (or immediate family member) has a financial relationship. The law prohibits an entity from processing a claim to Medicare or to any other person or other entity for DHS provided under a prohibited referral. No Medicare payment may be made for DHS rendered as a result of a prohibited referral, and an entity must timely refund any amounts collected for DHS performed under a prohibited referral. Further, CMS continues to examine arrangements that may appear to be a means of skirting the Stark law. Documentation that may be necessary to establish that a financial relationship with a referring physician satisfies an applicable Stark exception should be retained in the event that CMS denies a claim for DHS based on a prohibited referral, as it will be necessary for the DHS entity submitting the claim to establish that DHS was not produced pursuant to a prohibited referral.

When forming arrangements with physician organizations, DHS entities must verify whether a physician organization has non-titular physician owners (physician owners who have the ability or right to receive the financial benefits of ownership or investment), which would trigger the physician "stand-in-the-shoes" rules. If so, a direct compensation arrangement exception must be met. If a DHS entity is not able to verify if a physician organization has non-titular physician owners, the DHS entity may wish to structure the arrangement in a manner that satisfies a "direct compensation" exception. If a direct compensation exception is not used to protect a particular arrangement, a DHS entity should consider incorporating contractual provisions under which the physician organization represents that it does not have physician owners and further requires the physician organization to notify the DHS entity immediately if the physician organization becomes physician-owned.

Like the anti-kickback statute, there are certain exceptions. This is a strict liability statute; therefore, if the referral relationship does not meet every requirement of an exception, liability attaches. Each financial relationship must be evaluated for compliance with the Stark law based on its specific facts and circumstances. Some states have passed physician self-referral laws as well. Furthermore, continued amendments to the Stark law and its regulations have increased confusion in this already complex area and make it challenging for providers to feel secure with organizational changes. You should become aware of and familiar with the self-referral laws in any state in which you operate.

Q 20.9.1 Can a party self-disclose actual or potential Stark violations?

While there is no statute or regulation that explicitly requires the disclosure of a violation of the Stark law to the government, FERA amendments to the FCA require a provider to refund, on a timely basis, any amounts paid for services performed under a referral prohibited by Stark. The increased FCA exposure for overpayments received and not refunded as a result of inadvertent Stark violation has significantly complicated the decision of whether and how to self-report.

Enacted on March 23, 2010, PPACA provides for the establishment of a voluntary self-disclosure protocol, under which providers of services and suppliers may self-disclose actual or potential violations of the Stark law. In pertinent part, PPACA both (1) required the Secretary of HHS to establish a self-disclosure protocol under which providers can disclose discovered violations of Stark, and (2) gave HHS authority to compromise its claims under Stark to enable it to settle violations on reasonable terms. As a result, on September 23, 2010, CMS released its Voluntary Self-Referral Disclosure Protocol ("SRDP"), which provides a means for self-disclosing Stark violations in return for negotiating reduced repayment options. Such settlement ability provides a substantial benefit even without a guarantee that self-disclosure will result in reduced repayment obligations.

The SRDP sets forth certain factors that will be considered in reducing a repayment obligation, which include:

- nature and extent of the statutory violation;
- timeliness of self-disclosure;
- a party's cooperation in providing additional information related to the disclosure; and
- such other factors as the Secretary considers appropriate.[51]

Also a condition to self-reporting is the consent to re-open closed claims that involve the potential Stark violation(s), including those outside the relevant limitations period. Moreover, under the SRDP, CMS may refer the violations to the OIG or DOJ for resolution of possible claims under the FCA and other civil/monetary penalties.

It is important to distinguish between the SRDP—a self-disclosure program administered by CMS—and the OIG's Self Disclosure

Protocol. Participation in the SRDP is limited to actual or potential violations of the Stark law while the OIG's Self-Disclosure Protocol is available for disclosing conduct that raises potential liabilities under other federal criminal, civil, or administrative laws.[52] For example, conduct that raises liability risks under the Stark law may also raise liability risks under the OIG's civil monetary penalty authorities regarding the federal Anti-kickback Statute and should be disclosed through the OIG's Self-Disclosure Protocol. Disclosing parties should not disclose the same conduct under both the SRDP and OIG's Self-Disclosure Protocol.

Disclosing parties that currently have CIAs or CCAs with the OIG should also comply with any disclosure or reportable event requirements under such agreements. Effective September 23, 2010, a reportable event solely related to a Stark issue should be disclosed to CMS using the requirements set forth in the SRDP with a copy to the disclosing party's OIG monitor. Any further questions about any applicable CIA or CCA requirements should be directed to the disclosing party's OIG monitor.

> **TIP:** A careful analysis should be conducted in determining whether to self-report Stark violations and work with CMS to develop a settlement arrangement relating to over-payments received. If the Stark violation potentially also implicates the anti-kickback statute or other statutory or administrative penalty provisions, it should be carefully evaluated for possible self-disclosure through the OIG's Self-Disclosure Protocol.

HIPAA

Q 20.10 What is HIPAA?

The Health Insurance Portability and Accountability Act (HIPAA) applies to all healthcare providers and is very important to the compliance activities of all organizations. Due to the breadth of the regulations, it is covered separately in chapter 24, "HIPAA Security and Privacy," and should be reviewed by all healthcare compliance professionals.

EMTALA

Q 20.11 What is EMTALA?

The U.S. Congress passed the Emergency Medical Treatment and Active Labor Act (EMTALA) (42 U.S.C. § 1395dd) as part of the Consolidated Omnibus Budget Reconciliation Act of 1985 (COBRA). In recognition of the critical role that hospital emergency rooms play in our healthcare system, EMTALA is designed to ensure public access to emergency care regardless of an individual's ability to pay. At the time of EMTALA's enactment, Congress was responding to reports of some private hospitals refusing to treat indigent and uninsured patients and inappropriately transferring such patients to publicly funded hospitals. In an effort to stop this practice of "patient dumping," EMTALA was enacted.

Q 20.11.1 What are EMTALA's key requirements?

EMTALA requires Medicare-participating hospitals with dedicated emergency departments—including critical access hospitals—to provide a medical screening examination to any individual who comes to the emergency department and requests such an examination and prohibits such hospitals from refusing to examine or treat individuals with an emergency medical condition.[53] EMTALA does not apply, however, once a patient becomes an inpatient. In those circumstances, Medicare's Conditions of Participation would govern the hospital's responsibilities. In 2003, the Centers for Medicare and Medicaid Services (CMS) issued regulations that defined several EMTALA terms.[54] These definitions should be referred to in analyzing any EMTALA issue.

Hospitals are also required by EMTALA to do the following, at a minimum:

- Provide an appropriate medical screening examination to any individual who comes to the emergency department;
- Provide the patient with necessary stabilization treatment;
- Provide for an appropriate transfer to another facility if either the patient requests the transfer or the hospital does not have the capability or capacity to provide the treatment necessary to stabilize the patient's emergency medical condition;

- Not delay examination or treatment in order to inquire about the individual's insurance or ability to pay;
- Accept appropriate transfers of patients with emergency medical conditions if the hospital has a specialized capability that is not available at the transferring hospital and has the capacity to treat the patient;
- Obtain or attempt to obtain written and informed refusal or examination, treatment, or an appropriate transfer in the case of a patient that refuses examination, treatment, or transfer; and
- Not take adverse action against physicians who refuse to transfer an individual with an emergency medical condition, or against an employee who reports a violation of these requirements.

Q 20.11.2 How is EMTALA enforced and what are the penalties for an EMTALA violation?

EMTALA is enforced by the CMS regional offices, the OIG, the local professional review organization for medical issues, and each state's survey agency. CMS investigates EMTALA complaints and forwards confirmed violations to the OIG for the determination of possible penalties.

Violations of EMTALA can expose a hospital to civil monetary penalties of up to $50,000 per violation. The most significant penalty, however, is that the physician provider may be excluded from participating in federal healthcare programs. Hospitals in violation also risk civil suits brought by patients, which have no monetary cap.

Deficit Reduction Act

Q 20.12 What is the Deficit Reduction Act?

The Deficit Reduction Act of 2005 (DRA) was signed into law on February 8, 2006. Among other things, the DRA amends existing law on state medical assistance plans, 42 U.S.C. § 1396a.[55]

Q 20.12.1 Who may be affected by the DRA?

Healthcare providers and companies that receive Medicaid funds may be affected by the DRA. Specifically, any "entity" that receives $5 million a year or more from any state's Medicaid plan is required to train and educate its employees about existing federal and state false claims laws.

Q 20.12.2   What types of companies does the DRA apply to?

The DRA applies to healthcare "entities." An "entity" can include a governmental agency, organization, unit, corporation, partnership or other business arrangement (including any Medicaid managed care organization, irrespective of the form of business structure or arrangement by which it exists), whether for-profit or not-for-profit.

The law also applies to any organization that receives payments at more than one location or under more than one contractual or other payment arrangement if the aggregate payments to that organization meet the $5 million threshold, even if the organization uses one or more provider identification or tax identification numbers.

The determination as to whether this provision of the law applies will be made by looking at the preceding federal fiscal year (*e.g.*, an entity will have met the $5 million annual threshold as of January 1, 2007, if it received or made payments in that amount in federal fiscal year 2006).

Q 20.12.3   What does the DRA require?

In general, the law requires every state's plan for medical assistance to condition payments to entities receiving $5 million annually on whether those entities have taken certain steps to educate all of their employees about false claims laws.

Specifically, in order to continue to receive payment, entities must do the following:

A. Establish written policies for all employees, officers, contractors, and agents that "provide detailed information about the False Claims Act . . . , administrative remedies for false claims and statements . . . , any State laws pertaining to civil or criminal penalties for false claims and statements, and whistleblower protections under such laws, with respect to the role of such laws in preventing and detecting fraud, waste, and abuse in Federal health care programs";

B. Include in those written policies "detailed provisions regarding the entity's policies and procedures for detecting and preventing fraud, waste, and abuse"; and
C. Include in any employee handbook a discussion of all of the laws referenced in the written policies, as well as information about whistleblower protections and the company's "policies and procedures for detecting and preventing fraud, waste, and abuse."

Q 20.12.4 Do the policies required by the DRA have to be on paper?

It does not matter whether the policies are on paper or in electronic format, so long as they are readily available to all employees, contractors or agents.

Q 20.12.5 What if my company does not have a document called an "employee handbook"? Do we need to create one?

Centers for Medicare and Medicaid Services (CMS) has clarified that the DRA does not require companies to create an employee handbook if they do not have one. However, even if a company does not have a document called an "employee handbook," the information still must be disseminated to all employees. One efficient possibility would be to include the necessary information in a company's code of conduct, assuming that document is given out to all employees.

Q 20.12.6 What are the penalties for noncompliance with the DRA?

Although the relevant provisions of the Deficit Reduction Act do not set forth penalties or sanctions for those entities that fail to comply with the law's requirements, the language of the Act clearly conditions Medicaid payments upon compliance with these new requirements. Thus, if an entity fails to comply with every obligation of this new law, that entity may risk (1) not receiving future Medicaid funds or (2) forced repayment of previously received state Medicaid funds.

HITECH Act

Q 20.13   What is the HITECH Act?[56]

The Health Information Technology for Economic and Clinical Health Act (HITECH Act)[57] was signed into law as a portion of the American Recovery and Reinvestment Act (ARRA),[58] commonly known as the stimulus package. The HITECH Act encourages physicians and certain entities to adopt electronic health records (EHR) through the use of both incentive payments and penalties. The federal government's four stated goals to advance the use of health information technology when enacting the HITECH Act were:

- requiring the government to develop standards by 2010 that allow for the nationwide electronic exchange and use of health information;
- investing $20 billion in health information technology infrastructure and Medicare and Medicaid incentives to encourage doctors and hospitals to utilize health information technology;
- saving the government $10 billion through improvements in quality of care and care coordination, and reductions in medical errors and duplicative care; and
- strengthening federal privacy and security laws to protect identifiable health information from misuse as the healthcare sector increases use of health information technology.[59]

The Congressional Budget Office estimates that, as a result of the HITECH Act, approximately 90% of doctors and 70% of hospitals will be using comprehensive EHRs within the next ten years.

Q 20.13.1   What are the rules and requirements of the HITECH Act?

The exact rules and requirements of the HITECH Act are not yet certain. In early 2010, the Department of Health and Human Services released two of three coordinated rules implementing portions of the HITECH Act. Neither rule is final. The first rule, written by the Office of the National Coordinator of Health Information Technology (ONC), is an interim final rule outlining standards for creation, implementation, and certification of EHR.[60] The second rule, drafted by CMS, is a proposed rule addressing how CMS will implement and make operational the Medicare and Medicaid EHR incentives of the act.[61] The third rule, which will come from the ONC, was not yet released at the time of this writing.

A full analysis of the HITECH Act and its implications for various healthcare providers and organizations should be undertaken in preparation for the promulgation of the final rules. The rules above are lengthy and, as of this writing, have not been analyzed and vetted fully by most organizations. Still, chapter 24 of this book, "HIPAA Security and Privacy," addresses the implications of the HITECH Act on HIPAA obligations in greater detail. This information, however, is only a start, as the HITECH Act has much more far-reaching impacts. Healthcare organizations, most specifically physicians and hospitals, should analyze and take into account these rules and regulations when creating a comprehensive compliance program.

Notes

1. *See, e.g.*, Patient Protection and Affordable Care Act of 2010, H.R. 3590 [hereinafter PPACA], §§ 6102, 6401; CAL. HEALTH & SAFETY CODE §§ 119400–119402 and S.B. 1765.
2. *See generally* 45 C.F.R. pts. 160, 162, 164.
3. *See, e.g.*, PPACA §§ 6102, 6401.
4. The U.S. Sentencing Commission was created by Congress in 1984 to promulgate the U.S. Sentencing Guidelines for Organizations and the U.S. Sentencing Guidelines for Individuals to increase sentencing uniformity for violation of federal laws. To encourage good corporate citizenship, a punishment structure was developed based on the culpability of the organization and the seriousness of the crime.
5. Health Insurance Portability and Accountability Act, Pub. L. No. 104-191 [hereinafter HIPAA], § 203. *See also* False Claims Act, 31 U.S.C. § 3729 [hereinafter FCA].
6. *In re* Columbia/HCA Healthcare Corp. Qui Tam Litig., Civil Action No. 01-MS-50 (RCL) (D.D.C.).
7. www.oig.hhs.gov/fraud/complianceguidance.asp; *see also* www.stopmedicarefraud.com.
8. *Id.*
9. The OIG website is http://oig.hhs.gov.
10. *See* OIG Compliance Program Guidance for Individual and Small Group Physician Practices, 65 Fed. Reg. 59,434, 59,441 (Oct. 5, 2000).
11. U.S. SENTENCING GUIDELINES MANUAL § 8B2.1(a).
12. U.S. SENTENCING GUIDELINES MANUAL § 8B2.1(b).
13. False claims submitted in violation of the False Claims Act or Civil Monetary Penalties Law give rise to the OIG's permissive exclusion authority. *See* 42 U.S.C. § 1320a-7(b)(7).
14. *See* www.stopmedicarefraud.gov/heatsuccess/index.html.
15. Pub. L. No. 111-21.
16. Pub. L. No. 111-5.
17. H.R. 3590.
18. 42 U.S.C. § 1320 *et seq.*
19. 42 U.S.C. § 1396 *et seq.*
20. 5 U.S.C. §§ 8440, 8902, 8905, 8906.
21. For a more detailed discussion of the False Claims Act, please see chapter 11 of this book.
22. 31 U.S.C. § 3729(a).
23. For a more detailed discussion of state-specific laws and the relation to the DRA, see chapter 11, Q 11.24.
24. 31 U.S.C. § 3729(b).

25. U.S. *ex rel.* Norbeck v. Basin Elec. Power Coop., 248 F.3d 781, 792 (8th Cir. 2001).
26. 70 Fed. Reg. at 4,870.
27. 42 U.S.C. § 1320a-7b.
28. 42 U.S.C. § 1320a-7b(b) (emphasis added).
29. 42 U.S.C. § 1320a-7b(b)(1), (2).
30. 42 U.S.C. § 1320a-7b(b).
31. United States v. Starks, 157 F.3d 833 (11th Cir. 1998); United States v. Jain, 93 F.3d 436 (8th Cir. 1996); United States v. Anderson, 85 F. Supp. 2d 1047 (D. Kan. 1999); United States v. Neufeld, 908 F. Supp. 491 (S.D. Ohio 1995); Med. Dev. Network, Inc. v. Prof'l Respiratory Care, 673 So. 2d 565, 567 (Fla. 4th Dist. Ct. App. 1996).
32. *Id.*
33. Bryan v. United States, 524 U.S. 184 (1998).
34. *Id.* at 196.
35. *Id.* at 191.
36. OIG Advisory Opinions are available online at http://oig.hhs.gov/fraud/advisoryopinions/opinions.html.
37. *See* CARRIE VALIANT & DAVID MATYAS, LEGAL ISSUES IN HEALTH CARE FRAUD AND ABUSE: NAVIGATING THE UNCERTAINTIES 30 (National Health Lawyer Association 1997).
38. *See* Medicare and State Health Care Programs: Fraud and Abuse; Clarification of the Initial OIG Safe Harbor Provisions and Establishment of Additional Safe Harbor Provisions under the Anti-Kickback Statute, 64 Fed. Reg. 63,518, 63,519 (emphasis added).
39. United States v. Greber, 760 F.2d 68 (3d Cir. 1985).
40. *See* 42 U.S.C. § 1320a-7b(b)(7).
41. *See* 42 U.S.C. § 1320a-7a(a)(7).
42. *See* 31 U.S.C. § 3729 (2002).
43. 42 U.S.C. § 1320a-7b(b)(3).
44. *See* 42 C.F.R. § 1001.952 (1999).
45. *See generally* Preamble to Final Safe Harbor Regulations, 56 Fed. Reg. 35,952, 35,954 § III.A. (Response to Comments and Summary of Revisions) (July 29, 1991).
46. OIG Advisory Opinions are available online at http://oig.hhs.gov/fraud/advisoryopinions.html.
47. 56 Fed. Reg. at 35,954.
48. The personal services safe harbor allows providers to enter into agreements under which they provide services for another party. The contract cannot be a pretense for an illegal activity such as payments for referrals.
49. *See* OIG instructions for requesting advisory opinion, *available at* http://oig.hhs.gov/fraud/advisoryopinions/aofaq.html#7.
50. *See id.*
51. *See* PPACA § 6409.
52. *See* 63 Fed. Reg. 58,399 (Oct. 30, 1998); U.S. Dep't of Health & Human Services, Office of Inspector General, An Open Letter to Health Care Providers

(Mar. 24, 2009), available at http://oig.hhs.gov/fraud/docs/openletters/OpenLetter3-24-09.pdf.
    53. 42 U.S.C. § 1395dd.
    54. 68 Fed. Reg. 53,222 (Sept. 9, 2003).
    55. *See* Pub. L. No. 109-171, § 6081.
    56. For a more detailed discussion of the HITECH Act and, specifically, its relation to HIPAA, see chapter 24 of this book.
    57. Pub. L. No. 111-5, title IV.
    58. Pub. L. No. 111-5.
    59. *See* http://waysandmeans.house.gov/media/pdf/110/hit2.pdf.
    60. 4 Fed. Reg. 2,015; 42 C.F.R. pt. 170 (Jan. 13, 2010).
    61. 75 Fed. Reg. 1,844; 42 C.F.R. pts. 412, 413, 422, and 495 (Jan. 13, 2010).

21

Medicare Part D

Jeffrey W. Mittleman, Elizabeth Sanghavi & Jonathan E. Anderman

---

This chapter describes the compliance obligations for all stakeholders in the Medicare Part D prescription drug program. The stakeholders discussed include the Prescription Drug Plans, pharmaceutical manufacturers, and other healthcare providers. This chapter provides guidance for stakeholders on topics including sales and marketing, anti-kickback safe harbors, e-prescribing, compliance program requirements, and patient assistance programs.

Medicare Part D	677
The Basics	677
Potential Risks and Violations	679
Anti-Kickback Statute (AKS)	679
Patient Assistance Programs (PAPs)	680
Waivers of Coinsurance or Deductibles	682
Free or Discounted Drugs	683
Rebates and Other Price Concessions	683
Promotional Activities and Marketing Guidelines	684
AKS Safe Harbors	685
E-Prescribing Safe Harbor	685
E-Health Records Safe Harbor	686
Waiver or Reduction of Cost-Sharing	687
Compliance Programs	687
Required Elements	687
Audits and Prevention/Detection of Fraud and Abuse	691

Acronyms, initialisms, and abbreviations used in this chapter:

AKS	anti-kickback statute
CMS	Centers for Medicare & Medicaid Services
DAW	dispense as written
MA	Medicare Advantage
MAPD	Medicare Advantage Prescription Drug
MEDICs	Medicare Drug Integrity Contractors
MIPPA	Medicare Improvements for Patients and Providers Act
MMA	Medicare Prescription Drug, Improvement, and Modernization Act of 2003
OIG	Office of Inspector General

PAP	patient assistance program
PBM	pharmacy benefit manager
PDP	prescription drug plan
SPAP	State Pharmaceutical Assistance Program
TrOOP	True Out-of-Pocket Cost

Medicare Part D

The Basics

Q 21.1 What is Medicare Part D?

Medicare Part D was established by the Medicare Prescription Drug, Improvement, and Modernization Act of 2003 (MMA)[1] and its subsequent rules and regulations to provide outpatient prescription drug benefits for Medicare beneficiaries. Part D coverage is provided either through stand-alone prescription drug plans (PDPs) or through Medicare Advantage plans that offer both medical and prescription coverage (MAPDs). The program is estimated to cost $768 billion over ten years.[2]

Q 21.1.1 Is Medicare Part D mandatory?

Medicare Part D is a voluntary program, except for dual eligibles,[3] who must either enroll in a plan or become auto-enrolled by the government. All Medicare beneficiaries became eligible to enroll in the Part D program on January 1, 2006. At the end of the 2006 Part D enrollment period, approximately 22.5 million Medicare beneficiaries were enrolled in Part D plans.[4] In 2009, this number was up to nearly 27 million enrollees.[5]

Q 21.1.2 What benefits are provided under Part D?

Plans must offer a statutorily defined set of benefits, or in the alternative, a benefit package that is actuarially equivalent. In 2009, beneficiaries had a $295 deductible[6] and a 25% copayment, up to the initial coverage limit of $2,700 of total drug costs.[7] For total drug costs between $2,700 and $4,350 (the "doughnut hole"),[8] beneficiaries pay 100% of drug costs. After a beneficiary's total drug costs exceed $4,350, Medicare pays 95% of drug costs or copayment.[9]

Q 21.2 Why does my company need a compliance program for Medicare Part D?

Compliance programs are required for Medicare Part D plans. In addition, for reasons identified throughout this book, compliance programs reduce the risks that such plans will violate (among others) fraud and abuse laws.

Q 21.3 What is MIPPA and how does it impact Part D?

The Medicare Improvements for Patients and Providers Act (MIPPA)[10] was enacted on July 15, 2008. MIPPA cancels a reduction in Medicare's payment rates for physicians' services and extends other provisions governing the Medicare program. It also increases rates for physicians' services for 2009, expands eligibility for low-income beneficiaries, and reduces payments to Medicare Advantage Plans.

The various provisions of MIPPA impact entities that operate in Medicare Part D in several ways, including:

- *Incentives for electronic prescribing*—Providers who electronically prescribe ("e-Rx") are eligible to receive bonus payments based on a percentage of Medicare allowable charges through 2013. Beginning in 2014, penalty payments will become effective for providers who fail to use e-Rx.
- *Low-income subsidy*—MIPPA eliminates the Part D late-enrollment penalty for low-income beneficiaries and specifies that certain income and assets be disregarded in determining eligibility for the low-income subsidy program in Part D. MIPPA also provides additional funds to federal and state entities to increase outreach efforts to encourage eligible individuals to enroll in those programs.

- *Prompt pay*—Beginning in 2010, long-term care pharmacies will be required to submit Part D claims to PDPs no less than thirty days but no more than ninety days from the date the drugs are dispensed.
- *Formularies*—MIPPA expands the list of covered Part D drugs and offers CMS the authority to designate certain classes of drugs as having a protected status.

Potential Risks and Violations

Q 21.4 Generally, what kinds of risks does a Medicare D compliance program aim to mitigate?

The potential fraud and abuse that certain practices of plan sponsors, pharmacies, and PBMs can give rise to, such as:

- incorrect reporting of costs
- noncompliance with marketing guidelines
- dispensing of excluded drugs
- off-label dispensing
- prescriptions from excluded providers
- brand-name versus generic/dispense as written (DAW)
- Medical Secondary Payer/Coordination of Benefits Regulations

Note that this list is not exhaustive, and many other risk areas apply as well.

Anti-Kickback Statute (AKS)

Q 21.5 How are pharmacies and manufacturers at risk of violating the AKS?

One of the biggest potential risks under Medicare Part D is violation of the federal anti-kickback statute (AKS).[11] The anti-kickback statute makes it a criminal offense to knowingly and willfully offer, pay, solicit, or receive any remuneration, either directly or indirectly, in cash or in kind, to induce the referral or recommendation for a referral of business covered by a federal healthcare program.[12]

For example, pharmacies and manufacturers could violate the anti-kickback statute through, among other things, incorrect cost reports and related problems associated with:

a. patient assistance programs (PAPs);
b. waivers of coinsurance or deductibles;
c. free or discounted drugs;
d. rebates and other price concessions;
e. promotional and marketing activities.

Patient Assistance Programs (PAPs)

Q 21.6 What is a patient assistance program?

PAPs provide assistance to low-income individuals who do not have insurance coverage for drugs. A PAP may be structured in many different ways. PAPs may offer cash subsidies, free or reduced-price drugs, or both.[13] PAPs may offer assistance directly to patients, including Medicare enrollees, or offer drugs to pharmacies, clinics, hospitals, and other entities that provide drugs to patients that are not covered by an insurance program.[14] In addition, PAPs may be affiliated with a manufacturer or with an independent charitable organization.

Q 21.6.1 What are the AKS implications associated with a manufacturer-affiliated PAP?

The OIG, in its advisory opinions and in a special advisory bulletin,[15] has stated that pharmaceutical PAPs that subsidize Part D cost-sharing amounts present heightened risks under the anti-kickback statute.[16] The anti-kickback statute could be implicated because the manufacturer would be giving something of value to beneficiaries in exchange for their use of its product.[17] In addition, the OIG has expressed concern that the manufacturers might use subsidies to help beneficiaries meet their True Out-of-Pocket Cost (TrOOP) requirement.

Q 21.6.2 What is TrOOP?

TrOOP payments are used to determine when a beneficiary reaches the catastrophic out-of-pocket level. PAPs and other arrangements involving the discounting of drugs could increase the number of beneficiaries using manufacturers' products and therefore could hasten the point during the year at which beneficiaries reach the Medicare Part D catastrophic benefit.[18] Any arrangement that encourages such an accelerated push to the catastrophic level might have fraud and abuse implications, as it could increase federal healthcare spending.

Q 21.6.3 What are the AKS implications for PAPs affiliated with independent charities?

The OIG has found that cost-sharing subsidies by "bona fide, independent charities unaffiliated with pharmaceutical manufacturers should not raise anti-kickback concerns, even if the charities receive manufacturer contributions."[19] The charity, however, must not function as a "conduit for payments by the pharmaceutical manufacturer to patients and must not impermissibly influence beneficiaries' drug choices."[20]

Q 21.7 What are the AKS implications for PAPs operating outside of Part D?

The OIG has found that PAPs operating outside of the Part D benefit have a reduced risk of violating the anti-kickback statute, provided that:

- beneficiaries could not apply the assistance toward the TrOOP balance, therefore eliminating the concern that the PAP program would hasten the point during the coverage year at which a beneficiary reaches the catastrophic benefit;
- eligibility was based solely on uniform measures of need, not on choice of plan;
- the PAP provides assistance for the whole Part D coverage year (or the portion of the coverage year remaining after the beneficiary first begins receiving the PAP assistance);
- the PAP assistance remains available during the year, even if the beneficiary's use is periodic; and
- the PAP maintains accurate and contemporaneous records of the subsidized drugs to permit the government to verify the provision of drugs outside the Part D benefit.[21]

In addition, the OIG recommended that PAPs operating outside of the Part D benefit should coordinate with Part D plans to undertake appropriate drug utilization review and medication therapy management program activities.[22]

PAP sponsors that operate outside of the Part D benefit can still require their enrollees to pay nominal copayments. Copayments should be aggregated with TrOOP and total drug spend balances. Enrollees are responsible for submitting appropriate documentation to their plans. Any beneficiary payments structured as administration fees or premiums cannot be aggregated into Part D TrOOP and total drug spend balances.[23]

Q 21.7.1 Do PAPs run any risk of violating the AKS by offering services to uninsured patients?

Nothing in the Part D program or in any other laws or regulations prevents pharmaceutical manufacturers or others from providing assistance to uninsured patients.[24]

Waivers of Coinsurance or Deductibles

Q 21.8 How are waiver of coinsurance and deductible amounts regulated by the AKS?

Under the anti-kickback statute, the term "remuneration" includes the waiver of coinsurance and deductible amounts (or any part thereof) and transfers of items or services for free or for other than fair market value. The term does not, however, include the waiver of coinsurance and deductible amounts by a pharmacy, if:

(1) the waiver is not offered as part of any advertisement or solicitation;
(2) the pharmacy does not routinely waive coinsurance or deductible amounts; or
(3) the pharmacy:
   (a) waives the coinsurance and deductible amounts after determining in good faith that the individual is in financial need; or
   (b) fails to collect coinsurance or deductible amounts after making reasonable collection efforts.[25]

Note, if the individual for whom the subsidy is offered is a subsidy eligible individual, only factor (1) above applies.[26]

Free or Discounted Drugs

Q 21.9 How can pharmacies offer free or discounted drugs without violating the AKS?

Individuals can purchase drugs from a pharmacy offering a special or discount price that is lower than that available through the Part D plan. Beneficiaries must purchase the covered drug without using the Part D benefit or a supplemental card. The purchase price for the discounted drug would count toward the TrOOP balance, but the enrollee would be responsible for submitting appropriate documentation to the plan.[27] Plans would be responsible for adjusting the total drug spending and TrOOP balances consistent with established processes and clear enrollee instructions regarding paper-claim submissions. This policy only applies when an enrollee is within a coverage gap or deductible phase of his or her benefit.[28]

Some pharmacies (for example, Wal-Mart) offer lower prices at retail than are available under contracts with PDPs throughout a benefit year. These lower prices would be the pharmacy's "usual and customary" price and Part D sponsors would reimburse pharmacies based on this price and enrollees would pay a copay based on the appropriate percent under the plan.[29]

Rebates and Other Price Concessions

Q 21.10 How should pharmacies handle manufacturer rebates or other price concessions?

Rebates or other price concessions offered to Medicare Part D plan sponsors can both negate the cost-effectiveness goals of the MMA and implicate fraud and abuse laws, if not properly structured and reported.

Under Medicare Part D, Part D sponsors must negotiate maximum price concessions from pharmaceutical manufacturers in order to achieve cost-effectiveness, an overall goal of the MMA. These negotiated prices must reflect price concessions, such as discounts and rebates, for covered drugs. The MMA requires plans to disclose to the Secretary the aggregate negotiated price concessions made to the sponsor by a manufacturer.[30]

If a pharmacy receives rebates, it must pass this benefit through to beneficiaries. This cannot occur if the pharmacy does not disclose the rebate to the plan sponsor. Accordingly, pharmacies that receive rebates from a manufacturer with respect to Part D enrollees must pass this benefit on to beneficiaries by fully disclosing to the Part D plan sponsor that the rebates are being paid.[31] The plan sponsor must then account for this in its bid, and the price concessions would have to be netted out for the purposes of allowable reinsurance and risk corridor costs.[32]

In addition, CMS has specific concerns where, for example, a pharmacy receives rebates or discounts without the knowledge of the plan sponsor in order to obtain formulary access or to move the market, CMS has identified specific risks associated with these arrangements, including:

(1) increase program and beneficiary costs;
(2) induce demand for higher-tiered or non-formulary drugs; and
(3) create fraud and abuse concerns.[33]

Promotional Activities and Marketing Guidelines

CMS has developed marketing guidelines with which Medicare Plan Sponsors must comply. Under the marketing guidelines, plans must submit all marketing materials to CMS for approval.[34] Although many issues are addressed in these guidelines, **co-branding** and **patient steering** have raised particular concerns, according to CMS FAQs.

Q 21.11 What is co-branding?

Co-branding is defined as

> a relationship between two or more separate legal entities, one of which is an organization that sponsors a Medicare Plan. The organization displays the name(s) or brand(s) of the co-branding entity or entities on its marketing materials to signify a business arrangement. Co-branding arrangements allow an organization and its co-branding partner(s)

to promote enrollment into the plan. Co-branding relationships are entered into independently from the contract that the organization has with CMS.[35]

CMS has indicated that State Pharmaceutical Assistance Programs (SPAPs) can offer to co-brand with Part D plans by setting reasonable standards for co-branding. The co-branding standards, however, must be applied consistently to all Part D plans and may not establish selective standards that only some Part D plans can meet.[36] Both the SPAP and the Part D plans must notify CMS prior to co-branding. SPAPs or plans in co-branding relationships that involve remuneration between parties in a position to influence the referral of Medicare business must ensure compliance with fraud and abuse laws.[37]

Q 21.12 How does patient steering pose a risk?

While providers and pharmacies may provide prospective enrollees with information on the full range of Part D options available to them, they must not steer potential enrollees toward one particular plan nor may they receive any payment for referrals to any specific plan.[38] If a pharmacist or pharmacy is financially motivated to steer patients to a particular plan, the anti-kickback statute could be implicated.

AKS Safe Harbors

The anti-kickback statute contains two new safe harbors under the MMA that apply to electronic prescribing and electronic health records.

E-Prescribing Safe Harbor

Q 21.13 What is the electronic prescribing safe harbor?

The e-prescribing safe harbor protects certain arrangements involving the provision of nonmonetary remuneration in the form of technology that is necessary and used solely to transmit electronic prescription information. This safe harbor applies if the items and services are provided by

(1) a hospital to a physician who is a member of its medical staff;
(2) a group practice to a member healthcare professional; or
(3) a PDP sponsor or MA organization to pharmacists or pharmacies participating in the network and to prescribing healthcare professionals.

In addition, the exception only applies if:

(1) the donor does not take any action to limit or restrict the use of items or services with other electronic prescribing/electronic health records systems;
(2) neither the recipient nor the recipient's practice make the receipt of items or services or the amount or nature of the services a condition of doing business with the donor;
(3) the eligibility of the recipient is not determined in a manner that takes into account the volume or value of referrals or other business generated; and
(4) the donor and recipient have a written agreement.[39]

E-Health Records Safe Harbor

Q 21.14 What is the electronic health records safe harbor?

The e-health records safe harbor protects transfers of software, information technology and training services that are necessary and used predominantly to create, maintain, transmit, or receive electronic health records. The safe harbor protects arrangements involving donors (including individuals, health plans, or other entities that provide covered services and submit claims), and recipients (such as individuals or entities engaged in the delivery of healthcare). Donors cannot select recipients in a manner that directly takes into account the volume or value of referrals or other business. In addition, the recipient must contribute 15% of the donor's cost, and the cost and contribution must be documented in a written agreement.[40]

Waiver or Reduction of Cost-Sharing

Q 21.15 What is the waiver or reduction of cost-sharing exception to the AKS?

Medicare Part D provides a new exception to the anti-kickback statute whereby pharmacies are permitted to waive or reduce cost-sharing amounts for financially needy individuals and to individuals eligible for low-income subsidies.[41] To meet this exception, pharmacies cannot advertise waivers for financially needy individuals or for low-income subsidy recipients. Waivers for financially needy individuals also must be non-routine.[42]

Compliance Programs

Required Elements

Q 21.16 What are the elements of an effective Medicare Part D compliance program?

All sponsors of a Medicare D plan must have a comprehensive plan to detect, correct, and prevent fraud and abuse.[43] The elements of such a plan are similar to those outlined by the OIG for other healthcare entities such as hospitals, pharmaceutical manufacturers, and home health agencies.[44]

Each plan must include:[45]

(1) written policies and procedures and standards of conduct;
(2) compliance officer and compliance committee;
(3) training and education;
(4) effective lines of communication;
(5) enforcement of standards through well-publicized disciplinary guidelines;
(6) monitoring and auditing;
(7) corrective action procedures; and
(8) comprehensive fraud and abuse plans, including procedures to voluntarily self-report potential fraud or misconduct.

The establishment of a plan with these eight elements will allow sponsors to monitor themselves and their subcontractors with respect to contract regulations and compliance with applicable laws.[46]

Q 21.16.1 What should our written policies and procedures say?

A sponsor's written policies and procedures must clearly articulate the sponsor's commitment to comply with all federal and state statutory and regulatory requirements related to the Medicare program[47] and must state how the company will identify and reduce fraudulent or wasteful activity.[48] These policies and procedures should be updated to reflect statutory and regulatory changes.[49]

The polices and procedures must be comprehensive, including the following non-exhaustive list:

(1) procedures for identifying fraud and abuse;
(2) a process to conduct a timely inquiry into potential regulatory and statutory violations;
(3) a process to refer potential violations to the Medicare Drug Integrity Contractors (MEDICs)[50] and/or law enforcement for further investigation within a reasonable period;
(4) a process to ensure that the sponsor and subcontractors are marketing in accordance with the law;
(5) procedures for timely response to data requests by CMS, MEDICs, and law enforcement, or their designees;
(6) a process to identify overpayments and underpayments;
(7) a process to identify improper coverage determination;
(8) a process to identify any claims that were submitted for drugs that were prescribed by an excluded or deceased provider;
(9) a process to ensure full disclosure to CMS upon request of all sponsor pricing decisions; and
(10) policies and procedures for coordination and cooperation with CMS, MEDICs, and law enforcement agencies.[51]

In addition, the policies and procedures must include a code of conduct that is easy to read; that clearly articulates the sponsor's commitment to comply with all statutory, regulatory, and other Part D program requirements; and that outlines the expectation that employees, first-tier entities, and downstream entities act in an ethical and compliant manner. The code of ethics also should specify the disciplinary actions that can be imposed for noncompliance.[52]

Q 21.16.2 What requirements must be met to have an effective compliance officer and compliance committee?

An OIG study of sponsors to determine adherence to the eight required elements of a Part D Compliance Program found that many sponsors failed to designate a compliance officer or a compliance committee.[53] Having a compliance officer and compliance committee that is accountable to senior management is one of the elements of an effective compliance program. This element has four requirements:

(1) having a compliance officer in place;
(2) having a compliance committee in place;
(3) ensuring that the compliance committee is overseen by the compliance officer, advises the compliance officer, and assists in the implementation of the compliance program; and
(4) ensuring that the compliance officer is responsible for developing, operating, and monitoring the fraud, waste, and abuse program.[54]

Q 21.16.3 What do we need to do for training and education?

Compliance training should address relevant laws related to fraud and abuse issues and should be required of all individuals involved with the sponsor's administration of the Part D benefit. In its compliance manual, CMS has stated:

> The best training and education approach is to engage employees in substantive discussion to reinforce the organization's compliance with applicable laws, regulations, standards, and principles. In addition, training should be designed to ensure that employees understand what is expected of them. Sponsors should consider administering tests or quizzes during training sessions to ensure that employees understand the compliance goals of the organization. In addition, training should be incorporated into the organization's orientation of new employees.[55]

Employees with specific responsibilities regarding Medicare should be given specialized training specific to their positions. Such training may include marketing, calculating TrOOP, and submitting Part D data to CMS.[56]

Q 21.16.4 How can we develop effective lines of communication between individuals involved with compliance?

Sponsors must have a system to receive, record, and respond to compliance questions and reports of noncompliance. This system must be confidential. One of the common methods of communication is a hotline. Sponsors must provide prompt documentation and investigation of reports to hotlines.[57]

Q 21.16.5 How do we enforce our compliance standards?

Sponsors must have disciplinary guidelines that are well publicized and clearly supported by leadership. These guidelines would apply to employees. In addition, sponsors should have a provision in their contracts with other entities stating that violation of the guidelines would result in termination.[58]

Q 21.16.6 How do we effectively monitor and audit our program?

Sponsors' monitoring programs should include:

(1) an internal monitoring and auditing component;
(2) an auditing schedule and methodology; and
(3) a process to monitor and audit first-tier entities, downstream entities, and related entities.[59]

Q 21.16.7 What should our fraud and abuse plan look like?

CMS requires plan sponsors to develop fraud and abuse plans, either as separate programs, or as integrated components of the seven other elements of the compliance plans. CMS does not, however, provide any requirements for doing so.[60]

Q 21.16.8 Is self-reporting mandatory?

No. Self-reporting is voluntary.[61]

Q 21.17 Can compliance duties under a Part D contract be delegated?

Sponsors can delegate parts of its plan to control fraud, waste, and abuse to first-tier entities, downstream entities, and related entities. Sponsors, however, are ultimately responsible for complying with all Part D requirements and may not delegate the compliance officer or compliance committee responsibilities to any other related entity.[62] When a sponsor delegates any of its activities to another entity, the written arrangements for this delegation must specify that the delegation can be revoked or must state other available remedies when the entity has not performed the delegated activity satisfactorily.[63]

Audits and Prevention/Detection of Fraud and Abuse

Q 21.18 Can CMS audit plans?

CMS has contracted with private organizations, called Medicare Drug Integrity Contractors (MEDICs), to assist CMS with auditing and prevention and detection of fraud and abuse in the Part D benefit.

CMS is required to audit annually the financial records of at least one-third of the Part D Sponsors offering Part D drug plans.[64] CMS also may perform discretionary audits.[65] Sponsors and their subcontractors must allow CMS to audit records and must allow the federal government or CMS to conduct an on-site audit.[66] Sponsors, first-tier entities, downstream entities, and related entities must provide CMS and/or the MEDICs access to all requested facilities and records associated with the Part D program for ten years.[67]

Q 21.19 Has OIG audited plans?

Yes. OIG audited all seventy-six stand-alone PDPs operating in January 2006 to determine whether sponsors had compliance programs and, if so, whether they met the eight compliance elements listed above (see Q 21.16). OIG has independent authority to conduct audits and evaluations necessary to oversee Medicare reimbursement.[68]

In its audit, OIG found that, although most sponsors have compliance plans, many do not fully address all of the requirements that have been specified. In particular, sponsors' compliance plans did not adequately address the requirement to designate a compliance officer or compliance committee, or to create procedures for internal monitoring and auditing. In addition, for the other six required elements, sponsors generally did not provide details about how the plan would implement the requirements.[69]

Notes

1. Pub. L. No. 108-173.
2. OIG, Prescription Drug Plan Sponsors' Compliance Plans (OEI-03-06-0010), http://oig.hhs.gov/oei/reports/oei-03-06-00100.pdf.
3. A dual eligible is a beneficiary who, prior to the effective date of Medicare Part D, received prescription drug benefits through a state Medicaid program and also was eligible for Medicare.
4. Juliette Cubanski & Patricia Neuman, *Status Report on Medicare D Enrollment in 2006: Analysis of Plan-Specific Market Share and Coverage*, HEALTH AFFAIRS, vol. 26 no. 1 (Jan./Feb. 2007).
5. Particia Neuman & Juliette Cubanski, *Medicare Part D Update: Lessons Learned and Unfinished Business*, 361 NEW ENG. J. MED. 4 (July 23, 2009).
6. In 2010, the deductible will be $310. Letter from Jonathan Blum, Acting Director, Center for Drug and Health Plan Choice, to All Medicare Advantage Organizations, Prescription Drug Plan Sponsors, and Other Interested Parties ("Announcement of Calendar Year (CY) 2010 Medicare Advantage Capitation Rates and Medicare Advantage and Part D Payment Policies"), Attachment IV ("2010 Part D benefit Parameters") (Apr. 6, 2009), *available at* www.cms.hhs.gov/MedicareAdvtgSpecRateStats/Downloads/Announcement2010.pdf.
7. In 2010, the initial coverage limit will be $2,830. *Id.*
8. In 2010, the out-of-pocket threshold will be $4,550. *Id.*
9. The Kaiser Family Foundation, Medicare Primer, Mar. 2007, at 7.
10. H.R. 6331.
11. *See also* chapter 17 at Q 17.8 *et seq.*
12. 42 U.S.C. § 1320a-7b(b).
13. 70 Fed. Reg. 70,623–70,624 (Nov. 22, 2005).
14. *Id.*
15. *Id.* at 70,623.
16. *Id.*
17. *Id.* at 70,625.
18. *Id.* at 70,626.
19. *Id.* at 70,627.
20. *Id; see also* OIG Advisory Opinions No. 07-04 (Apr. 16, 2007), No. 06-14 (Sept. 26, 2006), and No. 06-03 (Apr. 18, 2006).
21. 70 Fed. Reg. 70,627.
22. *Id.*
23. CMS FAQ 7942 (Feb. 6, 2007), www.cms.hhs.gov/ (follow "Resources & Tools" hyperlink; then follow "Frequently Asked Questions" hyperlink; search all FAQs by ID number).
24. 70 Fed. Reg. 70,624.
25. 42 U.S.C. § 1320a-7b(b)(3)(G).

26. *Id.* Subsidy eligible is defined as a Part D eligible individual who (i) is enrolled in a prescription drug plan or MAPD plan; (ii) has income below 150% of the poverty line applicable to a family of the size involved; and (iii) meets certain resource standards. 42 U.S.C. § 1395w-114(a)(3).
27. CMS FAQ 7944 (Feb. 6, 2007).
28. *Id.*
29. *Id.*
30. CMS FAQ 6326 (Jan. 18, 2007).
31. CMS FAQ 5002 (Apr. 21, 2007).
32. *Id.* (citing 42 C.F.R. § 423.265 and 42 C.F.R. § 423.308).
33. CMS FAQ 6326.
34. MEDICARE MANAGED CARE MANUAL, ch. 3 (Medicare Marketing Guidelines), at 30.5 (Rev. 91, Aug. 7, 2009). Chapter 3 is available at www.cms.hhs.gov/manuals/downloads/mc86c03.pdf [hereinafter Marketing Guidelines].
35. Marketing Guidelines at 20.
36. CMS FAQ 5567 (Feb. 15, 2007).
37. *Id.*
38. Marketing Guidelines at 70.9.3.
39. 42 C.F.R. § 1001.952(x). A new Stark exception that parallels this safe harbor is at 42 C.F.R. § 411.357(v).
40. 42 C.F.R. § 1001.952(y). A new Stark exception that parallels this safe harbor is at 42 C.F.R. § 411.357(w).
41. 42 U.S.C. § 1320a-7b(b)(3)(G).
42. *Id.*
43. CMS Prescription Drug Benefit Manual [hereinafter Prescription Drug Benefit Manual], Chapter 9—Part D Program to Control Fraud, Waste and Abuse, at 8 (citing 42 C.F.R. § 423.504(b)(4)(vi)(H)).
44. *Id.*
45. For additional guidance on best practices and requirements in overall compliance and ethics program effectiveness, see chapter 2, *supra.*
46. Prescription Drug Benefit Manual at 9.
47. 42 C.F.R. § 423.504(b)(4)(vi)(A).
48. Prescription Drug Benefit Manual at 19.
49. *Id.*
50. CSM has contracted with MEDICs to aid in the oversight of the Part D benefit.
51. Prescription Drug Benefit Manual at 21.
52. *Id.*
53. *Id.* at 9.
54. OIG. *Prescription Drug Plan Sponsors' Compliance Plans*, OEI-03-06-00100 at 5 (Dec. 2006).
55. Prescription Drug Benefit Manual at 32.
56. *Id.* at 31.
57. *Id.* at 33–34.
58. *Id.* at 35–37.
59. *Id.* at 42.

60. *Id.* at 53.
61. 42 C.F.R. § 423.504(b)(4)(vi)(H).
62. Prescription Drug Benefit Manual at 15 (citing 2007 MA and PDP Call Letters (www.cms.hhs.gov/PrescriptionDrugCovContra/).
63. 42 C.F.R. § 423.505(i)(4)(iii).
64. 42 C.F.R. § 423.504(d).
65. 42 C.F.R. § 423.505(e)(2).
66. Prescription Drug Benefit Manual at 46; 42 C.F.R. § 423.505(e)(3).
67. Prescription Drug Benefit Manual at 46; 42 C.F.R. § 423.505(e)(4).
68. Prescription Drug Benefit Manual at 46.
69. OIG, *Prescription Drug Plan Sponsors' Compliance Plans*, OEI-03-06-00100 at iii–iv (Dec. 2006).

22

Managed Care Organizations

*Jeffrey W. Mittleman & Jonathan E. Anderman**

Managed care organizations (MCOs) are healthcare organizations that manage the financing, delivery, and payment of health services. MCOs control costs through management and contracts with healthcare providers and provider networks to deliver healthcare services and products. The concerns and liabilities faced by managed care systems are different from those of fee-for-service systems, including issues related to fraud and abuse, compliance, and liability under many federal statutes. In some respects, the compliance and liability risks for MCOs and those for traditional provider organizations come from opposite directions. Whereas the traditional providers can bring down the wrath of enforcement authorities by providing excessive, or medically unnecessary services, the MCO's risk comes from the potential for cost control procedures to lead to underutilization or denial of medically necessary services. Therefore, it is important for MCOs to

---

* The authors wish to acknowledge James Jacobson and Christopher A. Myers for their contributions to this chapter.

understand and address their particular compliance risks and not design a program that focuses on the risks that other kinds of organizations may face.

Managed Care Fraud and Abuse 698
    Federal Monitoring 698
    State Enforcement 700
MCO Compliance Programs.. 701
    Requirements 701
Liability Under the False Claims Act and Other Statutes 706
Physician Incentive Plans (PIPs).. 708
Managed Care Exceptions to the Anti-Kickback Statute 709
Prompt Payment and Denial of Care Compliance Issues...................... 709
Medicare Fraud and Abuse in Marketing 710

Managed Care Fraud and Abuse

Federal Monitoring

Q 22.1 What are the areas of focus in monitoring MCOs for fraud and abuse?

The Centers for Medicare and Medicaid Services (CMS) identifies four areas of scrutiny in looking at managed care integrity issues:

(1) ensuring correct beneficiary status categories to avoid overpayments and increased government administrative costs;
(2) augmenting review and validation of medical charges from "cost" contractors that receive more payment for providing more services;
(3) making sure that beneficiaries are receiving appropriate services; and
(4) ensuring that marketing is in line with CMS guidelines.[1]

The Office of Inspector General (OIG) has gone even further than CMS in its scrutiny, identifying twenty-one areas of focus:

(1) general and administrative costs, and making sure these costs are properly allocated to Medicare beneficiaries;
(2) enhanced payments and ensuring proper capitation payments to risk-based Medicare MCOs for certain beneficiary classifications;
(3) disclosure of physician incentive plans (PIPs) in managed care contracts that reward or penalize physicians based on utilization levels;
(4) costs of additional benefits offered by MCOs and whether or not beneficiaries are receiving these benefits;
(5) new adjusted community rate proposal (ACRP) processes requiring more detailed information submitted in support of ACRPs;
(6) cost-based MCOs and ensuring costs from these MCOs are properly allocated to Medicare;
(7) MCO profits comparing profitability of Medicare business versus other lines of business;
(8) evaluation of Medicare MCO marketing materials;
(9) examination of Medicare Advantage performance measures from a Medicare beneficiary's perspective;
(10) evaluation of CMS's efforts to educate beneficiaries about MA and their options under MA;
(11) assessment of potential financial incentives for Medicare MCOs to encourage enrollment for healthy beneficiaries and discourage enrollment for sick beneficiaries;
(12) prescription drug benefits and how limits on benefits are calculated for each beneficiary, which drugs are included, and how drug costs are calculated;
(13) MCO closings and the impact on beneficiaries' ability to access care;
(14) evaluation of the role of state health counselors in telling beneficiaries about their insurance options;
(15) monitoring Medicare MCO performance based on MA and risk programs;
(16) evaluation of the understanding by beneficiaries in MA MCOs of their extra benefits and financial responsibilities;
(17) MA compliance programs and the pros and cons of their implementation;
(18) fee-for-service (FFS) costs for MCO disenrollees and the reasons for high FFS costs by recent disenrollees;

(19) monitoring disenrollee feedback for insights into potential improvements;
(20) enrollee access to emergency services and whether protections for access are adequate with MCOs; and
(21) Medicaid managed care and their marketing, performance standards, and success in avoided FFP payments.[2]

Q 22.2 Do MCOs need to be concerned with fraud and abuse areas that do not involve under-utilization?

Yes. When the Department of Justice's (DOJ) Special Counsel for Health Care Fraud investigated fraud and abuse allegations made against MCOs, counsel found that the majority of allegations did not relate to under-utilization. Instead, investigations unearthed other types of fraud and abuse in MCOs, such as:

- fraudulent inflation rates resulting in different pricing for the same services in the same communities;
- bribes to win government-funded managed care contracts;
- intentionally failing to pay providers; and
- giving kickbacks to parent companies.[3]

State Enforcement

Q 22.3 What have states done to enforce regulations for MCOs?

States have increasingly looked into issues related to the delivery of managed care services, fraud and abuse, and operational issues, including "prompt payments."[4] This has included actions against MCOs under laws requiring MCOs to cover "medically necessary" drugs, and actions for misrepresentations and marketing abuses.[5]

States have increasingly regulated MCO anti-fraud activities, requiring MCOs to partake in anti-fraud investigative activities.[6] These measures can include creating special investigative units (SIUs) to investigate fraud and abuse claims, maintaining written anti-fraud plans, and reporting suspicious claims.[7] MCOs must research their states' regulations, as regulations and requirements may vary from state to state.

MCO Compliance Programs

Q 22.4 Why does our MCO need to adopt a compliance program?

MCOs should consider adopting compliance programs to ensure that the MCO is meeting all of its legal requirements. Utilizing a compliance program may also limit the possibility and severity of potential adverse actions against the MCO in the future.[8]

CMS also requires MCOs to have comprehensive compliance programs as a condition of participation in Medicare Advantage Plans (MA Plans) and Prescription Drug Plans. The compliance plans must have detailed procedures for disclosing misconduct to the government.

Q 22.5 Can our MCO implement the same compliance program as an FFS plan?

MCOs and FFS plans often have different considerations, especially related to fraud and abuse: While FFS concerns tend to center on over-utilization of services, MCO concerns focus instead on under-utilization of services.[9] As such, compliance programs for MCOs and FFS plans may need to be specifically tailored to address such concerns.

Requirements

Q 22.6 What are the CMS requirements for a compliance program?

CMS requirements for MA organizations and Part D drug plans fall into eight categories and are applicable to all MA organizations and MA-PDs, regardless of size:[10]

(1) written policies and procedures;
(2) designation of a compliance officer and a compliance committee;
(3) conducting effective training and education;
(4) development of effective lines of communication;
(5) auditing and monitoring;

(6) enforcement through publicized disciplinary guidelines and policies dealing with ineligible persons;
(7) response to detected offenses, development of corrective action initiatives and reporting to government authorities; and
(8) for MA-PDs, a comprehensive fraud and abuse plan to detect and prevent fraud.[11]

Q 22.6.1 What is required of a compliance plan's written policies, procedures, and standards?

It should "articulate the organization's commitment to comply with all applicable Federal and State standards."[12] CMS interprets this to require written standards to clearly articulate a commitment to comply with all applicable statutory, regulatory, and program requirements, and to show that MCO employees involved with Medicare business act ethically.[13]

These written standards should also speak to marketing, enrollment and disenrollment, under-utilization and quality of care, data collection, the anti-kickback statute, and other inducements and emergency services.

(1) The OIG would like MA MCOs to have policies on marketing materials and marketing personnel in addition to CMS's marketing requirements. MCOs should review their own marketing materials rather than simply relying on CMS approval as a stamp of accuracy and completeness. Marketing materials should include descriptions of rules, procedures, basic benefits and services, and the grievance and appeals process.[14]
(2) MCOs should have policies that prevent "cherry picking" and other selective enrollment practices. There should also be policies to protect against inappropriate disenrollment.[15]
(3) To prevent under-utilization, MCOs should implement policies to ensure quality care:
   (a) policies against physician "gag" rules;
   (b) policies to ensure that if the MA MCO is using a PIP, the PIP does not pay physicians to reduce medically necessary services; and
   (c) policies for selecting providers and appropriate credentialing and educational requirements.[16]

(4) MCOs should have policies regarding reporting and submission requirements under MA. Policies should ensure that submissions to CMS are accurate, timely and complete, especially for data determining CMS payments to MA MCOs.[17] Specifically, the OIG suggests
    (a) policies to ensure accuracy of the administrative component of the adjusted community rate (ACR); and
    (b) policies to ensure internal control of beneficiary status reporting.[18]
(5) MCOs should have policies to ensure that incentives fall within safe harbor provisions and that incentives for beneficiaries do not violate the anti-kickback statute or the CMP law prohibiting beneficiary inducements, codified at 42 U.S.C. § 1320a-7a(a)(5).[19]
(6) MCOs should have policies ensuring access for beneficiaries to emergency services in the MCO's network that is consistent with all regulations, regardless of insurance status.[20]

Q 22.6.2 What are the functions of the compliance officer and committee?

A compliance officer is the custodian of the MCO's entire compliance program and oversees every aspect of its implementation and performance. The compliance officer is accountable to senior management.[21] For the compliance officer to be accountable, CMS requires that the officer be employed at the organization holding CMS's Part C contract.[22] While the officer should have direct access to the CEO, senior management and the governing body, the officer should not report to the general counsel or other financial officers.[23] The compliance officer should be responsible for the following:

(1) overseeing the implementation of the compliance program;
(2) reporting regularly to the CEO and compliance committee;
(3) revising and adjusting the compliance program to stay current with applicable laws and regulations;
(4) reviewing employee certifications for receiving, reading and understanding the MCO's standards of conduct;
(5) developing compliance training;
(6) coordinating with human resources to ensure that the MCO does not employ excluded persons or entities;
(7) participating in internal compliance reviews;

(8) investigating compliance matters;
(9) creating policies for reporting of suspected fraud and abuse; and
(10) maintaining the effectiveness of the compliance program.[24]

The compliance committee is also accountable to senior management. The committee's responsibilities include:

(1) assessing policies to ensure they are consistent with regulations;
(2) developing standards of conduct and promoting the compliance program with MCO departments and affiliated providers;
(3) improving internal systems for better compliance; and
(4) creating systems to detect potential or suspected violations.[25]

Q 22.6.3 What kind of training should our MCO have?

CMS suggests that effective training requires that "all personnel, including contractors and agents, involved in Medicare programs receive general compliance training upon hire, or upon the initial adoption of a compliance program, and annually thereafter as a condition of employment."[26] Training should be documented and documentation should be maintained by the organization or MA or PDP.[27] Training should be both formal and informal, with mandatory attendance at formal training sessions.[28] Informal training may come in the form of newsletters, compliance-issue websites, or other appropriate forms.[29]

Q 22.6.4 What is meant by "effective lines of communication"?

CMS requires that the MCO compliance officer be able to communicate effectively with employees.[30] CMS interprets this to require the MA organization to show the compliance officer's ability to disseminate the compliance message to employees in effective ways.[31] This may come in the form of a hotline, newsletters, attendance at department staff meetings, visits to the various work units, intranet sites, or office displays to company leadership and employees.[32]

Q 22.6.5 What are the required procedures for internal monitoring and auditing?

CMS construes regulations requiring procedures for effective internal monitoring and auditing to require the organization to have an internal audit plan identifying audits to be performed, including a risk assessment regarding Medicare operations.[33] Audits should focus on these identified risk areas.[34] Monitoring should include reviewing compliance with state and federal regulations and the effectiveness of the compliance program itself.[35]

Q 22.6.6 How should standards be enforced through disciplinary guidelines?

CMS interprets the well-publicized disciplinary guidelines regulation to require that "written standards of conduct specify the disciplinary actions that can be imposed for noncompliance, including oral or written warnings or reprimands, suspensions, terminations, or financial penalties."[36] These standards should be approved by the organization's governing body or a committee of the governing body.[37]

Q 22.6.7 What procedures for corrective action should an MCO implement?

A compliance program should have procedures to correct program violations, like referral to criminal or civil law enforcement, corrective action plans, government reports and provider notification of discrepancies.[38] CMS specifically requires:

(1) a timely and reasonable inquiry into misconduct related to payment or delivery of items or services under the contract; and
(2) corrective actions in response to such misconduct.[39]

The development of corrective action initiatives require that the organization have policies and procedures that ensure corrective action initiatives have been taken, implemented, and the detected offenses have been corrected.[40] Additionally, MA MCOs should carefully document all attempts to comply with state and federal requirements.[41]

Q 22.6.8 What specific requirements are there for MA-PD plan compliance programs?

The program must detect, correct, and prevent fraud, waste, and abuse. The plan should "include procedures to voluntarily self-report potential fraud or misconduct related to the Part D program to the appropriate government authority."[42]

Q 22.7 What are the consequences of failing to comply with CMS's mandates?

Beginning in January 2007, CMS will conduct regular audits of MA organizations' compliance programs. Organizations that do not have an effective compliance program may face serious consequences, including sanctions. These consequences may include:

(1) suspension, termination or exclusion from participating in Medicare, Medicaid or other federal programs;
(2) preclusion from enrolling new beneficiaries;
(3) denial or recoupment of payments on behalf of beneficiaries already enrolled in their plans;
(4) recoupment of prior payments; or
(5) hefty fines.

Bear in mind that an ineffective compliance program may also lead to:

- enforcement actions;
- high investigation costs; and
- fines related to internal misconduct or big settlements of qui tam (whistleblower) cases for violations of fraud and abuse laws.

Liability Under the False Claims Act and Other Statutes

Q 22.8 Why should MCOs be concerned about the False Claims Act?

The False Claims Act (FCA)[43] holds the potential for severe MCO liability.[44] There has been increased federal enforcement of false claims, as well as recent amendments to the FCA, which may result in heavy monetary recoveries against MCOs. Although MCOs do not submit traditional claims to the federal government and their providers do not directly deal with the government, the FCA can apply to MCOs and many other types of arrangements, even those in which the participants do not intend to defraud the government.[45] In addition, the FERA changes to the FCA make this potential liability more explicit.[46] This can create considerable implications for managed care administrators and financial managers.[47]

Q 22.9 Who, in a managed care context, can liability be imposed on?

A person or entity who:

(1) knowingly presents, makes, or uses or causes to be presented, made, or used a false or fraudulent claim for payment or approval;

(2) knowingly makes a false statement or record to get a false or fraudulent claim paid or approved;

(3) conspires to defraud the government by getting a false or fraudulent claim allowed or paid; or

(4) knowingly or improperly avoids an obligation to pay the government.[48]

Q 22.9.1 What is required for liability under the FCA?

Actual knowledge, deliberate ignorance of the truth and falsity of the information, or reckless disregard of the truth or falsity of the information.[49]

Q 22.9.2 What penalties does the FCA provide for?

Liability may result in damages ranging from $5,000 to $10,000, plus treble damages.[50] Violations may also result in an MCO's mandatory exclusion from federal health care programs.[51]

Q 22.10 What other statutes might pose liability issues for MCOs?

MCO fraud and abuse might also lead to liability under several federal and state statutes. Among these statutes are the:

(1) Federal Health Care Program Anti-Kickback Act;[52]
(2) Health Care Fraud Act;[53]

(3) Obstruction of Health Care Investigations statute;[54]
(4) Theft or Embezzlement in Relation to a Health Care Benefit Program statutes;[55] and
(5) Racketeer Influenced and Corrupt Organizations Act (RICO).[56]

For further information on these statutes, see chapter 20, Healthcare Organizations and Providers.

Q 22.11 How are MA MCOs vulnerable to false claims liability?

Exposure to false claims liability may arise from errors in, among other areas:

(1) the adjusted community rate, representing the amount non-Medicare enrollees would be charged for Medicare-covered services and adjusted for greater use of services by Medicare enrollees;
(2) enrollment data certified and submitted monthly to CMS, and detailing new enrollments, disenrollments, and changes in institutional status of beneficiaries; and
(3) encounter data for encounters between Medicare enrollees and providers or suppliers used as a risk factor to adjust for health status.[57]

Physician Incentive Plans (PIPs)

Q 22.12 What liability issues can an MCO face related to Physician Incentive Plans?

PIP rules limit the situations where physicians are subject to financial incentives to deny medically necessary services to Medicare and Medicaid managed care patients.[58] The rule is applicable to MCOs that contract with CMS or state agencies to provide Medicare or Medicaid services. It covers physician compensation where the contracting is:

(1) directly between the physician and the MCO; and
(2) indirectly through a contract with an intermediary organization, like a physician hospital organization or an independent practice association.[59]

MCOs must furnish CMS with enough information to determine if the plan satisfies the requirements of 42 C.F.R. § 422.208 and if services not furnished by physicians are covered by the PIP.[60] MCOs must also carefully review the accuracy and completeness of physician incentive information provided by physicians to avoid false claims exposure based on false data. To decrease the potential for liability, MCOs should show their efforts to adhere to the PIP rules by employees, physicians, physicians groups, and intermediaries as part of its compliance program.[61]

Managed Care Exceptions to the Anti-Kickback Statute

The new exception to the AKS is discussed in chapter 21, Medicare Part D, at Q 21.15.

Prompt Payment and Denial of Care Compliance Issues

Q 22.13 What are CMS's prompt payment requirements?

MCOs are required to pay 95% of clean claims submitted by noncontracting providers within thirty days of receipt.[62]

Q 22.13.1 What is a "clean" claim?

A clean claim is a claim that:

(1) has no defect, impropriety, lack of any required substantiating documentation (consistent with section 422.310(d)) or particular circumstance requiring special treatment that prevents timely payment; and
(2) otherwise conforms to the clean claim requirements for equivalent claims under original Medicare.[63]

Q 22.13.2 What are potential consequences of failure to make prompt payments?

(1) Direct payment of the sums owed to providers, or MA private fee-for-service plan enrollees; and

(2) Appropriate reduction in the amounts that would otherwise be paid to the organization, to reflect the amounts of the direct payments and the cost of making those payments.[64]

Likewise, many states have enacted prompt payment statutes. State penalties may range from fines to substantial interest penalties for late payments.[65]

Q 22.14 When does denial or unavailability of care by an MCO constitute fraud and abuse?

The DOJ lists several factors it will consider in making these determinations, including:

(1) representations made to beneficiaries by the plan, physicians, sales representatives, customer service employees, contractors and plan documents;
(2) accounting and actuarial records systems that reveal the sources of MCO profits;
(3) incentives and bonuses;
(4) complaints from subscribers, providers, regulators, accreditation agencies and competitors;
(5) quality measurement;
(6) lack of articulated standards; and
(7) evidence that patients did not receive promised benefits.[66]

Q 22.14.1 What are potential consequences for denial of care?

In addition to being exposed to FCA liability, MCOs may also be sued by policyholders under state deceptive business practice laws.[67]

Medicare Fraud and Abuse in Marketing

Q 22.15 What are Medicare MCOs required to do in their marketing practices?

MCOs should be vigilant about not engaging in prohibited marketing activities, such as discouraging participation based on health status or inducing participation with gifts or payments.[68]

To ensure that beneficiaries receive accurate information about Medicare MCOs, prior to distributing marketing materials, MCOs must:

(1) submit marketing materials or forms to CMS for review at least forty-five days before the date of distribution (or ten days if using marketing materials that use, without modification, proposed model language as specified by CMS); and
(2) not receive a disapproval of the new materials or form from CMS.[69]

To aid MCOs in this process, CMS devised the *Medicare Managed Care National Marketing Guide*, which includes CMS regulations on marketing. These guidelines help MCOs and are intended to:

(1) expedite the process for CMS's review of marketing materials;
(2) conserve organization resources by avoiding multiple submissions/reviews of marketing materials prior to final approval;
(3) ensure consistent marketing review throughout the program;
(4) enable organizations to develop accurate, consumer-friendly marketing materials that will assist beneficiaries in making informed health care choices; and
(5) establish consistent review standards for all organizations, unless the marketing material is specific to a plan type.[70]

Notes

1. HEALTH CARE FRAUD AND ABUSE: PRACTICAL PERSPECTIVES 312 (Linda A. Baumann ed., ABA Health Law Section 2002) [hereinafter Baumann].
2. *Id.* at 314–23.
3. *Id.* at 324.
4. *Id.* at 326.
5. *Id.* at 326–27.
6. Kirk J. Nahra, Legal Issues in Fighting Fraud in a Managed Care Environment at 9, *available at* www.wileyrein.com/docs/publications/7851.pdf (accessed Mar. 25, 2007).
7. *Id.* at 11–13; Baumann at 327.
8. Baumann at 310.
9. *Id.* at 311.
10. *Id.* at 329.
11. 42 C.F.R. § 422.503(b)(4)(vi)(A)–(H), 42 C.F.R. § 423.504(b)(4)(i)–(vi).
12. 42 C.F.R. § 422.503(b)(4)(vi)(A).
13. Memorandum from David Lewis, Deputy Dir., Medicare Advantage Group Ctr. for Beneficiary Choices, Centers for Medicare and Medicaid Services, on Medicare Advantage, Medicare Advantage-Prescription Drug Plans CY 2007 Instructions (Apr. 4, 2006) [hereinafter Lewis], at 59, *available at* www.cms.hhs.gov/BenePriceBidFormPlanPackage/Downloads/2007CallLetter.pdf.
14. Baumann at 330–31.
15. *Id.* at 331–32.
16. *Id.* at 332.
17. *Id.*
18. *Id.* at 333.
19. *Id.* at 334.
20. *Id.*
21. 42 C.F.R. § 422.503(b)(4)(vi)(B).
22. Lewis at 59.
23. Baumann at 336.
24. *Id.*
25. *Id.* at 336–37.
26. Lewis at 59.
27. *Id.*
28. Baumann at 337.
29. *Id.*
30. 42 C.F.R. § 422.503(b)(4)(vi)(D).
31. Lewis at 59.
32. *Id.*

Managed Care Organizations

33. *Id.* at 60.
34. Baumann at 338.
35. *Id.*
36. Lewis at 60.
37. *Id.* at 60.
38. Baumann at 338.
39. 42 C.F.R. § 422.503(b)(4)(vi)(G)(1)–(2).
40. Lewis at 60.
41. Baumann at 338.
42. 42 C.F.R. § 423.504(b)(4)(vi)(H).
43. For more on the False Claims Act, see chapter 11.
44. For a more detailed discussion of the False Claims Act, see chapter 11.
45. Shelley R. Slade, *False Claims Act May Reach Managed Care Organizations*, HEALTHCARE FIN. MGMT., Jan. 1, 2002, *available at* www.allbusiness.com/personal-finance/health-care-health-plan/105286-1.html.
46. For a more detailed discussion of the FERA changes to the FCA, see chapters 11 and 20.
47. Slade, *supra* note 45.
48. 31 U.S.C. § 3729(a).
49. 31 U.S.C. § 3729(b).
50. 31 U.S.C. § 3729(a).
51. 42 U.S.C. § 1320a-7(a).
52. 42 U.S.C. § 1320a-7b(b).
53. 18 U.S.C. § 1347.
54. 18 U.S.C. § 1518.
55. 18 U.S.C. § 669.
56. 18 U.S.C. § 1961.
57. Baumann at 343–44.
58. *See* 42 U.S.C. §§ 1395mm(i), 1395w-22(j)(4).
59. Baumann at 345.
60. *Id.* at 346.
61. *Id.* at 350.
62. 42 C.F.R. § 422.520(a).
63. 42 C.F.R. § 422.500.
64. 42 C.F.R. § 422.520(c).
65. Baumann at 358.
66. *Id.* at 359 (citing 3 Health Care Fraud Rep. (BNA) 561 (June 30, 1999); 2 Health Care Fraud Rep. (BNA) 319 (May 6, 1998)).
67. *Id.* at 360.
68. *Id.* at 361.
69. 42 C.F.R. § 422.80(a).
70. *See* MEDICARE MANAGED CARE MANUAL, ch. 3 (Medicare Marketing Guidelines) (Rev. 91, Aug. 7, 2009). Chapter 3 is available at www.cms.hhs.gov/manuals/downloads/mc86c03.pdf.

23

Pharmaceutical and Medical Device Manufacturers

*Michael Manthei, William F. Gould, Patrick O'Brien & Jenna Phipps Bigornia**

This chapter assesses the major risk areas associated with the development and marketing of pharmaceuticals and medical devices—highly regulated industries whose regulatory structures present many compliance challenges. This chapter gives a high-level overview of the major risk areas; it does not attempt to catalogue every possible risk. Nor does it address in detail the FDA approval process itself. As a detailed discussion of the approval process is beyond the scope of this treatise, it is assumed that the reader has a basic understanding of the process.

This chapter focuses on labeling and advertising, sales, marketing, and pricing, and biomedical research/clinical trials.

---

* The authors wish to acknowledge Christopher A. Myers for his contributions to this chapter.

Overview	718
Labeling and Advertising	718
Labeling: The Basics	718
Labeling: Requirements	719
Advertising: The Basics	721
Advertising: Requirements	722
Table 23-1: Advertisements That Are False, Lacking in Fair Balance, or Otherwise Misleading	725
Table 23-2: Advertisements That May Be False, Lacking in Fair Balance, or Otherwise Misleading	728
Misbranding	731
"Off-Label" Use	733
Sales, Marketing, and Pricing	736
State and Federal Regulation	736
Table 23-3: Statutory and Non-Statutory Guidance Affecting Sales and Marketing of Pharmaceuticals and Medical Devices	737
Anti-Kickback Statute	738
False Claims Act	744
Prescription Drug Marketing Act	744
Biomedical Research/Clinical Trials	745
Conflicts of Interest	745
Table 23-4: Rules, Regulations, and Guidelines Governing Biomedical Research/Clinical Trials	746
Protection of Human Subjects	758
Informed Consent	762
Charging for Investigational Drugs	770
Medicare Coverage in Clinical Trials	771

Pharmaceutical and Medical Device Manufacturers

Acronyms, initialisms, and abbreviations used in this chapter:

AHRQ	Agency for Healthcare Research and Quality
AKS	anti-kickback statute
AMA	American Medical Association
ASP	average sales price
AWP	Average Wholesale Price
BLA	biologics license application
CDC	Centers for Disease Control
CMS	Centers for Medicare and Medicaid Services
DOD	Department of Defense
FDA	Food and Drug Administration
FDCA	Food, Drug and Cosmetic Act
GCP	good clinical practice
HHS	Health and Human Services
ICH	International Conference on Harmonisation of Technical Requirements for Registration of Pharmaceuticals for Human Use
IND	investigational new drug
IRB	Institutional Review Board
MDMA	Medical Device Manufacturers Association
NDA	new drug application
NIH	National Institutes of Health
NSF	National Science Foundation
OHRP	Office of Human Research Protection
OIG	Office of Inspector General
PDMA	Prescription Drug Marketing Act

PhRMA	Pharmaceutical Research and Manufacturers of America
PHS	Public Health Service
SBIR	Small Business Innovation Research
VA	Department of Veterans Affairs
WHO	World Health Organization
WMA	World Medical Association

Overview

Q 23.1 What are the major risk areas in the pharmaceutical and medical device industry?

The areas that present the most significant financial, operational, and reputational exposure include:

- labeling and advertising;
- sales, marketing, and pricing;
- goods manufacturing/quality compliance;
- product liability; and
- biomedical research/clinical trials.

Labeling and Advertising

Labeling: The Basics

Q 23.2 What is labeling?

The FDCA defines labeling to mean all labels and other written, printed, or graphic materials upon a regulated article (like a drug or medical device) or "accompanying such article" in interstate commerce. The Supreme Court interpreted the phrase "accompanying such article" broadly in *United States v. Kordel*, such that the labeling need not physically accompany the drug or medical device. Instead, material "accompanies" the regulated product "when it supplements or explains it, in the manner that a committee report of the Congress accompanies a bill."[1] A companion case makes clear that the holding in *Kordel* demands that written material be part of an integrated transaction in selling the drug or device,[2] although the government has attempted to read this requirement out of the FDCA by regulation:[3]

> [b]rochures, booklets, mailing pieces, detailing pieces, file cards, bulletins, calendars, price lists, catalogs, house organs, letters, motion picture films, film strips, lantern slides, sound recordings, exhibits, literature, and reprints and similar pieces of printed, audio, or visual matter descriptive of a drug and references published (for example, the "Physicians Desk Reference") for use by medical practitioners, pharmacists, or nurses, containing drug information supplied by the manufacturer, packer, or distributor of the drug and which are disseminated by or on behalf of its manufacturer, packer, or distributor are hereby determined to be labeling. . . .[4]

Labeling: Requirements

Q 23.2.1 What must a prescription drug label include?

The label and labeling for an approved prescription drug product must be identical to that approved by the FDA during the application process. The FDA will approve labeling for a drug found to be safe and effective where the general drug labeling requirements found at 21 C.F.R. § 202.1 *et seq.* as well as the specific prescription drug labeling requirements found at 21 C.F.R. §§ 202.60 *et seq.* and 202.100 are met.

Q 23.2.2 What must an over-the-counter drug label include?

The label and labeling for an over-the-counter drug must include information as approved by the FDA or as permitted under several final or draft product category monographs. Additionally, the label must include the general drug labeling requirements found at 21 C.F.R. §§ 202.1 *et seq.* and 201.60 *et seq.* with certain of that required information being in the format of a "Drug Facts" box.[5]

Q 23.2.3 What must a medical device label include?

The label and labeling for all medical devices must comply with the general labeling requirements found at 21 C.F.R. § 801.1 *et seq.* Specific labeling requirements for OTC devices can be found at 21 C.F.R. § 801.60 *et seq.*, for prescription medical devices at 21 C.F.R. § 801.109, and for *in vitro* diagnostic medical devices at 21 C.F.R. § 119.

Q 23.2.4 What happens if labeling does not comply with FDA requirements?

A drug or device is "misbranded" if its labeling does not contain all required contents, the label contents are not displayed as required (*e.g.*, type size, location on label, etc.) or the label contents are otherwise "false or misleading."[6] In particular, a drug or device is misbranded if the label does not contain adequate instructions for its intended use and required warnings.[7] (This requirement is complex and is important in "off-label" marketing, discussed elsewhere in this chapter.)

Q 23.2.5 What are the potential consequences of noncompliance with label requirements?

Introducing a misbranded drug or device into interstate commerce is a crime.[8] Penalties include imprisonment for up to a year for a first offense or up to three years for a subsequent offense or for any offense committed with the intent to defraud or to mislead.[9] Criminal fines of up to $10,000 per violation also may be imposed.[10]

The government also has at its disposal an array of civil sanctions. It may impose civil monetary penalties for certain violations.[11] It may seek an injunction restraining further violations of the FDCA labeling and advertising requirements.[12] Under certain circumstances, the FDA may seize the misbranded drugs or medical devices.[13]

Advertising: The Basics

Q 23.3 Generally speaking, how important is advertising/labeling compliance?

Advertising and labeling are fraught with compliance risk. The stakes are extremely high. Drug and device advertising and labeling expose the manufacturer *and* its officers and directors not only to simple regulatory risk, but also to potential criminal and civil liability under a variety of legal theories.

In recent years, manufacturers have paid billions of dollars in civil and criminal fines to state and federal authorities in order to settle claims arising from alleged advertising and labeling violations. In connection with these settlements, manufacturers (and in some instances, their officers) have been forced to plead guilty to criminal violations. Beyond mere fines, the finding of criminal liability can result in the so-called death penalty; that is, the manufacturer may be debarred, or excluded, from participation in all federal programs, including Medicare and Medicaid.

In an apparent effort to encourage corporate compliance, the government has recently been making a concerted effort to hold corporate executives, including corporate counsel, personally accountable. Specifically, the government has recently excluded corporate executives from participating in federally funded reimbursement programs after those executives, including a company lawyer, pled guilty to criminal misdemeanor misbranding.[14] As of this writing, the government has initiated proceedings to exclude the CEO of a pharmaceutical company where the company pled guilty to FDCA crimes although the CEO did not.[15] Additionally, the government has prosecuted, unsuccessfully, a corporate lawyer for obstruction of justice and for making false statements to the government after she oversaw an internal investigation concerning misbranding allegations. Notably, the court in that case acquitted the in-house lawyer observing that the case "should never have been prosecuted" by the government prosecutors.[16]

Q 23.4 What is "advertising"?

"Advertising," as used in the Food, Drug and Cosmetic Act (FDCA), includes both traditional advertising and advertising in "new media." Thus, it includes ads published in journals, magazines, other periodicals, and newspapers as well as information that is broadcast through media such as radio, television, and telephone communications systems. Similarly "advertising" can be conducted through fax machines, on computer programs, and through blogs, social networking sites such as Facebook or Twitter, and other web postings.[17]

Advertising: Requirements

Q 23.4.1 What are prescription drug advertisements required to include?

Advertisements must include:

- the established ("generic") name;
- the proprietary ("brand") name (if any);
- the formula showing quantitatively each ingredient;
- information in "brief summary" that discusses side effects, contraindications, and effectiveness;[18]
- for broadcast advertisements, the "brief summary" or an adequate alternative for disseminating the product's label in conjunction with the advertisement;
- for broadcast advertisements, a "major statement" of the product's most important risk-related information in the broadcast's audio or in the audio and visual parts of the broadcast;
- for all published direct-to-consumer advertisements, the statement, "You are encouraged to report negative side effects of prescription drugs to the FDA. Visit www.fda.gov/medwatch or call 1-800-FDA-1088." included conspicuously.

And advertising must be true, fairly balanced, and not misleading.

Q 23.4.2 What is the "brief summary" of side effects, contraindications, and effectiveness?

The "brief summary" required by the FDA regulations is familiar to all and often lampooned. In television and in radio advertisements it is the list of side effects, contraindications, warnings, precautions, special considerations, important notes, effectiveness, etc. included at the end of the advertisement.[19]

Recently the FDA issued draft guidance concerning an appropriate method for formulating the "brief summary" in consumer-directed print advertising. That draft guidance encourages companies advertising drugs with approved labeling containing a "highlights" section to disclose only those risks contained in the "highlights" section, translated into consumer-friendly language.[20] The draft guidance states the agency's belief that such a methodology increases consumer understanding of those risks that are most important to the consumer because they are not "drowned out" by less-important risk information. A decision to follow such guidance (as opposed to simply including all risks contained in the approved labeling) should be made with consideration of product liability implications.

Q 23.4.3 Must a broadcast advertisement contain the "brief summary" of side effects, contraindications, and effectiveness?

Advertisements broadcast through media such as radio, television, or telephone communications systems must include the "brief summary" in the audio or visual parts of the presentation unless adequate provision is made for dissemination of the approved or permitted package labeling in connection with the broadcast presentation.[21] The FDA has published a guidance document explaining a method to comply with the "adequate provision" requirement. That method involves providing for access to the approved package labeling through multiple opportunities such as web, print periodicals, and toll-free telephone numbers.[22] It should be noted that regulations and the FDA guidance for broadcast advertising require that major risks be disclosed in the broadcast advertisement itself. The FDA guidance terms this disclosure the "major statement."

Q 23.4.4 What does the FDA consider true, balanced, and not-misleading advertising?

Applicable regulations define these in the negative; that is, rather than describing the characteristics of ads that are true, fairly balanced, and not misleading, the regulations spell out a long list of characteristics of advertisements that are false, lacking in fair balance, or otherwise misleading (see Table 23-1). The regulations also include a long list of characteristics of advertisements that *may be* false, lacking in fair balance, or otherwise misleading (see Table 23-2).[23]

Q 23.4.5 Are there exceptions to these advertising requirements?

Yes, there are a few exceptions, but only to the requirement to provide a "brief summary" (as described above). The following are examples of exempt advertisements:

1. *Reminder advertisements*—advertisements intended to call attention to the name of the drug, but that do not contain indication statements or dosage recommendations.[24] Reminder advertisements must contain the proprietary (brand) name and established (generic) name of the drug and/or each active ingredient, and may contain quantitative ingredient statements, dosage forms, quantity of packages contents as sold, price, and the name and address of the manufacturer, packer, or distributor. While the advertisements can contain other information, there can be no other representations or suggestions relating to the drug being advertised. Reminder advertisements need not carry balancing information, prescribing information, or a brief summary. However, the agency broadly construes the prohibition on "other representations or suggestions about the drug" to include anything that is remotely related to the drug. The reminder advertisement exception does not apply to drugs carrying a boxed warning.[25]
2. *Advertisements of bulk-sale drugs*—sales of the drug in bulk packages to be processed, manufactured, labeled, or repackaged and that contain no claims for the therapeutic safety or effectiveness of the drug.
3. *Advertisements of prescription-compounding drugs*—ads that promote sale of a drug for use as a prescription chemical or other compound for use by registered pharmacists.[26]

TABLE 23-1
Advertisements That Are False, Lacking in Fair Balance, or Otherwise Misleading

A prescription drug advertisement *is* false, lacking in fair balance, or otherwise misleading if it:

(1) contains a representation/suggestion, not approved or permitted for use in the labeling, that a drug is better, more effective, useful in a broader range of conditions or patients (humans or, in the case of veterinary drugs, other animals), safer, has fewer, or less incidence of, or less-serious side effects or contraindications than substantial evidence/clinical experience has shown whether or not such representations are made by comparison with other drugs or treatments, and whether or not such a representation/suggestion is made directly or by using published or unpublished literature, quotations, or other references.

(2) represents/suggests that a drug is safer or more effective than another drug in some particular when substantial evidence/clin-ical experience has not demonstrated that.

(3) contains favorable information/opinions about a drug previously regarded as valid but that have been rendered invalid by contrary and more credible recent information, or contains references/quotations significantly more favorable to the drug than substantial evidence/clinical experience has shown.

(4) selectively presents information from published articles or other references that report no side effects or minimal side effects or otherwise make a drug appear to be safer than has been demonstrated.

(5) presents information from a study so as to imply that the study represents larger or more general experience with the drug than it actually does.

(6) refers to literature/studies that misrepresent the drug's effectiveness by not disclosing that claimed results may be due to concomitant therapy, or (in the case of ads promoting a drug for use by man) by not disclosing credible information available concerning the placebo effect on results.

(7) contains favorable data/conclusions from nonclinical drug studies (*e.g.*, in lab animals or in vitro), suggesting they have clinical significance when in fact no such significance has been demonstrated.

(8) uses an apparently favorable statement by a recognized authority but fails to refer to concurrent or more recent unfavorable data or statements from the same authority on the same subject(s).

(9) uses a quote or paraphrase out of context to convey a false or misleading idea.

(10) uses literature, quotations, or references that purport to support a claim but in fact do not support/have relevance to the claim.

(11) uses literature, quotations, or references for the purpose of recommending or suggesting conditions of drug use that are not approved or permitted in the drug package labeling.

(12) offers a combination of drugs for the treatment of patients suffering from a condition amenable to treatment by any of the components rather than limiting the indications for use to patients for whom concomitant therapy as provided by the fixed combination drug is indicated (unless such condition is included in the uses permitted by the regulations).

(13) uses a study on normal individuals without disclosing that they were normal, unless the drug is intended for use on normal individuals.

Pharmaceutical and Medical Device Manufacturers   Q 23.4.5

(14) uses "statistics" on numbers of patients, or counts of favorable results or side effects, derived from pooling data from various insignificant or dissimilar studies so as to suggest that such "statistics" are valid if they are not or that they are derived from large or significant studies supporting favorable conclusions when such is not the case.

(15) uses erroneously a statistical finding of "no significant difference" to claim clinical equivalence or to deny or conceal the potential existence of a real clinical difference.

(16) uses statements/representations that a drug differs from or does not contain a named drug/category of drugs, or that it has a greater potency per unit of weight, in a way that suggests falsely or misleadingly or without substantial evidence/clinical experience that the advertised drug is safer or more effective.

(17) uses data favorable to a drug derived from patients treated with dosages different from those recommended in approved or permitted labeling if the drug advertised is subject to section 505 of the act, or, in the case of other drugs, if the dosages employed were different from those recommended in the labeling and generally recognized as safe and effective.

(18) uses headline, sub-headline, or pictorial or other graphic matter in a misleading way.

(19) represents/suggests that properly recommended drug dosages for certain classes of patients or disease conditions are safe and effective for other classes of patients or disease conditions when they are not.

(20) presents required side-effect or contraindication information using a general term for a group in place of disclosing each specific side effect and contraindication (for example, employs the term "blood dyscrasias" instead of "leukopenia," "agranulocytosis," "neutropenia," etc.) (except as otherwise permitted).

TABLE 23-2
Advertisements That May Be False, Lacking in Fair Balance, or Otherwise Misleading

An advertisement *may be* false, lacking in fair balance, or otherwise misleading if it:

(1) contains favorable information/conclusions from a study that is inadequate in design, scope, or conduct to furnish significant support for such information/conclusions.

(2) uses "statistical significance" to support a claim that has not been demonstrated to have clinical significance or validity, or fails to reveal the range of variations around the quoted average results.

(3) uses statistical analyses and techniques on a retrospective basis to discover and cite findings not soundly supported by the study, or to suggest scientific validity and rigor for data from studies the design or protocol of which are not amenable to formal statistical evaluations.

(4) uses tables/graphs to distort or misrepresent the relationships, trends, differences, or changes among the variables or products studied; *e.g.*, by failing to label the abscissa (*X* axis) and ordinate (*Y* axis) thus creating a misleading impression.

(5) uses reports/statements represented to be statistical analyses, interpretations, or evaluations that are inconsistent with or violate the established principles of statistical theory, methodology, applied practice, and inference, or that are derived from clinical studies the design, data, or conduct of which substantially invalidate the application of statistical analyses, interpretations, or evaluations.

(6) contains claims concerning the mechanism or site of drug action that are not generally regarded as established by scientific evidence by experts qualified by scientific training and experience without disclosing that the claims are not established and the limitations of the supporting evidence.

(7) fails to provide sufficient emphasis for side-effect and contraindication information, when such information is contained in a distinct part of an advertisement, because of repetition or other emphasis in that part of the advertisement of claims for effectiveness or safety of the drug.

(8) fails to present side-effect and contraindication information with a prominence and readability reasonably comparable with that of information relating to the drug's effectiveness, taking into account typography, layout, contrast, headlines, paragraphing, white space, and any other techniques apt to achieve emphasis.

(9) fails to provide adequate emphasis (*e.g.*, by the use of color scheme, borders, headlines, or copy that extends across the gutter) for the fact that two facing pages are part of the same advertisement when one page contains side-effect and contraindication information.

(10) in an advertisement promoting use of the drug in a selected class of patients (*e.g.*, geriatric patients or depressed patients), fails to present with adequate emphasis the significant side effects and contraindications or the significant dosage considerations, when dosage recommendations are included in an advertisement, especially applicable to that selected class of patients.

(11) fails to present on a page facing another page (or on another full page) of an advertisement on more than one page side-effect and contraindication information when such information is in a distinct part of the advertisement.

(12) fails to include on each page or spread of an advertisement the side-effect and contraindication information or a prominent reference to its presence and location when it is presented as a distinct part of an advertisement.

(13) contains information from published or unpublished reports or opinions falsely or misleadingly represented or suggested to be authentic or authoritative.

Q 23.4.6 Does the FDA pre-approve advertising?

Any advertisement may be submitted to the FDA for comment prior to publication. FDA comments must be in writing. If the manufacturer is notified that the submitted advertisement is not in violation and, at some subsequent time, the FDA changes its opinion, the manufacturer is notified and will be given a reasonable time to correct the advertisement before any regulatory action is taken.[27]

Q 23.4.7 Is pre-approval of advertising ever mandatory?

If the FDA receives reliable information that has not been widely publicized that a drug may cause death or serious damage and it has notified the manufacturer of such information, then the manufacturer *might* need to get prior FDA approval for future advertisements. In this circumstance, the FDA will notify the manufacturer of the information and request that it submit a program for ensuring that such information will be publicized promptly and adequately to the medical profession in subsequent advertisements. If the manufacturer fails to submit a program, or if the FDA deems a proposed program to be inadequate, then the manufacturer *must* submit advertisements for the drug to the FDA for prior approval.[28] Once the information has been widely publicized to the medical profession, the FDA will notify the manufacturer that prior approval of advertising no longer is required.[29]

Drugs approved under the accelerated approval process (drugs approved to treat serious or life-threatening illnesses where the approval is usually based upon surrogate endpoints) are approved on condition that promotional materials must be submitted to the FDA thirty days in advance of use.[30] While these provisions do not require FDA approval, they do permit the FDA to object to the promotional materials before first use.

The FDCA has been amended to require prior submission of certain direct-to-consumer television advertisements for prescription drugs.[31] Implementation of these new provisions has been delayed in part due to statutory funding provisions of the legislation. However, it is likely FDA will soon issue guidance explaining which prescription drug products are subject to the prior submission requirements and the methods for making such submissions. Until such guidance issues, the agency does not have a mechanism enabling compliance with the statutory provisions, and marketers are not expected to comply. When these provisions are enabled by the agency, companies will be required to submit advertising in advance, but will not be required to obtain approval.

In some instances prior submission is required by operation of federal and state consent decrees resulting from enforcement action.

In the past, the FDA has stated in its drug approval letters that sponsors must submit copies of proposed launch materials to the FDA, in advance, for review. While the formal FDA position now appears to recognize that the agency generally cannot require such submissions (and in fact, the agency appears unwilling to even overtly encourage such submissions), the agency places a high priority on reviewing such draft launch material in an effort to enhance the probability of compliance. Many companies find such pre-launch submissions to be useful.

Q 23.4.8 Must advertisements be filed with the FDA?

Prescription drug sponsors must submit specimens of all labeling or advertising devised for promotion of the drug. Such materials must be submitted at the time of initial dissemination (for labeling material) and publication (for advertising material) under cover of FDA form 2253.[32]

Misbranding

Q 23.4.9 What happens if drug/device advertising does not comply with FDA requirements?

A drug or device that does not comply with FDA advertising requirements will generally be deemed to be misbranded. There are many ways a drug or medical device can become misbranded. In general, these consist of false or misleading statements on product labels or in product labeling, inadequate prominence or placement of required information in product labels or product labeling, inadequate or dangerous instructions for use, and omission of required labeling information from the product labeling or labels.[33] Additionally, false or misleading statements in prescription advertising or restricted medical device advertising may misbrand those products.[34] In recent years, a common allegation in misbranding cases is that a drug or medical device promoted for off-label use is misbranded because its approved labeling lacks adequate directions for the intended (off-label) use.

Q 23.4.10 What are the possible consequences of a misbranding violation?

Penalties include imprisonment for up to a year for a first offense or up to three years for a subsequent offense or for any offense committed with the intent to defraud or to mislead.[35] Criminal fines of up to $10,000 per violation also may be imposed.[36]

The government also has at its disposal an array of civil sanctions. It may impose significant civil monetary penalties of up to $500,000 for certain violations.[37] It may seek an injunction restraining further violations of the FDCA advertising requirements.[38] Finally, under certain circumstances, the FDA may seize the misbranded drugs.[39]

Typically, the FDA will send the manufacturer a warning letter or an "untitled letter" before taking more serious action such as seeking an injunction or seizing the drug. The letter will recite the alleged violations and will identify the language or other aspects of the ad or labeling that the FDA deems to be lacking fair balance, misleading, or otherwise inappropriate. The letter will demand specific action and a written response.

If the FDA considers the response to be adequate, then the matter may end there. However, it is important that the manufacturer respond. The failure to respond may result in the FDA seeking more severe sanctions.

Whether a manufacturer responds appropriately to a letter from the FDA or not, it may face liability from DOJ, OIG, individual states, or consumer groups. DOJ may enforce the FDCA misbranding provisions directly. OIG and the states may effectively do so by creative application of other laws such as the False Claims Act and various state consumer laws. The manufacturer's response letter should be carefully crafted to minimize the likelihood it will be used against the manufacturer in any subsequent proceedings.

"Off-Label" Use

Q 23.5 What is meant by "off-label"?

All drugs and medical devices are approved, cleared, or permitted for distribution containing adequate directions (or a similar requirement) in their labeling for their intended use. Uses other than those approved, cleared, or permitted intended uses are considered "off-label."

Q 23.5.1 Is it illegal for a physician to prescribe a drug "off-label"?

With the exception of the prescription and distribution of human growth hormone, it is not illegal for a physician to prescribe a drug or medical device "off-label." However, many payors will not reimburse the cost of drugs used off-label, or they might limit off-label reimbursement only to those off-label uses that have come to be generally accepted over time in the medical community.

Q 23.5.2 Is advertising or promotion of off-label uses permitted?

While there is no statute or regulation that specifically prohibits off-label promotion, the position of enforcement authorities tends to be that promotion of off-label uses is prohibited. When pressed on the interplay between the government's frequent assertion that "off-label promotion" and "off-label marketing" are illegal and the First Amendment requirements attendant to such speech restrictions, the government makes absolutely clear that off-label promotion is not a crime, but is instead evidence of intended use that can cause a drug or medical device to become misbranded.[40]

The FDA and others argue that off-label promotion violates the FDCA in two ways: first, that it constitutes the introduction into interstate commerce of an "unapproved new drug"; second, that it constitutes the illegal introduction into interstate commerce of a misbranded drug or device.

The FDCA prohibits the introduction of an unapproved drug, and the FDA contends a drug becomes a "new drug" if it is introduced in interstate commerce for a use different from the one for which the drug was approved (the "intended use"). Likewise, a drug is misbranded, the government contends, if its labeling does not include adequate directions for its intended use.

The government's assertion that "off-label" promotion is unlawful is particularly nettlesome, because the line between permitted activities and "promotion" is extremely unclear. For instance, FDA regulations state that the regulatory scheme is "not intended to restrict the full exchange of information concerning [a drug or medical device], including dissemination of scientific findings in scientific and lay media," but is intended to "restrict promotional claims of safety and effectiveness."[41] Additionally, notwithstanding the government's assertion that a drug or medical device must be introduced into interstate commerce with labeling sufficient to guide its intended use, the agency has issued a guidance permitting the distribution, including distribution by sales representatives, of reprints concerning certain unapproved uses of approved or cleared drugs and medical devices.[42]

While manufacturers and others disagree to a point, what can be said with certainty is that off-label promotion is a high priority for enforcement authorities, whose enforcement efforts have resulted in the government imposing fines totaling in the billions of dollars.

Q 23.5.3 How might off-label promotion constitute misbranding?

The FDA approves drugs and devices only after the manufacturer shows that the drug is safe and effective for the specific use described in the manufacturer's application for approval or clearance.[43] Once approved or cleared, the FDA requires that the product labeling, among other things, include adequate directions for all intended uses, absent which it is deemed to be misbranded.[44] While the government's argument is more complex than presented here, it essentially maintains that a product's approved labeling cannot contain "adequate directions" for an off-label use because the manufacturer cannot write "adequate directions" that were not approved by the FDA and that were not thereby proven to be safe and effective or that otherwise meet regulations for approval or clearance.[45]

Q 23.5.4 How might off-label promotion constitute the introduction of an unapproved new drug?

A "new drug" is defined as one that is not recognized as safe and effective for its intended use.[46] The intended use is demonstrated by the "objective intent of the persons legally responsible for the labeling of drugs."[47] The FDA ascertains a manufacturer's objective intent by looking at how the manufacturer distributes the drug, including the manufacturer's labeling claims, advertising materials, oral and written statements, and other circumstances surrounding the distribution of the drug.[48]

It is the FDA's position, therefore, that the manufacturer's promotion of a drug or device for an unapproved use creates a new "intended use." This new intended use has not been proven through the FDA approval process to be safe and effective. Consequently, the FDA reasons that promotion of the off-label use is the equivalent of introducing an unapproved "new drug" into interstate commerce in violation of the FDCA.[49]

Q 23.5.5 How does FDA determine the "intended use" of a regulated product?

The FDA has published regulations explaining how it determines "intended use" for drugs[50] and for medical devices.[51] Both of these regulations make clear that in determining the intended use of a product the FDA will look not only to the labeling and advertising of the regulated product, but also to the circumstances around the sale of the product, including the statements of the marketer's employees and even evidence that the seller knows the use to which a purchaser intends to put the product. The agency has variously made clear that it intends to exercise enforcement discretion in its interpretation, although it has declined to make clear those circumstances in which knowledge of the intention of a customer to use a product off-label will not misbrand the product on the argument that the product fails to contain adequate directions for the off-label use. Moreover, as explained elsewhere in this chapter, the agency permits the dissemination of off-label-use information by sales representatives under the agency's "Good Reprints Guidance Policy." Additionally, the agency has long made clear that drug and medical device manufacturers may answer unsolicited questions from customers and potential customers about off-label uses so long as the responses to those questions are concise, directed to the specific question asked, and accurate.

The ambiguity created by the government's discretionary approach to defining "intended use" is probably not consistent with constitutional due process requirements for criminal prosecutions.[52] Nonetheless, drug and medical device companies are generally reluctant to litigate such criminal prosecutions and, in fact, frequently settle them. Moreover, such due-process constraints are not likely to be relevant to related civil liability, such as the liability under the False Claims Act that frequently accompanies government claims of misbranding against medical device and prescription drug companies.

Sales, Marketing, and Pricing

State and Federal Regulation

Q 23.6 What laws and other guidance apply to the sale and marketing of pharmaceuticals and medical devices?

Other than the labeling and advertising rules discussed above, there are no federal statutes or regulations that exclusively regulate the sales and marketing practices of pharmaceutical and medical device manufacturers. Instead, there is a maze of federal and state laws, both criminal and civil, and a number of non-statutory guidance materials that serve to limit the sale and marketing activities of pharmaceutical and device manufacturers. These laws and guidance materials particularly impact the relationship between manufacturers on the one hand and prescribers, purchasers, and managed care organizations on the other. The main laws, other than the FDCA, used to restrict sales and marketing activities are the federal anti-kickback statute and the federal False Claims Act. (They are discussed in greater detail below.)

It is the enforcement of these laws, usually brought alongside criminal FDCA allegations, that has led to the many recent high-profile and high-dollar settlements between the federal and state governments and manufacturers. In addition to the advertising and labeling requirements discussed above, the laws and non-statutory guidance impacting the sales and marketing of pharmaceuticals and medical devices include those listed in Table 23-3.

Q 23.6.1 How do the states regulate sales and marketing practices?

As they face mounting budgetary constraints and are encouraged with financial incentives from the federal government, states are passing their own versions of the False Claims Act and of the anti-kickback statute. States also are using their consumer protection laws to address what they believe to be sales and marketing abuses. Finally, many states have passed, or are considering, statutes that require manufacturers to report the value of cash or items provided to physicians in a position to prescribe or to order the manufacturer's product.

TABLE 23-3
Statutory and Non-Statutory Guidance Affecting Sales and Marketing of Pharmaceuticals and Medical Devices

Laws affecting sales and marketing of drugs and devices
1. Federal Anti-Kickback Statute (42 U.S.C. § 1320a-7b(b))
2. Public Contracts Anti-Kickback Statute (41 U.S.C. § 52)
3. Federal False Claims Act (31 U.S.C. § 3729)
4. Civil Monetary Penalty Statute (42 U.S.C. § 1320a-7)
5. Robinson-Patman Act (15 U.S.C. § 13(c))
6. False Statements to a Federal Agent (18 U.S.C. § 1001)
7. Health Care Fraud (18 U.S.C. § 1035)
8. Patient Protection and Affordable Care Act (Pub. L. No. 111-148)
9. State anti-kickback statutes and false claims acts
10. State consumer protection laws
11. State reporting statutes

Non-statutory guidance
1. PhRMA Code[53]
2. AdvaMed Code[54]
3. AMA Ethics Opinion E-8.061
4. OIG Compliance Program Guidance for Pharmaceutical Manufacturers

Anti-Kickback Statute

Q 23.7 What is the federal anti-kickback statute?

The federal anti-kickback statute (AKS) is a federal criminal statute that prohibits the knowing or willful payment or receipt of any remuneration to induce or to recommend the referral of items or services that may be reimbursed in whole or in part by federal healthcare programs.[55] Violations of the AKS are punishable as felonies with fines of up to $25,000 per violation and imprisonment for up to five years.[56]

Remuneration broadly includes any benefit, either cash and "in-kind," and regardless of whether the benefit is provided directly or indirectly.[57] The AKS consequently implicates any payment or gift from a manufacturer to any person in a position to influence the prescription or purchase of the manufacturer's products.

Q 23.7.1 What are some of the key risk areas implicating the AKS?

There are several areas that the OIG has identified as being inherently risky for pharmaceutical and medical device companies, especially when marketing and promoting their products. This is not an exclusive list of problematic activities, nor does it mean that the described practices necessarily violate the AKS.

- Discounts
- Product support services
- Educational grants

- Research or other charitable donations
- Equipment and storage lease arrangements
- Formularies
- Pricing spreads
- Capital equipment pricing arrangements
- Product trainings, education, and sales meetings
- Gifts
- Switching arrangements
- Consulting arrangements

The key factor is the party's intent. Only those activities undertaken for the purpose (or at least a purpose) of inducing or rewarding referrals that result in federal healthcare program payments are prohibited.[58] To more clearly define the scope of the AKS, the OIG has created a number of "safe harbors" that identify financial relationships that will not be prosecuted as kickbacks.[59]

Q 23.7.2 What are the primary AKS considerations with regard to discounts?

Product discounts are permitted but only if properly documented and reported, and only if they constitute a reduction in the product's price. There is a specific safe harbor relating to discounts. The essential requirements are that the discount or rebate be stated on the face of the invoice or, in the case of a rebate, the formula is set forth in advance in writing. The discount cannot take into account the volume or value of referrals between the parties, and the records of the discount or rebate must be made available to HHS or reported on the entity's Medicare cost reports, if it is required to file one.

Q 23.7.3 ... product support services?

Product support services are "value-added" services offered in connection with the purchase of products. They may include billing, reimbursement, or other support. Provisions of these types of services can become problematic where the services eliminate a normal business cost or risk (*e.g.*, non-payment by insurance companies) or an expense to the customer.

Q 23.7.4 ... educational grants?

Companies often will sponsor educational conferences or make other grants to support education. This may include making donations to third-party educational, professional, charity groups for the advancement of medical or public health education. It might also mean providing grants to allow individuals to attend educational conferences. There are a few things to remember in providing these types of valuable community support:

- Educational grants should only be provided to organizations with bona fide educational purposes.[60]
- The grant should be made to the conference organizers and not to any individual.
- If the company is sponsoring a conference, the conference organizers and not the sponsoring company should be responsible for planning the content of the presentations selecting speakers and selecting invitees. Companies may buy space or booths to advertise their products at the event.[61]
- The non-drug or device company organizers must determine how to use the grant money, *i.e.*, to defray overall costs, to sponsor speakers, or to pay for hospitality.
- Grant-making functions within a company should be separated from marketing functions. Decisions on how to award grants should never be based on the actual or potential volume or value of products purchased by the grantee.[62]
- If the company is sponsoring students, fellows, or other healthcare workers to attend a conference, the donation should be made directly to an educational institution. The institution and not the pharmaceutical or medical device company should decide which individuals receive these funds.[63]

Q 23.7.5   ... research or other charitable organizations?

Companies making donations to various organizations with bona fide charitable purposes should ensure that the donations are well documented and are not connected to a request or promise for business.[64]

Pharmaceutical and medical device companies frequently fund research studies of independent investigators that investigate the effectiveness of those companies' products. It is acceptable to fund these studies, even where the party carrying out the research is or may become a purchaser of the product being studied, if carried out appropriately.[65] The research should be funded at fair market value and should be only for genuine significant scientific and medical purposes and not created as a pretext to generate sales or prescriptions. Research agreements should be in writing. Again, the research grant decisions should be kept separate from sales and marketing departments to reduce any possible implications of inducing business through the guise of donations.[66]

Studies conducted in support of an FDA application for marketing approval of a drug or device generally present fewer fraud and abuse risks, but relationships with investigators and institutions still should be scrutinized. All studies—especially "investigator initiated studies" conducted post-approval—should be carefully scrutinized and should be subject to internal compliance department and legal department review.

Q 23.7.6 ... equipment lease and storage agreements?

Equipment lease and storage agreements should be closely scrutinized to ensure that the terms offered are at fair market value. Determinations of fair market value should be documented.[67]

Q 23.7.7 ... price reporting?

Pharmaceutical and drug manufacturers have significant control over the price at which federal healthcare programs reimburse purchasers for their products. For instance, some programs still reimburse based on the AWP. This could implicate the AKS if the AWP is inflated such that purchasers receiving significant discounts are reimbursed at higher rates than what they actually pay for the product.[68] More commonly, average sales price (ASP) must be carefully and accurately reported quarterly with aggressive and appropriate customer negotiation. Some customers may wind up paying well below ASP, which creates a "spread."

OIG recommends the following to avoid problems in this regard:

- Be sure that price and price reporting are not based on an intent to create additional income for purchasers.
- Do not market the "spread" between the published price and the purchaser's price.[69]

Q 23.7.8   ... consultant training, education, and sales meetings?

A vital element of any pharmaceutical and medical device company's business is educating its current customers on how to use its products properly. Manufacturers also often hire healthcare practitioners as consultants to provide this education to their peers. These education and sales functions are still permitted if properly conducted.

Gatherings to train consultants or to provide product education and training should take place in environments conducive to learning or to effective product presentations or scientific discussions, such as in a conference room or in a quiet restaurant, so that the educational or business function is the focus of the meeting. Meetings should be held at business hotels and not at resorts.[70]

The company may provide attendees with occasional meals or other hospitality in connection with meetings so long as they are reasonable in value for the setting and region and are otherwise consistent with trade codes. A company representative should remain at the meeting; the representative may not simply purchase a meal for a group if the meal is not tied to an educational purpose.[71] Further, guests and spouses should not attend such meetings.[72]

Q 23.7.9   ... gifts?

The primary rule to remember here is that gifts may never be given for the purpose of inducing or rewarding customers for product purchases or referrals. Keeping this in mind, it may be acceptable, on infrequent occasions, to give some items of minimal value having a genuine educational value or patient benefit.[73] Gifts should never be in the form of cash.[74] The PhRMA Code gives guidance to pharmaceutical companies as to the types of gifts that are appropriate. Likewise, the AdvaMed Code and the MDMA Code[75] provide guidance to medical device companies as to the types of gifts that are appropriate.

Q 23.7.10   ... "switching arrangements"?

"Switching arrangements" refers to a pharmaceutical or medical device company providing remuneration to a clinician each time a patient's prescription is switched to one of the company's products.

OIG views these arrangements as highly suspect under the AKS, thus they usually should be avoided.[76]

Q 23.7.11 ... consulting arrangements?

Healthcare providers consult with companies in a variety of different ways. They speak on behalf of the company at promotional events; they provide scientific knowledge; they conduct clinical trials; they advise on matters related to marketing. Enforcement authorities, while recognizing the legitimate value of these relationships, also view them as ripe for abuse. Therefore, arrangements for bona fide business services with customers should be carefully crafted in the following ways in order to remain appropriate and to minimize anti-kickback implications:

- Do not make payments for clinicians to passively attend meetings or for ghostwritten papers or speeches.[77]
- Agreements should be in writing and should detail what services the clinician will provide.[78]
- Any compensation should be set in advance—not tied to amount of prescriptions or referrals—and reflective of fair market value for similar services.[79]

Selection of consultants must be based on the individual's qualifications, and not on the expected amount of prescriptions or referrals made by an individual consultant.[80] Selection of consultants must be made by those with the necessary skill and knowledge to assess the consultant's medical and scientific credentials. This means that sales and marketing personnel frequently will not be qualified to select consultants.

Consultants giving informational presentations on behalf of the company must disclose clearly that they are being paid by the manufacturer. All materials used for such presentations also should be marked clearly to indicate the manufacturer's sponsorship. The company also must educate consultants giving informational presentations about the prohibitions on off-label marketing and take steps to ensure that the presentation does not include off-label information except in response to unsolicited questions from program attendees.

False Claims Act

Q 23.8 What is the federal False Claims Act?

The False Claims Act establishes civil liability for anyone who knowingly presents or causes to be presented a false or fraudulent claim for payment by the federal government.[81] Civil penalties range from $5,000 to $11,000 per false claim, plus treble damages.[82]

Q 23.8.1 How does the marketing of drugs and devices implicate the False Claims Act?

Drug and device companies usually do not submit claims to government payors for their products. Nonetheless, the government has successfully argued that marketing materials or practices that are false or misleading can cause the submission of false claims and trigger liability under the FCA. Moreover, under recent revisions to the FCA, any claim for reimbursement of a drug or device that results from an illegal kickback is "false or fraudulent" and is subject to a claim under the FCA. (For a more complete treatment of the issues under the FCA, see chapter 11.)

Prescription Drug Marketing Act

Q 23.9 What is the Prescription Drug Marketing Act of 1987?

In 1987, Congress passed the Prescription Drug Marketing Act (PDMA) to regulate how prescription drugs are marketed and sold by many of the stakeholders in the drug supply chain. The PDMA, as amended by the Prescription Drug Amendments, modified sections 301, 303, 503, and 801 of the Federal Food, Drug, and Cosmetic Act (21 U.S.C. §§ 331, 333, 353, and 381) to:

1. ban the sale, purchase, or trade of, or the offer to sell, purchase, or trade, drug samples and drug coupons;
2. restrict re-importation of prescription drugs to the manufacturer of the drug product or for emergency medical care;
3. establish requirements for drug sample distribution and the storage and handling of drug samples;

4. require a wholesale distributor of prescription drugs to be state-licensed and require the FDA to establish minimum requirements for state licensing;
5. establish requirements for wholesale distribution of prescription drugs by unauthorized distributors;
6. prohibit, with certain exceptions, the sale, purchase, or trade of (or the offer to sell, purchase, or trade) prescription drugs that were purchased by hospitals or other healthcare entities, or donated or supplied at a reduced price to charities;
7. establish criminal and civil penalties for PDMA violations.

Q 23.9.1 Is it still permissible to provide free samples?

Yes, although manufacturers should be sure that samples are not later sold or billed to patients or to third-party payors. Pharmaceutical and device companies should train their sales associates to inform recipients that the samples are not to be sold. Further, all individual sample units and accompanying documentation should be clearly labeled stating that the units are samples and are not to be sold.[83]

Biomedical Research/Clinical Trials

Q 23.10 What are the major compliance risks arising from the conduct of biomedical research?

- Conflicts of interest;
- Protection of human subjects;
- Charging for investigational drugs;
- Medicare coverage.

Conflicts of Interest

Q 23.11 What rules and regulations govern conflicts of interest in clinical trials?

There are four sets of federal standards that address conflicts of interest in clinical research. Generally the conflicts rules and regulations require disclosure when an investigator has a financial interest in the sponsor or in the outcome of the investigation. They also impose requirements to limit conflicts of interest, and they preserve academic freedom. Finally, they set time frames for preservation of relevant documents.

A number of non-government professional and institutional associations publish their own guidelines. These industry guidance documents expand, augment, and interpret the official government regulations and guidance discussed above. The three non-government sets of guidelines discussed later in this chapter are the most well-known and widely recognized.

Failure to follow the conflicts-of-interest rules and regulations may result in delayed approval of products, rescission of federal grants, initiation of federal investigations, imposition of fines, debarment from future participation in federal grant and other programs, and ancillary litigation.

TABLE 23-4
Rules, Regulations, and Guidelines Governing Biomedical Research/Clinical Trials

Government Rules and Regulations

1. Public Health Service Rules
2. National Science Foundation Requirements
3. National Institutes of Health Guidelines
4. FDA Financial Disclosure Requirements

Association Guidelines

1. *Conflicts of Interest in Academic Health Centers, Policy Paper No. 1*, The Association of Academic Health Centers (1990)
2. *Conflicts of Interest in Institutional Decision Making*, The Association of Academic Health Centers Task Force on Science Policy (1994)
3. *Principles on Conduct of Clinical Trials and Communications of Clinical Trial Results*,[84] Pharmaceutical Research and Manufacturers of America (PhRMA) (rev. June 2004)

Q 23.12 What are the Public Health Service Rules?

These are standards established by the Public Health Service (PHS) (a division of the Department of Health and Human Services), codified at 42 C.F.R. § 50.601 *et seq.*, and aimed at avoiding conflicts of financial interest and at promoting objectivity in research funded by PHS grants.

Q 23.12.1 To whom do the PHS Rules apply?

The rules apply to each institution that applies for PHS research grants, except for Phase 1 Small Business Innovation Research applications.[85] Through the institution, the PHS Rules also apply to each investigator.[86] As used in the rules, a qualified "institution" is any domestic or foreign, private, or public entity or organization.[87]

Q 23.12.2 What do the PHS Rules require?

The PHS Rules require that each institutional applicant must maintain *and enforce* written conflict-of-interest policies (and inform each investigator of the policies) that, at a minimum, include provisions that do the following:[88]

1. Designate an institutional official to solicit and review financial disclosure statements from each investigator who is planning to participate in PHS-funded research.
2. Require and provide a mechanism for the disclosure by investigators and reporting to PHS of "significant financial interests" that would "reasonably appear to be affected by the research for which PHS funding is sought" and significant financial interests in entities whose own financial interests would reasonably appear to be affected by the research.
3. Provide a mechanism to update financial disclosures either annually or as new significant financial interests are obtained.
4. Include guidelines for the "designated official" to identify, manage, reduce, or eliminate conflicts of interest.
5. For three years after submission of the final grant expenditure report, maintain records of each financial disclosure and of the actions taken by the institution with respect to each conflicting interest.
6. Establish adequate enforcement measures and provide for sanctions where appropriate.

7. Certify to PHS that there are procedures in place to identify and to manage, reduce, or eliminate conflicts of interest.
8. Require that, before grant funds are expended, the institution report all then-existing conflicts of interest to the PHS awarding component with an assurance that the conflict has been managed, reduced, or eliminated.
9. Update conflict-of-interest reports as new significant financial interests are discovered or obtained.
10. Make available to HHS, upon request, information regarding all conflicting interests identified by the institution and how those interests have been managed, reduced, or eliminated to protect the research from bias.

Q 23.12.3   What is a "significant financial interest" under the PHS Rules?

"Significant financial interest" means anything of monetary value, including but not limited to:

- salary or other payments for services (*e.g.*, consulting fees or honoraria);
- equity interests (*e.g.*, stocks, stock options, or other ownership interests); and
- intellectual property rights (*e.g.*, patents, copyrights, and royalties from such rights).[89]

Q 23.12.4   What types of remuneration do *not* constitute a significant financial interest?

(1) Salary, royalties, or other remuneration from the applicant institution;
(2) Any ownership interests in the institution, if the institution is an applicant under the Small Business Innovation Research (SBIR) program;
(3) Income from seminars, lectures, or teaching engagements sponsored by public or nonprofit entities;
(4) Income from service on advisory committees or review panels for public or nonprofit entities;
(5) An equity interest that, when aggregated for the investigator and the investigator's spouse and dependent children, meets both of the following tests:

- It does not exceed $10,000 in value as determined through reference to public prices or other reasonable measures of fair market value, and
- It does not represent more than a 5% ownership interest in any single entity;

(6) Salary, royalties, or other payments that, when aggregated for the investigator and the investigator's spouse and dependent children over the next twelve months, are not expected to exceed $10,000.[90]

Q 23.12.5 Who is considered an "investigator" to whom the significant financial interest disclosure and other requirements apply under the PHS Rules?

"Investigator" means the principal investigator and any other person who is responsible for the design, conduct, or reporting of research funded by PHS or proposed for such funding. Importantly, for purposes of the requirements of the PHS Rules, "investigator" includes the investigator's *spouse and dependent children*.[91]

Q 23.12.6 What are the responsibilities of the designated institutional official?

The designated official(s) must:

(1) review all financial disclosures;
(2) determine whether a conflict of interest exists; and, if so,
(3) determine what actions should be taken by the institution to manage, reduce, or eliminate such conflict of interest.[92]

Q 23.12.7 What is a "conflict of interest" for purposes of the PHS Rules?

The PHS Rules state that a conflict of interest exists when the designated official(s) reasonably determine(s) that a significant financial interest could directly and significantly affect the design, conduct, or reporting of the PHS-funded research.[93] However, the institution can require that other conflicting financial interests be managed, reduced, or eliminated.[94]

Q 23.12.8 What mechanisms are available to "manage" conflicts of interest as required by the PHS Rules?

There are no specific requirements. The PHS Rules, however, give the following examples of conditions or restrictions that might be imposed to manage conflicts of interest:

(1) Public disclosure of significant financial interests;
(2) Monitoring of research by independent reviewers;
(3) Modification of the research plan;
(4) Disqualification from participation in all or a portion of the research funded by the PHS;
(5) Divestiture of significant financial interests; or
(6) Severance of relationships that create actual or potential conflicts.[95]

Q 23.12.9 What are the consequences for failing to comply with the PHS Rules?

Investigators: If the failure of an investigator to comply with the conflict-of-interest policy of the institution has biased the design, conduct, or reporting of the PHS-funded research, the institution promptly must notify the PHS awarding component of the corrective action taken or to be taken.

The PHS awarding component will consider the situation and, as necessary, take appropriate action, or refer the matter to the institution for further action, which may include directions to the institution on how to maintain appropriate objectivity in the funded project.[96]

If HHS determines that a PHS-funded project, the purpose of which is to evaluate the safety or effectiveness of a drug, medical device, or treatment, has been designed, conducted, or reported by an investigator with a conflicting interest that was not disclosed or managed as required by the PHS Rules, the institution must require the investigator(s) involved to disclose the conflicting interest in each public presentation of the results of the research.[97]

Institutions: If an institution fails to comply with the PHS Rules, the HHS may at any time inquire into the institutional procedures and actions regarding conflicting financial interests in PHS-funded research, including a requirement for submission of, or on-site review of, all records pertinent to compliance with the PHS Rules. The HHS may require that further corrective action be taken or that funding be suspended pursuant to 45 C.F.R. part 74 until the matter is resolved.

Q 23.12.10 Beyond suspension of funding or imposition of additional corrective action, what other consequences might there be for a failure to comply with the PHS Rules?

Civil Monetary Penalties: The PHS Rules specifically state that the provisions of 45 C.F.R. part 79 imposing civil penalties for fraud apply to violations of the PHS Rules. Thus, if a claim for original or ongoing grant funding is supported by a statement that is knowingly false, fictitious, or fraudulent, or that omits material information or that is supported by a written statement that includes any knowingly false, fictitious, or fraudulent statement, the HHS can institute proceedings to impose civil monetary penalties.[98]

Suspension and Debarment: A civil judgment for fraud can be the basis for a government-wide debarment or suspension of the investigator or of the institution from all non-procurement government programs.[99] This means that not only can the investigator or institution be debarred or suspended from receiving PHS grants, but also, because the debarment or suspension is "government-wide," that the debarment or suspension extends to participation in federal healthcare programs such as Medicare or Medicaid. It is thus a potential "death penalty" for institutions that also are participating Medicare or Medicaid providers or whose products otherwise are reimbursed by federal healthcare programs.

The federal False Claims Act: In short, the federal False Claims Act[100] prohibits the submission of false or fraudulent claims for payment to the federal government. If compliance with the PHS Rules is a condition of the grant award, then making statements regarding conflicts of interest that are knowingly false or fraudulent or that omit material information can violate the federal False Claims Act. Penalties include fines of up to $11,000 per false claim and treble the amount of the claim.

Q 23.13 What are the National Science Foundation requirements?

The National Science Foundation (NSF) requirements are conditions of grant awards, rather than regulations. They appear in the NSF *Grant Policy Manual*.[101] Amendments in 1995 to the NSF requirements conformed them to the PHS Rules. With two exceptions, the NSF requirements are essentially identical to the PHS Rules. First, the NSF requirements apply only to grantees having in excess of fifty employees. The second difference is that conflicts are reported to the NSF Office of General Counsel.

The "National Science Foundation Rules of Practice and Statutory Conflict-of-Interest Exemptions" are codified at 45 C.F.R. § 94.1 *et seq.* and 45 C.F.R. § 680.10 *et seq.*

Though the NSF requirements properly are "conditions," and not "rules" or "regulations," they have an equivalent force. Failure to comply with the NSF requirements can result in suspension of ongoing funding or disqualification from future grant funding.

Q 23.13.1 To whom do the NSF requirements apply?

To grantees with fifty or more employees.

Q 23.14 What are the National Institutes of Health Guidelines?

The National Institutes of Health (NIH) Guidelines, like the NSF requirements, are not formal regulations. They are guidelines for the development of sponsored research agreements. The formal title is "Developing Sponsored Research Agreements: Considerations for Recipients of NIH Grants and Contracts."[102] The NIH Guidelines provide NIH grantees with points for consideration when negotiating sponsored research agreements with commercial entities. "The intent is to assist Grantees in ensuring that those agreements comply with the requirements of the [Bayh-Dole Act] and NIH funding agreements while upholding basic principles of academic freedom."[103]

Q 23.14.1 What are the main "considerations" for sponsored research agreements?

The following are general considerations that apply to all agreements:

(1) Agreements should ensure preservation of academic freedom.
(2) Agreements should allow for timely dissemination of research findings.
(3) Grantees should encourage development and commercialization of technology resulting from NIH-funded research.
(4) Grantees must comply with the Bayh-Dole Act's U.S. manufacturing requirement and the requirement that, in the marketing of NIH-funded inventions, preference be given to small business firms (fewer than 500 employees).
(5) Grantees must timely notify NIH of inventions, patents, and licenses.

In addition, there are special considerations for nonprofit grant recipients (see Q 23.15.1). Finally, there are conditions that require "heightened scrutiny" (see Q 23.15.2).

Q 23.15 What is the Bayh-Dole Act?

The Patent and Trademark Act Amendments of 1980, commonly known as the "Bayh-Dole Act,"[104] provide the legal framework for transfer of university-generated, federally funded inventions to the commercial marketplace. The policy and objectives of the Bayh-Dole Act are to:

(1) promote collaboration between commercial concerns and nonprofit organizations, including universities;
(2) promote the utilization of inventions arising from federally supported research or development;
(3) encourage maximum participation of small business firms in federally sponsored research-and-development efforts;
(4) ensure that inventions made by nonprofit organizations and small business firms are used to promote free competition and enterprise;
(5) promote the commercialization and public availability of inventions made in the United States by U.S. industry and labor;

(6) ensure that the government obtains sufficient rights in federally sponsored inventions to meet the needs of the government and protect the public against non-use or unreasonable use of inventions; and

(7) minimize the costs of administering policies in this area.[105]

Bayh-Dole provisions have been implemented through regulations issued by the Department of Commerce and adopted by the Department of Health and Human Services.[106]

Q 23.15.1 What are the considerations for nonprofit grantees?

The following considerations are designed to aid nonprofit grantees in administering the Bayh-Dole Act and in complying with the requirements of NIH funding agreements:

(1) Grantees must ensure that the rights to inventions resulting from federal funding are not assigned without NIH approval. An exception to this is when the assignment is made to an organization that has as one of its primary functions the management of inventions, in which case, the assignee will be subject to the same provisions as the grantee.

(2) Grantees must share royalties collected on NIH-supported inventions with the inventors; and the balance of any royalties or income earned, after payment of expenses, including payment to inventors and incidental expenses to the administration of subject inventions, must be utilized for the support of scientific research or education.

(3) Grantees must employ reasonable efforts to attract licensees of subject inventions that are small business firms. Additionally, grantees must provide a preference to small business firms when licensing a subject invention if grantees determine that small business firms have plans or proposals for marketing the invention that, if executed, are equally as likely to bring the invention to practical application as any plans or proposals from applicants that are not small business firms. However, grantees must be satisfied that the small business firms have the capability and resources to carry out plans or proposals. The decision to give a preference in any specific case is at the discretion of the grantee.[107]

Q 23.15.2 What considerations require "heightened scrutiny"?

Grantees should subject their sponsored research agreements to heightened scrutiny when one or more of the following threshold criteria apply:

(1) The amount of financial support from the sponsor meets or exceeds $5 million in any one year or $50 million total over the total period of funding under the agreement;

(2) The proportion of funding by the sponsor exceeds 20% of the grantee's total research funding;

(3) The sponsor's prospective licensing rights cover all technologies developed by a major group or component of the grantee organization—such as a large laboratory, department or center—or the technologies in question represent a substantial proportion of the anticipated intellectual output of the grantee's research staff; or

(4) The duration of the agreement is for five or more years.[108]

If one or more of these criteria apply, the Department of Commerce considers it to be more likely that the proposed sponsored research agreement will adversely affect open commercial access, especially for small businesses, to a grantee's federally funded research activities and may delay or impede the rapid development and commercialization of technology.

Furthermore, recipients should be concerned and exercise special consideration if:

(1) The scope of the sponsored research agreement is so broad that the subsequent exclusive licensing of technology under the agreement provides a single sponsor with access to a wide array of grantee research findings and technologies that effectively exclude other organizations from reasonable access to a grantee's technology.

(2) The rights granted to the sponsor to review and license resulting technology or inventions are disproportionate to the amount of money the sponsor contributed.

(3) The sponsorship involves an unusual practice or stipulation that might generate public concern or undermine rather than serve the public interest.[109]

Q 23.16 What are the FDA Financial Disclosure Requirements?

In response to concerns about the integrity of clinical data in support of marketing applications that could be biased by financial conflicts of interest, the FDA issued its financial disclosure regulations.[110] The FDA may consider clinical studies and the resulting data inadequate if, among other things, appropriate steps have not been taken in the design, conduct, reporting, and analysis of the studies to minimize bias.

Anyone who submits to the FDA a marketing application for any drug, biological product, or device is required (1) to certify the absence of "disclosable" financial interests of, or arrangements with, clinical investigators; or (2) to disclose those financial interests.[111] This requirement applies to any clinical study submitted in a marketing application that the applicant or FDA relies on to establish that the product is effective, and any study in which a single investigator makes a significant contribution to the demonstration of safety.[112]

Q 23.16.1 What is a "disclosable" financial arrangement?

There are four categories of "disclosable" financial arrangements:

(1) *Compensation affected by the outcome of clinical studies* means compensation that could be higher for a favorable outcome than for an unfavorable outcome, such as compensation that is explicitly greater for a favorable result or compensation to the investigator in the form of an equity interest in the sponsor of a covered study or in the form of compensation tied to sales of the product, such as a royalty interest.[113]

(2) *Significant equity interest in the sponsor of a covered study* means any ownership interest, stock options, or other financial interest whose value cannot be readily determined through reference to public prices (generally, interests in a non-publicly traded corporation), or any equity interest in a publicly traded corporation that exceeds $50,000 during the time the clinical investigator is carrying out the study and for one year following completion of the study.[114]

(3) *Proprietary interest in the tested product* means property or other financial interest in the product including, but not

limited to, a patent, trademark, copyright, or licensing agreement.[115]

(4) *Significant payments of other sorts* means payments made by the sponsor of a covered study to the investigator or to the institution to support activities of the investigator that have a monetary value of more than $25,000, exclusive of the costs of conducting the clinical study or other clinical studies (*e.g.*, a grant to fund ongoing research, compensation in the form of equipment, or retainers for ongoing consultation or honoraria) during the time the clinical investigator is carrying out the study and for one year following the completion of the study.[116]

Q 23.16.2 What are the obligations of the investigator?

The investigator must provide information to the sponsor sufficient to allow it to file the certification or disclosure statement, as appropriate. The investigator also must update the sponsor promptly of any changes in the information provided.[117]

Q 23.16.3 What factors will the FDA consider in assessing the potential of a disclosable financial interest to bias a study?

The FDA will evaluate the information in each disclosure to determine the impact of the financial interest on the reliability of the study results. In assessing the potential of an investigator's financial interests to bias a study, the FDA will take into account the design and purpose of the study. Study designs that include safeguards against bias, such as multiple investigators (most of whom do not have a disclosable interest), blinding, objective endpoints, or measurement of endpoints by someone other than the investigator, may be deemed adequate to protect against any bias created by a disclosable financial interest.[118]

Q 23.16.4 What actions may the FDA take if it believes that the integrity of the research data may have been compromised by an investigator's financial interest?

First, the FDA will refuse to file any marketing application that does not include the required financial disclosure information or certification.[119] If the FDA determines that the financial interest of any investigator raises a serious question about the integrity of the data, the FDA will take any action it deems necessary to ensure the reliability of the data, including:

(1) initiating agency audits of the data derived from the clinical investigator in question;
(2) requesting that the applicant submit further analyses of data, *e.g.*, to evaluate the effect of the clinical investigator's data on overall study outcome;
(3) requesting that the applicant conduct additional independent studies to confirm the results of the questioned study; and
(4) refusing to treat the covered clinical study as providing data that can be the basis for an agency action.[120]

Protection of Human Subjects

Q 23.17 What rules govern the protection of human subjects?

Research involving human subjects is governed by a series of national legislation, agency regulation, and international declarations.

- The Common Rule
- FDA Regulations
- HHS Regulations
- ICH Guidance
- World Medical Association Declaration of Helsinki

Q 23.17.1 What is the Common Rule?

The Common Rule governs most federally funded research involving human subjects.[121] Fifteen federal agencies in addition to HHS have adopted the Common Rule. By executive order, the CIA also must comply with the Common Rule.[122] Its three basic requirements are aimed at protecting human research subjects. They are:

(1) Informed consent of research subjects;
(2) Review of proposed research by an Institutional Review Board (IRB); and

(3) Assurance of compliance with the regulations filed with the Office of Human Research Protection (OHRP).

Q 23.17.2 What are the FDA regulations concerning human-subject research?

The FDA regulates human-subject research that generates data to support a company's application for drug, device, or biologics marketing approval. Its regulations govern the form and scope of informed consent and also the structure of IRBs.[123] (See Q 23.18.4 for more about IRBs.)

While the FDA regulations are drafted to be consistent with the Common Rule, there are some major differences:[124]

(1) *Scope.* The Common Rule covers all research using federal funds, while the FDA regulations govern only research that supports marketing applications. Both regulations will apply to much research. But it is possible that some research will not be covered by either set of regulations and therefore that there would be no federal protection of human subjects.

(2) *Definitions.* The Common Rule specifically applies only to living human subjects; the FDA regulations do not. Only the FDA regulations define the concepts of "investigator" and "sponsor." In contrast, the Common Rule defines "institutions" and "research" that is subject to regulation.

(3) *Emergency use.* The FDA allows investigators to use test articles without consent in emergency situations.[125] HHS has adopted different emergency-use provisions that are incorporated into its version of the Common Rule.[126] But, the Common Rule as adopted by the other signatory agencies has no emergency-use provisions.

(4) *Financial conflicts of interest.* Both the Common Rule and FDA regulations provide that no IRB member may participate in initial or ongoing oversight of a study with respect to which the member has a financial conflict of interest.[127] However, only the FDA requires certification and disclosure of financial conflicts for *investigators*.[128]

(5) *International research.* The Common Rule allows a department or agency head to approve the substitution of foreign procedures if she determines that the substituted foreign procedures afford protections at least equivalent to the

Common Rule.[129] FDA regulations may not be waived in the conduct of foreign clinical trials used to support an investigational new drug (IND) application. (See Q 23.19.1 for more about INDs.) However, a non-IND study may be incorporated into "an application for marketing approval" (*e.g.*, an IND, a new drug application (NDA) or a biologics license application (BLA)) if the study was conducted in accordance with "good clinical practice" (GCP).[130]

(6) *Parental consent.* The Common Rule does not address parental consent. HHS-specific additions to its version of the Common Rule (discussed below) and FDA regulations generally require the consent of a parent or guardian and the assent of the child for the child to participate in a clinical trial.[131] The additional HHS regulations, but not the FDA regulations, state that the IRB may waive the requirement for parental consent if such consent is not reasonable to protect the subject (*e.g.*, abused or neglected children). In the event parental consent is waived, these additional HHS regulations provide an alternative mechanism to protect the child.[132]

Q 23.17.3 What are the HHS regulations concerning human-subject research?

The HHS version of the Common Rule is codified at 21 C.F.R. part 46, subpart A. In addition to adopting the basic Common Rule, HHS has adopted protections for specific populations as follows:

- *Subpart B.* Additional Protections for Pregnant Women, Human Fetuses, and Neonates Involved in Research.
- *Subpart C.* Additional Protections Pertaining to Biomedical and Behavioral Research Involving Prisoners as Subjects.
- *Subpart D.* Additional Protections for Children Involved as Subjects in Research.

These additional requirements are set forth clearly in the above-cited regulation, so they are not reported here.

Q 23.17.4 What is the ICH Guidance?

The International Conference on Harmonisation of Technical Requirements for Registration of Pharmaceuticals for Human Use (ICH)[133] comprises regulators and pharmaceutical industry representatives from the United States, the European Union, and Japan. There also are three "observers": The World Health Organization (WHO), the European Free Trade Association, and the International Federation of Pharmaceutical Manufacturers and Associations.

The purpose of the ICH "is to make recommendations on ways to achieve greater harmonisation in the interpretation and application of technical guidelines and requirements for product registration in order to reduce or obviate the need to duplicate the testing carried out during the research and development of new medicines."[134] Among its recommendations is the *E6 Good Clinical Practice: Consolidated Guidance* ("E6").[135]

E6 sets guidelines for the activities of both clinical trial sponsors and investigators. These guidelines address the composition, function, operation, and responsibilities of IRBs and so-called independent ethics committees (non-U.S. equivalents of IRBs).[136] In much the same terms as the Common Rule, E6 sets standards for the informed consent of human subjects.[137]

Additionally, E6 addresses a variety of other aspects of clinical trials that are not covered by the Common Rule. For instance, it recommends guidelines for development of clinical trial protocols. It also establishes a list of "Essential Documents."

> These are documents that individually and collectively permit evaluation of the conduct of a trial and of the quality of the data produced. These documents serve to demonstrate the compliance of the investigator, sponsor, and monitor with the standards of GCP and with all applicable regulatory requirements.[138]

Q 23.17.5 What is the World Medical Association Declaration of Helsinki?

The World Medical Association (WMA) is an international association of medical professionals. In 1964 it first adopted its *Declaration of Helsinki: Recommendations Guiding Medical Doctors on Biomedical Research Involving Human Subjects*. Most recently revised in 1989, the "Declaration of Helsinki" is a set of broad principles intended to guide physicians' professional judgment in the conduct of experiments involving human subjects. Its principles are not as detailed as the

Common Rule or E6. For instance, its "Basic Principle" regarding informed consent merely states:

> In any research on human beings, each potential subject must be adequately informed of the aims, methods, anticipated benefits and potential hazards of the study, and the discomfort it may entail. He or she should be informed that he or she is at liberty to abstain from participation in the study and that he or she is free to withdraw his or her consent to participation at any time. The physician should then obtain the subject's freely-given informed consent, *preferably in writing.*[139]

Informed Consent

Q 23.18 What are the general requirements for informed consent?

Generally, informed consent must be in writing and must be provided in a manner that minimizes the risk of coercion. It must be given in language that the subject can understand. It also may not include any exculpatory language that would release the institution, investigator, or sponsor from liability for negligence.

Beyond these basic requirements, the informed consent must contain all of the following elements:

(1) A statement that the study involves research and an explanation of the purpose of the research, the expected duration of the research, a description of the procedures to be followed, and an explanation of the procedures that are experimental;

(2) A description of the reasonably foreseeable risks or discomforts that the subject might endure;

(3) A description of any benefits to the subject or to others from the research;

(4) A disclosure of alternative procedures or treatments, if any, that might be beneficial to the subject;

(5) A statement of the extent to which records identifying the subject will be held confidential;

(6) If the study involves more than minimal risk, an explanation of any compensation being offered, an explanation of any

medical treatment that will be offered if an injury occurs, and a statement of where the subject may obtain further information;

(7) Identification of a contact person to whom the subject may address questions about the study and the subject's rights and identification of a person to whom the subject may report study-related injuries; and

(8) A statement that participation is voluntary, that there is no penalty for refusing to participate, and that the subject may withdraw from the study at any time without penalty or loss of benefits.[140]

Q 23.18.1 Are there exceptions to the informed consent requirements?

Yes. As noted, both the FDA regulations and the Common Rule contain exceptions for emergencies. Additionally, the Common Rule contains exceptions for certain studies that involve no more than a minimal risk.

Q 23.18.2 What are the "emergency exceptions" to the FDA's informed consent regulations?

The FDA regulations have two emergency exceptions. One sets standards for IRB approval of a protocol that does not require informed consent from all subjects. The other states the circumstances under which the investigator otherwise may proceed to administer the study agent without informed consent in life-threatening situations.

The IRB Exception. Under the first exception, the IRB may allow a study to proceed without requiring informed consent from all subjects upon finding that:

(1) the human subjects are in a life-threatening situation;
(2) available treatments are unproven or unsatisfactory;
(3) the collection of valid scientific evidence, which may include evidence obtained through randomized placebo-controlled investigations, is necessary to determine the safety and effectiveness of particular interventions; and
(4) the investigation could not be practicably carried out without the exception.[141]

Additionally, the IRB must determine that:

(1) obtaining informed consent is not feasible—for instance, because the subjects will be incapacitated, the likely subjects cannot be identified in advance (*e.g.*, in the study of emergency interventions or agents applied in cases of severe trauma), or the intervention must be administered before informed consent could be obtained; and

(2) there is the prospect of direct benefit to the subject.[142]

Notwithstanding the determination that obtaining informed consent may not be feasible, the protocol must include an informed consent document and procedure, and it must establish a therapeutic window based on scientific evidence during which the investigator will make an effort to obtain an informed consent. Further, the informed consent procedure must be followed in individual instances where it is in fact feasible to do so.[143]

Finally, the protocol must include at least the following additional protections:

(1) Consultation (including, where appropriate, consultation carried out by the IRB) with representatives of the communities in which the clinical investigation will be conducted and from which the subjects will be drawn;

(2) Public disclosure to the communities in which the clinical investigation will be conducted and from which the subjects will be drawn, prior to initiation of the clinical investigation, of plans for the investigation and its risks and expected benefits;

(3) Public disclosure of sufficient information following completion of the clinical investigation to apprise the community and researchers of the study, including the demographic characteristics of the research population, and its results;

(4) Establishment of an independent data monitoring committee to exercise oversight of the clinical investigation; and

(5) If obtaining informed consent is not feasible and a legally authorized representative is not reasonably available, a commitment by the investigator, if feasible, to attempt to contact within the therapeutic window the subject's family member who is not a legally authorized representative, and

asking whether he or she objects to the subject's participation in the clinical investigation. The investigator will summarize efforts made to contact family members and will make this information available to the IRB at the time of continuing review.[144]

The Investigator Exception. An investigator may administer the study agent without obtaining informed consent if, before the use of the study agent, both the investigator and a physician who is not otherwise participating in the clinical investigation certify in writing all of the following:

(1) The human subject is confronted by a life-threatening situation necessitating the use of the test article;
(2) Informed consent cannot be obtained from the subject because of an inability to communicate with, or obtain legally effective consent from, the subject;
(3) Time is not sufficient to obtain consent from the subject's legal representative; and
(4) No alternative method of approved or generally recognized therapy is available that provides an equal or greater likelihood of saving the life of the subject.[145]

If the investigator determines that the immediate use of the study agent is necessary to preserve the subject's life and that there is not enough time to obtain the independent evaluation described above, the investigator may administer the study agent. Then, within five working days after the use of the agent, the investigator's decisions must be reviewed and evaluated in writing by a physician who is not participating in the clinical investigation.[146]

Q 23.18.3 What are the exceptions to the Common Rule's informed consent regulations?

Emergency Exception. Under the Common Rule, assuming that the clinical trial is not also governed by the FDA regulations, the head of the agency that has incorporated the Common Rule may waive application of some or all of the provisions of the Common Rule to specific research activities or classes of research activities. Thus, the applicable agency head could waive the informed consent requirements in emergency situations.[147]

Other Exceptions. An IRB may approve a consent procedure that does not include, or that alters, some or all of the elements of informed consent set forth above, or waive the requirement to obtain informed consent provided the IRB finds and documents that:

- The research or demonstration project is to be conducted by or subject to the approval of state or local government officials and is designed to study, evaluate, or otherwise examine:
  (a) public benefit of service programs;
  (b) procedures for obtaining benefits or services under those programs;
  (c) possible changes in or alternatives to those programs or procedures; or
  (d) possible changes in methods or levels of payment for benefits or services under those programs; and
- The research could not practicably be carried out without the waiver or alteration.[148]

The same exception holds true, furthermore, if the IRB finds that:

- The research involves no more than minimal risk to the subjects;
- The waiver or alteration will not adversely affect the rights and welfare of the subjects;
- The research could not practicably be carried out without the waiver or alteration; and
- Whenever appropriate, the subjects will be provided with additional pertinent information after participation.[149]

Q 23.18.4 What are the membership requirements for IRBs?

IRBs are generally composed of volunteers who examine proposed and ongoing scientific research to ensure that human subjects are properly protected. The Common Rule requires that each IRB have the following:

- at least five members;
- members with varying backgrounds to promote complete and adequate review of research activities commonly conducted by the institution;
- members that are not entirely of one profession;

- at least one member whose primary concerns are in scientific areas and at least one member whose primary concerns are in non-scientific areas;
- at least one member who is not affiliated with the institution;
- a membership diverse in race, gender, and cultural backgrounds that is sensitive to community attitudes.

Furthermore, if an IRB regularly reviews research that involves a vulnerable category of subjects, such as children, prisoners, pregnant women, or handicapped or mentally disabled persons, consideration shall be given to the inclusion of one or more individuals who are knowledgeable about and experienced in working with these subjects.

Finally, members who have a conflict of interest may not participate except to provide requested information to the IRB.[150]

Q 23.18.5 What are the operational requirements for IRBs?

IRBs meet as necessary. Reviews must be conducted at convened meetings with a majority of the members present. At least one member whose primary concerns are in non-scientific areas must be present.[151]

The IRB must have written procedures:

(1) for conducting its initial and continuing review of research and for reporting its findings and actions to the investigator and the institution;
(2) for determining which projects require review more often than annually and which projects need verification from sources other than the investigator that no material changes have occurred since previous IRB review;
(3) for ensuring prompt reporting to the IRB of changes in research activity; and
(4) for ensuring that changes in approved research, during the period for which IRB approval has already been given, may not be initiated without IRB review and approval except where necessary to eliminate apparent immediate hazards to the human subjects.[152]

The IRB also must have written procedures for ensuring prompt reporting to the IRB, appropriate institutional officials, and the Food and Drug Administration of:

- any unanticipated problems involving risks to human subjects or others;
- any instance of serious or continuing noncompliance with these regulations or the requirements or determinations of the IRB; or
- any suspension or termination of IRB approval.[153]

Q 23.18.6   What are the criteria for IRB approval of research?

The IRB has the authority to approve, require modifications in (to secure approval), or disapprove all research activities under its jurisdiction. To approve research, the IRB must determine that all of the following criteria are satisfied:

(1) Informed consent is sought from each subject according to the requirements described above;
(2) Risks to subjects are minimized;
(3) Risks to subjects are reasonable in relation to anticipated benefits, if any, to subjects, and the importance of the knowledge that may reasonably be expected to result;
(4) The selection of subjects is equitable;
(5) When appropriate, the research plan makes adequate provision for monitoring the data collected to ensure the safety of subjects;
(6) When appropriate, there are adequate provisions to protect the privacy of subjects and to maintain the confidentiality of data; and
(7) If some or all of the subjects are likely to be vulnerable to coercion or undue influence, such as children, prisoners, pregnant women, mentally disabled persons, or economically or educationally disadvantaged persons, that the study has additional safeguards to protect the rights and welfare of these subjects.[154]

Q 23.18.7   What is "expedited review"?

Not every research project must be approved by the IRB through the formal process described above. The IRB may use "expedited review" procedures where it determines that the research presents no more than a *minimal risk* or that the research involves minor changes in previously approved research during the period for which the original approval was authorized.[155] An expedited review may be carried out by the IRB chairperson or by one or more experienced reviewers designated by the chairperson from among the members of the IRB. In reviewing the research, the reviewers may exercise all of the authorities of the IRB *except* that the reviewers may not disapprove the research. A research activity may be disapproved only after review in accordance with the non-expedited procedure.[156]

Q 23.18.8 What is "minimal risk"?

"Minimal risk" means that the probability and magnitude of harm or discomfort anticipated in the research are not greater in and of themselves than those ordinarily encountered in daily life or during the performance of routine physical or psychological tests.[157]

Q 23.18.9 What is an "assurance of compliance" with the Common Rule?

Each institution engaged in research governed by the Common Rule—that is, research supported by funds from a federal agency or department that has adopted the Common Rule—must provide written assurances satisfactory to the department or agency that it will comply with the Common Rule.[158] At a minimum, such assurance must include the following certifications:

(1) Designation of one or more IRBs established in accordance with the requirements of the Rule and for which provisions are made for meeting space and sufficient staff to support the IRB's review and record-keeping duties;

(2) Written IRB procedures for initial, continuing, and expedited review, and for ensuring prompt reporting of certain unanticipated problems;

(3) A statement of principles governing the institution for protecting the rights and welfare of human subjects of research conducted at or sponsored by the institution, regardless of whether the research is subject to federal regulation; and

(4) A list of IRB members identified by name; earned degrees; representative capacity; indications of experience such as board certifications, licenses, etc., sufficient to describe each member's chief anticipated contributions to IRB deliberations; and any employment or other relationship between

each member and the institution (for example, full-time employee, part-time employee, member of governing panel or board, stockholder, paid or unpaid consultant).[159]

Charging for Investigational Drugs

Q 23.19 Is it appropriate to charge for investigational drugs?

Charging for an investigational drug in a clinical trial under an IND application is not permitted without the prior written approval of the FDA. In requesting such approval, the sponsor must provide a full written explanation of why charging is necessary in order for the sponsor to undertake or to continue the clinical trial, for example, why distribution of the drug to test subjects should not be considered part of the normal cost of doing business.[160]

Q 23.19.1 What is a "treatment IND"?

A drug that is not approved for marketing may be under clinical investigation for a serious or immediately life-threatening disease or condition in patients for whom no comparable or satisfactory alternative drug or other therapy is available. During the clinical investigation of the drug, it may be appropriate to use the drug in the treatment of patients not in the clinical trials, in accordance with a treatment protocol or treatment IND.[161]

Q 23.19.2 Is it appropriate to charge for the study drug under a treatment IND?

A sponsor or investigator may charge for an investigational drug for a treatment use under a treatment protocol or treatment IND provided that:

(1) there is adequate enrollment in the ongoing clinical investigations under the authorized IND;
(2) charging does not constitute commercial marketing of a new drug for which a marketing application has not been approved;
(3) the drug is not being commercially promoted or advertised; and

(4) the sponsor of the drug is actively pursuing marketing approval with due diligence.[162]

Additionally, the sponsor must provide satisfactory evidence of the following criteria:

(1) The drug is intended to treat a serious or immediately life-threatening disease;
(2) There is no comparable or satisfactory alternative drug or other therapy available to treat that stage of the disease in the intended patient population;
(3) The drug is under investigation in a controlled clinical trial under an IND in effect for the trial, or all clinical trials have been completed; and
(4) The sponsor of the controlled clinical trial is actively pursuing marketing approval of the investigational drug with due diligence.[163]

The FDA must be notified in writing in advance of commencing any such charges. Authorization for charging goes into effect automatically thirty days after receipt by FDA of the information amendment, unless the sponsor is notified to the contrary.

Medicare Coverage in Clinical Trials

Q 23.20 Will Medicare pay for the healthcare services given to Medicare beneficiaries participating in clinical trials?

Yes. Effective for items and services furnished on or after July 9, 2007, Medicare covers the *routine costs* of qualifying clinical trials as well as reasonable and necessary items and services used to diagnose and treat complications arising from participation in all clinical trials. All other Medicare rules apply.[164]

Q 23.20.1 What does Medicare consider "routine costs"?

Routine costs of a clinical trial include all items and services that are otherwise generally available to Medicare beneficiaries (*i.e.*, there exists a benefit category, it is not statutorily excluded, and there is not a national non-coverage decision) that are provided in either the experimental or in the control arms of a clinical trial.

Routine costs do *not* include:

(1) The investigational item or service itself, unless otherwise covered outside of the clinical trial;
(2) Items and services provided solely to satisfy data collection and analysis needs and that are not used in the direct clinical management of the patient (*e.g.*, monthly CT scans for a condition usually requiring only a single scan); and
(3) Items and services customarily provided by the research sponsors free of charge for any enrollee in the trial.[165]

Routine costs in clinical trials *do* include:

(1) Items or services that are typically provided absent a clinical trial (*e.g.*, conventional care);
(2) Items or services required solely for the provision of the investigational item or service (*e.g.*, administration of a non-covered chemotherapeutic agent), the clinically appropriate monitoring of the effects of the item or service, or the prevention of complications; and
(3) Items or services needed for reasonable and necessary care arising from the provision of an investigational item or service—in particular, for the diagnosis or treatment of complications.[166]

Q 23.20.2 What is a "qualifying" clinical trial?

To qualify for coverage of routine costs, a clinical trial must meet the following three requirements and also have the additional "desirable characteristics" described below:

(1) The subject or purpose of the trial must be the evaluation of an item or service that falls within a Medicare benefit category (*e.g.*, physicians' service, durable medical equipment, diagnostic test) and is not statutorily excluded from coverage (*e.g.*, cosmetic surgery, hearing aids).
(2) The trial must not be designed exclusively to test toxicity or disease pathophysiology. It must have therapeutic intent.
(3) Trials of therapeutic interventions must enroll patients with diagnosed disease rather than healthy volunteers. Trials of diagnostic interventions may enroll healthy patients in order to have a proper control group.[167]

The three requirements above are insufficient by themselves to qualify a clinical trial for Medicare coverage of routine costs. Clinical trials also should have the following desirable characteristics; however, some trials, as described below, are presumed to meet these characteristics and are automatically qualified to receive Medicare coverage:

(1) The principal purpose of the trial is to test whether the intervention potentially improves the participants' health outcomes;
(2) The trial is well-supported by available scientific and medical information or it is intended to clarify or establish the health outcomes of interventions already in common clinical use;
(3) The trial does not unjustifiably duplicate existing studies;
(4) The trial design is appropriate to answer the research question being asked in the trial;
(5) The trial is sponsored by a credible organization or individual capable of executing the proposed trial successfully;
(6) The trial is in compliance with federal regulations relating to the protection of human subjects; and
(7) All aspects of the trial are conducted according to the appropriate standards of scientific integrity.[168]

Q 23.20.3 What types of clinical trials are deemed to automatically qualify for reimbursement of routine costs?

1. Trials funded by NIH, CDC, AHRQ, CMS, DOD and VA;
2. Trials supported by centers or cooperative groups that are funded by the NIH, CDC, AHRQ, CMS, DOD and VA;
3. Trials conducted under an IND application reviewed by the FDA; and
4. Drug trials that are exempt from having an IND under 21 C.F.R. § 312.2(b)(1) will be deemed automatically qualified until CMS develops specific qualifying criteria for these types of studies. At the time CMS promulgates such criteria, the principal investigator will need to certify that the trial meets such qualifying criteria. This certification process will affect only the future status of the trial and will not be used to retroactively change the earlier deemed status.[169]

Q 23.20.4 Does Medicare cover the costs of treating complications arising from the study?

Medicare will cover the costs of treating complications arising from clinical trials, assuming the services required in the treatment of the complication are otherwise covered.[170]

Notes

1. United States v. Kordel, 335 U.S. 345, 350 (1948).
2. United States v. Urbuteit, 355 U.S. 355 (1948); United States v. Kordel, 355 U.S. 345 (1948).
3. 21 C.F.R. § 202.1(*l*)(2).
4. 21 C.F.R. § 201.2(*l*)(2).
5. 21 C.F.R. § 201.66.
6. 21 U.S.C. § 352(a), (c).
7. *Id.* § 352(f).
8. *Id.* § 331(a).
9. *Id.* § 333(a).
10. *Id.*
11. *Id.* § 333.
12. *Id.* § 332(a).
13. *Id.* § 334.
14. *See* Friedman v. Sebelius, 755 F. Supp. 2d 98 (D.D.C. 2010).
15. Press Release, Forest Laboratories, Inc., Forest Laboratories Chairman and CEO to Challenge "Unwarranted and Unprecedented" Potential Action to Exclude Him from Federal Healthcare Programs (Apr. 13, 2011), *available at* www.frx.com/news/PressRelease.aspx?ID=1550242.
16. Transcript of Record at 10, United States v. Stevens, 771 F. Supp. 2d 556 (D. Md. 2011).
17. *See* 21 C.F.R. § 202.1(*l*)(1).
18. 21 U.S.C. § 352(n); 21 C.F.R. § 202.1(e)(1).
19. 21 C.F.R. § 202.1(e)(1).
20. *See* Guidance for Industry: Brief Summary: Disclosing Risk Information in Consumer-Directed Print Advertisements (Jan. 2004), www.fda.gov/downloads/Drugs/GuidanceComplianceRegulatoryInformation/Guidances/UCM069984.pdf; *see also* Example of Fictional Highlights of Prescribing Information (Based on Proposed Physician Labeling Rule) Translated in Consumer-Friendly Language and Formatted for Use in Consumer-Directed Advertisement, www.fda.gov/downloads/Drugs/GuidanceComplianceRegulatoryInformation/Guidances/ucm069987.pdf (for mock Brief Summary); Example of Fictional Highlights of Prescribing Information (Based on Proposed Physician Labeling Rule), www.fda.gov/downloads/Drugs/GuidanceComplianceRegulatoryInformation/Guidances/ucm069985.pdf (for mock "Highlights" section).
21. *Id.*
22. Guidance for Industry: Consumer-Directed Broadcast Advertisements (Aug. 1999), *available at* www.fda.gov/downloads/Drugs/GuidanceComplianceRegulatoryInformation/Guidances/UCM070065.pdf.
23. 21 C.F.R. § 202.1(e)(6), (e)(7).

24. *Id.* § 202.1(e)(2)(1).
25. *Id.*
26. 21 C.F.R. § 202.1(e)(2).
27. *Id.* § 202.1(j)(4).
28. *Id.* § 202.1(j)(1).
29. *Id.* § 202.1(j)(2).
30. 21 C.F.R. § 314.550.
31. 21 U.S.C. § 355(o).
32. 21 C.F.R. § 314.81(b)(3).
33. 21 U.S.C. § 352.
34. 21 U.S.C. § 352(n) (prescription drug advertising) and 21 U.S.C. § 352(q) and (r) (restricted medical devices).
35. 21 U.S.C. § 331(a).
36. *Id.*
37. *Id.* § 333.
38. *Id.* § 332(a).
39. *Id.* § 334.
40. Government Brief, United States v. Caronia, No. 09-5006, at 51 (2d Cir. Oct. 8, 2010).
41. 21 C.F.R. § 312.7(a).
42. *See* U.S. Food & Drug Admin., Guidance for Industry—Good Reprint Practices for the Distribution of Medical Journal Articles and Medical or Scientific Reference Publications on Unapproved New Uses of Approved Drugs and Approved or Cleared Medical Devices, *available at* www.fda.gov/RegulatoryInformation/Guidances/ucm125126.
43. 21 U.S.C. § 355(d).
44. *See* 65 Fed. Reg. 14,286, Decision in *Washington Legal Foundation v. Henney.* Adequate directions are "directions under which the layman can use a drug safely and for the purpose for which it is intended." 21 C.F.R. § 201.5.
45. *See* FDA, Notice, Decision in Washington Legal Foundation v. Henney, 65 Fed. Reg. 14,286 (Mar. 16, 2000) (citing United States v. Articles of Drug, 625 F.2d 665, 673 (5th Cir. 1980)).
46. 65 Fed. Reg. 14,286; 21 U.S.C. § 321(p)(1); "intended use" is discussed at Q 23.5 *et seq.*
47. 21 C.F.R. § 201.128; *see also* 62 Fed. Reg. 64,074.
48. 21 C.F.R. § 201.128; 62 Fed. Reg. 64,074.
49. 21 U.S.C. § 352(f); 65 Fed. Reg. 14,286.
50. 21 C.F.R. § 201.128.
51. 21 C.F.R. § 801.4.
52. *See* Kolender v. Lawson, 461 U.S. 352 (1983); Skilling v. United States, 130 S. Ct. 2896 (2010).
53. Pharmaceutical Research and Manufacturers of America, Code on Interactions with Healthcare Professionals (July 2008), *available at* www.phrma.org/sites/default/files/108/phrma_marketing_code_2008.pdf [hereinafter PhRMA Code].

54. Advanced Medical Technology Association, Code of Ethics on Interactions with Health Care Professionals (2009) [hereinafter AdvaMed Code]. The AdvaMed Code is published in PDF format on AdvaMed's website, www.advamed.org.
55. 42 U.S.C. § 1320a-7b(b).
56. Id.
57. 42 U.S.C. § 1320a-7b(b).
58. OIG Guidance, 68 Fed. Reg. at 23,734.
59. Id.
60. 42 C.F.R. § 1001.952.
61. Medical Device Manufacturers Association, MDMA Guidelines for Interactions with Customers (2006) [hereinafter MDMA Guidelines].
62. OIG Guidance, 68 Fed. Reg. at 23,735.
63. PhRMA Code at 9.
64. MDMA Guidelines.
65. OIG Guidance, 68 Fed. Reg. at 23,735.
66. OIG Guidance, 68 Fed. Reg. at 23,736.
67. Id.
68. PhRMA Code at 10–11.
69. Id.
70. MDMA Guidelines.
71. PhRMA Code at 9.
72. Id.
73. PhRMA Code at 19, 25.
74. MDMA Guidelines.
75. Medical Device Manufacturers Association, Revised Code of Conduct on Interactions with Healthcare Providers [hereinafter MDMA Code], *available at* www.medicaldevices.org/node/593.
76. OIG Guidance, 68 Fed. Reg. at 23,738.
77. PhRMA Code at 51.
78. MDMA Guidelines.
79. Id.
80. Id.
81. 31 U.S.C. § 3729.
82. Id. The False Claims Act is also discussed in chapters 8, 10, and 18.
83. OIG Guidance, 68 Fed. Reg. at 23,739.
84. www.phrma.org/files/Clinical%20Trials.pdf.
85. 42 C.F.R. § 50.602. These rules *do not* apply to individual applicants for PHS grants.
86. Id.
87. Id. § 50.603.
88. Id. § 50.604.
89. Id. § 50.603.
90. Id.
91. Id.
92. Id. § 50.605(a).

93. *Id.*
94. *Id.* § 50.605(b).
95. *Id.*
96. *Id.* § 50.606(a).
97. *Id.* § 50.606(c).
98. *Id.* § 50.607; 45 C.F.R. § 79.3.
99. 45 C.F.R. § 79.800.
100. The False Claims Act is also discussed in chapters 8, 10, and 18.
101. The National Science Foundation's *Grant Policy Manual* is available online at www.nsf.gov/pubs/manuals/gpm05_131/gpm05_131.pdf.
102. *Developing Sponsored Research Agreements: Considerations for Recipients of NIH Research Grants and Contracts*, NIH GUIDE, vol. 23, no. 25 (July 1, 1994) [hereinafter NIH GUIDE]. The NIH published a proposed draft at 59 Fed. Reg. 55,673 (June 27, 1994).
103. *Id.*
104. Pub. L. No. 96-517, ch. 38 (Dec. 12, 1980).
105. NIH GUIDE.
106. The Department of Commerce regulations are at 37 C.F.R. pt. 401 and supersede applicable portions of 45 C.F.R. pts. 6 and 8.
107. NIH GUIDE.
108. *Id.*
109. *Id.*
110. FDA Guidance: Financial Disclosure by Clinical Investigators, www.fda.gov/oc/guidance/financialdis.html. The regulations are codified at 21 C.F.R. § 54.1 *et seq.*
111. *Id.* § 54.4(a), § 54.5.
112. *Id.* § 54.2(e).
113. *Id.* § 54.2(a).
114. *Id.* § 54.2(b).
115. *Id.* § 54.2(c).
116. *Id.* § 54.2(f).
117. *Id.* § 54.4(b).
118. *Id.* § 54.5(b).
119. *Id.* § 54.4(c).
120. *Id.* § 54.5(c).
121. 45 C.F.R. pt. 46, subpt. A.
122. Agency for International Development (22 C.F.R. pt. 225); Department of Agriculture (7 C.F.R. pt. 1c); Consumer Product Safety Commission (16 C.F.R. pt. 1028); Department of Commerce (15 C.F.R. pt. 27); Department of Defense (32 C.F.R. pt. 219); Department of Education (34 C.F.R. pt. 97, subpt. A); Department of Energy (10 C.F.R. pt. 745); Department of Health and Human Services (45 C.F.R. pt. 46, subpt. A); Department of Housing and Urban Development (24 C.F.R. pt. 60); Department of Justice (28 C.F.R. pt. 46); Department of Veterans Affairs (38 C.F.R. pt. 16); Department of Transportation (49 C.F.R. pt. 11); Environmental Protection Agency (40 C.F.R. pt. 26); National Aeronautics and Space Administration (14 C.F.R. pt. 690); Central Intelligence Agency (Executive Order 12333).

123. 21 C.F.R. pt. 50 (protection of human subjects); 21 C.F.R. pt. 56 (Institutional Review Boards).
124. *See* Erin Williams, *Federal Protection for Human Research Subjects: An Analysis of the Common Rule and Its Interactions with FDA Regulations and the HIPAA Privacy Rule*, Congressional Research Service, Report for Congress (June 2, 2005).
125. 21 C.F.R. § 50.24.
126. 45 C.F.R. § 46.101(i).
127. 45 C.F.R. § 46.107(e) (HHS); 21 C.F.R. § 56.107(e) (FDA).
128. 21 C.F.R. pt. 54. *See also* the discussion earlier in this chapter of conflicts of interest rules.
129. 45 C.F.R. § 46.101(h).
130. 21 C.F.R. § 312.120(a)(i).
131. *Id.* § 50.55(e) (FDA); 45 C.F.R. § 46.408(b) (HHS).
132. *Id.* § 46.408(c).
133. The official website of the International Conference on Harmonisation of Technical Requirements for Registration of Pharmaceuticals for Human Use is www.ich.org.
134. www.ich.org/cache/compo/276-254-1.html.
135. The guidance is published at 62 Fed. Reg. 25,692 (May 9, 1997) and is available at www.fda.gov/cder/guidance/959fnl.pdf.
136. ICH E6, ch. 3.
137. *Id.* § 4.8.
138. *Id.* § 8.1.
139. World Medical Association Declaration of Helsinki, Sept. 1989 (emphasis added), *available at* www.wma.net/e/policy/pdf/17c.pdf.
140. 45 C.F.R. § 46.116; 21 C.F.R. § 50.20.
141. 21 C.F.R. § 50.24(a)(1), (a)(4).
142. *Id.* § 50.24(a)(2), (a)(3).
143. *Id.* § 50.24(a)(5), (a)(6).
144. *Id.* § 50.24(a)(7).
145. *Id.* § 50.23(a).
146. *Id.* § 50.23(b).
147. 45 C.F.R. § 46.101(i).
148. *Id.* § 46.116(c).
149. *Id.* § 46.116(d).
150. *Id.* § 46.107; 21 C.F.R. § 56.107; Williams, *supra* note 124, at 2–3.
151. 45 C.F.R. § 46.108(b); 21 C.F.R. § 56.108(c).
152. 45 C.F.R. § 46.103(b)(4); 21 C.F.R. § 56.108(a).
153. 45 C.F.R. § 46.103(b)(5); 21 C.F.R. § 56.108(b).
154. Williams, *supra* note 124, at 3–4; 45 C.F.R. § 46.111(a); 21 C.F.R. § 56.109.
155. 45 C.F.R. § 46.110(b); 21 C.F.R. § 56.110(b).
156. *Id.*
157. 45 C.F.R. § 46.102(i); 21 C.F.R. § 56.102(i).
158. 45 C.F.R. § 46.103(a).
159. 45 C.F.R. § 46.103(b).

160. 21 C.F.R. § 312.7(d).
161. 21 C.F.R. § 312.34(a).
162. *Id.*
163. *Id.* § 312.34(b).
164. NCD for Routine Costs in Clinical Trials, Publication No. 100-3 (July 9, 2007) (MEDICARE COVERAGE MANUAL § 310.1), *available at* www.cms.hhs.gov/ClinicalTrialPolicies/ (follow "Current Policy—July 2007 NCD" hyperlink).
165. *Id.*
166. *Id.*
167. *Id.*
168. *Id.*
169. *Id.*
170. *Id.*

24

HIPAA Security and Privacy

Shannon Hartsfield Salimone[*]

When it comes to the confidentiality of health information, the Department of Health and Human Services has stated that "security and privacy are inextricably linked."[1] The Privacy Rule and Security Rules contained in Title II of the Health Insurance Portability and Accountability Act of 1996 (HIPAA)[2] govern how health data of certain patients or health plan enrollees may be used, disclosed, or retained. Every entity that handles such information should be aware of these federal privacy and security rules. This chapter focuses on what compliance officers and in-house counsel should know about HIPAA's Privacy Rule and Security Rule, discusses the types of entities that are required to comply with HIPAA, and outlines some fundamental compliance activities that entities should undertake or periodically review and audit.

---

[*] The author wishes to acknowledge James Jacobson for his contributions to this chapter.

In 2009, Congress passed the American Recovery and Reinvestment Act. A portion of this act is known as the Health Information Technology for Economic and Clinical Health (HITECH) Act.[3] The HITECH Act makes several changes to HIPAA. For example, it created a new obligation to notify individuals if the privacy or security of their individually identifiable health information is compromised. The Department of Health and Human Services must also receive notice of breaches. The HITECH Act increases penalties for violations of HIPAA. These penalties can be as high as $1.5 million for multiple violations of a particular requirement in a calendar year. The HITECH Act also gives state attorneys general the power to bring enforcement actions. There are now new restrictions on selling information.

One of the more significant changes brought about by the HITECH Act is the fact that it broadened HIPAA's scope to apply to a greater number of individuals and entities. The new law made it clear that individuals can be held liable for HIPAA violations. Additionally, beginning on February 17, 2010, business associates are now obligated by law to comply with certain data security requirements.

Applicability of HIPAA	783
Privacy Overview	785
Security Overview	786
HIPAA Compliance	787
Risk Analysis	787
Assigned Security/Privacy Responsibility	788
Key Documents	788
Ongoing Compliance	789
Practice Tips	789
Job Aid: Key HIPAA Security and Privacy Standards Tasks	791
Table 24-1: JOB AID: Key HIPAA Security and Privacy Standards Tasks	792

Applicability of HIPAA

Q 24.1 Who must comply with HIPAA?

HIPAA applies to "covered entities," which includes health plans, healthcare clearinghouses, and most healthcare providers when they use protected health information (PHI) in connection with certain standard electronic transactions (such as payment or claims attachments).[4] PHI is discussed in more detail at Q 24.2 below. Beginning on February 17, 2010, under the HITECH Act, a business associate must comply with particular provisions of the HIPAA rules.[5]

Q 24.1.1 What is meant by "health plan"?

A "health plan" means an individual or group plan that provides or pays the cost of medical care, and includes group health plans, health insurance issuers, HMOs, and certain other plans and government programs.[6]

Q 24.1.2 Are employers considered covered entities?

Although employers as such are not covered entities,[7] an employer's group health plan, including a welfare plan governed by ERISA, is a covered entity; therefore, employers, especially those with self-insured group health plans, will need to take steps to ensure that those health plans comply with HIPAA. While some employers rely on their third-party administrators for HIPAA compliance, the employer, as the plan sponsor, must make sure that the plan is using and disclosing PHI in accordance with HIPAA.

Q 24.1.3 What is a business associate?

A "business associate" is a person or entity that, on behalf of a covered entity, performs or assists in the performance of a function or activity involving the use or disclosure of PHI.[8] Business associates include a wide variety of individuals and entities, including billing services, practice and medical management companies, third-party administrators, and even lawyers and accountants.

> **What is a covered entity?**
>
> *Example 1.* ACME Corp. operates a continuing care retirement community where residents receive long-term care in exchange for an up-front entrance fee and monthly service fee. ACME Corp. does not do any Medicare or Medicaid billing, nor does it transmit PHI electronically in connection with one of the "standard transactions" listed in HIPAA. ACME Corp. is licensed by the agency in its state that regulates insurers. ACME Corp. is authorized to engage in the business of insurance only for the purpose of selling its continuing care retirement community contracts. ACME Corp. would not be a covered healthcare provider under HIPAA because it does not engage in standard transactions. It is likely, however, that ACME Corp. would be covered under HIPAA as a "health plan" because it meets HIPAA's definition of a "health insurance issuer."
>
> *Example 2.* Newco has a number of self-insured employee benefit plans, including a health plan. Newco must ensure that its health plan, as a covered entity, complies with HIPAA, and that PHI held by that plan is not used for its other benefit plans (absent compliance with certain HIPAA exceptions, or patient authorization). Newco itself would not be a covered entity unless, aside from its self-insured employee health plan, it meets HIPAA's definition of a health plan, a covered healthcare provider, or a healthcare clearinghouse.

Q 24.1.4 Does HIPAA apply to business associates?

Prior to the HITECH Act, HIPAA allowed covered entities to disclose PHI to business associates as long as a written, HIPAA-compliant business associate agreement was in place. If a business associate failed to comply with an agreement, the business associate may have been guilty of a breach of contract, but the business associate was not directly subject to HIPAA. That changed with the HITECH Act, which makes business associates subject to many of

HIPAA's requirements beginning on February 17, 2010. For example, HIPAA's provisions on administrative, physical, and technical safeguards for PHI "shall apply to a business associate of a covered entity in the same manner that such sections apply to the covered entity."[9] Business associates must also document their policies and procedures relating to compliance with these requirements.[10]

What is a business associate?

Example 1. XYZ, Inc. provides disease management services to health plans. XYZ, Inc. does not transmit PHI electronically in connection with standard transactions, nor is it an individual or group plan that provides or pays for the cost of medical care. Instead, XYZ, Inc. assists health plans with their case management, utilization review, and other healthcare operations functions. XYZ, Inc. requires access to the health plans' PHI in order to perform these functions. XYZ, Inc. is a business associate.

Example 2. ABC, Inc. provides software used by hospitals to manage certain medical records and occasionally needs access to the hospitals' PHI to assist with troubleshooting, system setup, or other functions. ABC, Inc. is a business associate.

Privacy Overview

Q 24.2 What is the Privacy Rule?

HIPAA's Privacy Rule[11] restricts the use and disclosure of PHI.

Q 24.2.1 What is PHI?

"Protected health information" includes individually identifiable health information transmitted or maintained in any form or medium.[12] Individually identifiable health information is information that identifies the individual and is created or received by a healthcare provider, health plan, employer, or healthcare clearinghouse, and relates to the past, present, or future payment for the provision of healthcare to the individual.[13] It includes information that a layperson may not consider to be health-related, including demographic information.

Q 24.2.2 How are use and disclosure of PHI restricted by the Privacy Rule?

Generally, absent an individual's written authorization, PHI may be used and disclosed only for purposes relating to treatment, payment, or healthcare operations,[14] or as required by law.[15] In order to comply with the Privacy Rule, covered entities must develop appropriate administrative, technical, and physical safeguards relating to PHI.

Security Overview

Q 24.3 What is the Security Rule?

The Security Rule, which became enforceable for most covered entities in April 2005, governs electronic protected health information (ePHI).

Q 24.3.1 What is considered ePHI?

Electronic PHI is individually identifiable health information transmitted or maintained in electronic media.[16] The Security Rule applies to ePHI that is stored or at rest, as well as electronic PHI that is transmitted. The rule does not cover communication of information that is not in electronic form prior to transmission, such as person-to-person telephone calls, video conferencing, paper-to-paper faxes, and voice mail messages.

Q 24.3.2 What are covered entities required to do under the Security Rule?

Covered entities must comply with four primary requirements:

(a) Ensure the confidentiality, integrity, and availability of all electronic protected health information created, received, maintained, or transmitted;

(b) Protect against reasonably anticipated integrity or security threats or hazards;
(c) Protect against reasonably anticipated use or disclosures of electronic protected health information that are not allowed or required under the Privacy Rule; and
(d) Ensure workforce compliance.

When it designed the Security Rule, the Department of Health and Human Services had as one of its goals to "frame the standards in terms that are as generic as possible and which, generally speaking, may be met through various approaches or technologies."[17]

HIPAA Compliance

Q 24.4 As a covered entity or a business associate, where do we begin when approaching compliance measures?

You should conduct a risk analysis and design your security compliance program in light of its size, complexity, technical infrastructure, and probability of risk to critical PHI.[18] The Job Aid included at the end of this chapter may serve as a useful guide in assessing whether a covered entity or business associate has addressed basic privacy and security requirements. (See page 792.)

Risk Analysis

Q 24.4.1 What does a risk analysis involve?

Under the Security Rule, a risk analysis involves an accurate and thorough assessment of the potential risk and vulnerabilities to the integrity, confidentiality, and availability of ePHI.[19] An assessment of risks under the Privacy Rule should involve analyzing:

- how PHI flows into, through, and out of the organization;
- how it is used;
- who receives it; and
- why it is disclosed.

Conducting a risk analysis is important not only for entities just starting business, but also for existing entities that want to improve their privacy and security compliance.

Assigned Security/Privacy Responsibility

Q 24.4.2 Who is responsible for these compliance tasks?

Under the Privacy Rule and Security Rule, covered entities must appoint individuals to serve as privacy[20] and security officials.[21] Beginning on February 17, 2010, business associates are also required to appoint a security official.[22] These individuals will oversee compliance with standards and specifications, as well as develop and implement policies and procedures to protect PHI.

Key Documents

Q 24.5 What are some of the key documents that a covered entity or business associate needs?

1. Policies and procedures

Every entity that handles protected health information needs written policies and procedures to protect the data.[23] The Security Rule indicates that entities may change their policies and procedures at any time, provided that those changes comply with the regulations and are documented.[24] Policies and procedures must be retained six years from the date they were created or six years from the date they were last in effect, whichever is later.[25]

A critical aspect of a privacy and security compliance program is employee training. Employees must be trained not only on HIPAA's general requirements, but on the entity's actual policies and procedures.[26]

2. Business associate agreements

Both the Security Rule and the Privacy Rule impose specific requirements for the written agreements between covered entities and business associates. For example, the Security Rule requires these agreements to provide that the business associate will implement administrative, physical, and technical safeguards to protect ePHI.[27] The Privacy Rule lists numerous specific provisions that the contract must contain.[28] The HITECH Act requires that the additional provisions of the act related to privacy and security that apply to business associates be incorporated into the business associate agreements.[29]

3. Notice of privacy practices

Virtually everyone who has been a patient of any kind or who has patronized a pharmacy since 2003 has been made to sign an acknowledgement indicating that they have received a "Notice of Privacy Practices." Under the Privacy Rule, covered entities must develop these notices to allow the general public to understand how their PHI may be used or disclosed. The Privacy Rule contains specific provisions regarding what these notices must contain[30] and how they must be provided to patients and the general public. For example, if the covered entity has a website, the notice must be prominently displayed on the site.[31]

Ongoing Compliance

Q 24.6 **As a covered entity, we implemented a compliance program when the Rules became effective back in 2003, so we're all set; right?**

HIPAA compliance requires ongoing attention. You need to revisit your compliance efforts periodically. Employees should receive periodic privacy and security reminders. Policies and procedures should be reviewed to ensure that they continue to reflect your actual day-to-day operations. Privacy and security measures should be incorporated into a comprehensive and documented corporate compliance program.

Practice Tips

Q 24.7 **Do we need to be concerned about state law?**

State law still applies to PHI unless it is impossible to comply with both sets of laws and regulations and state law is less stringent than HIPAA. Therefore, state law will often contain requirements that will apply to a covered entity. For example, Florida law requires that physicians or other owners of records obtain a patient's written consent prior to disclosing medical records for certain purposes allowed by HIPAA, such as for payment or healthcare operations purposes.[32] Entities attempting to comply with HIPAA must also examine state law.

Q 24.8 As a covered entity, how should we handle subpoenas?

HIPAA allows covered entities to disclose PHI pursuant to a subpoena, but only if certain requirements are met.[33] Specifically, you must receive "satisfactory assurances" that the individual who is the subject of the information has been given notice of the request and the opportunity to object, or the party seeking the PHI has requested a protective order from the court.[34] You should also ensure that the party seeking the information has followed applicable state law. "Satisfactory assurances" require both a written statement and documentation supporting the statement.[35]

Q 24.9 What should happen if there is an improper disclosure?

If a covered entity makes an improper disclosure, quick action is critical. The covered entity needs to determine what information has been disclosed, and what action should be taken to mitigate any potential harm to the individual. Notice to law enforcement may be a reasonable and appropriate step to try to prevent further improper use or disclosure of the information. State law may also require notification to the individual if certain identifying information was stolen, such as Social Security numbers or driver's license numbers.

Under the HITECH Act, if there is a breach, the covered entity must notify each individual whose unsecured PHI has been, or is reasonably believed to have been, compromised.[36] If a business associate discovers a breach, that business associate must report the breach to the covered entity.[37] If a breach involves 500 or more individuals, the breach must be reported immediately to the Secretary of the Department of Health and Human Services.[38] If the breach involves less than 500 people, the covered entity may maintain a log of the breaches and report the log annually to the Secretary.[39] On August 19, 2009, the Department of Health and Human Services issued an interim final rule providing details about when a breach occurs and how it must be addressed.[40]

Job Aid: Key HIPAA Security and Privacy Standards Tasks

The Job Aid below (Table 24-1) cites some of the key requirements of the Security and Privacy Rules. Likewise, the Department of Health and Human Services has useful online resources that provide basic information about various HIPAA-related topics, including numerous "frequently asked questions."[41]

Use this table to assist in assessing whether an entity has addressed the basic requirements of the Privacy Rule and Security Rule. Note that this chart is not a comprehensive list of all requirements, nor is it a substitute for a thorough compliance plan.

TABLE 24-1
JOB AID: Key HIPAA Security and Privacy Standards Tasks

HIPAA Compliance Task	Responsible Personnel	Deadline	Specific Key Regulations (when applicable)
Determine whether entity is a covered entity or business associate.			45 C.F.R. § 160.103
Assess how PHI flows through the organization and where it is stored.			
Conduct a Security Rule risk analysis to identify potential risks and vulnerabilities of ePHI.			45 C.F.R. § 164.308(a)(1)
Implement a risk management system to reduce risk and vulnerabilities for ePHI.			45 C.F.R. §§ 164.308(a)(1), 164.306(a)

HIPAA Compliance Task	Responsible Personnel	Deadline	Specific Key Regulations (when applicable)
Build "firewalls" to protect PHI within the organization: (a) Identify employees with access to PHI. (b) Implement policies and procedures. (c) Restrict access to need-to-know basis, including implementation of workforce clearance procedures and termination procedures. (d) Develop nondisclosure or confidentiality acknowledgements/agreements for employees with PHI access and obtain signatures. (e) Develop a system for access authorization for ePHI. (f) Resolve instances of noncompliance.			45 C.F.R. §§ 164.308(a)(3), 164.308(a)(4)
Develop internal HIPAA policies and procedures (including, but not limited to, a system to track certain uses and disclosures; establishing a grievance procedure; developing procedures to deal with requests for restrictions).			45 C.F.R. §§ 164.316(a), 164.530(i)
Develop appropriate sanctions for workforce members who fail to comply.			45 C.F.R. § 164.308(a)(1)

HIPAA Compliance Task	Responsible Personnel	Deadline	Specific Key Regulations (when applicable)
Develop required Notice of Privacy Practices.			45 C.F.R. § 164.520
Develop system to obtain and record acknowledgement of receipt of Notice of Privacy Practices.			45 C.F.R. § 164.520
Appoint or hire a Privacy Official and Security Official.			45 C.F.R. § 164.308(a)(2)
Designate a person to handle grievances.			45 C.F.R. § 164.530(a)(1)(ii)
Identify all business associates.			45 C.F.R. § 160.103
Ensure business associates have appropriate written agreements in place.			45 C.F.R. §§ 164.314(a), 164.308(b)(1)
Train all personnel on HIPAA policies and procedures, and ensure training for all new hires. Develop a system for periodic security awareness training.			45 C.F.R. § 164.308(a)(5)
Implement procedures to regularly review records of information system activity, such as audit logs, access reports, and security incident tracking reports.			45 C.F.R. § 164.308(a)(1)

HIPAA Compliance Task	Responsible Personnel	Deadline	Specific Key Regulations (when applicable)
Develop procedures for protecting against malicious software; procedures for monitoring log-in attempts; and procedures for password management.			45 C.F.R. § 164.308(a)(5)
Develop procedures for identifying, mitigating, and documenting security incidents.			45 C.F.R. § 164.308(a)(6)
Establish and implement a data backup plan, contingency plan, disaster recovery plan, and emergency mode operation plan, including a data criticality analysis and testing and revision procedure.			45 C.F.R. § 164.308(a)(7)
Develop a system for ongoing evaluation and monitoring.			45 C.F.R. § 164.308(a)(8)
Develop facility access controls, including contingency operations procedures, a facility security plan, access control and validation procedures, and maintenance records.			45 C.F.R. § 164.310(a)(1)

HIPAA Compliance Task	Responsible Personnel	Deadline	Specific Key Regulations (when applicable)
Implement policies and procedures regarding workstation use, workstation security, device and media controls, media re-use, records of movements of hardware and software, and data backup and storage.			45 C.F.R. §§ 164.310(d)(1), 164.310(b)
Develop access controls, including unique user identification, emergency access procedures, and automatic logoff, and address encryption and decryption.			45 C.F.R. § 164.312(a)(1)
Implement electronic mechanisms to protect the integrity of electronic PHI through person and entity authentication and modification protection.			45 C.F.R. §§ 164.312(c)(1), 164.312(d), 164.312(e)(1)

Notes

1. Dep't of Health and Human Services, Office of the Secretary, 45 C.F.R. pts. 160, 162, 164, Health Insurance Reform, Security Standards, Final Rule, 68 Fed. Reg. 8334, 8335 (Feb. 20, 2003).
2. Pub. L. No. 104-191, 110 Stat. 1936 (Aug. 21, 1996).
3. 42 U.S.C. §§ 17921–17953.
4. 45 C.F.R. §§ 160.102, 160.103.
5. 42 U.S.C. § 17931.
6. 45 C.F.R. § 160.103.
7. *See, e.g.*, Dep't of Health and Human Services, Office of the Secretary, Standards for Privacy of Individually Identifiable Health Information, Final Rule, 65 Fed. Reg. 82,462, 82,485 (Dec. 28, 2000) ("Employers are not covered entities under the privacy regulation.").
8. 45 C.F.R. § 160.103.
9. 42 U.S.C. § 17931(a) (referencing 45 C.F.R. §§ 164.308, 164.310, 164.312, and 164.316).
10. *Id.*
11. *See* 45 C.F.R. pts. 160 and 164 (subparts A and E).
12. 45 C.F.R. § 160.103.
13. *Id.*
14. 45 C.F.R. § 164.502.
15. 45 C.F.R. § 164.512(a).
16. 45 C.F.R. § 160.103.
17. 68 Fed. Reg. 8336.
18. 45 C.F.R. § 164.306(b).
19. 45 C.F.R. § 164.308(a)(1)(ii)(A) (setting forth the risk analysis requirement under the Security Rule).
20. 45 C.F.R. § 164.530(a)(1)(i).
21. 45 C.F.R. § 164.308(a)(2).
22. 42 U.S.C. § 17931(a) (requiring business associates to comply with specific HIPAA provisions, including 45 C.F.R. § 164.308, which, among other things, requires the appointment of a security official); *see also* 45 C.F.R. § 164.308(a)(2).
23. 45 C.F.R. § 164.530(i).
24. 45 C.F.R. § 164.316(a).
25. *Id.*
26. *See* 45 C.F.R. § 164.530(b).
27. 45 C.F.R. § 164.314.
28. 45 C.F.R. § 164.504(e).
29. *See* 42 U.S.C. §§ 17931(a) and 17934(a).
30. 45 C.F.R. § 164.520.

31. 45 C.F.R. § 164.520(c)(3).
32. *See* FLA. STAT. § 456.057 (2008) (listing the specific limited situations in which medical information may be disclosed absent a patient's written consent).
33. 45 C.F.R. § 164.512(f).
34. 45 C.F.R. § 164.512(e)(1)(ii).
35. 45 C.F.R. § 164.512(e)(1)(iii).
36. 42 U.S.C. § 17932(a).
37. 42 U.S.C. § 17932(b).
38. 42 U.S.C. § 17932(e)(3).
39. *Id.*
40. *See* Breach Notification for Unsecured Protected Health Information, 74 Fed. Reg. 42,740 (2009) (to be codified at 45 C.F.R. pts. 160 and 164).
41. www.hhs.gov/ocr/privacy (visited Jan. 9, 2010); www.hhs.gov/ocr/privacy/hipaa/faq/index.html (last visited Jan. 9, 2010).

25

Ethical Conduct in Banking and Finance

Timothy N. Bergan & Michael Weissman[*]

Ethical conduct by bank officers and employees is critical to maintaining public confidence in the banking system. Indeed, it is considered so important and has achieved such a high priority among the federal bank regulators that it was the subject of a 2005 "Financial Institution Letter" from the Federal Deposit Insurance Corporation (FDIC) reminding all institutions subject to FDIC supervision of the importance of an effective internal corporate code of conduct.[1]

Yet, in developing effective corporate codes of conduct, banking institutions face challenges and circumstances that are unique among regulated businesses in the United States. The extensive mosaic of complicated state and federal laws, regulations, and guidance dealing with a bank's ethical conduct and regulatory responsibilities has made the design

---

[*] The authors wish to acknowledge Gregory Baldwin and Christopher A. Myers for their contributions to this chapter.

and implementation of a comprehensive and *effective* compliance and ethics program a most difficult and exacting venture. This chapter attempts to manage these inherent challenges by providing a roadmap for some of the more important considerations.

The Basics	800
The Reality of Ethics Breaches	800
Noncompliance: Risks and Consequences	801
Compliance and Ethics Programs	803
Program Structure and Policies	803
Regulatory Framework	805
Nonbanking Activities	809
Testing Compliance Programs	811
Maintaining Compliance	812

The Basics

The Reality of Ethics Breaches

Q 25.1 Why does my institution need a compliance and ethics program?

The simple answer is that it is a general counsel's job to protect the institution, and the best way to accomplish that is through a comprehensive, *effective* compliance and ethics program. Key to any compliance and ethics program is a realistic understanding and acceptance of the simple fact that it is easy for busy employees to make mistakes or to lose their moral compass. It's not the big things that are the cause; it's the little ones that, over time and left uncorrected, can cause the compass needle to deviate up to 180 degrees from true north.

Q 25.1.1 What are the consequences of ethics breaches?

Consequences include serious regulatory sanctions, as well as substantial civil money penalties, and even criminal liability. Sometimes all it takes is the failure of effective supervision and control over one employee to create ethics and legal risks with attendant civil liability for the entire company.

Noncompliance: Risks and Consequences

Q 25.2 What is compliance risk?

Compliance risk is:

> the risk of legal or regulatory sanctions, financial loss, or damage to reputation and franchise value that arises when a banking organization fails to comply with laws, regulations, or the standards or codes of conduct of self-regulatory organizations applicable to the banking organization's business activities and functions.[2]

Q 25.2.1 What are the consequences of noncompliance?

The cost of noncompliance is always far greater than the cost of prevention through the rigorous application of an effective, comprehensive compliance program. The costs can be counted in civil damages and, in especially severe cases, criminal prosecution. In addition, they can be counted in the damage to an institution's reputation, brand, and market value. Further, regulators have a wide range of enforcement tools available, both formal and informal, to address compliance deficiencies, and they do not hesitate to impose such sanctions. One recent case involved civil monetary penalties of $65 million.[3]

> **CASE STUDY:** *Groob v. Key Bank*[4]
>
> In 1997, John Scheve decided to sell Oldfield Equipment Co., his hydraulic pump rental and repair business. Jeffrey Groob and his wife were interested in purchasing Oldfield and signed a nondisclosure agreement with Scheve. They also undertook extensive market research to determine the feasibility of the proposed purchase. Groob sought financing from two banks, but because of his limited financial resources, both banks turned him down.
>
> Groob then brought Lowell Bowie in as the money partner for the proposed acquisition. They applied to Key Bank for financing. Key Bank was also Oldfield's bank. Groob and Bowie met with two bank officers, Kennedy and Sapinsley. A few days later, Groob was told that Key Bank declined to finance the deal. Groob and Bowie then abandoned their pursuit of Oldfield. However, within days of meeting Groob and Bowie, Sapinsley enlisted another Key Bank customer, Sarver, to purchase Oldfield. Sapinsley and Sarver sent Scheve an offer to purchase Oldfield similar to the one that Groob and Bowie had submitted. The offer was accepted, and the deal was consummated.
>
> Groob found out about the purchase two years later. Groob and Bowie sued both Sapinsley *and* Key Bank for breach of fiduciary duty. The key issues in the case were whether the bank had a fiduciary duty to Groob and Bowie, and whether the bank was liable, as Sapinsley's employer, for her misappropriation of the business opportunity. The court held against Key Bank on both issues.
>
> The court noted that a loan applicant's extensive disclosures to a bank create a duty of confidentiality on the bank's part traditionally recognized in the industry as a standard banking practice. When that duty of confidentiality is violated through a misappropriation of the loan applicant's information, the bank itself can be held liable for breach of fiduciary duty to the loan applicant. Even though Sapinsley used the information she obtained from Groob for her *personal* benefit rather than the benefit of the bank, the *bank* was nonetheless responsible for her misconduct because the bank had put her in a position that enabled her to "hijack [a] customer's business opportunities."[5]

Q 25.2.2 What's the difference between informal and formal sanctions?

Informal enforcement actions often take the form of a Memorandum of Understanding, in which an institution agrees to take specific actions to remedy compliance deficiencies. Formal enforcement actions are public sanctions imposed on an institution by regulators. Formal enforcement actions can include a Written Agreement, a Cease and Desist Order, and/or a Civil Money Penalty. Furthermore, the Department of Justice may seek to impose criminal sanctions, either immediately or under a Deferred Prosecution Agreement.

Regulatory sanctions also can severely limit an institution's ability to expand, including a prohibition on new branches or acquisitions. Even informal sanctions can have significant out-of-pocket costs. And, in most cases of significant compliance deficiencies, specific corporate governance requirements are imposed on the institution. Regulators acting to correct perceived failures by an institution do not hesitate to impose significant and *very* expensive additional investigative and monitoring responsibilities on management and the board of directors. It is not uncommon for regulators to require an institution to hire outside investigators, compliance monitors, auditors, or other consultants to conduct extensive forensic reviews of transactions, sometimes reaching back a number of years. To minimize *future* compliance deficiencies, extensive monitoring systems with frequent detailed reports to the regulators are routine for both regulatory enforcement actions and Deferred Prosecution Agreements.[6]

In short, designing and implementing a comprehensive compliance program, while challenging, pales in comparison to the extraordinarily difficult and intrusive requirements of formal or informal enforcement actions.

Compliance and Ethics Programs

Program Structure and Policies

Q 25.3 What is the best structure for a compliance and ethics program?

While there is no "one-size-fits-all" structure that works for all institutions, there are general principles that apply across the board:

Involvement of senior management. Most federal regulators are comfortable with a single chief compliance officer who has a dotted-line reporting relationship to the board of directors audit committee. The SEC and the Department of Justice prefer that the compliance department not be housed in the legal department. However, a variety of compliance structures, including one in which a small committee of very senior management takes responsibility and exercises authority for enterprise-wide compliance may be equally acceptable. The key is that the structure work in the particular business culture and operations of the institution. Whatever the structure, at a minimum it is essential that senior executives responsible for risk management and compliance be actively engaged.[7]

Custom tailoring. The day-to-day responsibility for implementation should be tailored to an institution's specific circumstances. For most institutions it makes sense to have dedicated compliance personnel embedded in each line of business. Similarly, compliance personnel usually are dedicated to specific compliance issues that affect the entire enterprise (for example, privacy). Ultimately, all compliance personnel should be included in an organizational framework by which they are accountable to a senior executive responsible for enterprise-wide compliance and independent from management.

Q 25.3.1   What specific policies should banks adopt?

The FDIC's 2005 Financial Institution Letter[8] set forth the following framework for a code of conduct or ethics policy:

- A corporate code of conduct or ethics policy should be implemented to provide employees, officers, directors, and agents with specific guidelines on acceptable and unacceptable business practices.
- The policies should cover the entire organization, including subsidiaries and specific business activities unique to an institution.
- The corporate code of conduct or ethics policy should adopt provisions that explain the general prohibitions of the "Federal Bank Bribery Law."[9]
- Management should require bank employees, officers, directors, and agents to sign a written acknowledgement of the institution's corporate code of conduct or ethics policy,

including written acknowledgment of any subsequent material changes to the code or policy.
- Management should provide periodic training about its corporate code of conduct or ethics policy.
- Compliance with the policies should be monitored. Violators should be subject to specific and appropriate actions to deter wrongdoing, compel accountability, and promote adherence to the policy.

Historically, regulatory scrutiny in the banking industry focused on compliance with traditional safety and soundness and consumer concerns. However, banks are now subject to a much wider array of federal and state laws and regulations.

Regulatory Framework

Q 25.4 What are some of the important federal regulations to consider?

The banking industry historically has been one of the most heavily regulated industries in the United States. Historically, regulatory scrutiny focused on compliance with traditional safety and soundness, in particular the safety of consumer deposits. Over time, consumer concerns related to home mortgages, privacy, and other practices that affect individuals have been addressed by statutes and regulations. In addition, statutes designed to achieve social objectives, such as the Community Reinvestment Act, have added considerable regulatory requirements for banking institutions. Finally, laws designed to achieve other national objectives, such as the Bank Secrecy Act[10] (as amended by the USA PATRIOT Act),[11] have substantially increased the regulatory burden imposed on banking institutions.

Virtually every aspect of an institution's activity is subject to some form of prudential or other regulation. Understanding this extraordinarily broad and deep regulatory framework is key to developing appropriate compliance programs and policies.

Q 25.4.1 What agencies regulate banks?

The universe of government agencies regulating banking institutions includes:

- the Federal Reserve System;

- the Federal Deposit Insurance Corporation;
- the Office of the Comptroller of Currency (OCC);
- the Office of Thrift Supervision (OTS);
- state banking departments; or
- some combination thereof.

Nonbanking activities are subject to regulation by securities and insurance regulators. (See Q 25.5 below.) Finally, banking institutions are subject to Financial Crimes Enforcement Network (FinCEN) and Office of Foreign Assets Control (OFAC) regulations and enforcement authority.

Q 25.4.2 Do we need a separate policy to cover each regulation?

Not necessarily. Consider, for example, the Federal Reserve's "alphabet soup" of regulations. The regulations range from Reg. A (extensions of credit by a Federal Reserve Bank to a depository institution) to Reg. Z (Truth-in-Lending), and even beyond to Reg. FF (Obtaining and Using Medical Information in Connection with Credit).[12] While a separate policy is not required for each Federal Reserve regulation, a bank must have policies that cover *all* regulations it is subject to. Additionally, since enactment of the USA PATRIOT Act, bank regulators have focused like a laser beam on Bank Secrecy Act/Anti-Money Laundering compliance.[13]

In some cases, a single policy will cover different products and services adequately. For example, a single Consumer Lending Compliance policy could cover a number of related laws and regulations, such as Equal Credit Opportunity (Reg. B); Home Mortgage Disclosure (Reg. C); Fair Credit Reporting (Reg. V); Truth-in-Lending (Reg. Z); Real Estate Settlement Procedures (HUD's Reg. X); Unfair or Deceptive Acts or Practices (Reg. AA); and/or others. A single policy for non-lending consumer compliance that covers Electronic Funds Transfers (Reg. E), Expedited Funds Availability (Reg. CC), Truth-in-Savings (Reg. DD), and others may be appropriate.

Several related regulations can be covered by the same well-constructed policy rather than by separate policies that address each individually.

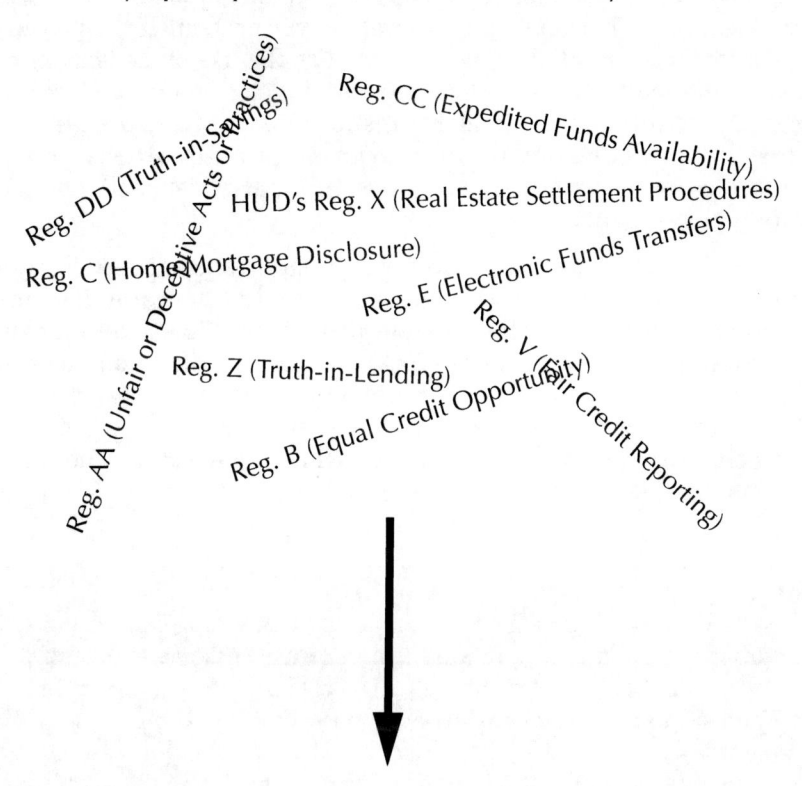

- Reg. DD (Truth-in-Savings)
- Reg. CC (Expedited Funds Availability)
- HUD's Reg. X (Real Estate Settlement Procedures)
- Reg. C (Home Mortgage Disclosure)
- Reg. E (Electronic Funds Transfers)
- Reg. AA (Unfair or Deceptive Acts or Practices)
- Reg. Z (Truth-in-Lending)
- Reg. V (Fair Credit Reporting)
- Reg. B (Equal Credit Opportunity)

↓

CONSUMER LENDING COMPLIANCE POLICY

Equal Credit Opportunity	(Reg. B)
Home Mortgage Disclosure	(Reg. C)
Fair Credit Reporting	(Reg. V)
Truth-in-Lending	(Reg. Z)
Real Estate Settlement Procedures	(HUD's Reg. X)
Unfair or Deceptive Acts or Practices	(Reg. AA)

NON-LENDING CONSUMER COMPLIANCE POLICY

Electronic Funds Transfers	(Reg. E)
Expedited Funds Availability	(Reg. CC)
Truth-in-Savings	(Reg. DD)

Further, a single policy might cover the use and confidentiality of customer information and could apply to all business lines, entities, and locations. This single policy could cover protecting the privacy of customer information (Reg. P) as well as the use of medical information in credit decisions (Reg. FF) and policies and procedures to prevent identity theft.[14] Similarly, institutions normally design policies for enterprise-wide concerns such as business continuity/disaster recovery, outsourcing/third-party transactions, and information security.

On the other hand, the visibility and importance of certain laws and regulations may merit separate or individual policies. For example, institutions often develop *specific* policies to focus on Community Reinvestment Act (CRA) and Fair Lending Compliance. Accordingly, it is important to first identify the laws and regulations that apply to each product and service offered by the bank. Doing so can help isolate, manage, and mitigate the legal, regulatory, and reputation risks inherent in these areas.

> **TIP:** Considerable judgment is involved in designing the breadth of a compliance program and the corresponding breadth of particular policies. It often makes sense to organize compliance policies in a manner consistent with the complexity, importance, and risk profile of specific products/services, lines of business, or markets. Furthermore, an institution should incorporate compliance considerations and compliance professionals as an integral part of the decision-making process for introducing new products/services, new lines of business, and entering new markets.

Q 25.4.3 Should policies for *state* laws and regulations also be included?

The answer depends in part on whether an institution is a national bank or a state-chartered bank. The OCC has promulgated regulations asserting that the National Bank Act preempts state laws with respect to the activities of operating subsidiaries of national banks.[15] Under this doctrine of preemption, certain activities of national banks and their operating subsidiaries—notably consumer finance and home mortgage lending activities—are not subject to state licensing, consumer protection, or predatory lending laws. (See the Case Study on the facing page for discussion of a recent Supreme Court case addressing preemption of state law.)

Nonbanking Activities

Q 25.5 How do nonbanking activities and affiliates fit into a compliance program?

Compliance policies applicable to nonbanking activities, whether conducted within the bank or by affiliates, are an integral part of the enterprise-wide compliance regime. These activities are subject to different statutes and regulations than banking activities. Accordingly, broker-dealer and insurance activities, for example, must comply with securities and insurance laws, respectively, as well as with the anti-money laundering regulatory requirements imposed on them through the Bank Secrecy Act.[16] In addition, policies and procedures are necessary to ensure that individuals engaged in activities that require a license have obtained and maintained the required licenses, and that people without licenses do not engage in those activities.

Q 25.5.1 What kinds of special compliance considerations do affiliates raise?

Aside from activities conducted *by* affiliates, transactions *among* affiliates merit a separate policy. Transactions between member banks and their affiliates (Reg. W) are subject to complex rules and limitations on certain types of credit transactions, including loans to affiliates and insiders. In addition, other transactions, such as contracts for goods and services between the bank and affiliates, must be "arm's-length" transactions. Finally, a specific anti-tying statute[17] applies to banks. In general, this statute prohibits a bank from conditioning the availability or price of one product on a requirement that the customer also purchase another nontraditional bank product from the bank or an affiliate.

> **CASE STUDY: *Watters v. Wachovia Bank, N.A.*[18]**
>
> In 2007, the U.S. Supreme Court confirmed the preemption of state law for operating subsidiaries of national banks, at least for the foreseeable future. The Court upheld the OCC regulations, holding that the mortgage business of a national bank, whether conducted by the bank itself or through the bank's operating subsidiary, is subject only to the OCC's supervision, and not to the licensing, reporting, and visitorial (*i.e.*, examination) powers of the states in which the subsidiary operates.
>
> However, the dissenting minority on the Court, certain key members of Congress, and consumer groups have expressed concern about the impact and implications of the decision, particularly on state regulatory regimes, which in some instances offer more comprehensive consumer protections in mortgage lending than federal law. Accordingly, it is expected that the Supreme Court decision will be an important consideration in federal legislative measures affecting mortgage lending, which has gained urgency due to the recent financial market turmoil, as well as increased pressure on the OCC and other federal bank regulators to more strictly regulate mortgage lending under Regulation Z or other federal regulations.
>
> On the other hand, a state-chartered institution is subject to the laws of the states in which it operates. Although state banks and their subsidiaries may be exempted under state law from certain regulations applicable to mortgage banks and other mortgage lenders, care should be taken to make sure that state-chartered institutions conform their policies and procedures to comply with applicable state laws.

Testing Compliance Programs

Q 25.6 Aren't audits and examinations enough?

Banks routinely and regularly undergo internal, external, and regulatory examinations and audits. Independent testing of the compliance program complements and supplements a bank's regular audits and examination.

For a *general* compliance program to be effective, it must meet the minimum requirements set forth in chapter 8 of the U.S. Sentencing Commission's Amended Sentencing Guidelines.[19] Among other things, the Guidelines require that "[t]he organization shall take reasonable steps . . . to ensure that the organization's compliance and ethics program is followed, including monitoring and auditing. . . ." Second, all banks are required to maintain anti-money laundering programs.[20] These programs must, at a minimum, include "an independent audit function to test programs."[21]

Thus, not only must a bank test its compliance program, but that testing must also be *independent* in order to comply with the Bank Secrecy Act. Independent testing *may* be conducted internally by the bank itself, as long as the persons involved are qualified and not involved in the function being tested. Alternatively, independent testing may be conducted by qualified outside auditors, consultants, or other independent parties. If conducted internally, however, it should be done by the bank's internal audit department and not by the bank's compliance officer.

Q 25.6.1 How often should independent testing be done?

While the frequency of independent testing is not specified in any regulation or statute, the Federal Financial Institutions Examination Counsel has stated that, for anti-money laundering programs at least, "a sound practice is for the bank to conduct independent testing generally every 12 to 18 months, commensurate with the BSA/AML risk profile of the bank."[22] This is a sound policy for independent testing of a bank's enterprise-wide compliance policies and procedures as well.

An effective compliance program that is regularly tested can help ensure that regulatory examinations—whether safety and soundness examinations or compliance examinations—are completed with favorable results. In this regard, the key to success is an effective system that assigns responsibility and accountability for correcting identified deficiencies and incorporates a process for escalating remediation issues to senior management to ensure that deficiencies are remediated in a timely fashion.

Maintaining Compliance

Q 25.6.2 What is the current emphasis in bank compliance?

The logical extension of bank regulators' emphasis on thorough risk assessments is the evolution and expansion of regulatory scrutiny to focus on compliance with *all* regulatory requirements. As regulators expand their compliance focus, there is a natural convergence that creates a nexus point between regulatory compliance and chapter 8 of the U.S. Sentencing Commission's Amended Sentencing Guidelines.[23] Indeed, this evolution strongly suggests that the emerging best practice for financial institutions is to implement a compliance and ethics program with a comprehensive regulatory compliance component within a framework that includes all of the elements of an "effective" compliance and ethics program as described in the Sentencing Guidelines. Implementing an effective compliance and ethics program is essential to minimizing and mitigating compliance risk, which directly damages the bank's reputation, brand, and market value.

Q 25.6.3 How can an institution keep up-to-date on changes to so many laws and regulations?

In addition to monitoring compliance with existing laws and regulations, it is critically important to closely monitor proposed, pending, or adopted changes to legislation and regulations (including enforcement actions). Such changes may have significant implications for the enterprise-wide compliance regime, as well as for the specific lines of business affected.

There are numerous sources of information that identify and monitor such developments. Sources range from national industry associations, like the American Bankers Association, to state and local industry associations and specialized compliance publications. Virtually all are available through online subscriptions that provide timely dissemination, frequently at a manageable cost. In addition, federal regulatory agencies (for example, FDIC, OTS, OCC and Federal Reserve) and most state agencies electronically distribute announcements that cover a vast amount of activity, including proposed rules and regulations, supervisory guidance, enforcement actions, and other decisions taken. You can receive this information by simply signing up on the agencies' websites for email distribution.

Q 25.6.4 Who should keep track of all the legal, legislative, and regulatory developments?

Two areas within the enterprise should monitor these developments. The first, and perhaps most important, is an individual or group of individuals possessing a substantive understanding of the issues and that must be responsible for bringing developments to senior management's attention for action. Normally, this role is performed by the legal department.

The second is the person (or department) responsible for a particular area of compliance. For example, the person in charge of compliance for the institution's privacy policy should subscribe to relevant sources of information as well as the regulators' electronic updates.

Effectively monitoring legal, legislative, and regulatory developments requires close coordination between the legal department and the relevant compliance professionals. Close coordination minimizes the risk that such developments will not be identified and addressed. It also provides an excellent opportunity to evaluate both the legal and operational implications of the developments.

Q 25.6.5 How can employees be motivated to embrace compliance?

Designing *incentives* to increase compliance performance is difficult: It is easier to punish poor compliance than to reward good compliance. At the same time, there are certain areas where compliance metrics can be linked to performance.

For example, extensive data are collected frequently and separately for Fair Lending and Community Reinvestment Act compliance. Normally, these particular areas are monitored very closely, with "exception reports" generated each month. After determining the institution's risk appetite for specific acceptable levels of exceptions, the appropriate personnel in the relevant business unit can be offered tangible rewards for achieving the acceptable levels of compliance. Indeed, compliance and ethical considerations should be included in position descriptions and performance reviews so that compliance will affect compensation and advancement.

In addition, creativity can help motivate employees to improve compliance. Reward good compliance by holding a free recognition lunch when a business unit makes a special effort, or by giving out tickets to concerts, sports, or other entertainment events for people who make exceptional contributions to identify a compliance risk or failure and then fix it.

For some institutions, embedding and rewarding good compliance in the business units is accomplished by requiring both the compliance function and the business unit to agree on a compliance staff performance evaluation, compensation, bonus, etc. For example, at one large international financial institution, the chief compliance officer's performance is evaluated jointly by the institution's chief risk officer and the head of the institution's business operations. Similarly, the compliance officer responsible for an individual business unit could be evaluated jointly by the head of the business unit and the chief compliance officer.

In the end, however, nothing gets the message across as effectively as simple, direct, powerful, and repeated messages from senior management and the board to the entire institution that effective compliance programs are not *suggestions*, they are *requirements* that *will be enforced by management*. And management must make clear that good compliance is motivated by enlightened self-interest. It is a very simple message:

> **TIP:** Bad compliance equals increased costs, which decreases profits, which decreases compensation and bonuses.

Employees must understand and believe that compliance and ethical business behavior are important to the organization. Compliance policies must be followed by all employees and management. The *culture* of the organization must be one that supports compliance and open communication. Employees must see that reports about compliance issues are followed up and investigated and that appropriate responses are made. If the culture supports the compliance program, the institution will be more likely to be able to discover problems early and correct them long before they become examination deficiencies or, worse, enforcement action.

Notes

1. FDIC Financial Institution Letter, Corporate Codes of Conduct, Guidance on Implementing an Effective Ethics Program, FIL-105-2005 (Oct. 21, 2005).
2. Federal Reserve Governor Mark Olson, Speech to the Financial Services Roundtable and the Morin Center for Banking and Financial Services, Washington, D.C. (May 16, 2006).
3. For example, see the Board of Governors of the Federal Reserve System's *Cease and Desist Order and Order of a Civil Money Penalty Issued Upon Consent Pursuant to the Federal Deposit Insurance Act, as Amended*, In the Matter of American Express Bank International, Docket No. 07-017-B-EC; Dep't of the Treasury, Financial Crimes Enforcement Network's *Assessment of Civil Money Penalty*, No. 2007-1; and United States v. American Express Bank International, Deferred Prosecution Agreement, Docket No. 07-20602-CR-ZLOCH/SNOW (S.D. Fla.).
4. The following facts are taken from the publicly reported case of Groob v. Key Bank, 801 N.E.2d 919 (Ohio Ct. App. 1st Dist. 2003).
5. *Id.* at 924.
6. For examples, see American Express Bank International enforcement actions *supra*.
7. *See* chapter 2, Implementation of Effective Compliance and Ethics Programs and the Federal Sentencing Guidelines, for detailed guidance on what is necessary for an "effective" compliance program.
8. FDIC Financial Institution Letter, Corporate Codes of Conduct, Guidance on Implementing an Effective Ethics Program, FIL-105-2005 (Oct. 21, 2005).
9. 18 U.S.C. § 215 *et seq.*
10. 31 U.S.C. § 5311 *et seq.*
11. "USA PATRIOT Act" is an acronym for the formal title of the Act, which is "Uniting and Strengthening America by Providing Appropriate Tools Required to Intercept and Obstruct Terrorism Act of 2001," Pub. L. No. 107-56, 115 Stat. 272–402 (2001). Title III of the Act, which is separately entitled "International Money Laundering and Anti-Terrorist Financing Act of 2001," Pub. L. No. 107-56, 115 Stat. 296–342 (2001), contains virtually all of the PATRIOT Act's anti-money laundering and anti-terrorist financing compliance provisions.
12. *See* www.federalreserve.gov/regulations/default.htm.
13. *See* chapter 26, Anti-Money Laundering. This focus on BSA/AML compliance has become a primary element of the supervisory strategy and regulators' expectations in examinations. Indeed, the publication of the Bank Secrecy Act Examination Manual institutionalizes this focus through its detailed, coordinated guidance, and by its emphasis on regular risk assessments.
14. *See* 72 Fed. Reg. 63,718 (Nov. 9, 2007), codified at 16 C.F.R. pt. 681.
15. 12 C.F.R. § 7.4006.
16. The Bank Secrecy Act regulatory requirements applicable to securities broker-dealers and insurance companies can be substantially different from those

imposed through the same Act on banks, while other regulatory requirements apply to all three equally. Whether preparing an enterprise-wide compliance program that includes such affiliates, or an affiliate-specific program, careful attention must be given to these regulations, which are generally found in 31 C.F.R. pt. 103 (2008).

17. 12 U.S.C. § 1972.
18. Watters v. Wachovia Bank, N.A., 127 S. Ct. 1559 (2007).
19. U.S. SENTENCING COMMISSION, GUIDELINES MANUAL § 8B2.1(b)(5)(A) (Nov. 2007).
20. *See* 31 U.S.C. § 5318(h) and 31 C.F.R. § 103.120 (2008). *See also* Federal Financial Institutions Examination Council, Bank Secrecy Act/Anti-Money Laundering Examination Manual, App. R: Enforcement Guidance (2007).
21. 31 U.S.C. § 5318(h)(1)(D).
22. Federal Financial Institutions Examination Council, Bank Secrecy Act/Anti-Money Laundering Examination Manual, at 30.
23. U.S. SENTENCING COMMISSION, GUIDELINES MANUAL § 8B2.1(b)(5)(A) (Nov. 2007).

26

Anti-Money Laundering

Gregory Baldwin *

Money laundering is the general term used to describe the process of concealing the true source, origin, ownership, destination, or use of money or property. It "is the criminal practice of processing ill-gotten gains, or 'dirty' money, through a series of transactions; in this way the funds are 'cleaned' so that they appear to be proceeds from legal activities."[1] The "dirty" money may have come from virtually any illegal activity, or it may be planned for an illicit purpose, like terrorism; but in every case it has one thing in common: to give money the appearance of having come from a legitimate source or being used for a legitimate purpose.

Many companies are required by law to implement anti-money laundering programs. Even for companies not required to have programs, the best defense against becoming unwittingly involved in a possible violation of the Money Laundering

---

* The author wishes to acknowledge Steven D. Gordon and Christopher A. Myers for their contributions to this chapter.

Control Act is to have an effective anti-money laundering compliance program. Such a program can be used to demonstrate that the business is a "good corporate citizen" that took reasonable steps to avoid involvement (through willful blindness or otherwise) in criminal money laundering activity.

Introduction	821
The Legal Framework	823
The Money Laundering Control Act	825
Key Definitions	825
Laundering of Money Instruments	828
Engaging in Monetary Transactions in Property Derived from Specified Unlawful Activity	831
The Bank Secrecy Act	832
Anti-Money Laundering Program Requirements	834
Customer Identification Programs (CIPs)	836
"Suspicious Transactions"	837
Information Sharing	839
Reporting Large Cash Transactions	844
Currency Transaction Reports	845
IRS Form 8300	846
Figure 26-1: Example: Multiple-Payment Transactions and Form 8300	849
BSA Record-Keeping Requirements	850
"Bulk Cash Smuggling"	851
Structuring	853
Transactions with Specially Designated Persons	853
Special Rules for MSBs	855
AML Compliance Programs	857
Compliance and Your Company	857
Components of an Effective Compliance Program	858
AML Compliance Officers	859
Employee Training	860
Independent Audit	861
"Know Your Customer" Procedures	862
Creating and Administering a Program	862

Introduction

Q 26.1   What are the goals of money laundering?

For the average criminal, money laundering is the process by which his or her criminal proceeds are made to look legitimate. For the average terrorist, money laundering is the process used to fund terrorist activity without revealing the true source, destination, or purpose of the money. These funds can only be used safely if the criminal or terrorist is able to place funds into the legitimate financial system, efficiently and securely move those funds in order to cover their source, ownership, or purpose, and then use the funds—all without attracting unwanted attention to the underlying criminal activity or purposes involved. Money laundering provides the vehicle for criminals and terrorists to operate and expand their criminal enterprises. To do so, they must exploit legitimate businesses. This is the only way they can make their money and themselves look legitimate.

> **money laundering,** *n.* The act of transferring illegally obtained money through legitimate people or accounts so that its original source cannot be traced.[2]

Q 26.1.1   How does money laundering work?

The methods and means of laundering money are limited only by the imagination of the money launderer. Although there are many different methods money launderers may use, there are three generally recognized and independent steps that can often occur simultaneously:

- placement
- layering
- integration[3]

Q 26.1.2 What is placement?

A great deal of criminal activity generates cash. Of course, criminal activity can also generate proceeds in forms other than cash, but if the proceeds are large amounts of cash, that creates a major problem for the criminal. Large amounts of cash can be hard to spend without attracting a lot of unwanted attention, hard to move around because cash is so bulky, and very difficult to hide. Regardless of the form of the proceeds, however, it is important for the criminal to disguise the true source and ownership of the money. The criminal has only one solution to these problems: get the criminal proceeds into the financial system, where it will be safer and much easier to move and disguise. The essential process of getting criminal proceeds into the financial system is known as the "placement" stage of money laundering. It is during the placement stage that criminal proceeds are most vulnerable to being identified and seized by law enforcement authorities.

Q 26.1.3 What is layering?

Once illicit funds have been placed into the financial system, the money launderer needs to conceal them as completely as possible. To accomplish this, the launderer moves the funds that have been placed in the financial system from business to business (often, but not always, a phony business), country to country, and continent to continent. This creates a trail that is extremely difficult and time consuming for law enforcement to follow—which is the entire point of the effort. Layering is the process of moving the money through a complicated, extended trail in order to conceal its source, ownership, or purpose.

Q 26.1.4 What is integration?

Once illicit funds have been hidden through the layering process, the money launderer is ready to use the money. To accomplish this, the money launderer will seek ways to efficiently "resurface" the money so that it looks completely legitimate—such as from the legal sale of products, employment, or consulting fees from apparently legitimate businesses, or the return on legal investments. This process of making the illicit funds available so that they look "clean" is known as the "integration" stage of money laundering.

Q 26.1.5 What forms aside from cash can funds for laundering take?

Money laundering and terrorist financing can involve every possible form that money and property can take in addition to cash:

- money orders
- checks
- cashier's checks
- bank drafts
- wire transfers
- traveler's checks
- letters of credit
- credit cards
- life insurance annuities
- real property
- precious stones and metal
- jewelry

The most common form for the funds in the placement stage is cash, although placement can also involve the deposit of checks and other fraudulently obtained monetary instruments. The layering and integration stages most commonly involve monetary instruments (such as wire transfers) and other forms of property.

The Legal Framework

Q 26.2 What are the federal anti-money laundering statutes?

There are several key federal statutes that together aim to detect and deter money laundering. Some apply only to certain types of businesses. Others apply to all businesses and all persons in the United States and, in some cases, even to persons and businesses located *outside* the United States.

The key laws are:

(1) the Money Laundering Control Act (MLCA);
(2) the Bank Secrecy Act (BSA);
(3) the federal laws requiring the reporting of large cash transactions; and

(4) the federal laws prohibiting transactions with "specially designated" persons, such as narcotics trafficking "kingpins," terrorists, and supporters of terrorist activity.

There are also special laws regarding "Money Services Businesses" (MSBs).

COMPLIANCE FACT

MSBs include: currency dealers or exchangers; check cashers; issuers, sellers, or redeemers of cashier's checks, traveler's checks, money orders, or stored value; and money transmitters.[4]

Q 26.2.1 To whom do these AML laws apply?

Some apply only to certain types of businesses. Others apply to all businesses and all persons in the United States and, in some cases, even to persons and businesses located *outside* the United States. But with all of these laws, it is important to keep in mind the general legal principle of "corporate liability." Under the law of the United States, every business is legally responsible for the acts or omissions of its employees and agents, as long as those employees or agents: (a) were acting within the scope of their employment; and (b) were acting for at least the partial benefit of their employer.

Thus, if the law requires some act to be performed and an employee purposely fails to perform that act because he or she thinks it may help the business, both that employee *and* the business can be criminally prosecuted for the failure to perform the act. Conversely, if the law prohibits some act and an employee performs that act anyway, then again, both that employee *and* the business itself can be criminally prosecuted for the employee's actions. It is therefore essential that every business and its employees scrupulously comply with the anti-money laundering laws.

The Money Laundering Control Act

Q 26.3 What does the MLCA provide?

The MLCA consists of two criminal statutes, 18 U.S.C. §§ 1956 and 1957. Generally, the MLCA makes it a federal crime to launder money. Violation of this law can result in up to twenty years' imprisonment for an individual and substantial fines for both an individual and a business. The MLCA applies not only to the person(s) who committed the underlying crime and are seeking to launder the illicit funds, but also to any person or business that knowingly assists or attempts to assist in the laundering. The MLCA applies to all persons and businesses in the United States. In addition, certain provisions of the MLCA are applicable to persons and businesses *outside* the United States.

As discussed below, the MLCA is complicated and involves numerous elements. Stripped to its barest essentials, however, the MLCA imposes liability on any person or business that "knows" or is "willfully blind" to the fact that funds or property involved in "a financial transaction" come from "some form of unlawful activity," and then engages in or attempts to engage in the financial transaction involving those funds or property, or transports, transmits, or transfers such funds or property, if the funds or property in fact come from or are intended to further a "specified unlawful activity."

Many of the terms used in both sections of the MLCA are specifically defined in the statute, and it is essential to understand those definitions in order to understand the scope of activity that can be considered criminal money laundering.

Key Definitions

Q 26.3.1 What does "some form of unlawful activity" mean under the MLCA?

"Some form of unlawful activity" means any activity that constitutes a felony under *any* federal law, *any* state law, or *any* law of a foreign country. All a person needs to know is that the funds or property have come from some illegal activity, even if he or she is ignorant or mistaken about the exact nature of the illegal activity. The law provides that no person or entity may get involved with funds or property they know is "dirty" money; it does not say the person or entity involved needs to know where the "dirt" came from.[5]

Q 26.3.2 What constitutes "knowledge" under the MLCA?

As interpreted by the case law, "knowing" the property comes from "some form of illegal activity" means not only *actual* knowledge but also "*deliberate indifference*," or "*willful blindness*." The term "deliberate indifference" is defined as "[t]he careful preservation of one's ignorance despite awareness of circumstances that would put a reasonable person on notice of a fact essential to a crime."[6] "Willful blindness" is the "[d]eliberate avoidance of knowledge of a crime, [especially] by failing to make a reasonable inquiry about suspected wrongdoing despite being aware that it is highly probable."[7]

Willful blindness occurs in situations in which one is aware of facts that would cause a reasonable person's suspicions to be aroused, but further inquiry is deliberately omitted because one wishes to remain in ignorance of the true facts.[8] It is the intentional "cutting off of one's normal curiosity by an effort of the will."[9] A person may not escape criminal liability by pleading ignorance "if he ... strongly suspects he is involved with criminal dealings but deliberately avoids learning more exact information about the nature or extent of those dealings."[10] Willful blindness creates an inference of *actual* knowledge of the factual element in issue. If a jury concludes that a person deliberately ignored the warning signs or "red flags" that funds or property involved in a transaction were derived from some form of illegal activity, the law will permit that jury to infer that the person *actually knew* that the funds or property were criminally derived.

In sum, one may not, simply to avoid learning the truth, turn a blind eye or ignore "red flags" indicating that funds or property are derived from some unlawful activity. Putting one's head ostrich-like in the sand will not provide a defense later.

Q 26.3.3 What is a "specified unlawful activity" for purposes of the MLCA?

Specified unlawful activities include violations of approximately 250 federal criminal laws as well as violations of certain *foreign* laws.[11] Given the broad definition, virtually any federal criminal offense can constitute "specified unlawful activity." The particular *foreign* laws that constitute "specified unlawful activity" include:

(1) violations of foreign drug laws;
(2) crimes of violence, such as murder, kidnapping, extortion, and terrorism;
(3) fraud by or against a foreign bank;
(4) public corruption, such as bribery, misappropriation or embezzlement of public funds;
(5) illegal arms dealing;
(6) sexual exploitation of children and "trafficking in persons" in general; and
(7) any act for which the United States would be obligated to extradite a person under a treaty with the nation in question.

Q 26.3.4 What are "financial transactions"?

A "financial transaction" is defined by the MLCA to include virtually every type of transaction that can be imagined. Specifically, the term covers: (1) a transaction that affects interstate or foreign commerce involving the movement of funds by wire, involving monetary instruments, or involving the transfer of title of any real property, vehicle, vessel, or aircraft; or (2) a transaction involving the use of a financial institution engaged in, or whose activities affect, interstate commerce.[12]

Q 26.3.5 What are "monetary instruments"?

Monetary instruments are defined, for purposes of the MLCA, as

> (i) coin or currency of the United States or any other country, traveler's checks, personal checks, bank checks and money orders, or (ii) investment securities or negotiable instruments, in bearer form or otherwise in such form that title thereto passes upon delivery.[13]

Q 26.3.6 What are "financial institutions"?

As used in the MLCA, the term "financial institution" means *much more than just banks*, although banks (including *foreign* banks) are certainly included. The term also includes all businesses listed as "financial institutions" under the BSA,[14] thus extending the meaning to include a host of other businesses as well.[15]

Laundering of Money Instruments

Q 26.4 What does section 1956 of the MLCA prohibit?

Section 1956 of the MLCA, entitled the "Laundering of Monetary Instruments,"[16] criminalizes three types of activity, which can generally be described as

(1) transaction money laundering,
(2) transportation money laundering, and
(3) transactions involving money used in sting operations.

Q 26.4.1 What is "transaction money laundering"?

The MLCA prohibits any person or entity from engaging or attempting to engage in a "financial transaction":

(1) "knowing" that the property involved in the transaction represents the proceeds of "some form of unlawful activity," and with
   (a) the intent to promote a "specified unlawful activity," tax evasion,[17] or fraud and false statements on a tax return or related documents,[18] or
   (b) the knowledge that the transaction is at least partly designed to conceal the true nature, location, source, ownership or control of the proceeds of a "specified unlawful activity," or to avoid a state or federal transaction reporting requirement;
(2) if the funds or property are in fact derived from a specified unlawful activity.[19]

Q 26.4.2 What is "transportation money laundering"?

Section 1956 of the MLCA prohibits any person or entity from transporting, transmitting or transferring, or attempting to do so, any "funds" or "monetary instrument" into, out of, or through the United States:

(1) with the intent to promote a "specified unlawful activity"; or
(2) knowing that the funds or instrument represent the proceeds of some form of unlawful activity, and that the movement is designed at least in part to either:
  (A) conceal the true nature, location, source, ownership or control of the proceeds of a "specified unlawful activity," or
  (B) avoid a federal or state transaction reporting requirement.[20]

Q 26.4.3 What are the prohibitions related to "sting" operations?

Section 1956 of the MLCA makes it a crime for any person or entity to conduct or attempt to conduct a "financial transaction" involving property "represented to be" the proceeds of a "specified unlawful activity," or property used to conduct or facilitate a "specified unlawful activity" with the intent to:

(1) promote the "specified unlawful activity";
(2) conceal the true nature, location, source, ownership or control of the proceeds of the "specified unlawful activity"; or
(3) avoid a federal or state transaction reporting requirement.[21]

The phrase "represented to be" means any representation made by a law enforcement officer or another person at the direction or with the approval of a federal law enforcement officer. Thus, funds in an undercover "sting" operation are considered to be the proceeds of a "specified unlawful activity" even if they are *not* derived from such activity, but an undercover agent *says* they are.

Q 26.4.4 What are the MLCA penalties for violation of section 1956?

Criminal: Any person or entity convicted of violating section 1956 of the MLCA may be sentenced to twenty years in prison and/or a criminal fine of $500,000 or twice the value of the property, whichever is *greater*.[22]

Civil: Section 1956 of the MLCA may also be enforced by civil penalty in the amount of $10,000 or twice the value of the property, whichever is *greater*.[23]

Forfeiture: Any real or personal property involved in a transaction or attempted transaction in violation of section 1956 of the MLCA, or any property traceable to such property, is subject to civil or criminal forfeiture by the United States.[24]

However, "tracing" the property to the offense is *not* required:

- if funds subject to forfeiture are deposited at a foreign bank and that foreign bank has an "interbank account" with a U.S. bank, a branch or agency of a foreign bank in the United States, or a broker or dealer registered with the SEC. In such cases, funds may be seized directly from the "interbank account," and neither the foreign bank nor the U.S. entity holding the "interbank account" has standing to contest the forfeiture.[25]
- in a civil forfeiture action in which the subject property consists of cash or monetary instruments in bearer form deposited into a financial institution, if the forfeiture action is commenced within one year of the offense that is the basis for the forfeiture.[26]

Q 26.4.5 What extraterritorial jurisdiction does section 1956 of the MLCA have?

The criminal provisions of section 1956 of the MLCA apply not only to persons and entities inside the United States, but also, under certain circumstances, to persons and entities located *outside* the United States.[27] The MLCA confers jurisdiction over criminal conduct that occurs in foreign countries if:

(1) the conduct is by a U.S. citizen, or is by a non-U.S. citizen and occurs at least in part in the United States; and
(2) the transaction or series of related transactions involves funds or monetary instruments of a value exceeding $10,000.

In addition, the U.S. government may initiate a civil action against any domestic or foreign person or entity for violation of section 1956 or section 1957 (discussed below) of the MLCA.[28] The civil penalty is the greater of (i) the value of the property or funds involved in the transaction; or (ii) $10,000. Federal courts have *personal* jurisdiction over the foreign person or entity when that person or entity:

(1) commits one of the three criminal offenses (see Q 26.4.1 through Q 26.4.3 above) involving a financial transaction that occurs in whole or in part in the United States;
(2) converts to his, her, or its own use property that has been forfeited to the United States by court order; or
(3) is a "financial institution" that maintains a bank account at a financial institution in the United States.[29]

The term "financial institution" includes any of the several dozen types of businesses defined as such in the BSA,[30] or any foreign bank.[31] For purposes of enforcing section 1956 of the MLCA, a U.S. court may issue a restraining order to ensure that any bank account or other property held in the United States by a defendant is available to satisfy a judgment. The courts have the authority to appoint a "federal receiver" to find and collect all of a defendant's assets, wherever located, to satisfy a civil or criminal judgment, or an order of forfeiture. The federal receiver is granted substantial powers to accomplish this task.[32]

Engaging in Monetary Transactions in Property Derived from Specified Unlawful Activity

Q 26.5 What does section 1957 of the MLCA provide?

Section 1957 of the MLCA[33] makes it illegal for any person or entity to knowingly engage or attempt to engage in a "monetary transaction" in "criminally derived property" of a value over $10,000, if the property is, in fact, derived from a "specified unlawful activity." The definition of "knowing" applicable to section 1957 of the MLCA applies also to this section of the MLCA. A "specified unlawful activity" has the same meaning as that used for purposes of section 1956 of the MLCA.[34]

Q 26.5.1 What is a "monetary transaction"?

It is the deposit, withdrawal, transfer, or exchange of funds or monetary instruments by, through, or to a "financial institution."[35] This provision essentially makes it illegal to *spend* funds in excess of $10,000 derived from "specified unlawful activity" without regard for the intent or purpose of the transaction.

Further, the government need not prove that the defendant knew that the offense from which the funds were derived was a "specified unlawful activity." It is enough for the defendant to know only that the funds were "criminally derived." Thus, any "financial institution" which *receives* funds in a transaction and knows, or is "willfully blind" to the fact that the funds come from criminal activity, potentially violates section 1957 of the MLCA.

Q 26.5.2   What is "criminally derived property"?

Any property, in whatever form, constituting or derived from proceeds obtained from a criminal offense.[36]

Q 26.5.3   Does the government have extraterritorial jurisdiction to prosecute violations of section 1957 of the MLCA?

A violation of section 1957 occurring *outside* the United States may be prosecuted if the defendant is a "United States person." A "United States person" includes a national of the United States, any resident alien, any person within the United States, any entity composed principally of nationals or permanent resident aliens of the United States, or any corporation organized under the laws of the United States, any state, the District of Columbia, or any territory or possession of the United States.[37]

Q 26.5.4   What are the penalties for violations of section 1957 of the MLCA?

Violations of this section are punishable by imprisonment for up to ten years and a fine of up to twice the amount of the value of the criminally derived property involved in the transaction. In addition, the forfeiture provisions described above also apply to violations of this section.

The Bank Secrecy Act

Q 26.6   What is the Bank Secrecy Act?

The BSA[38] is basically a *regulatory* statute that seeks to deter money laundering through regulations requiring certain business practices. Unlike the MLCA, the BSA applies only to certain types of businesses. The types of businesses it applies to are further limited by the implementing regulations issued by the Secretary of the Treasury. The Treasury regulations issued under the BSA are issued by the Financial Crimes Enforcement Network (FinCEN), a bureau within the Treasury Department whose mission is to deter and detect money laundering and terrorist financing. Although the BSA is a regulatory statute, violations of the BSA can be enforced through criminal prosecution against individuals and businesses.[39]

Q 26.6.1 To whom does the BSA apply?

With the exception of the cash reporting requirements (see Q 26.11.3, below), the BSA applies only to businesses classified as "financial institutions." It authorizes the U.S. Treasury Department to require those businesses to take certain anti-money laundering actions, including reporting large cash transactions (those over $10,000), making and keeping certain records, implementing a formal, written "anti-money laundering compliance program," and mandatory reporting of "suspicious activity" to the federal government.

Q 26.6.2 What is the definition of "financial institutions" for purposes of the BSA?

Under the BSA, the term "financial institution" includes *much more than banks*. The term is defined[40] to include the following (however, not all of these businesses have yet been regulated pursuant to the BSA (see below)):

(1) an insured bank;[41]
(2) a commercial bank or trust company;
(3) a private banker;
(4) an agency or branch of a foreign bank in the United States;
(5) any credit union;
(6) a thrift institution;
(7) a broker or dealer registered with the SEC under the Securities Exchange Act of 1934;
(8) any futures commission merchant, commodity trading advisor, or commodity pool operator registered or required to be registered under the Commodity Exchange Act;
(9) a broker or dealer in securities or commodities;
(10) an investment banker or investment company;[42]
(11) money services businesses (MSBs);[43]

(12) an operator of a credit card system;
(13) an insurance company;
(14) a dealer in precious metals, stones, or jewels;
(15) a pawnbroker;
(16) a loan or finance company;
(17) a travel agency;
(18) funds transmitters, both licensed businesses as well as informal networks of people engaged in facilitating domestic or international transfers outside the conventional financial system;
(19) a telegraph company;
(20) a business engaged in the sale of vehicles (including automobiles, airplanes, and boats);
(21) persons involved in real estate closings and settlements;
(22) the U.S. Postal Service;
(23) an agency of the U.S. government or of a state or local government carrying out a power or duty of a business described in 31 U.S.C. § 5312;
(24) a casino, a gambling casino, or gaming establishment with an annual gaming revenue of more than $1 million;
(25) any business engaging in an activity the secretary determines by regulation to be similar to, related to, or a substitute for any business described in 31 U.S.C. § 5312; and
(26) any other business designated by the secretary whose cash transactions have a high degree of usefulness in criminal, tax, or regulatory matters.

Anti-Money Laundering Program Requirements

Q 26.7 Which financial institutions must implement AML compliance programs, and which are exempted?

The Secretary of the Treasury has issued regulations implementing the BSA. All of those regulations were initially published at 31 C.F.R. part 103. Effective March 1, 2011, however, all regulations contained in part 103 were re-organized in new Chapter X of 31 C.F.R. The new Chapter X made no substantive changes in existing regulations, but existing regulations are now generally reorganized by financial industry.[44] References here to the BSA regulations will be to the new Chapter X, followed in parenthesis with the citation to former part 103.

The regulations issued by the Secretary only apply to *some* of the "financial institutions" listed in the BSA. Other BSA "financial institutions" have been exempted from regulation.

Currently, the "financial institutions" subject to specific implementing regulations are:

- all banks regulated by a federal regulatory agency;
- businesses regulated by the SEC;
- futures commissions merchants and introducing brokers in commodities;
- casinos and card clubs;
- credit unions regulated by the National Credit Union Administration;
- mutual funds;[45]
- MSBs;
- operators of credit card systems;
- some dealers in precious metals, precious stones, or jewels; and
- certain life insurance companies.[46]

All other businesses that fall within the definition of "financial institution" have been temporarily exempted from the provisions of the BSA, except for government agencies, which have been permanently exempted.[47]

A careful reading of the BSA regulations is important for all "financial institutions" because some types of businesses that fall within the general description (particularly life insurance companies and dealers in precious metals, stones, or jewels) may be excluded from the regulatory definitions.[48]

Q 26.7.1 What are the general regulatory requirements for subject financial institutions?

(1) Implementation of an anti-money laundering program;
(2) Implementation of customer identification programs (CIPs);
(3) Reporting of "suspicious transactions" to the Treasury Department;

(4) Reporting "large cash transactions"; and
(5) Certain record-keeping requirements.

Not all of these requirements are equally applicable to regulated "financial institutions," and accordingly, careful review of the applicable regulations is necessary.

Q 26.7.2 What are the BSA's requirements for anti-money laundering programs?

1. An anti-money laundering program must be in writing.
2. The "financial institution" must:
   (a) formally appoint an "anti-money laundering compliance officer" who is in overall charge of the program;
   (b) conduct periodic training of appropriate employees about the institution's anti-money laundering policies and procedures; and
   (c) conduct a periodic independent audit of the program to ensure it has been implemented and is being followed.[49]
3. Anti-money laundering programs must be "risk-based."

Q 26.7.3 What is a "risk-based" anti-money laundering program?

This means that each institution must carefully consider its customer base, products, services, geographic areas of operation, and market area in order to determine the degree of money laundering risk the institution faces and the degree of risk associated with each of these various categories. As a practical matter, this involves the preparation of a written "Risk Assessment" covering each of the factors just noted. Then, based upon that assessment, the institution must develop written policies and procedures specifically designed to address the degree of risk and detect, deter, and report money laundering or terrorist financing activity.

Customer Identification Programs (CIPs)

Q 26.8 What are the BSA's requirements regarding CIPs?

Customer identification programs are required only for some "financial institutions." These include:

- banks;
- savings associations;
- credit unions;
- securities broker dealers;
- futures commission merchants and introducing brokers; and
- mutual funds.[50]

The CIP must be in writing and, if the institution is also required to have an anti-money laundering program, the CIP must be included as part of that program. The CIP must include, at a minimum, procedures to verify the name, date of birth, address or principal place of business, and identification number of the customer. Verification may be done through documents specifically set forth in the program (generally, a government-issued photo identification for persons, or documents showing the legal existence of an entity). Verification may be made through non-documentary procedures, but the specific procedures to be followed must be specified in the program. The CIP must also prescribe the procedures to be followed by the institution when verification cannot be accomplished, including the circumstances under which an account must be closed for lack of verification. The institution must maintain copies of all records and documents used in the verification process.

"Suspicious Transactions"

Q 26.9 What is a "suspicious transaction"?

Generally, transactions are considered to be "suspicious" and subject to the reporting requirement where the institution knows, suspects, or has reason to suspect that a transaction:

(1) involves funds derived from illegal activities;
(2) is intended or conducted in order to hide or disguise funds or assets derived from illegal activities;
(3) is designed to evade any reporting or other requirements of the BSA or the BSA regulations;
(4) has no business or apparent lawful purpose;
(5) is not normal for the customer involved, and the institution knows of no reasonable explanation for the transaction; or
(6) involves the use of the financial institution to facilitate criminal activity.

Q 26.9.1 Who must report suspicious transactions?

Some financial institutions. Those required to report suspicious transactions in writing to the Treasury Department (specifically, to FinCEN) are:

(1) banks;[51]
(2) mutual funds;
(3) insurance companies covered under 31 C.F.R. § 103.137;
(4) brokers or dealers in securities;
(5) futures commission merchants and introducing brokers in commodities;
(6) MSBs; and
(7) casinos.[52]

No financial institution (or any officer, director, employee, or agent) may disclose a SAR, or any information that would reveal the existence of a SAR. Any financial institution that is subpoenaed or otherwise requested to disclose a SAR or any information that would reveal the existence of a SAR must refuse to provide that information and must notify FinCEN.[53]

However, *provided no person involved in the transaction is notified that the transaction has been reported*, disclosures *may* be made to

(1) FinCEN;
(2) any federal, state, or local law enforcement agency;
(3) any federal regulatory authority that examines the financial institution for compliance with the BSA; or
(4) any self-regulatory organization that examines the financial institution for compliance with its SAR reporting requirements, upon the request of the federal agency responsible for its oversight.

The regulations also allow: (i) the disclosure of the underlying facts, transactions, and documents upon which a SAR is based, including, but not limited to, disclosures related to filing a joint SAR and in connection with certain employment references or termination notices; and (ii) the sharing of a SAR, or any information that would reveal the existence of a SAR, within the corporate organizational structure of a financial institution for purposes consistent with the BSA, as determined by regulation or FinCEN guidance.[54]

Q 26.9.2   Doesn't reporting a suspicious transaction expose me and/or my company to legal risk?

The BSA provides a "safe harbor" for financial institutions (and their officers, directors, employees, and agents) reporting suspicious transactions or activity. No financial institution may he held liable to any person or entity under any federal statute or regulation, or under the constitution, law, or regulation of any state or political subdivision, for disclosing suspicious activity or for failing to notify the person or entity who is the subject of, or named in, the report.[55]

Q 26.9.3   What are the filing requirements for reports of suspicious transactions?

The form of the report depends upon the type of institution making it.[56] In all cases, however, the report must be filed within thirty days after the date of the detection of the facts that constitute grounds for filing. Filing may be delayed an additional thirty days in order to enable the institution to identify a suspect, but in no case may filing be delayed more than sixty days. Transactions involving ongoing money laundering schemes or terrorist financing must be verbally reported immediately upon suspicion to an appropriate law enforcement agency.

Information Sharing

Q 26.10   What is "information sharing"?

Information sharing, authorized by section 314 of the USA PATRIOT Act,[57] was designed to develop cooperative efforts among certain financial institutions, regulatory authorities, and federal law enforcement agencies through the exchange of information concerning possible participants in money laundering and terrorist financing. It consists of two distinct types, each subject to different regulations:

- section 314(a) "mandatory information sharing" between financial institutions and federal law enforcement agencies; and
- section 314(b) "voluntary information sharing" between financial institutions alone.

Q 26.10.1 What is section 314(a) mandatory information sharing?

Generally, section 314(a) mandatory information sharing consists of federal, state, local, or foreign law enforcement agencies[58] requesting, through FinCEN, financial institutions to state whether particular individuals, entities, or organizations:

(i) maintain a current "account" with the institution;
(ii) have maintained an "account" with the institution during the preceding twelve months; or
(iii) have been involved in any "transaction" or transmittal of funds by or through the institution during the preceding six months.

Law enforcement agencies are limited to requesting information only for investigations of terrorist activity or money laundering.[59] Section 314(a) requests for information may be made to financial institutions only through FinCEN, and a financial institution's response is provided to FinCEN only. Information provided to FinCEN in response to a section 314(a) request is reported by FinCEN to the law enforcement agency that initiated the FinCEN request.

Q 26.10.2 Who is subject to section 314(a) mandatory information sharing?

Mandatory information sharing applies to all "financial institutions" as defined by the Bank Secrecy Act.[60] In practice, however, the financial institutions subject to section 314(a) mandatory information sharing requests from FinCEN are limited to banks, credit unions, securities and commodities broker dealers, money services businesses, and casinos.[61]

Q 26.10.3 What must a financial institution do upon receipt of a section 314(a) mandatory information sharing request?

Financial institutions are required to immediately check their records upon receipt of the request and promptly respond within the time frame specified by FinCEN in the request (generally fourteen days).[62] Unless otherwise instructed in the request, the search must include:

(1) deposit account records;
(2) funds transfer records maintained pursuant to 31 C.F.R. § 103.33 to determine whether a suspect was an originator/transmitter or beneficiary/recipient of a funds transfer;
(3) records of the sale of monetary instruments (for example, cashier's checks, money orders, or traveler's checks) kept pursuant to 31 C.F.R. § 103.29;
(4) loan records;
(5) trust department account records;
(6) records of accounts to purchase, sell, lease, hold, or maintain custody of securities;
(7) commodity futures, options, or other derivatives account records; and
(8) safe deposit box records (but only if such safe deposit box records are searchable electronically).[63]

Positive matches must be reported directly and only to FinCEN. If the search does not uncover any matching account or transaction, the financial institution should not reply to the request. A positive report must include:

(i) the name of the individual, entity, or organization matched;
(ii) the number of each account or, in the case of a transaction, the date and type of the transaction; and
(iii) any Social Security or taxpayer identification number, passport number, date of birth, address, or other similar identifying information provided by the named suspect.

Reports should not provide any other details to FinCEN other than the fact that the financial institution has a match, together with the required information.[64]

Q 26.10.4 Should a positive response to a section 314(a) mandatory information sharing request include records?

No. A section 314(a) request is not a substitute for a subpoena or other legal process. But a financial institution submitting a positive report to FinCEN can expect to receive a grand jury subpoena or other legal process for documents relating to the suspect named in that report.

Q 26.10.5 Are section 314(a) mandatory information sharing requests and responses confidential?

Yes. Except to the extent necessary to comply with the request, a financial institution may not disclose to any person the fact that FinCEN has requested or obtained information. Each institution should have appropriate policies and procedures in place to ensure confidentiality.

Section 314(a) requests may, however, be disclosed to the institution's primary regulator, a *domestic* parent or holding company, and *domestic* subsidiaries and affiliates if those entities offer "account" or "transaction" services and are financial institutions as described in 31 U.S.C. § 5312(a)(2). The domestic parent or affiliate must maintain the confidentiality of the section 314(a) request.

Q 26.10.6 Should a section 314(a) mandatory information sharing request trigger the filing of a suspicious activity report if there is a positive match?

No. Mere inclusion in a section 314(a) list should not be the sole factor (but it may be one factor) used to determine whether to file a Suspicious Activity Report (SAR).[65] However, a financial institution that has a section 314(a) account or transaction should review that customer's activity in light of the section 314(a) request to decide whether to keep or close an account, engage in a proposed transaction, or file a SAR.

Q 26.10.7 What is section 314(b) voluntary information sharing?

Voluntary information sharing is the sharing of information between financial institutions about individuals, entities, organizations, or countries for the purposes of identifying and reporting activities that a financial institution suspects may involve possible terrorist activity or money laundering.[66]

Q 26.10.8 What information may be shared among financial institutions under section 314(b) voluntary information sharing?

The only information that may be exchanged under section 314(b) is information relating to identifying and reporting money laundering or terrorist activity. Section 314(b) may not be used to exchange information about other suspected criminal activity, or for general business purposes such as credit or lending decisions, locating defaulting borrowers or their assets, and so on.[67]

Q 26.10.9 Who may share information under section 314(b)?

Only those financial institutions that are required by regulation to have anti-money laundering programs are eligible to participate in voluntary information sharing.[68] This includes all banks and credit unions regulated by a federal regulatory agency, securities broker dealers, futures commissions merchants, and originating brokers in commodities, mutual funds, money services businesses, casinos, operators of credit card systems, dealers in precious metals, precious stones or jewels, and certain life insurance companies.[69]

Q 26.10.10 How does one participate in section 314(b) voluntary information sharing?

If a financial institution is eligible to participate, it must first submit a notification to FinCEN.[70] The notification is effective immediately and authorizes participation in voluntary information sharing for one year from the date of the notification. It must be renewed annually in order to continue to participate.

Q 26.10.11 Who may information be shared with?

Financial institutions may only share information with other eligible financial institutions that have themselves already filed the FinCEN notification.[71] Before engaging in voluntary information sharing, a financial institution must take reasonable steps to determine that the entity it is sharing with has also submitted the required notification to FinCEN.[72]

Q 26.10.12 Is information shared under 314(b) confidential?

Yes. Participating institutions must establish appropriate procedures to protect shared information, both internally and externally.

Q 26.10.13 Should a section 314(b) voluntary information sharing request trigger the filing of a SAR?

A financial institution may use information obtained under section 314(b) to determine whether to file a SAR, but the intention to prepare or file a SAR may not be shared with another financial institution. If a financial institution shares information under section 314(b), it should not include any reference to any SAR filing.

Q 26.10.14 May a financial institution that shares information under section 314(b) be sued civilly by the subject of the information?

Section 314(b) provides financial institutions with a "safe harbor" from civil liability for sharing information, and for not providing notice of such sharing to any person identified in the information shared if, and only if, the institution has fully complied with all of the voluntary information sharing regulations in 31 C.F.R. § 103.110(b)(2), (b)(3), and (b)(4).[73]

Reporting Large Cash Transactions

Q 26.11 Why does the government require large cash transactions to be reported?

Because cash transactions leave little or no documentary trail. Credit card transactions and check purchases leave records identifying the date and nature of the transaction as well as the names of the persons or entities involved. When a person engages in a cash transaction, there is rarely any record (other than a personal receipt) of the transaction's occurrence. A record showing the nature of the transaction or, more importantly, the persons involved in it, is even rarer still. Thus, in an effort to overcome this absence of a paper trail in cash transactions, federal laws require virtually all businesses in the United States to file reports with the federal government on all cash transactions over $10,000.

Q 26.11.1 What forms are used to report large cash transactions?

- Currency Transaction Report/FinCEN Form 104
- IRS/FinCEN Form 8300

Currency Transaction Reports

Q 26.11.2 What are the requirements for filing a Currency Transaction Report (CTR)?

The BSA authorizes the Secretary of the Treasury to require domestic financial institutions to report all cash transactions in excess of $10,000 that occur within a single business day by or on behalf of the same person.[74] "Cash transactions" are those involving the coin or paper money of the United States, as well as foreign currency.[75] A reportable cash transaction includes the aggregate of multiple cash transactions conducted at all of a reporting institution's branches and agencies on a single day if the transactions are conducted by or on behalf of the same person/entity. Reports must be made within fifteen days of the transaction to the IRS on a "Currency Transaction Report," FinCEN Form 104.[76]

The financial institutions required to report such transactions on a CTR include depository institutions such as banks, credit unions and thrift institutions, broker-dealers in securities, mutual funds, commodities futures traders, MSBs (that is, currency dealers or exchangers; check cashers; issuers or sellers of cashier's checks, traveler's checks, money orders, or stored value; and money transmitters), and casinos and card clubs.[77]

It is illegal to structure a cash transaction for the purpose of evading the reporting requirement.[78] It is illegal to fail to file a CTR, or to intentionally file one that is inaccurate or purposely omits required information. Negligent violations may be punished civilly; intentional failures may be punished civilly or criminally as violations of the BSA.

IRS Form 8300

Q 26.11.3 What are the requirements for filing an IRS Form 8300?

Both the BSA[79] and the Internal Revenue Code[80] require that any person who is engaged in a trade or business and who, in the course of such trade or business, receives more than $10,000 in currency in one transaction, or in two or more "related" transactions, is required to file a report of the transaction with FinCEN and the Internal Revenue Service. This requirement includes *all other* "financial institutions" not otherwise required to file CTRs, as well as *all other persons and businesses* in the United States, if they receive over $10,000 in "currency" in the course of their trade or business.[81]

Although required by two separate statutes, and subject to two separate (but virtually identical) sets of regulations,[82] reports are made on a single form, an IRS/FinCEN Form 8300, which is transmitted to the IRS.[83] A Form 8300 must be filed within fifteen days of the receipt of over $10,000 in currency.[84]

It is illegal to structure a cash transaction for the purpose of evading the reporting requirement.[85] It is illegal to fail to file a Form 8300, or to intentionally file one that is inaccurate or purposely omits required information. Negligent violations may be punished civilly, and intentional violations may be punished civilly and criminally, as violations of the BSA. Violations may also be punished civilly or criminally under the Internal Revenue Code.[86]

In addition to reporting currency transactions, every business must furnish a single, annual written statement to each person named on a Form 8300 that includes the name and address of the business, the total amount of currency reported to have been received in the calendar year from or on behalf of the person named in the form, and a statement saying that the information was reported to the IRS. The statement must be sent to each person named in the form on or before January 31 of the year following the calendar year in which the currency was received.[87]

Q 26.11.4 What constitutes "currency" for purposes of Form 8300?

Just as in the case of CTRs, "currency" includes U.S. currency, and the currency of any other country.[88] Unlike CTRs, however, "currency" for Form 8300 reporting purposes is not limited just to cash. "Currency" has a different meaning when the transaction involves the retail sale of a "consumer durable" or a travel or entertainment activity.[89] It includes cashier's checks (by whatever name called, including "treasurer's checks" and "bank checks"), bank drafts, traveler's checks, or money orders, *with a face value of under $10,000.*[90] The term does not include a personal check, regardless of the face value.

Q 26.11.5 What is a reportable transaction?

The law requires that if a business receives more than $10,000 in "currency" in one transaction or in two or more "related" transactions, it is required to file a Form 8300 with the IRS. A "transaction" means the underlying event precipitating the payer's transfer of currency to the recipient. This includes, but is not limited to the:

- sale of goods or services;
- sale of real property;
- sale of intangible property;
- rental of real or personal property;
- exchange of currency for other currency;
- establishment or maintenance of a custodial, trust, or escrow arrangement;
- payment of a pre-existing debt;
- conversion of currency into a negotiable instrument;
- reimbursement for expenses paid; or
- making or repayment of a loan.[91]

Any transactions between a business and the same customer that occur within a twenty-four-hour period are considered to be one transaction for reporting purposes.[92]

Q 26.11.6 When are transactions considered "related"?

Transactions are considered "related" for reporting purposes even if they occur over a period of more than twenty-four hours, if the receiving business knows or has reason to know that each transaction is one of a series of connected transactions.[93]

Q 26.11.7 How are multiple-payment transactions handled?

The receipt of "currency" deposits or installment payments for a single transaction are reported differently, depending on the amounts of cash paid in the initial and subsequent payments.[94]

If a customer's initial payment in one transaction is over $10,000 in "currency," that payment must be reported on Form 8300 within fifteen days of the transaction. If the initial payment is in "currency" but does not exceed $10,000, then the initial payment must be combined with subsequent "currency" payments made within one year. As soon as the total of "currency" payments on the transaction exceeds $10,000, a Form 8300 must be filed. If more "currency" payments on that transaction are later received within the one-year period, they must be separately reported every time they total over $10,000.

FIGURE 26-1

Example: Multiple-Payment Transactions and Form 8300

Joe Customer intends to purchase a $45,000 necklace from a business and pay over a five-month period. The $45,000 is a single transaction for cash reporting purposes. Joe pays $9,000 each month for five months; thus, if any part of any of the payments is made in cash, once the cash portions total over $10,000, a Form 8300 must be filed on the cash payments.

Monthly Payment	Form of Payment	File Form 8300?	Why/Why Not
1	$9,000 personal check	No	A personal check is not cash.
2	$9,000 cash	No	The amount of cash received by the company is still under $10,000.
3	$9,000 cashier's check	Yes	The business has now received, in one transaction, over $10,000 in cash—$9,000 in currency and $9,000 in a cashier's check (a "monetary instrument" that is the equivalent of cash).
4	$9,000 cash	No	After filing the first Form 8300, the $10,000 count starts over again.
5	$9,000 traveler's check	Yes	The business has again received, in one transaction (the original $45,000 transaction), over $10,000 in cash—$9,000 in currency and $9,000 in the traveler's check (again, the "monetary instrument" equivalent of cash).

BSA Record-Keeping Requirements

Q 26.12 What records must be made and kept under the BSA?

The BSA requires certain records of particular types of transactions must be made and kept. The record-keeping requirements of the BSA generally fall into three categories:

- those applicable to all businesses in general;
- those applicable to "all financial institutions"; and
- those applicable only to specific "financial institutions."

In general, the only record-keeping requirement applicable to all businesses in general is that copies of all reports of transactions involving "currency" over $10,000 (which are filed on IRS Form 8300) (see Q 26.11.3, above) must be maintained for five years from the date of filing.[95] It is important to note here that "currency" has a unique meaning that involves more than just cash; it can also include certain types of monetary instruments (see Q 26.11.4, above).

The BSA regulations also require that "all financial institutions" must keep records of:

- each extension of credit over $10,000 that is not secured by real property; and
- each advice, request, or instruction received or given that results in the transfer of funds, securities, or credit to or from any person, account, or place outside the United States.

These records must be kept for a period of five years.[96]

Although the record-keeping regulations apply to "all financial institutions," the regulatory definition of "financial institution" differs from the BSA statutory definition. For purposes of the regulations, "financial institutions" are banks, credit unions, MSBs, a telegraph company, brokers or dealers in securities, mutual funds, casinos and card clubs, futures commission merchants, and introducing brokers in commodities.[97]

The BSA record-keeping requirements applicable only to specific "financial institutions" apply to banks and credit unions, currency dealers or exchangers, brokers or dealers in securities, casinos, and MSBs.[98]

"Bulk Cash Smuggling"

Q 26.13 What is "bulk cash smuggling"?

It is the act of physically transporting, mailing, shipping, or causing the same, of any cash or "monetary instrument" into or out of the United States without filing the required report. For U.S. purposes, aggregate amounts exceeding $10,000 into or out of the United States must be reported to the U.S. Customs Service. The report must be made on a "Report of International Transportation of Currency or Monetary Instruments," also known as a "CMIR" or FinCEN Form 105.[99]

Q 26.13.1 What are the filing requirements for FinCEN Form 105?

The report must be filed before or at the time of the entry or departure into or from the United States. It may also be made by mail on or before the date of entry, departure, mailing, or shipping. However, as a practical matter, the report should be filed directly with U.S. Customs at the time or entry or departure.

A person or entity *receiving* cash or monetary instruments from outside the United States must file a FinCEN Form 105 within fifteen days of receipt if the form has not already been filed by the person sending or causing the sending of the funds.[100]

Q 26.13.2 What are the consequences of bulk cash smuggling?

The knowing and intentional failure to file this report may result in the seizure and civil or criminal forfeiture of the currency and monetary instruments being transported. If the currency or monetary instrument is concealed for the purpose of avoiding a report, the container or conveyance carrying the funds may also be seized. A knowing and intentional failure to report can be also punished criminally by imprisonment for up to five years.[101]

Q 26.13.3 For purposes of bulk cash smuggling, what are "currency" and "monetary instruments"?

For purposes of this law, "currency" means the coin or paper money of the United States, as well as the coin or paper money of a foreign country. Thus, the import or export of foreign currency whose value in U.S. dollars exceeds $10,000 must be reported.

The term "monetary instrument" means:

- traveler's checks in any form;
- all forms of negotiable instruments (including personal and business checks) that are either in bearer form, that may be endorsed without restriction, that are made out to a fictitious payee, or that are in any other form such that title passes upon delivery;
- incomplete instruments that are signed but with the payee's name left out; and
- securities or stocks in bearer form or whose title passes on delivery.[102]

Q 26.13.4 Are there any exceptions to this reporting requirement?

There are a number of them, including:

(1) banks, foreign banks, and securities broker-dealers shipping by mail or by common carrier;
(2) certain overland shipments by a domestic commercial bank or trust company for an established customer;
(3) common carriers of passengers with respect to funds carried by passengers;
(4) common carriers of goods with respect to funds shipments not declared to the common carrier;
(5) a non-U.S. citizen or resident for funds mailed or shipped from abroad to a bank or broker-dealer by mail or common carrier; and
(6) issuers of traveler's checks.[103]

Structuring

Q 26.14 What is structuring?

In order to avoid the large cash transaction reporting requirements, money launderers and terrorists frequently attempt to disguise one single cash transaction that exceeds $10,000 as multiple, separate transactions, each under $10,000. This type of activity, when designed to avoid the filing of applicable reports, is called "structuring."

Q 26.14.1 What are the penalties for structuring violations?

Structuring is illegal and punishable by imprisonment up to five years. Structuring violations, if committed while violating another law of the United States or as part of a pattern of any illegal activity involving over $100,000 in a one-year period are punishable by a fine of up to $500,000 and imprisonment for up to ten years.[104]

Transactions with Specially Designated Persons

Q 26.15 Who are the "specially designated persons" that federal AML statutes prohibit transactions with?

A number of federal laws impose severe restrictions and sanctions against:

(1) persons, groups, entities, and countries deemed to be supporters of terrorist activity;
(2) terrorists; and
(3) international narcotics traffickers and "kingpins."

The U.S. Treasury Department's Office of Foreign Assets Control (OFAC) maintains a list of these "Specially Designated Nationals" (SDNs) on its "OFAC List" (or "SDN List"). These sanctions are implemented through regulations issued by OFAC and apply to all "United States persons."

Q 26.15.1 Who is considered a "United States person"?

Generally, a "United States person" includes:

- a national of the United States anywhere in the world;
- any resident alien;
- any person within the United States;
- any entity composed principally of nationals or permanent resident aliens of the United States; or
- any corporation organized under the laws of the United States, any state, the District of Columbia, or any U.S. territory or possession.

Generally, for anti-money laundering and anti-terrorist financing purposes, the term does not include foreign subsidiaries of U.S. entities. However, the term *does* include, and the prohibitions *do* directly apply to, individual United States persons located anywhere in the world, regardless of who their employer is.[105]

Q 26.16 What kinds of transactions with SDNs are prohibited?

Generally, the OFAC regulations prohibit any United States person from conducting any business transaction or transfer of any funds or property, facilitating any business transaction, or providing any service to any person, group, or organization on the OFAC List. The regulations further generally require either that all property and assets of SDNs be "blocked" (that is, placed in an interest-bearing account not accessible to the SDN), or that any transaction involving any property or funds belonging to an SDN be rejected and promptly reported to OFAC. However, the precise prohibitions imposed by OFAC regulations against SDNs and the specific requirements imposed on United States persons vary according to the particular reason why the person, group, entity, or country has been placed on the OFAC List.[106] Accordingly, the names found on the list also refer to the particular reason for inclusion. It is thus important not only to identify SDNs, but also to know their specific designation in order to determine the precise requirements and prohibitions imposed on United States persons by the regulations.

Q 26.16.1 What are the consequences of conducting business with an SDN?

Violations can be punished by severe fines and imprisonment, depending upon the statute and sanctions program involved. Civil fines imposed by OFAC against United States persons violating OFAC regulations can be substantial, frequently involving hundreds of thousands—and in some cases millions—of dollars.[107]

Special Rules for MSBs

Q 26.17 What are the AML requirements for Money Services Businesses?

In addition to maintaining formal anti-money laundering programs and reporting "suspicious transactions," all MSBs are required to register with FinCEN.[108] Failure to register is a federal felony punishable by fine and imprisonment for up to five years.[109]

In addition, many *states* also require MSBs to register. Failure to register with a state, if required by state law, is a federal felony.[110] It is, therefore, essential for every such business not only to comply with the federal registration regulations, but also to check the laws of each state in which it does business. In some cases, an MSB may have to file multiple registrations. Care must be taken to closely examine the definition of the term "MSBs" under both the federal regulations and local state law, because they frequently differ. This can result in a business having to register in some states but not others, or with FinCEN but not with the state, or with the state but not with FinCEN.

Agents and branches of MSBs are not required by federal regulation to register with FinCEN, although the business must report information about its branch locations or offices, and must maintain a list of its agents. This list must include each agent's name, address, telephone number, type of service provided by the agent, the agent's bank, the year the agent first became an agent, the number of branches or sub-agents the agent has, and a listing of the months in the preceding twelve months in which the agent's gross transaction amount exceeded $100,000.[111]

Registration is valid for a two-year period, and a copy of the registration must be kept at a location in the United States for five years. If, however, the business is subject to a state registration requirement, then a change in control that requires re-registration with the state requires re-registration with FinCEN. In addition, the federal regulations also require re-registration with FinCEN if there is a transfer of more than 10% of the voting power or equity interest of the business. Further, if the business experiences a more than 50% increase in the number of its agents during any registration period, the business must re-register with FinCEN. Re-registration must be done within 180 days of the event triggering the re-registration requirement.[112]

Q 26.18 What are the AML requirements for *foreign* Money Services Businesses?

On July 18, 2011, FinCEN issued a final rule (effective in September 2011) clarifying the definition of MSBs to include *foreign* MSBs as well as domestic ones.[113] Specifically, FinCEN revised 31 C.F.R. § 1010.100(ff) so that an entity qualifies as an MSB based on its activity within the United States, not the physical presence there of one or more of its agents, agencies, branches, or offices. The new definition now states (in relevant part) that an MSB includes: "[a] person wherever located doing business . . . wholly or in substantial part within the United States. . . ."

The phrase "wholly or in substantial part within the United States" requires more than mere maintenance of a bank account in the United States by a foreign-located person or entity.[114] FinCEN has made it clear, however, that whether a foreign-located person's MSB activities occur within the United States

> depends on all of the facts and circumstances of each case, including whether persons in the United States are obtaining MSB services from the foreign-located person, such as sending money to or receiving money from third parties through the foreign-located person.[115]

The new definition does not include foreign banks or broker dealers. The new definition provides that foreign banks—as well as other foreign financial agencies that engage in financial activities that, if conducted in the United States, would require that agency to be registered with the SEC or CFTC—are not included in the new definition of MSB.[116]

As a result of the new definition, foreign MSBs will have the same registration, reporting, and record-keeping requirements as MSBs physically located in the United States and will be subject to the same civil and criminal penalties.[117] Foreign MSBs will also be required to designate a person who resides in the United States to act as an agent to accept service of legal process, including with respect to BSA compliance.[118]

AML Compliance Programs

Compliance and Your Company

Q 26.19   Why should my company care about having an anti-money laundering compliance program?

Any business that is a "financial institution" under the BSA and that is required to implement an anti-money laundering compliance program *must* care, because failure to implement the Program could expose the business to criminal, civil, and administrative penalties.[119] For such businesses, it is equally important to monitor changes in, or additions to, that requirement (for example, a requirement to report "suspicious transactions" or maintain certain types of records may be added to an already-existing compliance program requirement). Failure to comply with the applicable Treasury regulations can be punished both civilly and criminally under the Bank Secrecy Act and may also subject regulated "financial institutions" to severe administrative penalties imposed by their federal regulatory agency for failure to comply, or even for failure to fully and sufficiently comply.

Regardless of whether a business is a BSA "financial institution," for all businesses, the best defense against becoming unwittingly involved in a possible violation of the Money Laundering Control Act is to have an effective anti-money laundering compliance program. Such a program can be used to demonstrate that the business is a "good corporate citizen" that took reasonable steps to avoid involvement (through willful blindness or otherwise) in criminal money laundering activity.

Finally, the board of directors and senior management of every corporation, regardless of whether it is a BSA "financial institution," should consider whether it has a fiduciary duty to include anti-money laundering policies and procedures as part of its overall compliance program.[120] Management should consider the risk that money launderers may attempt to engage in laundering activities with the corporation.

Q 26.19.1 Our institution is currently exempted from anti-money laundering compliance program requirements. How can we keep track of changing regulations should our status change?

Businesses that are "financial institutions" under the BSA but that are exempt under 31 C.F.R. § 103.170 should closely monitor the *Federal Register* or FinCEN's website, www.fincen.gov, in order to determine whether the Treasury Department intends to issue regulations removing it from that exemption. In such cases, Treasury normally will issue a Notice of Proposed Rule Making in the *Federal Register*, explaining and stating the proposed regulations and inviting public comment. A Notice of Proposed Rule Making is a clear indication that the status of an exempted "financial institution" is about to change, although a substantial amount of time may elapse before a *proposed* rule is made a *final* rule. Further, sometimes a proposed rule imposing anti-money laundering requirements may be withdrawn by Treasury.[121]

Components of an Effective Compliance Program

Q 26.19.2 What are the elements of an effective anti-money laundering compliance program?

To restate the BSA's minimal requirements for a *mandatory* anti-money laundering program:

1. An anti-money laundering program must be in writing.
2. The financial institution must:
   (a) formally appoint an "Anti-Money Laundering Compliance Officer" who is in overall charge of the program;
   (b) conduct periodic training of appropriate employees about the institution's anti-money laundering policies and procedures; and

(c) conduct a periodic independent audit of the program to ensure it has been implemented and is being followed.[122]

3. Anti-money laundering programs must be "risk-based."[123]

In addition, a key element for the prevention and detection of money laundering and terrorist financing is to develop effective "Know Your Customer" procedures. In every transaction, each business should be diligent in knowing who it is dealing with and have reasonable grounds to believe that each customer is entirely legitimate and using funds derived from legitimate activity. This includes confirming an individual customer's true identity and, for customers that are businesses, ensuring that every entity with which one does business is, in fact, a legally established entity.

AML Compliance Officers

Q 26.19.3 What are the key considerations in appointing a compliance officer?

The compliance officer should be appointed by the board of directors or senior management. Although the actual title is not important, the compliance officer must have a level of authority and responsibility in the company sufficient to implement, supervise, and enforce the compliance program on a daily basis, and sufficient resources (budgetary and personnel) to perform his or her function.

The compliance officer must be a qualified person who is knowledgeable about money laundering and the Money Laundering Control Act. For "financial institutions," it is critical that the compliance officer also be fully knowledgeable about the Bank Secrecy Act and the implementing regulations that apply to the particular business. The compliance officer should also have a full knowledge of the business, its products, services, operations, general customer base, and money laundering risk assessment.

Finally, it is imperative that the compliance officer be of the highest integrity. Bad actors must be kept out of the position, and out of the overall supervision and operation of the compliance program. The board and senior management must take reasonable steps to screen out persons whom the company knows, or should know through the exercise of due diligence, have a history of engaging in illegal activity or other misconduct.

Employee Training

Q 26.19.4 What are the key considerations when approaching employee training?

For all BSA "financial institutions" that are required to maintain anti-money laundering programs, periodic employee training is mandatory. Periodic employee training is also necessary for any other business with an anti-money laundering compliance program because the failure to conduct periodic training will render the program ineffective.

All appropriate employees should be trained on money laundering in general and on the company's anti-money laundering policies and procedures. Who the "appropriate" employees are will vary from business to business and will also depend on the company's risk assessment, but at a minimum should include all employees whose duties could expose them to money laundering. Generally this will include management, sales, finance, and accounting personnel. Training should be tailored to the person's specific responsibilities. In addition, new staff should be given an overview of the compliance program during employee orientation. For "financial institutions," it is critical that employees be trained about the Bank Secrecy Act and the implementing regulations that apply to the particular business.

Training should be periodic (generally, annually) and include not only training on basic policies and procedures, but also current anti-money laundering developments and changes to any company policies and procedures. Important developments and changes should be disseminated on an ongoing basis, as needed.

The company should document its training program and keep accurate records of the dates of the periodic employee training, the content of the training, training and testing materials, and attendance records.

Independent Audit

Q 26.19.5 What are the key considerations regarding independent audits?

An anti-money laundering compliance program should be periodically tested independently to ensure it has been implemented, followed, and enforced. For all BSA "financial institutions" that are required to maintain anti-money laundering programs, periodic independent auditing of the program is mandatory. While the frequency of the independent audit is not prescribed, even for "financial institutions," it is generally a sound practice to conduct independent testing annually.

The periodic audit must be "independent" in the sense that it is conducted by persons who are not involved in or responsible for the program's operation. Thus, it may be conducted by the internal audit department, outside auditors, consultants, or other qualified persons.

The persons conducting the independent audit should be knowledgeable about the program, the policies and procedures included in the program, the business and its operations, and the company's money laundering risk assessment. For all BSA "financial institutions," the auditor(s) should also be knowledgeable about the BSA and the regulations applicable to the company. They should also be familiar with the company's money laundering risk assessment, because the audit should be "risk-based" and evaluate the quality of risk management for all operations and departments involved in applying the program's policies and procedures.

The persons conducting the independent audit should report directly to the company board of directors, or to a designated board committee. Deficiencies and corrective recommendations should then be conveyed to senior management and the compliance officer for correction and follow-up. Senior management should ensure, through the compliance officer, that identified deficiencies are promptly addressed and corrective recommendations implemented.

"Know Your Customer" Procedures

Q 26.19.6 How can we confirm a customer's identity?

For individual customers, verifying identity is normally done by means of a government-issued photo identification, and in appropriate cases by determining the customer's source of funds or wealth. For business customers, it normally means securing a copy of articles of incorporation, government-issued licenses, government tax identification numbers, trust documents, partnership registrations, or the like. It can also include procedures to verify business information by telephone or through publicly available information.

Q 26.19.7 What if verifying a customer's identity is not possible?

For some businesses, it is neither possible nor practical, from a cost or customer relations point of view, to secure such documentation for *every* customer. This is where the risk assessment comes into play. Depending upon the degree and type of risk, a business should determine when to require identification, what type of identification to secure, and what follow-up procedures are appropriate. The point to keep in mind is that, depending on the degree of risk and the volume of business being done, each business should attempt to establish, as effectively and efficiently as it can, that the individual or business it is doing business with is who it claims to be, is engaged in legitimate business activities, is using funds derived from legitimate business or legitimate sources of wealth and income.

Creating and Administering a Program

Q 26.19.8 What are the actual steps a company must take to create an effective anti-money laundering compliance program?

The regulations provide no guidance on *how* to create an effective anti-money laundering program. The U.S. Sentencing Guidelines, however, provide some direction that, at a minimum, a company should take:[124]

1. Establish policies, standards, and procedures to prevent and detect money laundering.

2. Ensure that the company's board of directors and senior management understand the content and operation of the compliance program and exercise reasonable oversight with respect to its implementation and effectiveness. Specific senior manager(s) should have overall responsibility to ensure the implementation and effectiveness of the program. A compliance officer should be delegated at the outset to conduct or supervise the risk assessment, develop appropriate procedures, and oversee the drafting, implementation and day-to-day operation of the program. This person should be afforded adequate resources and authority to accomplish these tasks.

3. Take reasonable steps to ensure that the compliance officer and his or her staff are adequately knowledgeable about the business, money laundering, and applicable statutes and regulations. Also ensure that company management and the compliance officer and staff are of the highest integrity by screening out persons whom the company knows, or should know through the exercise of due diligence, have a history of engaging in illegal activity or other misconduct.

4. Conduct a risk assessment based on the company's products, services, customer base and geographic location(s); prepare a written risk assessment; and develop specific risk-based procedures to meet the perceived risk areas. A risk assessment is *not* a one-time-only exercise. It is a continuing process that continually takes into account changes in methods of money laundering, new products or services offered by the company, changes in the company's customer base and geographic areas of operation, and changes in the law or applicable regulations.

5. Take reasonable steps to communicate periodically and in a practical manner the company's standards and procedures to all officers, employees, and, as appropriate, agents, through effective training programs and otherwise disseminating information.

6. Take reasonable steps to

    (a) ensure that the program is followed, including using monitoring and auditing to detect misconduct;
    (b) evaluate periodically the program's effectiveness; and
    (c) have a system in which employees and agents may report or seek guidance regarding potential or actual

misconduct without fear of retaliation (although a mechanism for anonymous reporting is not required).

7. Promote and enforce the program through appropriate incentives and disciplinary measures for engaging in misconduct and for failing to take reasonable steps to prevent or detect misconduct.

8. Take reasonable steps to respond appropriately to money laundering by customers and to prevent further similar conduct, including making any necessary modifications to the compliance and ethics program.[125]

Q 26.19.9 What is the relationship between a compliance program under the U.S. Sentencing Guidelines and an anti-money laundering compliance program?

Since enactment of the USA PATRIOT Act, bank regulators have focused heavily on Bank Secrecy Act/anti-money laundering compliance. The regulatory focus on BSA compliance has steadily evolved, and BSA compliance has become a primary element of the regulatory strategy and expectations in bank examinations. For banks in particular, the Federal Financial Institutions Examination Council (FFIEC) published the *Bank Secrecy Act/Anti-Money Laundering Examination Manual* in 2007, which institutionalizes this primary focus through its detailed, coordinated guidance, and with its emphasis on regular risk assessments.

The logical extension is the expansion of supervisory attention to other compliance areas. The Board of Governors of the Federal Reserve System has recognized this expansion, and the Board's Division of Banking Supervision and Regulation now organizes its Risk Section to include both BSA/AML compliance risk and *other* compliance risk. The Board expects banks to have effective *comprehensive* compliance and ethics programs as an essential component of the safety and soundness of their operations. These expectations are consistent with guidance from other regulatory agencies, including the SEC. Thus, BSA "financial institutions" are increasingly expected to have the overall comprehensive compliance program encouraged by Chapter 8 of the U.S. Sentencing Guidelines *in addition to* their BSA anti-money laundering compliance programs.

Q 26.19.10 Is there a standard anti-money laundering compliance program that my company can effectively use?

There is no such thing as a one-size-fits-all anti-money laundering compliance program. An effective program must be based on a risk assessment that is specific to each company. Each company must examine the nature of its business, its products and services, its customer base, and the areas in which it operates in order to determine and prioritize its potential exposure to money laundering, and the policies and procedures it adopts must be designed based on that company-specific analysis.

Q 26.19.11 How do we go about designing an anti-money laundering compliance program?

Initially, the company should determine whether the company is *required* to have an anti-money laundering compliance program. If so, it must satisfy the requirements of the applicable Bank Secrecy Act regulations. Compliance with those regulations should result in a basically sound compliance program that can then be tweaked and improved over time based upon the company's experience.

Even if the company is a "financial institution" that is not yet regulated under the Bank Secrecy Act or is not a "financial institution," the regulations still provide a good starting point for designing a compliance program. Although the specifics of the regulations vary somewhat from one industry to another, they are generally similar and provide overall guidance on what constitutes an effective program.

In addition to using the regulations as a blueprint for a compliance program, the following steps are essential:

Step One: Secure the support of the board of directors. This can be done by educating board members generally on the Money Laundering Control Act and, for "financial institutions," on the Bank Secrecy Act. The board should be made to understand that the best defense against involvement in criminal money laundering is an effective anti-money laundering compliance program.

Step Two: Have appropriate policies issued by the board directing senior management to publish company-wide policies and procedures stating the senior management's determination to comply with the law, to avoid involvement with money laundering, and to issue policies and procedures specifically designed to detect and deter such activity. These policies may provide for direct supervision and reporting to the board itself, or to a specially designated board committee.

Step Three: Develop, in association with outside consultants as deemed necessary, the specific duties, responsibilities, and authority of both senior management and the compliance officer regarding the implementation, operation, and enforcement of the compliance program.

Step Four: The board (or the designated board committee), in conjunction with senior management, should select and appoint a qualified anti-money laundering compliance officer and provide him or her with sufficient resources to implement, operate, and enforce a compliance program. The appointment of the compliance officer should be announced to all levels of management and to all employees. The announcement should make clear the compliance officer's scope of authority, as well as the board's and senior management's full support for the compliance officer in the performance of his or her mission.

Step Five: Under the supervision of the compliance officer, and in association with outside consultants as deemed necessary, prepare a written risk assessment which takes into account the areas of the business most vulnerable to money laundering activity. This should specifically include an analysis of the company's products, services, customer base, geographic locations and overall operations, and develop a risk assessment for each category. The results of the risk assessment should be reported to the board or the designated board committee.

It bears repeating that risk assessment is *not* a one-time-only exercise. It is a continuing process that takes into account changes in methods of money laundering, new products or services offered by the company, changes in the company's customer base and geographic areas of operation, and changes in the law or applicable regulations.

Step Six: Prepare a written set of procedures (based directly on the results of the risk assessment) that are specifically designed to deter and detect money laundering and that are practical in light of actual company operations and are as cost-efficient as possible. This process should occur under the supervision of the compliance officer and/or senior management, and in association with outside consultants as deemed necessary.

Step Seven: Issue a company-wide announcement of the compliance program, the appointment of the compliance officer, his or her duties, responsibilities and authority, and senior management's full expectation that every employee will fully comply with the program.

Step Eight: Conduct company-wide mandatory education of appropriate employees (as selected by the compliance officer) on money laundering, the company's anti-money laundering policies, and the company's specific anti-money laundering procedures contained in the compliance program. Employee training should be periodic and ongoing.

Step Nine: Establish a clear schedule for reporting by the compliance officer to the board and senior management on the progress of the implementation of the compliance program. Keep the board informed of the progress of the implementation of the program through direct reports to either the board or a designated board committee.

Step Ten: Select the independent audit team and establish dates for the commencement and completion of the initial periodic audit. For a newly established program, audits should be more frequent—about every six months until the program has been in place for a year or two. Well-established programs may be audited about every twelve to eighteen months.

Q 26.19.12 What are the basic considerations for the ongoing administration and enforcement of an anti-money laundering compliance program?

First, an effective compliance program changes with the environment in which the company operates; it is not static. Thus, one foundation of the program is ongoing risk assessment, which takes into account changes in methods of money laundering, new products or services offered by the company, changes in the company's customer base and geographic areas of operation, and changes in the law or applicable regulations. As new areas of vulnerability are identified, the program itself must evolve.

The second part of the foundation for an effective program is how the company administers and enforces it.

1. The company must conduct effective, periodic training programs and otherwise disseminate information about the compliance program to both officers and appropriate employees.

2. The company must establish and publicize a system by which employees know how to report not only suspected money laundering, but also internal violations of program policies and procedures.

3. The company must promptly and carefully investigate any reports of suspected money laundering or internal misconduct, and take corrective action as appropriate. This is particularly important for those Bank Secrecy Act "financial institutions" that are required to report "suspicious transactions" to FinCEN. Failure to identify and report such transactions can result in severe administrative, civil, and even criminal penalties.

4. The company also should provide feedback to employees who have reported suspected internal misconduct so that they know that their allegations were taken seriously and that an appropriate resolution was reached. Employees who believe that their complaints have been ignored by the corporation are far more likely to become "whistleblowers" who initiate litigation against the company than employees who believe that their complaints have been considered and addressed.[126]

5. The company should document suspected instances of money laundering and suspected violations of the program procedures *and* the steps that it takes to address them. Failure to keep such records makes it difficult or impossible to audit the operation of the program and severely hinders the company's ability to demonstrate its good faith and diligence should it ever become the target of scrutiny or accusation.

Q 26.19.13 Who should administer the anti-money laundering compliance program?

Several different departments within the company may have significant roles to play in the day-to-day operation of the compliance program, including the company audit or accounting department, the security department, human resources, and the legal department. However, their various compliance efforts must be coordinated as part of a single program, so the compliance officer should be responsible and accountable for overseeing the company's compliance efforts. Again, in order to accomplish this task and ensure the smooth and effective operation of the compliance program, the compliance officer needs to have sufficient line authority and resources.

Q 26.19.14 What role does top management have in administering the program?

The success of any compliance program depends upon the support and involvement of top management. Not surprisingly, the Treasury Department regulations requiring "financial institutions" to implement anti-money laundering programs expect the company's board of directors and senior management to issue the policies and procedures designed to implement the compliance program itself, as well as those designed to deter and detect money laundering. Top management is also expected to monitor, at least through the periodic independent audit, the operation of the program. While clearly not applicable to all businesses, the regulations establish a basic standard for the role of top management.

In addition to establishing the program and issuing the appropriate policies and procedures, the board of directors, or at least the senior management, should appoint the compliance officer. The compliance officer should report directly to senior management and the board.

It is the duty of the board and senior management to ensure that the compliance officer is qualified and that he or she has the necessary resources (in terms of budget and staff) to perform the assigned duties. The board and senior management need to understand the content and operation of the compliance program and exercise reasonable oversight with respect to its implementation and effectiveness. The board and senior management should supervise the compliance officer and receive periodic reports from him or her concerning the operation of the compliance program and any updates or changes needed in company policies and procedures. The individual delegated day-to-day operational responsibility should report periodically to senior management and should have direct access to the board of directors.

Again, because an effective compliance program is the best defense against becoming unwittingly involved in possible money laundering violations, senior management of every corporation—regardless of whether it is a "financial institution" required by law to comply—should consider the risk that money launderers may attempt to engage in laundering activities with the corporation, and thus whether to include anti-money laundering policies and procedures as part of its overall compliance program.[127]

Notes

1. FEDERAL FINANCIAL INSTITUTIONS EXAMINATION COUNCIL, BANK SECRECY ACT/ANTI-MONEY LAUNDERING EXAMINATION MANUAL (2010), at 12.
2. BLACK'S LAW DICTIONARY 1027 (8th ed. 2004).
3. *See, e.g.*, FEDERAL FINANCIAL INSTITUTIONS EXAMINATION COUNCIL, BANK SECRECY ACT/ANTI-MONEY LAUNDERING EXAMINATION MANUAL (2010), at 12.
4. 31 C.F.R. § 103.11(uu). *But see* FinCEN Proposed Rule at 74 Fed. Reg. 22,129 (May 12, 2009), which will, if adopted, clarify and expand the definition of each of these terms. This proposal has not yet been issued as a final rule.
5. 18 U.S.C. § 1956(c)(1).
6. BLACK'S LAW DICTIONARY 788 (8th ed. 2004) (at entry for "indifference").
7. *Id.* at 1630.
8. United States v. Murray, 154 F. App'x 740, 744, 2005 WL 3046549 (11th Cir. 2005).
9. United States v. Leahy, 464 F.3d 773, 796 (7th Cir. 2006).
10. United States v. Craig, 178 F.3d 891, 896 (7th Cir. 1999).
11. 18 U.S.C. § 1956(c)(7).
12. 18 U.S.C. § 1956(c)(3), (4).
13. 18 U.S.C. § 1956(c)(5).
14. 31 U.S.C. § 5312(a)(2).
15. 18 U.S.C. § 1956(c)(6). See Q 26.6.2 for the list of BSA "financial institutions."
16. 18 U.S.C. § 1956.
17. 26 U.S.C. § 7201.
18. 26 U.S.C. § 7206.
19. 18 U.S.C. § 1956(a)(1).
20. 18 U.S.C. § 1956(a)(2). In addition, for purposes of subsection (2), a defendant's knowledge can be established if: (i) a law enforcement agent states that the funds or monetary instruments represent the proceeds of "some form of unlawful activity"; and (ii) the defendant's subsequent statements or actions indicate that the defendant believed this to be true. *See* 18 U.S.C. § 1956(a)(2).
21. 18 U.S.C. § 1956(a)(3).
22. 18 U.S.C. § 1956(a).
23. 18 U.S.C. § 1956(b)(1).
24. 18 U.S.C. § 981(a)(1).
25. 18 U.S.C. § 981(k). An "interbank account" means any account held by a foreign bank in the United States primarily for the purpose of facilitating customer transactions. *See* 18 U.S.C. §§ 981(k)(4)(a) and 984(c)(2)(B).
26. 18 U.S.C. § 984.
27. 18 U.S.C. § 1956(f).
28. 18 U.S.C. § 1956(b)(1).

29. 18 U.S.C. § 1956(b)(2). On the key issue of federal *subject matter* jurisdiction over foreign entities, see United States v. Lloyds TSB Bank PLC, 639 F. Supp. 2d 314 (S.D.N.Y. 2009) (holding that the court lacked subject matter jurisdiction over a foreign bank sued by the United States for violation of the MLCA and dismissing the complaint).

30. 31 U.S.C. §§ 5312(a)(2), 5312(c).
31. 18 U.S.C. § 1956(c)(6).
32. 18 U.S.C. § 1956(b)(3)–(4).
33. 18 U.S.C. § 1957.
34. 18 U.S.C. § 1957(f)(3).
35. 18 U.S.C. § 1957(f)(1). The term specifically excludes, however, paying an attorney for representation in a criminal matter.
36. 18 U.S.C. § 1957(f)(2).
37. 18 U.S.C. §§ 1957(d)(2) and 3077(2).
38. 31 U.S.C. § 5311 *et seq.*
39. A willful violation of the BSA or a regulation prescribed under the BSA is punishable by a fine of up to $250,000 and imprisonment for up to five years. Such violations, if committed while violating another law of the United States or as part of a pattern of any illegal activity involving over $100,000 in a one-year period are punishable by a fine of up to $500,000 and imprisonment for up to ten years. Violations of section 5318(i) or (j) (relating to private banking and correspondent accounts), or any regulations or special measures imposed under section 5318(A), are punishable by a fine equal to not less than two times the amount of the transaction, but not more than $1 million. 18 U.S.C. § 5322.
40. *See* 31 U.S.C. § 5312(a)(2), (c).
41. *See* section 3(h) of the Federal Deposit Insurance Act, 12 U.S.C. § 1813(h), for the definition of insured bank.
42. FinCEN has included mutual funds as investment company "financial institutions," effective May 14, 2010. *See* 75 Fed. Reg. 19,241 (Apr. 14, 2010). Mutual funds are now included in the general definition of "financial institution" at 31 C.F.R. § 1010.100(t)(10) (formerly 31 C.F.R. § 103.11(n)(10)).
43. MSBs include: currency dealers or exchangers; check cashers; issuers or sellers of cashier's checks, traveler's checks, money orders, or stored value; and money transmitters. 31 C.F.R. § 1010.100(ff) (formerly 31 C.F.R. § 103.11(uu)). On July 18, 2011, FinCEN issued a final rule (effective in September 2011) clarifying the definitions of each of these terms. The definitions now include *foreign* MSBs as well as domestic ones, which means that foreign MSBs are now required to register with FinCEN and are subject to the same BSA/AML requirements as their domestic counterparts. *See* Final Rule: Bank Secrecy Act Regulations, Definitions and Other Regulations Relating to Money Services Businesses, 76 Fed. Reg. 43,585, at 43,589 (July 21, 2011). For further discussion on this rule, see also Q 26.18.
44. *See* 75 Fed. Reg. 65,806 (Oct. 26, 2010). Chapter X is organized as follows:

section 1010	general
section 1020	banks
section 1020	casinos and card clubs

Anti-Money Laundering

      section 1022   money services businesses
      section 1023   broker dealers
      section 1024   mutual funds
      section 1025   insurance
      section 1026   commodities/futures
      section 1027   dealers in precious metals, stones and jewels
      section 1028   credit card operators

A conversion table between the part 103 regulations and the Chapter X can be found at FinCEN's website.

    45. Although FinCEN has issued rules that apply to mutual funds (specifically, maintaining anti-money laundering programs, customer identification programs, and due diligence programs for correspondent and private banking accounts, and reporting suspicious transactions), FinCEN did not include mutual funds within the original definition of "financial institution" until April 2010. *See* 75 Fed. Reg. 19,241 (Apr. 14, 2010). Mutual funds are now required to file CTRs (instead of IRS Forms 8300, *see infra* Q 26.11.3), as previously required, and comply with other BSA record-keeping regulations such as the "Travel Rule" (*see* 31 C.F.R. § 1024.410 (formerly 31 C.F.R. § 103.33)) and other record-keeping and retention rules (*see* 31 C.F.R. §§ 103.33 and 103.38).

    46. *See variously* subsection .210 of each of 31 C.F.R. §§ 1020–28 (formerly 31 C.F.R. §§ 103.120, 103.125, 103.130, 103.135, 103.137, 104.140, and 103.64).

    47. 31 C.F.R. § 1010.205 (formerly 31 C.F.R. § 103.170). These include businesses such as agencies of federal, state, or local government carrying out a duty or power described in the definition of "financial institution"; loan or finance companies; travel agencies; telegraph companies; sellers of automobiles, airplanes, and boats; persons involved in real estate closings or settlements; private bankers; commodity pool operators; commodity trading advisors; some investment companies; some insurance companies; and some dealers in precious metals, stones, or jewels. *Proposed* regulations were published for "Unregistered Investment Companies" (*see* 67 Fed. Reg. 60,617 (Sept. 26, 2002)), Investment Advisers (*see* 68 Fed. Reg. 23,646 (May 5, 2003)), and Commodity Trading Advisers (*see* 68 Fed. Reg. 23,640 (May 5, 2003)). The Proposed Rules for Unregistered Investment Companies, Investment Advisers and Commodity Trading Advisers were *withdrawn* by FinCEN on October 20, 2008 (*see* 73 Fed. Reg. 65,568, 65,569 (Oct. 30, 2008)). A regulatory scheme for "persons involved in real estate closings or settlements" is apparently under consideration (*see* 68 Fed. Reg. 17,569 (Apr. 10, 2003)). Similarly, a regulatory scheme for non-bank residential mortgage lenders and originators is also apparently under consideration. *See* 74 Fed. Reg. 35,830 (July 21, 2009). No *final* rules have yet been issued for these categories of "financial institution."

    48. Regulations applicable to "dealers in precious metals, stones and jewels" are of limited application and generally exempt retail businesses. *See* 31 C.F.R. § 1027.100 (formerly 31 C.F.R. § 103.140). With regard to insurance companies, only those companies that are engaged within the United States as a business in the issuing of a permanent life insurance policy (other than group policies), annuity contracts (other than group contracts), and "any other insur-

ance product with features of cash value or investment" are required to implement anti-money laundering programs. *See* 31 C.F.R. § 1025.100 (formerly 31 C.F.R. § 103.137).

49. 31 U.S.C. § 5318(h).

50. *See variously* subsection .220 of each of 31 C.F.R. §§ 1020, 1023, 1024, and 1026 (formerly 31 C.F.R. §§ 103.121 through .123, and § 103.131).

51. "Banks" include all commercial banks, trust companies, savings or building and loan institutions and credit unions organized under federal or state law; private banks; institutions insured under the National Housing Act; savings banks; and foreign banks operating in the United States. 31 C.F.R. § 1010.100(d) (formerly 31 C.F.R. § 103.11(c)).

52. *See variously* subsection .320 of each of 31 C.F.R. §§ 1020–26 (formerly 31 C.F.R. §§ 103.15 through .21).

53. See subsection .320(e)(1)(i) of each of 31 C.F.R. §§ 1020–26 (formerly 31 C.F.R. §§ 103.18(e), .21(e), .20(e), .19(e), .15(e), .16(f), and .17(e), respectively).

54. See subsection .320(e)(1)(ii) of each of 31 C.F.R. §§ 1020–26 (formerly 31 C.F.R. §§ 103.18(e), .21(e), .20(e), .19(e), .15(e), .16(f), and .17(e), respectively). With regard to disclosure to corporate affiliates, see also FinCEN Guidance FIN-2010-G005 (Nov. 23, 2010), which can be found on FinCEN's website, www.fincen.gov.

55. 31 U.S.C. § 5318(g)(3). The "safe harbor" applies to any "financial institution" that makes either a mandatory or a "voluntary" disclosure. *Id.* Therefore, the "safe harbor" applies to *all* "financial institutions," even including those that are not *required* by regulation to make such reports.

56. Banks report on a Suspicious Activity Report (a SAR-DI, TDF 90-22.47); mutual funds, securities broker-dealers, futures commission merchants and introducing brokers report on a SAR-SF (FinCEN Form 101); insurance companies report on a SAR-SF for now, and on a SAR-IC (FinCEN Form 108) when it is published by FinCEN; MSBs report on a SAR-MSB (FinCEN Form 109); and casinos report on a SAR-C (FinCEN Form 102).

57. Uniting and Strengthening America by Providing Appropriate Tools Required to Intercept and Obstruct Terrorism Act of 2001 ("USA PATRIOT Act"), Pub. L. No. 107-56, Oct. 26, 2001, 115 Stat. 272–402. Section 314 was not included by Congress as a formal part of the BSA, although it clearly constitutes an integral part of an effective BSA anti-money laundering program. *See, e.g.,* FEDERAL FINANCIAL INSTITUTIONS EXAMINATION COUNCIL, BANK SECRECY ACT/ANTI-MONEY LAUNDERING EXAMINATION MANUAL (2006), at 89, *available at* www.ffiec.gov/pdf/bsa_aml_examination_ manual2006.pdf [hereinafter BSA/AML EXAMINATION MANUAL]. The full text of section 314 is also available as part of the Historical and Statutory Notes following 31 U.S.C. § 5311.

58. *See* 31 C.F.R. § 1010.520(a)(2) (formerly 31 C.F.R. § 103.100(a)(4)). Only foreign law enforcement in a country that provides U.S. law enforcement agencies reciprocal access to information may participate.

59. 31 C.F.R. § 1010.520(b)(1) (formerly 31 C.F.R. § 103.100(b)(1)).

60. 31 U.S.C. § 5312(a)(2). *See* Q 26.6.2, *supra*. This is unusual in that BSA regulations generally apply only to "financial institutions" as defined in 31 C.F.R.

Anti-Money Laundering

§ 1010.100(t) (formerly 31 C.F.R. § 103.11(n)), which is substantially narrower than the definition of "financial institution" found in 31 U.S.C. § 5312(a)(2) and (c).

61. Under 31 C.F.R. § 103.100(b)(1), section 314(a) requests may only ask whether an institution maintains an "account" (as defined in 31 C.F.R. § 1010.505(a) (formerly 31 C.F.R. § 103.90(c)) or has engaged in a "transaction" (as defined in 31 C.F.R. § 1010.505(d) (formerly 31 C.F.R. § 103.11(ii))) for, with or on behalf of a specified person or entity. Consequently, mandatory information sharing is limited to financial institutions that provide such services.

62. 31 C.F.R. § 1010.520(f)(3) (formerly 31 C.F.R. § 103.100(b)(2)); *see also* FinCEN General Instructions and Frequently Asked Questions [hereinafter FinCEN FAQs] for section 314(a) requests, available to financial institutions on the FinCEN section 314(a) Secure Information Sharing System.

63. *See also* FinCEN FAQs.
64. 31 C.F.R. § 1010.520(b)(3)(v) (formerly 31 C.F.R. § 103.100(b)(3)(v)).
65. *Id. See also* FinCEN FAQs; BSA/AML Examination Manual at 87.
66. 31 C.F.R. § 1010.540(b) (formerly 31 C.F.R. § 103.110).
67. 31 C.F.R. § 1010.540(b)(4) (formerly 31 C.F.R. § 103.110(b)(4)).
68. 31 C.F.R. § 1010.540(a)(1) (formerly 31 C.F.R. § 103.10(a)(2)).
69. 31 C.F.R. § 1010.520(a)(1) and (b). Only insurance companies that are engaged within the United States as a business in the issuing of a permanent life insurance policy (other than group policies), annuity contracts (other than group contracts) and "any other insurance product with features of cash value or investment" are required to implement anti-money laundering programs. *See* 31 C.F.R. § 1025.100 (formerly 31 C.F.R. § 103.137).
70. 31 C.F.R. § 1010.540(b)(2) (formerly 31 C.F.R. § 103.110(b)(2)). The notice is available on FinCEN's website, www.fincen.gov.
71. This does not include *foreign* financial institutions, even if they are parents, subsidiaries or affiliates of a participating financial institution because they do not meet the eligibility requirement of having to have an anti-money laundering program under the BSA regulations.
72. 31 C.F.R. § 1010.540(b)(3) (formerly 31 C.F.R. § 103.110(b)(3)). A list of participating institutions, including their related contact information, is periodically posted by FinCEN, and checking that list is deemed by the regulations to satisfy the verification requirement.
73. 31 C.F.R. § 1010.540(b)(5) (formerly 31 C.F.R. § 103.110(b)(5)); specifically, section 314(b) of the USA PATRIOT Act provides that a financial institution that "transmits, receives, or shares . . . information for the purposes of identifying and reporting activities that may involve terrorist acts or money laundering activities shall not be liable to any person under any law or regulation of the United States, any constitution, law or regulation of any State or political subdivision thereof, or under any contract or other legally enforceable agreement (including any arbitration agreement)" for disclosing information regarding possible terrorist activity or money laundering, or for failing to provide notice of the disclosure to the person who is identified in it. Pub. L. No. 107-56, tit. III, § 314(b), 115 Stat. 307 (Oct. 26, 2001).
74. 31 U.S.C. § 5313; 31 C.F.R. § 1010.310 (formerly 31 C.F.R. § 103.22).

75. 31 C.F.R. § 1010.100(*l*) (formerly 31 C.F.R. § 103.11(h)).
76. Casinos are required to use FinCEN Form 103.
77. Reporting for certain customers may be exempted under Treasury regulations. *See* 31 C.F.R. § 1020.315 (formerly 31 C.F.R. § 103.22(d)). While the *reporting* requirement applies to all "financial institutions," the reporting *form* to be used differs. Only the businesses listed in the text above should file Currency Transaction Reports ("CTRs"), and all of those businesses should use FinCEN Form 104, except for casinos and card clubs, which should use FinCEN Form 103. All other businesses, including those that are technically "financial institutions" under section 5312 of the BSA, and including insurance companies, dealers in precious metals, stones or jewels, and credit card operators, are required to report large cash transactions, but on IRS/FinCEN Form 8300.
78. 31 U.S.C. § 5324(a).
79. 31 U.S.C. § 5331.
80. 26 U.S.C. § 6050I.
81. *See generally* 31 C.F.R. § 1010.330 (formerly 31 C.F.R. § 103.30). Insurance companies, dealers in precious metals, stones or jewels, and credit card operators should refer to subsection .330 of 31 C.F.R. § 1025, § 1027, or § 1028, respectively. All other businesses that are not included in the BSA regulatory definition of "financial institution" at 31 C.F.R. § 1010.100(t) should follow the cash transaction reporting regulations at 26 C.F.R. § 1.6050I.
82. The BSA regulations for reporting large cash transactions by businesses other than those required to file CTRs are found at 31 C.F.R. § 1010.330 (formerly 31 C.F.R. § 103.130 *et seq.*). The Internal Revenue Code regulations for reporting large cash transactions by businesses other than those required to file CTRs are found at 26 C.F.R. § 1.6050I-1.
83. 31 C.F.R. § 1010.330(e) (formerly 31 C.F.R. § 103.30(e)); 26 C.F.R. § 1.6050I-1(e)(2).
84. 31 C.F.R. § 1010.330(e) (formerly 31 C.F.R. § 103.30(e)); 26 C.F.R. § 1.6050I-1(e).
85. 31 U.S.C. § 5324(b); 26 U.S.C. § 6050I(f).
86. 26 U.S.C. § 6721.
87. 26 C.F.R. § 1.6050I-1(f); the BSA regulations do not include this obligation.
88. 31 C.F.R. § 1010.330(c)(1)(i) (formerly 31 C.F.R. § 103.30(c)(1)(i)); 26 C.F.R. § 1.6050I-1(c)(1)(i).
89. A "consumer durable" means "an item of tangible personal property of a type that is suitable under ordinary usage for personal consumption or use, that can reasonably be expected to be useful for at least one year . . . and has a sales price of more than $20,000." 31 C.F.R. § 1010.330(c)(7) (formerly 31 C.F.R. § 103.30(c)(7)); 26 C.F.R. § 1.6050I-1(c)(2).
90. 31 C.F.R. § 1010.330(c)(1)(ii) (formerly 31 C.F.R. § 103.30(c)(1)(ii); 26 C.F.R. § 1.6050I-1(c)).
91. 31 C.F.R. § 1010.330(c)(12)(i) (formerly 31 C.F.R. § 103.30(c)(12)(i); 26 C.F.R. § 1.6050I-1(c)(7)).

92. 31 C.F.R. § 1010.330(c)(12)(ii) (formerly 31 C.F.R. § 103.30(c)(12)(ii); 26 C.F.R. § 1.6050I-1(c)(7)(ii)).
93. *Id.*
94. 31 C.F.R. § 1010.330(b) (formerly 31 C.F.R. § 103.30(b); 26 C.F.R. § 1.6050I-1(b)).
95. 31 C.F.R. § 1010.330(e) (formerly 31 C.F.R. § 103.30(e)).
96. 31 C.F.R. § 1010.410 (formerly 31 C.F.R. § 103.33).
97. 31 C.F.R. § 1010.100(t) (formerly 31 C.F.R. § 103.11(n)).
98. *See* 31 C.F.R. §§ 1010.415 and 1020.410 (formerly 31 C.F.R. § 103.29, .33(e), and .34, respectively) (banks); 31 C.F.R. § 1023.410 (formerly 31 C.F.R. § 103.35) (brokers or dealers in securities); 31 C.F.R. § 1021.410 (formerly 31 C.F.R. § 103.36) (casinos); 31 C.F.R. § 1022.410 (formerly 31 C.F.R. § 103.37) (currency dealers or exchangers).
99. 31 C.F.R. § 1010.340(a) (formerly 31 C.F.R. § 103.23(a)).
100. 31 C.F.R. § 1010.340(b) (formerly 31 C.F.R. § 103.23(b)).
101. 31 U.S.C. § 5332.
102. 31 C.F.R. § 1010.100(dd) (formerly 31 C.F.R. § 103.11(u)).
103. 31 C.F.R. § 1010.340(c) (formerly 31 C.F.R. § 103.23(c)). However, all exempted persons would be well advised to file the FinCEN Form 105 regardless of any supposed exemption, in order to avoid erroneous seizures by U.S. Customs officials. In addition, if an exempted business receives over $10,000 cash or monetary instruments from outside the United States, that business must report the receipt regardless of the exemption. *See* 31 C.F.R. § 1010.340(b) (formerly 31 C.F.R. § 103.23(b)).
104. 31 U.S.C. § 5324.
105. *See generally* 18 U.S.C. § 3077(2). However, the specific OFAC regulations should be checked for the precise application of the OFAC regulations, as they may be different depending upon the sanction program involved.
106. The OFAC regulations, which are voluminous, are generally found at 31 pts. 500–98. A useful reference for finding the specific regulatory prohibitions and requirements for specific sanctions programs can be found at 31 C.F.R. pt. 500, Appendix A to Chapter V, located immediately following 31 C.F.R. § 598.
107. OFAC has issued an interim final rule entitled "Economic Sanctions Enforcement Guidelines" as guidelines for persons subject to the requirement of U.S. sanctions statutes. *See* 73 Fed. Reg. 51,933 (Sept. 8, 2008).
108. 31 C.F.R. § 1022.380(a) (formerly 31 C.F.R. § 103.41(a)). Any person who owns or controls an MSB is responsible for registering the business, although only one registration for an MSB is required. *See* 31 C.F.R. § 103.41(c).
109. 18 U.S.C. § 1022.380(c) (formerly 31 C.F.R. § 1960(a)). On July 18, 2011, FinCEN issued a final rule (effective in September 2011) extending the registration requirement to *foreign-located* MSBs "doing business . . . wholly or in substantial part within the United States. . . ." *See* Final Rule: Bank Secrecy Act Regulations, Definitions and Other Regulations Relating to Money Services Businesses, 76 Fed. Reg. 43,585, at 43,589 (July 21, 2011). For further discussion on this rule, see also Q 26.18.
110. 18 U.S.C. § 1960(b).

111. 31 C.F.R. § 1022.380(d) (formerly 31 C.F.R. § 103.41(d)).

112. 31 C.F.R. § 1022.380(b) (formerly 31 C.F.R. § 103.41(b)).

113. Final Rule: Bank Secrecy Act Regulations, Definitions and Other Regulations Relating to Money Services Businesses, 76 Fed. Reg. 43,585, at 43,589 (July 21, 2011).

114. *See* FinCEN Ruling 2004-1, Definition of Money Services Business (Foreign-Located Currency Exchanger With U.S. Bank Account) (Mar. 29, 2004), *available at* www.fincen.gov/news_room/rp/rulings/pdf/fincenruling2004-1.pdf (a foreign-located currency exchanger whose only presence in the United States was a bank account was not deemed an MSB when the currency exchange transactions occurred solely in a foreign country for foreign-located customers and the use of the U.S. bank account was limited to issuing and clearing dollar-denominated monetary instruments). *See also* 74 Fed. Reg. 22,129 at 22,133 (May 12, 2009).

115. 76 Fed. Reg. 43,585 at 43,588 (emphasis added).

116. 31 C.F.R. § 1010.100(ff)(8).

117. 76 Fed. Reg. 43,585 at 43,589.

118. 31 C.F.R. § 1022.380(a)(2).

119. For businesses required to implement AML compliance programs, see Q 26.7, *supra*.

120. *See In re* Caremark Int'l, Inc. Derivative Litig., 698 A.2d 959, 970 (Del. Ch. 1996). *See also* Miller v. McDonald (*In re* World Health Alternatives, Inc.), 385 B.R. 576 (Bankr. D. Del. 2008) (applying *Caremark* duties to senior officers and in-house counsel).

121. See the discussion in Q 26.7 and at note 47.

122. 31 U.S.C. § 5318(h). For "financial institutions" *required* to have such programs, essential elements may also include Customer Identification Programs and procedures for identifying and reporting "suspicious transactions."

123. See Q 26.7.2 and Q 26.7.3, *supra*, for discussion of "risk-based" programs. See Bank Secrecy Act/Anti-Money Laundering Examination Manual (Federal Financial Institutions Examination Council, 2007), at 28–34, for an excellent overview of the components of an anti-money laundering program. Although specifically addressed to banks and credit unions, it offers "best practices" applicable to any business. The manual is available online at www.ffiec.gov.

124. U.S. SENTENCING GUIDELINES MANUAL § 8B2.1 (Nov. 2008).

125. *Id.* § 8B2.1(b).

126. The Bank Secrecy Act specifically provides for "whistleblower" protection. *See* 31 U.S.C. § 5328. *See also* Miller v. McDonald (*In re* World Health Alternatives, Inc.), 385 B.R. 576 (Bankr. D. Del. 2008).

127. *See In re* Caremark Int'l, Inc. Derivative Litig., 698 A.2d 959, 970 (Del. Ch. 1996).

27

The Troubled Asset Relief Program

Thomas Morante & Michelle T. Hess[*]

Following the enactment of the Emergency Economic Stabilization Act of 2008 (EESA) in October 2008,[1] the federal government has designed a number of programs to address the financial crisis and avert a possibly severe recession. Grouped broadly under the heading of the Troubled Asset Relief Program (TARP), these various remedies are part of the efforts to assist (among others) the financial, insurance, real estate, and auto industries, and to stabilize the economy.

The EESA granted the Secretary of Treasury broad authority to "restore liquidity and stability" to the U.S. financial system.[2] In the EESA, Congress authorized approximately $700 billion for the purchase of troubled assets through TARP.[3] The TARP legislation was set to expire on December 31, 2009, unless extended by the Secretary of Treasury through written certification to Congress.[4] On December 9, 2009, the Secretary of

---

[*] The authors wish to acknowledge Christopher A. Myers and William M. Pannier for their contributions to this chapter.

Treasury provided the required certification and extended TARP through October 3, 2010.[5] Immediately following initial enactment, TARP focused on emergency measures to "rescue" the financial system and encourage immediate recovery. Given nascent signs of an economic recovery, the focus for TARP has necessarily shifted—with Treasury now looking at TARP funding to stem real estate foreclosures, kick-start small business and community lending initiatives, and accommodate term asset-backed securities loan facility commitments.[6]

TARP was just part of the federal government's initiative to address the financial crisis. In addition to TARP, Congress enacted the American Recovery and Reinvestment Act of 2009 (Financial Recovery Act). The Financial Recovery Act, signed into law on February 17, 2009, was designed to jumpstart the economy by focusing on job creation and development of new industries. The Financial Recovery Act was described by Treasury as "[an] extraordinary response to a crisis unlike any since the Great Depression, and includes measures to modernize our nation's infrastructure, enhance energy independence, expand educational opportunities, preserve and improve affordable healthcare, provide tax relief, and protect those greatest in need."[7] While TARP is targeted primarily at financial institutions, the Financial Recovery Act focuses on jumpstarting the overall economy with federal spending.[8] The Financial Recovery Act created the Recovery Accountability and Transparency Board, which oversees the funds expended by the Act to prevent fraud, waste, and abuse.[9]

What Is TARP?	881
TARP Programs	881
Oversight and Enforcement	885
TARP Compliance	887
Identifying TARP Risks	887
Managing TARP Risks	889

What Is TARP?

Q 27.1 What is TARP?

TARP, the Troubled Asset Relief Program, was created by the Emergency Economic Stabilization Act of 2008[10] and authorized the Department of Treasury ("Treasury") to purchase up to $700 billion in troubled assets.[11] The legislation created the Office of Financial Stability (OFS) within Treasury to manage and distribute the TARP funds.[12] The OFS administers the TARP programs that are designed to stabilize the financial markets and address various industries affected by the financial crisis. Herbert M. Allison was confirmed on June 19, 2009, by the Senate to serve as Assistant Secretary for Financial Stability. In this role, he oversees the OFS and serves as counselor to the Secretary of the Treasury, Timothy F. Geithner.[13]

TARP Programs

Q 27.2 What are the TARP programs?

The TARP legislation includes a number of programs that were designed to address the financial crisis, including:

- Capital Purchase Program
- Systemically Significant Failing Institutions Program/AIG Investment Program
- Targeted Investment Program
- Asset Guarantee Program
- Term Asset-Backed Securities Loan Facility
- Public-Private Investment Program
- Unlocking Credit for Small Businesses/Small Business Administration Loan Support Initiative
- Automotive Industry Financing Program
- Auto Supplier Support Program
- Auto Warranty Commitment Program
- Making Home Affordable Program

Q 27.2.1 What is the Capital Purchase Program?

The Capital Purchase Program (CPP) aimed to strengthen viable financial institutions by directly injecting capital into healthy banks to facilitate lending. Through the CPP, Treasury purchased senior preferred shares from healthy banks and in return received dividend payments and warrants.[14] The application phase of the program closed on November 21, 2009, and additional funds will not be disbursed.[15] The program provided nearly $205 billion in capital to 692 financial institutions, including more than 300 community and small banks.[16] Approximately sixty banks have already repurchased their preferred shares, and as of March 1, 2010, Treasury has received approximately $130 billion in principal repayments.[17] Generally, the federal government has not bought back the warrants it holds at the time a bank has paid back its CPP capital injection.

Q 27.2.2 ... Capital Assistance Program?

The Capital Assistance Program (CAP) was designed to provide additional taxpayer support to financial institutions. CAP was intended to ensure that banks had a "sufficient capital cushion" should future losses exceed expectations.[18] If a bank determined it did require a "buffer," Treasury could provide additional capital.[19] The program was closed in November 2009 following the results of "stress tests," which demonstrated that eighteen of the nineteen participating banks did not require additional capital or had fulfilled their needs in the private market.[20]

Q 27.2.3 ... Systemically Significant Failing Institutions Program/AIG Investment Program?

The Systemically Significant Failing Institutions (SSFI) Program/AIG Investment Program aims to prevent the failure of financial institutions whose failure would impose significant losses on creditors, severely disturb financial markets, and raise borrowing costs for households and businesses.[21] AIG is the only participant in the program and has received approximately $70 billion from the federal government.[22] Secretary Geithner represented in early 2010 that AIG was performing substantially better than it had been at the same time in 2009.[23] Treasury anticipates that AIG will soon receive proceeds from the sale of some subsidiaries, with the federal government expecting to receive repayment for its financial support to AIG.[24]

Q 27.2.4 ... Targeted Investment Program?

The Targeted Investment Program provided funding from Treasury directly to financial institutions that were critical to the financial system.[25] Treasury spent approximately $40 billion to purchase senior preferred stock from Bank of America and Citigroup.[26] Unlike AIG, the federal government did not require Bank of America or Citigroup to make management changes.[27] Both banks have since repaid the funding, effectively terminating the program, although Treasury still holds the warrants—that is, the right, but not the obligation, to purchase a certain number of shares of common stock at a fixed price—it received from both banks.[28]

Q 27.2.5 ... Asset Guarantee Program?

The Asset Guarantee Program offered insurance-like loss protections on a select pool of mortgage-related or similar assets held by participants whose portfolios of distressed or illiquid assets posed a risk to market confidence.[29] Again, Citigroup was the only bank to receive loss protections under this program, and the program was terminated by agreement on December 23, 2009.[30] In return for the loss protection agreement, Treasury received approximately $4 billion in preferred stock, which Treasury intends to sell before the end of 2010.[31]

Q 27.2.6 ... Term Asset-Backed Securities Loan Facility?

Under the Term Asset-Backed Securities Loan Facility (TALF), the Federal Reserve Bank of New York provides non-recourse funding to any eligible borrower owning eligible collateral.[32] The loans are secured by certain types of asset-backed securities (ABS), such as credit card loans, auto loans, residential mortgage servicing advances, and commercial mortgage-backed securities.[33] On March 31, 2010, TALF was closed to all but non-recourse loans backed by newly issued commercial mortgage-backed securities. The program is scheduled to close completely in June of 2010.[34] There is some uncertainty as to how the markets will react to the termination of the TALF program.[35]

Q 27.2.7 ... Public-Private Investment Program?

The Public-Private Investment Program (PPIP) intended to remove troubled assets from the balance sheets of financial institutions in an attempt to restart the frozen credit market.[36] PPIP was announced in March 2009 and included two components: (1) purchase of troubled whole loans (legacy loans); and (2) purchase of troubled securities (legacy securities).[37] As of December 31, 2009, Treasury had signed final agreements with nine private fund managers with each managing a public-private investment fund (PPIF).[38] Through a combination of Treasury funds and private-sector capital, the PPIFs have almost $25 billion in purchasing power and will use those funds to purchase legacy assets, with approximately two-thirds of the funding coming from Treasury.[39] PPIF managers will invest in securities backed directly by mortgages that cover both the residential and commercial mortgage market.[40] Removing the legacy assets from banks and other financial institutions is intended to increase available credit and encourage lending.

Q 27.2.8 ... Unlocking Credit for Small Businesses/Small Business Administration Loan Support Initiative?

With this program, Treasury intends to purchase securities backed by loans from the Small Business Administration; but as of December 31, 2009, it had not disbursed any funds.[41] On February 3, 2010, Treasury announced terms for the Community Development Capital Initiative, which will invest lower-cost capital in Community-Development Financial Institutions that lend to small businesses in some of the country's hardest-hit areas.[42]

Q 27.2.9 ... Automotive Industry Financing Program?

The Automotive Industry Financing Program (AIFP) consisted of emergency loans to Chrysler, General Motors, and Chrysler Financial Services Americas LLC.[43] Treasury also purchased senior preferred stock from GMAC, Inc.[44] Treasury received an 8% pro forma equity stake in Chrysler and a 61% equity stake in GM as partial repayment of TARP funds.[45] As of December 31, 2009, Treasury had received approximately $1.3 billion in interest and dividend payments on the investments made in AIFP.[46] In addition, Chrysler has repaid its loan, and General Motors has entered into a payment plan with Treasury to repay its debt.[47]

Q 27.2.10 ... Auto Supplier Support Program?

The Auto Supplier Support Program (ASSP) targeted auto suppliers and ensured they were able to continue their operations.[48] Only General Motors and Chrysler received funds under this program, and the program terminated on April 5, 2010, for GM and April 7, 2010, for Chrysler.[49]

Q 27.2.11 ... Auto Warranty Commitment Program?

The Auto Warranty Commitment Program (AWCP) intended to bolster consumer confidence in automobile warranties on General Motors- and Chrysler-built vehicles and was terminated in July 2009 after Chrysler and General Motors satisfied their obligations under the program.[50]

Q 27.2.12 ... Making Home Affordable Program?

The Making Home Affordable Program (MHAP) was designed as a foreclosure mitigation plan and includes the Home Affordable Modification Program (HAMP), which will use up to $50 billion to prevent foreclosures by accepting some of the costs associated with modifying private mortgages and using TARP funds to provide incentives to loan holders and servicers.[51] With the additional funds received from TARP, Treasury hopes to prevent loan holders and servicers from resorting to foreclosures. As of February 25, 2010, nearly 1 million borrowers were in trial or permanent mortgage modifications, with a median savings of over $500 per month.[52] The program hopes to reach between 3 and 4 million homeowners through 2012.[53] In addition, over 4 million borrowers have refinanced their mortgages to more affordable levels.[54] The program continues to evolve and has received criticism because of the difficulty faced by homeowners in converting trial modifications to permanent modifications.[55]

Oversight and Enforcement

Q 27.3 Who oversees the EESA and, as a result, monitors TARP funding?

The wide variety of programs created by the EESA presented unique oversight and enforcement challenges for Treasury. Accordingly, the EESA created oversight bodies to monitor TARP funding and ensure transparency. The entities overseeing and enforcing EESA and monitoring TARP funding include:

- The Financial Stability Oversight Board
- The Office of the Special Investigator General TARP
- The Congressional Oversight Panel
- The Government Accountability Office

Q 27.3.1 What are the oversight and enforcement responsibilities of the Financial Stability Oversight Board?

The Financial Stability Oversight Board (FSOB) was established by section 104 of the EESA to assist in overseeing the TARP as well as the other authorities granted to the Secretary of Treasury under the EESA.[56] The members of the FSOB are:

- Secretary of Treasury;
- Chairman of the Board of Governors of the Federal Reserve System;
- Secretary of the Department of Housing and Urban Development;
- Chairman of the Securities and Exchange Commission; and
- Director of the Federal Housing Finance Agency.[57]

This board meets monthly to review and discuss TARP's progress and to promote transparency; it provides its meeting minutes to the public.[58]

Q 27.3.2 ... Office of the Special Investigator General TARP?

Office of the Special Investigator General TARP (SIGTARP) was created by section 121 of the EESA.[59] SIGTARP's role is to conduct audits and investigations of the purchase, sale, and management of TARP funds.[60] SIGTARP promotes transparency through civil and criminal enforcement of those who commit fraud, waste, or abuse with respect to TARP funds.[61] Through December 31, 2009, SIGTARP has opened eighty-six civil and criminal investigations that address a variety of abuses including accounting fraud, securities fraud, mortgage fraud, money laundering, obstruction of justice, and public corruption.[62] SIGTARP accepts tips and leads through its website and hotline and has acknowledged that a substantial number of its investigations were developed through its website and hotline.[63]

Q 27.3.3   ... the Congressional Oversight Panel?

The Congressional Oversight Panel (COP) was created by Congress to provide additional oversight of TARP.[64] The COP is authorized to hold hearings, review official data, and write reports on actions taken by Treasury and financial institutions and their effect on the economy.[65] On March 4, 2010, the COP held such a hearing on the assistance provided to Citigroup under the EESA and various TARP programs that provided capital to Citigroup.[66] Elizabeth Warren, Chair of the COP, discussed the "implicit government guarantee" afforded to Citigroup through the bailout it received.[67] The relationship between many financial institutions and the federal government changed as a result of the steps taken in the last year and a half to assist troubled institutions.

Q 27.3.4   ... the Government Accountability Office?

The Government Accountability Office was also tasked with TARP oversight responsibilities in EESA. The Comptroller General is required to report at least every sixty days on its efforts and present findings on its oversight efforts.[68] In addition, the Comptroller General is required to audit TARP's annual financial statements.[69]

TARP Compliance

Identifying TARP Risks

Q 27.4   What legal, compliance, and enforcement risks does a company face by participating in TARP?

A company considering TARP participation must realize that many rules and regulations exist that accompany funds from the federal government. Banks, PPIF managers, and other participants must recognize that in many respects they have become government contractors or grantees. Along with the benefits of participation in government programs come requirements to comply with often complex regulations. Notably, companies should be aware of significant risks created by the Fraud Enforcement and Recovery Act of 2009 (FERA) and the False Claims Act (FCA).

On May 20, 2009, President Obama signed FERA into law, which aims to "improve enforcement" of laws that prohibit fraud involving mortgage, financial institutions, and securities, and to facilitate the recovery of federal funds lost to those frauds.[70] Of particular interest to those considering participating in a TARP-related program are FERA's provisions that reclassify mortgage lenders as financial institutions and expand federal criminal liability for mortgage fraud, securities fraud, and major fraud against the United States involving TARP funds.[71] Also, specifically related to TARP, section 2(d) of FERA amends the law to prohibit participating in a scheme with the intention of obtaining money through false or fraudulent representations or promises made

> in any grant, contract, subcontract, subsidy, loan, guarantee, insurance, or other form of Federal assistance, including through the Troubled Asset Relief Program, an economic stimulus, recovery or rescue plan provided by the Government, or the Government's purchase of any troubled asset as defined in the Emergency Economic Stabilization Act of 2008.[72]

In addition, FERA amended the civil False Claims Act to greatly expand that statute's reach. Many financial institutions and real estate ventures may be unfamiliar with the FCA, which for decades has been used as the federal government's principal tool to combat fraud, waste, and abuse in government programs. Until now, the FCA generally did not apply to banks and other privately funded financial institutions; nor did it apply except in very limited situations to the real estate industry. With the proliferation of efforts to revive the real estate and financial sectors, those industries now are exposed to the potential for FCA liability when they participate in federally funded programs, including TARP. For further discussion of the FCA and FERA, please see chapter 11, The False Claims Act.

Managing TARP Risks

Q 27.5 What is the best way for my organization to manage the risks associated with participating in TARP?

As often happens with new government programs enacted to respond to a crisis, there is haste to get the money out the door, and in the early stages of the program controls are sometimes lacking. Later, different federal authorities, often with pressure from Congress, begin to examine with hindsight how the funds were spent. Even companies that have made good-faith efforts to do the right thing and help resolve the crisis often come under investigation for civil or criminal fraud. Simple, honest mistakes or failures to account for expenditures in accordance with regulations enacted after some funds have been disbursed and used by companies trying to do their best to implement an important government program can be misinterpreted and viewed as fraud by whistleblowers or federal prosecutors. These risks are increased further by the numerous states that have enacted their own False Claims Acts.

The most effective way your company can protect against these risks is to establish internal policies and controls that will allow you to effectively and fully explain how the government's funds were secured, accounted for, and used. Comprehensive compliance and ethics programs, including mandatory disclosure of various forms of wrongdoing, are now required of most government contractors, and those companies receiving TARP funding should anticipate similar requirements. Even if your company already has a compliance and ethics program, you should review your policies to insure that they incorporate the new compliance and enforcement risks affecting your business through its receipt and use of TARP funds.[73]

If your company is considering participation in TARP, be proactive in setting up systems and controls to detect and prevent fraud, as well as mistakes that the government or whistleblowers might interpret as fraud. In doing so, your company can develop a mutually beneficial business relationship with the government. Failing to take compliance and ethics programs and obligations seriously could cause serious even disastrous problems down the line.

Notes

1. Emergency Economic Stabilization Act of 2008, Pub. L. No. 110-343, 122 Stat. 3765 (2008) [hereinafter EESA].
2. *Id.* § 2.
3. Office of the Special Inspector General for the Troubled Asset Relief Program, Quarterly Report to Congress, Jan. 30, 2010, at 7, *available at* www.sigtarp.gov/reports/congress/2010/January2010_Quarterly_Report_to_Congress.pdf [hereinafter SIGTARP January Report].
4. EESA § 120.
5. SIGTARP January Report, *supra* note 3, at 33.
6. *Id.*
7. U.S. Department of Treasury, American Recovery and Reinvestment Act, www.ustreas.gov/recovery (last visited Mar. 3, 2010).
8. One industry benefiting from Recovery Act spending is the telecommunications industry. On February 26, 2010, the Department of Commerce announced a $7.25 million investment in digital literacy training in low-income communities in California. Press Release, National Telecommunications and Information Administration, Commerce Dept. Announces Recovery Act Investment in California to Expand Broadband Internet Adoption and Economic Opportunities (Feb. 26, 2010), *available at* www.ntia.doc.gov/press/2010/02262010_BTOP_CETF.html.
9. The American Recovery and Reinvestment Act of 2009, Pub. L. No. 111-5, § 1523, 123 Stat. 115 (2009).
10. EESA § 101.
11. SIGTARP January Report, *supra* note 3, at 7.
12. EESA § 101(a)(3).
13. U.S. Department of Treasury, About, www.financialstability.gov/about/staff.html (last visited Mar. 3, 2010).
14. U.S. Department of Treasury, Capital Purchase Program, www.financialstability.gov/roadtostability/capitalpurchaseprogram.html (last visited Mar. 3, 2010).
15. Congressional Oversight Panel, December Oversight Report: Taking Stock: What Has the Troubled Asset Relief Program Achieved?, at 18–19 (Dec. 9, 2009), *available at* http://cop.senate.gov/documents/cop-120909-report.pdf [hereinafter COP December Report].
16. COP December Report, *supra* note 15, at 19.
17. SIGTARP January Report, *supra* note 3, at 52–54; U.S. Department of Treasury, Office of Financial Stability, TARP Transactions Report for Period Ending February 25, 2010 (Mar. 1, 2010), *available at* www.financialstability.gov/docs/transaction-reports/3-1-10%20Transactions%20Report%20as%20of%202-25-10.pdf.

18. U.S. Department of Treasury, Capital Assistance Program, http://financialstability.gov/roadtostability/capitalassistance.html (last visited Mar. 6, 2010).
19. *Id.*
20. Press Release, U.S. Department of Treasury, Treasury Announcement Regarding Capital Assistance Program (Nov. 9, 2009), *available at* www.financialstability.gov/latest/tg_11092009.html.
21. U.S. Department of Treasury, Programs, www.financialstability.gov/roadtostability/programs.htm (last visited Mar. 3, 2010).
22. COP DECEMBER REPORT, *supra* note 15, at 22.
23. Timothy F. Geithner, Written Testimony Before the House Oversight and Government Reform Committee (Jan. 27, 2010).
24. *Id.*
25. U.S. Department of Treasury, Targeted Investment Program, www.financialstability.gov/roadtostability/targetedinvestmentprogram.html (last visited Mar. 3, 2010).
26. SIGTARP January Report, *supra* note 3, at 37.
27. COP DECEMBER REPORT, *supra* note 15, at 23.
28. SIGTARP January Report, *supra* note 3, at 37; COP DECEMBER REPORT, *supra* note 15, at 23.
29. U.S. Department of Treasury, Asset Guarantee Program, www.financialstability.gov/roadtostability/assetguaranteeprogram.htm (last visited Mar. 3, 2010).
30. SIGTARP January Report, *supra* note 3, at 37–38.
31. *Id.* at 72.
32. Federal Reserve Bank of New York, Term Asset-Backed Securities Loan Facility: Frequently Asked Questions, www.newyorkfed.org/markets/talf_faq.html#2 (last visited Mar. 3, 2010).
33. SIGTARP January Report, *supra* note 3, at 38.
34. Office of the Special Inspector General, Troubled Asset Relief Program, Quarterly Report to Congress, Apr. 20, 2010, at 38, *available at* www.sigtarp.gov/reports/congress/2010/April2010_Quarterly_Report_to_Congress.pdf [hereinafter SIGTARP April Report].
35. Jody Shenn, *End of TALF Spurs CIT, Sallie Mae Bond Sales*, BUS. WK., Mar. 3, 2010, *available at* www.businessweek.com/news/2010-03-03/end-of-talf-spurs-cit-sallie-mae-bond-sales-credit-markets.html.
36. U.S. Department of Treasury, Public-Private Investment Program, http://financialstability.gov/roadtostability/publicprivatefund.html.
37. *Id.*
38. SIGTARP January Report, *supra* note 3, at 83.
39. *Id.*
40. U.S. Department of Treasury, Legacy Securities Public-Private Investment Program, http://financialstability.gov/roadtostability/legacysecurities.html (last visited Mar. 8, 2010).
41. *Id.* at 89.

42. U.S. Department of Treasury, Community Development Capital Initiative, http://financialstability.gov/roadtostability/comdev.html (last visited Mar. 3, 2010).
43. SIGTARP January Report, *supra* note 3, at 39, 92–95.
44. *Id.*
45. *Id.*
46. *Id.* at 92.
47. *Id.* at 92, 95.
48. Press Release, U.S. Department of Treasury, Treasury Announces Auto Supplier Program (Mar. 19, 2009), *available at* http://financialstability.gov/latest/auto3_18.html.
49. SIGTARP April Report, *supra* note 34, at 41.
50. *Id.* at 40.
51. *Id.* at 96; U.S. Department of Treasury, Making Home Affordable, http://financialstability.gov/roadtostability/homeowner.html (last visited Mar. 3, 2010).
52. Written Testimony of Phyllis R. Caldwell, Chief of the Treasury Homeownership Preservation Office, House Committee on Oversight and Government Reform, Feb. 25, 2010, *available at* www.ustreas.gov/press/releases/tg566.htm.
53. U.S. DEPARTMENT OF TREASURY, MAKING HOME AFFORDABLE PROGRAM SERVICER PERFORMANCE REPORT THROUGH JANUARY 2010, *available at* www.financialstability.gov/docs/press/January%20Report%20FINAL%2002%2016%2010.pdf.
54. *Id.*
55. Nick Timiraos, *Is a Loan Modification Just Another Exotic Mortgage?*, WALL ST. J. BLOGS (Dec. 4, 2009), http://blogs.wsj.com/developments/2009/12/04/is-a-loan-modification-just-another-exotic-mortgage/tab/article/.
56. EESA § 104(a).
57. *Id.* § 104(b).
58. U.S. Department of Treasury, Oversight, http://financialstability.gov/about/oversight.html (last visited Mar. 3, 2010).
59. EESA § 121.
60. *Id.* § 121(c).
61. U.S. Department of Treasury, Oversight, http://financialstability.gov/about/oversight.html (last visited Mar. 3, 2010).
62. SIGTARP January Report, *supra* note 3, at 10.
63. *Id.*
64. EESA § 125.
65. *Id.*; Congressional Oversight Panel, About Us, http://cop.senate.gov/about/ (last visited Mar. 3, 2010).
66. Congressional Oversight Panel, COP Hearing on Assistance Provided to Citigroup Under TARP, http://cop.senate.gov/hearings/library/hearing-030410-citi.cfm (last visited Mar. 8, 2010).
67. Opening Statement of Elizabeth Warren, Chair of Congressional Oversight Panel, COP Hearing on Assistance Provided to Citigroup Under TARP (Mar. 4,

2010), *available at* http://cop.senate.gov/documents/statement-030410-warren.pdf (last visited Mar. 8, 2010).
    68. EESA § 116.
    69. *Id.*
    70. Fraud Enforcement and Recovery Act of 2009, Pub. L. No. 111-21, 123 Stat. 1617 (2009) [hereinafter FERA]. For additional details on the requirements of FERA and the FCA, see chapter 11 (The False Claims Act) and chapter 15 (Government Contractors).
    71. FERA § 2(a).
    72. FERA § 2(d).
    73. For further details on the design and implementation of an effective compliance and ethics programs, see chapters 1–5. *See also* chapters 11 (The False Claims Act) and 15 (Government Contractors).

28

Sarbanes-Oxley Act of 2002

Richard T. Williams & Jerome W. Hoffman[*]

Following the scandalous collapse of Enron and WorldCom and the attendant whirlwind of criticism by angry shareholders, Congress passed the Public Company Accounting Reform and Investor Protection Act of 2002 ("Sarbanes-Oxley" or SOX).[1] Its purpose was to restore investor confidence by improving the quality and transparency in financial reporting.

Congress intended that SOX will strengthen the authority and duties of boards of directors and their audit committees and make corporate management more accountable. It was anticipated that SOX will impose new regulations and obligations on attorneys and auditors, improve the quality of financial reporting, protect employee whistleblowers, and strengthen the powers of the U.S. Securities and Exchange Commission (SEC).

---

[*] The authors wish to acknowledge Jane K.P. Tam and Daniel Casey Flaherty for their contributions to this chapter.

Overview	897
Codes of Ethics	898
Boards of Directors/Audit Committees	899
Officers and Directors	902
Penalties	902
Insurance	903
Whistleblowers	904
Company Action	904
Consequences of Whistleblower Prevailing	906
State Law	906
Outside Auditors	906
Companies and Auditors	907
Audit Committees and Auditors	908
Procedures	908
PCAOB	910
Foreign Auditors	911
Lawyers	911
"Up-the-Ladder" Reporting	913
Supervisory and Subordinate Attorneys	914
Required Action	915
Credible Evidence and Material Violation	916
Qualified Legal Compliance Committees	918
CLO Responsibilities and Appropriate Responses	919
Foreign Lawyers	921
State Rules	922
Law Firm Training	923
Punishment	924
Insurance	924
General Counsel	925
SOX Effect	926
Tools	928
Investigations	930
Certification of Financial Statements	933
Requirements for Certification	933
Pre-Certification	936
Non-GAAP Reporting	937
Enforcement	938

Internal Controls	938
Manipulation of Financial Reports	942
Auditing Standards	946
Problems	948
Categorizing Problems	949
PCAOB Standards	951
Documentation	952
Continuing SOX Compliance	953
Disclosure Controls	956
The SEC	960
Private Rights of Action	962
SOX Provisions That Apply to Companies Other Than Issuers	964
Almost-Public Companies	965
Non-Public Banks and Insurance Companies	966
SOX and International Companies	967
Non-Profit Organizations	969

Overview

Q 28.1   To whom does SOX apply?

All SOX provisions apply to "issuers."[2] Issuers are entities that have registered (or are presently registering) securities with the SEC, or that are required to file periodic reports with the SEC.

Some SOX provisions apply to even privately held companies. These include the following:

- obstruction of any federal investigation;[3]
- protection of employee whistleblowers;[4]
- penalty enhancement provisions for white collar crimes;[5]
- debts incurred in connection with violation of securities laws are no longer dischargeable in bankruptcy.[6]

Q 28.2 Which companies are "issuers"?

Issuers include:

- all public companies in the United States whose securities are listed on any stock exchange or are otherwise publicly traded;
- all companies whose securities are registered under the Securities Exchange Act, regardless of whether or not they are listed on any stock exchange;
- all foreign companies whose securities are listed or traded in the United States;
- private companies whose debt securities are publicly offered; and
- all investment companies, mutual funds, closed-end investment companies, unit investment trusts, and issuers of asset-backed securities.

Q 28.3 Generally, what does SOX require?

SOX requires companies to adopt codes of ethics, and it increases the oversight responsibilities of directors, especially members of a board's audit committee. Particular types of loans and stock transactions are prohibited with respect to senior managers and directors. The chief executive officer and chief financial officer are required to certify the accuracy of financial reports and the fair presentation of other public disclosure. Jointly, the officers and directors must implement and maintain extensive disclosure controls and internal accounting controls. General counsel and legal departments are subject to SEC rules imposing investigative, reporting, and disclosure obligations upon them. Outside auditors must examine and certify management's representations concerning the adequacy and effectiveness of internal accounting controls.

Codes of Ethics

Q 28.4 What should a company put in its code of ethics?[7]

There are no specific language requirements. The SEC defines the term "code of ethics" broadly as:

... such standards as are reasonably necessary to promote—

(1) honest and ethical conduct, including the ethical handling of actual or apparent conflicts of interest between personal and professional relationships;
(2) full, fair, accurate, timely, and understandable disclosure in reports and documents that a company files with, or submits to, the SEC and in other public communications made by the company;
(3) compliance with applicable governmental laws, rules and regulations;
(4) the prompt internal reporting of violations of the code to appropriate person(s) identified in the code; and
(5) accountability for adherence to the code.[8]

Q 28.4.1 What does a company do with its code of ethics once it is adopted by the board?

The code must be filed with the SEC and also must be made publicly available, including being posted on the corporate Internet website.[9] The New York Stock Exchange (NYSE) and NASDAQ have adopted listing requirements that include a code of ethics.[10]

Companies must adhere to their codes of ethics, and any amendment to or waiver of provisions of the code must be promptly disclosed in a Form 8-K that must be filed with the SEC within four business days. Note that failure to "take action within a reasonable period of time regarding a material departure from a provision of the code of ethics that has been made known to an executive officer" would be deemed an implicit waiver of the code.

Boards of Directors/Audit Committees

Q 28.5 How does SOX affect boards of directors?

The boards of directors of issuers are now required to have a majority of their members be "independent."[11] An independent member is one who has not been employed or compensated by an issuer within the three years preceding his or her service on the board of directors. The exchanges have additional criteria for defining "independence."[12]

Q 28.5.1 Do boards have to act in a manner different from the way they did before SOX?

Boards of directors must now conduct executive sessions outside the presence of management and ensure that the audit committee, compensation committee, and nominating and governance committees are composed exclusively of independent directors.

Q 28.6 What does an audit committee do?

The audit committee meets with external auditors and recommends approval of financial statements to the full board of directors. The audit committee has the authority to engage and remove auditors. The SEC adopted rules directing the nation's stock exchanges to prohibit the listing of any security of a company that is not in compliance with the SOX audit committee requirements.[13]

COMPLIANCE FACT

Audit committee members and general responsibilities must be disclosed in annual reports or proxy statements of issuers.

Q 28.6.1 How does SOX affect the make-up of the audit committee?

Each member of an audit committee must now be an independent member of the board of the directors and may not receive any other compensation from the corporation, except for that given to any member of the board of directors and its committees. All members must be financially literate (able to read and understand the fundamental financial statements, including a company's balance sheet, income statement, and cash flow statement), and at least one member of the audit committee must be an "independent financial expert" (a person who has experience as a public accountant or auditor, or as a principal financial officer, comptroller, or principal accounting officer of a public company).

Q 28.6.2 What if no one in the company is an independent financial expert?

Individual companies may find it difficult to locate an independent financial expert among the ranks of their present directors or to be able to recruit quickly an appropriate candidate for election to their board of directors. In that case, the audit committee may engage appropriate professional experts as advisors for an interim period; without the obligations of decision-making imposed on board members, candidates for advisors to audit committees may be more plentiful.

COMPLIANCE FACT

Companies must disclose their audit committee financial expertise (or lack thereof) in their annual report.[14]

Q 28.6.3 Does SOX change the audit committee's responsibilities?

The audit committee is now directly responsible for the engagement and removal of any registered public accounting firm employed for the purpose of preparing or issuing audit reports. The audit committee is also responsible for resolution of disagreements between management and auditors regarding financial reporting. The audit committee has to establish procedures for dealing with complaints from employees about its accounting procedures. The audit committee must be given the authority to engage independent counsel and other advisors. Issuers are obligated to provide appropriate funding to compensate public accounting firms for their audit reports, and to pay advisors and counsel hired by the audit committee.

Officers and Directors

Q 28.7 What are the new requirements for officers and directors?

Congress included in SOX a series of specific prohibitions upon the conduct of officers and directors of issuers:

- prohibition of insider trading during pension fund blackout periods;[15]
- prohibition on certain personal loans;[16]
- prompt disclosure of insider stock transactions;[17] and
- prohibition on fraudulently influencing, coercing, manipulating, or misleading any independent auditors.[18]

Penalties

Q 28.8 What are the SEC's penalties for officers and directors if they violate SOX?

If restatement of financial statements occurs due to material noncompliance with SOX, the CEO and CFO may have to forfeit their bonuses and profits made on the sale of the company's securities.[19] In addition, they may be barred from serving as directors or officers of any public company.[20] In this regard, Congress has significantly lowered the standard for misconduct necessary to disqualify officers and directors.[21]

Q 28.8.1 Do officers and directors face any penalties beyond those imposed by the SEC?

SOX includes a significant number of civil and criminal penalty provisions. SOX encompasses a number of criminal statutes related to document destruction.[22] In addition, SOX has amended the Federal Sentencing Guidelines, extended statutes of limitation and dramatically increased fines and prison terms, which now reach up to twenty-five years.[23] Finally, the SEC has been given the power to petition for a judicial freeze of corporate assets in order to avoid last-minute looting by directors and officers.

Q 28.8.2 Have the SEC and law enforcement actually used these new powers?

The high-profile cases involving executives at Enron, WorldCom, HealthSouth, Gateway, Adelphia, Rite Aid, etc., are emblematic of the SEC's zealous pursuit of corporate malfeasance. In addition, the SEC has moved aggressively against overseas issuers and auditors such as the Italian company Parmalat, and the U.K. accounting firm Moore Stephens.[24]

Insurance

Q 28.9 Are violations of SOX by officers and directors generally covered by liability insurance?

Historically, private securities lawsuits have been alleged against issuers, directors, and officers with the expectation that a settlement will be funded from directors-and-officers liability insurance proceeds and corporate funds. Nowadays, directors and officers need greater insurance coverage as a result of their greater responsibilities imposed upon them by SOX; and, at the same time, insurers are more wary of providing such coverage. Far greater disclosure is necessary in the application and renewal process seeking insurance coverage. Moreover, constraining the insurer's ability to rescind coverage becomes of paramount importance to directors, although such restrictions in policy language are generally available only at additional cost.

Q 28.9.1 Other than insurers, who else is concerned with the effect SOX could have on officers and directors?

Underwriters also seek to develop an understanding and assess the quality of directors' and management's decision-making. The greater the commitment of an issuer to the "tone at the top" of its ethical conduct and its responsiveness to auditor and whistleblower allegations, the more comfortable an underwriter can be with an issuer's risk profile. Supplementing its evaluation by scrutinizing external business forecasts and analysis of finances and of corporate governance is very useful for underwriters, as are interviews of an issuer's senior management.

Whistleblowers

Q 28.10 How does SOX protect whistleblowers?

SOX is meant to encourage and protect employees who file complaints, give testimony, provide information or otherwise assist or participate in an internal corporate investigation or an SEC, Congressional, or law enforcement investigation.[25] Under SOX, no issuer may discharge, demote, suspend, threaten, harass, or, in any other manner, discriminate against an employee in the terms and conditions of employment because of any lawful act done by the whistleblower.

> **TIP:** An employee who believes he or she has been retaliated against in violation of this section may file a complaint with the Occupational Safety and Health Administration (OSHA) of the Department of Labor and, eventually, in federal court.

Q 28.10.1 What does a whistleblower employee need to show to prove that the company is taking retaliatory action against him or her?

The employee must show his or her specific whistleblowing activities, that unfavorable personnel action was taken against him or her, and that whistleblowing behavior was "a contributing factor" to the adverse personnel action.

Company Action

Q 28.10.2 What procedures should be in place to help stave off successful legal action by whistleblowers?

A company should have an effective corporate code of conduct in place that includes information on making anonymous reports of questionable accounting or securities disclosure matters and that affirms that the company will not retaliate against employees for making such reports. Furthermore, the company should train supervisors and managers, both in the human relations and financial management areas, on recognizing and responding to such complaints.

> **TIP:** It is important to always document performance failures that lead to employee discipline. This will help the employer demonstrate that the penalty imposed on an employee was not retaliatory and not related to his or her complaints under SOX.

Q 28.10.3 What should the company do once a complaint is filed?

Once a legitimate complaint is filed within the company, the employer must thoroughly—and immediately—investigate; typically, this is done by coordinated effort among the company's human resources staff, SOX compliance officer, and outside counsel. The accuracy and completeness of this investigation will pay great dividends in dealing with OSHA and the SEC and in restraining the potential for collateral damage to the company's reputation among investors. Records must be preserved concerning the investigation and underlying issues.

> **TIP:** In preparing investigation reports, keep in mind that both SEC staff and OSHA staff are likely to review the reports.

Consequences of Whistleblower Prevailing

Q 28.10.4   What happens if the whistleblower wins the case?

In the event the employee prevails, he or she may be awarded reinstatement with seniority, backpay with interest, compensation for special damages including for litigation costs, expert witness fees, and attorney fees.

Q 28.10.5   Are there any repercussions beyond what is owed to the whistleblower?

SOX provides for numerous civil remedies.[26] In addition, Congress adopted a broad criminal statute.[27] This statute punishes whoever knowingly and with the intent to retaliate takes action, including interference with employment, against any person "for providing to a law enforcement officer any truthful information relating to the commission or possible commission of any Federal offense." Violations are punishable by fines or imprisonment for up to ten years or both.

State Law

Q 28.10.6   Do states have similar protections for whistleblowers?

At the state level in the United States, individual states vary in their protection for whistleblowers, although forty-two states claim to have recognized at least some claims for retaliatory discharges. Some states are restrictive in their protection, such as in New York where financial improprieties are carved out of the protections.[28] In other jurisdictions, such as New Jersey, extensive litigation by whistleblowers is already occurring.

Outside Auditors

Q 28.11   The landscape has changed for public companies, but what about for accounting firms?

Congress dramatically overhauled the regulatory landscape for public accounting firms in SOX, creating an independent federal

Public Company Accounting Oversight Board (PCAOB) and requiring accounting firms to register with it to be eligible to prepare audit reports of issuers. Registrants promise to be governed by the PCAOB's accounting standards, approved by the SEC, and which take precedence over Generally Accepted Accounting Principles (GAAP).[29]

> **COMPLIANCE FACT**
>
> The PCAOB periodically inspects the performance of auditors and may discipline individual accountants as well as accounting firms.

Companies and Auditors

Q 28.12 Has SOX affected the relationship between the companies and auditors?

In a seismic shift from the past, Congress has prohibited auditors of an issuer from providing other services to their audit clients. The responsibilities of an issuer's management to install and maintain appropriate accounting systems and internal controls for the reliability of financial reporting have been underscored. Any former coziness between auditors and issuers is replaced by enforced independence and distance. In fact, the auditors are required under the Independence Standards Board Standard No. 1 to provide issuers' audit committee written disclosure about their provision of tax and other non-audit-related services, and their independence from the issuer.

Q 28.12.1 What about "one-stop shopping" for financial and accounting services?

No longer are public accounting firms permitted to be "one-stop shopping" venues for audit clients also desiring accounting, planning, information technology, control, and consulting services.[30] SOX flatly prohibits registered firms who are preparing audit reports for an issuer from contemporaneously providing "non-audit service," such as bookkeeping, designing or implementing financial information systems, rendering appraisal and valuation services, giving fairness opinions, providing actuarial or internal audit services, performing management or human resources functions,[31] broker-dealer services,[32] legal services,[33] or expert services unrelated to an audit.

Audit Committees and Auditors

Q 28.13 What is the relationship between the audit committees and the auditors?

All audit services must be pre-approved by the issuer's audit committee.[34] The audit firm is required to report to the audit committee all critical accounting policies and practices to be used in the audit. An audit committee may delegate to one or more designated independent director's authority to pre-approve work by an audit firm, subject to ratification by the audit committee at its next scheduled meeting. The audit committee's approval must be disclosed in periodic reports to investors.

Q 28.13.1 Can a company keep using audit partners with whom it has an established relationship?

An audit firm's lead partner on the engagement and the audit partner responsible for reviewing the audit must rotate out of the engagement at least once every five years.[35] In addition, a registered audit firm may not provide new audit services if an issuer's CEO, CFO, controller, or chief accounting officer was employed by that audit firm, and participated in any capacity at all in the audit of that issuer, during the preceding year.

Procedures

Q 28.14 What are new procedures that auditors must follow?

Congress specified certain requirements be included in PCAOB rules in SOX section 103:

- Audit firms must prepare and maintain for at least seven years audit work papers in sufficient detail to support the conclusions reached in a given audit report;
- A second partner who was not in charge of the audit must approve each audit report;
- In each audit report concerning an issuer's internal controls, the audit firm is to:
    - describe the scope of its testing of an issuer's structure and procedures for internal controls and present the findings from such testing, along with an evaluation of the internal controls and a description of material weaknesses in such internal controls, and of any material noncompliance found,
    - evaluate an issuer's maintenance of records that accurately and fairly reflect the transactions and disposition of its assets,
    - provide reasonable assurance that transactions are recorded as necessary to permit preparation of financial statements in accordance with GAAP, and
    - provide reasonable assurance that receipts and expenditures of the issuer are being made only in accordance with authorizations of management and directors of the issuer;
- Audit firms are to monitor their professional ethics and independence from issuers; and
- Audit firms are to provide:
    - procedures for internal consultation on accounting and audit questions;
    - for the supervision of audit work on behalf of which the firm issues audit reports;
    - for hiring and professional development of personnel;
    - procedures and standards for the acceptance and continuance of engagements; and
    - procedures for internal inspections.

PCAOB

Q 28.15 What powers does the PCAOB have over the auditors?

The PCAOB has investigatory and disciplinary powers over registered firms.[36] Those powers include requiring testimony from registered firms or their associated persons and the production of audit work papers and other documents from firms or associated persons. The PCAOB may sanction firms or associated persons who do not cooperate by suspending them from practice or suspending or revoking their registration with the PCAOB.

COMPLIANCE FACT

The PCAOB coordinates its investigations with the SEC and may seek SEC subpoenas to compel testimony or documents from any person, including audit clients.

Q 28.15.1 What can the PCAOB do if it uncovers a violation?

The PCAOB is authorized to impose disciplinary or remedial sanctions, including temporary suspension or permanent revocation of registration, suspension or bar of a person from further association with any registered firm, temporary or permanent limitations on the activities of a firm or person, and a civil penalty of up to $750,000 for an individual or $15 million for a firm.[37] These sanctions are available in cases of reckless or intentional misconduct. Censure and a requirement for additional professional training may be imposed for lesser violations.

Q 28.15.2 How have the new PCAOB rules changed audits?

Overall, these standards have emphasized the tightening of internal controls and proper documentation for transactions, more than making substantive changes in accounting principles. The relative frequency of enforcement actions by the SEC involving improper revenue recognition practices and misuse of reserves serves as a warning to issuers to be more cautious and conservative in applying and interpreting GAAP than before SOX. The vigor of the enforcement program, along with the pervasive impacts of this SOX revolution in the regulation of public accounting firms, has greatly altered the business, business methods, and even the daily professional activities of auditors. The combination of market scandals and SOX is forcing accountants to become gatekeepers for the public and the SEC.

Foreign Auditors

Q 28.16 What effect does SOX have on foreign auditors?

Foreign public accounting firms who prepare and furnish audit reports for issuers are subject to SOX to the same extent as U.S. public accounting firms, including registration with the PCAOB and inspections and discipline by PCAOB.[38]

Q 28.16.1 What if a U.S. accounting firm relies in part upon a foreign accounting firm?

If a registered U.S. public accounting firm, in issuing an audit report, chooses to rely in part upon an opinion or other material services furnished by a foreign public accounting firm, then the U.S. public accounting firm is deemed to have consented to supply the audit work papers of that foreign accounting firm to U.S. regulators on demand, and to have secured the agreement of that foreign public accounting to produce such work papers. Unless the U.S. public accounting firm secures such arrangements, it may not rely upon the work of a foreign public accounting firm in issuing audit reports.

Lawyers

Q 28.17 How does SOX affect lawyers for issuers?

While SOX does not impose a new oversight body upon the legal profession comparable to the PCAOB, the issuance and enforcement of rules for attorneys emanate directly from the SEC. Moreover, SEC standards pre-empt state bar regulation. Without formally deputizing attorneys as law enforcement employees of the federal government, the SEC nonetheless intrudes on traditional attorney-client relationship, privilege and even asserts the authority to second-guess the content and quality of a lawyer's legal advice.

Q 28.17.1 What responsibilities does the SEC impose upon lawyers under SOX?

The SEC views lawyers as gatekeepers. The SEC believes that lawyers, in particular in-house counsel, are in the best position to detect and stop fraudulent conduct by corporate managers and employees.

COMPLIANCE FACT

Lawyers are monitored by the SEC for their work in fraud prevention, not for their customary role as advocates for corporations.

Q 28.17.2 Which lawyers are affected by SOX?

The SEC's assertion of applicability of its rules to attorneys is very broad. Attorneys are not only persons who are admitted to practice law in the various states, but also include any person holding himself out as a lawyer and anyone otherwise qualified to be an attorney.[39] Likewise, the scope of work performed by attorneys that is subject to Rule 205 is defined very expansively. The preparation of documents to be filed with the SEC is covered, as is contributing information to such documents or advising issuers about them. Investigating a matter that is a subject of SEC reporting is also a form of practice before the SEC, as is formally appearing and representing a corporate client before the SEC.

Q 28.17.3 Are there any limitations on the applicability of the SEC rules on attorney conduct?

A few limitations are recognized, and the rules ordinarily do not apply to:

- attorneys who do not have an attorney-client relationship with an issuer; for example, attorneys performing a non-legal function or simply speaking before an audience of business persons who are not clients;
- attorneys for underwriters or other third persons are generally not considered attorneys for issuers;
- attorneys performing work for non-public clients who are not issuers or affiliates of issuers;
- foreign attorneys practicing foreign law in consultation with U.S. attorneys who are themselves appearing before the SEC.[40]

"Up-the-Ladder" Reporting

Q 28.18 What is "up-the-ladder" reporting?

If an attorney has identified "credible evidence" of a "material violation," he or she must report it to the top of the issuer corporation. The rules provide for a two-step internal reporting process regarding material violations.[41] First, a subordinate attorney must report the evidence to his or her supervisory attorney.[42] Second, a supervisory attorney must report evidence of a material violation up-the-ladder within the issuer company to the chief legal counsel (for example, the company's general counsel or chief legal officer (CLO)) or to the CEO.[43]

Q 28.18.1 Do the requirements depend on whether the attorney is in a supervisory position?

Although the scope of their "up-the-ladder" reporting obligations vary, both supervisory and subordinate attorneys, both inside an issuer and in law firms providing services to issuers, are subject to the rules.[44]

Q 28.18.2 What if an attorney has reason to believe that reporting to the CEO or CLO would be futile?

If the CEO or the chief legal counsel does not respond appropriately to the evidence or if the attorney reasonably believes that reporting to the chief legal counsel would be futile, the attorney must report the evidence to one of the following:

(1) the audit committee of the board of directors of the company;
(2) a committee of independent directors; or
(3) the full board of directors.[45]

Q 28.18.3 How do these requirements apply to outside counsel?

Outside counsel is also subject to this reporting duty. An attorney retained or directed by the chief legal officer to litigate a reported violation does not have a reporting obligation so long as he or she is able to assert a colorable defense on behalf of the issuer and the chief legal officer provides reports on the progress and outcome of the litigation to the issuer's board of directors.[46]

Supervisory and Subordinate Attorneys

Q 28.19 Who is a "supervisory attorney"?

Supervisory attorneys are those who oversee or direct another attorney in performing a task that is within the scope of practicing before the SEC on behalf of an issuer. A supervisory attorney is the one responsible for complying with the reporting requirements when he or she has received a report of evidence of a material violation from a subordinate attorney. A supervisory attorney who reasonably believes that information received from a subordinate attorney does not constitute evidence of a material violation need not report it to the issuer and has no further obligation under the SEC rules.

Q 28.20 Who is a "subordinate attorney"?

A subordinate attorney is one who is supervised by another attorney in performing a task that is part of practicing before the SEC. A subordinate attorney who reports evidence of a material violation, as described below, to his or her supervisory attorney has no further obligation under the SEC rules. If a subordinate attorney reasonably believes that the supervisory attorney to whom he or she reported the evidence has failed to comply with the SEC rules, then he or she is permitted to report the evidence directly to the issuer, thereby bypassing the supervisory attorney.

Q 28.20.1 As long as there is an attorney above you on the chain, are you a subordinate attorney?

An attorney (such as an assistant general counsel) who operates under a chief legal officer's supervision or direction is not considered a subordinate attorney under the rules. Such an attorney must go beyond reporting to a superior attorney and comply with the full panoply of rules.[47]

Q 28.20.2 Are the definitions of supervisory and subordinate attorney static?

Except for a corporation's chief legal officer and his or her direct reporting attorneys, one may be a supervising attorney for one task or matter and a subordinate attorney for another. To minimize confusion, it may be helpful for an issuer or its law firm to designate a formal chain of command within its legal department.

Required Action

Q 28.21 What do SOX and the SEC require of a lawyer?

Lawyers who practice before the SEC and become aware of credible evidence that any material violation of any federal securities law, or other federal or state law or breach of fiduciary duty, has taken place, is taking place, or is about to take place, must report it up the ladder until the lawyer receives an appropriate response.[48] If there is no appropriate response, the lawyer must take further reporting or action, including a "noisy withdrawal" (withdraw representation and notify the SEC of the withdrawal and the basis of its withdrawal, which is related to professional considerations) if necessary.

Q 28.21.1 How does this affect the attorney-client relationship?

Unquestionably, the SEC rules impose greater obligations upon lawyers with respect to public disclosure by issuers. In brief, they tend to command a lawyer: "When in doubt, report; when in doubt, disclose." They intend to narrow the confidences that issuer's counsel may protect, in what SOX and the SEC perceive as the greater objective of transparency and completeness in communications with investors.

Q 28.21.2 What sanctions are there for violations by an attorney of the SEC rules under SOX?

A violation of any rule issued by the SEC under SOX constitutes a violation of the Exchange Act of 1934.[49] Accordingly, a violation of the rule subjects the violator to all the remedies and sanctions available under the Exchange Act, including injunctions, and cease-and-desist orders. The SEC may deny, temporarily or permanently, the privilege of appearing or practicing before the SEC, including preparing and filing documents with the SEC.[50] The SEC may also bar an attorney from serving as an officer or director of a public company. Finally, a violation of disciplinary rules is routinely reported to other jurisdictions where the attorney is admitted, usually resulting in disciplinary proceedings in those jurisdictions as well.[51]

Credible Evidence and Material Violation

Q 28.22 What does "becoming aware of credible evidence" actually mean?

The information assessed by the attorney is credible evidence concerning a "material violation" if it would be unreasonable, under the circumstances, for a prudent and competent attorney not to conclude that it is "reasonably likely" (that is, more than a mere possibility, less than a probability) that a material violation has occurred or is about to occur.[52] The amount of information a reasonable and prudent attorney may determine to establish "credible evidence" may vary according to a given attorney's background, experience, seniority, and professional skills; the time constraints under which the attorney is acting; the attorney's previous experience and familiarity with the client; and the availability of other attorneys with whom he or she may consult.[53]

Q 28.22.1 How should companies define "credible evidence"?

Internally, an issuer or its outside law firm may elect to adopt a lower threshold for attorney reporting simply to assure that higher authority does not miss the opportunity to meet the minimum standards of the SEC.

Q 28.23 What constitutes a "material violation"?

What is to be reported upward is credible evidence concerning a material violation. What is "material" should be understood from the viewpoint of a reasonable investor. If there is a substantial likelihood that such an investor would see given information as significantly altering the total mix of information before him, that given information is material.

Information relating to integrity of management is always material, as are intentional misstatements, even a quantitatively small and non-intentional misstatement of a financial statement item, including:

- where a misstatement arises from an item capable of precise measurement or whether it arises from an estimate and, if so, the degree of imprecision inherent in the estimate;
- where a misstatement masks a change in earnings or other trends;
- whether a misstatement hides a failure to meet analysts' consensus expectations for the enterprise;
- where a misstatement changes a loss into income or vice versa;
- where a misstatement concerns a segment or other portion of the registrant's business that has been identified as playing a significant role in the registrant's operations or profitability;
- where a misstatement affects the registrant's compliance with regulatory requirements;
- where a misstatement affects the registrant's compliance with loan covenants or other contractual requirements; and

- where a misstatement has the effect of increasing management's compensation—for example, by satisfying requirements for the award of bonuses or other forms of incentive compensation.

Q 28.24 At what stage must a future possible violation be reported?

No case law or SEC guidance limits the prospective time horizon for incipient violations. The requirements for credible evidence and the reasonable likelihood of a material violation will provide screens to filter out speculation or gossip. However, the pressure upon attorneys for issuers deputizing them to report potential violations to top management, audit committees, or boards of directors is clear.

Qualified Legal Compliance Committees

Q 28.25 What is a qualified legal compliance committee (QLCC)?

An issuer may, but need not, establish a qualified legal compliance committee. A QLCC is a committee of the issuer's board of directors, consisting of at least one member of the audit committee (or its equivalent if the issuer does not have one) and two or more other independent members of the issuer's board who are not employed, directly or indirectly, by the issuer.

> **TIP:** The QLCC need not be a separate committee; the audit committee or another committee of the board of directors, appropriately composed, may be designated as the QLCC.[54]

Q 28.25.1 How is a QLCC established?

The QLCC must be formally established and must adopt written procedures for the confidential receipt, retention, and consideration of any report of evidence of a material violation. The QLCC must be established *before* receiving its first report of a material violation. If it is established in response to a report, it is not qualified to act with respect to that report. A QLCC acts by majority vote; upon receiving any report, it may initiate an investigation, will engage independent counsel to it, and may recommend that an issuer implement an appropriate response. If an issuer fails to implement an appropriate response recommended by the QLCC, the QLCC has authority to notify the SEC of the matter.

Q 28.25.2   How does the QLCC operate?

Typically, a QLCC will engage counsel to investigate on its behalf. An attorney retained or directed by a QLCC to investigate a reported violation has no reporting obligations other than to the QLCC. Similarly, an attorney retained or directed by a QLCC to litigate a reported violation has no reporting obligations except to the QLCC, provided he or she may assert a colorable defense on behalf of the issuer.

CLO Responsibilities and Appropriate Responses

Q 28.26   What steps must a CLO take when presented with a report of evidence of material violation?

The CLO is obligated to cause an inquiry to be conducted that he or she believes is appropriate to determine whether the reported material violation has occurred, is ongoing, or is about to occur. If the CLO determines there is no material violation, he or she must so notify the reporting attorney of the basis for such determination. If the CLO determines there is a material violation, he or she must take reasonable steps to ensure that the issuer adopts an appropriate response (which may include remedial measures and/or sanctions, and appropriate disclosures) and advise the reporting attorney accordingly. Alternately, the CLO or another supervising attorney may refer the report of a material violation to a QLCC. If the CLO makes such referral, the CLO must inform the reporting attorney of the referral. Once the report and referral occur, the CLO and supervising attorney are relieved of any further obligation (but also lose further control over the matter).[55]

Q 28.26.1 What kind of paper trail should the inquiry have?

The SEC excluded from its final rules requirements for documentation of reports of material violations, finding, for the present, that the risks and burdens associated with preparing and preserving documentation may outweigh the benefits. Probably, a determination by an attorney to report a material violation should be documented in writing to a higher authority. A preparatory inquiry or consideration of appropriate responses may be necessary. At this stage, excessive documentation may interfere with candid communications and/or impede the process and objective of ultimate transparency the rules seek to promote. It is likely this will be an unsettled area for the foreseeable future.

Q 28.26.2 What would be considered an "appropriate response"?

Following receipt of a report of a material violation, the CLO, CEO, audit committee, or QLCC must make an appropriate response. The response may take one of several forms:

- A determination that no material violation has occurred or is about to occur;
- The adoption of appropriate remedial measures to prevent any material violation that has yet to occur; or
- The issuer retains or directs an attorney to review the reported evidence of a material violation and either has implemented remedial recommendations made by such attorney or has been advised that such attorney may assert a colorable defense on behalf of the issuer.[56]

Q 28.26.3 How does a reporting attorney determine whether the response was appropriate?

Whether a response is appropriate must be evaluated under the particular circumstances of each report, considering the amount and weight of evidence of a material violation, the severity of the material violation, and the scope of the investigation that has been made following the report. In forming a belief concerning the appropriateness of a response, a reporting attorney may rely upon reasonable factual representations and legal determinations made by persons upon whom a reasonable attorney would rely.

Q 28.26.4 What does a reporting attorney do after the company has responded?

An attorney who receives what he or she believes is an appropriate response to a report need do nothing more.[57] However, an attorney who does not reasonably believe that the issuer has made an appropriate response, or who has not received an appropriate response within a reasonable time, must explain his or her reasons for disputing the appropriateness of the response to the CLO, CEO, or directors to whom the attorney first made his or her report.[58]

Q 28.26.5 In the absence of an appropriate response to a report of a material violation, what should a conscientious counsel do?

Initially, the SEC proposed a noisy withdrawal. As of today, the SEC has not adopted any final rules requiring further action by the reporting attorney.

Q 28.26.6 What options do lawyers currently have when a SOX violation may be occurring?

Apart from withdrawal, and breaking sharply from state regulations and case law, the SEC's rule authorizes an attorney to reveal facts to the SEC that the attorney believes are necessary to prevent an issuer from committing a material violation that would cause substantial injury, to prevent an issuer from committing perjury, or to rectify consequences of a material violation by the issuer.[59] An attorney may also use records made in the course of fulfilling reporting obligations to defend himself or herself against charges of misconduct.

Foreign Lawyers

Q 28.27 Does SOX also apply to foreign lawyers?

Foreign lawyers who assist companies issuing securities for sale in the United States with reporting documents to be filed with the SEC are practicing before the SEC and, in doing this work, they are subject to SOX and to the obligation to comply with the Rules of Professional Practice adopted by the SEC.

State Rules

Q 28.28 How do the SEC rules compare with American Bar Association and state rules?

The SEC views its rules as preemptive of any conflicting state provisions concerning lawyer behavior. Shortly after SOX, the American Bar Association amended its Model Rule 1.13 ("Organization as Client"). The amended rule is more general in content but closer in concept to SOX Rule 205. Model Rule 1.13(b) imposes an up-the-ladder reporting duty upon an attorney engaged by an organization who knows that an officer or employee is acting or intends to act in violation of law likely to result in substantial injury to the organization. The attorney "shall proceed as is reasonably necessary in the best interest of the organization" to refer the matter to higher authority in the organization, including to its highest authority.

> **COMPLIANCE FACT**
>
> More than forty states have included up-the-ladder reporting in adopting local versions of the model rules, but Delaware has not and the adopting states vary in the details of their requirement.

Q 28.28.1 What is the difference between the SEC and ABA and state rules?

Generally, Rule 205 is broader and more detailed than the model rules or states' disciplinary rules for lawyers. For example, some state provisions, such as California's Rule 3-100 of its Rules of Professional Conduct, do not permit a lawyer to report a client's fraud or imminent violation of law (unless it will cause death or severe bodily harm to an individual) outside the organization. Model Rule 1.13(f) parallels the provisions in SOX Rule 205 emphasizing that a lawyer for an organization represents the organization, which may have interests adverse to those of individual officers, directors, or employees.

In dealing with those individuals, an attorney is required to explain to them who is his or her client—and who is not.

Q 28.28.2 What is the relationship between the SEC and state rules?

Rule 205 supplements, but does not replace, most state rules of professional conduct for attorneys. It specifically permits additional and more rigorous regulation of lawyers by the states. Although there are no federal court decisions yet on the application of Rule 205, in analogous circumstances, it has been held that federal law regulating NASD arbitration preempts California's ethical standards for arbitrators.[60] By analogy, it is likely that the standards implementing SOX section 307 preempt inconsistent state ethical and disciplinary rules.

Law Firm Training

Q 28.29 How should law firms and lawyers adjust to the new standards?

The ever-changing and enlarging requirements of corporate compliance impose obligations on lawyers and their public companies and law firms for mandatory regular training. Given the breadth of the definition of practice before the SEC in the SEC's Rule 205, all attorneys should attend. Participants, whether in-house or in law firms, whether newly hired or long-tenured, should file written certifications of completion of training for inclusion in compliance files of the general counsel.

TIP: Training should take place at least once every year.

Q 28.29.1 What should the training entail?

The subjects of training should include at the very minimum:

- familiarization with the company's most updated compliance policy, governance documents, and code of ethics,

including the availability of anonymous telephone hotlines and websites and the protection afforded to whistleblowers;
- review of SEC rules, procedures, and enforcement actions, including the attorney conduct rules and enforcement actions. Lawyers must know the penalties for failures of compliance, including corporate disciplinary procedures for failure to perform up-the-ladder reporting; and
- review recent key disclosure documents for accuracy, completeness, and to make personnel aware of the scope of required disclosures.

Punishment

Q 28.30 Has the SEC punished lawyers for misconduct?

Yes. The SEC has proceeded vigorously against lawyers engaged directly in fraudulent or dishonest conduct. The SEC has named lawyers as respondents or defendants in more than thirty enforcement actions over the past two years.

Q 28.30.1 How has the SEC punished lawyers?

Civil actions commenced by the SEC against attorneys for violation of its attorney conduct rules have sought injunctive relief and monetary civil penalties, and administrative cease-and-desist proceedings. The SEC may notify a state bar of its disciplinary proceedings against an attorney. Beyond enforcing its rules of professional conduct, the SEC has also disciplined lawyers for inadequacy in the quality of their legal advice.[61]

Insurance

Q 28.31 How do the new SEC rules affect insurance for lawyers?

The gatekeeper responsibilities thrust upon lawyers by SOX and by the SEC's rules of attorney conduct make the general counsel and his staff more prominent to disgruntled investors and in greater need of insurance protection. Attraction and retention of capable legal officers requires an issuer to provide adequate insurance. Where the general counsel is covered, he or she should be protected even if other officers may have committed misconduct. Thus, the inability for the insurance company to rescind the coverage is especially important for the legal staff (and independent directors), as is severability (so that coverage of a class of insureds is not voided by allegations against one or more officers or directors). Separate and distinct policy limits for payment of defense expenses, and for settlements or judgments, are necessary.

General Counsel

Q 28.32 What should the role of the general counsel be in the new environment?

Under the collaborative model of corporate governance envisioned by COSO,[62] and assumed by the SEC in its SOX rulemakings, it is more important for an issuer than ever for the general counsel to be viewed as an advisor, with a greater range of topics on which he or she must present legal options to management and the directors. SOX compliance anticipates increasing communication among officers and directors, some of it formal (such as meetings with an audit committee), and much of it informal (such as designing, testing, and utilizing disclosure controls).

Q 28.32.1 How have the SEC rules changed the relations among general counsel, directors, and management?

SOX has substantially increased the accountability of directors and general counsel for oversight and disclosures of conduct by an issuer, necessarily adjusting the formal and informal relationships among them. In particular, these new responsibilities affect the functioning of the general counsel. Therefore, when speaking with individual officers, managers, and directors, the general counsel represents the issuer, whose interests may differ from, or even be adverse to, interests of those individuals. Depending on the circumstances, the general counsel may also be obligated under SOX to communicate with the board of directors over the objection of the CEO.

Q 28.32.2 How does the new environment affect the CEO vis à vis the general counsel?

With multiple dimensions ranging from SOX obligations, to certification programs for quality standards, such as ISO 9000, to due diligence reviews by insurers, lenders, regulators and in connection with business combinations, corporate compliance is becoming perpetual and pervasive. The independent obligations of directors, CEO, CFO, and the general counsel are forcing collaboration to accomplish effective corporate oversight. Accordingly, and at different paces in different companies but especially in larger public companies, the extent of the CEO's individual dominance is receding.

SOX Effect

Q 28.32.3 How has SOX changed the role of the general counsel?

Historically, general counsel often served as confidential advisors to management, counseling on strategy and business issues beyond questions of law. Under SOX, the general counsel's obligations for disclosure and for up-the-ladder reporting of evidence of material violations have caused some officers to view their general counsel as a deputy cop who cannot keep secrets, and whose first loyalty is external, rather than to his fellow officers. This can lead the general counsel sometimes to be informally screened from participating in strategic discussions.

Q 28.32.4 What new tasks does the general counsel have under SOX?

SOX prescribes an extensive list of tasks that will require intense involvement by an issuer's general counsel, some of which are new and others of which have wider scope of applications. The availability of electronic communications and the regulatory requirements for real-time disclosures pressure a general counsel for speedy handling of these tasks, which may reduce the time available for careful deliberation:

- Documenting corporate governance procedures—for example, charters for the audit committee, adoption of a code of ethics;

- Implementing rules against prohibited loans to officers;
- Investigating comments and complaints submitted via hotlines and websites;
- Assisting the CEO and CFO in acquiring and evaluating information from which they can determine whether to certify periodic financial reports under SOX sections 302 and 906;
- Assuring that internal controls for financial reporting have been documented, tested, and are being monitored;
- Preparing text for management's discussion and analysis of operations for investors and the SEC, and assuring the accuracy, fairness of presentation, and completeness of these disclosures;
- Overseeing the establishment, content, documentation, testing, monitoring, and improvement of disclosure controls;
- Administering nuts and bolts elements of the issuer's compliance program, including coordinating the performance of risk assessments and the evaluation of loss contingencies for audit and disclosure purposes;
- Communicating with internal auditors, external auditors, the CEO, CFO, and directors about a myriad of matters concerning independence of auditors, pre-approval of auditors' work, communications for audit verifications with third parties, and about credible evidence of material violations of law (if any);
- Dealing with external auditors and counsel on attestations under SOX section 404 and the recognition and amelioration of material weaknesses and significant deficiencies in the effective functioning of controls;
- Dealing, as appropriate, with regulators such as the SEC.

Q 28.32.5 How do the new SOX requirements interact with the need to protect privileged communications?

Because the general counsel sometimes fulfills executive functions apart from the performance of legal services, and because privilege often will not extend to non-legal tasks (unless incidental and ancillary to legal work), the organization of the legal function at an issuer in the post-SOX era is particularly important. It is increasingly appreciated that the risk assessment tasks that are part of the development and testing of internal controls and disclosure controls are appropriately performed by specialized professionals outside the law department of an issuer but communicating frequently with the general counsel, in a dotted-line relationship.

Tools

Q 28.32.6 What organizational steps and tools are out there to assist the general counsel?

Protection of a general counsel's scarce time can be improved through several mechanisms:

- Delegation of preparation of periodic report information and updates to a compliance officer;
- Assignment of a junior lawyer or legal assistant to initial review and investigation of hotline and anonymous complaints on the corporate website, reporting to the general counsel with summaries on a regular basis;
- Assignment of a liaison to the information technology department to provide access for the general counsel to automated reports on the operation of significant internal controls;
- Arranging for separate electronic mailboxes for strategic communications among senior management, for compliance communications with outside counsel and auditors, for compliance communications with directors and audit committee members;
- Regular meetings with operating and key administration department leaders to verify progress on development, testing, improvement of controls, and status of pending or potential reportable events;
- Assignment of a manager or officer to conduct and oversee risk assessments, taking guidance and providing reports to the general counsel, so that a broader span of loss contingencies and of operating, legal and financial risks are monitored, from overtime pay compliance, to environmental contamination and cleanup responsibilities, to adherence to domestic and foreign regulatory directives, etc.;
- Engaging outside specialist consultants to assist the risk assessment officer in undertaking specialized risk assessments, such as those involving evaluation of environmental liability exposure;

- Requiring monthly and quarterly subcertificates from managers of significant divisions, departments, and staff functions of the same attestations contained in SOX 302, with opportunities for comments and notes to be attached, so that compliance topics requiring the general counsel's attention will arrive earlier at his or her desk;
- Requiring all personnel to be familiar with up-the-ladder reporting and, in that connection, requiring quarterly subcertificates that none have failed to report information concerning potential violations of law or of compliance policies to the legal department, with the assurance that compliance in good faith will not subject the employee to discipline or dismissal;
- Requiring outside counsel to make quarterly certifications to the general counsel with respect to up-the-ladder reporting and any information or awareness of potential violations of law or of compliance policies;
- Instructing outside counsel as to the form and procedures for making reports to the general counsel and others within the company;
- Regular meetings with the CEO, CFO, and audit committee members reporting upon and discussing compliance topics so that an appropriate tone at the top is reinforced, a collaborative atmosphere is encouraged, and the risks of unanticipated crises minimized;
- Designing in advance, with the CEO and senior management, broad contingency plans so that, should crises arise, calm implementation of important early steps in investor and public communications, internal investigation and maintaining as much as possible business as usual in unaffected areas of corporate operations.

Q 28.32.7 How does a general counsel determine the best interests of the corporation?

The complexity inherent for a public company in competing in multiple product or service categories in domestic and overseas markets, each with multiple and evolving regulators, adds difficulty to a general counsel's fulfilling the fiduciary responsibility to recommend decisions in the best interests of the corporation. These matters illustrate the ever-increasing importance of involving the general counsel in strategic discussions at a public company, and the need for collaboration among management and directors, notwithstanding the disclosure obligations to regulators of the participants.

Investigations

Q 28.33 What factors are relevant to the SEC in the course of an investigation?

A general counsel should be mindful of guidance the SEC has published on how corporate behavior and cooperation influence its enforcement decisions:

1. What is the nature of the misconduct involved? Did it result from inadvertence, honest mistake, simple negligence, reckless or deliberate indifference to indicia of wrongful conduct, willful misconduct, or unadorned venality? Were the company's auditors misled?
2. How did the misconduct arise? Is it the result of pressure placed on employees to achieve specific results, or a tone of lawlessness set by those in control of the company? What compliance procedures were in place to prevent the misconduct now uncovered? Why did those procedures fail to stop or inhibit the wrongful conduct?
3. Where in the organization did the misconduct occur? Who knew about, or participated in, the misconduct? How high up in the chain of command were they? Did senior personnel participate in, or turn a blind eye toward, obvious indicia of misconduct? How systemic was the behavior? Is it symptomatic of the way the entity does business, or was it isolated?
4. How long did the misconduct last? Was it a one-quarter, or one-time, event, or did it last several years? In the case of a public company, did the misconduct occur before the company went public? Did it facilitate the company's ability to go public?
5. How much harm has the misconduct inflicted upon investors and other corporate constituencies? Did the share price of the company's stock drop significantly upon its discovery and disclosure?
6. How was the misconduct detected and who uncovered it?

7. How long after discovery of the misconduct did it take to implement an effective response?
8. What steps did the company take upon learning of the misconduct? Did the company immediately stop the misconduct? Are persons responsible for any misconduct still with the company? If so, are they still in the same positions? Did the company promptly, completely, and effectively disclose the existence of the misconduct to the public, to regulators, and to self-regulators? Did the company cooperate completely with appropriate regulatory and law enforcement bodies? Did the company identify what additional related misconduct is likely to have occurred? Did the company take steps to identify the extent of damage to investors and other corporate constituencies? Did the company appropriately recompense those adversely affected by the conduct?
9. What processes did the company follow to resolve many of these issues and ferret out necessary information? Were the audit committee and the board of directors fully informed? If so, when?
10. Did the company commit to learn the truth, fully and expeditiously? Did it do a thorough review of the nature, extent, origins, and consequences of the misconduct and related behavior? Did management, the board, or committees consisting solely of outside directors oversee the review? Did company employees or outside persons perform the review? If outside persons, had they done other work for the company? Where the review was conducted by outside counsel, had management previously engaged such counsel? Were scope limitations placed on the review? If so, what were they?
11. Did the company promptly make available to our staff the results of its review and provide sufficient documentation reflecting its response to the situation? Did the company identify possible violative conduct and evidence with sufficient precision to facilitate prompt enforcement actions against those who violated the law? Did the company produce a thorough and probing written report detailing the findings of its review? Did the company voluntarily disclose information the SEC did not directly request and otherwise

might not have uncovered? Did the company ask its employees to cooperate with our staff and make all reasonable efforts to secure such cooperation?
12. What assurances are there that the conduct is unlikely to recur? Did the company adopt and ensure enforcement of new and more effective internal controls and procedures designed to prevent a recurrence of the misconduct? Did the company provide our staff with sufficient information for it to evaluate the company's measures to correct the situation and ensure that the conduct does not recur?
13. Is the company the same company in which the misconduct occurred, or has it changed through a merger or bankruptcy reorganization?[63]

Q 28.33.1 Has the SEC indicated the areas of greatest concern?

The SEC has underscored the foregoing guidelines in recently announcing its intention to monitor closely the conduct of attorneys in their handling of internal investigations of alleged corporate wrongdoing. Internal investigations are typically performed under considerable time pressure and logistical obstacles by overworked teams of honest, bright, and diligent lawyers. It is, unfortunately, a further consideration in planning and conducting such an investigation to bear in mind that it may later be reviewed with the benefit of hindsight by the SEC.

In effect, the investigating lawyers must plan and document their audit program, double-check their facts and files, examining themselves while they investigate the conduct of others.

Q 28.33.2 What are the biggest obstacles to cooperation?

The management of archived computerized documents and of electronic mail presents logistics obstacles in every company. During an SEC inquiry, general counsel and outside counsel must make it a priority to retrieve such documents and to be candid with the SEC about its progress in responding to document requests. Delay, obfuscation, and unfounded excuses will frustrate the SEC and can only exasperate the situation.

> **CASE STUDY: *In re Lucent Technologies, Inc.*[64]**
>
> The SEC's May 2004 enforcement settlement with Lucent Technologies demonstrates the seriousness of inadequate attention to an investigation and the potential repercussions of delay in compliance with an SEC investigation. Lucent agreed to pay a $25 million penalty for its non-cooperation with an SEC investigation.

Certification of Financial Statements

Requirements for Certification

Q 28.34 What are SOX's certification requirements?

To enhance confidence in the reliability of financial reports and to place accountability squarely on the CEO and CFO of issuers, Congress required two certifications of financial statements and expressed the sense of the Senate that corporate tax returns should be signed by the CEO and CFO.[65] In addition, Congress required disclosure of accounting in an issuer's financial reports that does not correspond with GAAP.[66]

Q 28.34.1 What must the SOX 906 certificate contain?

The SOX section 906 certificate must be signed by the CEO and the CFO attesting that the report containing the financial statements fully complies with the reporting requirements in section 13(a) or 15(d) of the Securities Exchange Act of 1934[67] and the information contained in the report "fairly presents, in all material respects, the financial condition and results of operations of the issuer."

Q 28.34.2 What is the test for liability under the financial certificate requirements?

A corporate officer who knowingly makes a false certification by certifying a periodic report filed with the SEC that contains material false statements the officer knew to be false may be liable as a primary violator for securities fraud under section 10(b) of the Exchange Act as well as for criminal penalties.

Q 28.34.3 What else must the CEO and CFO do under SOX section 302?

SOX requires that the CEO and CFO have personal knowledge of the financial statements and impose responsibility on these executives to have established appropriate internal accounting controls and disclosure controls so that reliable financial statements may be prepared by the issuer. Under this requirement, the specificity of the promises and their basis in personal knowledge make it easier to demonstrate a violation.

Q 28.34.4 What must the CEO and CFO actually certify under SOX section 302?

(1) He or she has reviewed the report being filed;
(2) Based on his or her knowledge, the report does not contain any untrue statement of a material fact or omit to state a material fact necessary to make the statements made, in light of the circumstances under which such statements were made, not misleading with respect to the period covered by the report;
(3) Based on his or her knowledge, the financial statements, and other financial information included in the report, fairly present in all material respects the financial condition, results of operations and cash flows of the issuer as of, and for, the periods presented in the report;
(4) He or she and the other certifying officers are responsible for establishing and maintaining disclosure controls and procedures for the issuer and have:
 (i) Designed such disclosure controls and procedures to ensure that material information relating to the issuer, including its consolidated subsidiaries, is made known to them by others within those entities, particularly

during the period in which the periodic reports are being prepared,
(ii) Evaluated the effectiveness of the issuer's disclosure controls and procedures as of a date within ninety days prior to the filing date of the report ("Evaluation Date"), and
(iii) Presented in the report their conclusions about the effectiveness of the disclosure controls and procedures based on their evaluation as of the evaluation date;

(5) He or she and the other certifying officers have disclosed, based on their most recent evaluation, to the issuer's auditors and the audit committee of the board of directors (or persons fulfilling the equivalent function):
(i) All significant deficiencies in the design or operation of internal controls which could adversely affect the issuer's ability to record, process, summarize, and report financial data, and have identified for the issuer's auditors any material weaknesses in internal controls, and
(ii) Any fraud, whether or not material, that involves management or other employees who have a significant role in the issuer's internal controls; and

(6) He or she and the other certifying officers have indicated in the report whether or not there were significant changes in internal controls or in other factors that could significantly affect internal controls subsequent to the date of their most recent evaluation, including any corrective actions with regard to significant deficiencies and material weaknesses.[68]

Q 28.34.5 Does the CEO have to sign the company's federal tax returns?

SOX 1001 only sets forth the sense of the Senate that federal income tax returns of any corporation should be signed by the CEO.

Pre-Certification

Q 28.34.6 What should the CEO and CFO do prior to certifying a report under SOX?

Consistent with their affirmative responsibilities, before certifying a report under SOX section 302 or 906, a CEO and CFO should do no less than the following:

- Personally study the proposed report, looking closely at the financial statements, notes, and the discussion of financial matters and risk assessments, both financial and operating, in Management's Discussion and Analysis section;
- Require each member of the company's disclosure committee also to study personally the proposed report, thinking critically about the disclosures and notifying the CEO and CFO promptly of areas for consideration of further or modified discussion;
- With assistance from the disclosure committee, compare the proposed report with the company's recent filings with the SEC to identify instances where further amplification is appropriate in the proposed report;
- Specifically inquire of the disclosure committee and of all other members of management, the company's internal auditors, and outside auditors to report on the current status of any material weaknesses, significant deficiencies, and potential significant deficiencies, both financial and non-financial, in internal controls and disclosure controls that might impact the completeness and accuracy of the proposed report, including corrective steps planned or underway to relieve the weaknesses and deficiencies;
- Personally review with management and with outside auditors the current procedures undertaken to prepare the proposed report and to identify any issues appropriate for discussion in the report that were not raised by those procedures, as well as improvements in the information-gathering procedures;
- Obtain from other members of management and confirm with the audit partner(s) from outside auditors that none of them are aware of any material misrepresentations or omissions in the proposed report and, further, that the proposed

report fairly presents the financial condition, results of operations, and cash flows of the issuer, apart from the requirements of GAAP; and that the proposed report addresses every requirement for the particular report in SEC regulations and rules; and
- Meet with the audit committee to identify and resolve any disagreements regarding disclosures in the proposed report, and explain to the audit committee the due diligence performed by the CEO and CFO to enable their certification of the proposed report.

Non-GAAP Reporting

Q 28.35   What is non-GAAP reporting?

A non-GAAP financial measure is a numerical measure of a registrant's historical or future financial performance, financial position, or cash flow that (1) actually or effectively excludes amounts that are included in the most directly comparable measure calculated and presented in accordance with GAAP in the statement of income, balance sheet or statement of cash flows (or equivalent statements) of the issuer, or (2) actually or effectively includes amounts that are excluded from the most directly comparable GAAP measure that is so calculated and presented. Excluded from the definition of a "non-GAAP financial measure" are

(i) operating and other statistical measures; and
(ii) ratios or statistical measures calculated exclusively comprised of components calculated under GAAP.[69]

Q 28.35.1   How must a company report a non-GAAP financial measure?

The regulations require public companies that disclose or release non-GAAP financial measures to include in the disclosure (1) a presentation of the most directly comparable GAAP financial measure, and (2) a reconciliation of that measure with a GAAP measure.[70] A registrant must disclose its reasons why management believes that presentation of the non-GAAP measure is useful along with any additional purposes. The regulations prohibit any misleading use of non-GAAP measures or using titles or descriptions of non-GAAP financial measures that are the same as, or confusingly similar to, titles or descriptions used for GAAP financial measures.

> **TIP:** If a non-GAAP financial measure is released orally, telephonically, or by webcast or broadcast, the issuer may provide the required accompanying information by (a) the availability of the required accompanying information during its presentation, and (b) posting that information on its Internet website.[71]

Enforcement

Q 28.36 What enforcement action can the SEC take upon discovery of false certifications?

In addition to civil penalties and injunctions to cease and desist from violations, specific and significant governance requirements have been imposed by the SEC in its proceedings against issuers for false certifications of financial statements and periodic reports. The most extensive governance provisions to date were announced as part of a settlement with HealthSouth Corporation, following suits against fifteen officers of HealthSouth in which individual penalties were obtained. Along with a $100 million settlement was an unusually detailed permanent injunction.[72]

Internal Controls

Q 28.37 What internal controls does SOX require?

SOX section 404, as implemented by the SEC's rules, requires that a public company's annual report include an internal control report of management that contains:

- A statement of management's responsibility for establishing and maintaining adequate internal control over financial reporting for the company;

- A statement identifying the framework used by management to conduct the required evaluation of the effectiveness of the company's internal control over financial reporting;
- Management's assessment of the effectiveness of the company's internal control over financial reporting as of the end of the company's most recent fiscal year, including a statement as to whether or not the company's internal control over financial reporting is effective;
- The assessment must include disclosure of any material weaknesses in the company's internal control over financial reporting identified by management. Management may not qualify its conclusions with respect to the effectiveness of the company's internal control over financial reporting. Rather, management must take those problems into account when concluding whether the company's internal control over financial reporting is effective; and
- A statement that the registered public accounting firm that audited the financial statements included in the annual report has issued an attestation report on management's assessment of the registrant's internal control over financial reporting.[73]

Q 28.37.1   What is the scope of internal controls over financial reporting?

The SEC has summarized the scope of internal controls over financial reporting for this purpose, as including policies and procedures that:

- pertain to the maintenance of records that in reasonable detail accurately and fairly reflect the transactions and dispositions of the assets of the registrant;
- provide reasonable assurance that transactions are recorded as necessary to permit preparation of financial statements in accordance with GAAP, and that receipts and expenditures of the registrant are being made only in accordance with authorizations of management and directors of the registrant; and
- provide reasonable assurance regarding prevention or timely detection of unauthorized acquisition, use or disposi-

tion of the registrant's assets that could have a material effect on the financial statements.[74]

Q 28.37.2 What are the elements and scope of internal controls?

The COSO framework for internal controls consists of five very general components:

(1) the control environment;
(2) risk assessment;
(3) control activities;
(4) information and communication; and
(5) monitoring.[75]

Q 28.37.3 Is there a specified process for designing, monitoring, or testing internal controls?

The PCAOB and SEC have explained that controls must be customized to the individual business operations of each public company and are expected, therefore, to vary from one company to the next. The audit standards and rules implementing SOX do not prescribe any method or procedure to be followed by an issuer in designing its internal controls, nor in testing them, nor in evaluating their effectiveness.

Q 28.37.4 What can be expected from internal controls?

No matter how comprehensive an issuer's internal controls, nor how well they function, there are genuine, and often inadequately appreciated, limits to their effectiveness. Accordingly, the PCAOB and SEC limit their requirements for an effective internal control system to its providing reasonable assurance of reliability in financial statements.

Q 28.37.5 What is a "reasonable assurance"?

The concept of reasonable assurance is built into the definition of internal control over financial reporting and also is integral to the auditor's opinion. Reasonable assurance includes the understanding that there is a remote likelihood that material misstatements will not be prevented or detected on a timely basis. Although not absolute assurance, reasonable assurance is, nevertheless, a high level of assurance.[76]

Q 28.37.6 Whose responsibility is it to design and develop internal controls?

Under SOX section 404, it is management's responsibility to determine accounting principles, to design and implement internal controls, and to prepare financial statements. However, an auditor's giving advice to management, and even limited assistance, does not violate the auditor-independence rules. The SEC has acknowledged that "both common sense and sound policy dictate that communications must be ongoing and open in order to create the best environment for producing high quality financial reporting and auditing."[77]

Q 28.37.7 How do auditors advise on internal controls without violating the stringent requirements of auditor independence?

An issuer must keep in mind these basic principles on auditor independence:

(1) an auditor cannot function as management for an issuer,
(2) an audit firm cannot audit its own work,
(3) an audit firm cannot be an advocate for the issuer, and
(4) an auditor may not have a conflict of interest impairing its independence with respect to a client issuer.

Accordingly, the development of internal controls and internal audit work cannot be outsourced by the issuer to the auditor.[78] However, an auditor's discussing and exchanging views with management does not in itself violate the independence principles, nor does it fall into a prohibited category of services. An auditor may even assist management in documenting internal controls, provided management is actively involved in the process.[79]

Q 28.37.8 What are the processes for developing internal controls for financial reporting?

Conceptually, the design of individual controls for accuracy and reliability, however diverse their subject matter, involves the same steps:

(1) Specifying a clear purpose for a process or procedure;
(2) Mapping each step in that process or procedure to show the sources, travel, processing, and output of information, identifying each document and department through whose hands it passes;
(3) Declaring business rules to assure the consistency in the information and its processing; and
(4) Preparing tests and reports that monitor the application and enforcement of the business rules.

Manipulation of Financial Reports

Q 28.38 What areas of financial reporting appear to be most vulnerable to manipulation?

The SEC's enforcement activities reveal that certain parts of financial statements are especially vulnerable to manipulation and fraudulent schemes. *Repeatedly*, similar issues arise at different companies for the same elements of financial reporting. Accordingly, a public company should give special attention to strong internal controls in the areas of:

(1) revenue recognition;
(2) expense disclosure and recognition;
(3) asset valuations;
(4) contingent liability valuations; and
(5) transactions with special purpose entities.

Q 28.38.1 What aspects of revenue recognition should be considered in particular?

Companies have recorded revenues from fictitious transactions or expired agreements. They have also improperly accelerated the timing of revenue recognition, bringing future revenues into the current period. Some have entered into round-trip transactions with customers or vendors to stuff distribution channels in the current period, inflating revenues, and then secretly reversing or writing off the transactions in future periods.

Other companies have falsely represented that one-time transactions would yield recurring revenues in future periods, inflating revenues and earning projections. In other cases, senior management has required that unsubstantiated adjustments be made, inflating revenues and earnings. There have also been instances of inflated promotional allowances and discounts from vendors, inflating revenues, sometimes including inducing vendors to sign false confirmation letters to auditors attesting to the enhanced allowances. Finally, companies have improperly treated revenues resulting from improper formation or non-consolidation of Special Purpose Entities, inflating revenues and profits.

CASE STUDY: *SEC v. Robert Quattrone, et al.*

In January 2004, the SEC charged former executives and five customers of Suprema Securities in a $700 million fraud.[80] The heart of the Suprema scheme involved round-tripping transactions, in which Suprema, together with certain customers and vendors, created fictitious sales through false invoices and other fraudulent documentation. The effect of these transactions was to give the appearance that sales were made, when in actuality no products had been sold or shipped at all. The SEC went after both the issuer and the third parties.

Q 28.38.2 What aspects of expense accounting should be considered in particular?

It is not unusual for companies not to document or falsely support personal expenses. Some companies make improper overseas payments in violation of the Foreign Corrupt Practices Act. Companies also often fail to disclose payments to entities controlled by officers, directors, or their immediate family members. Companies may improperly capitalize operating expenses over several years, rather than charging in current period, thus reducing the charge against earnings in current period. Companies commonly fail to disclose payments for non-competition promises by officers and directors.

Q 28.38.3 What aspects of asset valuations should be considered in particular?

Companies use valuation methods not in compliance with GAAP resulting in values exceeding fair value, so as to avoid recognizing asset impairments and resulting write-downs. They also divert cash from proceeds of asset sales to officers and directors as well as understate expenses from acquisitions and restructuring.

Q 28.38.4 What aspects of contingent liability valuations should particularly be considered?

Companies have sometimes decreased values of reserves to inflate earnings. Valuation of balance sheet assets and liabilities necessarily involves judgments and may be devilishly complicated. Rendering them transparent in financial reporting can be quite difficult, the more so if not all levels of management are committed to such transparency.

Q 28.38.5 What aspects of special purpose entities should particularly be considered?

Especially since the collapse of Enron with its extensive use of mysterious complex Special Purpose Entities, the use of special purpose entities has become a red flag for investors and the SEC. If issuers choose to use a special purpose entity, they must provide the following disclosure:

- The nature and business purpose of the issuer's off-balance-sheet arrangements;
- The importance of the off-balance-sheet arrangements to the issuer for liquidity, capital resources, market risk or credit risk support, or other benefits;
- The financial impact of the arrangements on the issuer (*e.g.*, revenues, expenses, cash flows, or securities issued) and the issuer's exposure to risk as a result of the arrangements (*e.g.*, retained interests or contingent liabilities); and
- Known events, demands, commitments, trends, or uncertainties that affect the availability or benefits to the issuer of material off-balance-sheet arrangements.

Q 28.38.6 How should companies document internal controls?

Management of a public company must compile and maintain evidential matter including documentation, regarding both the design of internal controls and the testing processes to provide reasonable support for management's assessment of the effectiveness of internal control over financial reporting. This evidential matter should provide "reasonable support for the evaluation of whether the control is designed to prevent or detect material misstatements or omissions; for the conclusion that the tests were appropriately planned and performed; and that the results of the tests were appropriately considered."[81]

> **TIP:** The form and extent of documentation will vary from company to company but include paper and electronic files, policy manuals, process models, flowcharts, job descriptions, forms, and reports.

Q 28.38.7 What else is management required to do beyond developing, documenting, putting into operation, and using internal controls?

Under SOX section 404, management is also required to:

- accept responsibility for the effectiveness of the company's internal control over financial reporting;
- evaluate the effectiveness of the company's internal control over financial reporting using suitable control criteria;
- support its evaluation with sufficient evidence, including documentation; and
- present a written assessment of the effectiveness of the company's internal control over financial reporting as of the end of the company's most recent fiscal year.

Q 28.38.8 What should management use to assess their internal controls?

One way to understand the scope of management's assessment of the effectiveness of an issuer's financial controls is to examine what the PCAOB and SEC have prescribed for an outside auditor to do in evaluating management's assessment. Management should anticipate these audit steps, undertake many of them itself in addition to studying what self-assessment and ongoing monitoring of controls is done by its employees already.

Auditing Standards

Q 28.39 What are the auditing standards?

Auditors performing a SOX evaluation must first examine management's handling of each of the following elements:

- Determining which controls should be tested, including controls related to all significant accounts at all significant business units, locations, and activities, and disclosures in the financial statements, including:
  - controls over initiating, authorizing, recording, processing, and reporting significant accounts and disclosures in the financial statements,
  - controls over the selection and application of accounting policies consistent with GAAP,
  - antifraud programs and controls,
  - controls, such as computerized software, on which other controls are dependent,
  - controls over significant non-routine and non-systematic transactions, involving judgments and estimates,
  - company level controls including the control environment, and
  - controls over the financial reporting process, including controls over procedures used to close the books; to enter transaction totals into the general ledger; to initiate, authorize, record, and process journal entries in the general ledger; and to record adjustments to the financial statements (for example, consolidating adjustments, report combinations, and reclassifications);

- Evaluating the likelihood that failure of the control could result in a misstatement, the magnitude of such a misstatement, and the degree to which other controls ("compensating controls"), if effective, achieve the same control objectives;
- Evaluating the design effectiveness of controls;
- Evaluating the operating effectiveness of controls based on testing, internal audit, inspection of evidence of the application of controls, self-assessment, and ongoing monitoring, some of which might occur as part of management's ongoing monitoring activities;
- Identifying and determining deficiencies that are of such a magnitude and likelihood of occurrence that they constitute significant deficiencies or material weaknesses in internal control over financial reporting; and
- Documenting the foregoing process.[82]

Q 28.39.1   What should testing encompass?

The procedures for testing controls should include inquiry, observation, inspection of relevant documentation, and re-performance of the application of the control. Testing should include "walkthroughs" of a process described by an individual internal control. Most importantly, the person doing the testing should ask:

- What do employees do to determine if there is an error in the process?
- What is done when they find an error?
- What kind of errors have they found so far?
- What happened as a result of finding the errors?
- How were the errors resolved?

Q 28.39.2   What other inquiries should be made?

Management should also review all internal audit reports for the year related to internal controls as well as all complaints of violations of the code of ethics and other similar policy statements at the company. Management should also look back at what training employees were given with respect to the code of ethics. Finally, management should ascertain whether the audit committee acted independently during the year.

Problems

Q 28.40 What should management do if it finds problems with the internal controls?

Shortcomings in internal controls must be disclosed by management to the auditors and the more serious among them must be reflected in the public disclosure of an issuer. These shortcomings are graduated, and may be categorized as "control deficiencies," "significant deficiencies," and gravest of all, "material weaknesses" in internal controls.

Q 28.40.1 What is a "control deficiency"?

A control deficiency exists when the design or operation of a control does not allow management or employees, in the normal course of performing their assigned functions, to prevent or detect misstatements on a timely basis. A deficiency in *design* exists when (a) a control necessary to meet the control objective is missing or (b) the control operates as designed and the control objective is not always met. A control is deficient in *operation* when it does not operate as designed, or when the person assigned to perform it has not the qualifications or authority to do so effectively.

Q 28.40.2 What is a "significant deficiency"?

A significant deficiency is a control deficiency, or combination of control deficiencies, that adversely affects the company's ability to record, process, or report external financial data reliably in accordance with GAAP so there is more than a remote likelihood that a misstatement of the company's financial statements, that is more than inconsequential, will not be prevented or detected. A misstatement is *inconsequential* if a reasonable person would conclude, after considering the possibility of further undetected misstatements, that the misstatement, either individually or when aggregated with other misstatements, would clearly be immaterial to the financial statements.

> **TIP:** If a reasonable person could not reach such a conclusion regarding a particular misstatement, that misstatement is *more than inconsequential.*

Q 28.40.3 What is a "material weakness"?

A material weakness is a significant deficiency, or combination of significant deficiencies, that results in more than a remote likelihood that a material misstatement of the annual or interim financial statements will not be prevented or detected. In determining whether a control deficiency or combination of deficiencies is a significant deficiency or a material weakness, the auditor should evaluate the effect of compensating controls and whether such compensating controls are effective. The importance of categorizing a shortcoming as a material weakness is that the SEC requires that management and auditors disclose to the public each material weakness. Thus, an auditor may issue an unqualified opinion only when there are no identified material weaknesses and when there have been no restrictions on the scope of the auditor's work. The existence of a material weakness requires the auditor to express an adverse opinion on the effectiveness of internal control over financial reporting. Significant deficiencies should be disclosed to the Audit Committee and Board of Directors for remediation.

Categorizing Problems

Q 28.40.4 What factors should be considered in categorizing a shortcoming?

- The likelihood that a deficiency, or a combination of deficiencies, could result in a misstatement of an account balance or disclosure, and the magnitude of such a potential misstatement;

- The nature of the financial statement accounts; for example, suspense accounts and related-party transactions involve greater risk;
- The susceptibility of the related assets or liability to loss or fraud; that is, greater susceptibility increases risk;
- The subjectivity, complexity, or extent of judgment required to determine the amount involved (that is, greater subjectivity, complexity, or judgment, like that related to an accounting estimate, increases risk);
- The cause and frequency of known or detected exceptions for the operating effectiveness of a control;
- The interaction or relationship of the control with other controls (that is, the interdependence or redundancy of the control);
- The interaction of the deficiencies (for example, when evaluating a combination of two or more deficiencies, whether the deficiencies could affect the same financial statement accounts, amplifying or compensating for one another);
- The possible future consequences of the deficiency; and
- The dollar amounts or total number of transactions exposed to the deficiency.

Q 28.40.5 What kinds of deficiencies are least likely to be considered significant?

Deficiencies in the following areas are least likely to be considered significant:

(1) Controls over the selection and application of accounting policies that are in conformity with GAAP;
(2) Antifraud programs and controls;
(3) Controls over non-routine and non-systematic transactions; and
(4) Controls over the period-end financial reporting process, including controls over procedures used to enter transaction totals into the general ledger (that is, initiate, authorize, record, and process journal entries into the general ledger and record recurring and nonrecurring adjustments to the financial statements).

Q 28.40.6 What kinds of deficiencies are likely to be considered material?

(1) Restatements of previously issued financial statements to reflect the correction of an error or fraud;
(2) Identification by the auditor of a material misstatement in financial statements in the current period that was not initially found by management; and
(3) Whether the audit committee is evaluated as being ineffective.

Q 28.40.7 What should accompany the disclosure of material weaknesses?

Disclosure of material weaknesses by management should be accompanied by information about plans for remediation and also by contextual information. A disclosure will likely be more useful to investors if management differentiates the potential impact and importance to the financial statements of the various identified material weaknesses, distinguishing those material weaknesses that may have a pervasive impact on internal control over financial reporting from those material weaknesses that do not.

PCAOB Standards

Q 28.41 What is the PCAOB's auditing standard?

On May 24, 2007, the PCAOB adopted Auditing Standard No. 5, which superseded Auditing Standard No. 2. The SEC has published guidance for management in June 2007 generally consistent with Auditing Standard No. 5 and approved the new Auditing Standard in July 2007.[83] Auditing Standard No. 5 is designed to increase the likelihood that material weaknesses in internal control will be found before they result in material misstatement of a company's financial statements, and, at the same time, eliminate procedures that are not necessary. It also focuses the auditor on the procedures necessary to perform a high quality audit that is tailored to the company's facts and circumstances. Here are the four objectives Auditing Standard No. 5 has been designed to achieve:

- Focus the internal control audit on the most important matters with a top-down approach addressing risks of

fraud—it focuses auditors on those areas that present the greatest risk that a company's internal control will fail to prevent or detect a material misstatement in the financial statements;
- Eliminate procedures that are not necessary to achieve the intended benefits—the new standard does not include the previous standard's detailed requirements to evaluate management's own evaluation process and clarifies that an internal control audit does not require an opinion on the adequacy of management's process;
- Make the audit clearly scalable to fit the size and complexity of any company—the new standard includes notes on how to apply the principles in the standard to smaller, less complex companies; and
- Simplify the text of the standard—the new standard is shorter and easier to read.

Q 28.41.1 How important is documentation to an audit?

The PCAOB believes that the quality and integrity of an audit depends, in large part, on the existence of a complete and understandable record of the work the auditor performed, the conclusions the auditor reached, and the evidence the auditor obtained that supports those conclusions. Meaningful reviews, whether by the board in the context of its inspections or through other reviews, such as internal quality control reviews, would be difficult or impossible without adequate documentation.

Documentation

Q 28.42 What is the proper standard for documentation?

A proper standard is reviewability (keeping enough documentation to facilitate an external review). "Audit documentation related to planning, conducting, and reporting on the audit should contain sufficient information to enable an experienced auditor who has had no previous connection with the audit to ascertain from the audit documentation the evidence that supports the auditors' significant judgments and conclusions."[84] An experienced auditor is one who has a reasonable understanding of audit activities and has studied the company's industry as well as the accounting and auditing issues relevant to the industry.

Q 28.42.1 What are the relevant subjects for which management's records should be retained?

- Documenting testing of accounts, details, design of controls, operating effectiveness of controls, including walkthroughs;
- Documenting the inspection of terms and administration of significant contracts or agreements;
- Documenting related to significant complex or unusual transactions, accounting estimates, and uncertainties as well as related management assumptions;
- Sufficient information supporting conclusions of assessment;
- Significant information inconsistent with or contradicting conclusions of assessment;
- Selecting, applying, and consistency of accounting principles, including related disclosures;
- Scheduling of audit adjustments, including the nature and cause of each misstatement;
- Representations and communications between management and auditors;
- Communications with the audit committee;
- Identifying significant deficiencies and, separately, material weaknesses and including bases for determining these items to be deficient.

Continuing SOX Compliance

Q 28.43 What should a company do to sustain SOX compliance?

Beginning the second year of compliance with SOX, three project-like tasks must be given priority:

(1) Correction of material weaknesses reported in existing controls (these are disclosure events, as are the plan and progress for their remediation, and significant deficiencies that could become material weaknesses also need remedial attention);

(2) Establishment of an orderly process to assure that basic controls are in place for all significant locations, activities, and processes and that they are integrated into company-level controls; and
(3) Required quarterly reporting of disclosures of material changes in controls.

Q 28.43.1 What specific expectations does the SEC have regarding companies' ongoing compliance efforts?

Apart from clearing the decks with the foregoing tasks, sustainable compliance is the main task. The SEC envisions compliance as an ongoing, unending *process*, exactly like each of the traditional management functions and processes at a company. Every year, there should be a plan and budget, objectives, and staffing goals for the management of internal controls, just as there are for the managers of manufacturing and the managers of sales.

More specifically:

- The formal permanent organization structure of the issuer includes positions and committees for the oversight of compliance and risk assessment;
- The responsibilities of accounting, finance, information technology, internal audit, legal and general management functions, and personnel for developing, testing, monitoring, and assessing internal controls are specified in great detail and are closely coordinated;
- Adequate increased budget resources are routinely devoted to the work of these internal functions and personnel with respect to disclosure controls (smaller specific tasks will be outsourced to specialists and consultants);
- All employees are trained in their respective personal responsibilities in the compliance process (providing timely and accurate information, reporting mistakes and unauthorized behavior, and suggesting ways to optimize the processing of information);
- Periodic objectives for improving the quality of controls are set, and progress toward their attainment is monitored.

Q 28.43.2 What approach should a company take to achieve "optimization"?

Optimization includes pervasive integration of controls, quantitative monitoring, and feedback leading to continuous process improvement. The culture of the organization promotes continual improvement and change in all its processes, including controls. Management should apply a top-down approach, identifying from its knowledge, experience, and judgment the areas of financial statements for its business most susceptible to risk of material misstatement, and designing and testing controls at those levels. In performing future assessments, management may move back from a focus on individual controls to study the objective for batches of controls, testing their effectiveness in combination in meeting a broad control objective. It need not be the case that every individual step in a complex control is required to be tested in order to determine that the overall control is operating effectively.

Q 28.43.3 What is the advantage of a top-down approach?

A top-down approach prevents a management assessor or an auditor from spending unnecessary time and effort understanding a process or control that does not affect the likelihood that the company's financial statements could be materially misstated. Because of the pervasive effect of company-level controls, in this top-down approach, the auditor tests and evaluates the effectiveness of company-level controls first, because the results of this work will affect the auditor's testing strategy for controls at the process, transaction, and application levels.

Q 28.43.4 What can a company use to augment the top-down approach?

Risk assessment techniques should also be used, by management and auditors alike, in their respective work under SOX 404. A direct relationship is meant to exist between the degree of risk that a material weakness could exist or arise in a particular area of the company and the amount of assessment attention by management and audit attention by the auditor that should be devoted to that area. Identifying and discussing the areas of greatest risk will improve the focus and efficiency of both management's assessment and the auditor's evaluation of internal controls.

Q 28.43.5 What kinds of risk analysis should be used?

Both quantitative and qualitative methods for risk analysis may be applied. For valuing material loss contingencies, quantitative risk analysis identifies various potential outcomes, using a decision tree for example, and assigns to each a probability of occurrence and an estimate of potential loss. Multiplying each potential loss by its probability and summing the results for a given topic (for example, a lawsuit, or a potential dispute) will provide an overall loss expectancy. Events can be ranked by the magnitude of this overall risk expectancy. The obvious limitations of the process are the difficulties of assigning appropriate probabilities and omitting potential outcomes for evaluation.

Disclosure Controls

Q 28.44 What are disclosure controls?

Controls and procedures that are designed to ensure that information required to be disclosed in the reports filed under the Exchange Act is timely recorded, processed, summarized, and reported. Disclosure controls incorporate a broader concept of controls and procedures designed to ensure compliance with disclosure requirements generally. Disclosure controls address the quality and timeliness of disclosure.

Q 28.44.1 What are the certification requirements related to disclosure controls?

In quarterly and annual reports to the SEC on Forms 10-Q and 10-K, respectively, and on amendments to these reports, corporate CEOs and CFOs are each required by SOX section 302 to certify that he or she and the other certifying officers:

(1) are responsible for establishing and maintaining *disclosure controls* and procedures for the issuer and have:
- designed such *disclosure controls* and procedures to ensure that material information relating to the issuer, including its consolidated subsidiaries, is made known to them by others within those entities, particularly during the period in which the periodic reports are being prepared;

- evaluated the effectiveness of the issuer's *disclosure controls* and procedures as of a date within ninety days prior to the filing date of the report ("Evaluation Date"); and
- presented in the report their conclusions about the effectiveness of the *disclosure controls* and procedures based on their evaluation as of the Evaluation Date;

(2) have disclosed, based on their most recent evaluation, to the issuer's auditors and the audit committee of the board of directors (or persons fulfilling the equivalent function):
- all significant deficiencies in the design or operation of internal controls that could adversely affect the issuer's ability to record, process, summarize, and report financial data, and have identified for the issuer's auditors any material weaknesses in internal controls; and
- any fraud, whether or not material, that involves management or other employees who have a significant role in the issuer's internal controls; and

(3) have indicated in the report whether or not there were significant changes in internal controls or in other factors that could significantly affect internal controls subsequent to the date of their most recent evaluation, including any corrective actions with regard to significant deficiencies and material weaknesses.

Q 28.44.2 What exactly must the CEO and CFO certify about the disclosure controls?

An issuer must give reasonable assurance that the disclosure controls and procedures will meet their objectives.[85] If reasonable assurances cannot be given, then the issuer must clarify in Item 307 that the procedures are *designed* to give reasonable assurance.

Q 28.44.3 What is the purpose of disclosure controls?

Disclosure controls exist to require fair presentation in reports, which may require going beyond presenting financial information in conformity with GAAP. The essential elements include whether the accounting principles selected are appropriate in the circumstances and whether the disclosure is informative and reasonably reflects the underlying transactions and events.

Q 28.44.4 Is the procedure for disclosure important?

The SEC has emphasized that the procedure for disclosure is as important as the content of disclosure. In designing their disclosure controls, companies are expected to make judgments regarding the processes on which they will rely to meet applicable requirements. Some companies might design their disclosure controls and procedures so that certain components of internal control over financial reporting pertaining to the accurate recording of transactions and disposition of assets or to the safeguarding of assets are not included. Many companies will design their disclosure controls and procedures so that they do not include all components of internal control over financial reporting.

Q 28.44.5 What should the disclosure contain?

In content and subject matter, disclosure controls should identify and assure discussion of:

(1) known trends or known demands, commitments, events, or uncertainties that will result in or that are reasonably likely to have a material effect on financial condition, operating performance, or result in the registrant's liquidity increasing or decreasing in any material way;

(2) key performance indicators, including non-financial performance indicators, that their management uses to manage the business and that would be material to investors;

(3) a view of the company through the eyes of management, providing both a short- and long-term analysis of the business; and

(4) an assessment and evaluation of operational and regulatory risks may be necessary, along with disclosure of circumstances indicating a material violation of law.

Q 28.44.6 How should a company handle disclosure?

The very breadth of disclosure controls makes it prudent for compliance to be done through a company's disclosure committee, including the general counsel and other executive and financial officers designated as responsible for designing, maintaining, and evaluating disclosure controls. Such a committee should regularly meet with the CEO, CFO, and audit committee. The committee can prioritize its work and delegate responsibility for particular areas of controls.

Q 28.44.7 What should the disclosure controls consist of?

- Self-assessments at company and subordinate levels to identify and describe economic, financial, and operating trends and indicators used by management and to be considered for disclosure by the disclosure committee;
- Assessments by managers with the general counsel and risk assessment personnel of legal and regulatory risks, describing pending, threatened and potential claims, disputes, and proceedings, as well as those circumstances that present potential exposure for the company;
- Assessments and evaluation of contingencies and threats to company assets and operations from natural forces, man-made events (for example, power interruptions and competitors' behaviors);
- Procedures for communicating relevant information in timely fashion to the disclosure committee for review and transmittal to the CEO and CFO and, as appropriate, the audit committee;
- Drafting and review procedures to assure that discussion in proposed disclosure documents of the foregoing is accurate, adequate, and clearly articulated.

Q 28.44.8 How should a company sustain and enhance disclosure controls and enterprise risk management?

The same priority tasks as internal controls are needed beginning the second year of compliance with SOX:

(1) remediation of material weaknesses;
(2) checking the adequacy of disclosure controls for all significant locations, activities, and processes to address any situations neglected in the tumult of initial compliance; and
(3) disclosing material changes in controls and new controls.

The SEC

Q 28.45 How has SOX enhanced the powers of the SEC?

Congress has given the SEC the power to "promulgate such rules and regulations, as may be necessary or appropriate in the public interest or for the protection of investors, and in furtherance of this Act."[86] In addition, and no less sweeping, SEC was given power over the PCAOB. The SEC may review the discipline given by the PCAOB to auditors and accountants registered before it, and may deny them the privilege of practice before the SEC.[87] It may do the same with lawyers.[88] Congress also authorized that any violation of SOX or of the rules of the SEC thereunder and of the PCAOB may be treated as a violation of the Securities Exchange Act of 1934.[89]

Q 28.45.1 How much has the SEC grown under SOX?

Not surprisingly, the enactment of SOX in 2002 resulted in massive increases in budget and personnel at the SEC:

Fiscal Year	Budget (in millions)
2002	$514.0
2003	$745.5
2004	$811.5
2005	$888.0
2006	$888.0
2007	$877.0
2008	$905.3
2009	$960.0
2010	$1,100.0
2011	$1,143.0

Note that after 2005 the budget stabilized. For 2012, the administration has requested budget of $1.407 billion, a substantial increase that includes enlarged enforcement of SOX and also of Dodd-Frank (see endnote 2).

The staff of the SEC has also increased:

Fiscal Year	Number of Employees
2003	3,200
2006	3,600
2011	4,047

The SEC has requested an additional 780 positions for FY 2012.

Q 28.45.2 How has the increased budget affected enforcement?

These resources have permitted an enlarged level of reviews of disclosure reports filed by public companies and of enforcement investigations. In FY 2005, 4,500 reviews of reporting companies' filings were conducted, roughly 38% of all reporting companies; in FY 2006, the same number of companies' filings were examined. The SEC reported in 2006 that it is on track to review the filings of all public companies at least once every three years.

The volume of investigations increased through FY 2004, when the Enforcement Division launched 970 investigations, 375 administrative proceedings, and 260 civil proceedings in federal district courts; subsequently, it has stabilized. In FY 2006, the Enforcement Division conducted 914 investigations, 356 administrative proceedings, and 218 civil proceedings.

Q 28.45.3 Has the SEC expanded into any new areas?

In July 2004, the SEC established its Office of Risk Assessment, reporting to the chairman. That office and the Office of Compliance Inspections and Examinations have been identifying new or resurgent forms of fraud or questionable activities. More recently an upgrade of information technology systems at the SEC has resulted in more than 90% of required forms from regulated persons now being filed electronically. Risk assessment techniques have been integrated into the examination of electronically filed disclosure documents, enhancing the SEC's enforcement and disclosure review programs. As a result of the enactment in late 2010 of Dodd-Frank, the SEC has been instructed by Congress to regulate certain derivatives, hedge funds and other transactions and to increase its investor protection responsibilities.

Private Rights of Action

Q 28.46 Are there any express private rights of action under SOX?

In contrast to its aggressive empowerment of the SEC, Congress largely avoided creating new private causes of action under SOX. Indeed, Congress specifically forswore doing so in SOX section 804. Only two private rights of action were elsewhere established in SOX and neither has yet resulted in extensive litigation:

- SOX section 306 authorizes public companies, and their shareholders, to recover the proceeds from insider trading by officers and directors during pension blackout periods. Subject to a two-year statute of limitations, if an issuer fails to file suit against a violator within sixty days of being asked to do so, shareholders may bring a derivative action for recovery. This section responded to insider trading at Enron but has provoked few lawsuits, as most pension plans include blackout periods applicable to management, directors, and also to all participant employees.
- SOX section 806 protects whistleblowers, providing employees the opportunity for suits to recover compensatory damages, including backpay, and attorney fees for retaliatory termination, demotion, or ill treatment against employees reporting fraudulent conduct (mail fraud, wire fraud, bank fraud, or securities fraud) or giving testimony to state or federal law enforcement agencies. This provision is not limited to securities laws, or to public companies. Employees must first present a claim to the Secretary of

Labor and may not commence litigation until a statutory period has elapsed or the Secretary has undertaken enforcement of the claim. Congress reinforced the private right of action with criminal penalties against those who interfere with whistleblowers.[90]

Q 28.46.1 Did SOX enhance any existing private rights of action?

In SOX section 804, Congress enlarged the statute of limitations applicable to securities litigation claims for "fraud, deceit, manipulation or contrivance" from one year after discovery of facts amounting to fraud to two years, and from three years after the alleged violation took place to five years. It should be noted, however, this amendment does not extend the limitations period for other litigation under the Securities Act, the Investment Companies Act, or the Investment Advisers Act. As a further limit, this amendment applied to actions commenced on or after SOX was enacted and did not revive expired claims.

Q 28.46.2 Does SOX have any effect on private 10b-5 litigation?

SOX affected 10b-5 liabilities in a few ways. Certification by CEOs and CFOs of financial reports under SOX will improve the ability of plaintiffs to allege specific facts that give rise to a strong inference that defendants making false statements acted with scienter. Moreover, the detailed disclosure mandated by SOX, including discussions of material weaknesses and significant deficiencies in internal controls, will provide more information to plaintiffs to identify misleading statements in financial reports and to demonstrate their materiality.

Further, it is likely that the particular standards prescribed for officers and directors in SOX will be imported into additional requirements of fiduciary duties for defendants in shareholder suits, whether in state courts or as ancillary claims to federal securities cases. Faulty or outright false certifications of financial reports by a CEO may have greater traction in proving a breach of fiduciary duty than surmounting the pleading barriers of Rule 10b-5 litigation created by the Private Securities Litigation Reform Act of 1995.[91]

Q 28.46.3 Does SOX create a private right under which investors can file claims against the issuer's attorneys?

The SEC's Rules of Professional Conduct for lawyers apply to attorneys who assist in the preparation of documents filed with the SEC and made public, and prescribe obligations for the attorney. Though this should occur only in the most extreme circumstances, the knowledge possessed by an attorney, and the depth of his or her involvement in drafting and verifying registration statements, annual reports, and similar documents, all the time failing to correct misrepresentations, may implicate that attorney as the speaker making false representations to the public, or causing them to be made through the issuer. This drafting, reviewing, and commenting on a public company's statements was found sufficient to permit the law firm of Vinson & Elkins to be alleged to be a primary violator of the securities laws in the Enron litigation.[92] Quite apart from the risk that lawyers will be alleged to be primary actors and direct participants in private securities fraud cases, there is an additional risk of exposure for secondary actors: Racketeering Criminal Organizations (RICO) claims.

SOX Provisions That Apply to Companies Other Than Issuers

Q 28.47 What are the SOX penalty provisions that apply to also-private companies?

SOX provides new penalties for the destruction, alteration, or falsification of records in federal investigations and bankruptcies. Penalties include up to twenty years' imprisonment, fines, or both.[93] SOX further provides that any person who *attempts* to commit securities law crimes can be punished as if they had committed the crime.[94] SOX also increases the maximum penalty for mail and wire fraud from five to twenty years' imprisonment.[95] In addition, SOX requires that anyone who obstructs or tampers with an official proceeding be fined, imprisoned up to twenty years, or both.[96] Finally, SOX provides for a fine, imprisonment up to ten years, or both for retaliating against any corporate whistleblower.[97]

Q 28.48 What are the SOX record retention requirements that apply to all companies and persons?

SOX requires accountants conducting audits of any issuer to retain all audit or review paperwork for a period of five years. Penalties for violations include imprisonment up to ten years, fines, or both.[98]

Q 28.49 What are SOX's requirements for ERISA and notice of pension-fund blackout periods?

SOX increases penalties for ERISA violations. The maximum penalty for individual violations is increased from a $5,000 to a $100,000 fine and from one year to ten years' imprisonment. The maximum penalty for businesses is increased from a $100,000 to a $500,000 fine.[99] SOX requires employers to give employees thirty days' advance written or electronic notice of any pension-fund blackout period.[100]

Almost-Public Companies

Q 28.50 Does SOX apply to almost-public companies?

In addition to public companies for whom SOX is mandatory, many private companies are almost-public and should carefully consider acting as if SOX is mandatory for themselves, such as:

- private companies preparing for an initial public offering of securities;
- private companies preparing to sell divisions or affiliates to public companies;
- private companies with registered debt or equity securities;
- foreign operations of U.S. public companies;
- U.S. operations of foreign public companies whose securities are traded in the United States.

Q 28.50.1 How does SOX affect almost-public companies?

In order to complete a successful initial public offering, a private company will need to document and demonstrate its corporate governance consistent with SOX and its preparedness for SOX certifications and assessments of its internal controls and disclosures. Likewise, to make a division or part of its operations marketable at the highest price, a private company must consider preparing it for sale to a public company and facilitating the transition for that division to a SOX-compliant environment.

Non-Public Banks and Insurance Companies

Q 28.51 Does SOX cover non-public banks?

SOX applies, of course, to banks that are issuers of securities. Larger banks with assets of $500 million or more, regardless of whether they qualify as issuers, are subject to section 36 of the Federal Deposit Insurance Act and the FDIC's implementing regulations and guidelines. The FDIC's implementing guidelines reference and incorporate SOX provisions relating to auditor independence. Smaller, non-public banks are not subject to most SOX provisions, but the FRB and its fellow financial supervising agencies have long endorsed sound corporate governance practices and existing banking laws and guidelines already require or encourage all banking organizations to adhere to corporate governance and auditing practices that are similar in many respects to those reflected in SOX.

Q 28.52 Does SOX affect non-public insurance companies?

SOX enforcement has spilled over into insurance regulations applicable beyond public companies. For example, in the wake of American International Group's disclosure in April 2005 of finite reinsurance transfers admitted to be improperly accounted for, the New York Insurance Department has adopted and implemented a new rule requiring CEOs in such transactions to certify that legitimate risk transfer occurred, a SOX-like certification.[101] The NAIC promptly thereafter agreed on new model disclosure standards for finite reinsurance transactions for individual states to adopt.

SOX and International Companies

Q 28.53 What problems has SOX caused for international companies?

International public companies have faced very difficult compliance challenges with SOX:

- The adoption of SOX by Congress was done speedily and with little consultation with the European Union (EU) or its Member States, notwithstanding that SOX provisions and implementing rules were broad and clearly would apply to EU companies and EU operations of U.S. companies;
- Corporate governance in the EU's Member States is different structurally and culturally from that found in the United States. For example, directors may be collectively responsible for company management, but are not individually responsible; related-party transactions and off-balance-sheet transactions with special-purpose entities need not be publicly disclosed; further, company law varies among the Member States;
- Accounting principles differ in numerous details between the EU and the United States;
- Audit firms are not required to have the same independence or responsibilities in the EU as in the United States, and EU firms have not been subject to extra-territorial inspection or investigation.

Q 28.53.1 Has the EU responded to SOX with a law of its own?

The EU has recently passed the Eighth Company Law Directive, which prescribes audit committees, with independent members, to hire the auditors, oversee them, and communicate directly with auditors without going through management. Auditors would be given help in resisting inappropriate pressure from management during an audit. Auditors would follow new international auditing standards to be endorsed by the EU Commission; audit firms and staff would undergo compulsory continuing education in the new standards. Auditors and audit firms would undergo quality assurance reviews; audit firms for listed companies would issue annual reports including a description of the audit firm's operations, a governance statement, and a description of the internal quality control system and a confirmation of its effectiveness by the management of the audit firm.

Q 28.53.2   How has the EU coped with SOX?

The EU negotiated with the SEC for exemptions from SOX provisions covering overseas auditors. Particular points of contention have been the imposition on EU auditors of another layer of regulation—by the PCAOB—which was inconsistent with the laws in some EU member states and which could hinder the fulfillment of EU requirements based on emerging international standards. The EU has largely been unsuccessful in obtaining exemptions from SOX, though several provisions have been delayed in their implementation for foreign auditors and public companies.[102] PCAOB authorized itself to assist EU home country regulators in conducting inspections and investigations of auditors registered with PCAOB but located in the EU.

Q 28.53.3   Is there any hope for a convergence of EU and SEC standards?

On April 25, 2006, the EU Council of Ministers adopted the Statutory Audit Directive,[103] which somewhat parallels SOX and strengthens the EU framework of standards and public oversight for the audit profession. It replaces the Eighth Company Law Directive of 1984 (Directive 84/253/EC) and also amends the Fourth and Seventh Company Law Directives (Directives 78/660/EEC and 83/349/EEC) by introducing additional EU rules on the audit of company accounts.

Among other things, the Statutory Audit Directive introduces a requirement that European companies with transferable securities admitted to trading on a regulated market in any EU member state have an audit committee that meets certain requirements and performs certain functions set out in the directive. As to accounting standards, the FASB and the International Accounting Standards Board have aggressively pursued convergence for several years in drafting International Financial Reporting Standards (IFRS), with support from the SEC.[104]

Non-Profit Organizations

Q 28.54 How are non-profit governmental organizations treated under SOX?

Private non-profit organizations are not subject to most SOX requirements. The principal regulation for such organizations has come from the IRS's regulation and monitoring to assure each such organization operates as a legitimate charity, and from state laws and regulations, generally enforced by states' attorneys general, and, to an extent, through private litigation. Federal legislation, however, is likely to be forthcoming to regulate further the governance and financial reporting by non-profit organizations. New SOX-like regulations will likely cover:

(1) financial statements;
(2) Form 990 series tax returns;
(3) executive compensation;
(4) loans;
(5) related-party transactions;
(6) conflicts of interest;
(7) independent directors;
(8) bars to serving on boards of directors; and
(9) protection of whistleblowers.

Q 28.55 Does SOX apply to colleges and universities?

A particularly complex environment for compliance is presented by the subset of non-profits that are colleges and universities. Higher-education institutions are subject only to those sections of SOX applicable to all persons, and not to those portions regulating public companies. However, SOX concepts have permeated a dizzying array of compliance programs that do apply to colleges and universities. Thus, most colleges and universities receive some funding from state or federal agencies for research and programs, for which they are subject to audits and extensive requirements for internal controls.

Notes

1. Pub. L. No. 107-204, 116 Stat. 745 (2002) [hereinafter SOX].
2. 15 U.S.C. § 78c(a)(8). Section 989G of the Dodd-Frank Wall Street Reform and Consumer Protection Act of 2010, Pub. L. No. 111-203, 124 Stat. 1376 (Jan. 5, 2010) [hereinafter Dodd-Frank], permanently exempts public corporations with a market capitalization below $75 million from the internal controls provisions of SOX § 404(b). In April 2011, an SEC staff study required by the same section of Dodd-Frank recommended that public corporations with a market capitalization between $75 and $250 million continue to be subject to SOX § 404(b).
3. SOX §§ 802, 1102.
4. SOX §§ 806, 1107.
5. SOX §§ 897, 902.
6. SOX § 803.
7. SOX § 406. For a sample code see BOSTELMAN, BUCKHOLZ, JR. & TREVINO, PUBLIC COMPANY DESKBOOK (PLI 2009).
8. 17 C.F.R. § 229.406(b). An issuer may adopt separate codes of ethics for different officers. *Id.* §§ 229.406(d), 228.406(d).
9. 17 C.F.R. §§ 229.601(b)(14), 228.601(b)(14), 229.406(c)(2), 228.406(c)(2), 229.406(c)(3), 228.406(c)(3).
10. 17 C.F.R. §§ 228.406(a), 229.406(a).
11. SOX § 301.
12. *See* Standards Relating to Listed Company Audit Committees, SEC Rel. Nos. 33-8820, 34-47654, and IC-26001 (Apr. 9, 2003), 68 Fed. Reg. 18,788 (Apr. 16, 2003).
13. *Id.*
14. 17 C.F.R. § 229.401(h).
15. SOX § 306.
16. SOX § 402.
17. SOX § 403.
18. SOX § 303.
19. SOX § 304. In its first enforcement action under section 304, in July 2009, the SEC filed suit against M.L. Jenkins, former CEO of CSK Auto Corp. (SEC v. Maynard L. Jenkins, Case No. CV 09-1510-PHX-JWS (D. Ariz.), Litigation Rel. No. 21,149A (July 23, 2009)), demanding reimbursement by Mr. Jenkins to the company of more than $4 million in bonuses and stock-sale profits. The SEC complaint alleged that other former executives at the company engaged in accounting fraud that resulted in overstatement of pretax income for 2002 to 2004, requiring subsequent restatements of earnings. It was not alleged that Mr. Jenkins was a participant in, or aware of, the alleged wrongdoing, nor that the funds for which "clawback" was sought were related to the fraud, nor that, absent

the fraud, Mr. Jenkins would have been compensated any differently. In other litigation, no private right of action under section 304 has been found.
  20. 15 U.S.C. § 78u(d).
  21. SOX §§ 303, 1105; see SEC v. Levine, Fed. Sec. L. Rep. ¶ 94,320 (D.D.C. May 8, 2007).
  22. SOX §§ 802, 1102; 18 U.S.C. § 1520.
  23. SOX §§ 804, 805, 807.
  24. SEC v. Parmalat Finanziaria, S.p.A., Case No. 03 CV 10266 (PKC) (S.D.N.Y.); Litigation Rel. No. 18,803 (July 28, 2004); Accounting and Auditing Enforcement Rel. No. 2065 (July 28, 2004); Moore Stephens Chartered Accountants (United Kingdom) and Peter D. Stewart, A Partner, Litigation Rel. No. 18,695 (May 5, 2004); Accounting and Auditing Enforcement Rel. No. 2002 (May 5, 2004).
  25. SOX §§ 806, 1107. For more detailed information, see Moy, Neilan, Blostein & Kelley, *Whistleblower Claims Under the Sarbanes-Oxley Act of 2002, in* UNDERSTANDING THE SECURITIES LAWS 2009, at 573 (PLI Corporate Law & Practice, Course Handbook Series No. 1756, 2009). Whistleblower disclosures are protected when made to law enforcement or public authorities, but not when made to the press. *See* Tides v. Boeing Co., 2011 WL 1651245, 94 Empl. Prac. Dec. ¶ 44,168 (9th Cir. May 3, 2011) (No. 10-35238).
  26. SOX § 806.
  27. 18 U.S.C. § 1513(e).
  28. N.Y. LAB. LAW § 740.
  29. In Free Enter. Fund v. Pub. Co. Accounting Oversight Bd., 130 S. Ct. 3138 (2010), the U.S. Supreme Court found that SEC appointment of members to the PCAOB was lawful and that severing one part of a two-level provision for removal of such members, leaving removal in the hands of the SEC, would avoid a violation of the president's powers; the PCAOB was found otherwise constitutional.
  30. SOX § 201.
  31. 17 C.F.R. § 210.2-01(c)(4)(vi).
  32. 17 C.F.R. § 210.2-01(c)(4)(vii).
  33. 17 C.F.R. § 210.2-01(c)(4)(ix).
  34. SOX §§ 201(h), 202, 205(a).
  35. SOX § 203.
  36. SOX § 105.
  37. SOX § 106.
  38. *See* Rule 2105, Exchange Act Rel. No. 48,180; File No. PCAOB-2003-03 (July 16, 2003).
  39. *See* 17 C.F.R. § 205.2(b).
  40. *See* 17 C.F.R. § 205.2(a)(2).
  41. 17 C.F.R. § 205.3(b)(1).
  42. 17 C.F.R. § 205.5.
  43. 17 C.F.R. § 205.3(b)(2).
  44. SOX § 307.
  45. 17 C.F.R. § 205.3(b)(3), (4).
  46. 17 C.F.R. § 205.3(b)(7).
  47. 17 C.F.R. § 205.5.

48. SOX § 307.
49. SOX § 3; 17 C.F.R. § 205.6.
50. *See* 17 C.F.R. § 201.102(a).
51. 17 C.F.R. § 205.6.
52. 17 C.F.R. § 205.2(e).
53. 17 C.F.R. § 205.2(m).
54. 17 C.F.R. § 205.2(k).
55. 17 C.F.R. § 205.3(c).
56. 17 C.F.R. § 205.1(b).
57. 17 C.F.R. § 205.3(b)(8).
58. 17 C.F.R. § 205.3(b)(9).
59. 17 C.F.R. § 205.3(d).
60. *See* Credit Suisse First Bos. Corp. v. Grunwald, 400 F.3d 1119; Fed. Sec. L. Rep. (CCH) P93,125 (9th Cir. Mar. 2005).
61. *See* SEC v. John E. Isselmann, Jr., Case No. CV 04-1350 MO (D. Or.), Litigation Rel. No. 18,896 (Sept. 24, 2004). *See also* SEC v. Henry C. Yuen, et al., Civil Action No. CV 03-4376 MRP (PLAX) (C.D. Cal.), Litigation Rel. No. 19,047 (Jonathan B. Orlick) (Jan. 21, 2005). *See also* Tonya M. Grindon, *Regulating Ethics: A Review of Recent SEC Enforcement Actions Against Attorneys, in* SECURITIES FILINGS 2009, at 707 (PLI Corporate Law & Practice, Course Handbook Series No. 1767, 2009).
62. COSO refers to The Committee of Sponsoring Organizations (COSO) of the Treadway Commission, author of Internal Control—An Integrated Framework (1992) (the "COSO Report"). The COSO Report provides a widely accepted framework for the development and improvement of internal controls for financial reporting.
63. *See* "Report of Investigation Pursuant to Section 21(a) of the Securities Exchange Act of 1934 and Commission Statement on the Relationship of Cooperation to Agency Enforcement Decisions," Exchange Act Rel. No. 44,969; SEC Accounting and Auditing Enforcement Rel. No. 1470 (Oct. 23, 2001).
64. *See In re* Lucent Technologies, Inc., Litigation Rel. No. 18,715 (May 17, 2004); SEC Accounting and Auditing Enforcement Rel. No. 2016 (May 17, 2004).
65. SOX §§ 302, 906.
66. SOX § 401.
67. 15 U.S.C. § 78m or 15 U.S.C. § 78o(d).
68. 17 C.F.R. § 240.13a-15.
69. 17 C.F.R. §§ 228.10(h)(2) and (4), 229.10(e)(2) (Regs. S-K and S-B).
70. 17 C.F.R. § 244.100(a).
71. 17 C.F.R. § 244.100 (Reg. G), at n.1.
72. SEC v. HealthSouth Corp., 261 F. Supp. 2d 1298 (N.D. Ala. 2003).
73. *See* 17 C.F.R. §§ 240.13a-15(c), 240.15d-15(c).
74. 17 C.F.R. § 240.13a-15(f).
75. *See* COSO, "Internal Control—Integrated Framework" (1992) at "Executive Summary."
76. "PCAOB Rulemaking: Public Company Accounting Oversight Board; Notice of Filing of Proposed Rule on Auditing Standard No. 2, An Audit of Internal Control Over Financial Reporting Performed in Conjunction with an Audit of

Financial Statements," Exchange Act Rel. No. 49,544; File No. PCAOB-2004-03 (Apr. 8, 2004).
77. *See* Securities Act Rel. No. 8183 (Jan. 28, 2003).
78. *See* Item 2-01(c)(4) of Regulation S-X, 17 C.F.R. § 210.2-01(c)(4); Exchange Act § 10A(g).
79. *See* Securities Act Rel. No. 8183 (Jan. 28, 2003).
80. *See* SEC v. Robert Quattrone, et al., Civil Action No. 04-33(SRC) (D.N.J.); SEC Sues 10 Defendants for Securities Fraud Arising from $700 Million Round-Tripping Scheme at Suprema Specialties, Litigation Rel. No. 18,534; SEC Accounting and Auditing Enforcement Rel. No. 1938 (Jan. 7, 2004).
81. *See* Final Rule: Management's Reports on Internal Control over Financial Reporting and Certification of Disclosure in Exchange Act Periodic Reports, Securities Act Rel. No. 8238, Exchange Act Rel. 47,986 (June 11, 2003), at 15.
82. PCAOB's Audit Standard No. 2.
83. Commission Guidance Regarding Management's Report on Internal Control Over Financial Reporting Under Section 13(a) or 15(d) of the Securities Exchange Act of 1934 (SEC Rel. Nos. 33-8810, 34-55929, FR-77; File No. S7-24-06; June 20, 2007); Exchange Act Rel. No. 56,152 (July 27, 2007).
84. U.S. General Accounting Office, Government Auditing Standards, "Field Work Standards for Financial Audits" (2003 Revision), ¶ 4.22.
85. *See* Item 307 of Regulations S-K and S-B (Forms 10K) and Item 15 of Form 20-F and General Instruction B(6) to Form 40-F.
86. SOX § 3.
87. SOX §§ 107(c), 602.
88. SOX § 307.
89. SOX § 3(b).
90. SOX § 1107.
91. Pub. L. No. 104-67, 109 Stat. 737 (2004).
92. *See* Judge Harmon's denial of a motion to dismiss complaint as against Vinson & Elkins in *In re* Enron Corp. Sec., Derivative & ERISA Litig., 235 F. Supp. 2d 549, 704–05 (S.D. Tex. 2002).
93. SOX § 802(a) (codified at 18 U.S.C. §§ 1519–20).
94. SOX § 902(a) (codified at 18 U.S.C. § 1349).
95. SOX § 903(a)–(b) (codified at 18 U.S.C. §§ 1341, 1343).
96. SOX § 1102 (codified at 18 U.S.C. § 1512).
97. SOX § 1107(a) (codified at 18 U.S.C. § 1513(e)).
98. SOX § 306(b) (codified at 29 U.S.C. § 1021(i)).
99. SOX § 904 (codified at 29 U.S.C. § 1131).
100. SOX § 306 (codified at 29 U.S.C. § 1021).
101. *See* "AIG reinsurance problems likely to spur vast changes in industry practices, experts say," A.M. Best Co. "Bestwire" (Apr. 11, 2005).
102. *See, e.g.*, the PCAOB's Final Rules Relating to the Oversight of Non-U.S. Public Accounting Firms, PCAOB Rel. No. 2004-005 (June 9, 2004), in which the PCAOB agreed it may—but need not—rely on a European home country for inspections or investigations of auditors in the EU.

103. Council Directive 2006/43/EC, of the European Parliament and of the Council of 17 May 2006 on statutory audits of annual accounts and consolidated accounts, amending Council Directives 78/660/EEC and 83/349/EEC and repealing Council Directive 84/253/EEC (Text with EEA relevance), 2006 O.J. (L 157) 87–107, *available at* http://eur-lex.europa.eu/LexUriServ/LexUriServ.do?uri=OJ:L:2006:157:0087:01:EN:HTML.

104. *See* Concept Release on Allowing U.S. Issuers To Prepare Financial Statements in Accordance with International Financial Reporting Standards (Aug. 14, 2007), 72 Fed. Reg. 45,600. For recent developments, see www.IFRS.com.

# 29

The Law and Accounting:
The Convergence of Sarbanes-Oxley, COSO, the Federal Sentencing Guidelines, and *Caremark* Duties

*James D. Wing**

> Risk assessment, internal controls, and legal compliance are each essential components of a multi-faceted and inter-dependent process. Their goal is to ensure that the firm's objectives are met and its assets—including its brand—are safeguarded. Controls cannot be viewed as a segregated "bolt-on" process of compliance supervision and therefore solely a concern of external and internal audit. The companies that have been most successful in dealing with this are the ones that have made these principles part of every business unit manager's job description, so that the concepts are essentially driven into the firm's DNA.

---

* The author wishes to acknowledge Christopher A. Myers and Kwamina Thomas Williford for their contributions to this chapter.

The Federal Sentencing Guidelines and the Committee of Sponsoring Organizations of the Treadway Commission (COSO) frameworks, with their emphasis on careful risk assessment and design of appropriate internal control processes, share many attributes. As a result, their principles inform developing law allocating civil responsibility for breach of fiduciary duty by directors and officers due to violation of these standards. Civil, criminal, and regulatory law are converging.

Sarbanes-Oxley Act of 2002.. 976
Committee of Sponsoring Organizations of the
    Treadway Commission... 978
Reactions to SOX.. 981
    Effects of Financial Collapse... 983

Sarbanes-Oxley Act of 2002

Q 29.1   Is the Sarbanes-Oxley Act of 2002 (SOX)[1] primarily aimed at improving corporate governance and legal compliance?

Partly yes, and partly no. While legal compliance and improved corporate governance were certainly desired results of SOX, they are only subsets of the underlying and primary objective: improving the accuracy and reliability of financial reporting for investors and the public.

Q 29.1.1   How did SOX try to accomplish its goal?

First, by restructuring the entire accounting profession and its oversight so that accounting firms were no longer permitted to sell to their audit clients consulting and other non-audit services like IT implementations. Putting this in terms familiar to lawyers, it was the equivalent of the federal government's abolishing state bar association oversight of large law firms, putting them under the control and supervision of a federal regulator (here, the Public Company Accounting Oversight Board (PCAOB))—and then decreeing that any law firm that does SEC work for a client may no longer represent it in litigation, real estate, employment work, and just about everything else. The constitutionality of the law establishing the PCAOB has been upheld.[2]

Q 29.1.2   What prompted Congress to act?

In the wake of Enron, WorldCom, and other large frauds and audit failures, Congress felt that the quality and reliability of audits no longer met the expectations of public investors and the business community, not to mention juries. To improve the security of, and trust in, our capital markets, Congress decided to reduce potential conflicts of interest that it perceived had driven down the quality of audits. Needless to say, this "revolution" was not entirely bad for auditors; it increased their professional visibility and incomes and made it easier for them to jettison high-risk clients.

Q 29.1.3   What was the precise mechanism Congress used?

In addition to the conflict of interest provisions of SOX section 201, SOX section 404 directed the SEC to prescribe rules requiring each public company's annual report to contain an "internal control report." This report required management to assume responsibility for the firm's "internal control structure and procedures for financial reporting" and each year assess their effectiveness. The SEC implemented this directive by rule.[3] The term "internal controls over financial reporting" had a variety of meanings in different contexts. The SEC rule adopted a definition. At substantially the same time, the PCAOB created Auditing Standard No. 2. That standard required accounting firms to audit in a single integrated audit not only management's financial statements, but also the accuracy of management certifications as to the state of the company's internal financial controls and procedures. A subsequent Auditing Standard No. 5 reaffirmed the definition, while adopting an approach that reduced the scope and cost of section 404 audits.

Committee of Sponsoring Organizations of the Treadway Commission

Q 29.2 What is COSO?

COSO is the "Committee of Sponsoring Organizations of the Treadway Commission," established in 1985 by the private sector. The sponsoring organizations included the American Institute of Certified Public Accountants, the American Accounting Association, the Institute of Internal Auditors, the Institute of Management Accountants, and the Financial Executives Institute.

In 1992, this committee issued a report entitled "Internal Control—Integrated Framework." The SEC definition of "internal control over financial reporting" adopted the COSO definition: "a process . . . to provide reasonable assurance" that a company's financial statements are correct. This "process," in turn, required a "framework"; and COSO's "Internal Control—Integrated Framework" is the only such U.S. framework that meets the SEC's requirements. Thus, the COSO report was essentially written into the law through the back door.

Q 29.2.1 Does the COSO report relate only to details of financial reporting and concepts of accounting?

The COSO report is broader than that. The "Internal Control—Integrated Framework" document, otherwise known as "COSO I," specifically provides that internal control relates to the achievement of three objectives: "effectiveness and efficiency of operations; reliability of financial reporting; and compliance with applicable laws and regulations." Its fundamental premise is that the essential components for achieving appropriate internal control are:

- a good "control environment" (including the now-famous concept of "tone at the top");
- the adequacy of the company's program for assessing the risks that face the firm generally (including risk of internal fraud);
- the adequacy of the company's "control activities";
- the company's effectiveness at assembling useful and accurate information and its appropriate communication; and
- the company's ability to monitor and document its control activities.

Formally, auditors are only charged with reviewing the three COSO objectives insofar as they relate to the reliability of a company's financial reporting. But where does one draw the line? If a corporation's senior management pays no attention to the assessment of the company's legal risks, how can an auditor opine favorably on the firm's "control environment" and the adequacy of the company's program for assessing its business and operational risks, of which the use and/or dissemination of financial information is only one aspect? For example, in heavily regulated industries, such as healthcare, banking, or government contracting, compliance with complex legal and regulatory requirements may impact the company's right to maintain key contracts, receive payment, or even to remain authorized to conduct business operations. All of these factors could have a significant impact on the accuracy of financial statements. Yet, we are aware of no legal authority that has imposed on a firm's auditors a duty to note in a firm's audit report the absence of, or shortcomings in, a firm's legal compliance processes. Civil liability for failures in legal compliance rests on directors and compliance officers.[4]

Q 29.2.2 Have there been any subsequent developments since the first COSO report?

Yes. In 2001, COSO initiated a project to develop a broader framework that would be readily usable by managements to evaluate and improve their organizations' risk assessment and management practices. The result was a new document (COSO II) entitled "Enterprise Risk Management—Integrated Framework." This document incorporates COSO I and strongly challenges management "to move toward a fuller risk management process."

Three years later, in 2004, the U.S. Sentencing Commission, following a two-year study, issued revised guidance on the elements of an effective compliance and ethics program. Compliance with these guidelines reduces a company's exposure to criminal penalties. As explained in chapter 2, this new guidance incorporates many of the same considerations that led to the SEC's SOX section 404 regulations, as well as the requirements of COSO I and II as they bear on legal compliance.

Q 29.2.3 Is COSO II mandated by law?

No, but any management or board of directors that, having ignored COSO II's precepts, suffers a catastrophic failure or damage to its brand because of failures in legal compliance or internal financial controls is exposed to personal liability.

Q 29.2.4 What does COSO II's integrated framework recommend?

Its definition of "enterprise risk management" facially summarizes what a good management (and board) is supposed to do to safeguard its stakeholders' investments:

> Enterprise risk management is a process, effected by an entity's board of directors, management and other personnel, applied in strategy setting and across the enterprise, designed to identify potential events that may affect the entity, and manage risk to be within its risk appetite, to provide reasonable assurance regarding the achievement of entity objectives.[5]

It is to be applied to a firm's strategic goals, its operations, the reliability of its reporting, and its compliance with applicable laws and regulations.

Q 29.2.5 What are the specific components of COSO II?

They include:

- the company's internal environment/culture (its "tone at the top");
- the imperative for management to deliberately set objectives that are consistent with the entity's risk appetite;
- a formal process to identify events that affect achievement of the objectives;
- a formal process for analyzing and managing the risks that the entity faces;
- a formal process by which management selects the response to those risks; and
- formal attention to the COSO I requirements (namely, having documented policies and procedures, information assembly, and communication practices relevant to those procedures,

and a methodology both for monitoring whether these objectives are being fulfilled and for disciplining those who fail to execute the procedures).

The COSO I concept of internal control over financial reporting thus becomes only a smaller part of this larger risk management picture.

Q 29.2.6   What other principles guide risk management?

Any effective, comprehensive compliance and ethics program that uses the criteria outlined by the Sentencing Commission in its guidance must of necessity also be informed by a thorough risk assessment as the underpinning for the design of appropriate legal policies and procedures/internal controls to address the various risks affecting the organization.

This concept of "risk-based" programs that reduce the risk of violations associated with legal/ethical/regulatory/reputational and other standards is becoming the norm in guidance from a variety of regulatory agencies. The SEC, the Department of Justice, the Health and Human Services Office of Inspector General, the banking regulatory agencies, and others have all promulgated guidance with many of the same components. Companies would be wise to review the guidance documents carefully and design programs of internal control that incorporate portions that are relevant to their businesses.

Reactions to SOX

Q 29.3   Are these principles exclusively applicable to public companies, or do they have broader implications?

In the current environment, questions have frequently been asked why any regulatory organization, bank, or other person that must rely on the accuracy of a company's financial statements would ever be content in accepting a financial statement that is not premised upon the SOX standards. Anecdotal evidence from the marketplace suggests that at least "SOX-lite" audits are frequently demanded by those who do business with substantial non-public private and charitable entities. There are cases in which plaintiffs' lawyers have been able to introduce a management's failure to conform to COSO I and II as evidence of scienter.[6] In civil suits for damages against directors and officers for breach of fiduciary duty, these definitions of good management have been used by courts in measuring whether directors of corporations have engaged in mismanagement or gross negligence. These principles form the basis of so-called *Caremark* claims, which apply equally to public, private, for-profit, and not-for-profit entities.[7]

Q 29.3.1 Isn't there a massive political reaction against this, particularly given the huge cost to companies for instituting these programs?

Many companies, particularly smaller ones, complained that compliance with SOX section 404 is extremely costly and provides very little benefit. The SEC responded to these criticisms by issuing a "Guidance" in June 2007, followed by the adoption of a new Auditing Standard No. 5, to replace Auditing Standard No. 2. The new standard fundamentally restructured the approach to section 404 audits, thereby significantly reducing their scope and cost. Under section Dodd-Frank 989G and a related SEC rule, only large public companies now need comply.

In any case, the principles of COSO I and II, in conjunction with the Federal Sentencing Guidelines, SOX section 404, and developments in the common law of fiduciary duty, all converge on management's assessment of risk to a company's operations, brand value, and reputation as a key element of the accuracy of the company's financial statement assertions. The idea is that a carefully conducted risk assessment of key financial controls will enable management to focus on the areas that actually present significant risk to the organization so that auditors will therefore be able to reduce their audit procedures to focus on those areas. At the same time, corporate boards are mandated to ensure that similar procedures are in place in key areas of legal risk.

Effects of Financial Collapse

Q 29.4 Has the financial collapse of 2007-2008 interrupted recent developments in audits and compliance?

No. The movement toward better-quality audits and better legal compliance continues unabated. The 2009 decision in *In re Citigroup, Inc. Shareholder Derivative Litigation*[8] demonstrates that a well-constructed program of internal financial controls, legal compliance, and business risk assessment and controls serves to insulate corporate boards from personal liability for business losses in the harshest of economic environments.

Notes

1. *See* Sarbanes-Oxley Act of 2002, § 201, amending section 10A of the Securities and Exchange Act of 1934, 15 U.S.C. § 78j-1.
2. Free Enter. Fund v. Pub. Co. Accounting Oversight Bd., 130 S. Ct. 3138 (2010).
3. *See* Securities Act Rel. No. 8238, 17 C.F.R. pts. 210, 228, 229, 240, 249, 270, and 274.
4. *In re* Caremark Int'l, Inc. Derivative Litig., 698 A.2d 959 (Del. Ch. 1996).
5. *See* "Enterprise Risk Management—Integrated Framework Executive Summary," at 3, *available at* www.coso.org.
6. In one case the Department of Justice used alleged deficiencies in a company's compliance program as the basis for claiming that the company had submitted, or caused to be submitted, false claims for payment to the Medicare program with "reckless disregard" for their falsity, even though there was no allegation that upper management had actual knowledge of the improper claims. *See* United States v. Merck-Medco, LLC, 336 F. Supp. 2d 430, 440–41 (E.D. Pa. 2004).
7. *See, e.g., id.*; Caremark Int'l, Inc. Derivative Litig., 698 A.2d 959 (Del. Ch. 1996). Stone *ex rel.* AmSouth Bancorporation v. Ritter, 911 A.2d 362 (Del. 2006); *In re* Am. Int'l Group, Inc., 965 A.2d 763 (Del. Ch. 2009). A comprehensive overview of the development of case law in this area is set out annually in *Business Lawyer*, the magazine for the Business Section of the American Bar Association. The current discussion is found at Paul E. McGreal, *Corporate Compliance Survey*, 65 BUS. LAW. 125 (Nov. 2010).
8. *In re* Citigroup, Inc. S'holder Derivative Litig., 964 A.2d 106 (Del. Ch. 2009).

30

SEC Investigations of Public Companies

*Mitchell E. Herr**

The U.S. Securities and Exchange Commission (SEC or "Commission") is the law enforcement agency specifically charged by Congress with civil enforcement of the federal securities laws.[1] The SEC has authority to investigate all violations of the securities laws by any person or entity it believes may have committed a violation, including individuals, public companies, securities exchanges, broker-dealers, investment advisers, and mutual funds.[2]

This chapter explains how the SEC conducts investigations of public companies and their directors and officers and will help you understand what to expect during the course of such an investigation. While this chapter will help orient a nonspecialist to the process, the defense of an SEC investigation is best directed by an attorney with substantial experience in this specialty practice area.

---

* The author wishes to acknowledge Christopher A. Myers and Jennifer A. Short for their contributions to this chapter.

Overview of SEC Investigations 987
    The Basics 987
    Cooperation in Investigations 991
Related Investigations 999
    Coordination with Other Agencies 999
    Parallel Civil and Criminal Investigations 1000
Directors' and Officers' Policies 1003
    Coverage for Investigation-Related Expenses 1003
    Rescission of Coverage 1004
The Process of an SEC Investigation 1005
Document Requests 1007
    Obligation to Preserve Documents 1007
    Document Requests and Production 1010
    Selective Disclosure of Information to the SEC 1013
Witness Testimony 1015
    SEC Requests for Testimony 1015
    Witness Examination 1017
    Representation by Counsel 1019
    Joint Defense Agreements 1020
Wells Notice and Wells Submission 1022
    Wells Notice 1022
    Wells Submission 1022
    Charges and Remedies 1023
    Table 30-1: Monetary Penalties Against Corporations for
        Securities Violations 1026
    Table 30-2: Monetary Penalties Against Individuals for
        Securities Violations 1030
Settlement Negotiations 1031

Overview of SEC Investigations

The Basics

Q 30.1   What does the SEC investigate?

The SEC will initiate an enforcement investigation of a public company when it has reason to suspect that the company has violated the federal securities laws.[3] For instance, the SEC investigates potential securities fraud—that is, the making of false or misleading statements to the public through a company's financial statements, its periodic public disclosures (such as SEC Forms 10-Q and 10-K), or its press releases.

Today, any public company that restates its financial statements can expect an enforcement inquiry.[4] In recent years, some 25–30% of the SEC's enforcement investigations have concerned financial disclosures by public companies.[5] The SEC also may investigate a public company suspected of violating various other federal securities statutes or SEC regulations such as the registration requirements for the public issuance of new securities, the required disclosure of payments that violate the Foreign Corrupt Practices Act, and the prohibition against the selective disclosure of material information to the marketplace.

Q 30.1.1   What individuals are subject to investigation?

An SEC investigation of a public company typically involves scrutiny of all persons involved in the conduct in question. For example, in an investigation related to a company's financial statements, the SEC will examine the officers involved in the underlying conduct, the officers responsible for the financial statements (such as the Controller and the CFO), and the CFO and CEO who certified those financial statements under sections 302 and 906 of the Sarbanes-Oxley Act of 2002 (SOX).[6]

The SEC views attorneys as "gatekeepers" to our nation's financial markets and increasingly scrutinizes the role of corporate counsel. In a seminal speech in September 2004, the SEC's former Enforcement Director noted that:

> Consistent with SOX's focus on the important role of lawyers as gatekeepers, we have stepped up our scrutiny of the role of lawyers in the corporate frauds we investigate.[7]

Q 30.1.2 Who at the SEC is responsible for conducting investigations?

SEC investigations are conducted by its Division of Enforcement. The Enforcement Division has over 1,200 professional personnel (attorneys, accountants, and other staff) in its Washington, D.C. headquarters and eleven regional offices across the country.[8] Typically, the Enforcement Division office that begins an investigation sees it through to its conclusion, including the settlement or trial of any resulting enforcement action.

As part of efforts to revitalize the Division of Enforcement, in 2009 its newly appointed director, Robert Khuzami, eliminated an entire level of management (Branch Chiefs), allowing the Enforcement Division to devote additional seasoned attorneys to line investigative duties. In early 2010, Director Khuzami created the following specialized units that will focus enforcement efforts in particular areas of the securities laws; each unit is headed by a unit chief and staffed by enforcement personnel who have the relevant expertise.[9]

(1) Asset Management: issues involving investment advisers, investment companies, hedge funds, and private equity funds;
(2) Market Abuse: large-scale market abuses and complex manipulation schemes by institutional traders and market professionals;
(3) Structured and New Products: complex derivatives and financial products including credit default swaps, collateralized debt obligations, and securitized products;
(4) Foreign Corrupt Practices: violations of the Foreign Corrupt Practices Act, which prohibits U.S. companies from bribing foreign officials; and
(5) Municipal Securities and Public Pensions: issues concerning offering and disclosure fraud, tax or arbitrage-driven fraud, pay-to-play and public corruption violations, and pension accounting, disclosure, valuation, and pricing fraud.

It remains unclear how these specialized units will interact with the SEC's existing supervisory and reporting structure or how they will be staffed, but it is evident that these five areas will receive priority focus from the Enforcement Division.

Q 30.1.3   What triggers an SEC investigation?

The Enforcement Division obtains investigatory leads from a wide variety of sources including electronic and traditional news media, investor complaints, tips and bounty requests,[10] internal referrals from other SEC offices,[11] and referrals from self-regulatory organizations and other state and federal law enforcement and regulatory authorities. At the same time that the Enforcement Division established the five specialized units, it established an Office of Market Intelligence, responsible for the collection, analysis, and monitoring of the tens of thousands of tips, complaints, and referrals ("TCR") received by the SEC every year.[12] In September 2010 congressional testimony, Director Khuzami reported that the office is staffed with market surveillance specialists, accountants, attorneys, other support personnel, and an embedded FBI Special Agent. Director Khuzami further reported that the office is developing a centralized information technology system for tracking, analyzing, and reporting on the handling of TCRs. The office's TCR database is intended to help the division identify newly emerging techniques and trends in securities fraud, allowing the Enforcement Division to identify misconduct as early as possible in the life-cycle of a fraudulent scheme.[13]

Likewise, more frequent periodic reviews of corporate filings by the Division of Corporation Finance have led to an increased number of referrals to the Enforcement Division. Section 408 of SOX requires the SEC to review a public company's disclosures at least once every three years, which is considerably more frequently than in the past. In fiscal year 2006, the SEC reviewed the public filings of 4,485 (33%) public companies.

> **COMPLIANCE FACT**
>
> The SEC's 2011 budget request notes that it expects to receive over 85,000 investor complaints, tips, and forwarded email spam, and to open about 1,528 matters under inquiry (MUIs). The majority of these MUIs will become enforcement investigations. According to its 2011 budget request, the SEC expects to open roughly 1,258 enforcement investigations.[14] It is difficult to quantify what percentage of SEC investigations result in enforcement actions.[15]

Q 30.1.4 What is the difference between a "preliminary" investigation and a "formal" investigation?

The SEC may gather facts and make a charging decision either through a "preliminary" (or "informal") investigation or through a "formal" investigation. Both are serious. Indeed, preliminary investigations that never reach the formal stage still often result in SEC enforcement charges.

At the preliminary investigation stage, requests for documents or witness testimony are voluntary.[16] Of course, given the SEC's emphasis on cooperation, a corporation is likely to conclude that it is in its interests to respond to the staff's voluntary requests.

When the staff wants authority to subpoena documents or take witness testimony, it obtains a Formal Order of Investigation.[17] The Commission has delegated authority to approve Formal Orders of Investigation to the Director of the Division of Enforcement; this authority was sub-delegated to senior officers.[18] Under this delegated authority, the enforcement staff can obtain a Formal Order of Investigation within one day. The Director of Enforcement also has delegated authority to file an action in federal district court to enforce such subpoenas.[19]

Under the Commission's Rules Relating to Investigations, a person who is compelled to produce documents or testify has the right to be shown the Formal Order of Investigation; however, furnishing a copy of the formal order rests in the discretion of senior enforcement personnel.[20]

COMPLIANCE TIP

When compelled to produce documents or testify, it is useful to request a copy of the Formal Order of Investigation, as it may give some insight into the staff's concerns. However, while the formal order indicates the staff's concerns at the time it was issued, the staff subsequently may develop investigatory concerns that are not reflected in the formal order.

Q 30.1.5   Are all SEC investigations private?

Regardless of whether they are preliminary or formal, all SEC investigations are "non-public," meaning that neither the Commission nor the staff should acknowledge or comment on the investigation unless and until charges are brought.

However, parties under investigation may, and are sometimes obligated to, disclose the pendency of the investigation. SEC disclosure counsel may advise disclosing the investigation in the company's SEC filings, and companies may have to disclose the SEC investigation in response to other regulatory matters or in response to requests for proposals.

Cooperation in Investigations

Q 30.2   What are a company's obligations to its SEC defense counsel?

The company must be entirely candid with its SEC defense counsel. Counsel cannot adequately defend the company's interests (or the interests of its directors, officers, or employees) without the benefit of the complete, unvarnished truth.

It is critical that counsel know all of the relevant facts from the beginning. The company's SEC defense counsel may need to make certain factual representations to the SEC early in the investigation. If these representations turn out to be less than 100% accurate, the company will lose credibility and possibly be branded as uncooperative or obstructive. Thus, the company should disclose the full and complete truth—including facts that may be inconvenient or embarrassing—to its SEC defense counsel.

Q 30.3 What role does cooperation play in SEC enforcement investigations?

The SEC has stressed repeatedly the need for cooperation with its investigations. In its October 23, 2001 "Report of Investigation Pursuant to Section 21(a) of the Securities Exchange Act of 1934 and Commission Statement on the Relationship of Cooperation to Agency Enforcement Decisions" (the "Seaboard Report"),[21] the SEC articulated the role of self-policing, self-reporting, remediation, and cooperation with its investigations in its enforcement decisions relating to corporate actors.

In order to give proper consideration to a company's cooperation or lack thereof, senior Enforcement Division staff have publicly stated that the division keeps a running "scorecard" of cooperation during an investigation.

In an April 29, 2004 speech, the SEC's Director of Enforcement explained how cooperation can lead to more favorable outcomes for companies:

> The ... core factor, which will often prove decisive in our analysis [regarding what, if any, penalty to seek], is the extent of a violator's cooperation, as measured by the standards set forth in the Commission's 21(a) Report. ... [T]he provision of extraordinary cooperation ... including self reporting a violation, being forthcoming during the investigation, and implementing appropriate remedial measures (including, in the case of an entity, appropriate disciplinary action against culpable individuals), can contribute significantly to a conclusion by the staff that a penalty recommendation should be more moderate in size or reduced to zero.[22]

Similarly, in a January 4, 2006 statement concerning financial penalties, the SEC reiterated that "[t]he degree to which a corporation has . . . cooperated with the investigation and remediation of the offense, is a factor that the Commission will consider in determining the propriety of a corporate penalty."[23]

Q 30.4 What are the potential benefits of cooperation with the SEC?

In many instances, cooperation with an SEC investigation undoubtedly has mitigated what otherwise would have been a harsher outcome for the corporation. Of course, when the SEC believes that a corporate actor has been affirmatively uncooperative, it will mete out even harsher penalties than might otherwise be warranted by the underlying conduct.[24]

In the matter that gave rise to the Seaboard Report, the SEC refrained from taking any enforcement action against the company in light of its complete cooperation with the SEC investigation. As the SEC explained:

> We are not taking action against the parent company, given the nature of the conduct and the company's responses. Within a week of learning about the apparent misconduct, the company's internal auditors had conducted a preliminary review and had advised company management who, in turn, advised the Board's audit committee, that Meredith had caused the company's books and records to be inaccurate and its financial reports to be misstated. The full Board was advised and authorized the company to hire an outside law firm to conduct a thorough inquiry. Four days later, Meredith was dismissed, as were two other employees who, in the company's view, had inadequately supervised Meredith; a day later, the company disclosed publicly and to us that its financial statements would be restated. The price of the company's shares did not decline after the announcement or after the restatement was published. The company pledged and gave complete cooperation to our staff. It provided the staff with all information relevant to the underlying violations. Among other things, the company produced the details of its internal investigation, including notes and transcripts of interviews of Meredith and others; and it did not invoke the attorney-client privilege, work

product protection or other privileges or protections with respect to any facts uncovered in the investigation.

The company also strengthened its financial reporting processes to address Meredith's conduct—developing a detailed closing process for the subsidiary's accounting personnel, consolidating subsidiary accounting functions under a parent company CPA, hiring three new CPAs for the accounting department responsible for preparing the subsidiary's financial statements, redesigning the subsidiary's minimum annual audit requirements, and requiring the parent company's controller to interview and approve all senior accounting personnel in its subsidiaries' reporting processes.[25]

The Seaboard Report describes a level of self-policing, self-reporting, remediation, and cooperation that only a few companies have been able to achieve. The SEC has made clear that only the most complete cooperation will warrant a pass from any enforcement action.

Q 30.5 What are the potential benefits to an individual of cooperation with the SEC?

Although the SEC articulated standards for corporate cooperation in its October 2001 Seaboard Report, the SEC had not systematically addressed the question of individual cooperation. This led many practitioners to question whether the SEC would give cooperating individuals appropriate credit. In January 2010, the Commission issued a formal policy statement on individual cooperation that set forth the analytical framework the Commission will use to balance the tension between the objectives of holding individuals fully accountable for their misconduct and providing incentives for individuals to cooperate with law enforcement.

The framework sets forth four considerations that the SEC will examine:

(1) the assistance provided, which will include the quality of the information divulged and the amount of time and resources saved as a result of the cooperation;

(2) the nature of the individual's cooperation, including whether it was voluntary and whether the revealed information was requested or might not have been otherwise discovered;
(3) the importance of the underlying matter, including the character and importance of the investigation and the dangers to investors from the violations; and
(4) the societal interest in holding the individual accountable, including the severity of the individual's misconduct and the culpability of the individual.[26]

This framework signals the Commission's clear intent to appropriately reward individuals who cooperate with its enforcement investigations. The Enforcement Division is implementing the Commission's cooperation policy through a cooperation initiative that Director Khuzami has stated "has the potential to be a game-changer for the Enforcement Division."[27] The Enforcement Division's new January 2010 *Enforcement Manual*[28] sets forth five cooperation tools that offer a spectrum of relief:

- proffer agreements;
- cooperation agreements;
- deferred prosecution agreements;
- non-prosecution agreements; and
- immunity requests.

In employing each of these tools, the manual directs the staff to apply the analytic framework for cooperation described above.

Q 30.5.1   What is a proffer agreement?

A proffer agreement is an agreement with the Enforcement Division that a person's statements on a specific date will not be used against him by the Commission except as a source of investigative leads, impeachment, or rebuttal if he later testifies inconsistently. The staff is directed to use a proffer agreement first to determine whether the individual has information that is sufficiently worthwhile to offer any of the following more valuable cooperation tools. A proffer agreement offers the least amount of relief.

Q 30.5.2   ... a cooperation agreement?

A cooperation agreement is a written agreement with the division in which the division agrees to recommend to the Commission that the cooperator receive credit for cooperation in the enforcement action; in some cases, the division may even make specific enforcement recommendations. Cooperation agreements do not formally bind the Commission.

Q 30.5.3   ... a deferred prosecution agreement?

A deferred prosecution agreement is a written agreement with the Commission in which it agrees to forego an enforcement action if the cooperator complies with express prohibitions or undertakings during a specified period of time, generally not to exceed five years. Deferred prosecution agreements and non-prosecution agreements formally bind the Commission.

Q 30.5.4   ... a non-prosecution agreement?

A non-prosecution agreement is a written agreement in which the Commission agrees not to bring an enforcement action against the cooperator; the *Enforcement Manual* notes that such an agreement will almost never be proper for a recidivist and should not be entered at an early stage of the litigation. A non-prosecution agreement offers the greatest credit with respect to potential SEC civil liability.

Q 30.5.5   ... an immunity request?

The division's ability to encourage cooperation by individuals was further enhanced by the Commission's delegation to it of authority to seek immunity from criminal prosecution from the DOJ. With this authority, the Enforcement Division can offer a potential cooperator the prospect of immunity from federal criminal prosecution as well as specified relief from SEC civil liability.

CASE STUDY: *Homestore, Inc.*

In a 2002 investigation involving Homestore, Inc. and some of its senior executives, the SEC declined to pursue charges against the company, explaining that it

> would not bring any enforcement action against Homestore because of its swift, extensive and extraordinary cooperation in the Commission's investigation. This cooperation included reporting its discovery of possible misconduct to the Commission immediately upon the audit committee's learning of it, conducting a thorough and independent internal investigation, sharing the results of that investigation with the government (including not asserting any applicable privileges and protections with respect to written materials furnished to the Commission staff), terminating responsible wrongdoers, and implementing remedial actions designed to prevent the recurrence of fraudulent conduct. These actions, among others, significantly facilitated the Commission's expeditious investigation of this matter.[29]

🏛 CASE STUDY: *Putnam Fiduciary Trust Co.*

On January 3, 2006, the SEC announced it was filing charges against six former officers of Putnam Fiduciary Trust Company (PFTC), but said that it would not pursue PFTC "because of its swift, extensive and extraordinary cooperation" in the investigation. PFTC's cooperation consisted of:

> prompt self-reporting, an independent internal investigation, sharing the results of that investigation with the government (including not asserting any applicable privileges and protections with respect to written materials furnished to the Commission staff), terminating and otherwise disciplining responsible wrongdoers, providing full restitution to its defrauded clients, paying for the attorneys' and consultants' fees of its defrauded clients, and implementing new controls designed to prevent the recurrence of fraudulent conduct.[30]

🏛 CASE STUDY: *Apple, Inc.*

On April 24, 2007, the SEC filed charges against two former officers of Apple, Inc. for backdating stock options, but specifically stated that it:

> would not bring any enforcement action against Apple based in part on its swift, extensive, and extraordinary cooperation in the Commission's investigation. Apple's cooperation consisted of, among other things, prompt self-reporting, an independent internal investigation, the sharing of the results of that investigation with the government, and the implementation of new controls designed to prevent the recurrence of fraudulent conduct.[31]

Related Investigations

Coordination with Other Agencies

Q 30.6 Does the SEC coordinate investigations with other law enforcement authorities?

Yes; the SEC can share investigative information and coordinate its efforts with any number of foreign, federal, state, and local criminal, civil, or regulatory agencies.[32] In the post-Enron era, it has become commonplace for the SEC to coordinate its investigations with other law enforcement authorities, both civil and criminal. In recent years, there has been approximately a 400% increase in the number of SEC investigations that are coordinated with criminal authorities.[33]

Of the recent major securities fraud cases, most have been prosecuted both civilly and criminally:

- WorldCom
- Enron
- Qwest
- HealthSouth
- Adelphia Cable
- Rite Aid
- AIG/GenRe
- ImClone/Martha Stewart
- Tyco
- Comverse
- Brocade

Active coordination with enforcement authorities is not limited to major corporate fraud cases. For instance, in the spring of 2007, the SEC announced that it, the U.S. Attorney's Office, and the FBI had investigated and filed civil and criminal charges related to an alleged insider trading ring.[34]

The SEC also coordinates its investigations with various civil authorities. For instance, in 2006, the SEC jointly announced with the Office of Federal Housing Enterprise Oversight (OFHEO) that Fannie Mae had agreed to pay a $400 million penalty to settle fraud charges. The SEC acknowledged the assistance of OFHEO in the investigation.[35] Similarly, in the spring of 2007, the SEC announced a trading suspension of thirty-five companies allegedly engaged in email spam campaigns. In that case, the SEC thanked the National Association of Securities Dealers, the Royal Canadian Mounted Police, the British Columbia Securities Commission, and the Ontario Securities Commission for their assistance with the investigation.[36]

The SEC continues to increase its coordination with criminal authorities, having hired former federal criminal prosecutors to fill key positions in the Enforcement Division, including the new Director of the Division of Enforcement and his Deputy, as well as the heads of the SEC's New York City and Miami regional offices. With the Enforcement Division now staffed at key levels by former federal criminal prosecutors, 2009 saw increased coordination with criminal authorities and other regulators in approximately 75% of the SEC's highest-priority cases.[37] Consistent with this increase in coordination with criminal authorities, the SEC joined the DOJ, Treasury, and HUD in November 2009 in announcing the establishment of a Financial Fraud Enforcement Task Force.

The SEC's coordination with criminal prosecutors has also resulted in the employment of new tools to combat securities fraud. For instance, the Galleon hedge fund insider trading ring case of 2009 marked the first time that criminal authorities (working closely with the SEC) used wiretaps (which previously had been reserved for investigating organized crime and narcotics cases) to investigate insider trading.[38]

Parallel Civil and Criminal Investigations

Q 30.6.1 Do parallel civil and criminal investigations present additional risks?

The prospect of coordination between the SEC and other prosecutorial or regulatory authorities substantially increases the complexity of and risks attendant to an SEC investigation. The risks are often difficult to assess because, as a policy matter, the SEC will not confirm or deny whether parallel investigations are being conducted, but will direct counsel to inquire with whatever other prosecutorial authority she may be concerned about.[39] Additionally, in many cases the SEC will conclude its investigation and resulting enforcement action before the first sign of any criminal interest in the matter becomes visible.

As a practical matter, if the circumstances might be attractive to a criminal prosecutor (for example, if there is intentionally fraudulent conduct and significant investor losses), a company's safest course is to assume that there is or will be a parallel criminal investigation. In these circumstances, SEC defense counsel will often bring white-collar criminal defense counsel into the matter to help navigate the many difficult issues raised by parallel civil and criminal investigations.[40]

Q 30.6.2 Must the government disclose that there are parallel civil and criminal investigations?

It is well accepted that the government may conduct parallel investigations of conduct that potentially violates both the civil and criminal laws.[41] Still, the courts have long held that the "[g]overnment may not bring a parallel civil proceeding and avail itself of civil discovery devices to obtain evidence for subsequent criminal production."[42] An April 4, 2008, decision by the Ninth Circuit,[43] however, holds that the government has extremely wide latitude in conducting parallel investigations. Under the Ninth Circuit's reasoning:

- The government may use the SEC investigation as a stalking horse to obtain information for use in the criminal prosecution as long as it does not engage in outright deceit.
- SEC Form 1662 provides sufficient notice of the possibility of criminal prosecution, even if the government actively conceals that a criminal investigation is underway.
- If the SEC investigation is commenced first, no amount of criminal involvement with that investigation will justify a finding that the SEC investigation is being used impermissibly to obtain evidence for the criminal prosecution.

In practice, the Ninth Circuit decision makes it very difficult for defendants to successfully argue that the government's conduct of an undisclosed parallel criminal investigation violated their rights.

> **COMPLIANCE TIP**
>
> In any SEC investigation of conduct that might be of interest to a criminal prosecutor (all securities violations are *potentially* criminally prosecutable), defense counsel must assume that there is a parallel criminal investigation. Accordingly, defense counsel and their clients must make informed decisions as to whether witnesses should waive their Fifth Amendment rights and whether counsel should reveal defense theories to the SEC.

Q 30.6.3 Will both the criminal and civil proceedings proceed simultaneously?

Often, the government will announce joint civil and criminal prosecutions, only to move to stay the civil case to prevent the defendant from using civil discovery to gain a purportedly unfair advantage in the criminal matter in which it would not otherwise have broad discovery rights. Some federal courts have criticized this practice, holding that the usual rationales in favor of staying a civil case in favor of a pending criminal proceeding do not apply where the government has initiated both the civil and criminal proceedings.[44] For instance, in *SEC v. Saad*, in denying the government's motion to stay the SEC's civil case, the court observed that it was:

> strange[ ] . . . that the U.S. Attorney's Office, having closely coordinated with the SEC in bringing simultaneous civil and criminal actions against some hapless defendant, should then wish to be relieved of the consequences that will flow if the two actions proceed simultaneously.[45]

Directors' and Officers' Policies

Coverage for Investigation-Related Expenses

Q 30.7 **Can we rely on directors' and officers' policies to cover the costs of responding to an SEC investigation?**

A company's directors' and officers' (D&O) policy potentially could cover the costs of defending an SEC investigation that extends to an insured person.[46] Whether such coverage exists will depend on the precise policy language and, possibly, the type of investigation at issue. Covered "claims" under some policies may not include government investigations, and most policies exclude coverage for preliminary investigations.[47] Because coverage might exist, the company should give timely notice to its D&O carriers, including all excess layer carriers.

SEC investigations often proceed simultaneously with related shareholder litigation. When they do, both defenses become inextricably intertwined. For instance, the document productions will overlap, and inadequate preparation of witnesses for SEC testimony can create an evidentiary record that could prejudice the defense of the shareholder litigation. In these circumstances, at least some of the expenses related to the SEC investigation might be covered under policy language that defines a claim to include "costs, charges, and expenses incurred . . . *in connection with* any Claim."

COMPLIANCE TIP

Coverage questions can be complex. Even if, on the face of the policy, an SEC investigation does not appear to be covered, a company may have substantial arguments in favor of coverage. Thus, the company should engage an expert in D&O coverage issues to review its policies at the outset of the SEC investigation.

Q 30.7.1 What kinds of expenses related to an enforcement action might not be covered by a D&O policy?

D&O coverage might not extend to all of the relief that the SEC could seek in an enforcement action. For instance, many D&O policies do not cover penalties (in general, D&O policies do not cover fines, and many policies do not cover punitive damages) or disgorgement of ill-gotten gains. Likewise, many policies exclude coverage for intentional misconduct, fraud, dishonest or criminal acts, or acts that were undertaken for personal profit. But, because these exclusions do not apply unless there has been a final adjudication by a finder of fact (such as a judge or jury), defense costs incurred before a final adjudication should be covered.

Rescission of Coverage

Q 30.7.2 What other D&O policy issues/considerations are raised by SEC investigations?

The conduct underlying an SEC investigation can give rise to a risk that the company's D&O coverage may be rescinded. D&O new policy applications often require the company's officers to make representations concerning their knowledge of wrongful acts. If the SEC's investigation uncovers evidence that the officer who signed the application committed (and, therefore, was aware of) wrongful acts that were not disclosed on the application, the carrier may have grounds to rescind the D&O policy.

There is also a rescissionary risk if the company restates its financial statements. Because the carrier is, to some extent, underwriting the ability of the company to indemnify its directors and officers, the carrier will argue that it relied upon the company's financial statements (whether attached to the new policy application or filed with the SEC before a policy renewal) in determining whether to underwrite the risk. If the financials are restated, the carrier could argue that the original (but now admittedly incorrect) financial information was material to its underwriting decision, meaning that there was no "meeting of the minds" and, hence, no valid contract for insurance.

Q 30.7.3 How can we mitigate the risks of rescission of our D&O policy?

Consider obtaining expert assistance to negotiate the policy with a view to minimizing these above-described exclusions and rescissionary risks. Furthermore, be aware that, under the cooperation clause of most D&O policies, carriers can demand that their insureds turn over information relating to the SEC investigation. Because such information potentially could give rise to grounds for rescission, and because, moreover, providing such information to the carrier could waive the attorney-client privilege or work-product immunity, potentially prejudicing the company's defense of the SEC investigation as well as any shareholder or derivative action, your company must walk a fine line between sufficiently cooperating with its carrier to maintain coverage and not handing the carrier grounds to rescind the policy or prejudicing its defenses to the underlying action through a privilege waiver.

The Process of an SEC Investigation

Q 30.8 How is an SEC investigation conducted?

Typically, SEC investigations follow a predictable course:

- document requests;
- witness testimony;
- Wells Notice and Wells Submission;
- settlement negotiations.

Document requests. Most SEC investigations of public companies begin with a request for documents.[48] In an investigation of any consequence, the SEC likely will make several sets of document requests.

Witness testimony. If the SEC, after reviewing the company's document productions, continues to have an investigatory interest in the company, it will request sworn witness testimony.

Wells Notice and Wells Submission. After witness testimony has been completed, the SEC's investigative staff will review the evidentiary record to determine whether to recommend that the Commission institute charges. If the staff tentatively decides to make an enforcement recommendation to the Commission, in non-emergency cases it issues (typically by telephone and follow-up letter) a so-called Wells Notice to the proposed defendant.[49] The proposed defendant is given an opportunity (typically about three weeks) to respond with a Wells Submission—a memorandum or videotape explaining its position.

Settlement negotiations. If defense counsel does not succeed in convincing SEC staff that no enforcement action is warranted, counsel typically will engage the staff in settlement discussions to determine whether the matter can be resolved on mutually agreeable terms.

Q 30.8.1 Has the SEC disclosed how it conducts its investigations?

On January 13, 2010, the SEC's Division of Enforcement publicly released a revised version of its *Enforcement Manual*.[50] The *Enforcement Manual* provides valuable insight into the SEC's investigatory process and is required reading for any attorney dealing with an SEC enforcement investigation. Among other things, the *Enforcement Manual* explains how the Enforcement Division:

- ranks investigations and allocates scarce enforcement resources;
- reviews the status of pending investigations;
- handles referrals from the public, the PCAOB, state regulators, Congress, and the SROs;
- opens and closes investigations;
- obtains formal orders of investigations.

The *Enforcement Manual* also explains:

- the Wells Process;
- how the Commission considers enforcement recommendations;
- various investigative practices, including:
    - communications with senior SEC staff;
    - tolling agreements;
    - handling of parallel investigations;
    - document requests and subpoenas;
    - the requirement that settling parties confirm the completeness of document production;

- procedures for taking testimony;
- witness assurance letters, immunity orders, and proffer agreements;
- attorney-client, work-product, and Fifth Amendment assertions;
- inadvertent production or productions without privilege review;
- requests for waiver of the attorney-client privilege;
- confidentiality agreements;
- informal referrals to federal or state criminal agencies or others including state bars.

Finally, the *Enforcement Manual* contains a detailed explanation of how the Enforcement Division will employ the analytic framework for individual cooperation and cooperation tools described above at QQ 30.5.1 to 30.5.5.

Document Requests

Obligation to Preserve Documents

Q 30.9 What are a company's obligations regarding documents?

After learning of a *potential* SEC investigation, a company's foremost obligation is to preserve, without alteration, all potentially relevant documents, in both hard copy and electronic formats. The company and its employees must ensure that no copies of relevant electronic files, including emails, word-processing and spreadsheet files, and backups, are destroyed or overwritten, even inadvertently. The company must preserve all documents within its custody or control including, for instance, documents in the custody of its outside professionals, such as legal counsel.

Q 30.9.1 Are there special considerations for preserving electronic documents?

Electronic documents are particularly problematic because they are easily altered or deleted, often through routine electronic data policies. For example, a company might routinely delete emails of a certain age or recycle backup media, both of which destroy potentially relevant data. Moreover, often it is not obvious where relevant electronic documents may reside. Among the many possible places e-documents might reside are:

- file, email, and voicemail servers;
- desktop computers and laptops;
- personal digital assistants (*e.g.*, BlackBerry devices);
- temporary storage devices (*e.g.*, portable hard drives, USB flash drives); and
- backup media.

Q 30.9.2 What are the consequences of inadequate document preservation?

First, SOX provides for serious criminal penalties for document destruction intended to interfere with a governmental investigation. Section 802 of SOX provides for criminal penalties of up to twenty years' imprisonment for anyone who:

> knowingly alters, destroys, mutilates, conceals, covers up, falsifies, or makes a false entry in any record, document, or tangible object with the intent to impede, obstruct, or influence the investigation . . . of any matter within the jurisdiction of any department or agency of the United States. . . .[51]

Importantly, section 802 does not require that there be a pending investigation at the time of the conduct; a person can violate this section if he or she is aware of a *potential* governmental investigation. This prohibition applies to all persons; namely, companies, their employees, their directors, their legal counsel, their accountants, and other representatives.

Entirely apart from these criminal sanctions, the SEC can impose significant monetary penalties on companies that do not preserve and timely produce relevant documents. Section 802 of SOX (quoted above) also provides for fines of up to $10 million.

Q 30.9.3 What can our company do to make sure that it meets its preservation obligations?

A senior company official (preferably the general counsel) should instruct the information technology department to ensure that no potentially relevant electronic files, including backup media, are overwritten. These preservation efforts might well require alteration of the company's routine electronic data policies.[52] Similarly, company employees should be instructed to preserve all relevant electronic files, regardless of whether they reside on their desktop or laptop computers, home computers, personal digital assistants, or temporary storage devices.

Q 30.9.4 Should we preserve everything or only those documents we think the SEC will want produced?

Your document preservation efforts should be broad and inclusive. However, just because potentially relevant documents are being preserved does not mean they necessarily will be produced to the SEC. The company's SEC defense counsel will negotiate the scope of production with SEC staff and will review the company's and its employees' documents for responsiveness and privilege before producing documents to the SEC.

CASE STUDY: *AIG*

In a September 11, 2003 settlement with American Insurance Group, Inc., the SEC imposed a $10 million penalty, noting:

> AIG failed to produce a large quantity of documents that were called for by the staff's various requests and subpoenas. In part, this failure resulted from a woefully deficient document collection effort within AIG, in which AIG failed to search various locations in which responsive documents were likely to be found.[53]

> **CASE STUDY: Banc of America Securities, LLC**
>
> Similarly, in a March 10, 2004 settlement with Banc of America Securities, LLC (BAS), the SEC imposed a $10 million penalty solely for failing to promptly furnish documents requested during an enforcement investigation. The SEC did not allege that BAS had committed any substantive violations of the securities laws.[54]
>
> **CASE STUDY: Lucent Technologies, Inc.**
>
> Further underscoring the seriousness with which the SEC approaches this subject, in a May 17, 2004 settlement with Lucent Technologies, Inc., the SEC imposed a $25 million penalty for various acts of "non-cooperation," including incomplete document preservation and production in an enforcement proceeding.[55]

Document Requests and Production

Q 30.10 What can we expect from the document request process?

In SEC investigations, the staff routinely asks companies to produce a broad range of documents. The SEC typically requests production of electronic data,[56] such as documents from the company's file and email servers, hard drives, and other storage media. It may even request that the company restore certain backup media. It is often possible to negotiate the scope and sequence of a document production with the SEC staff.

At the beginning of the production, it can be difficult to accurately project a reasonable schedule for the document production because there are many difficult-to-estimate variables that must be taken into consideration, including the size of the document collection, the number of duplicates that will be eliminated, and the number of documents that will be responsive to key-word searches. If a company finds that it is falling behind its production schedule due to unforeseen circumstances (such as inaccurate estimates of the foregoing variables or difficulties in restoring backup tapes), it is important to notify the SEC to avoid appearing dilatory or uncooperative.

It is vital that SEC staff regard the producing party as making a timely and complete production of all non-privileged, responsive documents.[57] In larger document productions, the staff usually prefers to get the production started early and on a rolling basis. It is often easiest to begin the production with hard-copy documents.

The SEC frequently will follow up its initial document requests with additional document requests directed to individual directors, officers, and third parties that it believes may have relevant information (for example, auditors and parties to transactions that are under review), as well as with supplemental requests to the company. The SEC routinely requires company witnesses to testify to the completeness of the document production and their roles in the production process. Additionally, the SEC staff frequently requires producing parties to certify the adequacy of their searches for documents and the completeness of their productions.

COMPLIANCE TIP

Given the importance of complete document preservation and production, it is sound practice to document the steps that the company and its counsel have taken to preserve and produce responsive documents to the SEC.

Q 30.11 Can we negotiate with the SEC about our document production?

Counsel should negotiate the scope, sequence and timing of a document production with the SEC staff. Particularly in the case of an electronic document production, counsel should have a firm grasp of where and how documents are stored, the likely relevance of documents in various data sources, and the costs and time required to produce those documents. Armed with those facts, counsel can press the staff for reasonable limits on the scope and timing of a document production.

Counsel should consider whether it is in the company's interest to agree with the staff upon a production protocol that addresses which data sources and email boxes will be produced,[58] which backup media will be restored, the search terms or other search methodology that will be used to screen the data for relevance, and the format in which the SEC would like the data delivered. Agreement on these parameters will reduce the likelihood that the staff will find the production inadequate, deeming the company to be "uncooperative" and forcing it to bear the expense of a costly supplementation of its electronic production.

On the other hand, counsel may conclude that it is unwise to put the SEC in the position of dictating which data sources should be reviewed and which search terms should be used. Counsel may feel that opening these subjects to negotiation may result in the company's being required to engage in a more sweeping document production than it would otherwise make. Of course, failing to agree on these parameters at the outset puts the company at some risk that the SEC may later conclude that its electronic document production was inadequate.

There is certainly no "one-size-fits-all" solution to this quandary. Counsel will be guided by many factors, including her perceptions of the seriousness of the investigation and the staff's attitude toward the company.

Q 30.12 What are the advantages of hiring an outside e-discovery vendor?

Because electronic data productions are complex, expensive, and time-consuming, an outside vendor expert in electronic discovery can provide invaluable assistance. The vendor can help the company identify and preserve relevant data sources, copy electronic data in a forensically sound manner (with no alteration of metadata), eliminate duplicates, search the remaining document collection by key words, run preliminary privilege screens, host the electronic document collection online, provide a web-based review tool to facilitate attorney review, and, finally, properly format the documents for production to the SEC.[59]

Selective Disclosure of Information to the SEC

Q 30.13 Why is the question of selective disclosure of information in SEC investigations important?

The question of whether a company can "selectively disclose" privileged information to governmental authorities without waiving the privilege with respect to all others has come to the fore in recent years largely because of the confluence of two factors. Sarbanes-Oxley has put pressure on companies to uncover potential wrongdoing, resulting in an unprecedented number of internal investigations. At the same time, government enforcement authorities (such as DOJ and the SEC) have rewarded companies that "cooperate" by sharing their internal investigative findings. Indeed, in cases where the SEC has spared a company from any enforcement action, the company's cooperation included sharing the results of its internal investigation with SEC staff.[60] Companies have tried to maintain that they could "selectively disclose" such privileged information to governmental authorities, but not waive their privileges with respect to the rest of the world.

Q 30.14 Can privileged information be selectively disclosed to the SEC?

The DOJ and SEC have supported selective disclosure through various means. They have entered into confidentiality agreements with the disclosing company that purport to maintain the privilege with respect to third parties; they have accepted disclosures in forms that do not leave paper trails (such as oral disclosures or opportunities to review but not retain copies of documents); and they have supported the principle of selective disclosure in amicus briefs filed in private litigation.

The principle of selective disclosure garnered early support from the Eighth Circuit, which in 1978 held that the production of documents to the SEC did not result in a general waiver of the privilege despite the lack of a written confidentiality agreement.[61] Following this decision, several other courts of appeal indicated that they might apply the selective waiver principle where the producing party had a written confidentiality agreement with the government.[62]

However, by 2002, the Sixth Circuit described the law governing selective disclosure as being in a state of "hopeless confusion" and rejected the doctrine, refusing to limit waivers despite the existence of a written confidentiality agreement.[63] Since then, the trend has been decidedly against allowing companies to selectively waive the privilege to government agencies, regardless of whether a written confidentiality agreement is in place.[64]

CASE STUDY: *United States v. Reyes*[65]

In this particularly notable rejection of selective disclosure, the court rejected the principle even though confidentiality agreements were in place and the disclosing party did not produce any documents to the government, but limited their disclosures to oral briefings concerning their witness interviews and investigative findings. The court noted that its rejection of the principle was "[i]n accord with every appellate court that has considered the issue in the last twenty-five years...."[66]

Q 30.14.1 What is the outlook for selective disclosure?

Proponents of selective disclosure had hoped that the issue would be resolved by an amendment to the Federal Rules of Evidence. However, at its April 2007 meeting, the Advisory Committee on Evidence Rules to the U.S. Judicial Conference rejected an amendment to Rule 502 that would have protected selective disclosures to the government. The committee's report noted that the selective disclosure proposal was "very controversial" and "raised questions that were essentially political in nature."[67] Accordingly, the committee prepared language to assist Congress should it decide to proceed with independent legislation on selective disclosure, but refrained from recommending such an amendment. Rule 502, as adopted on September 19, 2008, does not speak to the question of selective disclosure.

Q 30.14.2 Should we consider disclosing privileged information?

Given the current state of the case law, the absence of rules or legislation that resolve the issue, and the fact that most companies can be subject to litigation in almost any jurisdiction in the country, companies should assume that *any* disclosure of privileged information to the government—regardless of whether a confidentiality agreement is in place and regardless of the form of the disclosure—runs a severe risk of waiving the attorney-client privilege and work-product immunity.

Witness Testimony

SEC Requests for Testimony

Q 30.15 From whom is sworn testimony likely to be requested?

The SEC likely will take sworn testimony from current and former employees, contractual counter-parties, and outside professionals, such as auditors. SEC staff often will begin with lower-level employees who can explain the organizational structure, the availability and location of documents, and basic information concerning the transactions or other matters under investigation. The staff will then proceed up the corporate hierarchy to those witnesses whose actions can be imputed to the company and who themselves might be the subject of an enforcement action.

Q 30.15.1 Should witnesses speak informally with SEC enforcement staff?

SEC enforcement staff occasionally try to engage witnesses in substantive discussions very early in the investigative process, often by telephone. Witnesses should be wary of engaging in any such discussion. These conversations often take place before the witness understands what is at issue and has had an opportunity to refresh her memory. The witness also will not have the benefit of representation by defense counsel.

Unfortunately, a witness's ill-advised comments made at this preliminary stage are not off the record. Typically, several SEC enforcement staff will participate in the conversation and will make detailed notes of the witness's statements, essentially locking in her testimony. Additionally, any inaccurate responses could later be interpreted as uncooperative conduct. Inaccurate responses, even though unsworn, might also expose the witness to criminal charges under 18 U.S.C. § 1001.

COMPLIANCE TIP

If SEC enforcement staff contact employees or corporate spokespersons and try to engage them in discussions, those employees or spokespersons should politely but firmly make clear that they will need to consult with counsel before speaking with the staff. This advice should be conveyed to potential witnesses in a manner that cannot be construed as an obstruction of justice.

Witness Examination

Q 30.16 How should we respond after a request for sworn witness testimony has been made?

Preparing a witness for testimony is perhaps the most important aspect of defending an SEC investigation. Sworn testimony is often a witness's best opportunity to explain her (and the company's) side of the story to SEC enforcement staff. The testimony will be a strong consideration in the staff's formulation of a charging decision and will lock in the witness's testimony in the event that charges eventually are brought.

Before holding preparation sessions with the witness, defense counsel will review all relevant documents that were written or received by the witness or which might help refresh the witness's memory. Experienced SEC defense counsel can anticipate the staff's lines of inquiry and can help the witness put herself and the company in the best possible light, offering testimony that is both inherently credible and consistent with the documents and other testimony the staff is likely to hear.

Q 30.17 What can we expect from an SEC witness examination?

Typically, several SEC enforcement staff participate in examining a witness. A staff attorney (the line-level investigator) usually leads the examination, with the branch chief (the first-level supervisor) and other enforcement staff (such as accountants) asking follow-up questions to ensure that a thorough record has been made. SEC investigative testimony is given under oath and on the record.[68]

Q 30.18 What rights do witnesses have?

Witnesses have the right to:

- obtain a copy of their transcript on payment of the appropriate fee (unless the Commission denies the request for good cause); and to inspect the official transcript of their own testimony.[69]
- see the formal order of investigation.[70]
- be accompanied, represented, and advised by counsel.[71]

Witnesses should be aware that their sworn testimony is subject to both the penalty for perjury[72] as well as to the penalties for false statements to the government.[73]

Q 30.18.1 Can a witness refuse to testify?

Witnesses have the right to refuse, under the Fifth Amendment to the U.S. Constitution, to give any information that may tend to incriminate her or subject her to a fine, penalty, or forfeiture. Witnesses should be aware, however, that the government will draw an "adverse inference" of wrongdoing from a refusal to testify, which can prejudice the witness's ability to defend against SEC civil charges.

Q 30.18.2 What are some important considerations in deciding whether or not to refuse to testify?

The decision as to whether a witness should testify in the SEC's civil investigation often comes down to a choice between the lesser of two evils. For example, a witness who is asked to testify in a civil proceeding may assert her Fifth Amendment rights to protect herself from criminal exposure, but doing so risks that civil authorities will draw an adverse inference of wrongdoing from her refusal to testify. Conversely, testifying holds risks for the witness. The witness may not be able to satisfactorily explain her conduct, thereby further exposing her to both civil and criminal charges for the underlying substantive offense. And, if the witness testifies inaccurately (even if due merely to faulty memory or inadequate preparation, rather than an intent to mislead), she may be exposed to criminal perjury or obstruction of justice charges.

Q 30.18.3 What is a witness's counsel permitted to do during an examination?

Counsel may:

(1) advise the witness before, during, and after the conclusion of such examination;

(2) briefly ask clarifying questions of the witness at the conclusion of the examination; and

(3) make summary notes during the examination.[74]

Q 30.19 What other important considerations should we keep in mind when anticipating a witness examination?

Because SEC investigations are fact-finding inquiries rather than evidentiary proceedings, the staff takes the view that it has greater latitude in conducting the examination (particularly in calling for speculation and opinion) than would be permitted under the Federal Rules of Evidence.

While a company may wish to cooperate with the staff's investigation, allowing speculation and lay opinion to creep into the record creates a risk. While such testimony may well be inadmissible in court, it can be used to support the staff's charging recommendation to the Commission. SEC defense counsel can minimize the amount of such inadmissible testimony through proper witness preparation and representation during the testimony.

Representation by Counsel

Q 30.20 Should the same counsel represent the company and its employees?

A company will often want the same counsel to represent both it and its current and former employees.

Q 30.20.1 What are the advantages of using the same counsel?

In a corporate investigation of any complexity, it is expensive for counsel to become sufficiently familiar with the issues, relevant documents, and witness testimony to be able to competently represent a single employee in SEC testimony. It would be unduly costly if the company were required to obtain separate counsel for each of its present or former employee witnesses. For this reason, the company typically will offer, at its expense, to have its defense counsel (in her capacity as the company's counsel) represent each of its employee witnesses at her SEC testimony.

Multiple representations also have the advantage of making company counsel privy to the testimony of all commonly represented employees. Because SEC investigations are confidential, only the counsel who represented the witness in testimony can order a copy of the witness's transcript. Indeed, if company counsel did not represent an employee during testimony, the staff usually will not allow company counsel to review the witness's testimony unless and until a Wells Notice (discussed below at Q 30.23) has been issued.

Q 30.20.2 Are there any limitations or provisions to using the same counsel?

Counsel may represent multiple witnesses in testimony provided that there are no actual or potential conflicts of interest amongst the company and each commonly represented employee witness.[75] The cooperation tools, however, may have an impact on multiple-representation scenarios. Unlike the white collar world, where it is rare for a criminal defense counsel to represent more than a single person, it has been common in SEC enforcement practice for a single defense lawyer to represent multiple witnesses, as long as no conflicts of interest between them existed. With the SEC's cooperation policies in effect, regardless of whether there are conflicts between witnesses, it may be in the interest of one client to be the first to report the misconduct to the SEC and offer cooperation. The SEC's new cooperation program is bound to heighten the ethical concerns of defense counsel and may lead to fewer multiple representations. It also may have the unintended consequence of driving up the cost of SEC investigations to corporate issuers who are indemnifying the defense costs of their employees. While the SEC will permit counsel, acting strictly in her capacity as company counsel, to represent present and former employees during their investigative testimony, the SEC typically notifies witnesses that they have a right to be represented during their testimony by their own personal counsel.[76]

Joint Defense Agreements

Q 30.21 What if an employee decides to retain separate personal counsel?

In the event that a present or former employee retains personal counsel, the company might partly secure the economic and informational advantages of a multiple representation through a joint defense agreement (JDA). Provided that the parties have a common interest in defending an SEC investigation, a JDA allows parties—even those who have potentially or actually conflicting interests—to share privileged communications and work product without fear of waiver. Thus, through a JDA, company counsel can help a separately represented employee more efficiently prepare for her SEC testimony by sharing work product with her counsel; company counsel can even participate in the preparation sessions. Likewise, through a JDA, company counsel may learn the substance of the testimony of a separately represented witness.

Because the SEC may ask about the existence of a JDA, counsel will not want to enter such an agreement with any witness whom the company likely will want to portray as a rogue whose actions were unauthorized.

Q 30.22 What are the opportunities for informal advocacy during the investigation?

During the investigation, SEC enforcement staff typically will not share its concerns with counsel. Nevertheless, there are numerous opportunities for informal advocacy during the course of the investigation.

Near the outset of the investigation, the company may ask its counsel to give the staff an overview of the matter, possibly even providing the staff with key documents. A presentation must be accurate and balanced if the company and counsel are to have credibility with the staff. Such a presentation can demonstrate a company's cooperation and, at the same time, present the company's views at an early date to SEC decision-makers who are more senior than those who will be involved in the day-to-day conduct of the investigation.[77]

As the investigation unfolds, counsel may find that the staff is laboring under a misapprehension of law, fact, or expert knowledge (for example, an arcane facet of Generally Accepted Accounting Principles). Counsel might find it advantageous to correct this misapprehension.

If, at the conclusion of the testimonial phase of the investigation, SEC staff makes a preliminary determination to recommend charges to the Commission, it will issue a Wells Notice (discussed in Q 30.23) to the proposed subject of such charges. On the other hand, if the staff does not issue a Wells Notice, a company may hear nothing about the status of the investigation for a long time, and can only guess the staff's intentions.[78]

Typically, a company will simply await further contact from the staff. However, in cases where the company believes that it has an especially strong position or where it is concerned that lower-level staff might not accurately summarize the investigatory record to their superiors, a company may consider providing more senior staff with its views on what the investigative record has established. This kind of "pre-Wells" submission must be approached cautiously, because the staff could re-open the record to fill any holes that the company has identified in the investigatory record.

Although a Wells Submission is the only opportunity for advocacy formally identified in the SEC's rules, experienced defense counsel will find ample opportunities during the investigative process to advance the client's views.

Wells Notice and Wells Submission

Wells Notice

Q 30.23   What is a Wells Notice?

The Wells Notice outlines the legal charges that the staff is prepared to recommend to the Commission and, sometimes, the factual basis for those charges. Although not required by the SEC's rules, the staff will usually give the proposed subject of enforcement charges an opportunity to review all relevant testimony and exhibits. Under Dodd-Frank, not later than 180 days after the SEC Staff provides a written Wells Notice to any person, the staff must either file an action against the person or provide notice to the Director of Enforcement of its intent not to file an action.[79]

Wells Submission

Q 30.24   What is a Wells Submission?

A Wells Submission is an opportunity for the proposed defendant to explain its position via a memorandum or (less commonly) videotape. A Wells Submission may argue that no enforcement action is warranted or that lower-level charges and less severe relief are appropriate; it may also argue in favor of a proposed settlement.[80]

Q 30.24.1 Should a Wells Submission automatically follow a Wells Notice?

No. While Wells Submissions can be effective defense tools, they must be approached with care. The SEC warns that "[t]he staff of the Commission routinely seeks to introduce [Wells] submissions . . . as evidence in Commission enforcement proceedings. . . ."[81] Additionally, they may be discoverable in civil litigation with third parties.[82] The SEC generally refuses to accept Wells Submissions under claims of privilege or as settlement materials.

Charges and Remedies

Q 30.25 What kind of charges can the SEC bring?

Broadly speaking, the SEC can bring two types of charges against a public company and its directors and officers with respect to the company's financial reporting. The SEC can bring such charges either against primary violators (*i.e.*, persons who directly commit the violation) or against secondary violators (*i.e.*, persons who assist the primary violation of another person).

Financial fraud. This is the more serious charge. To sustain a financial fraud charge, the SEC must show that the company, through its directors or officers, either knowingly issued materially misleading financial statements or was severely reckless as to whether its financial statements were materially misleading.[83] A financial fraud charge is significant not only because of its greater stigma, but because it also serves as the predicate for heavier penalties (discussed below) and other sanctions, including director and officer bars.

Violating the "books and records" and internal control provisions of the securities laws. These provisions require public companies to maintain accurate books and records and adequate internal control systems, and to file accurate periodic reports with the Commission. Unlike a financial fraud charge, these provisions generally do not require the SEC to prove that the company acted with intent or severe recklessness. When the SEC believes that it can prove financial fraud, it will invariably also charge books and records violations. However, where the evidence does not support a financial fraud charge, the SEC will limit the charges to books and records and internal control violations.

Secondary liability. The SEC's ability to pursue aiding-and-abetting charges was significantly enhanced by Dodd-Frank. Prior to Dodd-Frank, the SEC could only bring aiding-and-abetting charges under the Securities Exchange Act of 1934. Dodd-Frank allows the SEC to bring more aiding-and-abetting charges by authorizing such charges under both the Securities Act of 1933 and the Investment Company Act of 1940.[84] Dodd-Frank also made it easier for the SEC to prove aiding-and-abetting charges. Prior to Dodd-Frank, the SEC had to show that the defendant acted with "actual knowledge"; Dodd-Frank reduced this state of mind requirement to "knowingly or recklessly."[85] Dodd-Frank also made clear that the SEC has authority to charge "control persons" with liability,[86] enabling the SEC to charge corporate officers for their employer's violations.

Q 30.26 What remedies can the SEC obtain against a company?

Regardless of the nature of the charges it brings, the SEC may seek two kinds of relief against a public company:

(1) A federal court injunction or an administrative cease-and-desist order obligating the company to obey the law in the future.
(2) Two forms of monetary relief:
 (a) Equitable disgorgement (including pre-judgment interest); and
 (b) A civil money penalty.[87]

An order of equitable disgorgement requires a company to pay back any ill-gotten gains that it received as a result of its illegal conduct. Because it is usually difficult to quantify the company's receipt of ill-gotten gain in a financial reporting case, disgorgement usually is not a significant factor in these kinds of cases. Civil money penalties, however, have become a much more prominent feature of financial reporting enforcement cases.

Q 30.26.1 How large are civil monetary penalties?

Until recently, the SEC did not seek large penalties against public companies in financial fraud cases. For instance, the $10 million penalty imposed on Xerox on April 11, 2002, was then the largest penalty in the SEC's almost seventy-year history. Before Xerox, penalties rarely exceeded $1 million.

This has changed. Not only has the enforcement climate changed in the wake of this decade's corporate scandals, but SOX gives the SEC an incentive to obtain large penalties from public companies. The "fair funds" provision of SOX (section 308(a)) allows the SEC to add any penalties that it collects to a disgorgement fund for the benefit of the "victims" of the violation.

The securities laws provide a three-tiered penalty scheme, which is periodically increased to account for inflation. For violations occurring after February 14, 2005, the tiers are set forth in table 30-1.[88]

Because these penalties apply to each "violation" (which is not defined in the securities statutes), the SEC can argue that any given financial fraud involved multiple violations (*e.g.*, that each materially misstated financial statement entry constitutes a separate violation, and that each violation was repeated with every refiling or republication).

In an April 29, 2004 speech, the SEC's Director of Enforcement signaled his intent to continue to demand large civil penalties against corporations:

> Civil penalties against entities in the tens of millions of dollars are no longer rare; indeed, they seem to be expected by many. . . . I believe the ratcheting up of penalties is driven by both goals—increased accountability and enhanced deterrence.[89]

TABLE 30-1
Monetary Penalties Against Corporations for Securities Violations

Tier	Penalty per violation	When available
1	Not to exceed greater of gain to defendant or **$60,000**	Any violation
2	Not to exceed greater of gain to defendant or **$300,000**	Violations involving fraud, deceit, manipulation, or deliberate or reckless disregard of a regulatory requirement
3	Not to exceed greater of gain to defendant or **$600,000**	Same as Tier 2 *and* when such violation directly or indirectly resulted in substantial losses or created a significant risk of substantial losses

COMPLIANCE FACT

Since passage of the "fair funds" provision, the SEC has obtained a number of settlements in financial fraud cases that dwarf all prior civil monetary penalties:

WorldCom: $750 million

Vivendi: $50 million

Enron: Penalties ranging from $37.5 million to $65 million against financial services firms for aiding and abetting or causing Enron's accounting fraud

AIG: $800 million in disgorgement and penalties, which they agreed in 2006 to pay and which will be returned to investors through a "fair fund"

Fannie Mae: $350 million penalty as well as an additional $50 million to the Office of Federal Housing Enterprise Oversight, with whom the SEC jointly brought the case

In 2006, the SEC's enforcement cases resulted in a total of more than $3.3 billion in disgorgement and penalties.[90]

Q 30.26.2 What factors does the SEC consider in deciding on whether or not to assess a penalty on a company?

In January 2006, the SEC issued guidance regarding civil penalties against corporations. The SEC acknowledged that:

> The question of whether, and if so to what extent, to impose civil penalties against a corporation raises significant questions for our mission of investor protection. The authority to impose such penalties is relatively recent in the Commission's history, and the use of very large corporate penalties is more recent still. Recent cases have not produced a clear public view of when and how the Commission will use corporate penalties, and within the Commission itself a variety of views have heretofore been expressed, but not reconciled.[91]

After reviewing the legislative history of the Securities Enforcement Remedies and Penny Stock Reform Act of 1990, which gave the Commission authority generally to seek civil money penalties in enforcement cases, the SEC announced that the appropriateness of a penalty on a corporation turns principally on two considerations:

(1) *The presence or absence of a direct benefit to the corporation as a result of the violation.* The SEC explained that "the strongest case for the imposition of a corporate penalty is one in which the shareholders of the corporation have received an improper benefit as a result of the violation; the weakest case is one in which the current shareholders of the corporation are the principal victims of the securities law violation."[92]

(2) *The degree to which the penalty will recompense or further harm the injured shareholders.* The SEC explained that "[t]he presence of an opportunity to use the penalty as a meaningful source of compensation to injured shareholders is a factor in support of its imposition. The likelihood a corporate penalty will unfairly injure investors, the corporation, or third parties weighs against its use as a sanction."[93]

In its statement, the SEC identified the following additional factors that are properly considered in determining whether to impose a penalty on a corporation:

- the need to deter the particular type of offense;
- the extent of the injury to innocent parties;
- whether complicity in the violation is widespread throughout the corporation;
- the level of intent on the part of the perpetrators;
- the degree of difficulty in detecting the particular type of offense;
- presence or lack of remedial steps by the corporation; and
- extent of cooperation with commission or other law enforcement.[94]

Q 30.26.3 Does the SEC ever seek other remedies?

While the SEC is statutorily authorized to seek only the foregoing remedies against public companies, it frequently seeks other relief as a condition of settlement. For instance, the SEC may require a company to retain and follow the recommendations of an independent consultant charged with reviewing its accounting policies and procedures and internal control systems. The SEC will sometimes accept such undertakings in mitigation of the civil money penalty that it would otherwise require.

Q 30.27 What remedies can the SEC seek against directors and officers?

The SEC can seek both injunctive and monetary relief against individual corporate actors, including directors and officers.[95]

Q 30.27.1 What monetary penalties can the SEC seek against directors and officers?

The penalty amounts applicable to individuals are considerably lower than those against corporations. For violations occurring after February 14, 2005, the tiers are as follows:[96]

TABLE 30-2
Monetary Penalties Against Individuals for Securities Violations

Tier	Penalty per violation	When available
1	Not to exceed greater of gain to defendant or $6,500	Any violation
2	Not to exceed greater of gain to defendant or $60,000	Violations involving fraud, deceit, manipulation, or deliberate or reckless disregard of a regulatory requirement
3	Not to exceed greater of gain to defendant or $120,000	Same as Tier 2 *and* when such violation directly or indirectly resulted in substantial losses or created a significant risk of substantial losses

Q 30.27.2 What other kinds of relief can the SEC seek against directors and officers?

Where an individual has violated section 10(b) of the Exchange Act or any of the rules thereunder, the SEC can bar the individual (temporarily or permanently) from serving as a director or officer of a public company (a "D&O bar"). Prior to SOX, D&O bars were sparingly used in only the most egregious cases. Section 305 of SOX reduced the standard for imposing D&O bars from "substantially unfit" to serve as a director or officer of a public company to merely "unfit." Additionally, while the SEC previously could only seek a D&O bar in a federal court proceeding, section 1105 of SOX empowers the SEC to impose this remedy in an administrative cease-and-desist proceeding. In a February 11, 2004 speech, the SEC's Director of Enforcement warned "[Y]ou can expect us to continue to use this remedy aggressively."[97]

Under section 304 of SOX, if a company is required to restate its financials as a result of "misconduct," the CEO and CFO can be required to reimburse the company for (1) all bonuses and incentive- or equity-based compensation the officer received during the year following issuance of the restated document and (2) any profits from the sale of the issuer's securities during that year. Under section 304, the CEO and CFO need not have personally engaged in any misconduct to be liable. The year 2009 marked the SEC's first use of SOX section 304 to "claw back" compensation from an executive not charged with any violation of the securities laws. Section 304 does not apply to salary.[98]

Under section 1103 of SOX, the SEC is authorized during the course of an investigation to seek a forty-five-day freeze (which may be extended to ninety days) of any "extraordinary payments (whether compensation or otherwise)" to any of the company's directors, officers, partners, controlling persons, agents, or employees. If such an order is entered, the company is required to escrow those payments into an interest-bearing account. If the company or person is charged with a securities violation, the freeze remains in effect during the pendency of that proceeding.

Finally, if the subject of an investigation is an individual and a CPA who "appeared or practiced before the Commission" (for example, prepared or signed the company's SEC filings), the individual could be subject to a proceeding under SEC Rule of Procedure 102(e) to censure the individual or deny her, temporarily or permanently, the privilege of appearing or practicing before the Commission. On rare and egregious occasions, Rule 102(e) proceedings have been brought against attorneys.

Settlement Negotiations

Q 30.28   How does the SEC approach settlements?

At appropriate points in the enforcement process (during the fact-gathering stage, in connection with or following a Wells Submission, and even after an enforcement action has been commenced), a party can discuss settlement with the SEC staff.

The staff does not have independent authority to accept a settlement.[99] That said, settlement offers that do not have staff support are rarely accepted by the Commission.

A settlement reached prior to the commencement of an enforcement action often results in a reduction of the charges or relief that the staff would otherwise seek, whereas the range of compromise available post-commencement is usually more circumscribed.

The SEC routinely issues press releases when it brings and settles enforcement actions. Thus, when a matter is settled before an enforcement action is commenced, there is a single press event. When a matter is settled post-commencement, there are two press events: first, when the matter is brought; and second, when it is settled.

In any settlement with the SEC, the settling party neither admits nor denies the SEC's allegations. When a party settles a federal injunctive action, neither the court nor the SEC makes any factual finding. The SEC files a complaint making its allegations and the court enters a final judgment that enjoins the defendant and may order other relief, but makes no factual findings. However, when a party settles an SEC administrative action, the settling party (albeit without admitting or denying the SEC's charges) allows the SEC to make certain factual findings and conclusions of law.

Although all settlements are without admitting or denying the SEC's allegations, the SEC has a "no denial" policy that prohibits a settling party from denying the SEC's charges. At the same time, the settling party is permitted to defend itself in litigation with parties other than the SEC.[100]

Notes

1. *See* Securities Act of 1933 ("Securities Act") §§ 19 and 20, 15 U.S.C. §§ 77s, 77t; Securities Exchange Act of 1934 ("Exchange Act") § 21, 15 U.S.C. § 78u. Violations of the federal securities laws may also constitute criminal offenses. *See* Securities Act § 24, 15 U.S.C. § 77x; Exchange Act § 32(a), 15 U.S.C. § 78ff. However, the SEC does not have statutory authority to bring criminal prosecutions; all criminal prosecutions for federal securities offenses are handled by the U.S. Department of Justice ("DOJ"). *See* Securities Act § 20(b), 15 U.S.C. § 77t(b); Exchange Act § 21(d), 15 U.S.C. § 78u(d).

2. The SEC's civil enforcement jurisdiction extends beyond public companies to any person or entity that violates the federal securities laws. For example, the SEC has authority to enforce the securities antifraud rules against all issuers of securities, including private companies, partnerships, and individuals. The term "security" encompasses far more than stock; it also includes mutual funds, variable annuities, promissory notes, and investment contracts. Similarly, the SEC may enforce the nation's securities laws against individuals, such as persons who engage in insider trading.

3. *See, e.g.*, Exchange Act § 21(a), 15 U.S.C. § 78u(a) ("The Commission may, in its discretion, make such investigations as it deems necessary to determine whether any person has violated, is violating, or is about to violate any provision of this chapter.").

4. If, following a financial restatement, the company experiences a drop in its stock price, it can also expect to become the target of a securities class action and, possibly, a shareholder derivative suit. Accordingly, companies planning to restate their financial statements often retain experienced securities class action and SEC enforcement defense counsel to manage the restatement process to minimize such exposures.

5. *See* SEC Annual Performance and Accountability Reports, *available at* www.sec.gov/about.shtml (under "Annual Reports and Statistics").

6. Pub. L. No. 107-204, §§ 302, 906, 2002 U.S.C.C.A.N., 116 Stat. 745.

7. Stephen M. Cutler, Dir., Div. of Enforcement, U.S. Sec. & Exch. Comm'n, The Themes of Sarbanes-Oxley as Reflected in the Commission's Enforcement Program, Speech at UCLA School of Law (Sept. 20, 2004), *available at* www.sec.gov/news/speech/spch092004smc.htm.

8. Over 400 work in the SEC's Washington, D.C. headquarters, and more than 800 work in the various regional offices around the country.

9. Press Release No. 2010-5, U.S. Securities and Exchange Commission, SEC Names New Specialized Unit Chiefs and Head of New Office of Market Intelligence (Jan. 13, 2010), *available at* www.sec.gov/news/press/2010/2010-5.htm.

10. The Enforcement Division operates a bounty program for insider trading. *See* www.sec.gov/divisions/enforce/insider.htm.

11. Internal SEC referrals most often come from the Division of Corporation Finance (which reviews corporate disclosures), the Division of Trading and Markets (which regulates major market participants such as broker-dealers, self-regulatory organizations and transfer agents), the Division of Investment Management (which regulates investment companies such as mutual funds, closed-end funds, UITs, ETFs, and interval funds, as well as variable insurance products and federally registered investment advisers), and the Office of Compliance Inspections and Examinations (OCIE) (which conducts examinations of registered entities, including self-regulatory organizations, broker-dealers, transfer agents, investment companies and investment advisers). In fiscal year 2006, OCIE made 223 enforcement referrals, and the Division of Corporation Finance made 537 enforcement referrals. 2006 SEC Performance and Accountability Report at Exhibit 2.19, *available at* www.sec.gov/about/secpar/secpar2006.pdf#sec1.

12. Press Release No. 2010-5, U.S. Securities and Exchange Commission, SEC Names New Specialized Unit Chiefs and Head of New Office of Market Intelligence (Jan. 13, 2010).

13. Robert Khuzami, Dir., Div. of Enforcement, SEC, Testimony Concerning Investigating and Prosecuting Fraud After the Fraud Enforcement and Recovery Act, Before the United States Senate Committee on the Judiciary (Sept. 22, 2010), *available at* www.sec.gov/news/testimony/2010/ts092210rk.htm.

14. U.S. Securities and Exchange Commission, Investor Complaints and Questions: Fiscal Year 2009 Annual Complaint Data, www.sec.gov/news/data.htm (last visited Feb. 26, 2010).

15. The SEC does not publish this statistic, and it cannot be derived from comparing the number of investigations with the number of enforcement actions in a given year for two reasons: First, investigations precede enforcement actions by a year or more; second, a single investigation can lead to multiple enforcement actions (*e.g.*, a corporate investigation can lead to separate enforcement actions against the company, its employees, its auditors, and its outside counsel). Nevertheless, one can get some feel for the matter by looking at recent data. In fiscal year 2009, the SEC initiated 944 enforcement investigations and 664 enforcement actions. In fiscal year 2008, the SEC initiated 890 enforcement investigations and 671 enforcement actions.

16. Persons or entities regulated by the SEC, such as broker-dealer firms and investment advisers, however, must respond to preliminary requests for information.

17. *See* Exchange Act § 21(b), 15 U.S.C. § 78u(b); 17 C.F.R. § 202.5(a).

18. 17 C.F.R. § 200.30-4(a)(13).

19. 17 C.F.R. § 200.30-4(a)(10).

20. 17 C.F.R. § 203.7(a).

21. Exchange Act Rel. No. 44,969 (Oct. 23, 2001), *available at* www.sec.gov/litigation/investreport/34-44969.htm.

22. Stephen M. Cutler, Dir., Div. of Enforcement, U.S. Sec. & Exch. Comm'n, Remarks Before the 24th Annual Ray Garrett, Jr. Corporate & Securities Law Institute (Apr. 29, 2004), *available at* www.sec.gov/news/speech/spch042904smc.htm.

23. Press Release No. 2006-4, Statement of the Securities and Exchange Commission Concerning Financial Penalties, U.S. Securities and Exchange

Commission (Jan. 4, 2006), *available at* www.sec.gov/news/press/2006-4.htm. This statement discusses what factors the SEC will consider in connection with imposing a penalty on a company.

24. Similarly, in its April 11, 2002 settlement with Xerox Corporation, the SEC imposed a $10 million penalty, noting that "[t]he penalty . . . reflects, in part, a sanction for the company's lack of full cooperation in the investigation." Press Release No. 2002-52, U.S. Securities and Exchange Commission (Apr. 11, 2002), *available at* www.sec.gov/news/headlines/xeroxsettles.htm.

25. Exchange Act Rel. No. 44,969 (Oct. 23, 2001).

26. 17 C.F.R. § 202.12.

27. Robert Khuzami, Dir., Div. of Enforcement, U.S. Sec. & Exch. Comm'n, Remarks at SEC Press Conference (Jan. 13, 2010).

28. SEC, DIVISION OF ENFORCEMENT, ENFORCEMENT MANUAL (2010), *available at* www.sec.gov/divisions/enforce/enforcementmanual.pdf [hereinafter SEC ENFORCEMENT MANUAL].

29. Press Release No. 2002-141, U.S. Securities and Exchange Commission (Sept. 25, 2002), *available at* www.sec.gov/news/press/2002-141.htm. The *Homestore* investigation also illustrates the degree to which the SEC cooperates with other law enforcement authorities. The *Homestore* press release noted that the case was "the product of an investigation by the SEC, the Federal Bureau of Investigation, and the U.S. Attorney's Office for the Central District of California." *Id.* By the conclusion of this joint investigation, the SEC sued a total of sixteen individuals for their roles in the scheme, eleven of whom were criminally charged by the U.S. Attorney. *See* www.sec.gov/news/digest/dig050505.txt.

30. Press Release No. 2006-2, U.S. Securities and Exchange Commission (Jan. 3, 2006), *available at* www.sec.gov/news/press/2006-2.htm.

31. Press Release No. 2007-70, U.S. Securities and Exchange Commission (Apr. 24, 2007), *available at* www.sec.gov/news/press/2007/2007-70.htm.

32. Indeed, the standard form that the SEC provides to every individual and entity from whom it seeks either documents or testimony (Form 1662: "Supplemental Information for Persons Requested to Supply Information Voluntarily or Directed to Supply Information Pursuant to a Commission Subpoena") warns that "[t]here is a likelihood that information supplied by you will be made available to such agencies [federal and state prosecutors] where appropriate." The form goes on to list twenty-three categories of routine uses that the SEC might make of the supplied information. *See also* 17 C.F.R. § 240.24c-1 (2006) ("[t]he Commission may, in its discretion and upon a showing that such information is needed, provide nonpublic information in its possession to any of the following persons if the person receiving such nonpublic information provides such assurances of confidentiality as the Commission deems appropriate . . . federal, state, local or foreign government[s] or any political subdivision, authority, agency or instrumentality of such government. . . ."). The securities statutes expressly authorize the SEC to share investigative information with the DOJ. *See* 15 U.S.C. §§ 77t(b) and 78u(d)(1).

33. In the most recent pre-Enron years for which data is available, the SEC reported that criminal authorities brought seventy-four (fiscal year 1998) and

sixty-four (fiscal year 1999) indictments or informations in "SEC-related" cases. The numbers of criminal prosecutions dramatically increased after Enron. In fiscal year 2002, criminal charges were filed against 259 individuals or entities; in fiscal year 2003, criminal charges were filed against 246 individuals or entities; in fiscal year 2004, criminal charges were filed against 302 individuals or entities. *See* 2006 SEC Performance and Accountability Report, *available at* www.sec.gov/about/secpar/secpar2006.pdf#secl. While the SEC has not provided similar statistics for subsequent years, the SEC's 2006 annual report noted that during the past year it had enjoyed "an unprecedented high level of collaboration with our counterpart state and federal regulators and criminal authorities." *See id.* at 2.

34. Linda Chatman Thomsen, Dir., SEC Enforcement Div., U.S. Sec. & Exch. Comm'n, Statement Concerning SEC v. Guttenberg (Mar. 1, 2007), *available at* www.sec.gov/news/speech/2007/spch030107lct.htm.

35. SEC Litigation Rel. No. 19,710 (May 23, 2006), *available at* www.sec.gov/litigation/litreleases/2006/lr19710.htm.

36. Mark K. Schonfeld, Dir., SEC N.Y. Reg'l Office, *Remarks at "Operation Spamalot" Press Conference* (Mar. 8, 2007), *available at* www.sec.gov/news/speech/2007/spch030807mks.htm.

37. Testimony concerning Mortgage Fraud, Securities Fraud, and the Financial Meltdown: Prosecuting Those Responsible: Before the U.S. Senate Comm. on the Judiciary (Dec. 9, 2009) (testimony of Robert Khuzami, Director, Div. of Enforcement, U.S. Securities and Exchange Commission).

38. *See* Amended Complaint, SEC v. Galleon Mgmt. LP, 2009 WL 4837219 (S.D.N.Y. filed Nov. 5, 2009) (No. 09-CV-8811-JSR).

39. In a 2006 amicus curiae brief to the U.S. Court of Appeals for the Ninth Circuit, the SEC advised that, "[w]hen defendant Stringer's attorney asked whether the SEC was working in conjunction with the U.S. Attorney's Office of any jurisdiction, he was correctly advised that the SEC's policy was not to comment on such issues, but to direct the witness to inquire of the U.S. Attorney's Office if he chose to." Brief of the Securities and Exchange Commission, Amicus Curiae, in Support of Appellant's Brief Seeking Reversal and Remand, United States v. Stringer, 2006 WL 3225567 (9th Cir. Sept. 13, 2006) (No. 06-30100).

40. See Q 30.18.2, *infra*, for discussion of one such difficult issue: the decision as to whether or not a witness should testify in a civil investigation.

41. *See, e.g.*, United States v. Kordel, 397 U.S. 1 (1970) (no departure from proper administration of justice where defendant had to choose between either asserting Fifth Amendment rights or answering interrogatories, the responses to which were later used to convict him); SEC v. First Fin. Group of Tex., Inc., 659 F.2d 660, 666–67 (5th Cir. 1981) ("'[t]here is no general federal constitutional, statutory, or common law rule barring the simultaneous prosecution of separate civil and criminal actions by different federal agencies against the same defendant involving the same transactions. . . . The simultaneous prosecution of civil and criminal actions is generally unobjectionable because the federal government is entitled to vindicate the different interests promoted by different regulatory provisions even though it attempts to vindicate several interests simultaneously

in different forums.'"); SEC v. Dresser Indus., Inc., 628 F.2d 1368 (D.C. Cir. 1980) (courts should not intervene in parallel investigations unless the nature of the proceedings prejudices substantial rights).

42. United States v. Parrott, 248 F. Supp. 196, 202 (D.D.C. 1965).

43. United States v. Stringer, 521 F.3d 1189 (9th Cir. 2008). The Ninth Circuit's opinion expressly overruled United States v. Stringer, 408 F. Supp. 2d 1083 (D. Or. 2006), and rejected the reasoning of United States v. Scrushy, 366 F. Supp. 2d 1134, 1140 (N.D. Ala. 2005), two cases that had sharply criticized the government's conduct in conducting surreptitious parallel criminal investigations.

44. Indeed, Judge Rakoff of the Southern District of New York has termed the practice of the government initiating civil charges with the intent to stay those charges in favor of a parallel criminal proceeding as "a misuse of the processes" of the judicial system. *See* SEC v. Oakford Corp., 181 F.R.D. 269, 273 (S.D.N.Y. 1998); *see also* SEC v. Kornman, 2006 WL 1506954, at *4 (N.D. Tex. May 31, 2006) (following denial of motion to stay SEC civil action, SEC moved for voluntary dismissal without prejudice; court granted dismissal motion but allowed defendant to conduct requested discovery finding that requested dismissal was "an attempt to circumvent" the denial of the stay motion); SEC v. Yuen, No. 03-4376, slip op. at 5, 11–13 (C.D. Cal. Oct. 2, 2003) (denied motion to stay, in part, because government had chosen to bring both proceedings simultaneously); SEC v. Poirier, No. 97-3478, slip op. at 5 (N.D. Ga. Feb. 13, 1998) (same); SEC v. Tucker, 130 F.R.D. 461, 463 (S.D. Fla. 1990) (same).

45. SEC v. Saad, 229 F.R.D. 90, 91 (S.D.N.Y. 2005).

46. *See, e.g.*, Nat'l Stock Exch. v. Fed. Ins. Co., 2007 WL 1030293 (N.D. Ill. Mar. 30, 2007) (finding coverage for defense costs of officers from date of SEC's issuance of formal order of investigation to company).

47. A company might consider requesting that the SEC proceed by formal process to trigger its D&O coverage. Of course, the desire for D&O coverage must be balanced against the concern that formal investigations may be more likely to result in enforcement action because they have received attention both at high levels within the Enforcement Division, as well as from the Commission.

48. Occasionally, the SEC's initial contact with a company will be a request for an explanation of certain events, such as a financial restatement. The company's response could be in the form of either a written submission or a personal meeting. It is critical that counsel thoroughly prepare the company's response to ensure that its representations will withstand further investigative scrutiny. If the company's initial representations are discredited, both the company and its counsel will have credibility problems with the staff, which will make the investigation more protracted and costly.

49. *See* 17 C.F.R. § 202.5(c).

50. SEC ENFORCEMENT MANUAL, *available at* www.sec.gov/divisions/enforce/enforcementmanual.pdf.

51. 18 U.S.C. § 1519. Similarly, section 1102 of SOX makes it punishable by up to twenty years' imprisonment to "corruptly" alter, destroy, mutilate, or conceal a record to impair its integrity or availability for use in an official proceeding. 18 U.S.C. § 1512.

52. See chapter 5, *supra*, for a full discussion of records management programs and policies.
53. Press Release No. 2003-111, U.S. Securities and Exchange Commission (Sept. 11, 2003), *available at* www.sec.gov/news/press/2003-111.htm.
54. Admin. Proc. File No. 3-11425 (Mar. 10, 2004), *available at* www.sec.gov/litigation/admin/34-49386.htm.
55. Litigation Rel. No. 18,715 (May 17, 2004), *available at* www.sec.gov/litigation/litreleases/lr18715.htm. The SEC did make substantive allegations against Lucent in this matter.
56. See chapter 7 for an extensive discussion of e-discovery.
57. While a company may choose to disclose certain privileged documents to SEC staff in the interest of cooperating with the investigation, as discussed in Q 30.13 *et seq.*, the case law has become increasingly hostile to selective disclosures, holding that a disclosure to the SEC waives the attorney-client privilege with respect to all third parties.
58. One of the most efficient methods for managing e-discovery costs is to confine the number of sources, or custodians, to only those key individuals that are likely to have relevant electronic information.
59. The SEC's technical data delivery standards are constantly evolving. If the staff does not include its current data standards in its request for an electronic production, the responding party should request them.
60. The SEC's Enforcement Director stated at a national securities conference on May 4, 2007, however, that the SEC does not request waivers of the attorney client privilege:

> First, we do not—indeed we cannot—require waiver of the attorney/client privilege. Second, waiver of a privilege or protection is not a pre-requisite to obtaining credit in a Commission investigation. The credit given is based on, among other things, the factual information given, the timeliness of the provision of information and the usefulness of the information. Waivers may be, and often are, a means to that end but are not an end in and of themselves.

Linda Chatman Thomsen, Dir., Div. of Enforcement, U.S. Sec. & Exch. Comm'n, Remarks Before the 27th Annual Ray Garrett, Jr. Corporate and Securities Law Institute (May 4, 2007), *available at* www.sec.gov/news/speech/2007/spch050407lct.htm.

Indeed, the new SEC ENFORCEMENT MANUAL expressly directs that "*[t]he staff should not ask a party to waive the attorney-client or work product privileges and is directed not to do so.*" SEC ENFORCEMENT MANUAL § 4.3 (emphasis in original). Nonetheless, it remains to be seen whether any company that does not share the work product of its internal investigation will get a complete pass from any enforcement action.

61. *See* Diversified Indus., Inc. v. Meredith, 572 F.2d 596, 611 (8th Cir. 1978) (en banc).

62. *See, e.g., In re* Sealed Case, 676 F.2d 793, 824 (D.C. Cir. 1982); *In re* Steinhardt Partners, L.P., 9 F.3d 230, 236 (2d Cir. 1993); United States v. Billmyer, 57 F.3d 31, 37 (1st Cir. 1995); Dellwood Farms, Inc. v. Cargill, Inc., 128 F.3d 1122, 1127 (7th Cir. 1997); *In re* Keeper of Records, 348 F.3d 16, 28 (1st Cir. 2003).

63. *See In re* Columbia/HCA Healthcare Corp. Billing Practices Litig., 293 F.3d 289, 294–95 (6th Cir. 2002).

64. *See, e.g., In re* Qwest Commc'ns Int'l, Inc. Sec. Litig., 450 F.3d 1179 (10th Cir. 2006) (declining to allow selective disclosure even where a confidentiality agreement is in place); McKesson HBOC, Inc. v. Superior Court of S.F. County, 115 Cal. App. 4th 1229 (Cal. Ct. App. 2004) (rejecting selective disclosure under California law); McKesson Corp. v. Green, 266 Ga. App. 157, 164 (Ct. App. 2004) (rejecting selective disclosure under Georgia law); United States v. Bergonzi, 216 F.R.D. 487, 498 (N.D. Cal. 2003) (rejecting selective disclosure under federal common law). *But see* Aronson v. McKesson HBOC, Inc., 2005 WL 934331, at *10 (N.D. Cal. May 31, 2005) (allowing selective disclosure under federal common law where there was a written confidentiality agreement); Saito v. McKesson HBOC, Inc., 2002 WL 31657622, at *15 (Del. Ch. Nov. 13, 2002) (same).

65. United States v. Reyes, 239 F.R.D. 591 (N.D. Cal. 2006).

66. *Id.* at 603.

67. Report of the Advisory Committee on Evidence Rules (May 15, 2006), *available at* www.uscourts.gov/rules/Excerpt_EV_Report_Pub.pdf.

68. *See* 17 C.F.R. § 203.6.

69. *Id.*

70. *Id.* § 203.7(a).

71. *Id.* § 203.7(b).

72. 18 U.S.C. § 1621.

73. 18 U.S.C. § 1001.

74. 17 C.F.R. § 203.7(c).

75. Sometimes conflicts (or simply the advisability of having personal counsel) do not emerge until after the witness testifies or until after the SEC staff issues a Wells Notice advising of its preliminary charging recommendation. For this reason, it is not uncommon for certain witnesses to obtain personal counsel after testifying.

76. Indeed, SEC Form 1662, shown to every witness at the start of testimony, warns that multiple representations present a potential conflict of interest if one client's interests are or may be adverse to another's.

77. While testimony typically is not attended by staff above the Branch Chief (first level supervisor), overview presentations frequently will be attended by an Assistant Director (second level supervisor) or higher.

78. If the staff reaches a firm conclusion that it will not recommend enforcement charges, it has the discretion to advise the party that the investigation has been terminated. *See* 17 C.F.R. § 202.5(d). It is a matter of Enforcement Division policy to issue such letters, but the practice does not appear to be uniform. When they come at all, closing letters typically come long after (often more than a year) the conclusion of witness testimony.

79. Dodd-Frank Wall Street Reform and Consumer Protection Act of 2010, Pub. L. No. 111-203, 124 Stat. 1326, § 929U [hereinafter Dodd-Frank]. Certain complex actions may be extended 180 days with the approval of the Director of Enforcement and notice to the chairman of the commission; a further 180 day extension may be granted by the chairman.

80. See Mitchell E. Herr, *SEC Enforcement: A Better Wells Process*, 32 SEC. REG. L.J. 1 at 56 (Spring 2004), *available at* www.hklaw.com/content/white papers/SECEnforcementABetterWells.pdf.

81. SEC Form 1662. On the other hand, the SEC's Chief Administrative Law Judge, in a decision that may have continued vitality, held that Wells Submissions are inadmissible as protected settlement materials under Federal Rule of Evidence 408. See *In re* Allied Stores Corp., 52 SEC Docket (CCH) 451, 451–52 (1992).

82. See *In re* Initial Pub. Offering Sec. Litig., 2003 U.S. Dist. LEXIS 23102 (S.D.N.Y. Dec. 24, 2003).

83. Although less commonly invoked, the SEC may also charge non-scienter fraud under Securities Act § 17(a)(2) and (3), 15 U.S.C. § 77a(a)(2) and (3), for merely negligent conduct.

84. Dodd-Frank § 929M.

85. *Id.* §§ 929M, 929O.

86. *Id.* § 929P(c).

87. Dodd-Frank authorizes the SEC to impose monetary penalties in administrative cease-and-desist proceedings. *Id.* § 929P(a). This significantly enhances the SEC's enforcement options, because administrative proceedings are faster than federal court actions and do not allow for the expansive discovery available in federal district court.

88. 17 C.F.R. § 201.1003.

89. Stephen M. Cutler, Dir., Div. of Enforcement, Sec. & Exch. Comm'n, Remarks Before the 24th Annual Ray Garrett, Jr. Corporate and Securities Law Institute (Apr. 29, 2004), *available at* www.sec.gov/news/speech/spch042904smc.htm.

90. 2006 SEC Performance and Accountability Report at 8, *available at* www.sec.gov/about/secpar/secpar2006.pdf#sec1.

91. Press Release No. 2006-4, U.S. Securities and Exchange Commission, Statement of the Securities and Exchange Commission Concerning Penalties, *available at* www.sec.gov/news/press/2006-4.htm.

92. *Id.*

93. *Id.*

94. *Id.*

95. A director or officer cannot be held liable merely as a result of his or her position. To be held liable as a principal, the director or officer must have personally acted with the requisite scienter (*i.e.*, state of mind). Similarly, a director or officer cannot be held liable as a "control person" if he or she acted in good faith and did not directly or indirectly induce the violation.

96. 17 C.F.R. § 201.1003.

97. Stephen M. Cutler, Dir., Div. of Enforcement, U.S. Sec. & Exch. Comm'n, Remarks Before the District of Columbia Bar Association (Feb. 11, 2004), *available at* www.sec.gov/news/speech/spch021104smc.htm.

98. The year 2009 marked the SEC's first use of SOX section 304 to "claw back" compensation from an executive not charged with any violation of the securities laws. *See* Complaint for Violations of Section 304 of the Sarbanes-Oxley Act of 2002, SEC v. Jenkins, 2009 WL 2350797 (D. Ariz. July 22, 2009) (Case No. CV 09-1510-PHX-JWS).

99. In an April 13, 2007 speech, Chairman Cox signaled a potential shift in how the SEC approaches negotiating penalties against public companies. Christopher Cox, Chairman, U.S. Sec. & Exch. Comm'n, Address to the Mutual Fund Directors Forum, Seventh Annual Policy Conference, Washington, D.C. (Apr. 13, 2007), *available at* www.sec.gov/news/speech/2007/spch041207cc.htm. Heretofore, without prejudgment by the Commission, the staff negotiated the entire settlement with the company, subject to the Commission's subsequent approval. In the interest of fairness and "horizontal equity," Chairman Cox stated that going forward the staff may be required to obtain Commission approval prior to commencing settlement discussions. Under the new policy, if the staff then negotiates a settlement within the range of "guidance" provided by the Commission, the settlement will be eligible for summary approval through the Commission's seriatim procedure. This new policy raises issues for defense counsel who wish to have their views considered by the Commission before it issues settlement "guidance" to the staff. As of this writing the defense bar does not have sufficient experience with this new policy to understand precisely how it will be implemented or how it will affect the dynamics of settlement negotiations with the staff.

100. 17 C.F.R. § 202.5(e).

31

Executive Compensation

*Robert J. Friedman, Richard J. Hindlian,
David G. O'Leary & Meredith L. O'Leary*

This chapter is intended to assist corporate counsel by providing a roadmap through the many aspects of executive compensation. The chapter covers the basic elements of an executive compensation package and provides important information concerning the federal income tax and securities law rules that inform the executive compensation decisions and govern executive compensation awards.

Elements of Executive Compensation	1045
General Tax Rules	1048
Deferred Compensation	1055
Non-Qualified Deferred Compensation Plans	1056
Taxation of Deferred Compensation Under Code Section 409A	1059
Section 409A Exemptions	1062
Payment of Deferred Compensation	1068
Compliance/Reporting Requirements	1073
Offshore Non-Qualified Deferred Compensation Plans	1076
Golden Parachute Payments	1078
Equity and Equity-Based Compensation	1081
Types of Equity Awards	1082
Financial Accounting for Equity and Equity-Based Compensation	1086
Securities Law Issues	1087
Proxy Disclosure Rules	1088
Other Disclosure Rules for Executives and Directors	1095
Treatment of NQDC Plans As Securities	1097
Exemptions from Registration Requirements	1100
Disclosure and Reporting Requirements	1101
Shareholder Approval	1102
Profits Recovery/Restricting Insiders	1103
Limiting Resales of Stock	1105
Blackout Periods	1107

Elements of Executive Compensation

Q 31.1 How do employers generally provide and document executive compensation arrangements?

Executive compensation may be provided pursuant to an employment agreement or other type of plan or on an ad hoc basis.

Q 31.2 What types of compensation are usually provided by an employment agreement?

For publicly traded corporations, it is common for an employment agreement to provide one or more of the following compensation elements:

- Fixed cash compensation on an annual basis;
- Year-end cash bonus compensation based on various performance criteria, including individual, division, or company performance;
- Deferred compensation pursuant to the employment agreement or a related non-qualified plan, which may or may not include a rabbi trust;
- Restricted stock, stock options, or other stock awards, often with cashless exercise provisions that use built-up equity for the share purchase;
- Severance compensation under the agreement, or a related non-qualified severance compensation plan;
- Change-in-control compensation under the agreement or a related non-qualified plan, which becomes payable if the employer undergoes a change in control; and
- Other forms of employment-related benefits, including medical and life insurance, vacation or sick leave, or various forms of perquisites.

Q 31.2.1 What types of compensation are generally provided by a "plan"?

Employers generally provide tax-qualified plans and trusts under Internal Revenue Code ("Code") sections 401(a) and 501(a), such as a section 401(k) plan, defined benefit pension plan, profit sharing plan, employee stock ownership plan (ESOP), cash balance pension, and other forms of income tax–qualified plans and trusts for employees (including executives).

Other kinds of stock-, bonus-, and benefits-related non-qualified plans may vary widely from company to company and from industry to industry. Stock options or restricted share plans are generally not subject to title I of ERISA because they do not primarily provide retirement benefits.

The kinds of arrangements that are defined as "plans" will have varied definitions and legal and regulatory consequences depending on the particular applicable law.

Q 31.2.2 What types of compensation arrangements are not considered "plans"?

Under title I of ERISA, the U.S. Department of Labor (DOL) has issued regulations[1] providing that, if certain conditions and limitations are met, various kinds of compensation arrangements or programs will not be considered "plans" for purposes of title I of ERISA. Title I generally deals with the independent trust, funding, fiduciary responsibility, reporting, enforcement, and other requirements of title I of ERISA that otherwise apply to non-exempt retirement benefit plans.

For example, these DOL regulations exclude (and therefore permit) cash bonus compensation plans that are not viewed as an employee pension benefit plan when employee or executive bonuses are paid on a regular basis by the employer for work performed, unless the actual bonus payment is deferred until employment termination or beyond. Similarly, a severance pay plan providing for not more than two times an executive's recent annual compensation, which must be paid out in full within twenty-four months after employment termination and is not contingent on an employee's retiring, is also exempt from title I under this DOL regulation.

There are other forms of systematic benefits that are considered non-plans under these DOL regulations, but this regulatory exemption has nothing to do with the Code's treatment of a particular plan, with the benefits provided and enforced under the plan for local law purposes, or with respect to the application of other federal laws to the benefit or to the plan.

Q 31.2.3 What is severance pay?

A severance pay provision in an employment agreement or a severance pay program or plan typically provides for post-employment termination compensation to be paid to the executive in the event his or her employment is terminated by the company without cause. These benefits are typically of a short-term salary continuation nature. Frequently, the amounts payable will vary based on the duration of employment, compensation level, and the period over which the severance pay is to be paid. These benefits are unlike reduction in force benefit programs, which often are adopted to address a particular situation for a short interval.

Q 31.2.4 What is a change-in-control agreement or plan?

A change-in-control agreement or plan is quite different from a severance pay agreement or plan. Often, a change-in-control agreement is triggered, and compensation therefore becomes payable, if as part of a corporate transaction there is a change in control of the board of directors of the employer or if there is a change in the controlling stockholders. This change in control may occur in a sale, merger, private equity investment into the company, and many other forms of corporate transaction. A change-in-control agreement or plan might also be drafted to require a "double trigger" before the benefit is payable—where both (1) the change in control and (2) a termination of employment, diminution in the executive's role or title, change in the person to whom the executive reports, or other change in the executive's responsibilities following the change in control must occur.

Sometimes, when two public companies are combined in a so-called merger of equals, whether by merger or otherwise, the new board of directors is divided equally between representatives of the two constituent companies so that there will be no change in control. The change-in-control compensation covenants or plans are not triggered and do not become payable despite the fact that the shareholders from each constituent corporation are not equal in the merged entity. The liability to pay change-in-control compensation may trigger Code section 280G, which addresses the tax treatment to the executive of "excess" parachute payments. Treasury Regulations section 1.280G-1, Q&A-27(a) and -28 specifically refer to a greater-than-50% change-in-control transaction as being included within the section 280G provisions related to a change in control. The Securities and Exchange Commission (SEC) uses similar concepts for its own securities regulation and reporting requirements.

General Tax Rules

Q 31.3 What are the general rules that apply to taxation of executive compensation?

Individuals generally use the cash method of accounting for federal income tax purposes. This means that compensation paid becomes gross income and is subject to federal income tax when it is received by an executive. Even if it is not actually received in cash, income may be subject to taxation if the "constructive receipt" doctrine or the "economic benefit" doctrine becomes applicable. Constructive receipt of income occurs if the right to the income has been earned. The executive cannot postpone taxation of the income by deferring its receipt, beyond when it would otherwise be paid. The economic benefit doctrine becomes applicable if a taxpayer receives a non-cash economic benefit (such as the performance of services) that is considered to be gross income.[2]

Various Code sections also have been enacted to deal with the specialized income tax rules applicable to certain kinds of deferred income, such as Incentive Stock Options (ISOs), or to address and remedy certain perceived abuses. Code section 280G, which provides special rules for "excess" golden parachute payments made to executives, is an example of a Code provision that may impose an extra penalty tax on the employee executive. These situations may also be addressed through Treasury regulations and IRS notices. Regulations sections 1.61-22 and 1.7872-15 (adopted in September 2003), which relate to the "economic benefit" regime and "loan" regime alternatives for an executive split-dollar life insurance benefit program, are examples of a regulatory approach.

Code section 409A, enacted into law by Congress in October 2004 and often referred to as the "anti-Enron provision," applies equally to public, private, and tax-exempt employers.[3] Code section 409A applies to non-qualified deferred compensation plans (including individual employment agreements) that defer the receipt of earned income from one year to a later year. In its general application, when

Code section 409A has not been complied with, the employee is subjected to income taxation before the compensation is actually paid to the employee and an additional 20% penalty tax on the compensation amount in question. If the violation arises during a tax audit of an earlier year, then interest on back taxes, and various other penalties, may become payable, subject to applicable Code provisions for the possible abatement of penalties.[4]

Q 31.3.1 What are gross-up covenants?

It is common for various forms of compensation agreements and plans, such as change-in-control plans, phantom stock plans, and other stock-based or incentive compensation plans, to provide for supplementary amounts to be paid by the employer to the executive to compensate for an extra income tax or other tax or penalty. Payments under an incentive plan are sometimes intended to be after-tax payments to the executive. The employer secures the benefit of the income tax deduction for the payments it makes.

COMPLIANCE FACT

Gross-up amounts are themselves subject to federal, state, and local income taxes, if any, as additional compensation paid to the executive. As a result, the amounts paid in a gross-up need to be increased to account for the extra income taxes that become payable from the executive's receipt of the grossed-up amount.[5]

Example: In Massachusetts, it is not uncommon to see a gross-up of 37% to 38% of a phantom stock payment award (a form of deferred cash compensation), so as to account for federal income taxes, state income taxes, federal tax savings from the state income tax deduction, and other related items (such as the possible "alternative minimum tax" (AMT) liability, since state income tax deductions are an AMT tax preference item).

Q 31.3.2 What is an incentive stock option (ISO)?

An ISO is defined in Code section 422 to mean an option award that has been granted to an individual in connection with his or her employment to purchase stock but only if:

(a) the option is granted under a plan that is approved by the shareholders within twelve months before or after the plan is adopted and the plan sets forth the aggregate number of shares available;

(b) the option is granted to the employee within ten years after the plan is adopted, or the date it is approved by the shareholders, whichever is earlier;

(c) such option award is not exercisable after ten years from the date the option is granted to the employee;

(d) the option price to be paid on exercise is not less than the fair market value of the stock when the option was granted;

(e) such option is not transferable except by will or the laws of descent and the option is exercisable during his or her lifetime only by the employee; and

(f) such optionee, at the time of the grant of the option, does not own more than 10% of the total combined voting power of all stock of the corporation.

Code section 422(c) provides for good-faith valuation, and fair market value must be determined without reference to any restriction except those that by their terms will never lapse. Other special rules for disability, payment for stock purchased with stock options (that is, cashless exercise), etc., may also apply. Most importantly perhaps is the $100,000-per-year limitation on ISOs by which stock options that become exercisable are not treated as ISOs and are instead treated as non-qualified stock options to the extent they exceed the $100,000 limit. ISOs are not taxable when the option is granted to the employee, and on exercise the shares are subject to AMT in that year if they are substantially vested.[6] The AMT amount is the excess of the fair market value of such shares on the date of exercise over their exercise price.[7] Later gains on the sale of such shares are taxed at capital gain tax rates if the holding period for "qualified" sales has been met—that is, two years from the date the option was granted and one year after the option exercise date. The employer receives no income tax deduction from qualified stock sales.

Q 31.3.3 What is the AMT?

The alternative minimum tax (AMT) is a federal excise tax that is calculated as part of each taxpayer's annually filed income tax return. The AMT takes certain defined items of gross income, deductions, tax credits, exclusions, allowances, and other items, less applicable exemption amounts, from which is derived the AMT amount based on the AMT rate. If the AMT owed is less than the regular income tax liability for such tax year, no additional AMT amount is owed. If the AMT exceeds the regular income tax calculation, then the regular tax is increased by the applicable AMT amount owed.

Q 31.3.4 How should an executive prepare for the AMT?

It can be important for executives to be conscious of the AMT requirements under the Code whenever they face a one-time compensation event. A practical way to start to approach AMT is to take the prior year's federal income tax return, modify the amounts involved in the prior year for the one-time income event in question, and do a tax calculation for both the current year regular federal income tax and for the AMT. This can be especially important if ISOs are exercised triggering an AMT tax liability, which needs to be paid before the shares may be sold due to lock-up agreements, the twenty-four-month holding period required under Code section 422, or otherwise, and such shares may decline in value while owned. The executive will need other liquid assets if he does not promptly secure from the shares purchased the cash needed to cover the AMT tax.

For AMT purposes for individuals,[8] Code section 421 shall not apply to the transfer of shares acquired pursuant to the exercise of an ISO, as defined in Code section 422.[9] This means that, if an executive is granted an ISO for 10,000 shares of stock at its fair market value of $10 per share, and two years later the stock is selling for $20 per share when the executive exercises the option and pays $10 per share to buy the shares, there is an AMT adjustment item of $100,000 (or $10 × 10,000), which may cause an AMT tax liability to become payable, after exemptions and other adjustments, at the 26% AMT federal tax rate. This tax payment is largely a timing item, however, since if, for example, an AMT tax of $12,000 is paid for 2007, and the shares purchased are sold in 2009 at $25 per share, a long-term gain of $150,000 ($15 per share × 10,000 shares), the capital gains tax owed in 2009 is partially offset by the $12,000 AMT tax paid for 2007 on the exercise of the ISO.

Q 31.4 What is the general rule for the taxation of non-qualified deferred compensation?

An unsecured, unfunded promise by the employer to pay compensation in the future, which is entered into before the services are performed, should defer the receipt of the earned income until it is to be paid to the executive. Assuming that the requirements of Code section 409A are satisfied,[10] taxation of deferred compensation is postponed until payment is made to the executive even if the deferred compensation is earned and vested in an earlier year. The employer secures the benefit of the tax deduction on its corporate tax return at the same time that the executive receives and is subject to income tax on the payments received by the executive.

Q 31.4.1 Does a rabbi trust affect the treatment of a deferred compensation plan under the Code or ERISA?

Often a non-qualified deferred compensation plan is indirectly funded by what is called a rabbi trust. For income tax purposes, a rabbi trust is treated as a grantor trust (which means the employer owns the monies placed in the trust and the earnings on the trust investments are taxable to the employer). Since the employer's creditors may reach the trust's assets in the event of employer insolvency, thereby depriving the executive of the security of the trust's assets, this arrangement is considered by the IRS to be an unfunded promise to pay deferred compensation.

Q 31.4.2 How does Code section 83, concerning transfers of property as compensation for services, affect executive compensation?

Code section 83(a) provides detailed rules (including section 83(b) election) for the taxation of property, including employer stock, transferred in connection with the performance of services. This Code section requires inclusion in income of the fair market value of property (less any amount paid by the employee) transferred to an employee or independent contractor, when such property becomes substantially vested (that is, is not subject to a substantial risk of

Executive Compensation Q 31.4.3

> **COMPLIANCE FACT**
>
> ERISA provides that a "top hat" plan—that is, an unfunded non-qualified deferred compensation plan which covers only a select group of highly compensated or managerial personnel—is excluded from being subject to several aspects of ERISA that are applicable to pension plans. A top hat plan will not be considered a funded plan for purposes of ERISA because it is indirectly funded with a rabbi trust.[11]

forfeiture). Code section 83(e)(1) makes stock option transactions that are subject to Code section 421 (which relates to Code section 422 and to ISOs) not subject to taxation under section 83(a).

Q 31.4.3 How does Code section 422, concerning ISOs, affect executive compensation?

Under Code section 422, special federal income tax treatment applies to ISOs. If:

(a) no disposition of the shares is made by the employee within two years from the date of the granting of the ISO nor within one year after such shares are transferred to him or her by exercise of the ISO, and

(b) at all times from the date of the ISO grant and ending three months before the date of exercise, the option holder was an employee of either the granting corporation, a parent or subsidiary, or a corporation that assumes the stock option in a section 424(a) transaction,[12]

then generally the employee will recognize a capital gain or loss from the sale or other disposition of the stock acquired pursuant to the exercise of the ISO.

Under Code section 421, when Code section 422(a) has been complied with, an ISO:

1053

(a) results in no income to the employee on exercise of the option and purchase of the shares;
(b) results in no business expense deduction for compensation paid by the employer corporation with respect to the shares transferred to the employee; and
(c) results in no amount to be paid to the corporation except the purchase price paid by the employee.

A disqualifying disposition of the shares by the employee (which occurs when the ISO holding period has not been complied with) results in ordinary income to the employee and a business expense deduction to the employer for the amounts involved.

Q 31.4.4 What are the general tax rules for non-qualified stock options?

A non-qualified stock option, like an ISO, results in no income realized by the employee on the grant of the option assuming that the options do not have a readily ascertainable fair market value at that time, as defined in Treasury regulations section 1.83-7(a).[13] However, the exercise of the non-qualified stock option and purchase of the shares results in ordinary income equal to the fair market value of the shares purchased less the amount paid to purchase the shares. In many cases, when an executive faces an income tax liability when he or she purchases shares, it is often recommended that share sales be promptly considered so as to raise cash proceeds to pay the taxes owed, particularly if the market value of the shares is at all volatile. This is true even when the AMT tax does not apply since the options are not ISOs.[14] The employee has a corresponding income tax deduction in the same year the ordinary income is reported by the employee from his exercise of such non-qualified options.

Q 31.4.5 Are there adverse tax consequences from mispriced stock options?

In addition to all of the accounting, fiduciary, SEC, and negative publicity issues raised by discounted and backdated stock option awards, Code section 409A is also implicated when stock option awards are priced at below fair market value on the date of the grant. Therefore, this practice triggers the 20% penalty and back taxes issues.

> **COMPLIANCE FACT**
>
> In 2007, the IRS provided limited transitional relief for innocent rank-and-file employees who received the benefit of share option awards that were backdated and violated the fair market value at grant requirements of the Code and that had been exercised by the employees in 2006.[15] In addition, in IRS Initiative 2007-18, the IRS allowed companies to come forward voluntarily to pay the section 409A 20% penalty tax and interest owed on back taxes by one or more such employees (other than insiders and top executives) as defined in the securities laws. The program, however, expired on February 28, 2007, with notice to affected employees required to be provided by March 15, 2007. The extra 20% penalty tax paid to the IRS by the employer relieved the employee of his or her penalty burden, plus interest, but such amount was to be treated as additional compensation paid to the employee for the then current tax year. Presumably, the IRS will provide similar relief for 2007 as well.

Deferred Compensation

Q 31.5 What is deferred compensation?

Another mechanism for providing valuable compensation and benefits to corporate executives is through the use of deferred compensation. Deferred compensation refers to cash compensation that will be paid to the executive at some point in the future. There are many different types of deferred compensation plans. For example, there are **qualified deferred compensation plans** (such as a traditional pension plan or a 401(k) plan) and **non-qualified deferred compensation plans**. There are many variations of non-qualified deferred compensation plans, as non-qualified deferred compensation provides companies with greater flexibility for design purposes in terms of how contributions are made and participant vesting.

Non-Qualified Deferred Compensation Plans

Q 31.6 What are the general attributes of a non-qualified deferred compensation plan?

A non-qualified deferred compensation plan has greater flexibility than a qualified plan. In general, a non-qualified deferred compensation plan has no limits on the amount of compensation that can be deferred. A non-qualified deferred compensation plan will be subject to Code section 409A. Generally, a participant is not subject to taxation on any of the compensation deferred under the plan until receipt. In such a situation, however, the company would not be entitled to a deduction for the compensation paid until the date of distribution.[16]

Q 31.6.1 What types of non-qualified deferred compensation plans are there?

The most common types of non-qualified deferred compensation plans include the "excess plan" and the "supplemental executive retirement plan" (SERP).

Excess plan. An "excess plan" typically allows executives and highly compensated employees to defer money or to accrue benefits in excess of the amounts they accrue under the company's qualified plans. Many times, an executive is limited from deferring amounts under the company's qualified plans due to Code limitations on compensation and non-discrimination testing.

SERP. A SERP refers to a non-qualified deferred compensation plan that is provided to a select group of management and highly compensated employees. This plan is also sometimes referred to as a "top hat" plan. A SERP is a non-qualified deferred compensation plan that is not tied to a company qualified plan. Subject to Code section 409A,[17] a company has discretion to determine most of the plan terms and features.

Q 31.6.2 How does an excess plan work?

The following example demonstrates how: Assume that the chief executive officer of a company earns $750,000 annually and intends to defer 10% of her compensation into the company's 401(k) plan. Unfortunately, there are three problems with this scenario:

(1) In 2007, the CEO could only defer $15,500 into the company's 401(k) plan plus an additional $5,000 as a catch-up contribution if over fifty years old;

(2) Under the Code, there is a $225,000 limit on compensation for determining benefits under qualified retirement plans; and

(3) Any amounts deferred may be further reduced as a correction method if the non-discrimination tests for the 401(k) plan failed.

However, if the company had an excess SERP, the CEO would be able to contribute the full 10% of her salary. The CEO's contributions would first be used to "max out" the 401(k) plan and then any spillover contributions due to Code or plan limits would be contributed to the excess plan. The same principles can apply with respect to defined benefit plans.

Q 31.6.3   Are there any requirements with respect to SERP?

A top hat plan refers to an unfunded plan offered to a select group of management and highly compensated employees of the company. If structured correctly, a top hat plan could provide for unlimited, tax-free deferral opportunities that would grow on a tax-free basis. Although a top hat plan is subject to ERISA's reporting and disclosure requirements, the DOL has provided that such a plan could meet all of those requirements by filing a statement with the Secretary of Labor that includes the following information: the name and address of the employer; the employer's IRS identification number (EIN); a statement declaring that the employer maintains the plan or plans primarily for the purpose of providing deferred compensation for a select group of management or highly compensated employees; and a statement listing the number of such plans and the number of employees in each such plan.[18] Contributions into a top hat plan may be contributed to a rabbi trust.[19]

Q 31.6.4   What is a select group of management and highly compensated employees?

The U.S. DOL has never formally answered the question of what constitutes a select group of management and highly compensated employees. Based on case law, it appears that a conservative estimate would be 5%–10% of the senior management and highest paid employees of the company. A greater number of participants could result in a challenge by the DOL and the loss of the three statutory exemptions.[20]

Q 31.6.5   May a deferred compensation plan be funded?

A non-qualified deferred compensation plan may be funded or unfunded. A funded non-qualified plan is one where the employer maintains the plan by making contributions to a trust or by paying premiums into an annuity contract. The employee may or may not have to pay current income tax on the contributions depending on the employee's vested rights in the contributions. Funding a non-qualified deferred compensation plan may subject the plan to the various participation, vesting, funding, fiduciary responsibility, and plan termination insurance provisions under ERISA.[21]

One way in which deferred compensation may be funded is through the use of life insurance products. Typically, the deferred amounts can be used to pay premiums on cash value life insurance. The cash value may then be available at retirement to supplement other income or, if the insured dies before retirement, the insured's designated beneficiary would receive the insurance policy's death benefit.

If a non-qualified plan is unfunded, the plan merely involves the employer's present promise to pay amounts to the employee in the future. The employee is taxed only when those amounts are actually or constructively received by the employee or beneficiary.[22] One main concern with an unfunded plan from the executive's standpoint is that the payments are only conditioned on the company's promise to pay in the future. Often, particularly in the context of a change in control, the executives worry that the new company will not follow through on the promised benefits. Funding a rabbi trust is not considered funding for this purpose because creditors of the employer may reach the assets of the rabbi trust if the employer becomes insolvent, and for income tax purposes, the profits and losses earned by the trust before payout of the benefits to the executive occurs are reported on the employer's federal tax return since the trust is treated as a grantor trust under Code section 671 due to the company creditor's access to the trust assets in an insolvency.[23]

Q 31.6.6 What is split-dollar insurance?

Split-dollar insurance is insurance in which the premiums for the policy on an employee are split between the insured employee and his or her employer. The typical form of split-dollar insurance provides that the employer pays the portion of the premium that relates to the yearly build-up in the cash value of the policy, while the employee pays the portion that relates to the insurance protection.

Q 31.6.7 How is split-dollar insurance taxed?

The way that split-dollar insurance is taxed was changed in 2003. Currently, the taxation of split-dollar insurance depends on who owns the policy. If the employee owns the policy, the employer's premium payments are treated as loans to the executive. Thus, the executive is required to pay the employer market-rate interest on the loan (the "loan regime") or the executive will be taxed on the difference between market-rate interest and the actual interest. If the employer is the owner of the policy, the employer's premium payments are treated as providing a taxable economic benefit to the executive (the "economic benefit regime"), which includes both the executive's interest in the policy's cash value and current life insurance protection.[24] The IRS has ruled that, if the "loan regime" applies to a split-dollar arrangement, Code section 409A does not apply to the split-dollar arrangement with an employee.

Taxation of Deferred Compensation Under Code Section 409A

Q 31.7 What rules does Code section 409A impose?

In response to actual and perceived abuses, Congress enacted sweeping changes to the taxation of benefits under non-qualified deferred compensation plans. The American Jobs Creation Act of 2004 added Code section 409A, which significantly impacted the design and operation of such plans. Code section 409A, which became effective January 1, 2005, affects all employers, whether public, private, or tax-exempt. Code section 409A imposes rules on the deferral elections, distributions, and funding with respect to deferred compensation arrangements. Failure to comply with the requirements of Code section 409A may result in significant adverse tax consequences to the service provider.

After the enactment of Code section 409A, the IRS permitted employers and other plan sponsors to delay the amendment of the plan or arrangement until the issuance of final regulations, provided that they administer the plan or arrangement in good-faith compliance with the requirements of section 409A during the interim period. Final regulations were issued in April 2007 and all affected plans and arrangements had to be amended to conform to the requirements of Code section 409A by December 31, 2007. This deadline was later extended to December 31, 2008.

Q 31.7.1 What is a non-qualified deferred compensation plan for purposes of Code section 409A?

Generally, the term "non-qualified deferred compensation plan" means any plan or arrangement between a service provider and a service recipient that provides for the deferral of compensation by the service provider. It includes any agreement, method, or arrangement, including an agreement, method, or arrangement that applies to one person or individual. A plan may be adopted unilaterally by the service recipient or may be negotiated among or agreed to by the service recipient and one or more service providers or service providers' representatives.[25]

Q 31.7.2 What is a deferral of compensation?

In general, Code section 409A provides that a deferral of compensation has occurred if, during a taxable year, under the terms of the plan or arrangement and the relevant facts and circumstances, the service provider has a legally binding right to compensation that has not been actually or constructively received but is payable in a future year.[26] A service provider does not have a legally binding right to compensation if that compensation can be unilaterally reduced or eliminated by the service recipient or other person after the services have been performed. The customary payroll practice in which a service provider is paid after the end of an employee's taxable year is not considered a deferral of compensation.

Q 31.7.3 What is a "service provider"?

A service provider is a person who performs services for a service recipient. The term "service provider" includes:

(1) an individual, corporation, Subchapter S corporation, or partnership;
(2) a personal service corporation (as defined in Code section 269A(b)(1)), or a non-corporate entity that would be a personal service corporation if it were a corporation; or
(3) a qualified personal service corporation (as defined in Code section 448(d)(2)), or a non-corporate entity that would be a qualified personal service corporation if it were a corporation. A service provider may be either an employee of the service recipient or an independent contractor.[27]

Q 31.7.4 What is a "service recipient"?

A service recipient is a person for whom services are performed and with respect to whom the legally binding right to compensation arises. The term "service recipient" includes the person who is the service recipient and all persons with whom such person would be considered a single employer under Code sections 414(b) (employees of controlled group of corporations) and 414(c) (employees of partnerships, proprietorships, etc., which are under common control).[28]

Q 31.7.5 Which non-qualified deferred compensation plans are subject to Code section 409A?

Code section 409A applies to all plans and arrangements that provide for the deferral of compensation, unless such plans and arrangements are specifically exempted.[29] Examples of the types of plans that are generally subject to the rules of section 409A are:

- unfunded, secured deferred compensation plans;
- excess benefit plans;
- equity-based compensation arrangements, such as stock appreciation rights, restricted stock, and phantom stock;
- supplemental executive retirement benefits (SERPs);
- plans that cover only one person, such as employment agreements and severance agreements; and

- non-qualified stock options having a below-market exercise price or deferral features, other than the right to exercise the option.

Section 409A Exemptions

Q 31.8 What types of plans and arrangements are generally exempt from the requirements of Code section 409A?

Certain deferred compensation plans and arrangements are specifically exempt from the requirements of Code section 409A.[30] These exemptions are:

- short-term deferrals;
- statutory stock options and employee stock purchase plans;
- certain non-statutory stock options;
- certain stock appreciation rights;
- restricted property and stock plans covered by Code section 83;
- qualified employer plans;
- welfare benefit plans and arrangements;
- certain foreign plans;
- certain severance payments;
- arrangements if both service provider and service receiver use the accrual method of accounting; and
- arrangements with independent contractors actively engaged in a trade or business.

Q 31.8.1 What are short-term deferrals?

One of the most important exemptions from Code section 409A is the short-term deferral. A common example is annual bonuses or other annual compensation amounts paid after the close of the tax year in which the services were performed. A short-term deferral occurs if compensation is actually or constructively received by the service provider by the later of:[31]

(1) the fifteenth day of the third month after the end of the service provider's first taxable year in which the amount is no longer subject to a substantial risk of forfeiture; or

(2) the fifteenth day of the third month after the end of the service recipient's first taxable year in which the amount is no longer subject to a substantial risk of forfeiture.

However, a payment not made within the two-and-a-half-month short-term deferral period may still qualify as a short-term deferral if, as a result of unforeseeable circumstances, it was administratively impractical to make the payment, or the payment would have jeopardized the solvency of the service recipient, and the payment is made as soon as is reasonably practicable.[32]

Q 31.8.2   What are statutory stock options and employee stock purchase plans?

Statutory stock options and employee stock purchase plans include plans that provide for the grant of an ISO, as described in Code section 422, and the grant of an option under an employee stock purchase plan described in Code section 423.

Q 31.8.3   What non-statutory stock options are exempt from the section 409A requirements?

A non-statutory stock option is exempt from Code section 409A only if:

(1) the exercise price may never be less than the fair market value of the underlying stock on the date the option is granted;
(2) the receipt, transfer, or exercise of the option is subject to tax under Code section 83; and
(3) the option does not include any separate feature for the deferral of compensation, other than the deferral of the recognition of income on the exercise of the option.[33]

Q 31.8.4   What kinds of stock appreciation rights are exempt from the section 409A requirements?

The grant of stock appreciation rights is exempt from Code section 409A only if:

(1) the compensation payable under the stock appreciation right does not exceed the difference between the fair market

value of the stock on the date of the grant and the fair market value of the stock on the date of exercise;
(2) the stock appreciation right exercise price does not exceed the fair market value of the underlying stock on the date of grant; and
(3) the stock appreciation right does not include any feature for the deferral of compensation other than the deferral of the recognition of income on the exercise of the stock appreciation right.[34]

Q 31.8.5 What are restricted property and stock plans covered by Code section 83?

Code section 409A does not apply to restricted property and stock plans covered by Code section 83 if (a) the restricted property is non-transferable and subject to a substantial risk of forfeiture and is therefore not currently includable in income under Code section 83 by the service provider, or (b) the restricted property is includable in income under section 83 solely because a valid election was made under section 83(b) by the service provider.[35]

Q 31.8.6 What are qualified employer plans?

Qualified employer plans include qualified retirement plans described in Code section 401(a), tax deferred annuities, simplified employee pension plans, SIMPLE plans, eligible deferred compensation plans described in Code section 457(b) and certain governmental excess benefit arrangements.

Q 31.8.7 What are welfare benefit plans and arrangements?

Welfare benefit plans and arrangements include bona fide vacation or sick leave, compensatory time, disability pay, or death benefit plans. It also includes certain health/medical savings and reimbursement arrangements.[36]

Q 31.8.8 What kinds of foreign plans are exempt from the section 409A requirements?

Certain foreign plans include certain nondiscriminatory plans sponsored by foreign entities that cover a wide range of employees, substantially all of whom are non-resident aliens.[37]

Q 31.8.9 What kinds of severance payments are exempt from section 409A requirements?

Separation payments made on account of a service provider's involuntary separation from service or participation in a "window program" are exempt from Code section 409A if:

(a) the amount is not more than two times the lesser of: (i) the service provider's annual compensation, or (ii) the maximum amount that can be taken into account under a qualified plan pursuant to Code section 401(a)(17) for such year ($245,000 for 2009); and

(b) the payment is made no later than December 31 of the second calendar year following the calendar year in which the separation occurs. Certain reimbursements of expenses are also permitted.[38]

A "window program" is a program established by the service recipient for a limited period of time (no more than a year) to provide separation pay to service providers who separate from service.

Q 31.8.10 What happens if the service provider uses the accrual method of accounting?

Arrangements between a service provider and a service recipient are exempt from Code section 409A if the service provider uses the accrual method of accounting for federal income tax purposes.[39]

Q 31.8.11 What if the service provider is actively engaged in the trade or business of providing substantial services?

Arrangements between a service provider and a service recipient are *not* deferred compensation if:[40]

(a) the service provider is actively engaged in the trade or business of providing substantial services, other than: (i) as an employee, or (ii) as a director of the corporation; and
(b) the service provider provides such services to two or more unrelated service recipients. There are special rules for determining whether the service provider and the service recipient are related.

COMPLIANCE FACT

If the service provider is an officer of, or performs management functions for, a service recipient, the service provider is considered related to the service recipient and therefore subject to the provisions of Code section 409A.

Q 31.8.12 Why is fair market value of stock important and how is it determined?

An accurate determination of fair market value of stock is necessary when determining if stock options, stock appreciation rights, and other equity-based compensation agreements are exempt from Code section 409A. Section 409A has specific rules for determining fair market value. In general, if the stock is readily tradable on an established securities market, the fair market value of the stock may be determined with respect to actual transactions immediately before or after the grant or exercise, so long as the determination is made on a reasonable basis, consistently applied. In addition, an average price during a specified time period within thirty days before or after the grant or exercise, can be used, if the commitment to grant the stock right based on such valuation method is irrevocable before the beginning of the specified period, and the valuation method is consistently applied. In the case of stock that is not readily tradable on an established securities market, the value must be determined by the reasonable application of a reasonable valuation method. The final regulations under Code section 409A set forth several permissible valuation methods.[41]

Q 31.8.13 If a deferred compensation plan or arrangement is not exempt from section 409A, what restrictions are necessary to prevent immediate taxation to the service provider?

Amounts deferred under a non-qualified deferred compensation plan or arrangement that is not exempt from Code section 409A currently will be includable in a service provider's gross income unless: (a) the amounts are subject to a substantial risk of forfeiture, or (b) the plan or arrangement satisfies certain requirements.[42]

Q 31.8.14 What constitutes a "substantial risk of forfeiture"?

Compensation is subject to a substantial risk of forfeiture if the service provider's receipt of the compensation is conditioned upon (i) the performance of substantial future services by any person, or (ii) the occurrence of a condition related to the purpose of the compensation, and the possibility of forfeiture is substantial.[43] An amount will not be considered subject to a substantial risk of forfeiture beyond the time in which the service provider could have elected to receive the compensation. An amount is not subject to a substantial risk of forfeiture merely because the right to the amount is conditioned, directly or indirectly, upon the service performer refraining from performance of services for others (that is, a noncompete agreement).

A substantial risk of forfeiture will be disregarded if it is used to manipulate the timing of the inclusion of income or if it is illusory. It will also be disregarded if the enforcement of the forfeiture is not likely to occur. This is a possible problem if the service provider is a substantial shareholder or exercises control over the service recipient.

Q 31.8.15 If there is no substantial risk of forfeiture, what requirements must be satisfied?

If the plan does not provide that compensation deferred under the plan is subject to a "substantial risk of forfeiture," then, in order to avoid the compensation being included in the service provider's gross income under Code section 409A, the plan must impose restrictions on: (a) the time and form of distributions, and (b) the making of initial and subsequent deferral elections.[44]

Payment of Deferred Compensation

Q 31.8.16 Does section 409A restrict the time and form of payments of deferred compensation?

One of the most significant effects of Code section 409A has to do with the time and form of payments. One of the most common provisions of deferred compensation plans and agreements was to provide the service provider or the service recipient (sometimes both) with substantial discretion as to when and how deferred compensation would be paid. This discretion has been substantially restricted.[45]

Q 31.9 What are permitted "distributable events" under Code section 409A?

If a plan is subject to Code section 409A, compensation deferred under the plan may be paid only on account of one or more of the following events:

(1) separation from service;
(2) service recipient becomes disabled;
(3) the arrival of a specified time or fixed schedule for payment described in the plan;
(4) death of the service provider;
(5) a change in control; or
(6) occurrence of an unforeseeable emergency.[46]

Q 31.9.1 When has an employee separated from service?

Generally, an employee is deemed to have separated from service with the service recipient when the employee dies, retires, or otherwise has terminated employment with the service recipient. An independent contractor is deemed to have separated from service with the service recipient upon the expiration of the contract (or, if more than one contract, all contracts) under which services are performed for the service recipient if the expiration constitutes a good-faith complete termination of the contractual relationship.[47]

Q 31.9.2 When is a service recipient considered disabled?

A service recipient is considered disabled if:

(1) he is unable to engage in any substantial gainful activity by reason of any medically determinable physical or mental impairment that can be expected to result in death or that can be expected to last for a continuous period of not less than twelve months; or

(2) he is, by reason of any medically determinable physical or mental impairment that can be expected to result in death or that can be expected to last for a continuous period of not less than twelve months, receiving income replacement benefits for a period of not less than three months under an accident and health plan covering employees of the service recipient.[48]

Q 31.9.3 What are the requirements for specified-time or fixed-schedule payments?

To qualify, these amounts must be paid at a specific time or pursuant to a fixed schedule that is objectively determinable at the time the amount is deferred. Any subsequent change in the fixed time or schedule will constitute a change in the time and form of payment, subject to the subsequent deferral election requirements.

Q 31.9.4 What constitutes a change in control?

The regulations under Code section 409A define what constitutes a change in control. A change in control can be:

(1) a change in ownership interests of the company whereby a person acquires 50% or more of such ownership interests;

(2) a change in effective control, such as a change in the company's board of directors; or

(3) a sale of 50% or more of the assets of the company.[49]

Q 31.9.5 How is an "unforeseeable emergency" defined?

An "unforeseeable emergency" is a severe financial hardship to the service provider resulting from an illness or accident of the service provider or his immediate family. An unforeseeable emergency also includes loss of property due to casualties or similar extraordinary and unforeseeable circumstances arising as the result of events beyond the control of the service provider. Amounts payable as an unforeseeable emergency must not exceed the amount necessary to satisfy such emergency, plus applicable taxes on such payment.[50]

Q 31.10   When can deferred compensation be paid?

The plan or arrangement must specify when deferred compensation is to be paid. Deferred compensation may be paid upon the occurrence of a distributable event, or at an objectively determinable time following the event (for example, three months following the death of the service provider). The compensation can also be paid during the calendar year in which the event occurred or within three months following the year in which the event occurs (for example, during the first three months of the calendar year following the calendar year in which the service provider dies). However, the service provider must not be permitted to designate the year in which payment is to be received. The plan may provide for the payment upon the earlier or latest of more than one event.[51]

A payment is treated as having been made on the date specified if it is made on such date, or upon a later date within the same calendar year, or if later, by the fifteenth day of the third calendar month following the specified date.[52]

Q 31.10.1   When must payments to key employees of a public company be delayed?

A plan subject to Code section 409A must prohibit payments on account of separation from service to a "specified employee" prior to a date that is six months after the date of such employee's separation from service (or, if earlier, the date of death of the specified employee).[53] A specified employee is generally defined to mean a key employee (as that term is defined under Code section 416(i)) of a publicly traded corporation. Code section 416(i) provides that a key employee generally includes up to fifty officers of the employer having annual compensation greater than $130,000 (indexed, $145,000 for 2007), 5% owners, and 1% owners having annual compensation from the employer greater than $150,000.

Q 31.10.2 Under what conditions may a plan permit the acceleration of the time or schedule of any payments under the plan?

Code section 409A generally provides that no acceleration of the time or schedule of any payment may be allowed, except for:[54]

(1) payments pursuant to a domestic relations order, as defined in Code section 414(p)(1)(b);
(2) payments pursuant to a certificate of divestiture, as defined in Code section 1043(b)(2);
(3) a de minimis amount if the payment is not greater than $10,000 and represents the payment of a participant's entire benefit;
(4) payments of FICA taxes on vested balances;
(5) payments made to avoid a non-allocation year under Code section 409(p); and
(6) payments linked to qualified plans.

If a plan or arrangement is terminated, acceleration of payments is permitted if:[55]

(1) all like plans or arrangements are terminated;
(2) no payments are made for twelve months following the termination date;
(3) all distributions occur within twenty-four months following plan termination; and
(4) no similar type plan or arrangement is adopted for five years following the date of termination.

Q 31.10.3 Under what circumstances can payments be delayed?

Generally, under Code section 409A, delay of payments is not permitted. However, if the payment would violate loan covenants or other contractual terms that would cause material harm to the service provider, the payment may be delayed. Also, payments may be delayed in the event of bona fide disputes between the service provider and the service recipient or upon the dissolution or bankruptcy of the service provider.[56]

Q 31.10.4 Does section 409A provide rules affecting initial and subsequent deferral elections?

Yes. Another significant effect of Code section 409A has to do with the timing and effective date of elections to defer compensation and subsequent changes to those elections.

Q 31.10.5 When must an initial deferral election be made?

Generally, a plan must require initial deferral elections for the deferral of compensation to be made no later than the immediately preceding taxable year. In the case of a person who first becomes eligible to participate in a plan, the election to defer compensation with respect to services to be performed subsequent to the election may be made within thirty days after the person becomes eligible to participate in the plan.[57]

Q 31.10.6 What are the special rules for an initial deferral election related to performance-based compensation?

An exception to the general rule is provided for performance-based compensation. If the services are performed over a "performance period" of at least twelve months, an initial deferral election may be made at any time up to six months prior to the end of the performance period, provided the service provider's right to compensation has not become both substantially certain to be paid and readily ascertainable. Performance-based compensation is defined as compensation which is contingent on the satisfaction of pre-established organizational or individual performance goals.[58]

Q 31.10.7 What is the effect of changes to an existing election?

Code section 409A permits "subsequent elections." Subsequent elections are elections that are made after compensation has been deferred that changes either the time or form of distribution. A subsequent election must meet the following requirements:[59]

(a) The subsequent deferral election must not take effect until at least twelve months after the date on which the subsequent election is made;

(b) If the subsequent election relates to a distribution payable upon
   (i) the service provider's separation from service,
   (ii) a specified time, or
   (iii) a change of control,
   then the first payment with respect to which such election is made must be deferred for a period of at least five years from the date the payment otherwise would have been made; and
(c) If the subsequent election relates to a distribution that otherwise was to be paid at a specified time or pursuant to a fixed schedule, the election must be made at least twelve months before the date of the first scheduled payment.

Q 31.10.8 What effects does Code section 409A have on the use of rabbi trusts?

Rabbi trusts are often used by service recipients to provide service providers with protection against third-party claims against the assets of the service recipient. Generally, the use of rabbi trusts does not cause the value of the trust assets to be taxed to the service provider under Code section 83. However, under Code section 409A, if an offshore rabbi trust is used, or if a rabbi trust containing provisions permitting its conversion into a trust whose assets are not treated as owned by the service recipient, the assets of the trust will be treated as property transferred in connection with the performance of services and taxable to the service recipient under Code section 83.[60]

Compliance/Reporting Requirements

Q 31.11 What are the penalties for failure to comply with Code section 409A?

Failure to comply with the requirements of Code section 409A may result in substantial penalties for employees and other service providers who are parties to deferred compensation plans and arrangements. Service providers may be liable for:

(1) income taxes on all amounts deferred in the current and prior years;

(2) interest on the tax from the date the amount was first deferred or vested; and

(3) additional penalties equal to twenty percent (20%) of the deferred amounts included in the service provider's income.

If, *at any time* during the taxable year, a non-qualified deferred compensation plan fails to meet the requirements of Code section 409A, or it is not operated in accordance with those requirements, all amounts deferred for the taxable year, and all preceding taxable years, are includable in gross income of the service provider for such taxable year, to the extent not subject to a substantial risk of forfeiture and not previously included in gross income. Such amounts are also subject to interest and an additional income tax. Interest is computed at the IRS underpayment rate, plus one percentage point. The additional income tax is equal to 20% of the compensation required to be included in gross income.

Q 31.11.1 What are the reporting requirements?

Code section 409A requires that deferred compensation be reported to the IRS for the year deferred on the service provider's Form W-2 or Form 1099, even if the amounts are not currently includable in income by the service provider. Also, any amounts required to be included in income under Code section 409A are subject to normal reporting and withholding requirements.[61]

Q 31.11.2 What is the effective date of Code section 409A?

Code section 409A is effective for amounts deferred or amounts that became vested and nonforfeitable in tax years beginning after December 31, 2004. Compensation deferred under a plan or arrangement during tax years beginning prior to January 1, 2005, and earnings thereon, are "grandfathered" and not subject to the new rules unless the plan or arrangement is "materially modified" after October 3, 2004. An amount is considered deferred prior to January 1, 2005, if, before that date, the service provider has a legally binding right to receive the amount and the amount is earned and vested.

Q 31.11.3 What is a "material modification" of a plan?

A plan is "materially modified" if a benefit or right existing on October 3, 2004 is enhanced or a new benefit or right is added. Amending a plan to conform to the requirements of Code section 409A is not considered a material modification. However, amending a plan to add a provision permitted by section 409A, such as permitting distributions upon a change in control, if the provision was not previously in the plan, is considered a material modification.

Q 31.11.4 What relief from section 409A violations can be sought under the IRS "Voluntary Compliance Program"?

If a deferred compensation plan is subject to section 409A, the plan document must comply with section 409A and the plan must be operated in accordance with section 409A. Failure of the plan document to contain the necessary provisions is referred to as a "document failure." Failure of the plan to be operated in accordance with the requirements of section 409A is referred to as an "operational failure." The IRS has established a Voluntary Compliance Program for taxpayers to self-correct certain unintentional document and operational failures, thereby obtaining relief from part or all of the additional taxes imposed for violating the provisions of section 409A.

In Notice 2007-100,[62] the IRS provided transition relief and guidance on how to correct operational failures. It then issued Notice 2008-113,[63] which clarified and expanded the guidance provided by Notice 2007-100, and Notice 2010-6,[64] which set forth guidance with respect to correction of document failures. Notice 2010-6 was intended to encourage employers to review their non-qualified deferred compensation plan documents and to promptly correct those provisions that are not in compliance with section 409A. Notice 2010-6 also provided transition relief for certain document failures corrected prior to December 31, 2010, and clarified certain aspects of Notice 2008-113 related to operational failures. It is expected that future notices will provide additional guidance.

Generally, a taxpayer seeking relief under the Voluntary Compliance Program has the burden of demonstrating that it is eligible for the relief and that the requirements for the relief have been met. Relief is not available if a federal income tax return for the service recipient or service provider is under examination with respect to a non-qualified deferred compensation issue for any taxable year in which a failure exists. Relief is also not available for intentional failures or if the failure is directly or indirectly related to participation in a listed transaction under Treasury regulations section 1.6011-4(b)(2).

Offshore Non-Qualified Deferred Compensation Plans

Q 31.12 Are there any special rules that apply to offshore non-qualified deferred compensation plans?

Yes. The Emergency Economic Stabilization Act of 2008[65] added Code section 457A. This section imposes significant restrictions on the ability of offshore entities to defer income beyond twelve months following the year in which compensation is earned. Section 457A applies to agreements or arrangements that defer income and that

(1) are "nonqualified deferred compensation plans";
(2) are maintained by a "nonqualified entity"; and
(3) do not include a "substantial risk of forfeiture."

Q 31.12.1 What is a "nonqualified deferred compensation plan" under section 457?

Under section 457, a non-qualified deferred compensation plan is defined with reference to the broad definition in section 409A, as described earlier in this chapter, and includes certain partnership arrangements and equity appreciation plans. A plan will be a non-qualified deferred compensation plan if it is sponsored (in whole or in part) by a non-qualified entity (as defined below) as of the last day of such non-qualified entity's taxable year.

Non-qualified stock options granted at fair market value do not constitute non-qualified deferred compensation plans for purposes of section 457A.

Q 31.12.2 What is a "nonqualified entity"?

A non-qualified entity includes:

(1) any foreign corporation unless substantially all its income is
   (a) connected to a U.S. trade or business or
   (b) is subject to a comprehensive foreign income tax scheme; and
(2) any partnership unless substantially all of its income is allocated to persons other than
   (a) foreign persons with respect to whom such income is not subject to a comprehensive foreign income tax and
   (b) organizations that are exempt from tax under title 26 of the U.S. Code.

Independent contractors are not non-qualified entities for purposes of section 457A if they would not constitute service providers under section 409A.

Q 31.12.3   What is a substantial risk of forfeiture?

A service provider's rights are subject to "substantial risk of forfeiture" only if they are conditioned upon the future performance of substantial services by the service provider. Section 457A also defines service provider with reference to the broad definition in section 409A, which includes both individuals and corporate entities.

Q 31.12.4   What rules does section 457A impose?

Section 457A prohibits offshore non-qualified deferred compensation plans from paying compensation more than twelve months following the year in which compensation is earned—that is, it permits the deferral of income only for twelve months following the tax year in which it was earned.

Section 457A provides that, if the compensation cannot be determined and paid out within this time period, the compensation becomes includable in the service provider's income at the time that the compensation becomes determinable and, at such time, is subject to a premium interest charge computed back to the year in which the compensation was earned, plus a 20% federal penalty tax (in addition to any other applicable taxes such as ordinary income tax, capital gains tax, or tax pursuant to section 409A).

Q 31.12.5 Are there any exceptions to the requirements of section 457A?

Yes. Compensation paid within the twelve months following the year in which compensation is no longer subject to a substantial risk of forfeiture is exempt from section 457A (although it may still be subject to section 409A). Additionally, to the extent compensation remains subject to a substantial risk of forfeiture, it is exempt from section 457A and is earned when such risk of forfeiture has ended, at which point it becomes taxable. Additionally, there is an exception for single assets directly held by investment funds which are not actively managed by the fund or a related person.

Golden Parachute Payments

Q 31.13 What are golden parachute payments?

Many executive compensation agreements provide that the executive will receive significant additional compensation payments in the event the executive loses his or her job as a result of a change in control of the employer. Such payments are referred to as "golden parachute payments" and may include a package consisting of payments of cash bonuses, vesting of stock rights and other benefits. If the value of the payments exceeds a certain amount (that is, amounts deemed to be excess parachute payments), the payments are not deductible by the corporation,[66] and the executive is subject to a 20% excise tax.[67]

Q 31.13.1 What types of payments are considered parachute payments?

The rules for golden parachute payments are set forth in Code section 280G and the related Treasury regulations. An executive does not have to terminate employment for the rules to apply. Basically, a payment to (or for the benefit of) an executive is a parachute payment if:

(a) the executive is a "disqualified individual";
(b) the payment is "in the nature of compensation";
(c) the payment is contingent on a change in the ownership or effective control of the corporation (or a change in the

ownership of a substantial portion of the assets of the corporation); and

(d) the aggregate present value of all such payments equals or exceeds three times the executive's "base amount."

Parachute payments may also include certain compensation payments made to an executive, if the IRS is able to establish that the agreements violate generally enforced securities laws and regulations.[68]

Q 31.13.2 What types of payments are exempt?

Code section 280G and the accompanying regulations provide that certain payments are exempt from the golden parachute rules:

(a) payments to an executive made by a small business corporation (generally an S corporation);

(b) payments to an executive made by corporations that are not publicly traded before the change in control if the payment was approved by shareholders in control of at least 75% of the outstanding shares prior to the change;

(c) payments to an executive made from tax-qualified retirement plans and arrangements; and

(d) payments to an executive that constitute reasonable compensation for services rendered before, on, or after the date of the change in control. The taxpayer has the burden of proof to establish by clear and convincing evidence that the payment is reasonable compensation.[69]

Q 31.13.3 What are "excess parachute payments"?

Parachute payments are considered excess parachute payments to the extent the present value of the aggregate amount of the parachute payments to the executive equals or exceeds the executive's base amount. If there are multiple payments, the base amount is allocated proportionally to the amount of each payment.[70]

Q 31.13.4 What is an executive's "base amount"?

An executive's "base amount" is the executive's average annual compensation during the five years preceding the year in which a change in ownership or control occurs.[71]

Q 31.13.5 Which executives are "disqualified individuals"?

An executive is a "disqualified individual" if he or she is an individual who is an employee, independent contractor, or other person specified in the regulations who performs personal services for the corporation and who is an officer, shareholder, or highly compensated individual of the corporation. Personal service corporations and similar entities are generally treated as individuals for this purpose.

In general, for purposes of determining who is a disqualified individual:[72]

(a) an officer is defined as an administrative executive who is in regular and continued service to the corporation; however, no more than the lesser of (i) fifty employees, or (ii) the greater of (A) three employees, or (B) 10% of the employees of the corporation, can be officers;

(b) a shareholder is defined as an individual who owns more than 1% of the value of all outstanding stock of the corporation; and

(c) a highly compensated individual is defined as an employee (or former employee) who is among the highest paid one percent of employees of the corporation (or an affiliated corporation) or, if less, the employee is among the 250 highest paid employees of the corporation (or member of its affiliated group).

Q 31.13.6 What are "payments in the nature of compensation"?

In general, payments in the nature of compensation include all payments that arise out of an executive's employment relationship and are related to his or her performance of services. They include wages, salary, bonuses, severance pay, fringe benefits, stock options, and other similar payments. The payments may be made by the acquired or acquiring corporation.[73]

Q 31.13.7 What payments are considered "contingent on a change in ownership or control"?

In general, a payment is contingent on a change in ownership or control if the payment would not have been made to the executive "but for" (a) the change in ownership or control of the corporation or the ownership of its assets, or (b) an event that is closely associated with or materially related to a change in such ownership or control.[74]

There is a rebuttable presumption that any payments made to an executive pursuant to an agreement entered into or amended within one year of a change in ownership or control, is a payment that is considered contingent on a change in ownership or control.

Q 31.13.8 Is there a minimum "threshold" for change-in-control payments to be considered excess parachute payments?

If the aggregate present value of the compensation payments to an executive as a result of a change in control does not equal or exceed three times his or her base amount, the payments are not considered parachute payments and therefore, there is no "excess" parachute payment.[75]

Q 31.13.9 How are excess parachute payments taxed?

Excess parachute payments are fully taxable to the executive and are subject to Federal Insurance Contributions Act (FICA) and Federal Unemployment Tax Act (FUTA) taxes. Code section 4999 provides that an executive who receives excess parachute payments will also be liable for a 20% excise tax on the amount of such payment. The employer is required to deduct and withhold the excise tax, as well as income and employment taxes, from payments made to the executive.

In addition, Code section 162(m) provides that the $1 million limitation on the executive's compensation is reduced by the amount of any excess parachute payments.

Equity and Equity-Based Compensation

Q 31.14 What are the advantages of equity-based compensation?

Companies have a broad range of options in compensating their employees. Offering equity-based compensation to executives accomplishes two main goals:

(1) The recipients of equity compensation will be interested in creating value to the company and increasing the value of the company's stock; and
(2) The nature of offering equity compensation to executives lends itself as a retention tool because of vesting periods and the time needed to create value in the equity compensation.

Types of Equity Awards

Q 31.14.1 What are the different types of equity compensation plans?

Any company has the ability to grant equity awards to its employees, officers, directors, and consultants. Equity awards can take the form of stock options, stock awards, and performance awards. An award of stock options can be either a grant of qualified stock options (called ISOs) or non-qualified stock options. Stock awards typically consist of grants of restricted stock, deferred stock, or stock appreciation rights. Performance awards or performance units are awards that are typically granted to certain executives in order to comply with Code section 162(m).

Q 31.14.2 Do equity awards have to be issued pursuant to a plan?

Equity awards are typically granted pursuant to a plan. In certain cases, such plans must be approved by shareholders, as discussed later in this chapter. Occasionally, equity awards are granted outside of a plan, although these grants are awarded in conjunction with another form of agreement, such as an employment agreement. A commonly used form of equity plan is called an "omnibus" plan that provides the company with discretion to grant all the different types of equity awards, rather than have a separate plan for each type of equity award.

Q 31.14.3 What are the main differences between granting an ISO and a non-qualified stock option?

The main difference between an ISO and a non-qualified stock option is how the company and the recipient of the option is taxed.

Q 31.14.4 What are the rules with respect to ISOs?

Unlike non-qualified stock options, section 422 provides the other requirements for an option to qualify as an ISO. (See Q 31.3.2.)

Q 31.14.5 What are the rules with respect to non-qualified options?

Unlike ISOs, there are only a few important rules to remember when dealing with grants of non-qualified options. First, all options that are granted at a discount to the fair market value of the stock on the date of grant (except for options granted pursuant to a qualified employee stock purchase plan under Code section 423) will subject the option to Code section 409A. Second, if a discounted option is granted whereby the option price is far less than the fair market value of the company stock on the date of grant (typically at least 50% or less than the fair market value of the company stock on the date of grant), the award of options actually may be considered a purchase of the company stock, which would cause different taxation to the recipient.

Q 31.14.6 What is a grant of restricted stock?

A grant of restricted stock provides the recipient with shares of stock of the company that are subject to a substantial risk of forfeiture, until such time as the recipient vests in the stock. Vesting conditions for restricted stock usually fall into one of two categories: time-based vesting and performance vesting (based on subjective and/or objective individual and/or corporate goals). A combination of these conditions can also be used as a vesting condition. A grant of restricted stock typically will provide the recipient with a choice in taxation and will not be subject to Code section 409A.[76]

Q 31.14.7 What is a stock appreciation right (SAR) and how do SARs work?

A SAR is an award that provides the recipient with the ability to recognize gain based on the appreciation in value of a set number of shares of company stock over a set period of time. Like a stock option, the valuation of a stock appreciation right operates in that the employee benefits from any increases in stock price above the price set in the award, except that the employee will not be required to pay an exercise price to exercise them. The recipient just receives the net amount of the increase in the stock price in either cash or shares of company stock, depending on the plan terms. SARs are sometimes granted in tandem with stock options (either ISOs or NSOs) to help finance the purchase of the options and/or pay tax if any is due upon exercise of the options (sometimes referred to as "tandem options").

SARs are granted at a set price, and generally have a vesting period and an expiration date. Once a SAR vests, the recipient can exercise it at any time prior to its expiration. The value of SARs does not reflect stock dividends or stock splits. Generally, SARs must be granted with a grant price equal to the fair market value of the company stock on the date of grant, or the SAR will be subject to Code section 409A.[77]

Q 31.14.8   What is phantom stock?

Phantom stock (sometimes referred to as restricted stock units) is the company's promise to pay a bonus in the form of the equivalent of the value of company shares. Unlike SARs, phantom stock can reflect dividends, typically through a mechanism called dividend equivalent units, which can be paid out immediately to the recipient or converted into additional phantom stock shares that are paid out on vesting. Phantom stock payments are usually made at a fixed, predetermined date. Phantom stock is subject to Code section 409A.[78]

Q 31.14.9   Can a company reissue stock options if the price goes down?

Until December 1998, a company was able to cancel underwater options (options that have a negative value because the current stock price is lower than the exercise price) and replace them with new options without much consequence. However, under Interpretation No. 44, Accounting for Certain Transactions Involving Stock Compensation, which was adopted by the Financial Accounting Standards Board (FASB) on March 31, 2000, and made retroactively effective to December 15, 1998, a repricing of an underwater option resulted in the exercise price being treated as variable for the remaining life of the option.

For this purpose, the variable accounting treatment meant that the difference between the revised exercise price and the value of the underlying stock when the repriced option was exercised, forfeited or expired unexercised had to be recognized as a compensation expense for financial accounting purposes. In addition, as the company's stock price increased, a periodic charge to earnings was required to be reported. The variable accounting treatment under Interpretation No. 44 discouraged option repricings and led employers to use alternatives to compensate executives, such as cashing out the options.

FASB changed the accounting treatment of option repricings when it issued Statement No. 123 (revised 2004), *Share-Based Payment* (FAS 123(R)), effective for most public companies for reporting periods that start after June 15, 2005, and for nonpublic companies for fiscal years beginning after December 15, 2005. FAS 123(R) applies the fair value method of accounting to option repricing. This means that the fair value of the option immediately before the repricing is compared to the fair value of the option immediately after the repricing and if the fair value of the option after the repricing is higher, the company must recognize the incremental value of the repriced option over the remaining service period. Accordingly, the total compensation charge related to the repricing will be fixed at the time of the repricing.

Q 31.14.10 What are the concerns about backdated stock options?

The headlines have been filled recently with stories about backdated stock options. Backdating options refers to the practice that some companies have used to manipulate the dates of option grants. The manipulation typically occurs in one of three ways:

(1) The grant date is set to a time when the stock was selling at a historical low point;
(2) The grant date is set to a time right before a news release that is expected to have a positive effect on the market price of the stock; and
(3) The grant date is set to a time right after the release of negative news that has a negative effect on the market price of the stock.[79]

Backdated stock options can create significant problems for the company and the recipient of a backdated stock option. The SEC has come down very hard on senior executives of companies who have backdated options, with penalties being levied against the responsible parties reaching into the millions of dollars. Additionally, backdated option recipients will be subject to Code section 409A and the penalties thereunder. Finally, in most cases, audited and unaudited financial statements will have to be restated to reflect the correct accounting for the backdated options.

Financial Accounting for Equity and Equity-Based Compensation

Q 31.15 What are the general rules about accounting for options?

Accounting for options is now governed by FAS 123(R). Under FAS 123(R), companies are required to show the fair value of their stock option awards on their income statements. The fair value is typically determined by using an option-pricing model, such as Black-Scholes or Monte Carlo simulation, to determine the value of the stock options. The valuation of fair value must, at a minimum, take into account:

(1) the exercise price of the option;
(2) the expected term of the option;
(3) the current price of the underlying shares;
(4) the expected volatility of the price of the underlying shares for the expected term of the option;
(5) the expected dividends on the underlying shares; and
(6) the risk-free interest rate.

With respect to options with a graded vesting schedule, FAS 123(R) allows companies to account for the award on a straight-line basis over the service period covered by the entire award. With respect to performance-based awards, FAS 123(R) makes them equivalent to other forms of equity compensation as long as they do not vest based on increases in a company's stock price. Performance-based awards based on length of service or general financial goals can be "trued up" at the end of the vesting period. This means that the company only expenses the shares that actually vest. A company whose performance awards vest based on the company stock price must show the cost of all awards as an expense.

Q 31.15.1 How are SARs and phantom stock accounted for?

The company must record a compensation charge on its income statement as the employee's interest in the award increases. So from the time the grant is made until the award is paid out, the company records the value of the percentage of the promised shares or increase in the value of the shares, pro-rated over the term of the award. In each year, the value is adjusted to reflect the additional pro-rata share of the award the employee has earned, plus or minus any adjustments to value arising from the rise or fall in share price.

Unlike accounting for variable award stock options, where a charge is amortized only over a vesting period, with phantom stock and SARs, the charge builds up during the vesting period, then after vesting, all additional stock price increases are taken as they occur when the vesting is triggered by a performance event, such as a profit target. In this case, the company must estimate the expected amount earned based on progress towards the target. The accounting treatment is more complicated if the vesting occurs gradually. Each tranche of vested awards is treated as a separate award. Appreciation is allocated to each award pro-rata to time over which it is earned.

The accounting treatment is different if the SARs or phantom stock awards are settled in shares. In this case, the company must use a formula to estimate the present value of the award at grant, making adjustments for expected forfeitures.

Securities Law Issues

Q 31.16 What kinds of obligations and limits do the securities laws place upon companies and executives?

Federal securities laws affecting executive compensation impact companies and executives. The specific laws involved include the Securities Act of 1933, the Securities Exchange Act of 1934, and the Sarbanes-Oxley Act of 2002 and the SEC's rules and regulations issued pursuant to such statutes. These laws:

- impose disclosure obligations on companies in the form of periodic reports and proxy statements,
- require registration of company securities offered or sold in connection with executive compensation plans and arrangements,
- require shareholder approval of certain benefit plans,
- restrict the ability of company insiders to profit from the trading of company securities,
- limit the ability of certain executives to resell company securities received under compensation arrangements, and
- impose certain trading blackouts when other company employees are not permitted to sell securities held in a Code section 401(k) or other company-sponsored individual account retirement plan.

Proxy Disclosure Rules

Q 31.16.1 How do the SEC's 2006 Proxy Disclosure Rules affect the company's disclosure obligations with respect to executive compensation?

Under SEC rules, information concerning the compensation of executives and directors of publicly traded companies must be included in certain registration statements and in the employer's proxy and information statements and reports. New Proxy Disclosure Rules were issued by the SEC on August 11, 2006,[80] and were amended in December 2006.[81] The Proxy Disclosure Rules can be found in Item 402 of Regulation S-K. The new rules generally are effective December 15, 2006. The Proxy Disclosure Rules prescribe requirements for the content of the information that must be disclosed. In addition, the disclosure must be provided in "plain English," which requires, among other things, presentation of information in clear, concise sections, paragraphs, and sentences; use of short sentences; use of definite, concrete, everyday words; use of descriptive headings and subheadings; and avoiding the use of explanations that are overly generic.

Q 31.16.2 Are there special rules for small business issuers?

Small business issuers, that is, certain U.S. or Canadian companies with annual revenues of less than $25 million, are exempt from a number of specific disclosures required under the Proxy Disclosure Rules.[82]

Q 31.16.3 Are there other classes of companies that are subject to special disclosure rules?

Foreign private issuers[83] and registered investment companies[84] are subject to special disclosure rules.

Q 31.16.4 What is the Compensation Discussion and Analysis?

Under the Proxy Disclosure Rules, the company must include a Compensation Discussion and Analysis (CDA), which is a narrative overview of the company's compensation objectives and policies for named executive officers. The CDA must be presented without resorting to boilerplate disclosure. The CDA must discuss the material elements of the compensation awarded to, earned by, or paid to the named executive officers. The discussion must be designed to answer and provide material information concerning the following questions:[85]

- What are the compensation program's objectives?
- What is the compensation program designed to reward?
- What is each element of compensation?
- Why does the company choose to pay each element?
- How is each element determined (amount and, where applicable, the formula)?
- How do each element and the company's decisions regarding that element fit into the company's overall compensation objectives and affect decisions regarding other elements?

Other required disclosures will vary based on facts and circumstances, but the SEC has identified the following list of potential material information which, among other items, may need to be discussed in the CDA, if applicable to the company:[86]

- Policies for allocating between long-term and currently paid out compensation;

- Policies for allocating between cash and non-cash compensation, and among different forms of non-cash compensation;
- For long-term compensation, the basis for allocating compensation to each different form of award;
- How the determination is made as to when awards are granted, including awards of equity-based compensation such as options;
- What specific items of corporate performance are taken into account in setting compensation policies and making compensation decisions;
- How specific elements of compensation are structured and implemented to reflect these items of the company's performance and the executive's individual performance;
- How specific forms of compensation are structured and implemented to reflect the named executive officer's (NEO's) individual performance and/or individual contribution to these items of the company's performance, describing the elements of individual performance and/or contribution that are taken into account;
- Policies and decisions regarding the adjustment or recovery of awards or payments if performance measures are restated or adjusted in a manner that would reduce the award or payment;
- The factors considered in decisions to increase or decrease compensation materially;
- How compensation or amounts realizable from prior compensation are considered in setting other elements of compensation (for example, how gains from prior option or stock awards are considered in setting retirement benefits);
- With respect to any contract, agreement, plan, or arrangement, whether written on unwritten, that provides for payments at, following, or in connection with, any termination or change in control, the basis for selecting particular events as triggering payment;
- The impact of accounting and tax treatments of a particular form of compensation;
- The company's stock ownership guidelines and any policies regarding hedging the economic risk of such ownership;

- Whether the company engaged in any benchmarking of total compensation or any material element of compensation, identifying the benchmark and, if applicable, its components (including component companies); and
- The role of executive officers in the compensation process.

Q 31.16.5 What period does the CDA cover?

The CDA must cover compensation for the last fiscal year, but the company may also be required to discuss post-termination compensation arrangements, ongoing compensation arrangements, and policies that the company will apply on a going-forward basis. The company should also address actions that were taken after the last fiscal year's end, and, in some situations, the SEC has indicated it may be necessary to discuss prior years in order to give context to the disclosure provided.[87]

Q 31.16.6 Which executives are covered by the Proxy Disclosure Rules?

The company's executive compensation disclosure must cover the "named executive officers" (NEOs), which include:

- each individual who served as the Principal Executive Officer (PEO) during the last fiscal year;
- each individual who served as the Principal Financial Officer (PFO) during the last fiscal year;
- the three other highest paid executive officers employed as of fiscal year end; and
- up to two additional executives who would have been among the top three highest paid if they had been employed by the company as of fiscal year end.

Notwithstanding the general rule above, no disclosure is required with respect to an executive other than the PEO or PFO if salary and bonuses paid to such individual did not exceed $100,000.[88]

Q 31.16.7 What if compensation policies differ among the NEOs?

The company is required to identify material differences in the company's compensation policies for each individual NEO. Where compensation policies and decisions are materially similar, NEOs may be grouped together. If, however, compensation policies or decisions are materially different for a particular NEO (such as the principal executive officer), his or her compensation policy and decision should be described separately.[89]

Q 31.16.8 What if performance targets/goals contain sensitive information?

Award targets that contain confidential commercial or business information are not required to be disclosed in the CDA. The company is not required to formally seek confidential treatment of omitted information, but omitted information will be subject to the same standards as information a company requests be treated as confidential. The company must also disclose how difficult it will be for the executive and/or how likely it will be for the company to achieve the undisclosed target.[90]

Q 31.16.9 What are the "tabular disclosures" that must accompany the CDA?

The "tabular disclosures" that must accompany the CDA fall into three basic categories:

(1) Compensation with respect to the last three fiscal years (for example, Summary Compensation Table and Grants of Plan-Based Awards Table);

(2) Holdings of equity-related interests that relate to compensation or are sources of future gains (for example, Outstanding Equity Awards at Fiscal Year-End Table and Option Exercises and Stock Vested Table); and

(3) Pension, deferred compensation, and other post-employment payments and benefits (for example, Pension Benefits Table, Non-qualified Deferred Compensation Table and Director Compensation Table).[91]

Q 31.16.10 Are narratives required with respect to the tabular disclosures?

Yes, narrative disclosures that supplement the tabular disclosures are required of any material factors necessary to an understanding of the information disclosed therein. In addition, narrative disclosure is required for each contract, agreement, plan, or arrangement that provides for a payment at, following, or in connection with any termination or change in control or change in an executive's responsibilities. Such disclosure must quantify the amount of such payments and benefits.[92]

Q 31.16.11 What is a perquisite or personal benefit?

An item is *not* a perquisite or personal benefit if it is integrally and directly related to the performance of the executive's duties. The SEC views the "integrally and directly related" requirement as being a narrow one and does not extend it to items that facilitate job performance.[93]

An item that is not integrally and directly related to the performance of duties is a perquisite or personal benefit if it confers a direct or indirect benefit that has a personal aspect, without regard to whether it may be provided for some business reason or for the convenience of the company, unless it is generally available on a nondiscriminatory basis to all employees.

The SEC releases relating to the new Proxy Disclosure Rules contain a number of examples of items that, in the SEC's view, constitute and do not constitute perquisites under the foregoing analysis.

Q 31.16.12 Must perquisites and personal benefits be disclosed?

Under the Proxy Disclosure Rules, the perquisites and personal benefits paid or made available to the NEOs must be identified in a footnote and included in the "All Other Compensation" column of the Summary Compensation Table if, in the aggregate, they exceed $10,000. If any single perquisite has a value exceeding the greater of $25,000 or 10% of total perquisites, its value also must be separately disclosed in a footnote. Perquisites are required to be valued on the basis of the aggregate incremental cost to the company and its subsidiaries of providing the perquisite.[94]

Q 31.16.13 What disclosures are required for grants of stock options and stock appreciation rights?

The Summary Compensation Table must include the portion of the fair value of an award (determined as of the date of grant), attributable to service during the fiscal year (in a manner similar to FAS

123(R)), of options, stock appreciation rights, and similar instruments that have option-like features.

The Grants of Plan-Based Awards Table must include the fair value as of the date of grant, as determined under FAS 123(R), of options, stock appreciation rights and other stock-based awards, and the number of options granted in the last fiscal year. The table must show the full grant date fair value on a grant-by-grant basis. The company also must disclose each instance in which the grant date differs from the date on which the compensation committee takes action or is deemed to take action to grant an award. If the exercise price is different from the closing market price on the date of grant, the company must explain the methodology for determining the exercise price in a footnote or a textual narrative and must show the closing market price in a special column in the table.

In the CDA, the company must discuss the aspects of its option grant program, plan, or practice relating to the timing and pricing of option grants. With respect to timing, the discussion should include:

(1) how its option grant program or practice is coordinated with the release of material nonpublic information;
(2) how its option grant program or practice with respect to executives fits with its program or practice with respect to grants to employees more generally;
(3) the role of the compensation committee in approving and administering such program or practice, including the information taken into account by the compensation committee in determining whether and in what amount to make the grants and whether the compensation committee delegated any aspect of the actual administration of such program or practice to any other person;
(4) the role of executives in the company's program or practice of option timing;
(5) whether the company sets the grant date of option grants to new executives in coordination with the release of material nonpublic information; and
(6) whether the company plans to time, or has timed, its release of material nonpublic information for the purpose of affecting the value of executive compensation.[95]

With respect to option pricing, the decision should address whether the option grant program or practice allows the company to set the exercise price based on the stock's price on a date other than the actual grant date and whether such program or practice allows the company to grant options with an exercise price based upon average prices (or lowest prices) of the company's stock in a period preceding, surrounding, or following the grant date.

Q 31.16.14 What disclosures are required for director compensation?

Under the Proxy Disclosure Rules, the company must include a Director Compensation Table in its disclosure. The Director Compensation Table is similar to the Summary Compensation Table. If a NEO is also a director and his or her compensation for service as a director is fully reflected in the Summary Compensation Table, then no disclosure is required for such individual in the Director Compensation Table.[96]

Other Disclosure Rules for Executives and Directors

Q 31.16.15 Are there other SEC-required disclosure rules that relate to executives and directors?

At the time that the SEC issued the new Proxy Disclosure Rules in 2006, the SEC issued revised disclosure rules in the areas of related-person transactions, director independence, and certain other corporate governance matters.

Q 31.16.16 What are the disclosure requirements regarding related-party transactions?

The company must disclose information regarding any transaction since the beginning of the company's last fiscal year, or any currently proposed transaction, in which the company was or is to be a participant, involving an amount in excess of $120,000, and in which a related person had or will have a direct or indirect material interest. In connection with related-party transactions, the company must provide:

- the name of the related person and the basis on which such person is a related person;

- the related person's interest in the transaction with the company;
- the approximate dollar amount involved in each transaction;
- in the case of indebtedness, the largest amount of principal outstanding for the period reported, the amount of principal and interest paid during the period reported and the rate of interest payable on the indebtedness; and
- any other information that is material to investors.[97]

Companies are also required to disclose their policies and procedures for approving related-party transactions. Such disclosure includes:

- the types of transactions covered by such policies and procedures;
- the standards applied pursuant to such policies and procedures;
- the persons or groups of persons who are in charge of applying such policies and procedures; and
- whether such policies and procedures are in writing and, if not, how such policies and procedures are evidenced.[98]

In addition, the company must disclose any transaction required to be disclosed under the rules that was not required to be reviewed under the company's related-party transaction policies and procedures or where such policies and procedures were not followed.

Q 31.16.17 What are the disclosure requirements regarding other corporate governance matters?

Companies also are required to disclose as part of their corporate governance-related disclosure their processes and procedures for the consideration and determination of executive and director compensation, including the scope of authority of the compensation committee, the role of the executive officers in determining the amount or form of executive and director compensation, and the role of compensation consultants in determining or recommending the amount or form of executive and director compensation.[99]

In addition, a company must file or furnish a Form 8-K upon the occurrence of certain triggering events. The Form 8-K disclosures may include information relating to executive pay and benefits.

Q 31.16.18 Are company disclosures required to include a Compensation Committee Report?

Under the SEC's disclosure rules, the Compensation Committee Report (CCR) is part of the company's corporate governance disclosure. The CCR must be furnished once during the fiscal year and must be included or incorporated by reference through a company's proxy statement into the company's Form 10-K. The CCR is required to state whether the compensation committee reviewed and discussed the CDA with management and whether, based on the review and discussions, the compensation committee recommended to the board that the CDA be included in the annual report, proxy statement, or information statement.[100]

Q 31.16.19 Do the CEO and CFO certifications apply to the CDA and the CCR?

Under the SEC's rules, the CDA is "filed" for security law purposes and, therefore, the CEO and CFO certifications apply to the CDA. The CCR is "furnished" for security law purposes and, therefore, the CEO and CFO certifications do not apply to the CCR.[101]

Treatment of NQDC Plans As Securities

Q 31.17 For purposes of registration requirements under the Securities Act of 1933, what is a "security"?

The basic definition of "security" includes any note, stock, treasury stock, bond, debenture, participation in a profit-sharing arrangement or investment contract. Under this definition, in the context of executive compensation, shares of stock offered in connection with a benefits plan and options to purchase stock are "securities." Participation interests in employee benefit plans, including plans that do not involve any purchase of employer stock, may be considered securities under certain circumstances.[102]

Q 31.17.1 Is an interest in a non-qualified deferred compensation plan treated as a "security" under federal securities law?

The SEC's current position with respect to the treatment of non-qualified deferred compensation (NQDC) plans was established in 1991. Prior to such time, the SEC took "no-action" ruling positions on NQDC plans where the interests in the plans were not registered under the Securities Act of 1933. In 1991, in the SEC's "Current Issues and Rulemaking Projects," the SEC provided its current view on NQDC plans. In the report, the SEC stated that it would no longer grant requests for no-action. The determination of whether the participant's interest in a NQDC plan is a security is to be made by the company and to the extent that such interests are securities, registration would be required unless the interests would qualify for an exemption.

The interests in a NQDC plan are not generally treated as securities that are subject to registration under the provisions of the Exchange Act of 1934 and the Investment Company Act of 1940.

Q 31.17.2 When might a participant's interest in a NQDC plan be treated as a "security" under federal securities law?

The definition of "security" under the Securities Act of 1933 includes, among other things, investment contracts. The issue with respect to NQDC plans is whether such plan is an investment contract. The U.S. Supreme Court established the test for determining whether an investment contract is a security in *SEC v. W.J. Howey Co.*[103] Under the *Howey* case, a financial interest will be an investment contract if

(1) there is an investment of money,
(2) in a common enterprise,
(3) with an expectation of profits,
(4) principally derived from the efforts of others.

The SEC held that interests in an employee benefit plan are considered securities by the SEC if the plan is both voluntary and contributory, because the action on the part of the participant under such plan would be sufficient to meet the test under *Howey*.[104]

Arguably, NQDC plans fail to meet the test for an investment contract established in *Howey* because

(1) the participants are deferring compensation for tax savings purposes, rather than making an investment,
(2) there is no expectation of profit in the investment sense,
(3) there is no investment in a common enterprise because each participant has a separate account, and
(4) there is no profit derived from the effort of others (other than possibly the company's continued solvency).

Q 31.17.3 Does the Securities Act of 1933 require registration of sales of stock in connection with employee stock plans?

In general, the Securities Act of 1933 requires the registration of the offer or sale of stock in connection with employee stock plans, including stock option plans and other stock rights plans that are settled in stock. Registration must be effective by the earliest date on which an option or other stock right may be exercised.[105]

Q 31.17.4 Does the Securities Exchange Act of 1934 require registration of sales of stock in connection with employee stock plans?

The registration requirement under section 12(g) of the Securities Exchange Act of 1934 might be triggered if the company has more than $1 million in assets and has a class of stock held of record by 500 or more persons. The SEC has granted relief from this requirement for companies that have granted options to more than 500 employees if certain requirements are met.[106]

Exemptions from Registration Requirements

Q 31.18 Are there any exemptions from the registration requirements of the Securities Act of 1933 that apply to interests in a NQDC plan or the stock sold to a participant in connection with an employee stock plan?

There are four exemptions from registration that may apply to the interests in a NQDC plan or an employee stock plan.

Rule 701 provides an exemption to private companies for securities issued pursuant to certain compensatory benefit plans and contracts. For purposes of Rule 701, "securities" includes interests in a NQDC plan or an employee stock plan. A "compensatory benefit plan" is any purchase, savings, option, bonus, stock appreciation, profit sharing, thrift, incentive, deferred compensation, pension, or similar plan. No filing with the SEC is required to apply the Rule 701 exemption.

Section 4(2) of the Securities Act of 1933 provides an exemption that may apply to certain top-hat NQDC plans. Section 4(2) transactions do not involve a public offering and are made to a sophisticated group that has a relationship to the company, which alleviates the need for the safeguards of the Securities Act of 1933.

Regulation D provides three different exemptions, each of which depends on meeting maximum dollar limits. The three exemptions are summarized as follows:

- Rule 504: an exemption for sales up to $1 million within a twelve-month period by a private company.
- Rule 505: an exemption for sales up to $5 million within a twelve-month period to an unlimited number of accredited investors and up to thirty-five non-accredited investors.
- Rule 506: an exemption for an unlimited amount of sales to no more than thirty-five purchasers (other than accredited investors and sophisticated investors).

Section 3(a)(11) is the "intrastate offering exemption." Section 3(a)(11)'s exemption is available if the offer or sale of securities involves residents of a single state by a company that is incorporated in the same state and conducts substantial business activity in the state. A safe harbor for meeting the exemption is available pursuant to Rule 147.

Q 31.18.1 What form should be used to register interests in NQDC plans and the stock sold pursuant to employee stock plans?

Employers that have previously registered stock under the Securities Act of 1933 typically use Form S-8 to register interests in NQDC plans and the stock to be sold in connection with an employee stock plan. The employer company must have filed all required reports due under the Securities Exchange Act of 1934 during the past twelve months. The Form S-8 may be used only if the participants are employees, nonemployee directors, consultants, and advisors and the offer and sale is made pursuant to an employee benefit plan.

Disclosure and Reporting Requirements

Q 31.18.2 If a NQDC plan or employee stock plan is registered, what disclosures must be made to plan participants?

The company must provide participants with a prospectus or documents constituting a prospectus that meets the requirements of section 10 of the Securities Act of 1933. The company is not required to file the prospectus with the SEC if Form S-8 is used.

Rule 428 under the Securities Act of 1933 provides requirements applicable to Form S-8 prospectuses, including timing for delivery of the prospectus, the persons who should receive the prospectus, and the documents to be delivered with the prospectus.

Q 31.18.3 If a NQDC plan or employee stock plan is not registered, are there any disclosure requirements?

If a private company is relying on a Rule 701 exemption, the company must give all participants a copy of the benefit plan or contract and certain other information if the amount sold exceeds $5 million in any twelve-month period.

If the company is relying on an exemption under Rules 505 and 506 of Regulation D, the company must give all nonacccredited investors the information set forth in Rule 502(b).

Q 31.18.4 Do the anti-fraud provisions of federal securities law apply to disclosures in connection with NQDC plans and employee stock plans?

Yes. The company must avoid a misstatement or omission of material information.

Q 31.18.5 Are there other disclosures to the SEC required in connection with NQDC plans and employee stock plans?

Companies are required to file certain reports and exhibits when establishing or amending an employee benefit plan that is deemed to be a "material contract." The term "material contract" is defined under Item 601 of Regulation S-K. Generally, plans, agreements, and arrangements for the benefit of executives and/or directors will be "material contracts" unless they are available to all employees generally and provide for a uniform method of the allocation of benefits that does not favor management participants.

Form 8-K must be filed by the company within four business days of the adoption or amendment of a "material contract." In addition, benefit plans that are deemed to be "material contracts" must be filed as exhibits to a company's Forms 10-K and 10-Q, and other periodic reports under the Securities Exchange Act of 1934, and to registration statements under the Securities Act of 1933.

Shareholder Approval

Q 31.18.6 What plans must be approved by shareholders pursuant to stock exchange requirements?

Certain plans must be approved by shareholders under the rules of the New York Stock Exchange, the American Stock Exchange, and the Nasdaq Stock Market. In general, these markets require shareholder approval for plans that provide for the issuance or delivery of equity securities to directors, officers, employees, or other service providers. In addition, the shareholder approval requirement will apply when a material amendment is made to such plans, including a material increase in the number of shares to be issued under the plan and a material increase in the class of participants eligible to participate in the plan. Plans involving phantom stock or that merely track stock performance and are settled in cash only are not subject to shareholder approval requirements.[107]

Q 31.18.7 What plans are exempt from the shareholder approval requirements of the stock markets?

Generally, the following plans or arrangements are not subject to shareholder approval:[108]

- Plans available to shareholders generally, such as dividend reinvestment plans.
- Tax-qualified plans that meet the requirements of Code section 401(a) or 423.
- Certain excess plans for key employees that allow for benefits in excess of the limits under Code section 402(g).
- Grants to a person not previously an employee or director of the company, or following a bona fide period of non-employment, as an inducement material to the individual's entering into employment with the company, provided such issuances are approved by either the issuer's independent compensation committee or a majority of the issuer's independent directors. Promptly following an issuance of any employment inducement grant, a company must disclose in a press release the material terms of the grant, including the recipient(s) of the grant and the number of shares involved.

Profits Recovery/Restricting Insiders

Q 31.18.8 What is the profit recovery rule of section 16(b) of the Securities Exchange Act of 1934?

Section 16(b) of the Securities Exchange Act of 1934 provides that any profit earned by an insider by reason of the purchase and sale (or sale and purchase) of employer stock within a period of less than six months must be repaid to the employer.

Q 31.18.9 Who are "insiders" under section 16(b)?

The three categories of insiders are 10% shareholders, directors, and officers. Generally, the company's officers include the president, the PFO, the principal accounting officer or controller, vice presidents in charge of a principal business of the company, and any other officer who performs a significant policy-making function.

Q 31.18.10 What happens if a person becomes an insider within six months of a stock purchase or sale transaction?

Transactions that occur within six months of the date on which a person becomes an officer or director are subject to section 16(b) only in limited circumstances. If a person is a 10% shareholder and is not an officer or director, there is liability under section 16(b) only if both the purchase and sale occurred while the person was a 10% shareholder.

If a person becomes a 10% shareholder, the transaction that caused such person to become a 10% shareholder is not subject to section 16(b).

Q 31.18.11 What filings are required by an insider under section 16(a) of the 1934 Act?

Insiders must make the following filings:

- Form 3 must be filed within ten days of becoming an insider.
- Form 4 must be filed within two business days after the day on which a transaction is executed that changes an insider's ownership of the employer.
- Form 5 must be filed within forty-five days of the employer's fiscal year end. Form 5 must disclose certain stock holdings and transactions not covered by a Form 3 or Form 4 that was previously filed and can be used to report holdings and transactions that should have been included in a previously filed Form 3 or Form 4.

Q 31.18.12 What transactions are exempt under Rule 16(b)-3 from the profit recovery rule of section 16(b)?

Transactions involving a tax-qualified retirement plan, an excess benefit (non-qualified) plan, or an employee stock purchase plan, other than certain discretionary transactions described below, are exempt from the section 16(b) profit recovery rule and section 16(a)'s filing requirements.

The following transactions are exempt from the section 16(b) profit recovery rule, but not from section 16(a)'s filing requirements:

(1) grants, awards, and other acquisitions of securities from the company, other than discretionary transactions, if:
  (a) the transaction is approved in advance by the board, the compensation committee, or the shareholders, or
  (b) the transaction is ratified by the shareholders at the next meeting after the transaction, or
  (c) the acquired securities are held for at least six months;
(2) dispositions to the company, other than discretionary transactions, if the transaction is approved in advance by the board, the compensation committee, or the shareholders; and
(3) discretionary transactions in which the insider makes a volitional intra-plan transfer into or out of a fund invested in company stock or receives a cash distribution that is funded by a disposition of company stock (such as transactions within a 401(k) plan) within a plan or disposes of company stock for cash, but only if the transaction occurs pursuant to an election made by the insider at least six months after the date of the most recent opposite-way transaction under any of the company's plans.

Limiting Resales of Stock

Q 31.18.13 Under what circumstances and conditions can a plan participant resell public company securities purchased or otherwise received through an employee benefit plan?

The rules for resales of stock received under an employee benefit plan are different depending upon whether the stock is registered or unregistered and whether the participant is an affiliate or a non-affiliate.[109] For non-affiliates, resales of unregistered stock are permitted if either:

- (i) (a) the company is a reporting company under the Securities Exchange Act of 1934,
       (b) the stock to be resold is actually traded, and
       (c) the number of shares that is resold is small compared to the total number of shares of that class issued and outstanding;
- (ii) the participant satisfies the conditions of Rule 144; or
- (iii) the participant has held the shares for at least two years and meets certain other conditions of a Rule 144(k) transaction.

Resales of registered stock are permitted without restriction.

For affiliates, resales of unregistered stock are permitted if the participant satisfies the conditions of Rule 144. Resales of registered stock are permitted if either:

- (i) the participant satisfies the conditions of Rule 144;
- (ii) the transaction is a private sale; or
- (iii) the shares are registered by the participant using a reoffer prospectus.

Q 31.18.14 Who is an affiliate for purposes of resales?

Rule 144(a)(1) provides that an affiliate is a person that directly, or indirectly through one or more intermediaries, controls, or is controlled by, or is under common control with, the employer company.

Q 31.18.15 What are the conditions that must be met under Rule 144?

Rule 144 imposes the following conditions:

- The employer is subject to the reporting requirements of section 13 of the Securities Exchange Act of 1934 for at least ninety days preceding the sale of stock.
- The employer has filed all reports required under section 13 for the twelve months preceding the sale of the stock.
- The participant has held the stock for at least one year.

- The amount of stock sold by the participant during a three-month period does not exceed the greater of one percent of the outstanding shares or the average weekly reported volume of trading in the stock for the four calendar weeks preceding the participant's notice of sale that is filed with the SEC.
- A Rule 144 sale must be effected in a broker's transaction or directly with a market maker.
- Notices must be filed with the SEC and the national exchange on which the employer stock is traded.

Blackout Periods

Q 31.18.16 Does Sarbanes-Oxley prohibit trading by executives of a company stock during pension blackout periods?

Yes. Section 306(a) of the Sarbanes-Oxley Act of 2002 prohibits directors and executive officers from trading company stock and derivative securities during any blackout period when at least 50% of the company's 401(k) plan participants are blacked-out from buying or selling company stock in their plan accounts. The prohibition applies only to stock acquired by the director or officer in connection with his or her service for the company. The SEC issued Regulation BTR to provide rules governing the section 306(a) prohibition.

Q 31.18.17 Does Regulation BTR provide any exemptions to the trading prohibition?

Yes. Regulation BTR provides a number of exemptions. The exemption transactions include:

- acquisitions under dividend reinvestment plans;
- purchases or sales in connection with tax-qualified plans (other than a transaction involving a discretionary transaction under the section 16 rules);
- grants or awards under an option or other stock rights plan that provides a formula or that occur automatically;
- acquisitions or dispositions pursuant to a gift transaction or a post-death transfer; and
- acquisitions or dispositions pursuant to a domestic relations order.

Q 31.18.18 Is there a notice requirement relating to the trading prohibition?

The company must give the directors and officers and the SEC notice that a blackout period is going to occur. The notice is timely only if it is given no later than five business days after the company receives notice of the blackout period from the plan administrator. If the company does not receive such notice, the company's notice must be given at least fifteen days before the first day of the blackout period. The company also must file a Form 8-K.[110]

Q 31.18.19 What remedies apply to a violation of the trading prohibition?

The violation is subject to an SEC enforcement action. In addition, the company, or a shareholder on behalf of the company, may bring an action to recover any profit made by the director or executive officer as a result of a prohibited transaction.[111]

Q 31.18.20 Does Sarbanes-Oxley impose any other restrictions impacting executive compensation?

Under Sarbanes-Oxley, a company's chief executive officer and chief financial officer must forfeit bonuses and other incentive compensation if the company is required to prepare an accounting restatement due to material noncompliance or misconduct relating to financial reporting requirements. In addition, the law allows the SEC to freeze certain payments to directors and executives during an investigation of the company for securities law violations. Sarbanes-Oxley also prohibits loans by the company directly or indirectly to executives and directors.[112]

Executive Compensation

Notes

1. 29 C.F.R. § 2510.3-2.
2. *See, e.g.*, Treas. Reg. § 1.61-2(d) and Rev. Rul. 79-24, 1979-1 C.B. 60.
3. Additional Code sections and Treasury regulations apply to tax-exempt entities, which goes beyond the scope of this chapter.
4. After the enactment of Code section 409A, the IRS permitted employers and other plan sponsors to delay amendment of a plan or arrangement until the issuance of final regulations, provided they administered the plan or arrangement in good-faith compliance with the requirements of section 409A during the interim period. Final regulations were issued in April 2007 and all affected plans and arrangements had to be amended to conform to the requirements of section 409A by December 31, 2007.
5. Treas. Reg. § 1.61-2(d); Safe Harbor Water Power Corp. v. United States, 303 F.2d 928 (Ct. Cl. 1962); Rev. Rul. 74-75, 1974-1 C.B. 19, as modified in Rev. Rul. 86-14, 1986-1 C.B. 304; Rev. Rul. 68-507, 1968-2 C.B. 485; Old Colony Trust Co. v. Comm'r, 279 U.S. 716 (1929).
6. I.R.C. § 56(b)(3).
7. I.R.C. § 83(a).
8. I.R.C. § 56(b)(3).
9. *See* Q 31.3.2.
10. *See* Q 31.7.
11. *See* Q 31.6.1.
12. A section 424(a) transaction is a corporate merger, consolidation, acquisition of property or stock, separation, reorganization, or liquidation if an ISO is assumed or a substitution for an old option occurs with a new option that is issued and certain aggregate value tests are met when tested before and after the transaction occurs.
13. I.R.C. § 83(a).
14. Treas. Reg. § 1.83-7(a).
15. *See* IRS News Release IR-2007-30.
16. I.R.C. §§ 61, 162, 402(b), and 451.
17. *See* Q 31.7.
18. 29 U.S.C. §§ 1051(2), 1081(a)(3), and 1101(a)(1); in providing statutory exemptions, the statute uses phrase "unfunded" and a "select group of managerial or highly compensated employees." U.S. Dep't of Labor Advisory Opinion 90-14A (May 8, 1990) is instructive in its content, even though it was informally withdrawn by the DOL and may not be relied upon.
19. *See* Q 31.4.1.
20. *See* 29 U.S.C. §§ 1051(2), 1081(a)(3), 1101(a)(1); *see also* Demery v. Extebank Deferred Compensation Plan (B), 216 F.3d 283 (2d Cir. 2000) (where 15% was allowed for an exempt plan where all participants were in management *and* were

highly compensated); Foley v. Am. Elec. Power, 425 F. Supp. 2d 863 (S.D. Ohio 2006); *but see* Carrabba v. Randalls Food Mkts., 252 F.3d 721 (5th Cir. 2001) (holding that a group of "all" management could not, by definition, be viewed as a "select" group).

21. *See In re* IT Grp., Inc., 305 B.R. 402 (Bankr. D. Del. 2004), *aff'd*, 448 F.3d 661 (3d Cir. 2006).
22. Treas. Reg. § 1.451-2(a); Ross v. Comm'r, 169 F.2d 483 (1st Cir. 1948).
23. *See* I.R.C. § 671 and Treas. Reg. § 1.671-1 and -2.
24. Treas. Reg. §§ 1.61-22 and 1.7872-15.
25. Treas. Reg. § 1.409A-1(a)(1).
26. Treas. Reg. § 1.409A-1(b)(1).
27. Treas. Reg. § 1.409A-1(f).
28. Treas. Reg. § 1.409A-1(h)(3).
29. Treas. Reg. § 1.409A-1(a)(1).
30. Treas. Reg. § 1.409A-1(a).
31. Treas. Reg. § 1.409A-1(b)(4).
32. Treas. Reg. § 1.409A-1(b)(4)(ii).
33. Treas. Reg. § 1.409A-1(b)(5)(i)(A).
34. Treas. Reg. § 1.409A-1(b)(5)(i)(B).
35. Treas. Reg. § 1.409A-1(b)(6).
36. Treas. Reg. § 1.409A-1(a)(5).
37. Treas. Reg. § 1.409A-1(a)(3).
38. Treas. Reg. § 1.409A-1(b)(9).
39. Treas. Reg. § 1.409A-1(f)(1).
40. Treas. Reg. § 1.409A-1(f)(2).
41. Treas. Reg. § 1.409A-1(b)(5)(iv)(B).
42. I.R.C. § 409A(a)(1)(A).
43. Treas. Reg. § 1.409A-1(d).
44. I.R.C. § 409A(a)(1)(A)(i)(I).
45. I.R.C. § 409A(a)(2).
46. I.R.C. § 409A(a)(2)(A).
47. Treas. Reg. § 1.409A-1(h).
48. Treas. Reg. § 1.409A-3(d)(4).
49. Treas. Reg. § 1.409A-3(i)(5).
50. Treas. Reg. § 1.409A-3(i)(3).
51. Treas. Reg. § 1.409A-3(d).
52. *Id*.
53. Treas. Reg. § 1.409A-3(i)(2).
54. Treas. Reg. § 1.409A-3(j)(4).
55. Treas. Reg. § 1.409A-3(j)(4)(ix).
56. Treas. Reg. § 1.409A-2(b)(7).
57. Treas. Reg. § 1.409A-2(a).
58. Treas. Reg. § 1.409A-2(a)(8).
59. Treas. Reg. § 1.409A-2(b).
60. I.R.C. § 409A(b)(1).
61. I.R.S. Notice 2005-1, 2005-1 C.B. 274, Q&A-29.

62. I.R.S. Notice 2007-100, 2007-52 I.R.B. 1243 (Dec. 26, 2007).
63. I.R.S. Notice 2008-113, 2008-51 I.R.B. 1305 (Dec. 22, 2008).
64. I.R.S. Notice 2010-6, 2010-3 I.R.B. 275 (Jan. 9, 2010).
65. The Emergency Economic Stabilization Act of 2008 is Division A of Pub. L. No. 110-343, 122 Stat. 3765 (Oct. 3, 2008).
66. I.R.C. § 280G(a).
67. I.R.C. § 4999(a).
68. I.R.C. § 280G(b)(2).
69. Treas. Reg. § 1.280G-1, Q&A-5.
70. I.R.C. § 280G(b)(1).
71. I.R.C. § 280G(b)(3).
72. I.R.C. § 280G(c).
73. Treas. Reg. § 1.280G-1, Q&A-11(a).
74. Treas. Reg. § 1.280G-1, Q&A-22.
75. I.R.C. § 280G(b)(2)(A).
76. *See* I.R.C. § 83(a) and (b), I.R.S. Notice 2005-1, 2005-1 C.B. 274.
77. *See generally* I.R.S. Notice 2005-1, 2005-1 C.B. 274.
78. *Id.*
79. *See, e.g., Testimony Concerning Optional Backdating, Before the U.S. Senate Committee on Banking, Housing and Urban Affairs* (Sept. 6, 2006) (statement of Christopher Cox, Chairman, U.S. Securities and Exchange Commission), *available at* www.sec.gov/news/testimony/2006/ts090606cc.htm.
80. Executive Compensation and Related Person Disclosure, Securities Act Rel. No. 8732A.
81. Securities Act Rel. No. 8765 (Dec. 22, 2006).
82. Regulation S-K, Item 402(a)(1)(i).
83. Regulation S-K, Item 402(a)(1).
84. Securities Act Rel. No. 8732A (Aug. 29, 2006) [hereinafter 2006 Adopting Release], pt. VII.
85. Regulation S-K, Item 402(b)(1)(i)–(vi).
86. Regulation S-K, Item 402(b)(2).
87. Regulation S-K, Item 402(b), instruction 2.
88. Regulation S-K, Item 402(a)(3), instruction 1.
89. 2006 Adopting Release at 35.
90. Regulation S-K, Item 402(b), instruction 4.
91. Regulation S-K, Item 402(b).
92. Regulation S-K, Item 402(j).
93. Exchange Act Rel. No. 53,185 (Jan. 27, 2006).
94. Regulation S-K, Item 402(c)(2)(ix), instruction 4.
95. Regulation S-K, Item 402(b)(2).
96. Regulation S-K, Item 402(k).
97. Regulation S-K, Item 402(a).
98. Regulation S-K, Item 402(b)(1).
99. Regulation S-K, Item 407(e).
100. Regulation S-K, Item 407(e)(5).

101. Securities Act Rel. No. 8732A, Exchange Act Rel. No. 54,302A (Aug. 29, 2006).
102. Securities Act of 1933 § 2(1).
103. SEC v. W.J. Howey Co., 328 U.S. 293 (1946).
104. Securities Act Rel. Nos. 6188 (Feb. 1, 1980), and 33-6281 (Jan. 15, 1981).
105. 17 U.S.C. § 77a *et seq.*
106. 17 C.F.R. § 240.12h-1.
107. NYSE Listed Company Manual § 303A.08; NASD Rule 4350(i).
108. *Id.*
109. Securities Act of 1933, Rule 144, 17 C.F.R. § 230.144.
110. Rule 104 of Regulation BTR, 17 C.F.R. § 245.104.
111. Sarbanes-Oxley Act of 2002 § 306(a)(2).
112. *Id.* § 402.

32

Institutions of Higher Education

*Kwamina Thomas Williford, Paul Lannon &
Nathan Adams*[*]

Colleges, universities, and other institutions of higher education[1] operate within special environments regulated by federal, state, and local laws. These regulations govern a broad range of activities, including admissions, financial aid, sponsored research, intellectual property, campus safety, and privacy, to name just a few. Consequently, the compliance concerns are vast and constantly changing. Instead of attempting the Sisyphean task of cataloguing each one, this chapter highlights and addresses in depth the more prominent federal compliance obligations.

---

*The authors wish to acknowledge Ieuan G. Mahony, Maximillian Bodoin, Ronald A. Oleynik, and Antonia I. Tzinova for their contributions to this chapter.

Overview	1115
Compliance Programs	1115
Risk Assessment	1118
Diversity in Admissions	1119
Disability	1123
Student Assistance/Federal Student Aid	1126
Institutional Eligibility	1126
Program Eligibility	1127
Participation Requirements	1128
Incentive Compensation	1129
Preferred Lender Lists	1131
Code of Conduct	1132
Student Loan Information Notification and Disclosure	1133
Counseling for Borrowers	1134
Private Lenders	1135
Penalties	1135
Campus Safety and Security	1136
Privacy of Student Education Records/ Information—FERPA	1141
Privacy Rights	1142
FERPA Investigations	1143
FERPA Violations	1143
"Education Records"	1144
Student Access to Records	1146
Exceptions to Student Consent	1147
Outsourcing Records	1154
Enforcement	1155
Record-Keeping Requirements	1156
Security/Privacy of Student Medical Records—HIPAA	1158
Intellectual Property and Copyright Protection	1159
Copyright Basics	1159
The Work-for-Hire Doctrine	1161
The Academic Exception	1162
The Fair-Use Doctrine	1165
Copyright Policy	1166
Liability for Copyright Infringement	1167
Export Controls	1172
Deemed Exports	1173

Foreign Students 1173
Regulation of Teaching 1175
Regulation of Research 1177
Teaching Abroad and Foreign Campuses........................... 1180
Export Controls Compliance... 1180
Federally Sponsored Research... 1182
Accounting and Reporting Effort and Costs 1183
Human-Subject Research 1185
Stimulus Funds 1186
Patentable Inventions.. 1187
False Claims Act Considerations... 1188

Overview

Compliance Programs

Q 32.1   Is it necessary for an institution to have a compliance program?

Yes. The sheer number of regulations governing the activities of higher education, as well as the gravity of violating many of those regulations, necessitates a comprehensive and well-maintained compliance program. Moreover, depending on the activity, a particular statute may mandate a specific compliance program. For example, if an institution has been awarded a government contract of $5 million or more and the contract has a performance period of 120 days or longer, then the Federal Acquisition Regulation (FAR)[2] requires a compliance and ethics program in connection with that contract.[3] Likewise, if an institution offers a preferred lender list in connection with a student's choice for financial aid, then the Higher Education Act (HEA) requires that institution to develop a code of conduct for its financial aid personnel to comply with.[4]

More generally, institutions are responsible for ensuring that their faculty and staff comply with their mounting legal requirements, many of which are referenced and discussed in this chapter. Creating an effective compliance program serves as a sword, prompting education and training about an institution's particular requirements.[5] If implemented properly, the compliance program may also operate as a shield, helping to protect an institution from enhanced enforcement and fines. As explained in chapter 2, the Federal Sentencing Guidelines permit corporate entities, including institutions of higher education, to use implementation of a compliance program as a mitigating factor for fines if an employee engages in wrongdoing or violates a compliance obligation in his work on behalf of the institution.[6]

Q 32.1.1 What should a compliance program for a higher education institution entail?

An institution's compliance program should aim to prevent and detect criminal conduct and promote an organizational culture and "tone from the top" that encourages ethical conduct and a commitment to compliance with the law.[7] Ideally, the program should encompass the several basic components set forth within the Federal Sentencing Guidelines and discussed in chapter 2. These components include:

(1) assessment of the compliance risks;
(2) adoption of standards and internal controls for compliance that will prevent or deter wrongdoing;
(3) designation of a point person with overall responsibility to oversee the program;
(4) communication and training;
(5) periodic auditing and monitoring;
(6) a confidential means for people to raise compliance issues without fear of retaliation;
(7) prompt and appropriate investigation of compliance-related issues; and
(8) periodic assessment and modification of the program in response to weaknesses or new risks.

Q 32.1.2 Who should be involved in the implementation of a compliance program at institutions of higher education?

An effective compliance program requires a comprehensive approach with strategic participation from the institution's governing board, president, compliance officer and committee, as well as the specific operational units within the institution.[8] A breakdown of the types of responsibilities and potential designation of responsibilities is set forth below.[9]

Governing Board. The governing board should be responsible for setting the "tone from the top" and establishing a culture of compliance that recognizes compliance as an institutional value that is the responsibility of every employee. This may be accomplished through broad expressions of support for the institution's compliance efforts and "doing what is right," allocating sufficient resources to develop and address compliance concerns, and authorizing swift corrective action when negative compliance incidents occur. Ultimately, the governing board should have oversight responsibility for the compliance program.[10]

President/Office of the President. The office of the president should assist in efforts to cultivate a culture of compliance by reinforcing the tone from the top as one that places a high value on institutional compliance. The office should serve as the spokesperson for the institution, capitalizing on opportunities to deliver its message of compliance. It should be kept apprised of the institution's compliance activities and have oversight responsibility in connection with training, monitoring, and auditing.[11]

Compliance Officer and/or Compliance Committee. The compliance officer and committee serve as the backbone of the compliance program. They have intimate knowledge of the legal and regulatory requirements and compliance activities of the institution. They should meet regularly to review compliance activities and make recommendations for improvements. In addition, they should have the authority to receive, review, and investigate issues and reported violations. They should have direct reporting access to the governing board to enable swift action if necessary. They also should keep the governing board and office of the president apprised of compliance activities and potential breaches.

Operations Units. The various divisions, departments, and other operations units within an institution are closest to the regulatory and legal issues faced by the institution. The issues are embedded in their daily operations, and as such, the employees within these operational units often have the best insight into heightened compliance concerns that they encounter on a daily basis. It is also more likely that they have a hands-on understanding of which training and monitoring methods will work best with their units. Operations units should share this knowledge with the compliance officer to help shape a strategic plan for compliance objectives and training methods. The units should be involved in the training as well. In addition, the operations units should review and investigate issues and reports made regarding compliance concerns.

COMPLIANCE FACT

Compliance is not one-size-fits-all.

When organizing a compliance program at a higher educational institution, there is no one-size-fits-all model to follow. The key to an effective compliance program is ensuring that controls are in place to prevent and detect wrongdoing, and instilling an organizational culture that encourages ethical conduct.

Risk Assessment

Q 32.2 What are the greatest areas of risk for institutions?

The level of risk faced by an institution varies greatly based on the institution and its activities. To determine which areas generate the greatest risks, each institution should conduct a risk assessment of its activities. A risk assessment looks at the institution's level of activity within a specified area, the number of compliance violations sustained by the institution in the specified area, potential penalties and other consequences for noncompliance, whether internal controls, such as policies, training, and monitoring are in place, and the attention or activity of enforcement authorities.[12]

Many of the more salient risk areas are referenced within this chapter and include:
- diversity in admissions,
- disability,
- student assistance/federal student aid,
- campus security,

- privacy/security of student records and information,
- copyright protection,
- ownership of intellectual property,
- government-sponsored research, and
- false claims.

Diversity in Admissions

Q 32.3   May academic institutions take race and gender into account when making admissions decisions?

Academic institutions may take race into account when making admissions decisions, but only after undertaking a searching inquiry into compliance with, as applicable, the Equal Protection Clause[13] or Title VI.[14] Race-based admissions decisions are presumptively unconstitutional[15] and, therefore, must satisfy strict scrutiny or, in other words, must further a "compelling governmental interest" in the "least restrictive" or most "narrowly tailored" manner.[16] Even private institutions must meet these standards if they participate in federal financial aid programs, because Title VI applies to all programs in a college that receives federal financial assistance.[17]

The standard for gender-based admissions policies is at least that of intermediate scrutiny. The Equal Protection Clause applies to public universities and requires affected institutions to demonstrate an "exceedingly persuasive justification" to take gender into account.[18] For this, the institutions must show at least that the "discriminatory means employed" are substantially related to important governmental objectives.[19] In addition, Title IX[20] applies to public undergraduate institutions and public and private institutions of vocational, professional, and graduate education, except certain religious educational institutions.[21] Some federal courts have granted female students greater protection under Title IX than under the Equal Protection Clause by applying strict scrutiny to evaluate academic policies.[22] Some states have also adopted statutes that prohibit sex discrimination at educational institutions.[23]

Q 32.3.1 When do institutions have a compelling interest to consider race in admissions?

An institution may have a compelling interest in attaining a diverse student body.[24] An institution may consider race and gender critical to this, but efforts to achieve racial balancing have been struck down. The concept of diversity is broader than quotas or balancing tests.[25] Diversity is understood to comprise a wide variety of demographic factors, such as religion, income, and national origin. Diversity also encompasses unusual travel abroad, intellectual achievement, leadership qualities, community service, overcoming personal adversity or special needs, language fluency, employment and military experience, and extraordinary awards and honors.[26]

The institution must clearly articulate the pedagogical justification for why achieving diversity (including racial and gender diversity) is at the heart of the institution's educational mission.[27] Justifications for race-sensitive policies approved by the courts include

- promoting cross-racial understanding;
- helping to break down racial stereotypes;
- enabling students to better understand persons of different races;
- achieving a "critical mass" of students;
- preparing students to function in a multi-cultural workforce;
- cultivating the next set of leaders;
- recruiting a sufficient number of minorities to secure the educational benefits that diversity is designed to produce;
- enabling frequent, comfortable, and normal inter-group interaction; and
- avoiding racial isolation.[28]

The pedagogical justification must correspond to the level of diversity sought, and that level must be identified prospectively.[29] Consequently, a periodic study will ordinarily be essential to determine the level of diversity attained at the institution, the extent to which diversity-conscious admissions decisions are achieving the institution's pedagogical objectives, and the continued need for the diversity-conscious policies. As an example of periodic study, academic institutions have examined diversity on university-wide, degree program, department, and classroom bases to determine the extent of under-enrollment of minority and female students.[30]

Q 32.3.2 When is an institution's implementation of a race-conscious admissions policy narrowly tailored?

A race-conscious admissions policy is narrowly tailored consistent with the strict scrutiny standard when:

(1) race is merely a "plus" factor in admissions, not a quota;[31]
(2) applicants are not isolated by race in pools or otherwise;[32]
(3) applicants are given a highly individualized, holistic review;[33]
(4) race-neutral alternatives to increase diversity are considered;[34] and
(5) the race-conscious policy has a limited duration and depends for renewal on periodic review of the program.[35]

Impermissible pooling of minority applicants occurs when minorities are considered separately from non-minorities.[36] Mechanical and predetermined bonus points linked to race or ethnicity are the antithesis of individualized review.[37] Additionally, a system is not holistic if it is not "flexible enough to consider all pertinent elements of diversity in light of the particular qualifications of each applicant, and to place them on the same footing for consideration, although not necessarily according them the same weight."[38]

An academic institution need not exhaust race-neutral alternatives to race-conscious admissions policies, but it must take seriously employing as many alternatives as feasible; for example, by increasing the pool of minority applicants through community outreach efforts (*e.g.*, adopt-a-minority high school programs) and scholarship programs (*e.g.*, first-in-family scholarships).[39] Sunset provisions contingent upon evaluation of the importance of a race-sensitive admissions policy in light of the pedagogical reasons for the program and the success of the program are also required to implement a narrowly tailored constitutional policy.[40]

Q 32.3.3 In what circumstances may the consideration of gender in admissions be constitutional?

The U.S. Supreme Court has not yet ruled on when gender-based admissions policies are constitutional, but it has held that a "gender-based classification favoring one sex can be justified if it intentionally and directly assists members of the sex that is disproportionately burdened."[41] The justification must be genuine, not hypothesized or invented *post hoc* in response to litigation.[42] An asserted need for "gender diversity" that is no more than "a front for . . . gender balancing" is insufficient.[43]

In addition, the justification for a gender-sensitive policy should not rely on "archaic and stereotypic notions" about the sexes or have as its purpose to "exclude or 'protect' members of one gender because they are presumed to suffer from an inherent handicap or to be innately inferior. . . ."[44] An admissions system that awards automatic points on the basis of gender without any individualized assessment may be no less objectionable than one that does so on the basis of race.[45] In fact, it is likely that in gender-based admissions cases a court will consider many of the same factors weighed in race-based admissions cases.[46]

Q 32.4 What are the consequences of a noncompliant admissions policy?

Institutions that fail to ensure that their race- or gender-sensitive admissions policies comply with the Equal Protection Clause risk investigation by state and federal departments of education and state and federal civil rights commissions. In addition to public enforcement, institutions risk private enforcement efforts by accrediting agencies or individuals and advocacy groups opposed to affirmative action in admissions. Successful actions brought under 42 U.S.C. § 1983 entitle plaintiffs to attorney fees and costs.

> **CASE STUDY**
>
> In December 2009, the U.S. Commission on Civil Rights subpoenaed roughly nineteen public and private, religious and secular, and historically black institutions in the mid-Atlantic region,[47] based on reports that those institutions were admitting men at greater rates than women. The commission explained that their investigation grew out of anecdotal stories that admissions officials were discriminating against women to promote a more even gender mix.[48]

Disability

Q 32.5 What obligations regarding disability should an institution be aware of?

Title II and Title III of the Americans with Disabilities Act (ADA)[49] and section 504 of the Rehabilitation Act of 1973 (the "Rehabilitation Act")[50] impose similar requirements[51] and apply to public and private institutions.[52] Title II of the ADA prevents a disabled person, as defined by the statute, who is "otherwise qualified" for the benefit in question from being excluded from the benefit on the basis of a disability.[53] Title III and the Rehabilitation Act also require that institutions reasonably accommodate a disabled person who is otherwise qualified academically, as long as the institution is a private entity that owns, leases, or operates a place of public accommodation (for ADA purposes) and receives federal funding (for Rehabilitation Act purposes). The institution would not be required to make an accommodation that would "fundamentally alter the nature of the public accommodation."[54]

In 2008, Congress amended the ADA and Rehabilitation Act in a manner likely to expand their applicability to the admissions, employment, and other practices of post-secondary institutions.[55] The ADA Amendments Act of 2008 (ADAAA)[56] stated that the definition of disability must be "construed in favor of broad coverage of individuals under this Act, to the maximum extent permitted by the terms of this Act."[57] The ADAAA includes a non-exhaustive list of major life activities subject to impairment, which is likely to expand available legal protection to include the following activities:[58]

caring for oneself	walking	learning
performing manual tasks	standing	reading
seeing	lifting	concentrating
hearing	bending	thinking
eating	speaking	communicating
sleeping	breathing	working

The ADAAA also covers individuals with episodic impairments such as epilepsy and asthma.[59]

Altogether, these changes appear to have expanded the class of protected individuals.[60] To illustrate, before the ADAAA, "learning" was identified as a major life activity that could be substantially limited, but the Department of Justice issued guidance indicating that the degree of limitation posed should be evaluated in relation to "most people."[61] As a result, lower courts held that plaintiffs with learning disabilities seeking extra time to take the medical bar exam and a separate testing room were not protected because they showed a history of significant scholastic achievement as compared to most people.[62] This led some to conclude that a plaintiff's status as a graduate student itself negated class membership on the basis of a learning disability. The congressional record relating to the ADAAA[63] lends support to the view that Congress meant to reject these holdings in favor of *Bartlett v. N.Y. State Bd. of Law Examiners*,[64] where the court held that a university must take an individualized look at the method and manner in which the plaintiff achieved academic success to decide whether in select ways the student may in fact be disabled.[65]

Q 32.5.1   How should institutions respond to the ADAAA?

The ADAAA reaffirms the principle that disabled students may not compel institutions "to eliminate academic requirements essential to the instruction being pursued by a student." Essential academic requirements may include both academic and technical requirements, "with technical requirements embracing all 'nonacademic admissions criteria that are essential to participation in the program in question.'"[66] Although universities do not need to lower these standards, the burden is upon them to demonstrate that they considered alternative means (including their feasibility, cost, and effect) and came to a rationally justifiable conclusion that the alternatives would either lower academic standards or require substantial program alteration.[67]

Select legislative reports confirm that colleges should be willing "to make modifications in order to enable students with disabilities to meet . . . academic requirements."[68] Modifications may include changes in the length of time permitted for the completion of degree requirements, substitution of specific courses required for the completion of degree requirements, and adaptation of the manner in which specific courses are conducted.[69] An institution is financially responsible for auxiliary aids and services unless it can demonstrate that the cost is an undue burden.[70] Higher education institutions must have appropriate policies and procedures proffering accommodations and give the utmost care to record keeping.

In the wake of tragedies like the April 2007 massacre at Virginia Tech (see Q 32.9.3 below), applicants and students with known psychiatric disabilities create especially acute challenges. Although institutions need not admit or continue to serve students who present a direct threat to self, others, or property—such students are "not otherwise qualified"—institutions must still take care to engage in individualized and objective assessment, sound evidence of probable and proximate injury, and consideration of reasonable mitigating policies, practices, or procedures.[71]

Student Assistance/Federal Student Aid

Institutional Eligibility

Q 32.6 What are the eligibility requirements for an institution to participate in federal student aid (FSA) programs?

The U.S. Department of Education (DOE) must certify the eligibility of all institutions participating in FSA programs under Title IV of HEA. Institutional eligibility requirements can be found in the 34 C.F.R. § 600 *et seq.* and in the second volume of the *Federal Student Aid Handbook*.[72]

The DOE recognizes three types of eligible institutions:

(i) institutions of higher education,
(ii) proprietary institutions of higher education, and
(iii) post-secondary vocational institutions.

Institutions of higher education and post-secondary vocational institutions may be public or private, but they must be non-profit. By contrast, a proprietary institution of higher education must be private and for-profit.

To be eligible, an institution must:

(a) have state authorization to provide a post-secondary education program in that state;
(b) have accreditation by a nationally recognized accrediting agency or have met the alternative requirements, if applicable; and
(c) admit as regular students only individuals with a high school diploma or its recognized equivalent, or individuals beyond the age of compulsory school attendance in the state where the institution is located.

Proprietary and post-secondary vocational institutions must also comply with the "two-year rule," which requires institutions to demonstrate that they have been legally authorized to provide (and have been continuously providing) the same post-secondary instruction for which they now seek FSA for at least two consecutive years (with allowances for changes to program length and subject matter made because of new technology or requirements of other federal agencies).

Program Eligibility

Q 32.7 What are the requirements for an academic program to be eligible for FSA?

At institutions of higher education, programs eligible for FSA must:

(a) lead to an associate's, bachelor's, graduate, or professional degree,
(b) be at least a two-academic-year program that is acceptable for full credit toward a bachelor's degree, or
(c) be at least a one-academic-year training program that leads to a degree, certificate, or other recognized educational credential and that prepares a student for gainful employment in a recognized occupation.[73]

For proprietary and vocational institutions, there are three types of programs eligible for FSA. Each program must provide training for gainful employment in a recognized occupation and meet at least one of the following criteria:

(1) require at least a fifteen-week (instructional time) undergraduate program of 600 clock hours, sixteen semester or trimester hours, or twenty-four quarter hours;
(2) require at least a ten-week (instructional time) program of 300 clock hours, eight semester or trimester hours, or twelve quarter hours; or
(3) require at least a ten-week (instructional time) undergraduate program of 300 to 599 clock hours.[74]

Within a type-1 program, institutions may accept students without an associate's degree or the equivalent. A type-2 program is for graduate or professional students and may accept only students with an associate's degree or the equivalent. A type-3 program, known as a short-term program, is limited to FFEL and the Federal Direct Loan Program (DL)[75] financial aid and must admit as regular students some persons who have not yet completed an associate's degree or the equivalent. Short-term programs must also satisfy the following additional requirements:

(a) have verified completion and placement rates of at least 70%;
(b) not be more than 50% longer than the minimum training period required by state or federal agencies, if any, for the occupation for which the program of instruction is intended; and
(c) have operated for at least one year.[76]

Specific FSA programs will have further eligibility requirements.

Participation Requirements

Q 32.8 What requirements must an institution comply with in order to participate in FSA programs?

To participate in FSA programs, an institution must have a current Program Participation Agreement (PPA),[77] signed by the institution's president or chief executive officer and by an authorized representative of the Secretary of Education. By signing the PPA, an institution certifies that it will comply with the program statutes, regulations, and policies governing the FSA programs. Failure to meet the terms of a PPA could result in suspension or termination from FSA programs. Failure to meet the terms of a PPA has also triggered False Claims Act liability.[78]

An institution seeking FSA must comply with certain statutory obligations, including compliance with the Campus Security Act (also known as the Clery Act, discussed below); certain federal civil rights and anti-discrimination laws, including Title VI of the Civil Rights Act of 1964,[79] and its implementing regulation,[80] which prohibit discrimination on the basis of race, color or national origin;[81] specific preferred lender arrangement disclosures to students borrowing under the Federal Family Educational Loan Program (FFEL)[82] as required by the Secretary of Education;[83] and a written copyright protection plan designed to educate students and staff about the proper use of copyrighted materials, prevent the unauthorized distribution or use of copyrighted materials, and provide notice to students that the unauthorized distribution of copyrighted materials, including peer-to-peer file sharing, is unlawful and may subject them to civil or criminal penalties.[84]

The HEA sets forth many additional specific obligations for institution participation in Title IV programs, including requirements related to:

- incentive compensation and employment compensation for recruitment activities;
- preferred lender lists;
- an institution code of conduct;
- private education loan disclosures;[85]
- institutional and financial assistance information for students;[86]
- exit counseling for borrowers; and
- private lenders' relationships and activities with institutions and students.

Incentive Compensation

Q 32.8.1 What limitations are there on the compensation of student recruiters?

Title IV of the HEA strictly prohibits compensating student recruiters, admissions officers, and financial aid administrators based on their success in securing enrollments or financial aid.[87] The purpose of this compensation restriction is to diminish the financial incentives for enrolling unqualified students. This restriction only applies to Title IV programs. Thus, it does not apply, for example, to the recruitment of foreign students residing in foreign countries who are not eligible to receive federal student assistance.

Q 32.8.2 What types of compensation plans are permitted for student recruiters under Title IV?

The DOE has recognized twelve safe harbors that describe specific payment arrangements that do not violate the incentive compensation prohibition. In the DOE's view, the safe harbors are acceptable because they reflect situations that do not pose a significant risk of fraudulent or unscrupulous procurement of federal funding. These safe harbors are summarized as follows:

1. *Fixed compensation.* Fixed annual salaries may be adjusted up or down twice in twelve months, provided the adjust-

ment is not based "solely" on the number of students recruited, admitted, enrolled or awarded financial aid.[88]
2. *Non-Title IV course work.* The incentive compensation prohibition does not apply to the recruitment of students who enroll only in programs ineligible for Title IV funds, such as product training courses.[89]
3. *Employer contracts.* Employer-sponsored programs are exempt, provided that the employer pays more than 50% of the costs, there is no contact between the recruiter and the enrolled employees, and the recruiter's compensation is not based on the number of enrolled employees or the amount of revenue generated thereby.[90]
4. *Profit sharing.* Profit-sharing plans are exempt, provided that payments are substantially the same amount or percentage of salary or wages and made to substantially all of the institution's full-time professional and administrative staff at one or more organizational levels, except that a level may not consist predominantly of recruiters, admissions staff or financial aid staff.[91]
5. *Program completions.* It is permissible to compensate recruiters based on students successfully *completing*, as opposed to merely enrolling in, educational programs or one academic year of an educational program.[92]
6. *Pre-enrollment clerical staff.* The incentive compensation restrictions do not apply to persons who are support staff for recruiters and are not themselves recruiters. These support activities must be clerical in nature and do not include, for example, soliciting students for interviews, which is considered a core recruiting activity.[93]
7. *Certain managers and supervisors.* The institution may provide incentive compensation to managers and supervisors who do not directly manage or supervise employees directly involved in recruiting, admissions, or financial aid activities.[94]
8. *Token gifts.* Single, non-monetary gifts worth $100 or less are exempt.[95]
9. *Profit distributions.* The institution may distribute profits proportionately based upon an individual's ownership interest in the institution.[96]

10. *Internet support.* Incentive compensation is permissible for "Internet-based recruitment and admission activities that provide information about the institution to prospective students, refer prospective students to the institution, or permit prospective students to apply for admission on-line."[97]
11. *Third parties (unrestricted activities).* To the extent third parties do not participate in any recruiting, financial aid, or admissions activities, there are no restrictions on their compensation.[98]
12. *Third parties (restricted activities).* Incentive payments to third parties providing recruiting, admissions, or financial aid services are permissible, provided that the third parties adhere to the same restrictions that apply to the institution.[99]

Preferred Lender Lists

Q 32.8.3   What requirements and limitations are there on institutions providing students with a list of preferred lenders?

Institutions may provide students with a list of preferred or recommended lenders, but only if the list:

(a) does not limit a borrower's choice of lenders,
(b) contains no fewer than three lenders unaffiliated with each other, and
(c) does not include lenders that offer the institution any financial or other benefits in exchange for inclusion on the list.[100]

An institution choosing to offer a preferred lender list must:

(i) disclose the method and criteria for selecting the lenders;
(ii) provide comparative information to prospective borrowers about interest rates and other benefits offered by the lenders;
(iii) include a prominent statement that students are not required to use any of the listed lenders;
(iv) not assign a first-time borrower's loan to a particular lender; and
(v) not delay the certification of loans for borrowers who choose to use a lender not on the preferred list.

The institution must update the preferred lender list at least annually.[101]

The method and criteria used to select preferred lenders must include payment of origination or other fees for borrowers, competitive terms of conditions, including interest rates, and high-quality servicing and benefits beyond the standard terms. If the institution endorses private loans, the list must include at least two lenders that are not affiliates of one another. For each lender, the list must disclose affiliates and describe the affiliation.[102] The institution must include a statement indicating on its website and in any publications, mailings, or electronic messages distributed to prospective or current students or their families discussing financial aid opportunities that the institution may not deny or impede a borrower's loan certification if he or she chooses a lender not on the preferred lender list.[103]

State laws may add further limitations, particularly regarding consumer protection and truth in lending.

Code of Conduct

Q 32.8.4 What are an institution's obligations regarding a code of conduct?

Institutions participating in Title IV programs must develop, publish, and comply with a code of conduct for its financial aid personnel.[104] The code must be published on the institution's website and annually to those who have FSA responsibilities. At a minimum, the code of conduct must contain provisions prohibiting:

- conflicts of interest;
- revenue sharing arrangements;
- the solicitation or acceptance of gifts, receipt of fees, payments, or other financial benefits for consulting services by anyone in the institution with responsibilities for student loans, assistance with call centers, or staffing;
- the acceptance of funds to be used for private loans in exchange for providing concessions to a private lender; and
- the acceptance of anything of value except reimbursement for reasonable expenses by an employee with responsibilities for financial assistance that sits on a lender's advisory board or commission.

Student Loan Information Notification and Disclosure

Q 32.8.5 What are an institution's disclosure and notification obligations regarding student loan information?

When an institution is lending Title IV funds, it must notify the borrower, in easy-to-understand terms, what the borrower's rights and responsibilities are, and what the consequences of default are, including the disclosure of the default to consumer credit agencies.[105] The borrower must receive this information when the loan is first approved. Thereafter, the institution must make several additional disclosures, either in written or electronic form, before disbursing the loan.[106] Among the required disclosures are:

- a prominent statement that the loan must be repaid;
- the principal amount of the loan;
- charges associated with the loan;
- the interest rate;
- information regarding the payment of interest while the borrower is in school, if applicable;
- repayment information including the types of repayment plans available and an estimate of the borrower's monthly payment, consolidation, or refinancing options;
- information on deferral, forbearance, and loan forgiveness options; and
- information on the consequences of default.[107]

Not less than thirty days or more than 150 days before the borrower's first loan payment is due, institutional lenders must disclose, among other things:

- the name of the lender or loan servicer, and the payment address;
- the date repayment begins and a repayment schedule;
- an estimate of the balance owed;
- interest rate information;
- fees associated with repayment;
- the borrower's prepayment rights;
- repayment options, and benefits;
- consolidation and refinancing options; and

- additional resources for the borrower to receive advice on loan repayment.[108]

During the repayment term, institutional lenders must provide each borrower with a bill for each payment. The bill must detail:

- the original principal;
- the current balance;
- the interest rate;
- the total amount paid in interest;
- the aggregate amount paid on the loan;
- a description of any fees charged to the borrower during the preceding payment period;
- the next payment due date;
- the lender's or servicer's address and toll-free phone number; and
- a reminder that the borrower has the option of changing repayment plans.[109]

If a borrower notifies the institution about a difficulty making loan payments on time, the institution must provide information on available repayment plans, the requirements for a forbearance, and other options available to avoid default.[110] For borrowers that are sixty days or more delinquent, institutional lenders must disclose the date on which the loan will default, the minimum payment the borrower must make to avoid default, options available to avoid default, discharge options, and additional resources where the borrower may receive assistance.[111]

Institutions should also review applicable state lending laws.

Counseling for Borrowers

Q 32.8.6 What obligations does an institution have regarding financial counseling for students?

Institutions must provide entrance and exit counseling to a student borrower.[112] The counseling can be done in person, online, or through documents that the borrower acknowledges having received and reviewed.[113] The counseling must address the loan's effect on the student's eligibility for other federal financial assistance, the ability to pay interest on some loans while in school, descriptions of loan forgiveness plans and forbearance requirements, and debt management techniques.[114]

Private Lenders

Q 32.8.7 What requirements and limitations are there on the activities of private lenders?

The Private Student Loan Transparency and Improvement Act (Title X of the HEA), which amends the Truth in Lending Act (TILA), making it applicable to all private student loans, prohibits a private student loan lender from offering gifts to an institution or its employees or agents in exchange for any advantage in providing private loans to the institution's students. A private lender may not use an institution's name, logo, mascot, or any other representation of the institution to market its loans. An institution's financial aid personnel may not receive anything of value for serving on an advisory board for a lender, aside from reimbursement for reasonable expenses. Private lenders may not penalize borrowers for prepayment of their loans.[115] Furthermore, any private lender that has a preferred lender arrangement with an institution must provide an annual report to that institution, including a copy of the disclosures required to be made when a loan is approved[116] for each type of private loan the lender plans to offer to a student at the institution.[117]

Penalties

Q 32.8.8 What are the penalties for violating Title IV student aid regulations?

The regulations concerning an institution's PPA with the DOE specifically require the institution to agree that it is liable for all "improperly spent or unspent funds received under Title IV . . . programs . . . and . . . [r]efunds that the institution . . . may be required to make."[118] Title IV expressly authorizes the DOE to impose civil fines of up to $27,500 for each violation of the statute or regulations.[119] A separate violation can occur each time Title IV financial aid is disbursed improperly. In the case of students recruited under illegal incentive-based compensation schemes, the DOE has taken the position that a separate violation occurs each time one of those students obtains federal financial aid. In contrast, the DOE will count "the total of violations caused by a repeated mechanical systemic unintentional error as a single violation," unless there was prior notice of the problem and the servicer failed to correct it.[120] The DOE can also order "corrective actions," which may include payment to the DOE of any Title IV funds "improperly received, withheld, disbursed, or caused to be disbursed."[121] The monetary penalties, consequently, can be enormous.

Compromise is built into the system. The DOE is expressly authorized to "compromise" any civil penalty proposed by the OIG.[122] The DOE is also required to weigh the appropriateness of the penalty against the size of the institution and the gravity of the violation.[123] Penalties are appealable.[124]

Violations may also lead to suspension or termination from Title IV programs.[125] The suspension may not exceed sixty days unless a longer suspension is agreed to, or the DOE begins a limitation or termination proceeding against the institution.[126] A termination ends an institution's participation in a Title IV program.[127] Termination is typically reserved for situations where an institution has consistently violated Title IV and the implementing regulations, and attempts to remedy the situation have failed.[128]

Short of terminating an institution, the DOE may limit participation in Title IV programs.[129] Limitations can be applied to:

(1) the number or percentage of students enrolled in an institution who may receive Title IV funds;
(2) the percentage of an institution's total receipts from tuition and fees derived from Title IV program funds;
(3) the requirements for a surety, in a specified amount; and
(4) other conditions that the DOE deems reasonable and appropriate.[130]

Campus Safety and Security

Q 32.9 What liability does an institution have for violence on campus?

The general rule is that an institution has no duty to control the conduct of a third person so as to prevent that person from causing physical harm to another.[131] However, exceptions to this rule prevail when there is a special relationship between the institution and third person such as exists between:

- employee and employer;[132]
- landlord and tenant;[133]
- business and invitee;[134] and
- in a minority of jurisdictions, college and student.[135]

A duty may also arise if a person voluntarily assumes the duty,[136] or by virtue of a contract.[137]

When there exists a legal duty of care between an academic institution and an injured third person, the next inquiry under negligence law is to determine the standard of care due under the relevant circumstances. In making that determination, the institutions should consider the custom and practice within the academic community and expert testimony. If that standard was breached, the next question is whether there is a direct causal connection between the breach of duty and damages to another.

Foreseeability is a factor in determining both duty and proximate cause.[138] Harm is foreseeable when there is knowledge of a specific threat.[139] Foreseeability can also arise from like-kind threats or general threats within the same scope as the injury.[140] Lastly, foreseeability can be imputed when an institution is not actually aware of a risk but reasonably should have been.[141]

Q 32.9.1 What are the requirements of the Clery Act?

The Jeanne Clery Disclosure of Campus Security Policy and Campus Crime Statistics Act (the "Clery Act")[142] (originally known as the Crime Awareness and Campus Security Act) requires institutions participating in FSA programs to:

(1) publish an annual security report detailing certain crimes committed on campus and at affiliated locations for the previous three calendar years,[143]
(2) disclose campus safety policies,[144]
(3) compile and disclose campus crime statistics,[144]
(4) report to the campus community crimes that represent a threat to students and/or employees "in a manner that is timely and will aid in the prevention of similar crimes,"[146] and

(5) maintain and disclose daily crime log information.[147]

The annual security report must describe campus policies concerning the following subjects:

(1) procedures and facilities for students and others to report criminal activity or other emergencies occurring on campus and policies concerning the institution's response to such reports;
(2) policies concerning security and access to campus facilities and security considerations used in the maintenance of campus facilities;
(3) policies concerning the enforcement authority of campus law enforcement units and their relationship with state and local police agencies;
(4) policies relating to the monitoring and recording through local police agencies of criminal activity at off-campus student organizations that are recognized by the institution;
(5) policies regarding the possession, use, and sale of alcoholic beverages, enforcement of under-age drinking laws, and the possession, use, and sale of illegal drugs; and
(6) policies regarding sexual assault and procedures to follow when a sex offense occurs.[148]

Proposed amendments to the federal rules interpreting the Clery Act would:

- expand the list of hate crimes to be reported;
- require a statement of policy regarding the emergency response and evacuation procedure in the annual security report and how it will be annually tested;
- mandate immediate notification of the campus community about confirmation of an emergency or dangerous situation and require follow-up information "as needed";
- require adoption of a missing student policy and procedure; and
- mandate publication of an annual fire safety report.[149]

Q 32.9.2 What are the repercussions for failing to comply with the Clery Act?

The Clery Act does not create a private right of action, nor is it supposed to establish a standard of care,[150] but it may certainly be influencing the non-statutory standard of care by requiring policies that themselves create a threshold standard of care. In addition, the DOE is authorized to impose civil fines of up to $27,500 per violation on an educational institution that has "substantially misrepresented" the nature of the crimes required to be reported.[151] It may also limit, suspend, or terminate the institution's participation in federal financial aid programs.[152]

Q 32.9.3 What are some best practices for preventing and responding to campus violence?

In the wake of incidents such as the April 2007 massacre at Virginia Tech, where a senior at that school killed thirty-two people in two separate shooting attacks, and the February 2008 shooting at Northern Illinois University, where six people were killed, states and universities have investigated and issued multiple reports establishing best practices for preventing and responding to campus violence.[153] Due to the Clery Act and for other reasons, most schools have complied with the most rudimentary of these national standards by adopting an all-hazards emergency response plan (ERP), implementing an emergency mass notification and communications system, and providing on-campus mental health services for students.[154] The policy for use of the mass notification system should indicate the kinds of events that would initiate the use of the system, who is authorized to launch the system, the parties that should be notified, and what information should be provided.[155] Redundant means of mass communication are also important.[156]

A slightly smaller percentage of colleges have put in place a multi-disciplinary "threat assessment team" (TAT), begun training personnel regarding privacy and information sharing laws and policies such as FERPA and HIPAA, agreed to a memorandum of understanding or a mutual aid agreement with community partners such as law enforcement agencies and mental health providers, and begun to train students, faculty, and staff about mass notification systems and their roles and responsibilities in an emergency.[157] The TAT should meet weekly and include members from campus police, residential life, counseling services, faculty, and the graduate and undergraduate school deans.[158]

Additional recommended steps for preventing and responding to campus violence include:

- Repair/replace exterior doors.[159]
- Conduct an inquiry of school applicants (especially graduate students) about unusual academic histories, criminal records, and disciplinary actions.
- Include public safety as part of the school orientation process.
- Conduct annual vulnerability assessments of the campus and regular reviews of the ERP.
- Educate faculty, staff, and students about recognizing and responding to signs of mental illness and potential threats.
- Adopt a policy outlining how and to whom faculty and staff should refer students who may be threatening.
- Have multiple reporting systems to enable the reporting of threatening behavior anonymously and conveniently.
- Have an interoperable communication system with all area responders.
- Ensure that all responder agencies are trained in the National Incident Management System (NIMS) and the Incident Command System (ICS).
- Install CCTV cameras and electronic access control systems.
- Provide "active shooter response training" to campus police.
- Provide on-campus or off-campus, by agreement, specialized mental health services (*e.g.*, substance abuse, eating disorders, suicide).
- Submit potentially violent writings, drawings, and other forms of expression for forensic behavioral review.
- Ensure adequate campus safety staffing levels.
- Provide lethal weapons to campus police, training in the use of personal and specialized firearms, and the means to gain forcible entry to locked spaces.
- Drill emergency preparedness.
- Establish a trained behavioral health trauma response team.
- Develop plans to stand-up a joint information center with a public information officer.
- Plan for victim services in the aftermath of a tragic event including short- and long-term counseling for first responders, students, staff, and their families.[160]

Q 32.9.4 What is the role of legal counsel in improving campus security?

Legal counsel should be consulted in the drafting of campus security documents. In addition, counsel should either be on a school's threat assessment team or be readily available to the TAT. As one campus violence report explained:

> Attorneys can play an integral role in threat assessment and violence prevention and should be involved early in the process of dealing with more severe and credible threats. These professionals are familiar with privacy and confidentiality issues. They can also facilitate obtaining judicial injunctions and Temporary Restraining Orders, and assist in preparing legal documents to handle potentially dangerous persons or situations.[161]

Privacy of Student Education Records/ Information—FERPA

Q 32.10 What is FERPA?

The Family Educational Rights and Privacy Act (FERPA) is a federal law designed to protect the privacy of student education records.[162] FERPA first came into effect on November 19, 1974 and has gone through several amendments.[163] FERPA applies to all secondary and post-secondary schools that receive funds from any program administered by the DOE, whether public or private, including funding from federal financial aid programs.[164] FERPA's protections cover elementary school, high school, and post-secondary records. In elementary and high school, the privacy rights created by FERPA mostly flow to parents; however, once a student turns eighteen and enrolls in an institution of higher education, all of the FERPA rights transfer to the student.[165] FERPA does not protect records that only contain information about an individual generated after the student has left the college or university.[166] Accordingly, alumni and fundraising records generally fall outside FERPA.[167] On the other hand, information that was part of the individual's education record while at the institution is still protected by FERPA after graduation, as are any records produced after graduation that directly pertain to an individual's previous attendance at the institution.[168]

Privacy Rights

Q 32.10.1 What are the privacy rights students have under FERPA?

FERPA confers three privacy rights upon parents/students:

(1) The right to inspect and review their own individual education records.[169]
(2) The right to request that the college amend any information in the education record that the student believes is inaccurate, misleading, or otherwise in violation of his or her privacy rights.[170] The college then must follow further FERPA regulations to determine whether the record needs amendment. That process is discussed further below.
(3) The right to consent before an institution may disclose personally identifiable information in the student's education records.[171] The consent must specify the records to be disclosed, state the purpose of the disclosure, and identify the party or parties who will receive the disclosure.[172] The right to nondisclosure without consent is subject to several exceptions, discussed in detail below.[173]

Q 32.10.2 Who enforces FERPA?

The DOE's Family Policy Compliance Office (FPCO) enforces FERPA.[174] The Secretary of the DOE designates the FPCO to investigate, process, and review complaints and FERPA violations, as well as to provide technical assistance to ensure FERPA compliance.[175] The FPCO may require a college to submit reports, information on policies and procedures, annual notifications, training materials, or other information needed to carry out its enforcement responsibilities.[176]

Q 32.10.3 Can a student bring a lawsuit against an institution for FERPA violations?

No. In *Gonzaga University v. Doe*, the Supreme Court determined that FERPA creates no private right of action.[177] The *Gonzaga* decision means that students may not sue colleges or universities in state or federal court for purported FERPA violations.[178] Instead, individuals must file a written complaint with the FPCO to assert any alleged violations.[179]

FERPA Investigations

Q 32.10.4 What is the process for FERPA investigations by the FPCO?

The FPCO enforces FERPA by investigating complaints that a college violated an individual's protected rights.[180] However, the FPCO may also decide to investigate a college's FERPA compliance on its own initiative even when no complaint is pending.[181] It may also decide to continue with an investigation if a complaint is filed but later withdrawn.[182] If a complaint is filed, it must contain specific allegations that give a reasonable basis to believe a FERPA violation occurred.[183] When such a complaint is received, the FPCO reviews the complaint, any information the college submits on its behalf, and other relevant information.[184] It may also permit the parties to submit further written or oral arguments and information pertaining to the alleged violation.[185] After the investigation, the FPCO will give the individual who filed the complaint, if any, and the college or university a written notice of its decision and the reasons why it came to the determination.[186]

The FPCO may not find that an institution violated FERPA based on a "single instance" of releasing a protected record without student consent.[187] The institution must have a "policy or practice" of allowing the release of protected student records before the FPCO will take enforcement measures.[188]

FERPA Violations

Q 32.11 What are the consequences of a FERPA violation?

If the FPCO determines that a FERPA violation exists, the FPCO will send the institution a list of conditions to meet within a certain timeframe.[189] If the institution complies, the complaint is resolved. If the institution does not comply, the FPCO may take any of the following actions:

(1) withhold further payments under any applicable federal program;
(2) issue a complaint to compel compliance through a cease-and-desist order; or

(3) terminate the institution's eligibility to receive federal funding.[190]

"Education Records"

Q 32.12 How does an institution determine what constitutes "education records" covered by FERPA?

Understanding what documents are protected by FERPA is essential to ensuring compliance with the regulations.[191] FERPA broadly defines "education records" as those records that are: (1) directly related to a student, and (2) maintained by an educational agency or institution or by a party acting for the agency or institution.[192] Protected information can be recorded in "any way including, but not limited to, handwriting, print, computer media, video or audio tape, microfilm, and microfiche."[193]

Subject to the exceptions discussed below, FERPA protects all "personally identifiable information" in the student record.[194] "Personally identifiable information" is anything that makes a student's identity "easily traceable," including the name of the student's parents, the family address, a "personal identifier" (such as the student's Social Security number or student number), "indirect identifiers" (such as date of birth, place of birth, mother's maiden name), information "linked or linkable to a specific student" that would allow someone to identify the student with "reasonable certainty," or information from a student record when disclosed to someone believed by the institution to know the student's identity.[195]

Q 32.12.1 What information is excluded from the definition of "education records"?

FERPA explicitly excludes several categories of documents from the education record.[196] The following categories of records are not FERPA-protected and may be disclosed without student consent:

(1) Records that are kept in the sole possession of the maker, used only "as a personal memory aid," and are not accessible or revealed to any other person, except someone serving as a temporary substitute for the person that made the record.[197] That includes the personal notes kept by a

teacher that are not accessible to anyone else at the university or college.

(2) Records of the institution's campus safety department kept in the course of its duties to protect the security and safety of the campus community.[198] The records must be created by a law enforcement unit, for a law enforcement purpose, and maintained by the law enforcement unit.[199] Records created as part of college or university disciplinary actions against a student are still protected as part of the student's education record and are not part of this exception.[200] In addition, records created by a law enforcement unit for a law enforcement purpose but maintained by another office in the university or college are still considered part of a student's education record and protected by FERPA.[201]

(3) The employment records of a student who is employed by the college or university, as long as those records are made and maintained in the regular course of business, relate exclusively to the student's status as an employee of the school, and are not available for any other purpose.[202] Employment records of a student who is employed by the college or university as a result of the student's status as a student are still considered education records and are not part of this exception.[203]

(4) Student medical and mental health records that are
   (i) made or maintained by a physician, psychiatrist, psychologist, or other recognized medical professional;
   (ii) made, maintained, or used only in connection with treatment of the student; and
   (iii) disclosed only to those who are providing the treatment.

Treatment does not include remedial educational activities that may be part of a program at the college or university.[204]

(5) Records created or received by an institution after an individual no longer attends the institution are not part of the education record; however, records that directly relate to the individual's earlier attendance at the institution remain protected.[205]

(6) Grades on peer-graded papers before they are collected and recorded by a teacher are not protected.[206]

Student Access to Records

Q 32.13 When must an institution allow a student to view his or her education records?

Under FERPA, students must be given the opportunity to inspect and review their education records.[207] An institution must comply within a reasonable period of time, not to exceed forty-five days after receipt of the student's request.[208] In addition, FERPA requires institutions to respond to a student's reasonable requests for explanation or interpretation of the contents of the record.[209] If the student cannot exercise the right to inspect and review the records, the institution must either provide the student with a copy of the records requested or identify another means that allows the student to review them.[210] An institution may charge a fee for copying student records, as long as the fee does not effectively prevent a student from exercising the right to review his or her education records.[211] FERPA does not allow the school to charge for searching for or obtaining the records, only to copy them.[212] The regulations bar institutions from destroying any education records that a student has requested an opportunity to view.[213] Finally, an institution is not required to give a student access to medical treatment records, but a student may request that the institution provide the record to a physician or other appropriate professional of the student's choice.[214]

Q 32.13.1 Are there any limits on a student's rights to access to his or her education records?

There are some limits on the inspection rights FERPA gives to students. First, if an education record details information about more than one student, a student may only inspect and review the information specific to that particular student.[215] An institution may refuse to allow a student to inspect and review financial records, including the financial documents relating to the student's parents.[216] A student is excluded from viewing confidential letters of recommendation in the file, as long as the student signed a waiver of the right to inspect the letters and they are related to the student's admission, application for employment, or receipt of an honor.[217] The names of the individuals who provided letters of recommendation must still be provided upon request to a student who waived the right to inspect them, and the institution may only use those letters for their intended purpose.[218] A student can revoke his or her waiver of the right to view confidential letters of recommendation, but the revocation only covers subsequent letters; the student still cannot inspect any letters sent before the waiver was revoked.[219]

Q 32.13.2 Can students amend their education records after inspecting them?

Once a student inspects the contents of his or her education record, FERPA confers on the student the right to request the amendment of any information in the record that the student finds inaccurate, misleading, or otherwise in violation of his or her privacy rights.[220] If the institution determines that the student is correct, the institution must amend the record and notify the student in writing of the change.[221] On the other hand, if the school determines that the information in the education record is not inaccurate, misleading, or otherwise in violation of the student's privacy rights, it must tell the student of his or her right to place a statement in the file commenting on the contested information and/or noting disagreement with the school's decision.[222] The amendment right is interpreted to apply only to things like typographical errors and is not means for a student to challenge decisions made by teachers, such as the criteria a teacher used to determine the final grade in a class.[223]

Exceptions to Student Consent

Q 32.14 When is student consent not required for disclosure?

There are several situations where FERPA breaks from the general rule that student consent is needed before disclosing personally identifiable information in education records, including:

- when the information is not deemed to harm privacy interests (such as directory information);
- when the student is a dependent for federal tax purposes;
- when disclosure is to certain outside institutions for educational purposes;
- when disclosure is between schools; and
- when there is a court order or subpoena.[224]

Similarly, FERPA allows protected information to be disclosed in certain situations of health or safety emergency. Each situation where consent is not required for disclosure is discussed below.

Q 32.14.1 What is disclosable "directory information"?

"Directory information" means information in a student record that would not cause harm to a student or violate privacy rights if disclosed.[225] Directory information in a student record includes, but is not limited to:

- name, address, telephone number;
- email address;
- photograph;
- date and place of birth;
- major field of study;
- grade level;
- enrollment status;
- attendance data;
- participation in officially recognized school activities and sports;
- height and weight of members of athletic teams;
- degrees received;
- most recent educational institution attended; and
- honors and awards received.[226]

Directory information does not include a student's Social Security or student ID number.[227]

The general requirement that information in a student record may not be disclosed without consent does not apply to "directory information."[228] Institutions must give public notice to enrolled students of the type of personally identifiable information designated as directory information before that information may be disclosed.[229] Students must also receive public notice of the right to refuse to let the institution designate any or all of that information as directory information and the time period within which the student must notify the school in writing that the information may not be disclosed without consent.[230] An institution does not have to give former students public notice and the opportunity to refuse consent, unless the former student refused consent while still in attendance.[231]

Q 32.14.2 When can parents view education records without the student's consent?

Institutions may choose to disclose education records without student consent to parents who still claim the student as a "dependent" for federal tax purposes as defined in section 152 of the Internal Revenue Code.[232] If a student is under twenty-one years old, institutions do not need to obtain consent to disclose education records to the student's parents relating to a violation of drug or alcohol rules.[233]

Q 32.14.3 Does FERPA allow a student's former high school to send records to a university or college?

FERPA allows a student's former high school to transfer records to the post-secondary institution where the student is enrolled, upon the institution's request.[234] The student's former high school must make a reasonable attempt to notify the student at his or her last known address before transferring records to the college or university, unless the former school's annual FERPA notice provides that it forwards education records to other schools where the student seeks or intends to enroll upon the new school's request or unless the transfer is initiated by the student.[235] Upon request by the student, the former school must also give the student a copy of the record it disclosed.[236] If these conditions are met, an institution may receive any information in the education record of a student's former school, as long as the record is forwarded because of the student's enrollment at the college or university.[237]

Q 32.14.4 What types of outside institutions can access student education records?

Institutions can sometimes disclose education records to outside institutions without first obtaining student consent.[238] The following types of organizations qualify to receive education records without student consent:

(1) A contractor, consultant, volunteer, or other party that provides outsourced institutional services or functions that would normally be performed by college or university employees.[239] The college or university may disclose personally identifiable information to such a party only for the function that party provides to the institution, and only on the

condition that the third party will not disclose the information to any other party without the student's prior consent.[240] The use and maintenance of the education records must remain under the college's or university's direct control.[241] The third party may only use the protected information for the purpose designated by the college or university when it disclosed the record.

(2) Information may be disclosed to another school, school system, or institution of postsecondary education where a student seeks or intends to enroll, or where the student is already enrolled. The disclosure must be related to the student's enrollment or transfer.

(3) Student records may be disclosed to government agencies, including the Comptroller General of the United States, the Attorney General of the United States, the Secretary of the DOE, or state and local educational authorities.[245] The disclosure to these agencies may only be in connection with an audit or evaluation of federal or state education programs, or the enforcement of federal legal requirements relating to education programs.[246] Information collected must be protected so that the students are not personally identified by anyone other than the officials or agencies that received the records, unless the student gives written consent for the disclosure or the collection of the personally identifiable information is specifically authorized by federal law.[247]

(4) An institution may disclose information to an outside institution in connection with a student's application for financial aid.[248] The disclosure must be necessary to determine aid eligibility, amount, conditions of the aid, or aid terms and conditions.[249]

(5) Disclosure may be made to state and local officials specifically authorized to receive information relating to reporting or disclosure under the regulations of the juvenile justice system and the system's ability to service the student who is the subject of the record.[250] The officials and authorities that receive the records must certify in writing to the institution that the information will not be disclosed to any other party, except as provided under state law, without the written consent of the student.[251]

(6) An institution may also disclose information to organizations conducting studies for, or on behalf of, educational agencies or institutions to develop, validate, or administer predictive tests, administer student aid programs, or improve instruction.[252] The institution must enter into with the organization a written contract that specifies the purpose, scope, and duration of the study and the information to be disclosed; requires the organization to use personally identifiable information only to meet the study's purposes; requires the study to be conducted in a manner that does not permit personal identification of parents or students by anyone other than representatives of the organization with legitimate interests in the study; and specifies that the information must be returned or destroyed when no longer needed for the study.[253] The institution does not have to initiate the study or agree with or endorse its results.[254]

(7) Finally, disclosure may be made to accrediting organizations for the purposes of an institution's accreditation.[255]

Q 32.14.5 Can college and university officials share information in the education record with each other?

FERPA allows protected information in student records to be shared without student consent with college officials, including teachers, who the institution determines have a "legitimate educational interest" in the student record.[256] The institution must publish a description of the criteria it uses to determine who is a "school official" and what is considered a "legitimate educational interest."[257]

Q 32.14.6 What if there is a court order or subpoena for information in a student's education record?

Institutions may disclose education records without consent to comply with a judicial order or lawful subpoena.[258] Before disclosing the information, the institution must make a reasonable effort to notify the student about the order or subpoena to give the student an opportunity to seek protective action.[259] Prior notice to the student is not required if disclosure is made in compliance with a federal grand jury subpoena or any other subpoena issued for a law enforcement purpose where the court orders that the contents of the subpoena or information obtained in response to it must not be disclosed, or if information is requested in regard to an act of domestic or international terrorism as defined by federal law.[260]

Q 32.14.7 What happens to protected records when there is a legal action between the student and the educational institution?

If a student initiates legal action against an educational institution, the institution may disclose relevant information in the education record to the court, without the student's consent, for the purpose of defending itself.[261] Should the institution initiate legal action against a student, the institution may also disclose, without the student's consent, information in the student's record that is relevant to prosecuting its claims.[262]

Q 32.14.8 What is the health or safety emergency exception?

FERPA allows records to be disclosed without a student's consent "in connection with an emergency, [to] appropriate persons if the knowledge of such information is necessary to protect the health or safety of the student or other persons."[263] The ability to release information in case of a health or safety emergency is subject to the regulations adopted by the DOE.[264] The DOE will not substitute its judgment for that of the college or university if the information available to school officials at the time of the release creates a rational basis for the determination a health or safety emergency exists.[265] The institution must keep a record in the student file of reasons for invoking the health or safety emergency exception and list the parties that received the information.[266]

Over the years, the DOE adopted regulations strictly construing the emergency exception.[267] FERPA's 2009 amendments removed the strict construction requirement in an attempt to provide "greater flexibility and deference" to administrators who seek to invoke the emergency exception to effectively protect the health or safety of an individual or the greater campus community.[268] Accordingly, FERPA now states that colleges may take into account "the totality of the circumstances" surrounding a threat to the health or safety of a student or others.[269]

FERPA requires the college or university to determine that there is an "articulable and significant threat" before information may be disclosed under the emergency exception.[270] The "articulable" threat does not mean that the threat must be verbal, but that the school must be able to articulate the nature of the threat when it makes its disclosure record.[271] The DOE explains that a significant threat may be "a threat of substantial bodily harm, to any person," including threats of "a terrorist attack, a natural disaster, a campus shooting, or the outbreak of an epidemic such as e-coli."[272] It can also be "a situation in which a student gives sufficient, cumulative warning signs that lead [the institution] to believe the student may harm himself or others at any moment."[273] The emergency exception is not intended to apply to the mere threat of an emergency (such as emergency preparedness activities), unless there is a determination that the emergency is imminent.[274]

Q 32.14.9 To whom may institutions disclose information in case of health or safety emergency?

The health or safety emergency exception gives institutions the ability to disclose a student education record without consent to "appropriate" parties if that information is necessary to protect the health or safety of the student or others.[275] The individuals who receive the disclosure do not have to be the parties responsible for protecting the student or the community.[276] Instead, disclosure may be made to any party who will be able to help the college gather necessary information to address the threat.[277]

The DOE affirms that the following parties may receive information under the emergency exception:[278]

(1) Current or prior peers of the student or mental health professionals who can provide the institution with information to assist in protecting against the threat.

(2) A potential victim and the parents of a potential victim as "other individuals" whose health or safety needs to be protected.

(3) Other institutions that the student previously attended. The other institution may rely on the current institution's determination that an emergency exists to also disclose personally identifiable information from the student's former

education records to the student's current institution to help address the threat.
(4) Law enforcement officials whom the institution determines can be helpful to provide appropriate protection from the threat.
(5) The student's parents or legal guardians.

The institution must make its own determination about which officials may disclose student records to appropriate parties, like the student's parents, whose knowledge of the record is necessary to protect the health or safety of the student or others.[279] The DOE recommends that institutions create a policy identifying the officials who will access and disclose information under the emergency exception.[280] Institutions are encouraged to create a "threat assessment program" that includes creating a "threat assessment team" made up of individuals with a wide degree of expertise, including law enforcement.[281]

Outsourcing Records

Q 32.15 When does FERPA allow outsourcing of information in student education records?

The 2009 FERPA amendments provide that information in the student records may be outsourced without student consent to contractors, consultants, volunteers, and other outside service providers whom an institution uses as "school officials" to perform institutional services and functions.[282] Information may only be outsourced when it is the type of service that would normally be performed by institution employees.[283] The DOE made the change to its regulations to support its policy that FERPA does not require institutions to provide all institutional services and functions "on an in-house basis."[284] Institutions may outsource information for such activities as fund raising, debt collection, enrollment and degree verification, transcript distribution, and information technology services.[285] Information in student records may not be outsourced for the purpose of a service that the institution would not otherwise provide; for instance, it may not be outsourced to outside parties for marketing purposes.[286]

Q 32.15.1 What steps must be taken to comply with FERPA when student education records are outsourced?

Institutions must ensure that they comply with FERPA requirements before choosing to outsource information in the student record. Outsourced information must stay under the direct control of the disclosing school.[287] For purposes of FERPA, "direct control" means retaining control over the outside institution's maintenance and use of information from student records; it does not affect the outside institution's status as an independent contractor.[288] The institution may outsource information to the outside institution only on the condition that the outside institution will not re-disclose it to any other party.[289] The outside institution may only use the protected information for the purpose designated by the college or university when it disclosed the record.[290]

Enforcement

Q 32.16 What guidance does the DOE provide for protecting access to student records within an institution?

The FERPA amendments, effective January 8, 2009, sought to specify the steps an institution must take to enforce the requirement that only college officials with a "legitimate educational interest" may view information in the education record.[291] The amendments were made because parents and students expressed concern that college officials have unrestricted access to students' education records, particularly when they are maintained electronically.[292] Institutions also reported confusion about proper methods to safeguard student records with electronic record-keeping.[293] The final regulations responded to the issue by requiring colleges to use "reasonable methods" to ensure that teachers and other institution officials only have access to the records in which they have a legitimate educational interest.[294] The "reasonable methods" requirement applies whether an institution chooses physical, technological, or administrative controls to restrict access to education records.[295]

The preamble to the latest FERPA revision defines "risk of unauthorized access" as the likelihood that records may be targeted for compromise and cause resulting harm.[296] Methods to protect records are "reasonable" if they reduce the risk those particular records will be targeted.[297] The greater the potential harm from unauthorized access, the greater the protection required.[298] High-risk records, like Social Security numbers or information that could be used to steal a student's identity, should receive greater protection than medium- or low-risk records, such as those that simply contain directory information.[299] The DOE provides that "reasonableness depends ultimately on . . . the usual and customary good business practices of similarly situated institutions," which means institutions must undertake "ongoing review and modification of methods and procedures as standards and technologies change."[300]

Institutions that already use "role-based security features" that grant access to electronic records based on an institution official's professional responsibilities should be in compliance with the "reasonable methods" requirement.[301] Institutions that do not currently implement those security features should use the DOE's recent guidance to ensure they are in compliance with the new regulations.[302] An institution does not have to use physical or technological access controls; it can also use an effective administrative policy that restricts access to student records to only those officials with a legitimate educational interest.[303] If a student complains an unauthorized official gained access to the student's records, the burden is on the institution to prove the official in question had a legitimate educational interest in the record.[304]

Record-Keeping Requirements

Q 32.17 What records does FERPA require an institution to keep after it discloses information in a student education record?

When an institution discloses personally identifiable information in a student record, it must make a separate record documenting the disclosure.[305] The record of disclosure must be maintained in the file with the student's education records and kept for as long as the student records are maintained.[306] Disclosure records must identify the parties who requested or received personally identifiable information from the education record and the legitimate interest the parties had in obtaining the information.[307] For example, if the record is disclosed as part of a health or safety emergency, then the institution must record the threat to health or safety that formed the basis for the disclosure and the parties who received the information.[308]

A record of disclosure does not have to be made if the disclosure was made to the student or parent of a dependent student, a college official with legitimate educational interests, a party with written consent from the student to receive the information, a party seeking directory information, or to comply with a judicial order or lawfully obtained subpoena.[309]

Q 32.17.1 What should the institution include in its annual FERPA notice?

Institutions are required to file an annual notice that provides students with notice of their FERPA rights.[310] The notice must include information about the right to

(1) inspect and review education records;
(2) seek to have records the student believes to be inaccurate, misleading, or otherwise in violation of the student's privacy rights amended;
(3) consent to disclosures of personally identifiable information, except to the extent that FERPA authorizes disclosure without consent; and
(4) file a complaint with the FPCO within the DOE if the student believes that the institution violated any of the student's privacy rights.[311]

The notice must include the procedure for exercising the right to inspect and review records and for requesting record amendment.[312] If the institution seeks to routinely disclose information in a student record to other institution officials with a "legitimate educational interest" without student consent, the notice must also indicate the criteria the institution uses to determine who is a "school official" and what creates a "legitimate educational interest."[313]

The institution may provide the notice by any means "reasonably likely" to inform students of their rights, including students with disabilities.[314] A useful model notification of rights under FERPA is available on the FPCO website at www2.ed.gov/policy/gen/guid/fpco/ferpa/ps-officials.html.

Security/Privacy of Student Medical Records — HIPAA

Q 32.18   How are student health/medical records protected by institutions?

The Health Insurance Portability and Accountability Act of 1996 (HIPAA) is another major federal statutory scheme that seeks to protect the privacy of records.[315] HIPAA applies exclusively to information contained in health records.[316] An institution that provides healthcare to students "in the normal course of business" is considered a healthcare provider under HIPAA.[317] If the institution conducts electronic transactions covered by HIPAA, then it is a "covered entity" subject to "HIPAA Administrative Simplification Rules for Transactions and Code Sets and Identifiers."[318] For a detailed rendition of HIPAA, as well as its consequences if violated, refer to chapter 24, HIPAA Security and Privacy.

Q 32.18.1   How does FERPA interact with HIPAA?

Even when an educational institution is a covered entity under HIPAA, it is not required to comply with HIPAA if the only health records the institution maintains are "education records" or "treatment records" as defined by FERPA.[319] FERPA defines "education records" as records that are "directly related" to a student and "maintained" by the school.[320] "Treatment records" are those made about a student eighteen years or older, attending an institution of higher education, by a physician, psychiatrist, psychologist, or other recognized professional or para-professional acting in that capacity, used only in connection with providing treatment to a student, and not available to anyone other than those providing the treatment, except that a student may request the records also be reviewed by another medical professional.[321] Student treatment records are excluded from the protected education record; however, the moment that an institution discloses treatment records for any purpose other than treatment, they are subject to all FERPA requirements, including student rights to consent to disclosure and to inspect the records.[322] To disclose treatment records for any purpose, an institution must obtain student consent or meet one of the exceptions to student consent, as discussed in the FERPA section above (see Q 32.14 *et seq.*).[323]

Most of the medical records created by an institution will be subject to FERPA's regulations, not to HIPAA.[324] The HIPAA Privacy Rule "specifically excludes" records protected by FERPA.[35] However, if an institution also provides healthcare to individuals who are not students, those records must still comply with the HIPAA Privacy Rule.[326] An institution that operates a clinic open to staff or the public must comply with FERPA with respect to health records of student patients and the HIPAA Privacy Rule for the health records of non-student patients.[327] Patient records created by a hospital affiliated with a university are subject to HIPAA rules because hospitals provide services "without regard to the person's status as a student" and do not provide services to students on behalf of the university.[328] If a university-affiliated hospital runs the student health clinic on behalf of the university, those records are subject to FERPA, not HIPAA.[329]

Q 32.18.2 When are student records protected under HIPAA?

When a student's treatment records are disclosed to a third-party healthcare provider for the purpose of providing treatment to the student, or when the student requests the records be reviewed by another medical professional, the records become subject to the HIPAA Privacy Rule if the third-party healthcare provider is a HIPAA-covered entity.[330] Accordingly, the third-party provider must follow the HIPAA regulations to protect all "individually identifiable health information" related to the individual's past, present, or future physical or mental health, information related to its provision or healthcare, and the past, present, or future payment for the provision of healthcare to the individual.[331] Detailed information about compliance with requirements of the HIPAA Privacy Rule is available on the Department of Health and Human Services website, at www.hhs.gov/ocr/privacy/hipaa/understanding/summary/index.html, as well as in chapter 24, HIPAA Security and Privacy.

Intellectual Property and Copyright Protection

Copyright Basics

Q 32.19 What does the Copyright Act protect?

The Copyright Act protects "original works of authorship fixed in any tangible medium of expression."[332] The act identifies categories of original works of authorship, which include, among other things, books, sound recordings, movies, plays, choreographic works, photographs, sculptural works, websites, and architectural works.[333]

Q 32.19.1   How is a copyright created?

Creating a copyright is relatively simple. All that is needed is an "original" work of authorship that is fixed in a tangible medium of expression.[334] Very little originality is required for something to be considered an "original" work. Authors are not obligated to produce a new or novel work, but the work should display "at least some minimal degree of creativity."[335] As low as the bar for originality is, facts themselves do not constitute originality. Copyright law protects the *expression* of facts and ideas in an underlying work, and not the facts or ideas themselves. For example, while a professor's particular depiction of the Battle of Waterloo may be protectable under copyright law, the fact that it took place is not protectable. The bar for having a work "fixed in a tangible medium of expression" is also low and extends to creations accessible via computer memory and not simply tangible, physical embodiments of works.[336]

COMPLIANCE FACT

No Formalities Required

A copyright is created the instant an original work of authorship is "fixed" under the Copyright Act. U.S. law no longer requires authors to register a copyright or provide notice to create a copyright. Although registration and notice have been removed as prerequisites, there is still value to registering a copyright and providing notice. Registration is required in the United States if the copyright owner wishes to sue a potential infringer.[337] In addition, if an author registers his or her work within three months of its publication or an infringement, then the author may also be entitled to seek reasonable attorney fees and statutory damages.[338] Statutory damages range from a minimum of $750 up to $30,000, and as high as $150,000 for willful infringement.[339]

Q 32.19.2 What benefits does a copyright holder enjoy?

The Copyright Act extends certain exclusive rights to copyright holders, including:

- the right to copy the copyrighted work;
- the right to distribute the copyrighted work;
- the right to perform the copyrighted work;
- the right to display the copyrighted work;
- the right to create derivatives of the copyrighted work (such as making adaptations of, or modifications to, the copyrighted work); and
- the right to make digital audio transmissions (in the case of sound recordings).[340]

Authors of copyrighted works have the ability to grant rights, or transfer ownership, in portions or all of the exclusive rights listed above to other parties.[341] For example, the author of a novel could grant or transfer all of her rights in the novel to a film producer, so that the latter could make a movie based on it. The exclusive rights, however, may be diminished through statutory exceptions[342] that allow the protected work to be used without the owner's approval.

The Work-for-Hire Doctrine

Q 32.20 Who owns the copyright in faculty-produced work?

The answer depends on the circumstances in which the work was produced. Generally, a copyright is owned by the author of the protected work. The Copyright Act, however, recognizes situations in which another entity owns the copyright. One such situation is "work made for hire," which is defined as

(1) "a work prepared by an employee within the scope of his or her employment,"
    or
(2) a "work specially ordered or commissioned for use. . . ."[343]

Thus, when an employee prepares protectable work within the scope of his or her employment, the employer typically owns the copyright.[344]

Institutions may be able to secure ownership in applicable copyrights if the work was specially ordered or commissioned by the institution. An example of this would be a new website that a university engaged an outside vendor to develop. However, only certain works specially ordered or commissioned by an institution are owned by the institution, including:

- a contribution to a collective work;
- a part of a motion picture or other audiovisual work;
- a translation, supplementary work, compilation, instructional text;
- a test, as well as answer material for a test; or
- an atlas.[345]

Moreover, simply commissioning a work that falls within the above categories is *not* sufficient; the parties must expressly agree *in writing* that the work shall be considered a "work made for hire."[346] Institutions should consider these requirements when engaging an independent contractor to prepare a foreword to a book or a documentary about the institution. An institution should also consider including contract provisions in any agreement it enters into with an independent contractor whereby the latter assigns all of its right, title, and interest in and to the commissioned work, including all associated intellectual property rights. In doing so, the institution may capture more than it would otherwise receive under the work-for-hire doctrine.

The Academic Exception

Q 32.20.1 Are there any exceptions to the work-for-hire doctrine?

The application of the work-for-hire doctrine in the academic setting may not be as straightforward. Some courts traditionally recognized a so-called academic exception, under which academic writing was presumed not to be a work made for hire.[347] The exception was based on the assumption that the "work" created by the professor was not rendered "within the scope" of his or her employment because higher education institutions did not supervise their faculty in the preparation of academic books and articles. It was further assumed that the institutions were poorly equipped to exploit the works.[348] Accordingly, under this rule, if a professor chose to reduce his or her lectures to writing, the professor, and not the institution employing the professor, would own the copyright in the lectures.[349]

> **TIP: Sample contract language for commissioned work**
>
> The categories of work falling under "work specially ordered or commissioned" is a fairly restrictive list. For example, computer software usually falls outside of the work-for-hire doctrine. In addition to relying on statutory protections, institutions should consider securing their rights in copyrighted material contractually. An institution might consider using the following template contract language to obtain an assignment of commissioned work:
>
>> VENDOR hereby irrevocably assigns and transfers to INSTITUTION all of VENDOR's right, title, and interest in and to the WORK PRODUCT, including all associated intellectual property rights. For the avoidance of doubt, this assignment includes (but is not limited to) the exclusive right to enforce, sue upon, obtain relief, and recover damages for infringement of the WORK PRODUCT.

The continued strength of the academic exception, however, is questionable in light of amendments to the Copyright Act.[350] Commentators, moreover, have pointed out weaknesses in the reasoning underlying the exception.[351] More importantly, the academic exception is based on the assumption that the work falls "outside" the instructor's duties, as the instructor is hired to instruct—not to create—academic works. Where an instructor is hired specifically to create an online course, the basis for the exception disappears, and the copyright would most likely belong to the institution.

> **TIP**
>
> *Faculty contracts:* Institutions should be cognizant of any provision in its policies or in a faculty member's employment agreement that effectively undermines the copyright interests that the institution may otherwise enjoy and establishes copyright ownership with the faculty member.
>
> *Student work:* Students are neither employees of an institution nor independent contractors; consequently, institutions likely do not have a copyright claim to student works unless the student is also an employee and the work falls within the work-for-hire doctrine.

Q 32.20.2 Can a faculty member use copyrighted materials without permission from the copyright owner?

Yes. In addition to the fair-use doctrine discussed below, the following exceptions exist that permit a faculty member to use copyrighted materials without permission from the owner.

The face-to-face teaching exemption. The Copyright Act allows faculty and students to perform or display copyrighted work without the permission of the copyright holder if the performance or display is done "in the course of face-to-face teaching activities of a nonprofit educational institution."[352] Moreover, the particular performance or display must be done in a classroom or similar place devoted to instruction.[353] If the previous requirements are met, teachers and students can play television programs, movies or sound recordings, perform plays, or read novels, provided, however, that the particular copy of the motion picture or other audiovisual work was not unlawfully made or the person responsible for the display or performance knew or had reason to believe that the copy was not lawfully made. The face-to-face teaching exemption *only* addresses performance and displaying of copyright work and does not include things like copying, distributing, and making derivative works. Moreover, institutions should note that the exemption is limited to the classroom and other similar places and would not cover, for example, school performances, graduation ceremonies, or other general school events.

The TEACH Act. Recognizing that the face-to-face teaching exemption fails to address the advent of technologies that bring faculty and students together without the need for a physical presence, Congress introduced the Technology, Education and Copyright Harmonization Act of 2001 (the "TEACH Act"). While the face-to-face teaching exemption is limited to classrooms and similar settings, the TEACH Act provides for the performance and display of certain works on websites and in distance education settings without obtaining permission from the copyright holder.[354] Moreover, unlike the broad exemption afforded under the face-to-face teaching exemption, the TEACH Act has specific limitations on what materials may be used, the manner in which they may be used, and the technological restrictions that must be in place to protect the utilized materials from improper access.[355]

The Fair-Use Doctrine

Q 32.21 What is "fair use," and does it apply to institutions of higher education?

The fair-use doctrine allows a copyrighted work to be used, in certain circumstances, without permission from the copyright owner.[356] The Copyright Act states that "fair use of a copyrighted work . . . for purposes such as criticism, comment, news reporting, teaching . . . is not an infringement of copyright."[357] Four factors are used when determining whether a particular use of copyrighted material is a "fair use" under the Copyright Act, including:

(1) The purpose and character of the use, including whether such use is of a commercial nature or is for nonprofit educational purposes;

(2) The nature of the copyright work (Where is the copyrighted work on a spectrum of fact to fantasy?);

(3) The amount and substantiality of the portion used in relation to the copyrighted work as a whole; and

(4) The effect of the use upon the potential market for or value of the copyrighted work.

Fair use is an affirmative defense to a claim of copyright infringement and a fact-intensive investigation that is conducted in a legal proceeding. The above factors must be considered as a whole and cannot be evaluated in isolation. Although each factor appears straightforward in the Copyright Act itself, a large body of case law has developed a variety of nuances that must be examined. Ultimately, there is no bright-line test.

COMPLIANCE FACT

Agreement on Guidelines for Classroom Copying in Not-for-Profit Educational Institutions:

During debate over the 1976 Copyright Act, guidelines were included in the House of Representatives Report on the pending bill.[358] Backed by content holders and industry supporters, the guidelines were advertised as intending to help educators better understand the fair-use provisions relating to copying protected work for educational use. It should be emphasized, however, that the guidelines *are not legally binding*. Moreover, while they appear to provide some certainty for the fair-use doctrine, critics point out the guidelines are very rigid and much more restrictive than what is available under the fair-use doctrine.

Copyright Policy

Q 32.22 Should an institution implement a copyright policy?

Yes. Implementing an institution-wide copyright policy may provide certain protections that institutions would not otherwise be entitled to enjoy. For example, under the Copyright Act, courts shall

> remit statutory damages in any case where an infringer believed and had reasonable grounds for believing that his or her use of the copyrighted work was a fair use under section 107, if the infringer was ... an employee or agent of a nonprofit educational institution, library, or archives

acting within the scope of his or her employment who infringed by reproducing the work in copies or phonorecords....[360]

Given the potential reduction in exposure that a nonprofit educational institution may enjoy under section 504 of the Copyright Act, institutions should take steps to ensure that their faculty are familiar with the fair-use doctrine, which can be achieved by introducing a copyright policy.

> **TIP:** Fair use is a *defense* to an allegation of copyright infringement. Institutions should consider other options before simply relying on the fair-use defense, such as:
>
> - whether the institution has a statutory right to use the copyrighted materials, such as those rights afforded by the face-to-face teaching exemption or the TEACH Act;
>
> - whether the institution should seek express permission from the copyright holder to use the protected material, which may be difficult if the copyright holder cannot be found or demands compensation;
>
> - whether a license for the material is available through copyright brokers;[359] or
>
> - whether there are grounds for asserting that the institution has an implied right to use the protected work, which may be the case if the surrounding circumstances suggest that the copyright owner gave the institution permission to use the protected material.

Liability for Copyright Infringement

Q 32.23 What exposure does an institution face if found liable for copyright infringement?

A party defending against claims of copyright infringement faces a number of possible penalties including the actual damages suffered by the copyright owner, as well as profits made by the infringer as a result of the infringing activity.[361] Instead of actual damages, a copyright holder may seek statutory damages, which gives courts the flexibility to award from $750 to $30,000 per infringed work.[362] Moreover, if a court concludes that the infringement was committed willfully, the ceiling of the statutory damage award is raised to $150,000.[363] In addition to monetary relief, an injured party can request an injunction, through which a party asks the court to order another party to act, or refrain from acting, in a particular manner.

Q 32.23.1 Can an institution be liable for copyright infringement based on the acts of its students or faculty?

As a general proposition, an institution can be held liable for the acts of its students or faculty under a theory of indirect liability. (As discussed elsewhere in this chapter, there are steps that an educational institution can take to reduce the potential liability for copyright infringement based on the actions of its students or faculty.) Indirect liability comprises two separate theories: contributory infringement and vicarious liability. Contributory infringement rests on the premise that a third party, such as a university, can be liable for the actions of the copyright infringer if the university (1) knew or should have known of the infringing activity, and (2) provided a material contribution in the form of assistance or inducement to the alleged infringement. Vicarious liability can be found where a party has (a) the right and ability to control another party, and (b) receives a direct financial benefit from allowing the infringement to occur. Consider a student using the computer networks provided by his university to illegally share music files with other students as an example of potential contributory infringement. Institutions could be held vicariously liable for the actions of its faculty, unless protected under the Digital Millennium Copyright Act (discussed below).

In addition to contributory infringement and vicarious liability, institutions present an attractive target due to joint and several liability. Under joint and several liability, a plaintiff can seek to recover the full damage amount from multiple defendants, regardless of each defendant's relative responsibility. The case of a copyright holder suing a student and his college for copyright infringement presents a good example. The copyright holder is awarded a $1 million judgment, and the court finds that the student is 98% responsible for the infringement and the college is 2% responsible. Under joint and several liability, the copyright holder could seek to enforce the judgment against the college alone, requiring it to pay the total amount. The college's recourse would then be to sue its own student to recover $980,000. The theory behind joint and several liability is that defendants are better able to allocate damages among themselves. It protects the injured party against the possibility that one of the defendants is unable to pay the allocated portion of his or her liability. Unless the student is independently wealthy, it is safe to assume that a plaintiff will be focusing on the institution to collect when joint and several liability applies.

Q 32.23.2 Can an institution limit its exposure from students who use the institution's computer network to commit copyright infringement?

Although institutions that provide Internet access to their students face exposure for transmitting copyrighted material through an institution's networks, this exposure can be mitigated through affirmative steps. In 1999, Congress enacted the Digital Millennium Copyright Act (DMCA)[364] to establish a safe harbor from copyright infringement for Internet service providers (ISPs). Institutions, if acting as ISPs, can qualify for the safe harbor protections afforded under the DMCA and avoid contributory infringement for copyright infringement committed by their students.[365]

Provided that all of the DMCA's requirements are met, an institution acting as an ISP may be granted immunity from suit for the following four types of activities:

(1) **Transitory digital network communications.**[366] The transitory safe harbor addresses situations in which students are using a university's network to illegally share copyrighted material. The DMCA provides a safe harbor for the automatic transmission of material through the ISP's network if the transmission was initiated by someone other than the service provider; the transmission, storage, routing, or provision of connections is provided through an automatic technical process without selection of material by the service provider; the service provider does not select recipients or modify the content; the material as stored for no

longer than is necessary, and the material is not generally accessible to others besides the intended recipient.[367]

(2) **System caching.**[368] System caching is the process through which data and information can be accessed by a computer faster by saving a copy of the data locally instead of requiring the requesting party to go back to the original source of the data.

(3) **Information residing on systems or networks at the direction of users.**[369] This safe harbor protects against infringement resulting from the posting of copyrighted material on a network controlled by an institution. To qualify for this safe harbor, the institution must
  (i) have no actual knowledge that the material is infringing;
  (ii) not be aware of facts or circumstances from which infringing activity is apparent;
  (iii) take action expeditiously to remove the material;
  (iv) not receive a financial benefit directly attributable to the infringing activity in cases in which the university has the right to control the activity;
  (v) designate an agent to receive notifications of claimed infringement;
  (vi) make certain information about the designated agent available on its website;
  (vii) provide certain information to the Copyright Office; and
  (viii) comply with the requisite notice and take-down procedures after receiving a proper notification from the copyright holder (or a party acting on the authority of the copyright holder) that the material is infringing copyrighted work.[370]

(4) **Information location tools.**[371] The DMCA also provides a safe harbor for ISPs for referring or linking users to online locations containing infringing material through hypertext links or other information location tools, provided, of course, the ISP complies with the necessary requirements.

To qualify for any of the safe harbors, an ISP or host must also adopt, implement, and inform users of its policy that provides for the termination of user access to the ISP's system or network where the user is a repeat infringer.[372] Such a policy may include features that would allow an institution to monitor user activity and note repeated complaints about a particular user's actions. The policies should be published and publicized so that students are aware of the monitoring that is taking place and understand the consequences of infringement.

> **TIP: Compliance with the DMCA**
>
> The DMCA is a valuable resource for protecting against certain liability threatening institutions due to the growing popularity of computer networking and file sharing. Protection under the DMCA, however, is not automatic, and coming into compliance to enjoy the benefits of the safe harbor is not easy. An institution wishing to meet the requirements of the DMCA should seek legal counsel.

Q 32.23.3 Does the DMCA address copyright infringement by faculty and graduate students?

The DMCA contains provisions stating that, under certain circumstances, faculty members and graduate students employed by an institution that acts as an ISP will not be deemed employees of that institution for purposes of liability and their knowledge or awareness of their infringing activities will not be attributed to the institution.[373] To qualify for this status, the following conditions must be met:

- The faculty member's or graduate student's infringing activities must not involve the provision of online access to instructional materials that are or were required or recommended within the proceeding three-year period by that faculty member or graduate student;
- The institution has not, within the preceding three-year period, received more than two notifications under the DMCA that the faculty member or graduate student was infringing; and
- The institution provides all of its system and network users with informational materials that accurately describes and promotes compliance with U.S. copyright laws.

Export Controls

Q 32.24 Why should U.S. institutions of higher education be concerned with export controls?

One does not intuitively connect universities with the highly technical and complex system of U.S. export controls. The word "export" in its common usage might lead some to believe that concerns about export controls arise only when they are shipping something abroad. Generally, the U.S. export controls regime is shaped by economic, national security, and foreign policy interests, and places restrictions on the shipping of defense items or dual-use items (items that have both commercial and military applications) and on most types of dealings with sanctioned persons and destinations under U.S. embargoes.[374] The controls do not stop at the actual hardware, but encompass information necessary for the design, production, development, or use of the controlled item.

Universities are in the business of expanding knowledge through teaching and research and—with the unlikely exception of test equipment and the more likely reality of traveling abroad with a personal laptop—rarely ship anything abroad. But as institutions that share and transfer knowledge, universities have come into the sights of U.S. export enforcement personnel and are struggling to square the nightmarish restrictions of export controls when it comes to teaching and sharing information and knowledge in an open academic environment.

Export controls present unique challenges to an institution of higher education because they require balancing concerns about national security and U.S. economic vitality with traditional concepts of unrestricted academic freedom and publication and dissemination of research findings and results. University researchers and administrators need to be aware that these laws may apply to research, whether sponsored or not. However, it also is important to understand the extent to which the regulations do not affect normal university activities.[375]

Deemed Exports

Q 32.24.1 What is an "export"?

Under current U.S. laws, an "export" is any transfer of an item, *tangible or intangible*, to a foreign country or to a foreign person wherever located. One quirk of the export regime not sensed intuitively is what the industry calls "deemed exports." The definition of "export" includes the transfer of controlled *information or services* to foreign nationals even when the transfer takes place within the territory of the United States; hence, an export is deemed to have taken place even though no physical border has been crossed. Under this definition, an export is not only the physical shipment from the United States, but can also be:

- an electronic transfer by email or fax;
- discussions or telephone conversations;
- information posted on an internal or external website.

Foreign Students

Q 32.24.2 What do export controls concerns related to the defense and high-technology sectors have to do with institutions of higher education?

U.S. national security and economic interests are heavily dependent on technological innovation and advantage. Many of the nation's leading-edge technologies, including defense-related technologies, are being discovered by U.S. and foreign national students and scholars in U.S. university research and university-affiliated laboratories. As the Department of Defense invests less and less of its funding on in-house research and development, university-based discoveries are becoming increasingly vital to national security and other U.S. interests.

U.S. policymakers recognize that foreign students and researchers have made substantial contributions to U.S. research efforts, but the potential transfer of knowledge of controlled defense or dual-use technologies to their home countries could have significant consequences for U.S. national interests. As a result, a fine balance has been set up between export controls in general and university endeavors like teaching and research in administering export controls as they relate to universities. The U.S. export controls agencies place the onus on universities to understand and comply with the regulations.[376]

> **COMPLIANCE FACT**
>
> Some 671,616 international students attended U.S. institutions in 2008–09, an increase of almost 8% from a year earlier. In 2008–09, there were 269,874 international undergraduate students and 283,329 graduate students. Of these approximately 62% came from Asia, with India and China, which predominantly send graduate students, rising to become the top two suppliers of international students to American colleges. Peggy Blumenthal, executive vice president of the Institute of International Education, notes that international students contribute an estimated $17.6 billion to the U.S. economy.[377]

Q 32.24.3 Who is a "foreign student" for purposes of export controls?

A foreign student is any person who is not a U.S. person—that is, any person who is not a U.S. citizen, a person lawfully admitted for permanent residence in the United States (or a green card holder), or a protected individual under the Immigration and Naturalization Act (8 U.S.C. § 1324b(a)(3), certain classes of asylees).[378]

Q 32.24.4 Can an institution's treatment of foreign students differ from that of U.S. students?

Generally, you cannot refuse to hire someone because of national origin or citizenship status (as long as they are lawfully in the United States). Title VII of the Civil Rights Act prohibits discrimination based on race, creed, color, and national origin.[379] The Immigration Reform and Control Act of 1986 (IRCA) fills the gap to add "alienage" (for example, an individual's current citizenship status).[380] However, under a narrow exception to IRCA, discrimination is allowed based on citizenship status which is otherwise required in order to comply with law, regulation, or executive order, or required by Federal, State, or local government contract, or which the attorney general determines to be essential for an employer to do business with an agency or department of the Federal, State, or local Government.[381]

If U.S. citizenship or permanent resident status is required for a job, then it is a legitimate question to ask for citizenship status.

Q 32.25 What institution activities may fall under the export controls?

Generally, the following activities should be considered with respect to export controls:

- teaching
- university research
- foreign campuses and teaching abroad

Regulation of Teaching

Q 32.26 Is all information taught at universities subject to export controls?

It is important to note that many of the activities that a U.S. institution engages in are not subject to export controls or, even if controlled, do not require licensing. Both the ITAR and the EAR have special provisions relating to publicly available information that is not subject to export controls, including limited exemptions regarding the release of information in the context of university research and educational activities. Additionally, the embargo regulations have exceptions for certain information and informational materials.

Q 32.26.1 What information qualifies as "publicly available" and thus not subject to export controls?

The ITAR and the EAR do not control information that is published and generally accessible or available to the public. Even though the two regimes have similar scope, the ITAR and the EAR vary in the specific information that qualifies as publicly available.

ITAR provision: The ITAR describes such information as information in the *public domain*.[382] The information in the public domain may be obtained through:

- sales at newsstands and bookstores;
- subscription or purchase without restriction to any individual;
- second-class mailing privileges granted by the U.S. government;
- libraries open to the public;
- patents available at any patent office;
- conferences, meetings, seminars, trade shows, or exhibitions in the United States that are generally accessible to the public;
- public release in any form after approval of the cognizant U.S. government agency; and
- fundamental research in the United States (see Q 32.27, below).

EAR provision: The EAR does not control publicly available technology if it is already published or will be published.[383] Information is published when it becomes generally accessible to the interested public in any form, including:

- publication in periodicals, books, print, etc., available for general distribution free or at cost;
- readily available at libraries open to the public or university libraries;
- patents and open patents applications available at any patent office; and
- release at an open conference, meeting, seminar, trade show, or other gathering open to the public.[384]

Differences between the two regimes appear in the concept of intent to publish; whether the publication is distributed for a fee; and whether the conference or trade show takes place in the United States or not.

Q 32.26.2 How is educational information subject to export controls?

Both the ITAR and the EAR address the issue of general educational information that is typically taught in schools and universities.

Such information, even if it relates to items included on the USML or the CCL, does not fall under the application of export controls.

ITAR provision: The ITAR specifically provides that the definition of "technical data" does not include information concerning general scientific, mathematical, or engineering principles commonly taught in schools, colleges, and universities.[385]

EAR provision: The EAR provides that publicly available "educational information" is not subject to the EAR if it is released by instruction in catalogue courses and associated teaching laboratories of academic institutions.[386]

Therefore, a university graduate course on design and manufacture of very-high-speed integrated circuitry will not be subject to export controls, even though the technology is on the CCL. The key factor is the fact that the information is provided by instruction in a catalogue course. Foreign students from any country may attend this course because the information is not controlled.

Under the fundamental research exception, the information will not be controlled even if the course contains recent and unpublished results from laboratory research, so long as the university did not accept separate obligations with respect to publication or dissemination, for example, a publication restriction under federal funding.[387] (See detailed discussion of the fundamental research exception at Q 32.27.)

Regulation of Research

Q 32.27 Are the results of fundamental research subject to export controls?

No. Both the ITAR and the EAR provide that information published and generally accessible to the public through fundamental research at an accredited U.S. university is not subject to export controls. However, there are certain restrictions. In order to take advantage of this exemption:

- Such information must be produced as part of basic and applied research in science and engineering *and* must be broadly shared within the scientific community (that is, no

restrictions on publication/dissemination of the research results);[388]
- It is essential to distinguish the information or product that *results* from the fundamental research from the *conduct* that occurs within the context of the fundamental research;
- While the *results* of the fundamental research are not subject to export controls, an export license may be required if during the *conduct* of the research export-controlled technology is to be released to a foreign national; and
- Such export-controlled technology may come from the research sponsor, from a research partner institution, or from a previous research project conducted at the university.[389]

Q 32.27.1 How does an institution apply the fundamental research exception in practice?

It is helpful to think of a research project in terms of three phases:

(1) pre-existing information;
(2) conduct of research; and
(3) research results.

The researcher must then perform a two-step analysis:

1. Will there be any restrictions on publication or dissemination of the research results?

If yes, the research does not qualify as fundamental. If no, then the research qualifies as fundamental and the end results may be released to foreign nationals.

2. Did the researcher use any pre-existing controlled data in conducting the fundamental research?

If yes, no foreign nationals may participate in the conduct of the research even if they may receive the end results. If no, foreign nationals may participate in the research itself.

Q 32.27.2 What are the limitations on publication or dissemination of the research results?

Research performed at universities will not qualify as fundamental if the university (or the primary investigator) has accepted publication or other dissemination restrictions. The fundamental research exception does not apply to research whose results are restricted for proprietary reasons or specific U.S. government dissemination and national security controls.[390] University-based research is not considered fundamental research if the university or its researchers accept restrictions (other than review to ensure no release of sponsor-provided proprietary or patent information) on publication of scientific and technical information resulting from the project.[391]

Pre-publication review by a sponsor of university research solely to ensure that the publication would not inadvertently divulge proprietary information that the sponsor has initially furnished, or compromise patent rights, does not constitute restriction on publication for proprietary reasons. Examples of "specific national security controls" that will trigger export controls include requirements for pre-publication review by the government with right to withhold permission for publication; restriction on prepublication dissemination of information to non-U.S. citizens or other categories of persons; or restrictions on participation of non-U.S. citizens or other categories of persons in the research.[392]

Q 32.27.3 What are some pitfalls to avoid in negotiating research grants or funding?

Perform extensive screening of an external funding contract's terms to ensure that the sponsor will provide explicit notice that a specific technology/data is export-controlled and will not place any restrictions on publication or dissemination of the research results. Actively inquire whether foreign nationals may participate.

With respect to government contracts, there are several restrictions that you should look for: provisions that declare all information export-controlled; provisions that restrict access to U.S. citizens or even representatives of foreign persons; provisions "incorporated by reference"; flow-down clauses. Often this is caused by lack of knowledge by the government procurement official. Remember that not all clauses are mandatory flow-down clauses and you may seek a modification or removal. If you are a subcontractor, review the scope of the flow-down clauses to ascertain the scope of possible export controls restrictions.

Teaching Abroad and Foreign Campuses

Q 32.28   Can a U.S. university professor teach abroad?

A U.S. professor can teach abroad provided that the material is limited to educational information, that is, information that is generally taught in a catalog course at a U.S. university. Similarly, a U.S. professor may disclose the *results* of fundamental research performed at a U.S. university. With respect to embargoed countries, the information and informational materials exception would cover the information generally released in a catalog course; however, providing a service in an embargoed country is prohibited under U.S. embargo regulations, and services such as awarding a degree would be prohibited.

Q 32.29   Are there limitations on setting up a foreign campus?

Generally, educational information is not subject to U.S. export controls, and therefore, a class can be taught at a foreign campus provided that such a course is generally taught at a U.S. university. However, there are limitations with respect to fundamental research (for example, the ITAR only recognizes fundamental research if performed at an accredited institution of higher education in the United States). Another limitation on foreign campuses is that a U.S. university may not set up a campus in a country under a U.S. economic sanctions embargo, such as Cuba, Iran, or Sudan.

Export Controls Compliance

Q 32.30   How can an institution set up successful screening and compliance procedures?

- ❏ Minimize limitations on publication and keep an open learning environment.
- ❏ Screen against barred entities lists and determine export controls on a project or course material basis.
- ❏ Develop a technology control plan for each controlled project and brief the principal investigator, as well as all students involved in the project, of their obligations under

U.S. export controls laws and the specific restrictions associated with the project.
☐ Designate an export compliance officer with sufficient resources to implement export controls procedures and direct access to the legal department and senior management.

> **CASE STUDY:** *The Roth Case*
>
> On July 1, 2009, John Reece Roth, a seventy-one-year-old retired University of Tennessee Emeritus professor of electrical engineering, was sentenced to four years in prison for illegal exports of military technical information after a trial that had been followed closely by academic institutions. Roth was convicted of conspiring with Atmospheric Glow Technologies, Inc., a private company, to unlawfully export defense articles to one of his Chinese students in violation of the Arms Export Control Act, 22 U.S.C. § 2778. The Chinese student was enrolled at the University of Tennessee and was hired by Professor Roth as a research assistant for a project on plasma actuators that were being developed for use in U.S. Air Force drones. What is most intriguing about the Roth case is that even though the university compliance officer was instructing the professor that the involvement of the Chinese student was in violation of export controls, the professor chose to continually and stubbornly disregard the advice. While it is sometimes difficult to convince faculty that they must comply with export controls laws—making an effective and working compliance program even more needed—the fact that the University of Tennessee had an export compliance program and compliance personnel who were actively trying to protect the controlled information determined the results of the case. Roth was convicted and sentenced to jail, while the university was neither charged nor penalized.

Federally Sponsored Research

Q 32.31 What specific requirements pertaining to research sponsored by a federal grant or contract should institutions be aware of?

Conducting research with federal dollars comes with hefty federal obligations. Most of these obligations are set forth within the grant or contract funding documents itself. However, the Office of Management and Budget (OMB) issues circulars that set forth numerous demands on a recipient institution.[393] The three most significant circulars for institutions are:

- OMB Circular A-21: Cost Principles for Educational Institutions;
- OMB Circular A-110: Uniform Administrative Requirements for Grants and Agreements with Institutions of Higher Education, Hospitals, and Other Non-Profit Organizations; and
- OMB Circular A-133: Audits of States, Local Governments, and Non-Profit Organizations (and applicable compliance supplements).

In addition, specific regulations from the agency administering the funding often require various internal control and reporting obligations.[394] Other federal statutory and regulatory obligations exist that impose compliance obligations on recipients of federal funds, such as the civil False Claims Act.

Among the obligations that present the greatest concerns to many institutions are:

- time and effort reporting;
- summer salary calculations and reporting;
- cost transfers; and
- cost sharing.

Additionally, institutions should be aware of issues related to federally funded human-subject research, research supported by "stimulus" money, and patentable inventions created with the help of federal funds.

Accounting and Reporting Effort and Costs

Q 32.31.1 What are an institution's obligations regarding time and effort reporting?

Many grant agreements support faculty time and effort on research projects. Often the salaries charged to a sponsored project are set initially on the basis of an estimate before the work is performed. The institution must then submit some form of "after-the-fact" confirmation, affirming the distributed costs represent actual costs, unless some other satisfactory alternative method is reached with the federal agency. If a faculty member's time deviates "substantially" from the estimates provided, then the federal granting agency's prior approval is required. "Substantially" has been recognized as a faculty member's effort reduced by 25% or work not performed for a period of three or more months.[395] It is not necessary to report short fluctuations in a faculty member's workload as long as the distribution of time is reasonable over the longer term (such as an academic period).

These requirements have proven problematic for many institutions when faculty and principal investigators report greater progress made than they actually achieved. This "over-reporting" may violate the terms of the grant, as well as the civil False Claims Act, because it may be viewed as a knowing submission of a false claim for payment with federal dollars. The implications of the civil False Claims Act in this area are discussed in detail below.

Q 32.31.2 ... summer salary calculations and reporting?

The accounting of summer salaries for faculty working on sponsored research is an aspect of effort reporting that poses significant challenges to institutions. The cost accounting regulations make clear that stipends from grant funding are not in addition to a faculty member's salary.[396] Stipends must be included as a part of the faculty member's total salary: The faculty member's base rate of pay received from the institution must be equal to or more than the rate paid under the grant or contract. For example, where a faculty member is paid a base salary of $90,000 for working a nine-month school year, that faculty member has a $10,000-per-month base salary rate. If she conducts research pursuant to a federal grant during the remaining three summer months, then her allowable compensation may not exceed her base salary rate of $10,000 per month.[397] She cannot be compensated more than $10,000 per month or $30,000 for working the months of June, July, and August.

In addition, an institution must be careful to ensure that the base rate encompasses the compensation for all the work that the faculty member does during the summer months. In instances where a faculty member conducts the sponsored research 70% of her time during the summer months and during the remaining 30% she continues to engage in other institutional or administrative activities, such as proposal writing, then the institution may not charge 100% of an individual's salary to a federally sponsored research project. Only the percentage of the faculty member's time that is allocated to the research may be charged to the research grant. In the example provided, it would be up to 70%, or $7,000 per month.

Q 32.31.3   ... cost transfers?

Cost transfers refer to the moving of a transaction cost from one sponsored project to another. The cost accounting standards for higher educational institutions require cost transfers be reasonable, allocable, and permissible under the sponsored research agreement.[398] Many grant agreements prohibit the moving of one transaction from one sponsored project to another, except in specified circumstances. Some institutions have encountered problems with this requirement due to shortages in grant funding that may exist. An improper cost transfer may violate the terms of the grant agreement as well as implicate the civil False Claims Act, as described in detail below.

Q 32.31.4   ... cost sharing?

Cost sharing is most often represented as an institution's financial contribution toward a sponsored project. The uniform administrative requirements for institutions of higher education set the threshold standard for what may be allocated as a cost-share expense.[399] The cost must

(a) be verifiable from the recipient's records,
(b) not be included as contributions from any federal program,
(c) be necessary and reasonable for the objectives of the program,

(d) be an allowable cost under the terms of the grant itself,
(e) not be paid by the federal government under another award, except when authorized by statute,
(f) be provided for in an approved budget when required by the federal awarding agency, and
(g) not be unrecovered indirect costs unless prior approval is received from the agency.

Three forms of cost sharing exist: mandatory, voluntary committed, and voluntary uncommitted. Mandatory cost sharing are those costs required by the federal agency sponsor and that are documented and agreed to within the awarding document. These costs must be documented and reported to the federal sponsoring agency. Voluntary committed cost sharing encompasses the sharing that the sponsor did not require yet the proposal nevertheless included and subsequently became a condition of the award. These costs must be documented but not necessarily reported to the agency unless specifically requested. Voluntary uncommitted costs include the cost sharing that the institution expended on a project but that was neither required by the federal sponsoring agency, nor was it included in the proposal documentation. Neither documentation nor reporting requirement usually exists for this category of uncommitted costs.[400] Institutions encounter problems with these costs as they determine which costs are allowable and how they should be categorized, documented, and reported.

Human-Subject Research

Q 32.31.5 ... human-subject research?

The Department of Health and Human Services requires numerous basic protections in connection with human-subject research.[401] An institution's internal review board (IRB) must comply with standards relating to

- membership;[402]
- written procedures;[403]
- written assurances;[404]
- IRB review;[405]
- maintenance of records for a minimum three-year period;[406] and
- early research termination.[407]

In addition, the IRB is required to have specific procedures for protection of:

- pregnant women involved in research;[408]
- human fetuses and neonates involved in research;[409] and
- prisoners involved in biomedical and behavioral research.[410]

Stimulus Funds

Q 32.31.6 ... receiving American Recovery and Reinvestment Act funding?

Institutions that receive grants or contracts to perform research funded with appropriations from the American Recovery and Reinvestment Act ("Recovery Act")[411] must comply with enhanced accounting and reporting requirements. Recipients of grants or contracts that are funded in whole or in part by Recovery Act money must report quarterly on their use of the Recovery Act funds to include:

(1) an accounting of funds received and expended;
(2) a project information narrative description, which must include the project name, objective and status of completion;
(3) employment information on the estimated number of jobs created or retained as a result of the project; and
(4) compensation information for the five most highly compensated officers.

If the institution contracts with a third party as a subcontractor or sub-grantee to work on a research project funded with Recovery Act funds, then the same information must be obtained from subcontractors/sub-grantees.

To properly report upon Recovery Act activities, award recipients must also separately track and account for the Recovery Act funding. Commingling Recovery Act funds with other funding sources is not permitted. If not already in place, procedures must be established that will allow government auditors to determine with specificity what has been done with each federal dollar provided.

Patentable Inventions

Q 32.31.7 ... patentable inventions created with federal money?

The Bayh-Dole Act,[412] also known as the University and Small Business Patent Procedures Act, sets forth guidelines that provide protection and ownership rights of inventions created by institutions with the help of federal funds. The act is important because it reversed a long-standing presumption of title and permits an institution to elect to pursue ownership of an invention ahead of the government. The act applies to all inventions conceived or first actually reduced to practice in the performance of a federal grant, contract, or cooperative agreement. This is true even if the federal government is not the sole source of funding for either the conception or the reduction to practice.[413] The act does not apply to federal grants that are primarily for the training of students and post-doctoral scientists. It sets forth various requirements in connection with the protection of intellectual property rights.[414] Some of the more salient requirements fall into three broad categories related to disclosure, title requirements, and reporting.

Relating to disclosure, the act requires an institution to disclose its invention to the funding agency within two months after it is disclosed internally to the institution.[415] Procedures must be in place to ensure that inventions are promptly identified and timely disclosed.[416] This includes a written agreement with faculty and technical staff requiring disclosure and assignment of inventions.[417] The act also requires the designation of a point of contact for communications on matters relating to patent rights.[418]

Relating to the retention of title, the act provides that an institution must adhere to a specific decision timeline in connection with expressing its intent to retain title in an invention.[419] It also requires an institution to execute and promptly deliver to the agency all instruments necessary to establish or confirm government rights in inventions that the institution elects to retain and then to convey title to the agency when requested so that the government may obtain patent protection throughout the world.[420]

Finally, the Bayh-Dole Act requires the submission of periodic reports regarding the utilization of the invention in accordance with the funding agency's request.[421]

False Claims Act Considerations

Q 32.32   How does False Claims Act liability affect institutions?

Civil False Claims Act liability is one of the most significant consequences of inaccurate certifications and reporting. Institutions that receive or administer federal funding may subject themselves to liability under the civil False Claims Act (FCA)[422] if they make inaccurate certifications or reports to the government. This act creates liability for the "knowing" submission of false or fraudulent claims to the U.S. government. "Knowing" can include both actual knowledge and "reckless disregard" or "deliberate ignorance" of compliance obligations. Violators can be required to pay treble damages plus civil penalties of up to $11,000 for each false claim submitted. The FCA also permits private citizens with information about the submission of false claims to file a civil false claims action on behalf of, and in the name of, the United States. These actions are referred to as *qui tam* (or "whistleblower") lawsuits, and the person who brings them is permitted by statute to share in any recovery that is obtained for the government. Another potential consequence of violating the FCA is the possibility of being suspended, debarred, or excluded from future participation in government-funded programs.[423]

Since the inception of the FCA, the government has—as have whistleblowers—aggressively pursued FCA cases against government contractors, healthcare providers, and pharmaceutical manufacturers, while many institutions of higher education were not "on enforcement's radar." However, since the mid 1990s, institutions increasingly have become targets of False Claims Act enforcement. The up-tick in activity is best seen in the areas of improper medical billing, certifications regarding adherence to state and federal laws, and federally sponsored research. As discussed below, numerous multi-million-dollar settlements have been reached to settle False Claims Act allegations.

Q 32.32.1 How does improper medical billing expose institutions to False Claims Act liability?

Teaching hospitals and universities have been targeted for allegations related to improperly billing medical services to a federally funded program, such as Medicaid or Medicare. Liability may attach when the institution submits a false claim for payment or reimbursement for medical services provided. This may occur when services are "knowingly" or "recklessly" billed inaccurately, often causing the federal agency to pay more than what the institution was required to receive. Some of the more prominent settlements are set forth below.

> **CASE STUDIES:** *FCA Settlements Involving Institutions and Medical Billing*
>
> **The Clinical Practices of The University of Pennsylvania (Dec. 1995).**[424] A $30 million settlement of allegations that the institution submitted false Medicare bills for services performed by hospital residents when they were allegedly performed by faculty teaching physicians. The government claimed, among other things, that attending physicians may receive Medicare reimbursement only if they are personally involved in the care of Medicare beneficiaries being treated by residents. The settlement also resolves allegations of billing errors, as well as coding errors regarding the level of services provided by attending physicians.
>
> **The University of Texas Health Science Center at San Antonio (June 1998).**[425] A $17.2 million settlement of allegations that the center submitted false claims for reimbursement to several federally funded healthcare insurance programs. A component of the university allegedly submitted claims to Medicare, Medicaid, and other federal programs between January 1990 and December 1995 without possessing sufficient documentary evidence to support those claims.

> **The University of California (Feb. 2001).**[426] A $22.5 million settlement of allegations that physicians at teaching hospitals at UCLA and four other campuses over-billed the government in filing Medicare claims. The payment was to compensate for overcharges for physician services at the medical centers between 1994 and 1998.
>
> **New Jersey University Hospital (June 2009).**[427] A $2 million settlement of allegations that the hospital submitted duplicate claims for payment under Medicaid when it submitted claims for outpatient physician services that physicians working in the hospital's outpatient centers also billed.
>
> **Robert Wood Johnson University Hospital (Hamilton) (Mar. 2010).**[428] A $6.35 million settlement of allegations that the hospital fraudulently inflated its charges, in the form of supplemental outlier payments, to Medicare patients in order to obtain larger Medicare reimbursements.

Q 32.32.2 How do certification requirements regarding adherence to federal and state laws expose institutions to False Claims Act liability?

Civil False Claims Act liability has begun to gain greater traction within the higher-education community as it pertains to certifications made by institutions in connection with the receipt of government funding. In particular, in 2006, the Ninth Circuit confirmed that an institution could face False Claims Act liability when it falsely certifies compliance with a statute or regulation that is a condition to government payment.[429] Ultimately, the court entertained claims of liability as long as a certified statement is knowingly false when made and that statement is a condition to payment by the government.[430] "Knowingly" includes claims or certifications that are made in "reckless disregard" of their accuracy. Therefore, certifications that are made without confirmation regarding the accuracy could potentially lead to significant liability. Below are a few examples of cases where significant settlements were reached in the face of alleged false certification of adherence to federal and state laws.

> **CASE STUDIES:** *FCA Settlements Involving Institutions and Certifications of Adherence to Federal/State Laws*
>
> **Alta Colleges, Inc. (Apr. 2009).** A $7 million settlement of allegations that Alta made false representations to receive federal financial student aid. In particular, it was alleged that it misrepresented that it met Texas state licensing requirements related to: (a) state job-placement reporting and (b) program compliance with professional license requirements. The government alleged that Alta obtained the requisite state licensing by misrepresenting to the state licensing agency that they complied with these requirements.[431]
>
> **University of Phoenix (Dec. 2009).**[432] A $78.5 million settlement of a long-running False Claims Act qui tam suit that alleged the institution unlawfully rewarded recruiters for enrolling students. This suit came after a 2006 Ninth Circuit decision that held that an institution could be liable when it falsely certifies compliance with any statute or regulation that is a condition of government funding.
>
> **Rush University Medical Center (Mar. 2010).**[433] A $1.5 million settlement of allegations that Rush violated the False Claims Act by entering into impermissible financial arrangements with physicians in the form of rent concessions on medical office space leased to those physicians. The government took the position that to submit bills to Medicare and Medicaid for services referred by the physicians with whom Rush had impermissible financial relationships constituted false claims under the civil False Claims Act. According to the government, the Stark Law prohibited Rush from billing Medicare and Medicaid for those services, and Rush improperly certified in its cost reports that the services were provided consistent with applicable law.

Q 32.32.3 How has federally sponsored research exposed institutions to False Claims Act liability?

False Claims Act liability within the context of federally sponsored research is largely attributed to inaccurate reporting of costs and effort expended by its faculty members and principal investigators. The government's theory has been that the institution inaccurately represented to the government the status of the faculty's effort and cost expended and, therefore, improperly received funding based on these false submissions. In several instances, the institutions reached settlements with the government to resolve these allegations. Some of the more prominent case studies of False Claims Act settlements related to federally sponsored research funding are set forth below.

CASE STUDIES: *FCA Settlements Involving Institutions and Federally Sponsored Research*

University of Minnesota (Nov. 1998).[434] A $32 million settlement, $4.7 million of which went to resolve inflated billings related to federal grants, of allegations that the university illegally profited by selling an unlicensed drug, failed to report to the National Institutes of Health income from selling the drug, improperly tested the drug on patients without their informed consent, and inflated billings on twenty-nine federal grants. The university also allegedly charged salaries and supplies to federal grants for employees who did not work on the grant and for supplies that were not used toward the research funded with the grant.

Northwestern University (Feb. 2003).[435] A $5.5 million settlement of allegations that the university violated the False Claims Act related to federally sponsored medical research grants. The university allegedly overstated the percentage of its researchers' work effort that it was able to devote to the grant and failed to comply with the grant's requirement that a specified percentage of the researchers' effort be devoted to the grant.

Johns Hopkins University (Feb. 2004).[436] A $2.6 million settlement of allegations that the university overstated its principal investigator's effort on federal projects—the work amounted to more than 100% of the individual's time.

Harvard University (July 2004).[437] A $3.3 million settlement of allegations that the university over-charged federal grants by seeking reimbursements for the salary of researchers who did not work on the grant or who did not meet citizenship requirements, and for equipment and supplies not used on the grant projects.

Florida International University (Feb. 2005).[438] An $11.5 million settlement of allegations that the university improperly billed researchers' salaries, travel, and administrative expenses during a seven-to-ten-year period.

University of Alabama at Birmingham (Apr. 2005).[439] A $3.39 million settlement of allegations that the university and two related entities overstated the percentage of work effort that the researchers were able to devote to the grant. It was also alleged that Medicare was improperly billed for clinical research trials that were also billed to the sponsor of research grants.

St. Louis University (July 2008).[440] A $1 million settlement of allegations that the university engaged in a scheme to defraud the government by overstating the time certain faculty members were spending on grants received from the Centers for Disease Control and Prevention. The university allegedly failed to comply with federal requirements to maintain a system that accurately tracked hours worked on by federal grants.

Yale University (Dec. 2008).[441] A $7.6 million settlement for allegations to resolve two types of claims related to the False Claims Act and related common law requirements in the management of more than 6,000 federally funded research grants. The first allegation concerned some improper cost transfers. Researchers were allegedly motivated to carry out these transfers when the federal grant was near its expiration date, and

> the remaining funding had to be expended or returned to the government. The second allegation concerned researchers submitting time and effort reports for summer salaries paid from federal grants. They allegedly falsely charged 100% of their summer effort to federal grants when, in fact, they expended significant effort on other unrelated work.
>
> **Weill Medical College of Cornell (Mar. 2009).**[442] A $2.6 million settlement of allegations of false statements made to the National Institutes of Health and the Department of Defense in connection with Weill's federal grant applications. An investigator allegedly failed to disclose the full extent of her various active research projects, depriving the government of its ability to assess the investigator's ability to perform the projects in the grant application. Weill allegedly knew, or should have known, that this investigator failed to fully disclose her active research projects in the grant applications, because the totality of her research commitments exceeded 100% of her available time.

Q 32.32.4 Are public institutions immune from claims under the False Claims Act?

Public institutions are not immune from claims brought by the federal government; however, they may be immune from suits by private citizens unless state law authorizes the claim. The Eleventh Amendment prohibits suits in federal courts against public institutions of higher education and other state government entities by a state's own citizen or citizens of another state or foreign country.[443] However, the Eleventh Amendment does not bar the United States itself from bringing suit against a state in federal court.[444] Therefore, a public institution is not immune from suit when the federal government itself intervenes in a private suit brought under the False Claims Act.

However, when the federal government does not intervene and the suit is brought by a qui tam plaintiff, the institution's jurisdiction may dictate its immunity exposure under the False Claims Act. The

Fifth Circuit and D.C. Circuit have made it clear that a False Claims Act suit against a public institution will be barred under the Eleventh Amendment when the federal government has not actively intervened in the action.[445] However, the Fourth Circuit and Eighth Circuit have held that, since a qui tam suit against a state is essentially a suit by and for the United States, then the Eleventh Amendment does not preclude a qui tam suit in federal court.[446] Until the Supreme Court or Congress weighs in definitively, it is important for public institutions to be aware of the perils of the False Claims Act and to be just as vigilant as private institutions to ensure the accuracy and reliability of their accounting and reporting.

COMPLIANCE FACT

Despite the Eleventh Amendment's immunity protections, public institutions of higher education remain exposed to False Claims Act liability. Even though some jurisdictions are more lenient than others in their view of who is permitted to bring suit, the various False Claims Act settlements against public universities demonstrate that a public institution's exposure to False Claims Act liability is real and should be taken seriously.

Q 32.33 How can an institution limit its exposure to False Claims Act liability?

Establishing a compliance program that has checks in place for accuracy in reporting and adherence to accounting and tracking standards will help to limit an institution's exposure to the False Claims Act. For example, the program should set forth affirmative policies and procedures related to the accounting and tracking of bills submitted related to work performed and costs expended. The institution also should educate and train its faculty and staff on the procedures and periodically audit submissions being made to federal agencies. Moreover, the institutions should develop a confidential means for faculty and staff to bring potentially inappropriate billing and reporting practices to the institution's attention to be addressed before they create a foundation for False Claims Act allegations.

When an institution has an effective compliance program in place, it may argue more convincingly that it did not knowingly submit false claims, but rather that any such claims either were innocent mistakes or were the independent and unauthorized acts of faculty or staff.[447]

Notes

1. For ease of reference, colleges, universities, and higher-education institutions are referred to herein as "institutions."
2. The FAR is codified in 48 C.F.R. pts. 1–53. See chapter 15, Government Contractors, for a thorough discussion of compliance programs and the FAR.
3. The compliance and ethics program is required to: (1) have a written code of business ethics and conduct; (2) have the code available to all employees involved in performance of the contract; (3) encourage "due diligence" to prevent and detect improper conduct; (4) promote an organizational culture that encourages ethical conduct and a commitment to compliance with the law; (5) promote the timely disclosure, in writing, to the agency Office of the Inspector General (OIG), with a copy to the contracting officer, whenever the contractor has credible evidence of a violation of federal criminal laws or a violation of the civil False Claims Act (31 U.S.C. § 3729 et seq.); and (6) promote the full cooperation in government audits, investigations, or corrective actions relating to contract fraud and corruption.
4. Higher Education Act of 1965, Pub. L. No. 89-329, 79 Stat. 1219 (Nov. 8, 1965) (codified at 20 U.S.C. § 1001 et seq.), amended by The Higher Education Opportunity Act, Pub. L. No. 110-315, 122 Stat. 3078 (Aug. 14, 2008). References hereinafter to "HEA" and sections thereof are to the Higher Education Act of 1965 as amended. See HEA §§ 153(c)(3), 487(a)(25), 487(e).
5. This was recognized in 2005 when draft compliance guidance was submitted by the Office of Inspector General (OIG) for recipients of Public Health Service (PHS) research awards. The draft guidance elaborated on the fundamental principles of a compliance program for colleges, universities, and other recipients of PHS awards for biomedical and behavioral research. The proposed guidance emphasized written policies, review at regular intervals, and broad promulgation. See 70 Fed. Reg. 59,292 (2005).
6. U.S. SENTENCING GUIDELINES MANUAL § 8C2.5(f).
7. U.S. SENTENCING GUIDELINES MANUAL § 8B2.1(a).
8. See, e.g., Thomas A. Butcher, Compliance: A Practical Protocol of the Entire Campus and Beyond, at 10–11 (Seminar Material for NACUA 48th Annual Conference, June 22-25, 2008).
9. See id. at 7–10.
10. Id. at 7.
11. Id. at 10.
12. See chapter 4, Risk Assessments and Gap Analyses.
13. U.S. CONST. amend. XIV ("no state shall . . . deny to any person within its jurisdiction the equal protection of the laws").
14. Title VI states, "No person in the United States shall, on the ground of race, color, or national origin, be excluded from participation in, be denied the

benefits of, or be subjected to discrimination under any program or activity receiving federal financial assistance." 42 U.S.C. § 2000d.

15. Fullilove v. Klutznick, 448 U.S. 448, 537 (1980); Adarand Constr., Inc. v. Peña, 515 U.S. 200, 223 (1995).

16. Grutter v. Bollinger, 539 U.S. 306, 326 (2003); Gratz v. Bollinger, 539 U.S. 244, 270 (2003).

17. *Grutter*, 539 U.S. at 343; *Gratz*, 539 U.S. at 247.

18. *See* United States v. Virginia, 518 U.S. 515, 524 (1996) (citing Miss. Univ. for Women v. Hogan, 458 U.S. 718, 724 (1982)) [hereinafter *VMI*].

19. *VMI*, 518 U.S. at 533; *Hogan*, 458 U.S. at 724; Craig v. Boren, 429 U.S. 190, 197 (1976).

20. Title IX states, in pertinent part, "No person in the United States shall, on the basis of sex, be excluded from participation in, be denied the benefits of, or be subjected to discrimination under any education programs or activity receiving Federal financial assistance...." 20 U.S.C. § 1681(a).

21. 20 U.S.C. § 1681(a)(1), (3).

22. *See* Klinger v. Dep't of Corr., 107 F.3d 609, 614 (8th Cir. 1997); Jeldness v. Pearce, 30 F.3d 1220, 1227 (9th Cir. 1994); Cannon v. Univ. of Chi., 648 F.2d 1104, 1106 (7th Cir.), *cert. denied*, 454 U.S. 1128 (1981), and 460 U.S. 1013 (1983); Johnson v. Bd. of Regents of Univ. Sys. of Ga., 106 F. Supp. 2d 1362, 1367 (S.D. Ga. 2000), *aff'd on other grounds*, 263 F.3d 1234 (11th Cir. 2001).

23. *See, e.g.*, CAL. EDUC. CODE § 6625 (West 2002); COLO. REV. STAT. § 22-7-403 (2005); D.C. CODE § 2-1402.41 (2001); ME. REV. STAT. ANN. tit. 5, § 4602(1) (2001); MINN. STAT. §§ 363A.03, 363A.13, 363A.23 (2001); MONT. CODE ANN. § 49-2-307 (2006); 24 PA. STAT. ANN. § 5004 (West 2001); S.D. CODIFIED LAWS § 20-13-22 (2002).

24. *Grutter*, 539 U.S. at 328.

25. Parents Involved in Cmty. Schs. v. Seattle Dist., 127 S. Ct. 2738, 2753 (2007) (citing *Grutter*, 539 U.S. at 330).

26. *See Grutter*, 539 U.S. at 338.

27. *Id.*

28. *See generally id.*, 539 U.S. at 319–20, 330–33.

29. *Cf. Parents Involved*, 127 S. Ct. at 2757.

30. *See* Fisher v. Univ. of Tex., 645 F. Supp. 2d 587, 593–94 (W.D. Tex. 2009).

31. *Grutter*, 539 U.S. at 334.

32. *Cf. Gratz*, 539 U.S. at 254–56.

33. *Grutter*, 539 U.S. at 337.

34. *Id.* at 339.

35. *Id.* at 342.

36. *Gratz*, 539 U.S. at 254–56.

37. *Id.* at 274.

38. *Grutter*, 539 U.S. at 337.

39. *Id.* at 339; *cf. Parents Involved*, 127 S. Ct. at 2760.

40. *Grutter*, 539 U.S. at 342.

41. *Hogan*, 458 U.S. at 728 (citing Schlesinger v. Ballard, 419 U.S. 498 (1975)).

42. *VMI*, 518 U.S. at 533.

43. *Johnson*, 106 F. Supp. 2d at 1375–76 & n.10 ("The desire to 'help out' men who are not earning baccalaureate degrees in the same numbers as women . . . is far from persuasive.")

44. *Hogan*, 458 U.S. at 725; *accord VMI*, 518 U.S. at 533.

45. *See Johnson*, 106 F. Supp. 2d at 1371.

46. *See* Debra Franzese (Comment), *The Gender Curve: An Analysis of Colleges' Use of Affirmative Action Policies to Benefit Male Applicants*, 56 AM. U. L. REV. 719, 739–48 (2007).

47. The colleges are: Howard University, Lincoln University, Virginia Union University, and the University of Maryland Eastern Shore (all historically black); Catholic University, Loyola University, and Messiah College (all religious); Georgetown, Johns Hopkins, and Gettysburg (all "highly selective"); University of Richmond (considered "very selective"); York College, Goucher College, Goldey-Beacom College, and Washington College (all private and "moderately selective"); and Shepherd University, Shippensburg University, University of Delaware, and University of Maryland Baltimore County (all public and "moderately selective").

48. *See* Kathy Matheson, *Civil Rights Commission Probes Possible Gender Bias at Colleges*, DIVERSE (Dec. 18, 2009), *available at* http://diverseeducation.com/article/13278/civil-rights-commission-probes-possible-gender-bias-at-colleges.html.

49. Under Title II of the ADA, "no qualified individual with a disability shall, by reason of such disability, be excluded from participation in or be denied the benefits of the services, programs, or activities of a public entity, or be subjected to discrimination by any such entity." 42 U.S.C. § 12132. Under Title III of the ADA, "[n]o individual shall be discriminated against on the basis of disability in the full and equal enjoyment of the goods, services, facilities, privileges, advantages, or accommodations of any place of public accommodation." 42 U.S.C. § 12182(a).

50. Section 504 of the Rehabilitation Act of 1973 provides, "No otherwise qualified individual with a disability . . . shall solely by reason of her or his disability, be excluded from the participation in, be denied the benefits of, or be subjected to discrimination under any program or activity receiving Federal financial assistance. . . ." 29 U.S.C. § 794(a). "Program or activity" includes a college, university, or other post-secondary institution or a public system of higher education. 29 U.S.C. § 794(b)(2)(A).

51. *See* Manickavasagar v. Va. Commonwealth Univ. Sch. of Med., 667 F. Supp. 2d 635, 643 (E.D. Va. 2009) (citing Baird *ex rel.* Baird v. Rose, 192 F.3d 462, 468 (4th Cir. 1999)); Mershon v. St. Louis Univ., 442 F.3d 1069, 1076 n.4 (8th Cir. 2006); Betts, II v. Rector & Visitors of Univ. of Va., 145 F. App'x 7, 2005 WL 1870049, at *10 (4th Cir. 2005); Ernest v. Univ. of Phoenix, 2009 WL 4282006, at *3 (S.D. Cal. Nov. 25, 2009).

52. Title II of the ADA applies to public post-secondary institutions. 42 U.S.C. § 12132. Title III of the ADA applies to private places of public accommodation to include an undergraduate or postgraduate private school, but excludes religious organizations or entities controlled by religious organizations. 42 U.S.C. §§ 12181(7)(J), 12182, and 12187. Title III authorizes only a suit for injunctive relief. *See* Kahn v. N.Y. Univ. Med. Ctr., 328 F. App'x 758, 2009 WL 2171322, at *1 (2d

Cir. July 21, 2009). The ADA does not have a federal funding requirement. *See Mershon*, 442 F.3d at 1076 n.4. In contrast, the Rehabilitation Act applies only to public or private post-secondary institutions receiving federal financial assistance. 29 U.S.C. § 794(a), (b)(2)(A). Some courts require that the federal dollars fund the particular program at issue in the plaintiff's claim. *See* Datto v. Harrison, 2009 WL 3104988, at *2 (E.D. Pa. Sept. 28, 2009).

53. *Manickavasagar*, 667 F. Supp. 2d at 643–44 (citing *Betts*, 2005 WL 1870049, at *10); *accord* Brettler v. Purdue Univ., 408 F. Supp. 2d 640, 662 (N.D. Ind. 2006) (to establish claim under Title II of ADA, plaintiff must prove: (1) that he is a qualified individual, (2) with disability, (3) that he was excluded from participation in or denied benefits of services, programs, or activities of public entity, or was otherwise discriminated against by any such entity, (4) by reason of his disability).

54. *Mershon*, 442 F.3d at 1076 (citing Amir v. St. Louis Univ., 184 F.3d 1017, 1027 (8th Cir. 1999) (as discussed above, the ADA does not require federal funding, but the Rehabilitation Act does; and Title III may be alleged against a public institution without the federal funding requirement)); *accord Manickavasagar*, 442 F. Supp. 2d at 644 (citing Baucom v. Potter, 225 F. Supp. 2d 585, 591 (D. Md. 2002)).

55. Many courts are declining to apply the ADAAA to events occurring before its effective date. *See* Herzog v. Loyola Coll. in Md., Inc., 2009 WL 3271246, at n.3 (D. Md. Oct. 9, 2009).

56. ADA Amendments Act of 2008, Pub. L. No. 110-325, 122 Stat. 3553, § 2 (2008).

57. *Id.* § 4.

58. *Id.* § 4.

59. *Id.* § 2(a)(4)–(5).

60. *See* Jenkins v. Nat'l Bd. of Med. Exam'rs, 2009 WL 331638 (6th Cir. Feb. 11, 2009).

61. *See* 28 C.F.R. pt. 36, app. B (2008); *see also* Wong v. Regents of Univ. of Cal., 379 F.3d 1097, 1109 (9th Cir. 2004).

62. *See* Price v. Nat'l Bd. of Med. Exam'rs, 966 F. Supp. 419 (S.D. W. Va. 1997); *accord* Wong v. Regents of Univ. of Cal., 379 F.3d 1097 (9th Cir. 2004); Steere v. George Wash. Univ. Sch. of Med. & Health Sci., 439 F. Supp. 2d 17 (D.D.C. 2006); Dixson v. Univ. of Cincinnati, 2005 WL 2709628 (S.D. Ohio Oct. 21, 2005).

63. *See* 154 CONG. REC. H8290-91 (daily ed. Sept. 17, 2008); Singh v. George Wash. Univ. Sch. of Med. & Health Sci., 597 F. Supp. 2d 89 (D.D.C. 2009).

64. Bartlett v. N.Y. State Bd. of Law Exam'rs, 156 F.3d 321 (2d Cir. 1998), *cert. granted and vacated*, 527 U.S. 1031 (1999), *remanded*, 226 F.3d 69 (2d Cir. 2000).

65. *See* 226 F.3d at 82. In *Bartlett*, plaintiff, a Ph.D. who had also completed her law degree, claimed that she had dyslexia and repeatedly applied to take the New York State Bar exam, requesting that she be given unlimited or extended time, permission to tape-record her essays, and permission to circle her test answers in the booklet rather than on the testing sheet. Each time, the board denied the request, finding that she did not have a legal disability.

66. Tips v. Regents of Tex. Tech Univ., 921 F. Supp. 1515, 1518 (N.D. Tex. 1996).

67. *See* Wynne v. Tufts Univ. Sch. of Med., 932 F.2d 19 (1st Cir. 1991).
68. Statement of the Managers to Accompany S. 3406.
69. *See* Wendy F. Hensel, *Rights Resurgence: The Impact of the ADA Amendments Act on Schools and Universities*, 25 GA. ST. U. L. REV. 641, 680 (2009) (citing H.R. REP. NO. 110-730, pt. 1, at 11 (2008)).
70. *See* United States v. Bd. of Trs. for Univ. of Ala., 908 F.2d 740 (11th Cir. 1990).
71. *See* Karin McAnaney, *Finding the Proper Balance: Protecting Suicidal Students without Harming Universities*, 94 VA. L. REV. 197, 223 (2008) (citing Letter from Michal Gallagher, Team Leader, Office for Civil Rights, U.S. Dep't of Educ., to Dr. Jean Scott, President, Marietta Coll. 3 (Mar. 18, 2005)).
72. *See* 2009–2010 Federal Student Aid Handbook (U.S. Dep't of Educ. 2009), vol. 2, ch. 1, "Institutional Eligibility," at 2-1. The entire 909-page handbook, comprising an index, the Application and Verification Guide, and six numbered volumes, can be downloaded from the DOE's Information for Financial Aid Professionals (IFAP) website. *See* http://ifap.ed.gov/fsahandbook/attachments/0910FSAHandbookIndex.pdf.
73. 34 C.F.R. § 668.8(c)(1)–(3).
74. 34 C.F.R. § 668.8(d).
75. *See* 34 C.F.R. § 685.402.
76. 34 C.F.R. § 668.8(e)(1).
77. *See* 34 C.F.R. § 668.14.
78. *See* Hendow v. Univ. of Phoenix, 461 F.3d 1166, 1176–77 (9th Cir. 2006) (holding that an institution can be liable under the False Claims Act when it falsely certifies compliance with a statute or regulation that is a condition of government funding received in connection with an institution's program participation agreement).
79. 42 U.S.C. § 2000d *et seq.*
80. 34 C.F.R. pt. 100.
81. Title IX of the HEA, 20 U.S.C. § 1681 *et seq.*, which prohibits gender discrimination in any academic program or activity receiving federal financial assistance, and section 504 of the Rehabilitation Act of 1973, 29 U.S.C. § 794, and its implementing regulation, 34 C.F.R. pt. 104, which prohibits discrimination on the basis of disability.
82. *See* 34 C.F.R. § 682.401.
83. *See* HEA § 152(a)(1)(A).
84. *See* HEA § 485(a)(1)(P).
85. *See* HEA § 152(a)(1)(B).
86. *See* HEA § 485.
87. 34 C.F.R. § 668.14(b)(22)(i); 20 U.S.C. § 1094(a)(20) (stating that an institution "will not provide any commission, bonus, or other incentive payment based directly or indirectly on success in securing enrollments or financial aid to any persons or entities engaged in any student recruiting or admission activities or in making decisions regarding the award of student financial assistance, except this paragraph shall not apply to the recruitment of foreign students residing in foreign countries who are not eligible to receive Federal student assistance").

88. *See* 34 C.F.R. § 668.14(b)(22)(ii)(A).
89. *See* 34 C.F.R. § 668.14(b)(22)(ii)(B).
90. *See* 34 C.F.R. § 668.14(b)(22)(ii)(C).
91. *See* 34 C.F.R. § 668.14(b)(22)(ii)(D).
92. *See* 34 C.F.R. § 668.14(b)(22)(ii)(E).
93. *See* 34 C.F.R. § 668.14(b)(22)(ii)(F); Federal Student Aid Programs, 67 Fed. Reg. 67,053, 67,056 (Nov. 1, 2002).
94. *See* 34 C.F.R. § 668.14(b)(22)(ii)(G).
95. *See* 34 C.F.R. § 668.14(b)(22)(ii)(H).
96. *See* 34 C.F.R. § 668.14(b)(22)(ii)(I).
97. *See* 34 C.F.R. § 668.14(b)(22)(ii)(J).
98. *See* 34 C.F.R. § 668.14(b)(22)(ii)(K).
99. *See* 34 C.F.R. § 668.14(b)(22)(ii)(L).
100. *See* 34 C.F.R. § 682.212(h).
101. *Id.*
102. *See* HEA § 487(h).
103. *See* HEA § 153(c)(3).
104. *See* HEA §§ 493(a)(25), 493(e).
105. HEA § 433(c).
106. HEA § 433(a).
107. *Id.*
108. HEA § 433(b).
109. HEA § 433(e)(1).
110. HEA § 433(e)(2).
111. HEA § 433(e)(3).
112. HEA § 485(b)(1).
113. *Id.*
114. *Id.*
115. *See* TILA § 140(a)–(e).
116. *See* TILA § 128(e).
117. *See* TILA § 128(e)(5), (11).
118. *See* 34 C.F.R. § 668.14(b)(25).
119. *See* 20 U.S.C. § 1094(c)(3)(B); 34 C.F.R. § 668.84(a).
120. 34 C.F.R. § 668.92(a)(5)(i).
121. 34 C.F.R. § 668.95(b).
122. *See* 20 U.S.C. § 1094(c)(3)(b)(ii).
123. *See id. See also* 34 C.F.R. § 668.92.
124. *See* 34 C.F.R. §§ 668.90, 668.91, and 668.98.
125. *See* 34 C.F.R. § 668.85.
126. *See* 34 C.F.R. § 668.85(a)(3).
127. *See* 34 C.F.R. § 668.94.
128. *See* Matter of Yorktowne Bus. Inst., 1993 WL 591773, at *1 (Dep't of Educ. Office of Hearings & Appeals July 1, 1993).
129. *See* 34 C.F.R. § 668.86.
130. *See* 34 C.F.R. § 668.93.
131. Restatement (Second) of Torts § 315.

132. RESTATEMENT (SECOND) OF TORTS § 314A (1965).
133. *See* Cutler v. Bd. of Regents of Fla., 459 So. 2d 413 (Fla. 1st DCA 1984) (college had a duty to student as tenant in her dormitory as a landlord to protect her from assault and rape); Nero v. Kan. State Univ., 253 Kan. 567, 861 P.2d 768 (1993) (providing housing to students conferred upon the university all the rights and responsibilities that any landlord would have); Miller v. New York, 467 N.E.2d 493 (N.Y. 1984) (college liable for rape of student by a third party for failing to lock outer door to dormitory).
134. *See* Furek v. Univ. of Del., 594 A.2d 506 (Del. 1991) (college students are invitees, and universities owe them a duty to "regulate and supervise" student activities that are foreseeable and within the university's control).
135. Most courts have rejected the university-college student relationship alone as a basis for liability. *See* Bradshaw v. Rawlings, 612 F.2d 135 (3d Cir. 1979), *cert. denied*, 446 U.S. 909 (1980); Beach v. Univ. of Utah, 726 P.2d 413 (Utah 1986); Booker v. Lehigh Univ., 800 F. Supp. 234 (E.D. Pa. 1992), *aff'd*, 995 F.2d 215 (3d Cir. 1993); Campbell v. Bd. of Trs. of Wabash Coll., 495 N.E.2d 227 (Ind. Ct. App. 1986); Crow v. State of California, 222 Cal. App. 3d 192 (Cal. Ct. App. 1990); Hartman v. Bethany Coll., 778 F. Supp. 286 (N.D. W. Va. 1991); Leonardi v. Bradley, 253 Ill. App. 3d 685 (Ill. App. Ct. 1993), *appeal denied*, 155 Ill. 2d 565 (Ill. 1994); Millard v. Osborne, 611 A.2d 715 (Pa. Super. Ct. 1992), *appeal denied*, 532 Pa. 656 (Pa. 1992); Murrell v. Mt. St. Clare Coll., 2001 WL 1678766 (S.D. Iowa 2001); Rothbard v. Colgate Univ., 235 A.D.2d 675, 652 N.Y.S.2d 146 (App. Div. 1997); Tanja H. v. Regents of Univ. of Cal., 228 Cal. App. 3d 434 (Cal. Ct. App. 1991). But there are exceptional circumstances when the court finds a special relationship between college and student. *See* Schieszler v. Ferrum Coll., 236 F. Supp. 2d 602 (W.D. Va. 2002) (college had special relationship with student who hanged self where, *inter alia*, college officials were aware that student had emotional problems and indicated intent to commit suicide); Shin v. Mass. Inst. of Tech., 19 Mass. L. Rptr. 570, 2005 WL 1869101 (Mass. Super. Ct. 2005) (university had special relationship with student who committed suicide because university was well aware of student's suicidal ideation). The trend appears to be toward an expansion of this type of liability especially in the area of suicidal ideation.
136. Nova Se. Univ., Inc. v. Gross, 758 So. 2d 86 (Fla. 2000) (since university had control over graduate student's conduct by requiring her to do mandatory internship and by assigning her to specific location, it assumed correlative duty of acting reasonably in making that assignment); *see also* Mullins v. Pine Manor Coll., 389 Mass. 47 (1983) (college undertook a duty to provide students in dormitories with protection from criminal acts of third parties, in this case rape).
137. *See, e.g.*, Duarte v. State, 88 Cal. App. 3d 473, 151 Cal. Rptr. 727 (Cal. Ct. App. 4th Dist. 1979) (claim stated for breach of warranty of habitability in residence contract when state university student was raped and murdered in her residence hall); Cutler v. Bd. of Regents of Fla., 459 So. 2d 413 (Fla. 1st Dist. Ct. App. 1984) (allowing plaintiff to amend complaint to attach her rental contract with the university to attempt to state a claim for breach of warranty of habitability).

138. *See, e.g.*, McCain v. Fla. Power Corp., 593 So. 2d 500, 502 (Fla. 1992) ("The duty element of negligence focuses on whether the defendant's conduct foreseeably created a broader 'zone of risk' that poses a general threat of harm to others. . . . The proximate causation element, on the other hand, is concerned with whether and to what extent the defendant's conduct foreseeably and substantially caused the specific injury that actually occurred. In other words, the former is a minimal threshold *legal* requirement for opening the courthouse doors, whereas the latter is part of the much more specific *factual* requirement that must be proved to win the case once the courthouse doors are open. As is obvious, a defendant might be under a legal duty of care to a specific plaintiff, but still not be liable for negligence because proximate causation cannot be proven.") (emphasis original).

139. *See, e.g.*, Jesik v. Maricopa County Cmty. Coll. Dist., 611 P.2d 547 (Ariz. 1980) (reversing summary judgment against community college when student was shot by third party who he reported twice to security guard as threatening him); Peterson v. S.F. Cmty. Coll., 685 P.2d 1193 (1984) (college had a duty to prevent attempted rape on a stairway in the college's parking lot where prior attacks happened); Schieszler v. Ferrum Coll., 236 F. Supp. 2d 602 (W.D. Va. 2002) (college liable when student committed suicide after campus police aware of student's prior attempt merely asked him to sign a statement promising not to harm self); Tarasoff v. Cal. Bd. of Regents, 551 P.2d 334 (Cal. 1976) (college liable when treating psychotherapist failed to warn a third party whom a student patient had threatened).

140. *See, e.g.*, Duarte v. State, 88 Cal. App. 3d 473, 151 Cal. Rptr. 727 (Cal. Ct. App. 4th Dist. 1979) (liability arose from rape and murder of student in dorm because university had knowledge of a chronic pattern of violent assaults, rapes, and attacks on female members of the university community); Mullins v. Pine Manor Coll., 389 Mass. 47, 449 N.E.2d 331 (1983) (women's college liable to student who was raped on campus by intruder who took her from her dormitory where director of student affairs had warned students during freshman orientation of dangers inherent in being housed at a women's college near metropolitan area short distance from bus and train lines to Boston).

141. *See* Collins v. Sch. Bd. of Broward County, 471 So. 2d 560 (Fla. 4th Dist. Ct. App. 1985) (school liable for sexual assault of student in shop class when teacher left room; had teacher been at desk he would have seen the assault).

142. 20 U.S.C. § 1092.

143. 20 U.S.C. § 1092(f)(1); 34 C.F.R. § 668.46(b).

144. 20 U.S.C. § 1092(f)(1), (8)(B).

145. 20 U.S.C. § 1092(f)(1)(F); 34 C.F.R. § 668.46(c).

146. 20 U.S.C. § 1092(f)(3); 34 C.F.R. § 668.46(e); Havlik v. Johnson & Wales Univ., 509 F.3d 25, 28 (1st Cir. 2007).

147. 20 U.S.C. § 1092(f)(4)(A), (B); 34 C.F.R. § 668.46(f). Campus law enforcement records are excluded from coverage under the Family Educational Rights and Privacy Act of 1974 (FERPA). 20 U.S.C. § 1232g.

148. 20 U.S.C. § 1092(f)(1), (8); 34 C.F.R. § 668.46(b).

149. 74 Fed. Reg. 42,395 *et seq.* (Aug. 21, 2009).

150. 20 U.S.C. § 1092(14)(A). In addition, evidence regarding compliance or noncompliance with the Clery Act is not admissible except with respect to an action to enforce it. 20 U.S.C. § 1092(14)(B).

151. 20 U.S.C. §§ 1092(13), 1094(c)(3)(B).

152. 20 U.S.C. § 1094(c)(3)(A).

153. *See, e.g.*, APPLIED RISK MANAGEMENT, REPORT TO MASSACHUSETTS DEPARTMENT OF HIGHER EDUCATION, CAMPUS VIOLENCE PREVENTION AND RESPONSE: BEST PRACTICES FOR MASSACHUSETTS HIGHER EDUCATION, at 45 (June 2008), *available at* www.arm-security.com/pdf/ARM_MA_Colleges_Campus_Violence_Prevention_ And_Response.pdf [hereinafter CAMPUS VIOLENCE]; MASS SHOOTINGS AT VIRGINIA TECH APRIL 16, 2007: REPORT OF THE VIRGINIA TECH REVIEW PANEL (Aug. 2007), *available at* www.vtreviewpanel.org/report/index.html [hereinafter VTRP REPORT]; STATE OF ILLINOIS CAMPUS SECURITY TASK FORCE REPORT TO THE GOVERNOR (Apr. 15, 2008), *available at* www.ready.illinois.gov/pdf/CSTF_Report_Part1.pdf [hereinafter CAMPUS SECURITY].

154. *See* CAMPUS VIOLENCE, *supra* note 153, at ii, 13–14.

155. *Id.* at 39.

156. *Id.* at 39.

157. *Id.* at 14–16.

158. *Id.* at ii, 44–45.

159. *Id.* at iii, 33–34. Replace doors that can be chained one to another to prevent access and escape. *Id.* at 33.

160. *Id.* at i–vi, 31–46; VTRP REPORT, *supra* note 153, at 146; *see generally* CAMPUS SECURITY, *supra* note 153, at Prevention and Mental Health Committee Findings & Recommendations (unpaginated).

161. CAMPUS VIOLENCE, *supra* note 153, at 45.

162. U.S. Dep't of Education, Family Educational Rights and Privacy Act (FERPA), www.ed.gov/policy/gen/guid/fpco/ferpa/index.html.

163. Legislative History of Major FERPA Provisions (June 2002), www.ed.gov/policy/gen/guid/fpco/pdf/ferpaleghistory.pdf; Family Educational Rights and Privacy Act, codified at 20 U.S.C. § 1232g, 34 C.F.R. pt. 99.

164. Family Educational Rights and Privacy Act (FERPA), Final Rule, 34 C.F.R. pt. 99, Section-by-Section Analysis (Dec. 2008) [hereinafter FERPA Section-by-Section Analysis], www.ed.gov/policy/gen/guid/fpco/pdf/ht12-17-08-att.pdf; U.S. Department of Education, Office of Communications and Outreach, Guide to U.S. Department of Education Programs 2009, at 66–80 (2009), *available at* www.ed.gov/programs/gtep/gtep.pdf.

165. 34 C.F.R. § 99.5.

166. 34 C.F.R. § 99.3.

167. FERPA Section-by-Section Analysis, *supra* note 164, at 3.

168. Steven J. McDonald, *The Fundamentals of Fundamental FERPA*, *in* NEW FERPA REGULATIONS: COMPLIANCE FOR COLLEGES AND UNIVERSITIES, at 54–55 (NNACUA, Virtual Seminar Handouts, Jan. 29, 2009); FERPA Section-by-Section Analysis, *supra* note 164, at 3.

169. 20 U.S.C. § 1232g(a)(1)(A).

170. 20 U.S.C. § 1232g(a)(2); 34 C.F.R. §§ 99.20–99.22.

171. 20 U.S.C. § 1232g(b)(2)(A); 34 C.F.R. §§ 99.30–99.31.
172. 34 C.F.R. § 99.30(b)(1)–(3).
173. 34 C.F.R. § 99.31.
174. 34 C.F.R. § 99.60.
175. 34 C.F.R. § 99.60(b)(1)–(2).
176. 34 C.F.R. § 99.62.
177. Gonzaga Univ. v. Doe, 536 U.S. 273, 286 n.5 (2002).
178. *Id.*
179. 34 C.F.R. § 99.63.
180. 34 C.F.R. § 99.64(b).
181. *Id.*
182. *Id.*
183. 34 C.F.R. § 99.64(a).
184. 34 C.F.R. § 99.66(a).
185. *Id.*
186. 34 C.F.R. § 99.66(b).
187. E. Theuman, *Validity, Construction, and Application of Family Educational Rights and Privacy Act of 1974 (FERPA)*, 112 A.L.R. FED. 1, § 12[c] (1993) (citing 20 U.S.C. § 1232(a), (b), (e); Commonwealth v. Buccella, 751 N.E.2d 373 (Mass. 2001)).
188. Gonzaga Univ. v. Doe, 536 U.S. 273, 288 (2002) (citing 20 U.S.C. §§ 1232g(b)(1)–(2)) (noting the FERPA prohibits funding an educational institution with a policy or practice of permitting the release of education records).
189. 34 C.F.R. § 99.66(c).
190. 20 U.S.C. § 1232g(b)(2), (f); 34 C.F.R. § 99.67.
191. *See* Owasso Indep. Sch. Dist. v. Falvo, 534 U.S. 426, 431, 434 (2002) (finding that the determination of whether there is a FERPA violation turns on the definition of what is considered part of a student record).
192. 20 U.S.C. § 1232g(a)(4); 34 C.F.R. § 99.3.
193. 34 C.F.R. § 99.3.
194. 20 U.S.C. § 1232g(b)(1).
195. 34 C.F.R. § 99.3.
196. 20 U.S.C. § 1232g(a)(4)(B)(i)–(iv).
197. 34 C.F.R. § 99.3.
198. 34 C.F.R. §§ 99.3, 99.8.
199. 34 C.F.R. § 99.8.
200. 34 C.F.R. § 99.8(b)(2)(ii).
201. 34 C.F.R. § 99.8(b)(2)(i).
202. 34 C.F.R. § 99.3.
203. *Id.*
204. *Id.*
205. *Id.*
206. *Id.*
207. 34 C.F.R. § 99.10(a).
208. 34 C.F.R. § 99.10(b).
209. 34 C.F.R. § 99.10(c).
210. 34 C.F.R. § 99.10(d)(1)–(2).

211. 34 C.F.R. § 99.11(a).
212. 34 C.F.R. § 99.11(a)–(b).
213. 34 C.F.R. § 99.10(e).
214. 34 C.F.R. §§ 99.3, 99.10(f).
215. 34 C.F.R. § 99.12(a).
216. 34 C.F.R. § 99.12(b)(1).
217. 34 C.F.R. § 99.12(b)(3).
218. 34 C.F.R. § 99.12(c)(2)(i).
219. 34 C.F.R. § 99.12(c)(3)(i)–(ii).
220. 20 U.S.C. § 1232g(a)(2); 34 C.F.R. §§ 99.20–99.22.
221. 34 C.F.R. § 99.21(b)(1).
222. 34 C.F.R. § 99.21(b)(2).
223. Steven J. McDonald, *The Fundamentals of FERPA, in* NEW FERPA REGULATIONS: COMPLIANCE FOR COLLEGES AND UNIVERSITIES, at 67 (NACUA, Virtual Seminar Handouts, Jan. 29, 2009), citing Adatsi v. Mathur, 934 F.2d 910 (7th Cir. 1991), Tarka v. Cunningham, 741 F. Supp. 1281, 1282 (W.D. Tex.), *aff'd*, 917 F.2d 890 (5th Cir. 1990).
224. 34 C.F.R. § 99.31.
225. 34 C.F.R. § 99.3.
226. *Id.*
227. *Id.*
228. 20 U.S.C. § 1232g(b)(1).
229. 34 C.F.R. § 99.37(a)(1).
230. 34 C.F.R. § 99.37(a)(2)–(3).
231. 34 C.F.R. § 99.37(b).
232. 34 C.F.R. § 99.31(a)(8).
233. 34 C.F.R. § 99.31(a)(15).
234. 20 U.S.C. § 1232g(b)(1)(B); 34 C.F.R. § 99.34(b).
235. 20 U.S.C. § 1232g(b)(1)(B); 34 C.F.R. § 99.34(a)(1).
236. 34 C.F.R. § 99.34(a)(2).
237. 34 C.F.R. § 99.31(a)(2).
238. 34 C.F.R. § 99.31.
239. 34 C.F.R. § 99.31(a)(1)(i)(B)(1).
240. 34 C.F.R. § 99.33(a)(1).
241. 34 C.F.R. § 99.31(a)(1)(i)(B)(2).
242. 34 C.F.R. § 99.33(a)(2).
234. *Id.*
244. *Id.*
245. 34 C.F.R. § 99.31(a)(3).
246. 34 C.F.R. § 99.35(a)(1).
247. 34 C.F.R. § 99.35(a)(2).
248. 34 C.F.R. § 99.31(a)(4).
249. 34 C.F.R. § 99.31(a)(4)(A)–(D).
250. 34 C.F.R. § 99.31(a)(5).
251. 34 C.F.R. § 99.38(b).
252. 34 C.F.R. § 99.31(a)(6)(i).

253. 34 C.F.R. § 99.31(a)(6)(ii)(A)–(C).
254. 34 C.F.R. § 99.31(a)(6)(iii).
255. 34 C.F.R. § 99.31(a)(7).
256. 20 U.S.C. § 1232g(a)(7)(B)(h)(1)–(2); 34 C.F.R. § 99.31(a).
257. 34 C.F.R. § 99.7(a)(3)(iii).
258. 34 C.F.R. § 99.31(a)(9)(i).
259. 34 C.F.R. § 99.31(a)(9)(ii).
260. 34 C.F.R. § 99.31(a)(9)(ii)(A)–(C).
261. 34 C.F.R. § 99.31(a)(9)(iii)(B).
262. 34 C.F.R. § 99.31(a)(9)(iii)(A).
263. 20 U.S.C. § 1232g(b)(1)(I).
264. *Id.*
265. 34 C.F.R. § 99.36(c).
266. 34 C.F.R. § 99.32(a)(5)(i)–(ii).
267. FERPA Section-by-Section Analysis, *supra* note 164, at 13.
268. *Id.*
269. 34 C.F.R. § 99.36(c).
270. *Id.*
271. Family Educational Rights and Privacy, Final Regulations, 73 Fed. Reg. 74,838 (Dec. 9, 2008) (codified at 34 C.F.R. pt. 99).
272. *Id.*
273. *Id.*
274. *Id.*
275. 20 U.S.C. § 1232g(b)(1)(I).
276. 73 Fed. Reg. 74,838 (Dec. 9, 2008).
277. *Id.*
278. *Id.*
279. *Id.*
280. *Id.*
281. *Id.*
282. FERPA Section-by-Section Analysis, *supra* note 164, at 5.
283. 34 C.F.R. § 99.31(a)(1)(i)(B)(1).
284. FERPA Section-by-Section Analysis, *supra* note 164, at 5.
285. *Id.*
286. *Id.*
287. *Id.*; 34 C.F.R. § 99.31(a)(1)(i)(B)(2).
288. FERPA Section-by-Section Analysis, *supra* note 164, at 6.
289. 34 C.F.R. § 99.33(a)(1).
290. 34 C.F.R. § 99.33(a)(2).
291. FERPA Section-by-Section Analysis, *supra* note 164, at 6.
292. *Id.*
293. *Id.*
294. *Id.*; 34 C.F.R. § 99.31(a)(1)(ii).
295. FERPA Section-by-Section Analysis, *supra* note 164, at 6.
296. *Id.*
297. *Id.*

298. *Id.*
299. *Id.*
300. *Id.*
301. *Id.*
302. *Id.*
303. 34 C.F.R. § 99.31(a)(1)(ii).
304. FERPA Section-by-Section Analysis, *supra* note 164, at 6.
305. 34 C.F.R. § 99.32(a)(1).
306. 34 C.F.R. § 99.32(a)(2).
307. 34 C.F.R. § 99.32(a)(3)(i)–(ii).
308. 34 C.F.R. § 99.32(a)(5)(i)–(ii).
309. 34 C.F.R. § 99.32(b)(d)(1)–(5).
310. 34 C.F.R. § 99.7(a)(1).
311. 34 C.F.R. § 99.7(a)(2)(i)–(iv).
312. 34 C.F.R. § 99.7(a)(3)(i)–(ii).
313. 34 C.F.R. § 99.7(a)(3)(iii).
314. 34 C.F.R. § 99.7(b).
315. U.S. Dep't of Health and Human Services, Health Information Privacy, www.hhs.gov/ocr/privacy/index.html.
316. *Id.*
317. U.S. Department of Health and Human Services & U.S. Department of Education, Joint Guidance on the Application of the Family Educational Rights and Privacy Act (FERPA) and the Health Insurance Portability and Accountability Act of 1996 (HIPAA) to Student Health Records, at 3 (Nov. 2008), *available at* www2.ed.gov/policy/gen/guid/fpco/doc/ferpa-hipaa-guidance.pdf.
318. *Id.*
319. *Id.*; 45 C.F.R. § 160.103(2)(i)–(ii).
320. *Id.* at 6; 34 C.F.R. § 99.3.
321. *Id.* at 6–7; 34 C.F.R. § 99.3.
322. *Id.* at 7; 34 C.F.R. § 99.30.
323. *Id.* at 7; 34 C.F.R. §§ 99.30, 99.31(a).
324. *Id.* at 3, 7.
325. *Id.* at 8.
326. *Id.* at 7.
327. *Id.* at 7.
328. *Id.* at 9.
329. *Id.* at 9.
330. *Id.* at 8.
331. U.S. Department of Health and Human Services, Health Information Privacy: Summary of the HIPAA Privacy Rule, www.hhs.gov/ocr/privacy/hipaa/understanding/summary/index.html.
332. 17 U.S.C. § 102.
333. *See id.*
334. *See id.*
335. Feist Publ'ns, Inc. v. Rural Tel. Serv. Co., 499 U.S. 340, 345 (1991).
336. *See* Midway Mfg. Co. v. Artic Int'l, Inc., 547 F. Supp. 999 (N.D. Ill. 1982).

337. 17 U.S.C. § 411.
338. 17 U.S.C. §§ 504–05.
339. 17 U.S.C. § 504(c).
340. 17 U.S.C. § 106.
341. 17 U.S.C. § 201.
342. *See* Q 32.21.
343. 17 U.S.C. § 101.
344. The Supreme Court identified certain factors that characterize what constitutes the "employer-employee" relationship for purposes of determining whether an individual should be considered an "employee" for purposes of a work made for hire. *See* Cmty. for Creative Non-Violence v. Reid, 490 U.S. 730 (1989). Although the Court did not provide an exhaustive list, most of the factors characterize a regular, salaried employment relationship. *See id.*
345. 17 U.S.C. § 101.
346. *Id.*
347. *See* Hayes v. Sony Corp. of Am., 847 F.2d 412, 416 (7th Cir. 1988); *see also* Dreyfuss, *The Creative Employee and the Copyright Act of 1976*, 54 U. CHI. L. REV. 590, 597–98 (1987).
348. *Hayes*, 847 F.2d at 416. For example, in rejecting a publisher's contention that a professor was an employee, and his work a "work for hire," a California court held that:

> [t]his contention calls for some understanding of the purpose for which a university hires a professor and what rights it may reasonably expect to retain after the services have been rendered. A university's obligation to its students is to make the subject matter covered by a course available for study by various methods, including classroom presentation. It is not obligated to present the subject by means of any particular expression. As far as the teacher is concerned, neither the record in this case nor any custom known to us suggests that the university can prescribe his way of expressing the ideas he puts before his students. Yet expression is what this lawsuit is all about. No reason has been suggested *why a university would want to retain the ownership in a professor's expression.* Such retention would be useless except possible for making a little profit from a publication and for making it difficult for the teacher to give the same lectures, should he change jobs.

Williams v. Weisser, 273 Cal. App. 2d 726, 78 Cal. Rptr. 542 (1969) (emphasis added). *See generally* RAPP, 5 EDUCATION LAW § 14.01[2][a][r] (Bender 1999).
349. *See* M.B. NIMMER & D. NIMMER, 1 NIMMER ON COPYRIGHT § 5.03[B][1][b] at 5-32 (Bender 1999).
350. *Hayes*, 847 F.2d at 416; Weinstein v. Univ. of Ill., 811 F.2d 1091, 1093–94 (7th Cir. 1987) ("the statute [17 U.S.C. §201(b)] is general enough to make every academic article a 'work for hire' and therefore vest exclusive control in universities rather than scholars").

351. *See, e.g.*, Simon, *Faculty Writings: Are They "Works for Hire" Under the 1976 Copyright Act?*, 9 J.C. & U.L. 45, 495–99 (1982).
352. 17 U.S.C. § 110(1).
353. *See id.*
354. *See* 17 U.S.C. § 110(2).
355. *See id.*
356. 17 U.S.C. § 107.
357. *Id.*
358. H.R. REP. NO. 94-1476, at 65–74.
359. Several companies have compiled large portfolios of copyrighted material through negotiations with authors, which can then be licensed by other end users. For example, the Copyright Clearance Center handles text-based works. *See* www.copyright.com. The benefit to this model is that end users do not need to track down individual authors, and authors do not need to negotiate separate agreements with each end user.
360. 17 U.S.C. § 504(2).
361. *See* 17 U.S.C. § 504(b).
362. 17 U.S.C. § 504(c). As sated above, the statutory damages are calculated on a "per work" basis. For example, if a defendant made one million copies of the same novel, then a successful plaintiff could receive up to $30,000 (assuming the infringement was not willful) in statutory damages as only one copyrighted work was involved.
363. 17 U.S.C. § 504(c). Copyright violations are also considered federal crimes when the infringement is done willfully with intent to profit. The penalties vary with prison sentences of up to ten years in some instances. *See* 18 U.S.C. § 2319.
364. Digital Millennium Copyright Act, Pub. L. No. 105-304, 112 Stat. 2860 (Oct. 28, 1998) [hereinafter DMCA].
365. Although the DMCA can shield a university from contributory liability, it does not protect against vicarious liability—the safe harbor does not extend to *employees* of the university.
366. 17 U.S.C. § 512(a).
367. *See id.* Although section 512(a) (like the other safe harbors) provides a list of requirements for the transitory safe harbor, it should be noted that the DMCA contains obligations *in addition* to those listed for each safe harbor.
368. 17 U.S.C. § 512(b).
369. 17 U.S.C. § 512(c).
370. *See id.*
371. 17 U.S.C. § 512(d).
372. 17 U.S.C. § 512(i)(1)(A).
373. 17 U.S.C. § 512(e).
374. For a general and more detailed overview of U.S. export controls, see chapter 18. Three principal agencies regulate exports from the United States: The U.S. Department of State Directorate of Defense Trade Controls (DDTC) administers export control of defense exports under the International Traffic in Arms Regulations (ITAR); the U.S. Department of Commerce Bureau of Industry and

Security ("BIS") administers export control of so-called dual-use technology exports under the Export Administration Regulations (EAR); and the U.S. Department of the Treasury Office of Foreign Assets Control (OFAC) administers exports to embargoed countries and designated entities under OFAC regulations.

375. *See* Council on Governmental Relations, Export Controls and Universities—Information and Case Studies (Jan. 2, 2004), *available at* www.cogr.edu/viewDoc.cfm?DocID=151612.

376. *See* U.S. GOVERNMENT ACCOUNTABILITY OFFICE, REPORT TO THE COMM. ON THE JUDICIARY, EXPORT CONTROLS: AGENCIES SHOULD ASSESS VULNERABILITIES AND IMPROVE GUIDANCE FOR PROTECTING EXPORT-CONTROLLED INFORMATION AT UNIVERSITIES (Dec. 2006), *available at* www.gao.gov/new.items/d0770.pdf.

377. *See* Karin Fischer, *Number of Foreign Students in U.S. Hit a New High Last Year*, CHRON. OF HIGHER ED., Nov. 16, 2009, *available at* http://chronicle.com/article/Number-of-Foreign-Students-in/49142/.

378. ITAR § 120.15; EAR § 734.2(b). A special question arises with foreign persons who are dual nationals. While BIS looks at the person's most recent citizenship or permanent residence, DDTC also looks at the person's country of origin (*i.e.*, country of birth). Therefore, under the ITAR, an export that generally may not require a license to a citizen of an EU country will still require licensing if the EU citizen was born in an embargoed country, such as Iran.

379. 42 U.S.C. § 2000e-2.

380. Pub. L. No. 99-603 (1986).

381. 8 U.S.C. § 1324(2)(C).

382. ITAR §§ 120.10(a)(5) and 120.11.

383. EAR §§ 734.3(b)(3) and 734.7.

384. For guidance on BIS interpretation of "published" information, see EAR Supplement No. 1 to Part 734, Questions A(1)–B(6).

385. ITAR § 120.10(a)(5).

386. EAR §§ 734.3(b)(3) and 734.9.

387. EAR Supplement No. 1 to Part 734, Questions C(1)–(6).

388. ITAR § 120.11(a)(8); EAR §§ 734.3(b)(3) and 734.8(a).

389. *See* BIS Revisions and Clarification of Deemed Export Related Regulatory Requirements, 71 Fed. Reg. 30,840, 30,844 (May 31, 2006). (This interpretation of fundamental research by BIS, while not binding, is instructive as to how DDTC might interpret its regulations.)

390. ITAR §§ 120.11(a)(8) and 120.10(a)(5); EAR § 734.8(a).

391. *See* EAR § 734.8(b)(5). However, once the sponsor has reviewed and approved the release, the results may be published as fundamental research.

392. EAR § 734.11(b). While the ITAR does not contain such descriptive provisions, the EAR is instructive as to interpreting the limitations on fundamental research.

393. All OMB circulars are available at www.whitehouse.gov/omb/circulars/.

394. *See, e.g.*, Department of Defense Grant and Agreement Regulations, 32 C.F.R. § 21.100 *et seq.*

395. *See* OMB Circular A-110, Uniform Administrative Requirements for Grants and Agreements with Institutions of Higher Education, Hospitals, and Other Non-Profit Organizations.
396. *See* OMB Circular A-21, Cost Principles for Educational Institutions, 2 C.F.R. § 215, 220, section J10.
397. Council on Government Relations, Policies and Practices: Compensation, Effort Commitments and Certification, at 23 (Mar. 1, 2007).
398. *See* OMB Circular A-21, section C4.
399. *See* OMB Circular A-110, section A-110.23.
400. *See* OMB Memorandum M-01-06, Joshaua Gotbaum, Exec. Assoc. Dir. & Controller, Office of Mgmt. & Budget, Clarification of OMB A-21 Treatment of Voluntary Uncommitted Cost Sharing and Tuition Remission Costs (Jan. 5, 2001), *available at* www.whitehouse.gov/omb/memoranda_m01-06/ (last visited Mar. 24, 2010).
401. *See* 45 C.F.R. § 46.
402. *See* 45 C.F.R. § 46.107 (noting that the review board must have five members, with varying backgrounds to promote complete and adequate review of research activities commonly conducted by the institution).
403. *See* 45 C.F.R. § 46.108.
404. *See* 45 C.F.R. § 46.103.
405. *See* 45 C.F.R. §§ 46.109, 46.501.
406. *See* 45 C.F.R. § 46.115.
407. *See* 45 C.F.R. § 46.123.
408. 45 C.F.R. § 46.201.
409. *Id.*
410. *See* 45 C.F.R. § 46.301.
411. American Recovery and Reinvestment Act, Pub. L. No. 111-5, 123 Stat. 115 (Feb. 17, 2009) [hereinafter Recovery Act].
412. Bayh-Dole Act, 35 U.S.C. §§ 200–12.
413. *See* 37 C.F.R. § 401.1.
414. *Id.*
415. 35 U.S.C. § 202(c)(1); 37 C.F.R. § 401.14(c)(1).
416. *See* 37 C.F.R. § 401.5(h).
417. *See* 37 C.F.R. § 401.14(f)(2).
418. *See* 37 C.F.R. § 401.5(b) (referencing section 401.14, Standard Patent Rights Clauses).
419. *See* 35 U.S.C. § 202(c); 37 C.F.R. § 401.14(c).
420. *See* 37 C.F.R. § 401.14(f)(1).
421. *See* 35 U.S.C. § 202(c)(5); 35 U.S.C. § 205 (agency has discretion to withhold); 37 C.F.R. § 401.8; 37 C.F.R. § 401.14(h), 37 C.F.R. § 401.13(c).
422. False Claims Act, 31 U.S.C. § 3729 *et seq.* [hereinafter FCA].
423. In practice, the FCA is enforced against institutions through civil actions. However, criminal penalties do exist. The government may seek criminal penalties for basically the same behavior that forms the basis of a civil False Claims Act action. *See* 18 U.S.C. § 287. As in civil actions, the government is required to demonstrate that the violation was "knowing." Unlike civil actions,

however, the government is required to prove the allegation beyond a reasonable doubt, rather than to the lesser civil standard of "preponderance of the evidence." Violations are punishable by up to five years in prison and fines of up to $500,000 for organizations and $250,000 for individuals. *See* 18 U.S.C. §§ 287, 3559, 3571. The government might instead seek an "alternative fine" of twice the gain or loss that resulted from the conduct, which may be above the applicable statutory maximums. *See* 18 U.S.C. § 3571.

424. *See* Medicare Fraud Case Settled for $30 Million, HEALTHCARE FIN. MGMT., Feb. 1, 1996, *available at* http://findarticles.com/p/articles/mi_m3257/is_n2_v50/ai_18711041/.

425. *See* Press Release No. 98-278, U.S. Department of Justice, Health Center in San Antonio Will Pay US $17.2 Million to Settle False Claims Act Case, *available at* www.justice.gov/opa/pr/1998/June/278.html.

426. *See* Kenneth R. Weiss, *UC to Pay $22.5 Million in Medicare Investigation*, L.A. TIMES, Feb. 3, 2001, *available at* http://articles.latimes.com/2001/feb/03/local/me-20621.

427. *See* Press Release No. 09-566, U.S. Department of Justice, New Jersey University Hospital to Pay Additional $2 Million to Resolve Fraud Claims That Facility Double Billed Medicaid (June 9, 2009), *available at* www.justice.gov/opa/pr/2009/June/09-civ-566.html.

428. *See* Press Release No. 10-293, U.S. Department of Justice, New Jersey Hospital to Pay $6.35 Million to Resolve Allegations of Inflating Charges to Obtain Higher Medicare Reimbursement (Mar. 19, 2010), *available at* www.justice.gov/opa/pr/2010/March/10-civ-293.html (noting the settlement and explaining that, "[i]n addition to its standard payment system, Medicare provides supplemental reimbursement, called 'outlier payments,' to hospitals and other health care providers in cases where the cost of care is unusually high. Congress enacted the supplemental outlier payments system to ensure that hospitals have the incentive to treat inpatients whose care requires unusually high costs.").

429. *See* Hendow v. Univ. of Phoenix, 461 F.3d 1166, 1176–77 (9th Cir. 2006); *see also* United States *ex rel.* Main v. Oakland City Univ., 426 F.3d 914 (7th Cir. 2005).

430. *See id.*

431. *See* Press Release No. 09-367, U.S. Department of Justice, Alta Colleges to Pay $7 Million to Resolve False Claims Act Allegations (Apr. 29, 2009), *available at* www.justice.gov/opa/pr/2009/April/09-civ-367.html.

432. *See* Kate Moser, *Qui Tam Suit Against University Nets $78.5 Million Settlement*, RECORDER (CALLAW), Dec. 15, 2009, *available at* www.law.com/jsp/article.jsp?id=1202436337644&Qui_Tam_Suit_Against_University_Nets__Million_Settlement#; *Hendow*, 461 F.3d at 1176–77.

433. *See* Press Release No. 10-240, U.S. Department of Justice, Chicago Hospital to Pay More Than $1.5 Million to Resolve Medicare False Claims Act Allegations (Mar. 9, 2010), *available at* www.justice.gov/opa/pr/2010/March/10-civ-240.html.

434. *See* Press Release No. 98-549, U.S. Department of Justice, University of Minnesota Pays $32 Million to Settle Allegations of Selling an Unlicensed Drug and

Mishandling NIH Grant Funds (Nov. 17, 1998), *available at* www.justice.gov/opa/pr/1998/November/549civ.htm.

435. *See* Press Release No. 03-076, U.S. Department of Justice, Northwestern University Will Pay $5.5 Million to Resolve False Claims Act and Common Law Allegations (Feb. 6, 2003), *available at* www.justice.gov/opa/pr/2003/February/03_civ_076.htm.

436. *See* Jeffrey Brainard, *Johns Hopkins Settles Charges of Overbilling*, CHRON. OF HIGHER EDUC. (Mar. 12, 2004), *available at* http://chronicle.com/article/Johns-Hopkins-Settles-Charges/35473.

437. *See* Jeffrey Brainard, *Accounting for Researchers' Time: Recent Legal Settlements Are Highlighting a Longstanding Conflict Between Universities and the Federal Government*, 50 CHRON. OF HIGHER EDUC. 45 (July 16, 2004), at A20, *available at* www.cga.msu.edu/effortreportingarticle.htm.

438. *See Florida International U. Agrees to $11.5-Million Settlement with Government over Grants Accounting*, CHRON. OF HIGHER EDUC., Feb. 15, 2005.

439. *See* Press Release No. 05-194, U.S. Department of Justice, University of Alabama-Birmingham Will Pay U.S. $3.39 Million to Resolve False Billing Allegations (Apr. 14, 2005), *available at* www.justice.gov/opa/pr/2005/April/05_civ_194.htm.

440. *See* Press Release, Department of Justice, U.S. Attorney's Office, Northern District of Georgia, St. Louis University Agrees to Pay $1 Million to Settle Federal False Claims Act Allegations (July 8, 2008), *available at* www.justice.gov/usao/gan/press/2008/07-08-08.pdf.

441. *See* Press Release, U.S. Attorney's Office, District of Connecticut, Yale University to Pay $7.6 Million to Resolve False Claims Act and Common Law Allegations (Dec. 23, 2008), *available at* www.justice.gov/usao/ct/Press2008/20081223-1.html.

442. *See* Press Release No. 09-051, U.S. Attorney's Office, Southern District of New York, Weill Medical College of Cornell University to Pay over $2.6 Million to Settle Federal Civil Fraud Charges (Mar. 6, 2009), *available at* www.justice.gov/usao/nys/pressreleases/March09/weillmedicalcollegesettlementpr.pdf.

443. *See, e.g.*, Seminole Tribe of Fla. v. Florida, 517 U.S. 44 (1996) (prohibits suits in federal courts against state governments by its citizens); ERWIN CHEMORISKY, FEDERAL JURISDICTION 394 (4th ed. Aspen 2003) (prohibits suits in federal courts against state governments by citizens of another state or by a citizen of a foreign country).

444. *See* United States v. SCS Bus. & Tech. Inst., Inc. 173 F.3d 870, 882 (D.C. Cir. 1999) (citing West Virginia v. United States, 479 U.S. 305, 311 (1987)).

445. *See* United States *ex rel.* Foulds v. Tex. Tech Univ., 171 F.3d 279, 294 (5th Cir. 1999) (reasoning that the decision by the United States to maintain a passive role compels us to conclude that the private citizen, not the United States, has "commenced or prosecuted" the suit); United States *ex rel.* Long v. SCS Bus. & Tech. Inst., Inc., 173 F.3d 870, 882–84 (D.C. Cir. 1999) (holding that "a state is not a person who may be held liable [by a citizen] under [the] False Claims Act" and

explaining that a qui tam relator was a "real party in interest" against the state because the federal government did not intervene).

446. *See* United States *ex rel.* Berge v. United States, 104 F.3d 1453, 1458–59 (4th Cir. 1997) ("[S]tates have no Eleventh Amendment immunity against the United States ab initio. Therefore, there is no reason Congress would have displaced it in the False Claims Act."); United States *ex rel.* Rodgers v. Arkansas, 154 F.3d 865, 868 (8th Cir. 1998); United States *ex rel.* Milam v. Univ. of Tex. M.D. Anderson Cancer Ctr., 961 F.2d 46, 50 (4th Cir. 1992).

447. *See* chapter 11, The False Claims Act.

33

Environmental Law

Bonni F. Kaufman & Stacy Watson May[*]

This chapter discusses the key federal environmental statutes and regulations governing business operations in the United States.[1] These regulations are applicable to industrial, manufacturing, and business operations, universities, farms, feeding lots and agricultural operations, municipal and state governments, as well as construction companies, developers, and property owners. Essentially any business that generates, stores, or uses hazardous substances—such as petroleum, cleaning solvents, grease, and lubricating oils—as well as businesses that engage in construction, renovation, and development are subject to detailed environmental laws.

The purpose of this chapter is to identify and briefly describe the applicable federal laws and the compliance obligations that companies subject to environmental laws must be aware of. In addition, each state has its own authority to enact and enforce the environmental laws as long as the state's law is not

---

[*] The authors wish to acknowledge Christopher A. Myers for his contributions to this chapter.

in conflict with federal law. However, state environmental laws generally follow federal law and must mirror the basic federal requirements that are discussed in this chapter. For questions regarding compliance with state laws, each state's environmental regulations and statutes must be reviewed.

Federal Statutes and Regulations 1221
Resource Conservation and Recovery Act 1222
    Storage and Accumulation of Hazardous Waste 1224
    Release of Hazardous Waste 1225
    Compliance and Enforcement 1226
CERCLA/Superfund 1227
    Release Reporting 1227
    Property Cleanup Liability 1228
    Recycling and SREA 1229
    Enforcement 1230
    Defenses 1230
Hazardous Chemical Emergencies and EPCRA 1231
    Compliance and Enforcement 1231
Clean Air Act (CAA) 1233
    Compliance/Permits 1235
    Violations and Penalties 1237
Clean Water Act (CWA) 1237
    NPDES Permits 1238
    Storm Water Discharges 1239
    Publicly Owned Treatment Works 1240
    Wetlands Regulation and Development/Dredge
        and Fill Permits 1241
    Spill Prevention Control and Countermeasures 1241
    Enforcement 1243
Toxic Substances Control Act 1244
    Reporting Requirements 1245
    Regulation of Asbestos 1245
    Regulation of Lead-Based Paint 1246
    Regulation of Polychlorinated Biphenyls (PCBs) 1247
    TSCA Enforcement 1249
Other Pertinent Regulations 1249
    Homeland Security Chemical Storage Rules 1249

Environmental Law

SEC Environmental Liability Disclosure Requirements 1250
    Contingent Remediation Liabilities 1250
    Environmental Legal Proceedings 1251
    Description of Business Disclosures 1252
    Management Discussion and Analysis 1252
    Conditional Asset Retirement Obligations............................. 1252
    Climate Change Disclosures.. 1253

Acronyms, initialisms, and abbreviations used in this chapter:

BOD	biochemical oxygen demand
CAA	Clean Air Act
CERCLA	Comprehensive Environmental Response, Compensation, and Liability Act
CFATS	Chemical Facility Anti-Terrorism Standards
CWA	Clean Water Act (Federal Water Pollution Control Act)
DHS	Department of Homeland Security
EPA	U.S. Environmental Protection Agency
EPCRA	Emergency Planning and Community Right-to-Know Act
FASB	Financial Accounting Standards Board
HAP	hazardous air pollutant
LEPC	local emergency planning committee
LLP	Landowner Liability Protections
MACT	maximum achievable control technology
MD&A	Management Discussion and Analysis
MSDS	material safety data sheet
NAAQS	national ambient air quality standards
NCP	National Oil and Hazardous Substances Pollution Contingency Plan
NESHAP	National Emission Standards for Hazardous Air Pollutants

NPDES	National Pollutant Discharge Elimination System
NPL	National Priorities List
NRC	National Response Center
NSPS	New Source Performance Standards
NSR	New Source Review
OSHA	Occupational Safety and Health Administration
PCBs	polychlorinated biphenyls
PMN	pre-manufacture notice
POTW	publicly owned treatment work
RCRA	Resource Conservation and Recovery Act
SARA	Superfund Amendments and Reauthorization Act of 1986
SEC	U.S. Securities and Exchange Commission
SERC	state emergency response commission
SIP	State Implementation Plan
SPCC	Spill Prevention Control and Countermeasures
SREA	Superfund Recycling Equity Act
TRI	Toxic Release Inventory
TSCA	Toxic Substances Control Act
TSS	total suspended solids
UST	underground storage tank

Federal Statutes and Regulations

Q 33.1 How are environmental issues regulated in the United States?

The U.S. Environmental Protection Agency (EPA) is the federal administrative agency responsible for enforcement of federal environmental laws in the United States. EPA is divided into ten regions, with its headquarters in Washington, D.C. Each region is responsible for administering and enforcing the environmental laws in the states located in its region.

Federal laws are implemented in two stages. First, the statute is passed setting forth the federal requirements, which can be found in the final form in the United States Code. Second, for more technical environmental statutes, EPA is authorized, and often expressly required, to implement regulations (also known as rules) further defining the technical aspects of the law, which are contained in the Code of Federal Regulations. Both the statute and the regulations must be complied with. Where there is a conflict, the statute controls.

Q 33.2 What are the major federal environmental laws with general application to business operations that we need to be aware of and comply with?

Resource Conservation and Recovery Act	regulates use and disposal of hazardous substances;
CERCLA (or Superfund)	requires reporting of spills and other accidental or intentional "releases" of hazardous substances;
Clean Air Act	governs emissions of air pollutants from industrial and manufacturing sources as well as automobiles and other modes of transportation;
Clean Water Act	regulates discharge of pollutants into navigable waters of the United States, including discharges of storm water and filling of wetland areas; and

Toxic Substances Control Act	regulates manufacture and importation of chemicals in the United States as well as disposal and use of asbestos, PCBs, and lead-based paint.

Other environmental laws that regulate specific areas of the environment include the Endangered Species Act, the Federal Insecticide and Fungicide Regulation Act, and the Oil Pollution Act. But because these laws do not have general application to business operations, they are outside the scope of this chapter. Furthermore, be advised that all environmental laws and regulations are subject to frequent revision; the most current versions must be reviewed.

Resource Conservation and Recovery Act

Q 33.3 What is the Resource Conservation and Recovery Act?

The Resource Conservation and Recovery Act (RCRA)[2] regulates the solid and hazardous waste management practices of generators and transporters of solid and hazardous waste, and owners and operators of solid and hazardous waste treatment, storage, and disposal facilities. RCRA establishes a "cradle-to-grave" system governing hazardous waste from the point of generation to disposal. RCRA is a federal statute, but almost all states administer the RCRA hazardous waste program themselves.

The implementing regulations regarding hazardous waste[3] require the entity or person generating the hazardous waste (the "generator") to determine whether its waste is hazardous.[4] If a waste is hazardous, the generator must comply with regulations[5] and properly manage and dispose of it.

Q 33.3.1 What is "hazardous waste"?

Solid waste—garbage, construction debris, sludge, or other discarded material—will be considered a hazardous waste if it is:

(1) solid waste that is "listed" as a hazardous waste in the regulations is a hazardous waste;[6]

(2) solid waste that exhibits one or more hazardous waste characteristics—such as ignitability, corrosivity, reactivity, or toxicity;
(3) solid waste that becomes a hazardous waste after being mixed with any listed hazardous waste;
(4) solid waste generated from the treatment, storage, or disposal of a listed hazardous waste.

Q 33.3.2 How does a generator properly manage and dispose of hazardous waste?

If a waste is determined to be hazardous, the generator must and properly manage and dispose of it by taking the following steps:

(1) Obtain an identification number from EPA (or the state that is implementing RCRA under delegated authority).[7]
(2) Prepare a manifest for the waste to be disposed of by a licensed hazardous waste transporter.[8]
(3) Ensure proper packaging, labeling, and placarding of the waste.[9]
(4) Meet standards for waste accumulation units.[10]
(5) Maintain proper records of its waste generation.[11]
(6) Prepare a biennial report by March 1 of each even-numbered year of hazardous waste generated that was shipped off-site for storage, treatment, or disposal (within the United States) for the prior year.[12]

Q 33.3.3 What are the reporting requirements for hazardous waste generators?

Each type of hazardous waste generator has different reporting requirements. Hazardous waste generators are divided into three categories, according to how much they generate in a calendar month:

- **Large quantity generators:** generate more than 1,000 kg of hazardous waste per month or more than 1 kg of acutely hazardous waste per month.
- **Small quantity generators:** generate more than 100 kg, but less than 1,000 kg of hazardous waste per month, or less than 1 kg of acutely hazardous waste per month.

- **Conditionally exempt small quantity generators:** generate less than or equal to 100 kg of hazardous waste per month or less than or equal to 1 kg of acutely hazardous waste per month.[13]

Storage and Accumulation of Hazardous Waste

Q 33.3.4 What are the allowances for hazardous waste storage?

The length of time a generator is allowed to store hazardous waste on-site depends on the generator's classification. For example, a Large Quantity Generator may accumulate any quantity of hazardous waste on-site for ninety days without a permit or interim status authorization. Small quantity generators may accumulate no more than 6,000 kg. Generators count the amount of waste generated by adding up the total weight of all quantities of hazardous waste generated at a particular facility. If waste is accumulated for more than ninety days (for up to 100 kg) or more than 180 days (for up to 1,000 kg), the facility will be deemed to "treat, store, or dispose of hazardous waste" and will be required to obtain a hazardous waste facility permit.[14] Extremely onerous requirements, including financial insurance, detailed record keeping, and numerous inspections, are imposed on hazardous waste treatment, storage, and disposal facilities.

Q 33.3.5 How are underground storage tanks (USTs) for hazardous waste regulated?

The regulations for underground tanks containing petroleum and hazardous substances[15] provide for tank design and release detection requirements, as well as financial responsibility and corrective action standards for USTs. Most states have their own underground storage tank regulations and many states also regulate above-ground tanks.

As of December 22, 1998, all existing UST systems had to be upgraded or closed as set forth in the regulations.[16] Newly installed USTs and related piping must be designed to prevent releases due to structural failure, corrosion, or spills and overfills.[17]

The owner or operator of a facility with underground tanks must notify the implementing agency (typically the state environmental agency) of the following:

1. The installation of a new UST, using EPA Form 7530-1 (Appendix I, 40 C.F.R. pt. 280),[18] which contains a certification of compliance attesting to the proper installation.
2. All releases or suspected releases,[19] spills and overfills,[20] and confirmed releases, exceeding the quantity limits,[21] within twenty-four hours.
3. Corrective actions planned or taken to address a release or spill.
4. Permanent closure or change-in-service.[22]

USTs must have spill and overfill prevention equipment such as a catch basin at the connection of the transfer hose to the fill pipe, as well as equipment such as an automatic shut-off at 95% full or a 90% high-level alarm.[23] USTs and related piping must also have methods of release detection.[24] These methods can include inventory control, manual or automatic tank gauging, tank tightness testing, vapor monitoring, ground water monitoring, and interstitial monitoring. Records of USTs' installation, maintenance, and closure must be available for inspection upon request.

Release of Hazardous Waste

Q 33.3.6 What am I required to do if I release hazardous waste?

Releases or suspected releases must be reported to the implementing agency within twenty-four hours, as well as reported to local and state emergency response commissions as specified at Q 33.6. Suspected releases must be immediately investigated to confirm the suspected release. All spills and releases must be cleaned up immediately.

If a confirmed release exceeds the reportable quantity of a hazardous substance under CERCLA,[25] the facility owner or operator must initiate an RCRA Corrective Action.[26] This includes:

1. Initial abatement measures and site check.
2. Initial site characterization.
3. Free product removal.
4. Investigations for soil and ground water cleanup.
5. Corrective action plan submittal if required.

6. Public participation regarding the corrective action plan, if required.

UST owners or operators must demonstrate financial responsibility to take necessary corrective action and to compensate third parties for bodily injury and property damage. Financial responsibility may be demonstrated by different mechanisms such as satisfying the financial test of self insurance, by providing a guarantee, surety bond, or insurance coverage.[27]

Q 33.3.7 Is used oil subject to RCRA regulation?

Generators of used oil are subject to storage standards and state and local requirements. Entities that offer storage, transportation, burning, processing, or re-refining of used oil are subject to additional regulatory requirements under both federal and state programs.[28] Generators of used oil must also comply with EPA's Spill Prevention, Control, and Countermeasures.[29] If used oil is stored in underground storage tanks, generators are subject to UST standards.[30]

Q 33.3.8 Is lead-based paint subject to RCRA regulation?

RCRA defines lead-based paint debris as hazardous waste unless it is generated during abatement, renovation, and remodeling of homes or other residences such as apartment buildings. Regulations promulgated pursuant to the Toxic Substances Control Act govern the treatment and disposal of lead-based paint and are discussed below at Q 33.11.

Compliance and Enforcement

Q 33.3.9 What are the penalties for RCRA violations?

Violators of RCRA may be subject to an administrative order, a civil judicial action, and/or a criminal enforcement action.[31] Specifically, EPA or an authorized state can issue orders requiring compliance with RCRA requirements and can assess civil penalties up to $25,000 per day for each day of the violation. Persons convicted of RCRA crimes are subject to fines up to $50,000 per day of violation or imprisonment of up to five years.

It is important to note that any employee, including a plant manager, who fails to comply with any aspect of the RCRA regulations may be held *personally* liable for civil and criminal penalties. To comply with RCRA, all facilities should take care to dispose of all hazardous substances properly and responsibly. Proper disposal means sending materials to the properly permitted facilities, segregating the waste to ensure it is transferred to the appropriate disposal or recycling vendor, properly storing and packaging the waste, and preparing hazardous waste manifests.

CERCLA/Superfund

Q 33.4   What does CERCLA provide?

The Comprehensive Environmental Response, Compensation, and Liability Act (CERCLA), a 1980 law commonly known as "Superfund," authorizes EPA to respond to releases (or threatened releases) of hazardous substances that may endanger public health or welfare, or the environment.[32] CERCLA also enables EPA to force parties responsible for environmental contamination to clean it up or to reimburse the Superfund for response costs incurred by EPA. The Superfund Amendments and Reauthorization Act of 1986 (SARA) revised various sections of CERCLA, extended the taxing authority for the Superfund, and created a free-standing law, the Emergency Planning and Community Response Act (discussed below). In 2002, Congress passed the Small Business Liability Relief and Brownfields Revitalization Act, which expanded EPA's brownfields development program, expanded and created certain defenses for innocent purchasers of contaminated property, and gave liability relief to certain small businesses and municipalities that generated and disposed of de minimis amounts of hazardous wastes.[33]

Release Reporting

Q 33.4.1   What are CERCLA's hazardous substance release reporting requirements?

CERCLA regulations[34] require the *person in charge of a facility* to immediately report to the National Response Center (NRC) any environmental release of a hazardous substance that exceeds a reportable quantity.[35] A release report may trigger a response by EPA or by one or more federal or state emergency response authorities. Failure to provide notice of a release as required by CERCLA, or providing false or misleading information in such notification, may subject the violator to criminal penalties, including fines and imprisonment up to five years.

> **TIP:** Each state has separate state reporting obligations when there is a release of hazardous substances. Furthermore, there are separate obligations pursuant to the Emergency Planning and Community Right-to-Know Act that require release reporting to local municipal agencies. (See Q 33.6.1, below.)

Property Cleanup Liability

Q 33.4.2 How does CERCLA govern cleanup of property containing hazardous substances?

EPA implements cleanup according to procedures outlined in the National Oil and Hazardous Substances Pollution Contingency Plan (NCP).[36] The NCP includes provisions for permanent cleanups—known as "remedial actions"—and other more short-term cleanups—referred to as "removals." EPA generally conducts remedial actions only at sites on the National Priorities List (NPL). Both EPA and states can act at other sites; however, EPA generally requires responsible parties to conduct removal and remedial actions and encourages community involvement throughout the Superfund response process.

Q 33.4.3 Who is subject to CERCLA liability for release of a hazardous substance?

(1) Current owners or operators of a vessel or facility,
(2) Past owners or operators of a facility at the time a release occurred,
(3) Transporters of hazardous substances to a facility, and
(4) Persons who arrange for the treatment or disposal of hazardous substances at a facility.[37]

Q 33.4.4 Is anyone exempted from liability?

Yes. A "person who arranged for recycling of recyclable material"[38] is expressly exempted from CERCLA liability by the Superfund Recycling Equity Act, as well as persons who qualify for liability defenses discussed at Q 33.5.3.

Recycling and SREA

Q 33.5 What is the Superfund Recycling Equity Act?

The Superfund Recycling Equity Act (SREA) was enacted November 29, 1999. The purpose of the Act, among other things, is to promote the reuse and recycling of scrap material and to reduce waste while protecting human health and the environment.

Q 33.5.1 What is "recyclable material"?

"Recyclable material" is:

> scrap paper, scrap plastic, scrap glass, scrap textiles, scrap rubber (other than whole tires), scrap metal, or spent lead-acid, spent nickel-cadmium, and other spent batteries, as well as minor amounts of material incident to or adhering to the scrap material as a result of its normal and customary use prior to becoming scrap [except certain shipping containers and materials containing certain levels of PCBs].[39]

Q 33.5.2 What does the SREA consider "recycling"?

A "recycling" arrangement must meet the following criteria under the SREA:

(1) The recyclable material met a commercial specification grade.
(2) A market existed for the recyclable material.
(3) A substantial portion of the recyclable material was made available for use as feedstock for the manufacture of a new saleable product.
(4) The recyclable material could have been a replacement or substitute for a virgin raw material, or the product to be

made from the recyclable material could have been a replacement or substitute for a product made, in whole or in part, from a virgin raw material.
(5) The generator exercised reasonable care to determine that the recycling facility was in compliance with substantive provision of any environmental law or compliance order.
(6) If recycling scrap metal, the metal cannot be melted prior to providing it to the recycler.[40]

In addition, for transactions involving scrap metal, it will only be deemed "arranging for recycling" if the person can also demonstrate that he or she was in compliance with any applicable regulations associated with the recycling of scrap metal (after November 29, 1999) and did not melt the scrap metal prior to the transaction.[41]

Enforcement

CERCLA liability is imposed regardless of fault and regardless of whether the disposal or release of a hazardous substance was authorized by law at the time. In addition to liability for cleanup of releases, facilities may be subject to liability for:

- Punitive damages (up to three times the cost of cleanup) for willful misconduct.[42]
- Natural resource damages.[43]
- Citizen injuries to person or property.[44]
- Criminal penalties, including fines, and imprisonment up to five years, for failure to provide notification of a release of a reportable quantity to the NRC.

Defenses

Q 33.5.3 What are some defenses to CERCLA liability?

The Small Business Liability Relief and Brownfields Revitalization Act provides two defenses to CERCLA liability, in addition to the existing "innocent landowner defense," collectively referred to as the Landowner Liability Protections (LLP). The statute added the contiguous property exemption and the "bona fide prospective purchaser" defense.

Pursuant to these provisions of CERCLA, a property owner will not be responsible for contamination that migrates onto his property

from an adjacent site or that pre-existed his purchase. In both cases, the property owner must demonstrate that:
1. he is not responsible for causing the environmental impacts or affiliated with the entity who is;
2. he took reasonable steps to address the threat of release;
3. he is in compliance with any land use restrictions;
4. he did not know of the release prior to purchase and that he properly investigated the property, except that a bona fide prospective purchaser may know of the contamination prior to purchase as long as the other conditions are met.

Hazardous Chemical Emergencies and EPCRA

Q 33.6 What is the EPCRA?

The Emergency Planning and Community Right-to-Know Act (EPCRA), also known as SARA Title III, was created by SARA. EPCRA is designed to improve community access to information about chemical hazards and to facilitate the development of chemical emergency response plans by state and local governments. EPCRA required the establishment of state emergency response commissions (SERCs) responsible for coordinating certain emergency response activities and for appointing local emergency planning committees (LEPCs).

Compliance and Enforcement

Q 33.6.1 How does the EPCRA regulate hazardous chemicals?

Manufacturing facilities that store or manage specified chemicals must comply with EPCRA and the EPCRA regulations[45] by providing the following:

- *Extremely Hazardous Substance Notification.* A facility that stores or uses any "extremely hazardous substance" in excess of the substance's "threshold planning quantity" must notify the SERC and LEPC of the presence of the substance. The facility must also appoint an emergency response coordinator.[46]
- *Release Notification.* The facility must notify the SERC and the LEPC in the event of a release exceeding the reportable

quantity of a CERCLA hazardous substance or any quantity of an EPCRA extremely hazardous substance.[47]
- *Hazardous Chemical Inventory and MSDS.* A facility must submit to the SERC, LEPC, and local fire department material safety data sheets (MSDSs) or lists of MSDSs and hazardous chemical inventory forms (also known as Tier I and II forms) if the facility has a "hazardous chemical," as defined by the Occupational Safety and Health Act, present in an amount exceeding a specified threshold.[48]
- *Annual Toxic Chemical Release Report ("Form R").* A facility with ten or more employees that uses specified chemicals in amounts greater than the threshold quantities must submit an annual toxic chemical release report.[49] This report, commonly known as the Form R, covers releases and transfers of toxic chemicals to various facilities and environmental media and allows EPA to compile the national Toxic Release Inventory (TRI) database.[50] Pursuant to the Pollution Prevention Act of 1990, also known as "P2," section 8 of Form R requires reporting of waste minimization efforts for each reportable chemical, how much the chemical was reduced, the reduction amount, and how much chemical waste was sent off-site for recycling.

COMPLIANCE FACT

All information submitted pursuant to EPCRA regulations is publicly accessible, unless protected by a trade secret claim.

Q 33.6.2 What are the penalties for noncompliance with EPCRA?

Violations of EPCRA's reporting requirements may be subject to civil and administrative penalties up to $32,500 per day for each violation.

Clean Air Act (CAA)

Q 33.7 What is the intent of the Clear Air Act?

The Clean Air Act and its amendments, including the Clean Air Act Amendments of 1990 (collectively CAA), are designed to "protect and enhance the nation's air resources so as to promote the public health and welfare and the productive capacity of the population." The CAA consists of six titles, which direct EPA to establish national standards for ambient air quality. It requires EPA and the states to implement, maintain, and enforce these standards through a variety of mechanisms. State and local governments oversee, manage, and enforce many of the CAA requirements.[51]

Q 33.7.1 What kinds of air pollutants does the CAA aim to clean up?

The most common are:

- particulate matter,
- ground-level ozone,
- carbon monoxide,
- nitrogen oxides,
- sulfur oxides, and
- lead.

EPA regulates these six "criteria pollutants" using science-based guidelines to set permissible levels. The CAA also identifies 188 hazardous air pollutants (HAPs).[52] The source of pollutants can be stationary (such as gas stations, chemical plants, and power plants) or mobile[53] (such as cars, trucks, buses, and planes).

Q 33.7.2 How does the CAA regulate criteria pollutants?

Pursuant to the CAA, EPA has established national ambient air quality standards (NAAQS) to limit criteria pollutant levels. Geographic areas that meet NAAQS for a given pollutant are classified as "attainment areas"; those that do not meet NAAQS are classified as "non-attainment areas." Non-attainment areas must develop a strategy to bring the areas into attainment of the NAAQS. One useful tool in developing such a strategy is the State Implementation Plan (SIP). Under section 110 of the CAA, each state must develop a SIP to identify sources of air pollution and to determine what reductions are required to meet federal air quality standards. The SIPs contain permitting requirements, source-specific emission standards, and numerous other air-related requirements.

Q 33.7.3   What are some of the ways the CAA regulates HAPs?

EPA establishes and enforces National Emission Standards for Hazardous Air Pollutants (NESHAP), which are national uniform standards designed to control particular HAPs. The CAA requires EPA to develop a list of sources that emit HAPs and to develop regulations for these categories of sources.

EPA has listed numerous categories and developed a schedule for the establishment of emission standards. The emission standards are based on "maximum achievable control technology" (MACT), defined as the control technology achieving the maximum degree of reduction in the emission of the HAPs.

The CAA also authorizes EPA to establish New Source Performance Standards (NSPS), which are nationally uniform emission standards for new stationary sources falling within particular industrial categories. NSPS are based on the pollution control technology available to that category of industrial source but allow the affected industries the flexibility to devise a cost-effective means of reducing emissions.

The CAA also establishes a sulfur dioxide emissions program designed to reduce the formation of acid rain. Reduction of sulfur dioxide releases will be obtained by granting to certain sources limited emissions allowances.[54]

In an effort to protect stratospheric ozone, the CAA also provides for the phasing-out of the manufacture of ozone-depleting chemicals and the restricting of their use and distribution.[55]

Q 33.7.4   How does the CAA regulate greenhouse gas emissions?

In December 2009, EPA issued an endangerment finding under the Clean Air Act that greenhouse gases (that is, gases from combustion processes) present an endangerment to the environment, allowing federal regulation of greenhouse gas emissions under the Clean Air Act.[56]

In addition, on January 1, 2010, the EPA began to require mandatory reporting for large emitters of greenhouse gases. The EPA's rule requires over 10,000 facilities to collect and report data with respect to their greenhouse gas emissions, which covers 85% of gas emissions in the United States.[57]

EPA will likely issue new regulations covering emissions of greenhouse gases in the next one to two years. The regulations may require mandatory reductions in emissions, which in turn, may increase the cost of fuel, utilities, and petrochemical products for downstream customers.

California and other states have already begun to regulate greenhouse gas emissions, and many cities (such as the District of Columbia) are imposing "green building" requirements on new construction.[58] These require building owners to use sustainable materials, alternate forms of energy, and energy-efficient lighting and HVAC systems in commercial and, in some cases, residential buildings.

Compliance/Permits

Q 33.7.5 What kinds of CAA reporting/compliance requirements should businesses be aware of?

New Source Review (NSR). New major sources of air emissions must apply for a permit prior to construction of a source. New sources in attainment areas must obtain a "prevention of significant deterioration permit." A new major source in a non-attainment area must obtain an NSR permit and is subject to stricter control technology requirements, the lowest achievable emissions rate for that industry.

Title V Operating Permit. The CAA requires the following sources (*i.e.*, facilities and equipment) to have a Title V operating permit:[59]

- any major source;[60]
- any source, including area sources, subject to a new source performance standard (NSPS) under section 111 of the CAA;
- any source, including area sources, subject to a standard for air toxics, except if the source is only subject to the stan-

dard because of the risk management program applicability under section 112(r) of the CAA;
- electric utilities that are regulated under the acid rain provision (Title IV of the CAA);
- any sources subject to non-attainment area source review or prevention of significant deterioration programs;
- any other stationary source in an industry category EPA designation pursuant to the regulation.

One purpose of the operating permit is to include in a single document all air emissions requirements that apply to a given facility. States have developed the permit programs in accordance with guidance and regulations from EPA. Once each state's program is approved by EPA, permits are issued and monitored by that state. No state operating permit can be less stringent than the federal requirements. EPA has veto authority over all state-issued operating permits.

Each Title V operating permit will have facility-specific requirements that must be consulted and followed at each facility.

Risk Management Programs. Section 112(r) of the CAA requires facilities to reduce releases of hazardous chemicals into the air, reduce the severity of any accidents that may occur, and improve communication between facilities and the community. The CAA requires all stationary sources that handle extremely hazardous substances or listed substances above certain quantities[61] to take steps to prevent releases or minimize the consequences of such releases. Facilities must generally do the following:

- identify hazards that may result from accidental releases;
- design and maintain a safe facility;
- take steps necessary to prevent releases and to minimize the consequences of such accidental releases.

Facilities that use a listed or extremely hazardous substance in a process[62] must prepare a Risk Management Program and maintain documentation of the program at the facility.[63]

Record-Keeping Requirements. The record-keeping requirements of the air regulations range from two to five years in most cases. Each permit and applicable regulations should be consulted to determine the appropriate document retention period.

Violations and Penalties

Q 33.7.6 What constitutes a violation of the CAA?

- A knowing violation of a state implementation plan.
- A knowing violation of an air toxics, acid rain, non-attainment, or stratospheric ozone provision.
- A knowing violation of a standard associated with a permit.
- A knowing omission of material information on a record required under the CAA.
- A knowing failure to report or notify as required.
- A knowing alteration or concealment of data or files.
- A failure to maintain files or records.
- A knowing failure to install required monitoring devices.

Q 33.7.7 What are the penalties for CAA violations?

Violation of the CAA may be subject to a civil judicial or administrative order, and/or civil or criminal penalties that may include fines of up to $25,000 per day of violation or imprisonment of up to five years.[64] "Knowing Violations" are subject to criminal liability.

Clean Water Act (CWA)

Q 33.8 What is the aim of the Clean Water Act?

The Federal Water Pollution Control Act,[65] commonly known as the Clean Water Act (CWA), is intended to restore and maintain the chemical, physical, and biological integrity of the nation's waters. It directs the EPA to minimize the effects of chemical pollution on fish, shellfish, wildlife, recreation, biological diversity, productivity, and stability.

Q 33.8.1 What kinds of pollutants are regulated by the CWA?

The CWA regulates "priority" pollutants, including various toxic pollutants; "conventional" pollutants, such as biochemical oxygen demand (BOD), total suspended solids (TSS), fecal coliform, oil and grease, and pH; and "non-conventional" pollutants, including any pollutant not identified as either conventional or priority.

Q 33.8.2 How does the CWA protect the nation's waters?

The CWA authorizes the EPA to establish maximum "effluent limitations" for discharges of pollutants from "point sources." It creates various enforcement and permitting mechanisms to achieve effluent limitations, including the National Pollutant Discharge Elimination System (NPDES), which makes it unlawful to discharge a pollutant to "waters of the United States" without first obtaining a permit and complying with its terms.

Q 33.8.3 What are point source discharges?

The CWA regulates both direct and indirect discharges. The NPDES program[66] controls direct discharges into navigable waters. Direct discharges, or "point source" discharges, are from sources such as pipes and sewers.

Q 33.8.4 What are nonpoint sources?

Certain sources of pollution such as storm water runoff from industrial sources or municipal storm drains, agricultural storm water discharges, and irrigation return flows are considered "nonpoint sources." While some of these nonpoint sources are exempted from permit requirements, others—such as certain kinds of storm water discharges—are not. (See the discussion of Storm Water Discharges at Q 33.8.7, below.)

NPDES Permits

Q 33.8.5 What is an NPDES permit required for?

NPDES permits, issued by either EPA or an authorized state, contain industry-specific, technology-based, and/or water quality-based limits, and establish pollutant monitoring and reporting requirements. A facility that intends to discharge into the nation's waters must obtain a permit prior to initiating its discharge.

Q 33.8.6 What are the requirements for a discharging facility to be issued an NPDES permit?

A permit applicant must provide quantitative analytical data identifying the types of pollutants present in the facility's effluent. The permit will then set forth the conditions and effluent limitations under which a facility may make a discharge.

A NPDES permit may also include discharge limits based on federal or state water quality criteria or standards that are designed to protect designated uses of surface waters, such as supporting aquatic life or recreation. These standards, unlike the technological standards, generally do not take into account technological feasibility or costs. Water quality criteria and standards vary from state to state and site to site, depending on the use classification of the receiving body of water. Most states follow EPA guidelines that propose aquatic life and human health criteria for many of the 126 priority pollutants.

For an NPDES permit, facilities must provide the results of biological toxicity tests and any information on its "effluent characteristics." Specific facilities in specific industries must test for certain parameters. For example, the electronics/computer industry must test for all 126 priority pollutants listed in 40 C.F.R. § 122, Appendix D. Facilities must provide quantifiable data only for discharges of priority pollutants which the applicant knows or has reason to believe will be greater than trace amounts.

All manufacturing facilities must satisfy the technology-based effluent limitation guidelines.

Storm Water Discharges

Q 33.8.7 Which kinds of storm water discharges require an NPDES permit?

Facilities that meet certain criteria, such as storing products, inventory, equipment, or hazardous materials outside, must apply for an NPDES permit for its storm water discharges. Storm water discharge associated with industrial activity directly related to manufacturing, processing, or raw materials storage areas at an industrial plant must have a storm water permit.[67]

Agricultural storm water discharges and irrigation return flows do *not* require a permit. Also exempted from permit requirements are storm water discharges from areas located on lands separate from the plant's industrial activities, such as office buildings and accompanying parking lots, as long as the drainage from the excluded areas is not mixed with storm water from the industrial areas. Storm water discharges from construction activities—including clearing, grading, and excavation—that disturb one acre or more *are* subject to the storm water permit program.

EPA has delegated storm water permitting programs in most states, but has retained enforcement authority so that both EPA and the applicable state may bring enforcement action for non-permitted storm water discharges.

Publicly Owned Treatment Works

Q 33.8.8 What kind of permits are required for municipal sewage treatment plants?

The CWA also regulates discharges to publicly owned treatment works (POTWs). Industrial users of POTWs must comply with the national pretreatment program[68] that controls the discharge of pollutants to POTWs. Facilities regulated under section 307(b) must meet certain pretreatment standards. The goal of the pretreatment program is to protect municipal wastewater treatment plants from damage that may occur when hazardous, toxic, or other wastes are discharged into a sewer system and to protect the quality of sludge generated by these plants.

Discharges to a POTW are regulated primarily by the POTW itself, rather than by the state or EPA. EPA has developed technology-based standards for industrial users of POTWs. Different standards apply to existing and new sources within each category. "Categorical" pretreatment standards applicable to an entire industry on a nationwide basis are also developed by EPA. "Local limits" are also developed by the POTW in order to assist the POTW in achieving the effluent limitations in its NPDES permit.

Regardless of whether a state is authorized to implement either the NPDES or the pretreatment program,[69] a state may develop and enforce requirements more stringent than federal standards.

Wetlands Regulation and Development/Dredge and Fill Permits

Q 33.8.9 What other permits are required by the CWA?

Section 404 of the Clean Water Act is administered by the U.S. Army Corps of Engineers and regulates the discharge of dredged and fill material into the waters of the United States, which include wetlands in many circumstances. Therefore, any person planning to engage in activities that involve the filling of wetlands (such as construction of buildings in wetland areas) must apply for a permit from the appropriate regional office of the Army Corps of Engineers and present a mitigation plan for any damage to the wetlands.[70]

Spill Prevention Control and Countermeasures

Q 33.8.10 What regulations should facilities dealing with oil be aware of?

Facilities that have above-ground oil storage capacity of greater than 1,320 gallons or underground oil storage capacity greater than 42,000 gallons may be subject to Spill Prevention Control and Countermeasures (SPCC) regulations.[71] The CWA requires facilities that store more than 1,320 gallons of petroleum products to prepare a written Spill Prevention Control and Countermeasures plan that requires measures to be implemented to prevent releases of petroleum to navigable waters. The SPCC plan sets forth a facility's response to a discharge of oil. The plan ensures that owners and operators of facilities develop and implement containment and other countermeasures that prevent oil spills that could reach navigable waters. SPCC plans provide for facility practices to reduce the number and volume of spills, such as tank lead detection, spill-overfill protection, external pipe protection, and secondary containment.

Q 33.8.11 What does the SPCC consider "oil"?

The CWA definition of "oil" includes non-petroleum oils as well as petroleum and petroleum-refined products. "Oil" means oil of any kind or in any form, including, but not limited to:

- fats, oils, or greases of animal, fish, or marine mammal origin;

- vegetable oils, including oils from seeds, nuts, fruits, or kernels; and
- other oils and greases, including petroleum, fuel oil, sludge, synthetic oils, mineral oils, oil refuse, or oil mixed with wastes other than dredged spoil.[72]

Q 33.8.12 What must an SPCC plan include?

The plan must include following components:[73]

- Physical layout of the facility, including facility diagram, marking the location and contents of each container (even if exempted), transfer stations, and piping.
- The type of oil in each container and its storage capacity.
- The discharge prevention measures, including procedures for routine handling of products such as loading, unloading, and facility transfers.
- The discharge or drainage controls such as secondary containment around containers and other structures, equipment, and procedures for the control of a discharge.
- Any countermeasures for discharge discovery, response, and cleanup, including those performed by a contractor.
- Methods of proper disposal of recovered materials.
- Contact list and phone numbers for the facility response coordinator, National Response Center, cleanup contractors, and all appropriate federal, state, and local agencies who must be contacted in case of a discharge.
- Details about conducting inspections, required tests, and related record keeping.
- Security procedures for the operation, such as fencing, lighting, security of valves, locks on oil pumps, and secure loading/unloading connections of pipelines and piping.
- Proper certification by a licensed professional engineer, unless the facility qualifies as a small business.[74]
- Signature of approval by management.

The SPCC plan must be kept at the facility (except in some cases, it may be kept at the nearest field office).[75]

Q 33.8.13 What other requirements do the SPCC regulations impose?

Each covered facility must train oil-handling personnel in the operation and maintenance of equipment to prevent discharges, procedure protocols, applicable pollution control laws and regulations, general facility operations, and the contents of the SPCC plan.[76] Such training includes an annual discharge prevention briefing for oil-handling personnel to ensure adequate understanding of the SPCC plan for the facility. Each facility must designate a person who is accountable for discharge prevention and who reports to facility management. SPCC plans must be amended whenever there is a change in the facility's design, construction, operation, or maintenance which materially affects the facility's potential for a discharge of oil to or upon waters of the United States or adjoining shorelines.[77]

COMPLIANCE FACT

Discharge of Oil regulations, also known as the "Sheen Rule," require that certain releases of oil that reach the waters of the United States must be reported under the Clean Water Act if they cause a film or sheen upon or discoloration of the surface of the water or adjacent shoreline.

Enforcement

Q 33.8.14 What are the penalties for CWA violations?

Most states have enforcement authority under the CWA and may enforce similar or more stringent penalties. Federal penalties may be in the form of an administrative order, an action for civil penalties, an injunction, or an action for criminal penalties. Federal penalties may include:

- *Administrative penalty.* Any owner, operator, or person in charge of any vessel may be liable for a discharge of

hazardous substance or the failure to comply with any regulation under the CWA[78] by administrative penalty up to $11,000 per day up to $157,500.
- *Civil penalty.* Any owner, operator, or person in charge of any vessel may be liable for a discharge of hazardous substance or the failure to comply with any regulation under the CWA by civil penalty up to $32,500; and may be subject to a civil penalty three times the costs incurred by the Oil Spill Liability Trust Fund for failure to comply with a removal order of the EPA; and may be subject to a minimum penalty of $130,000 for grossly negligent or willful misconduct resulting in a release.
- *Criminal penalty.* Any person in charge of a facility from which oil or a hazardous substance is discharged who fails to immediately notify the appropriate federal or state agency shall be fined (in accordance with title 18) or imprisoned for not more than five years, or both.

Toxic Substances Control Act

Q 33.9 What is the intent of the Toxic Substances Control Act?

The Toxic Substances Control Act (TSCA) grants EPA authority to create a regulatory framework to collect data on chemicals in order to evaluate, assess, mitigate, and control risks that may be posed by their manufacture, processing, and use.[79] TSCA provides a variety of control methods to prevent chemicals from posing unreasonable risk. TSCA standards may apply at any point during a chemical's life cycle.

Q 33.9.1 What substances does the TSCA address?

Under TSCA section 5, EPA has established an inventory of "existing chemicals" whose manufacture or importation is permitted. (Certain substances including food, drugs, cosmetics, and pesticides are generally excluded.) Substances not on the inventory of existing chemicals are referred to as "new chemicals," which are subject to review and regulation by the EPA.

Among the specific chemicals regulated by the TSCA are polychlorinated biphenyls (PCBs), asbestos, chlorofluorocarbons, radon, and lead-based paint.

Q 33.9.2   Are all substances not on the inventory of existing chemicals banned?

Not necessarily. If a chemical is not already on the inventory and has not been excluded by TSCA, a pre-manufacture notice (PMN) must be submitted to EPA for review prior to manufacture or import. The PMN must identify the chemical and provide available information on health and environmental effects. Depending on the risk to human health and the environment, the EPA can ban the manufacture or distribution in commerce, limit the use, require labeling, or place other restrictions on chemicals that pose unreasonable risks. If available data are not sufficient to evaluate the chemical's effects, EPA can impose restrictions pending the development of information on its health and environmental effects. EPA can also restrict significant new uses of chemicals based upon factors such as the projected volume and use of the chemical.

Reporting Requirements

Q 33.9.3   What reporting requirements does TSCA impose?

Under TSCA section 8, EPA requires the producers and importers (and others) of chemicals to report information on the chemicals' production, use, exposure, and risks. Companies producing and importing chemicals can be required to report unpublished health and safety studies on listed chemicals and to collect and record any allegations of adverse reactions or any information indicating that a substance may pose a substantial risk to humans or the environment.

Unless companies manufacture, produce, or import chemicals that are restricted by EPA, they will have no reporting obligations under TSCA.[80]

Regulation of Asbestos

Q 33.10   How is asbestos regulated?

The EPA has passed regulations prohibiting the manufacture, importation, processing, and distribution in commerce of asbestos-containing products[81] due to the health risks from exposure to asbestos. Also, the EPA and OSHA have promulgated regulations for the use and disposal of asbestos, particularly asbestos that is removed from buildings as a result of asbestos abatement projects and/or renovations. OSHA regulates employees' exposure to asbestos and requires specific work practices and engineering controls for removing and handling asbestos. Many states have also established asbestos requirements, particularly for abatement and renovation activities and disposal. Most of the regulations require notice to the appropriate state agency before commencement of asbestos abatement projects and specific work practices to protect building occupants and asbestos removal workers. Building owners with knowledge of asbestos in their buildings are required to comply with other provisions of the OSHA standards, such as maintenance personnel training, signs, and warning labels.

Regulation of Lead-Based Paint

Q 33.11 How is lead-based paint regulated?

EPA has promulgated regulations governing the use, abatement, and disposal of lead-based paint to prevent lead-based paint hazards in buildings, residences, and soils. Although the manufacture of lead-based paint was prohibited in 1978, lead-based paint remains in housing units and buildings constructed before that time. Renovation of such buildings is problematic because scraping of paint results in the release of lead-based paint chips and dust. Emission of lead from cars, smelters, and other industrial sources has also resulted in the contamination of soils in urban areas.

EPA's regulations require lead-based paint that has been released from walls, window frames, and door frames, among other areas, to be abated so that it does not affect human health.[82] The Department of Housing and Urban Development has also promulgated lead-based paint disclosure regulations that require sellers and landlords of pre-1978 housing to disclose any knowledge or information regarding lead-based paint present in the housing to purchasers and all residential tenants.[83]

Regulation of Polychlorinated Biphenyls (PCBs)

Q 33.12 How are PCBs regulated?

With a few exceptions, EPA has banned the manufacture, processing, and distribution of PCBs at concentrations of 50 ppm (parts per million) or greater because they present an unreasonable risk of injury to health within the United States.[84]

Q 33.12.1 What uses of PCB-containing materials/equipment are permitted?

The EPA ban of PCBs does not prevent the use of PCB-containing equipment in which the PCBs are "totally enclosed," such as non-leaking transformers, capacitors, electromagnets, voltage regulators, switches, circuit breakers, reclosers, and cable.

The following uses of PCBs, which are not "totally enclosed," are among those authorized by EPA, subject to certain conditions as noted in the regulation:

- Use in and servicing of transformers.
- Use in mining equipment at concentrations <50 ppm.
- Use in heat transfer systems at concentrations <50 ppm.
- Use in hydraulic systems at concentrations <50 ppm.
- Use in and servicing of circuit breakers, reclosers, and cable at any concentration subject to certain conditions.[85]

The regulation should be consulted prior to the use of any PCB-containing material.

Q 33.12.2 What are some of the requirements for permitted uses of PCBs?

PCB Marking. Materials containing PCBs must be marked as set forth in the regulations.[86] This requirement applies to

- PCB containers,
- PCB transformers,
- PCB large high- or low-voltage capacitors,
- Equipment containing a PCB transformer or a PCB large high- or low-voltage capacitor,
- electric motors using PCB coolants,

- hydraulic systems using PCB hydraulic fluid,
- heat transfer systems, and
- PCB article containers.

Importantly, each storage area used to store PCBs and PCB Items for disposal, as well as vehicles carrying more than 45 kg of liquid PCBs at concentrations at 50 ppm or higher, must be properly marked.

PCB Storage. Proper storage of PCBs and PCB items with concentrations of 50 ppm or greater is set forth in the regulations.[87] PCBs may only be stored for one year prior to disposal.

PCB Disposal.[88] PCB transformers may be disposed of in an incinerator that complies with 40 C.F.R. § 761.70 or in a chemical waste landfill if all of the free-flowing liquid is properly removed. PCB capacitors that contain PCBs must be disposed of in an incinerator that complies with 40 C.F.R. § 761.70. Other articles that contain PCBs at 500 ppm or greater must be disposed of in an incinerator that complies with 40 C.F.R. § 761.70 or in a chemical waste landfill that complies with 40 C.F.R. § 761.75, provided that all free-flowing liquid PCBs have been properly removed before disposal.

PCBs or PCB items with concentrations greater than 50 ppm may not be exported for disposal without an exemption from EPA.[89]

PCB Waste Manifests. A waste manifest, EPA Form 8700-22, or comparable state form must be properly completed for all PCB waste that is offered for transport for off-site storage or disposal.[90] If the generator is not required to have a storage identification number, the generator should use the generic identification number of "40 C.F.R. Part 761" on the manifest.

PCB Record Keeping. The record-keeping requirements are more stringent for generators of larger quantities of PCB waste.[91] If a facility stores at least 45 kg of PCB waste, one or more PCB transformers, or fifty or more PCB large high- or low-voltage capacitors, the generator shall develop and maintain all annual records and the written annual document log of the disposition of PCBs and PCB items. The log must be prepared for each facility by July 1 for the previous calendar year and shall be retained at the facility for at least three years after the facility ceases using or storing PCBs and PCB items in the quantities set forth in 40 C.F.R. § 761.180. That section should be consulted for the specific content required in the annual log.

TSCA Enforcement

Q 33.13 What are the penalties for violations of the TSCA?

Failure to comply with a TSCA regulation such as properly maintaining records or submitting reports may be subject the violator to civil or criminal penalties[92] up to $25,000 per day for each violation, or imprisonment for up to one year, or both.

Other Pertinent Regulations

Homeland Security Chemical Storage Rules

Q 33.14 What other federal regulations should businesses be aware of when considering environmental issues and compliance?

The Department of Homeland Security (DHS) recently developed Chemical Facility Anti-Terrorism Standards (CFATS), a comprehensive new regulatory program governing security at chemical facilities.[93] CFATS' scope is large because the definition of "chemical facility" is broad and encompasses many facilities that would not traditionally be thought of as chemical facilities, such as warehouses. CFATS covers any establishment that possesses or plans to possess a quantity of a chemical substance determined by DHS to be potentially dangerous ("chemical of interest").

Q 33.14.1 What are covered facilities required to do under CFATS?

- Prepare and submit security vulnerability assessments and site security plans to DHS for approval;
- Update security vulnerability assessments and site security plans;
- Comply with record-keeping requirements;
- Protect chemical terrorism vulnerability information;
- Conduct background checks.

Q 33.14.2 How does DHS enforce these standards?

DHS may enforce the program through audits and inspections and orders. Administrative penalties of up to $25,000/day can be assessed for noncompliance. On November 20, 2007, DHS published the final Appendix A of the regulations in the *Federal Register*. With the publication of a final Appendix A, all provisions of 6 C.F.R. pt. 27 are operative and in effect.

SEC Environmental Liability Disclosure Requirements

Q 33.15 What other compliance obligations related to environmental issues should businesses be aware of?

The SEC requires five disclosures related to environmental liabilities. Compliance with the SEC rules governing these disclosures typically requires input from both accounting and environmental professionals.

- Contingent Remediation Liabilities—Rule FASB 5 (and SOP-96-1 and Staff Action Bulletin 92 "SAB-92")
- Environmental Legal Proceedings—Regulation S-K 103 (17 C.F.R. § 229.103)
- Description of Business—Regulation S-K 101 (17 C.F.R. § 229.101(c)(xii))
- Management Discussion and Analysis (MD&A)—Rule S-K 303(a) (17 C.F.R. § 229.303)
- Accounting for Conditional Asset Retirement Obligations—FIN 47

Contingent Remediation Liabilities

Q 33.15.1 What are Contingent Remediation Liabilities?

Examples of probable remediation liabilities requiring disclosure could be (1) cost of cleaning up a spill as a result of an accident or other company operation; (2) the company's anticipated share of remedial costs at a CERCLA Superfund site in which records show that the company sent hazardous substances to the site.

The SEC requires contingent environmental remediation liabilities to be disclosed and, if possible, estimated and accrued each quarter. Accrual is required if liability is probable and estimable. A company must accrue the best estimate, if one exists. If no estimate is better than any other and there is a range of estimates, the company must accrue the low end of the range. If only part of the remedial activity can be estimated (*e.g.*, investigation), it should be accrued.[94]

Environmental Legal Proceedings

Q 33.15.2 What kinds of environmental legal proceedings must be disclosed?

The SEC requires disclosure each quarter of any pending administrative or judicial proceeding (or one contemplated by the government) arising under environmental laws that meet any of the following criteria:

(1) is "material" to the company's business or financial condition or

(2) involves a claim for damages, or involves potential monetary sanctions, capital expenditures, deferred charges, or charges to income, and the amount involved exclusive of interest and costs exceeds 10% of the current assets of the company and its subsidiaries on a consolidated basis or

(3) has a governmental authority as a party and "such proceeding involves potential monetary sanctions" for which the company reasonably believes the sanctions (not including remedial costs or other costs) will be $100,000 or more.

Examples of administrative or judicial proceedings include (1) formal or informal negotiations with a government agency regarding potential sanctions for an alleged violation; and (2) an administrative proceeding initiated by the company to challenge a permit requirement under an environmental law.

Description of Business Disclosures

Q 33.15.3 What are "Description of Business" disclosures?

The SEC requires annual disclosure of the material effects that compliance with environmental laws may have upon the capital expenditures, earnings, and competitive position of the registrant. The registrant must disclose material estimated capital expenditures for environmental control facilities for the remainder of its current fiscal year, succeeding fiscal year, and further periods the registrant may deem material.

Examples of such expenditures are (1) upgrades to underground storage tanks; and (2) upgrades to a wastewater treatment facility.

Management Discussion and Analysis

Q 33.15.4 What are MD&A disclosures?

The SEC requires a company to disclose and discuss in the MD&A of its annual report "known trends . . . events or uncertainties that are reasonably likely" to have a material impact on liquidity, capital resources, or operating results (even if disclosed elsewhere in the filing)—for example, the potential impact of proposed legislation or regulations. (A company is not required to disclose optional forward-looking information by anticipating a future trend or event.)

Conditional Asset Retirement Obligations

Q 33.15.5 What are "Conditional Asset Retirement Obligations" disclosures?

Financial Interpretation No. 47 (FIN 47) was issued March 2005 and became effective December 15, 2005. FIN 47 is an interpretation and clarification of FASB Statement No. 143, which requires companies to disclose on their financial statements environmental liability that will be realized at a future date. FIN 47 requires an asset retirement activity where the timing and/or method of settlement of an environmental liability are conditional on a future event that may or may not be within the control of the company, such as environmental remediation costs associated with closing or selling a facility. FIN 47 explains that a company is required to recognize an environmental liability for the fair value of a conditional asset retirement obligation at the time it is identified so long as the environmental liability's fair value can be estimated.

An asset retirement obligation can be reasonably estimated if:

(1) it is evident that the fair value of the retirement obligation is included in the acquisition price,
(2) an active market exists for the transfer of the obligation, or
(3) information exists to determine the expected present value, which incorporates uncertainty about the timing and method of settlement into the fair value.

Retirement obligation includes sale, abandonment, recycling, or disposal of a conditional asset. The characteristics of a liability are:

(1) An entity has a present duty to another entity that entails settlement by probable future transfer or use of assets at a specified or determinable date, on occurrence of a specified event, or on demand;
(2) A duty obligates an entity, leaving little or no discretion to avoid the future sacrifice; and
(3) The event obligating an entity has already occurred. Only present obligations are relevant.

Climate Change Disclosures

Q 33.16 What does the SEC require companies to report with respect to the impact of climate change?

On February 2, 2010, the SEC published an interpretive release entitled "Commission Guidance Regarding Disclosure Related to Climate Change."[95] The interpretive guidance does not create new disclosure requirements, but clarifies existing Regulation S-K reporting obligations, particularly existing requirements with respect to the impact of climate change on business operations and profitability. The relevant rules cover a company's climate change disclosure obligations in the risk factors, business description, legal proceedings, and management's discussion and analysis (MD&A) sections in SEC filings.

Notes

1. This chapter addresses only legally required programs. Voluntary programs, such as recycling or energy-reduction initiatives, are not included in the chapter.
2. 42 U.S.C. § 6901 *et seq.*
3. Subtitle C of RCRA, contained in 40 C.F.R. pts. 260–99.
4. 40 C.F.R. pt. 261.
5. 40 C.F.R. pt. 262.
6. 40 C.F.R. § 261.3(a)(2).
7. 40 C.F.R. § 262.12.
8. 40 C.F.R. § 262.2 to .23.
9. 40 C.F.R. § 262.30 to .33.
10. 40 C.F.R. § 262.34.
11. 40 C.F.R. § 262.40. Records of hazardous waste handling must generally be retained for three years from the date the waste was received or shipped off-site.
12. 40 C.F.R. § 262.41 to .44.
13. Not all states recognize conditionally exempt small quantity generators.
14. As set forth in 40 C.F.R. pt. 270.
15. Subtitle I of RCRA, 40 C.F.R. pt. 280.
16. 40 C.F.R. § 280.21.
17. The type of permissible UST construction is specified in 40 C.F.R. § 280.20.
18. 40 C.F.R. § 280.22.
19. 40 C.F.R. § 280.50.
20. 40 C.F.R. § 280.53.
21. 40 C.F.R. § 280.61.
22. 40 C.F.R. § 280.71.
23. 40 C.F.R. § 280.20(c).
24. 40 C.F.R. § 280.40 to .44.
25. 40 C.F.R. pt. 302.
26. *See* 40 C.F.R. § 280.60 to .67.
27. 40 C.F.R. § 280.94.
28. 40 C.F.R. § 279.20 to .24.
29. *See* Q 33.8.10 *et seq., infra.*
30. 40 C.F.R. pt. 280. *See* Q 33.3.5, *supra.*
31. 42 U.S.C. § 6928.
32. 42 U.S.C. § 9601 *et seq.*
33. EPA's Superfund, TRI, EPCRA, RMP, and Oil Information Center answers questions and provides references to EPA guidance pertaining to the Superfund program. Call them at (800) 424-9346.

34. 40 C.F.R. pt. 302.
35. Reportable quantities are defined and listed in 40 C.F.R. § 302.4-5a. The NRC number is (800) 424-8802; fax (202) 267-2165.
36. 40 C.F.R. pt. 300.
37. 42 U.S.C. § 9607(a).
38. 42 U.S.C. § 9627.
39. 42 U.S.C. § 9627(b).
40. *See* 42 U.S.C. § 9627(c).
41. 42 U.S.C. § 9627(d).
42. 42 U.S.C. § 9607.
43. 42 U.S.C. § 9607(f).
44. 42 U.S.C. § 9659.
45. 40 C.F.R. pts. 350–72.
46. EPCRA § 302. (The list of extremely hazardous substances is in 40 C.F.R. pt. 355, Appendices A and B.)
47. EPCRA § 304.
48. EPCRA §§ 311, 312.
49. EPCRA § 313.
50. *Id.*
51. CAA regulations appear at 40 C.F.R. pts. 50–99. EPA's Control Technology Center, at (919) 541-0800, provides general assistance and information on CAA standards.
52. CAA § 112(b), as amended.
53. Reformulated gasoline, automobile pollution control devices, and vapor recovery nozzles on gas pumps are a few of the mechanisms EPA uses to regulate mobile air emission sources.
54. Since 1995, these allowances have been set below previous levels of sulfur dioxide releases.
55. Production of Class I substances, including fifteen kinds of chlorofluorocarbons (CFCs), was to be phased out entirely by the year 2000, while certain hydrochlorofluorocarbons (HCFCs) are to be phased out by 2030.
56. *See* Climate Change—Regulatory Initiatives: Endangerment and Cause or Contribute Findings for Greenhouse Gases under Section 202(a) of the Clean Air Act, http://epa.gov/climatechange/endangerment.html.
57. 40 C.F.R. pt. 98.
58. The Green Building Act of 2006, D.C. Law 16-234 (Mar. 8, 2007).
59. This requirement was created by title V of the 1990 Amendments.
60. As defined at 40 C.F.R. § 70.2.
61. 40 C.F.R. § 68.130.
62. 40 C.F.R. § 68.115.
63. 40 C.F.R. pt. 68.
64. 42 U.S.C. § 7413.
65. 33 U.S.C. § 1251 *et seq.*
66. CWA § 402.
67. 40 C.F.R. § 122.26(b)(14).
68. CWA § 307(b).

69. The general pretreatment requirements that must be followed are found at 40 C.F.R. pt. 413, subpart B.

70. *See* 40 C.F.R. pt. 230.

71. SPCC regulations are found at 40 C.F.R. pt. 112. Questions about SPCC regulations can be answered by EPA's Superfund, TRI, EPCRA, RMP, and Oil Information Center at (800) 424-9346.

72. 40 C.F.R. § 112.2.
73. 40 C.F.R. § 112.7(a).
74. 40 C.F.R. § 112.3.
75. *Id.*
76. 40 C.F.R. § 112.7.
77. 40 C.F.R. § 112.3(b).
78. 33 U.S.C. § 1321.
79. 15 U.S.C. § 2601 *et seq.*
80. If you are unsure about the status of a chemical, consult the Toxic Substances Control Act Hotline (202-554-1404), which answers questions and distributes guidance pertaining to TSCA standards, Monday through Friday, from 8:30 A.M. to 5:00 P.M. (Eastern).
81. Identified in 40 C.F.R. pt. 763.
82. 40 C.F.R. pt. 745.
83. For further information regarding lead-based paint, consult www.epa.gov/lead/pubs/n.lic.htm.
84. 40 C.F.R. § 761.20.
85. 40 C.F.R. § 761.30.
86. 40 C.F.R. § 761.40.
87. 40 C.F.R. § 761.65.
88. Proper disposal of PCB-containing materials is set forth in Subpart D of 40 C.F.R. pt. 761.
89. 40 C.F.R. § 761.97.
90. 40 C.F.R. § 761.207.
91. 40 C.F.R. § 761.80.
92. 15 U.S.C. § 2615.
93. 6 C.F.R. pt. 27.
94. Rule FASB 5 (SOP-96-1 & SAB-92).
95. Securities Act Rel. No. 9106 (Feb. 2, 2010), *available at* www.sec.gov/rules/interp/2010/33-9106.pdf.

34

Labor and Employment Law

Mark E. Baker*

An extensive and complicated labyrinth of federal, state, and local laws governs the relationship between companies and their employees. The task of maintaining a program for compliance with these myriad requirements falls upon management at all levels, typically with the human resources department taking the lead in coordinating the compliance efforts. A detailed prescription for a compliance program focused on labor and employment requirements could fill many volumes. Rather than attempt to offer such a prescription here, which is not possible given the scope of this book, this chapter provides an overview[1] that is intended to enable compliance officers to identify those principal areas of labor and employment law compliance on which they should focus.

The substantive discussion in this chapter is limited exclusively to federal labor and employment law requirements. A discussion of the many requirements imposed by state and local

---

* The author wishes to acknowledge Christopher A. Myers for his contributions to this chapter.

governments—even at a relatively superficial "issue spotting" level—would far exceed the confines of this book. However, managers charged with compliance responsibility must be mindful of the fact that state and even local governments have become increasingly active and aggressive in adopting and enforcing their own laws for regulating the workplace. While many state and local labor/employment laws are patterned on federal laws, they often expand upon the federal regulatory scheme.[2] This means that companies must be careful to explore and understand the labor and employment law nuances of the jurisdictions in which they operate.

Employment Eligibility and Verification 1260
    Eligibility Verification Form I-9 1260
    Credit Reports and Background Checks 1261
Employment Discrimination—Statutory Framework 1262
    Race, Color, Religion, Sex, Pregnancy,
      and National Origin Discrimination 1262
    "Disparate Impact" Discrimination 1263
    "Association" Discrimination 1263
    Religious Discrimination and Accommodation
      of Religious Beliefs 1264
    Pregnancy Discrimination 1264
    National Origin Discrimination 1265
    Age Discrimination 1266
    Disability Discrimination 1266
    Gender-Based Pay Discrimination 1269
Employment Discrimination—General Compliance Issues 1270
    Prohibited Actions 1270
    Affirmative Accommodation 1270
    Written Policies 1271
    Retaliation 1272
    Workplace Harassment 1272
Wage-and-Hour Issues 1275
    Fair Labor Standards Act 1275
    FLSA Exemptions 1277
    Working Hours 1280
    Compliance Policies 1281

Labor and Employment Law

Benefits 1282
    ERISA 1282
    HIPAA 1283
Family/Medical Leave 1283
    The Family and Medical Leave Act 1283
    Eligibility 1284
    "Serious Medical Condition" 1285
    Parental Leaves 1285
    Notice/Application Requirements 1286
    Pay and Benefits During Leave 1287
    Returning from Leave 1287
    Military Caregiver Leave 1288
    Compliance Programs 1288
Military Leave 1289
    Uniformed Services Employment and
        Reemployment Rights Act 1289
    Notice Requirements 1289
    Pay and Benefits During Leave 1289
    Returning from Leave 1290
Medical Insurance Coverage 1290
    COBRA 1290
Plant Shutdowns and Mass Layoffs 1291
    Worker Adjustment Retraining and Notification Act 1291
Polygraphs 1292
    Employee Polygraph Protection Act 1292
Unions 1293
    National Labor Relations Act 1293
Government Contracting 1295
    Affirmative Action Plans 1295
    Wages and Benefits 1296

Employment Eligibility and Verification

Q 34.1 What are an employer's obligations regarding documentation of an employee's legal authorization to work in the United States?

The Immigration Reform and Control Act of 1986 (IRCA),[3] which prohibits the employment of individuals who are not legally authorized to work in the United States, requires employers to verify each new employee's work authorization by completing an Employment Eligibility Verification Form I-9 for the employee.

Eligibility Verification Form I-9

Q 34.1.1 What are the Form I-9 filing requirements?

All employers are subject to the I-9 requirement. A separate Form I-9 must be completed for each employee. The form must be fully completed within the first three days of employment.

The form requires the employee to submit certain specified information establishing his or her identity and authorization to work. A variety of types of identification and authorization documentation may be submitted. Employers should ensure that they are familiar with employment eligibility verification documentation requirements, including which documents are "acceptable I-9 documents" under current regulations.

Q 34.1.2 What are the consequences of failure to file?

Federal regulators at the U.S. Department of Labor and other agencies make a review of I-9 forms a routine part of any audit or investigation they conduct. Employers who fail to comply with the I-9 and related requirements or who knowingly employ illegal workers are subject to fines and, in some circumstances, criminal prosecution.

> **TIP:** Most employers find that, to be prepared for a review of I-9 forms in an audit or investigation by the DOL or other agency, it is administratively simpler to retain I-9 forms in separate files that are designated for that purpose—usually alphabetically by employee name. It is easier to collect requested I-9 forms from such files than it is to pull them from each individual's personnel file.

Credit Reports and Background Checks

Q 34.1.3 What federal laws/regulations governing employment background checks must an employer comply with?

The Fair Credit Reporting Act (FCRA)[4] applies whenever an employer uses, for any employment-related purpose, certain credit bureau reports and background checks furnished by individuals or entities who are in the business of providing such reports and checks. (Note that state laws may impose more stringent requirements on employment background checks.) FCRA's definition of the types of reports and checks that trigger its requirements is broad, encompassing not only true credit reports but also reports on such matters as driving records, criminal records, work histories, interviews with personal acquaintances, etc.

Q 34.1.4 What does the FCRA require?

Whenever the FCRA is triggered, the employer must make certain written disclosures to the affected applicant or employee and obtain the applicant's or employee's written consent prior to obtaining and using FCRA-covered information about that individual. Additional disclosures are required if the covered information is a factor in an adverse employment decision; for example, a refusal to hire, denial of a promotion, or disciplinary action.

Employment Discrimination—Statutory Framework

Q 34.2 What federal laws govern employment discrimination?

The broadest nondiscrimination statute is Title VII of the Civil Rights Act of 1964,[5] which prohibits discrimination on the basis of race, color, religion, sex, pregnancy, and national origin. Among the others, which are discussed in more detail below, are:

- Pregnancy Discrimination Act
- Age Discrimination in Employment Act
- Americans with Disabilities Act
- Equal Pay Act.

Q 34.3 What types of discrimination are prohibited?

A variety of federal statutes prohibit discrimination against job applicants and employees based on the following:

- race
- color
- religion
- sex
- pregnancy
- national origin
- genetic information
- age
- disability
- "disparate impact"
- "association".

Race, Color, Religion, Sex, Pregnancy, and National Origin Discrimination

Q 34.4 How does Title VII protect against discrimination?

Title VII requires that job applicants and employees not be treated differently because of their protected characteristics; for example, an employee cannot be given a lower-paying job or different benefits or harder assignments, and cannot be subjected to jokes, cartoons, or derogatory comments, because she is Hispanic. Title VII prohibits employers from acting on stereotypes and assumptions—rather than facts—about an applicant's or employee's abilities, traits, or performance. "Majority" employees and employees suspected of being minorities also are protected; for example, employers cannot discriminate against white male employees because of race or gender, and employers may commit national origin discrimination by disadvantaging employees thought to be Hispanic (even though they are not Hispanic in fact). Title VII protects employees regardless of American citizenship if they are working in the United States.

"Disparate Impact" Discrimination

Q 34.4.1 What is "disparate impact" discrimination?

It is discrimination arising from neutral policies or practices that have a disproportionate adverse effect on minority employees but that are not reasonably related to the necessities of the business. In addition to prohibiting intentional discrimination, Title VII also prohibits such unintentional "disparate impact" discrimination. An employer likely would commit disparate impact discrimination against minority employees by requiring a high school diploma for minimum-skill entry-level manual-labor jobs that, in fact, require no education to perform their tasks (because, statistically, minority employees have a lower high school graduation rate).

"Association" Discrimination

Q 34.4.2 What is "association" discrimination?

It is discrimination against another because he or she is married or related to, or associated with, a person or persons in a protected class. Title VII also protects applicants and employees from such discrimination. For example, an employer cannot refuse to hire an otherwise-qualified job applicant because she is a white woman dating or married to a black man.

Religious Discrimination and Accommodation of Religious Beliefs

Q 34.4.3　How must an employer protect an employee's rights regarding religion?

Title VII's prohibition on religious discrimination means that employers must allow employees to practice their own religious beliefs and cannot endorse, promote, or require specific religious practices or beliefs against an employee's wishes. In addition, employers must ensure that employees are not harassed because of their religious beliefs.

Beyond prohibiting religious discrimination, Title VII requires employers to make requested reasonable accommodations to the religious practices of employees, so long as the accommodation does not impose an "undue hardship" on the employer's business. Such accommodations might include time off for religious observances. An accommodation might create an "undue hardship" for an employer if it would require the employer to bear unreasonable expenses, diminish the efficiency of performance of other jobs, cause coworkers to carry the accommodated employee's share of potentially hazardous or burdensome work, or if less disruptive or burdensome accommodations would achieve the same result.

Pregnancy Discrimination

Q 34.4.4　What are the rules regarding a pregnant employee?

Discrimination based on pregnancy, possible pregnancy, or pregnancy-related conditions is a prohibited form of sex discrimination under amendments to Title VII enacted by the Pregnancy Discrimination Act (PDA).[6] An employer cannot refuse to hire and cannot fire, transfer, reduce benefits to, or otherwise take adverse action against a woman because she is pregnant or thought to be pregnant, planning to become pregnant, or been pregnant or chosen (or not chosen) to end the pregnancy.

Women who are pregnant or affected by pregnancy-related conditions must be treated in the same manner as other applicants or employees with similar limitations. An employer must respond to the temporary incapacities of pregnant employees in the same manner that it would respond to the temporary incapacities of male employees. For example, if the employer would modify the job duties, transfer the worker to a different job, or offer unpaid leave to a temporarily incapacitated male employee, those same opportunities must be extended to a pregnant employee. In addressing pregnant employees' need for leaves and returns to work during and after the pregnancy, employers must follow their customary procedures for requiring medical documentation and must hold jobs open for pregnant employees who are on leave if the jobs would be held for male employees who are out on leave. Employers cannot restrict pregnancy benefits to pregnant employees who are married. Pregnant employees must be allowed to work (or return to work) as long as they are able to perform their jobs.

National Origin Discrimination

Q 34.4.5 What are indications of discrimination based on national origin?

Title VII's prohibition of national origin discrimination means that employers cannot treat employees or applicants differently because they are (or are thought to be) of different ancestry or culture (such as Italian-American) or because they "look foreign," have an accent, or are not fluent in English (unless, of course, the absence of an accent or fluent English are legitimate job requirements). Requiring only job applicants who "look foreign" or "sound foreign" to verify their eligibility to work in the United States would be a form of national origin discrimination.

Q 34.4.6 Can an employer insist that English be spoken in the workplace?

Title VII prohibits employers from imposing requirements that only English be spoken in the workplace, absent a legitimate business reason for the rule. Even when there is a legitimate reason for such a rule, the requirement to speak "English only" cannot extend to breaks, meal periods, or other conversations unrelated to work activities.

Age Discrimination

Q 34.5 What are an employer's compliance obligations regarding discrimination based on age?

The Age Discrimination in Employment Act (ADEA)[7] protects persons who are at least forty years old against age discrimination. An employer may not refuse to hire or discharge someone based merely on the suspicion that age makes that individual unfit for a job. In addition, most mandatory retirements based on age are illegal, although retirement eligibility programs in which age is a factor can be legal under certain circumstances.

As with Title VII, the ADEA prohibits both intentional discrimination and, in some instances, disparate impact discrimination.

Disability Discrimination

Q 34.6 How is a disability protected in the workplace?

The Americans with Disabilities Act (ADA)[8] prohibits employment discrimination against a "qualified individual with a disability." The ADA makes it illegal to refuse to hire or to discharge someone based merely on the suspicion that a disability or suspected disability makes that person unfit for a job.

Q 34.6.1 What is the ADA's definition of "disability"?

The ADA's definition of "disability" is very broad, encompassing applicants and employees if they:

- have a physical or mental impairment that substantially limits one or more major life activities (for example, caring for oneself, performing manual tasks, seeing, hearing, eating, lifting, bending, speaking, breathing, learning, reading, concentrating, thinking, communicating, and working); or
- have a record or history of such physical or mental impairment; or
- are regarded (accurately or inaccurately) as having such an impairment.

In addition to readily detectable impairments such as deafness, blindness, or paraplegia, the ADA protects persons suffering from less obvious impairments such as long-term diseases (for example, AIDS, emphysema, cancer) and mental illnesses (for example, major depression).

Q 34.6.2 What qualifies a person to be protected under the ADA?

To be protected by the ADA, an applicant or employee must be a "qualified individual with a disability" by (1) having the required education, experience, and skills for the job, and (2) being able to perform the essential functions of the job with or without reasonable accommodations for the disability. The "essential functions" are the fundamental duties of the job. For example, a secretary's "essential functions" typically would include typing, filing papers, and taking and making telephone calls, but typically would not include sharpening pencils. Thus, the employer would have to consider providing accommodations to allow a secretary to type and file despite a disability (and likely could take her out of that position if the accommodations were unsuccessful) but it would not have to accommodate a disability preventing pencil-sharpening (and could not take action against the secretary for the inability to sharpen pencils).

Q 34.6.3 How does ADA protection extend to an employee's family?

The ADA protects applicants and employees from discrimination because they are married or related to, or associated with, an individual with a disability. An employer cannot refuse to hire an otherwise qualified job applicant because she has a severely disabled minor child who might impose a financial burden on the group medical plan if the child were enrolled.

Q 34.6.4 How must an employer assist a disabled individual?

The ADA requires employers to provide "reasonable accommodations" to qualified applicants or employees with known disabilities to enable the applicants to apply for jobs and the employees to perform the essential functions of their jobs, *unless* the accommodations would pose an undue hardship on the employer. Such accommodations may involve modifications to equipment, working conditions, schedules, reassignment or relocation to different jobs or locations, or provision of unpaid leaves or supportive devices to assist persons with hearing, vision, or speech limitations. For individuals with mental disabilities, different supervisory methods may be required in some circumstances. The ADA does not require that an applicant's or employee's preferred accommodation be adopted if equally effective but less expensive or less disruptive alternatives are available, nor does the ADA require that employers provide personal use items such as glasses and hearing aids.

Q 34.6.5 What kind of standards can employers maintain for disabled employees?

The ADA permits employers to select the best qualified applicants for employment or promotion—that is, employers may make decisions based on reasons unrelated to the existence or consequences of a disability. Further, the ADA does not require that employers lower production or behavior standards for persons with disabilities, nor does it require employment of persons who are direct threats to the health or safety of themselves or coworkers. The ADA allows employers to prohibit the use of alcohol at the workplace and to hold illegal drug users and alcoholics to the same standards of performance and behavior as other employees.

Q 34.6.6 What compliance issues arise during the hiring process when disabled applicants are involved?

The ADA requires that employers provide reasonable accommodations to job applicants who are known to be disabled to allow them to participate in the application/interview process. Employers cannot ask about the existence, nature, or severity of any disability before extending an offer of employment, but employers can tell applicants about the specific duties of the job, ask how the applicant would perform specific tasks, and ask if the applicant can perform the essential functions of the job being sought. Employers cannot require medical examinations or tests searching for information about physical or mental disabilities before a job offer is extended, but such tests may be required *after* a job offer is made if they are required of all new hires into the same job classification. The ADA also permits employers to test applicants (after a job offer has been made) and employees for illegal drug use or to ensure that they meet legitimate job qualifications, and to require physical examinations of classes of employees to ensure that they are fit for duty. Offers of employment may be conditioned on successful completion and passing of any post-offer examinations or tests that the employer utilizes.

Q 34.6.7 What are the ADA's confidentiality requirements?

The ADA requires that employers keep sensitive employee medical information in confidential files separate from the regular personnel files. Access to these confidential files must be restricted to persons with a legitimate need to have access to them.

Gender-Based Pay Discrimination

Q 34.7 What are the rules governing pay differences between men and women?

While all of the discrimination prohibitions discussed above apply to discrimination in pay, the Equal Pay Act (EPA)[9] prohibits discriminatory pay practices based on gender and imposes specific guidelines for assessing pay differences between men and women. Under the EPA, male and female employees working in the same establishment must be paid equally if they are performing "equal work"—that is, work that requires equal skill, effort, and responsibility and that is performed under similar working conditions. Because job *content* and not job *titles* is the critical focus under the EPA, these requirements apply even if the men and women have different job titles. The EPA also prohibits gender-based pay differences between persons who now hold and once held the same job—a woman cannot be replaced in a job by a higher-paid male employee unless the pay differential is warranted by some factor other than sex.

Q 34.7.1 What kinds of pay differences are allowed?

The EPA permits male-female pay differentials if they are based on seniority, merit, quality or quantity of production, or other factors other than sex.

> **COMPLIANCE FACT**
>
> The EPA prohibits an employee's pay from being lowered to correct a gender-based pay differential. To correct the problem, the wages of the lower-paid employee must be *increased*.

Employment Discrimination—General Compliance Issues

Prohibited Actions

Q 34.8 What types of employment-related actions are subject to the discrimination prohibitions?

The prohibitions on discrimination in employment extend to both applicants and employees and to all aspects of the employment relationship. Discrimination is prohibited in recruiting, testing, hiring, wages and benefits, promotions, application of policies, use of employer facilities, participation in employer-sponsored events, training, discipline, working conditions, layoffs, terminations, and all other aspects of the employment relationship.

Affirmative Accommodation

Q 34.9 What affirmative accommodation obligations are imposed by employment discrimination laws?

Most employment discrimination laws are prohibitive in nature—that is, they specify what employers may *not* do rather than affirmative steps that the employer must take. The two principal exceptions to this general approach are the affirmative duty to make requested accommodations to religious practices and the duty to accommodate disabled applicants and employees.

In both instances, the employer need only make "reasonable" accommodations that do not impose an "undue hardship" on the employer's business. What actions are "reasonable" and what constitutes "undue hardship" are highly fact-specific determinations that should be made only with the assistance of personnel or counsel who are experienced in these matters. These determinations should not be left to lower-level, front-line managers. A coordinated, consistent approach should be adopted.

The failure to make accommodations that are reasonable and that do not create an undue hardship can constitute a violation of Title VII (for religious accommodations) or the ADA (for disability discrimination) with the same consequences as intentional acts of discrimination.

Written Policies

Q 34.10 What written statements and policies should be adopted to help assure nondiscrimination compliance?

Employer recruiting materials, advertisements, applications, and related materials should state that the employer is an equal employment opportunity (EEO) employer and should, where appropriate, note the protected characteristics on the basis of which discrimination will be prohibited. Similar statements should be included in employee handbooks, policy manuals, postings, union contracts, and other employment-related written materials. Postings for job openings, promotion opportunities, etc., should also contain such statements.

All of the above types of materials should, where appropriate, invite disabled individuals to make their needs for reasonable accommodations known if the accommodations are necessary to permit the individual to complete the application process or to perform the essential duties of the job.

Q 34.11 What notice requirements are imposed by employment discrimination laws?

Title VII, the ADEA, the ADA, the PDA, and the EPA all require that employers display certain posters informing employees of their rights to be free from discrimination and how to contact the Equal Employment Opportunity Commission (EEOC) to file claims of discrimination. In addition, although such policies are not directly required, it is beneficial for employers to include nondiscrimination policy statements in their various employment-related documentation as discussed in response to the preceding question.

Retaliation

Q 34.12 What compliance issues are triggered by discrimination claims or other assertions of employee rights?

Employers may not retaliate in any manner against employees who oppose or complain about suspected discrimination, or who participate in investigations or other proceedings dealing with discrimination claims, regardless of whether the opposition, complaint, or participation is inside the employer's operations or external (with the EEOC or a court). For example, an employee cannot be discharged or moved to a less desirable job because that employee opposed what he or she reasonably believed to be sexual harassment, because the employee complained to a supervisor that minorities are mistreated at the company, or because the employee asserted that older workers were disproportionately selected for layoff.

Retaliation claims are often made in conjunction with underlying claims of discrimination, and they are often more difficult to defend than the underlying claim. Employers must proceed carefully in dealing with individuals who oppose, complain about, or otherwise support processes relating to alleged discriminatory acts. A finding of actual underlying discrimination is not necessary for a related retaliation claim to prevail.

Workplace Harassment

Q 34.13 What types of harassment are prohibited?

Harassment based on any of the characteristics protected by the employment discrimination laws discussed above (race, color, religion, sex, pregnancy, national origin, age, or disability) is a prohibited form of discrimination. In addition, a harassing or hostile work environment directed at a particular individual or group because of that individual's or group's protected characteristic may be grounds for a claim of discrimination, even if the content of the harassment or hostility is not tied to the protected characteristic. For example, if a supervisor singles out women or Hispanic employees for harsher treatment relative to other employees (for example, in the form of more onerous work assignments, yelling, belittling comments, etc.), that conduct may be found discriminatory.

Sexual harassment is the most common form of harassment claim. Sexual harassment may occur between individuals of different genders or individuals of the same gender, regardless of the positions of the individuals within the organization. In addition to "hostile environment" harassment, "*quid pro quo*" harassment is prohibited. *Quid pro quo* harassment occurs when there are demands for sexual favors or for submission to sexually related conduct as a condition of employment, or when employment-related actions are based on submission to or rejection of such conduct.

In addition to sexual harassment, claims of racial and religious harassment are a growing area of liability for employers. Employers should have an active commitment to keeping their workplaces free of verbal, physical, visual, or electronic content based on sex, race, religion, or other legally protected characteristics.

COMPLIANCE FACT

An employer may be held liable for harassing conduct of managers, employees, contractors, vendors, customers, or anyone else who is present in the workplace. Regardless of the source of the harassing conduct, the employer has a duty to take appropriate steps to address it.

Q 34.13.1 What kinds of conduct constitute harassment?

Among the conduct that can give rise to claims for unlawful harassment are unwelcome and offensive:

- comments,
- depictions,
- touching,
- gestures,
- jokes, or
- other verbal or physical behavior based on an individual's protected (or suspected) characteristic.

In general, the harassing conduct must be "severe and pervasive" to be actionable, but the determination of what satisfies the required threshold of severity and pervasiveness is highly fact-specific, and employers should not assume that an isolated or seemingly trivial incident of harassment can be safely ignored. A "zero-tolerance" policy toward harassment based on legally protected characteristics is the most prudent course.

Q 34.13.2 What policies should be adopted to address harassment concerns?

Employers are required to take steps to prevent, investigate, and correct harassment. Employers should adopt and prominently publish and circulate written policies that define what constitutes harassing conduct, how and to whom harassment complaints may be raised, and how such complaints will be investigated and resolved. The policy should make clear that corrective action, up to and including termination of employees found to have engaged in harassing conduct, will be taken in response to harassment incidents.

Confidentiality is a common concern with respect to harassment matters. The employer's written harassment policy should address confidentiality and make clear that, while an alleged harassment victim's confidentiality will be considered, the need for a thorough investigation and for proper remediation of harassment incidents does not permit any guarantees of confidentiality.

Q 34.13.3 Are there particular notice requirements that must be met to address harassment concerns?

In addition to the postings that are required by the nondiscrimination laws discussed above, as well as the policies that are described in response to the preceding question, training on harassment should be a regular part of the employer's human resources functions. Both management and non-management employees should receive training, with management personnel given specific training on how to respond to and address harassment complaints.

Q 34.13.4 What compliance concerns does the threat of retaliation raise?

Employers may not retaliate in any manner against employees who oppose or complain about suspected harassment, or who participate in investigations or other proceedings dealing with harassment claims, regardless of whether the opposition, complaint, or participation is inside the employer's operations or external (with the EEOC or a court). In addition, individuals alleged to have engaged in harassing conduct may not retaliate against employees who assert harassment claims. When an employer receives a harassment complaint, the alleged harasser should be warned against any kind of retaliatory, coercive, or threatening conduct toward the alleged harassment victim.

COMPLIANCE FACT

A finding of unlawful harassing conduct is not required for a related retaliation claim to prevail.

Wage-and-Hour Issues

Fair Labor Standards Act

Q 34.14 What minimum wage and overtime requirements apply generally to employees?

The Fair Labor Standards Act (FLSA)[10] requires that employers pay a specified minimum wage and overtime pay for hours in excess of forty hours per work week to employees who are not otherwise "exempt" from the requirements. Overtime must be paid at the rate of one and one-half times the employee's "regular" hourly rate. In computing the "regular" hourly rate, most forms of pay beyond the employee's straight hourly rate (for example, most types of bonuses, shift differentials, premiums, and other cash payments) must be considered.

Although the minimum wage requirement is specified in terms of an hourly rate, the FLSA does not require that non-exempt employees (those subject to the minimum wage and overtime requirements) be paid only on an hourly basis. Certain types of salary and piece-rate pay plans are acceptable if, when reduced to an hourly rate, they provide pay that is at or above the specified minimum rate.

Employees cannot waive their rights to minimum or overtime wages.

COMPLIANCE FACT

The required minimum wage was raised from $6.55 per hour to $7.25 as of July 24, 2009.

Q 34.14.1 Which employees and employers are subject to the minimum wage and overtime requirements?

All employees that are engaged in interstate commerce and that are not otherwise subject to an exemption—by virtue of either the type of industry in which they work or the type of job they perform—are subject to the FLSA's minimum wage and overtime requirements.

Although the FLSA has a complex exemption scheme, most employers engaged in interstate commerce are, for some or all of their employees, subject to its requirements.

FLSA Exemptions

Q 34.14.2 Who is exempt from the minimum wage and overtime requirements?

Lines of business in which there are full or partial exemptions from FLSA requirements include transportation, bulk oil distribution, domestic service, forestry, and agriculture. Employers operating in these industries should carefully determine the extent to which they may be exempt from FLSA requirements before assuming that any exemption applies.

The most common exemptions, which are from both the minimum wage and the overtime requirements, extend to "white collar" workers such as executives, administrators, and professionals. Specific rules apply in determining whether an exemption applies, and the exemption determination must be carefully made by personnel who are experienced and knowledgeable in such matters.

> **TIP:** The misapplication and overuse of minimum wage and overtime exemptions is the most common source of claims, investigations, backpay liability, and other penalties and losses under the FLSA. Employers should use great care in making exempt/nonexempt classifications under the FLSA.

Q 34.14.3 What are the rules for application of the "white-collar" exemptions?

Two sets of requirements must be met for an employee to qualify for one of the "white collar" exemptions. First, the employee must perform duties that qualify under the rules for the exemption. Second, the employee must be paid on a "salary basis," as discussed more fully in the question below.

To qualify as an exempt "executive," the employee's primary duty must be the management and supervision of two or more full-time equivalent employees in a discrete, recognized unit of the business.

An exempt "administrative" employee is one whose primary duties involve (i) non-manual work that is directly related to the management or general business operations of the employer or the employer's customers, and (ii) the exercise of discretion and independent judgment with respect to matters of significance.

To qualify as an exempt "professional," the employee's primary duties must (i) require the use of advanced knowledge in a field of science or learning customarily acquired through a prolonged course of specialized education and instruction, and (ii) be primarily intellectual in character and require the consistent exercise of discretion and judgment. Neither job titles nor written job descriptions should be relied upon in making exemption determinations. While those items may be helpful, the most important determinant of whether an employee is exempt under one of the "white collar" exemptions is what the employee actually spends his or her work time doing. The employee's day-to-day duties must be carefully examined.

Q 34.14.4 How must exempt employees be paid to ensure that they are paid on a "salary basis," as required for their exempt status?

In addition to meeting the specified duties requirements, an employee must be paid on a "salary basis" to qualify for one of the white collar exemptions. "Salary basis" pay means that the employee is paid a predetermined salary of at least $455 per week that is not subject to any deductions or variations, except in the very limited circumstances permitted under FLSA regulations. For example, the salary may not be subject to deductions or variations based on the quality or quantity of the employee's work, partial day absences, absences occasioned by the employer (for example, absences caused by an employer shutting down operations for a day due to low demand for its goods or services), or absences for jury or witness duty.

In general, if the exempt employee works any portion of a work day, he or she must be paid the full salary attributable to that work day. Similarly, if the employee works any time during the week, he or she must be paid the predetermined salary for the entire week unless one of the limited exceptions for making full-day deductions applies. Full-day absences initiated by the employee for purely personal reasons, and full-day absences for personal sickness or disability that are not covered by a bona fide sickness or disability leave policy because the terms of the policy do not extend paid leave for the absence, are generally the only types of absences for which full-day deductions are permitted.

Merely paying a salary without strict adherence to the various technical rules that govern "salary basis" pay does not satisfy the FLSA requirements. Moreover, even policies or practices that make the salary subject to permissible deductions can, in some instances, result in a finding that the "salary basis" requirements have not been met, which in turn results in loss of the exemption.

Employers should carefully examine their policies and practices pertaining to pay and leave charging for exempt employees to ensure that the salary basis pay requirements are being satisfied.

Q 34.14.5 Who qualifies for the "computer-related professionals" exemption?

The FLSA provides a narrow exemption for certain computer-related professionals. The exemption applies only to computer systems analysts, computer programmers, software engineers, and other highly skilled workers in the computer field who have extensive expertise and involvement with software-related functions. Employees who deal principally with computer hardware or who merely use computers in performing other functions do not qualify for the exemption.

To qualify for the exemption, a computer-related professional must be engaged in: the application of systems analysis techniques and procedures, including consulting with users to determine hardware, software, or system design specifications; designing, developing, documenting, analyzing, creating, testing, or modifying computer systems or programs, including prototypes based on and related to user or system design specifications; designing, documenting, testing, creating, or modifying computer programs related to machine operating systems; or any combination of the above duties that requires the same level of skills.

Employees who meet the requirements must either be paid on a salary basis, as described in response to the prior question, or be paid a rate of at least $27.63 per hour.

Q 34.14.6 Can "compensatory time" be provided in lieu of overtime pay?

Except in one limited circumstance, "compensatory time" or "time off" may never be used as a substitute for overtime pay. Under rulings of the U.S. Department of Labor's Wage Hour Administrator, the sole exception permitting use of compensatory time applies when (a) time off is granted during *the same pay period* in which the overtime was worked, and (b) the time off is granted at the rate of one and one-half hours for each hour of overtime worked. Thus, if an employee works forty-five hours in the first week of a two-week pay period, the employee could be given 7.5 hours of compensatory time (working only 32.5 hours of the normal forty-hour work week) in the second week of that same pay period in lieu of overtime pay for the five hours of overtime in the first week. If the overtime were worked in the second week of the pay period, compensatory time in the following week would not be an acceptable substitute for overtime pay because that following week is in a different pay period than the one in which the overtime was worked.

Working Hours

Q 34.14.7 What are compensable hours of work?

The FLSA imposes numerous technical requirements for determining what are "hours of work" for purposes of the minimum wage and overtime requirements. In general, all time during which the employee is performing any services for the employer, is engaged to wait to perform services and is not otherwise free to use the time predominantly for his or her own benefit, or is required by the employer to commit to work-related activities (for example, a mandatory training class) is compensable work time. Time worked at home is also compensable.

Employees cannot be required to work "off the clock" or to underreport their time. Such practices, even if committed at the direction of lower-level supervisors contrary to higher-management directives, are a violation of the FLSA.

A variety of technical rules apply to travel time, training time, on-call time, sleeping time (for jobs where extended presence on the employer's premises is required), waiting time, and other activities.

Employers should examine their employees' work and timekeeping practices carefully to ensure that all compensable time is captured on time records.

Compliance Policies

Q 34.14.8 What policies should be adopted to assure compliance with wage/hour laws?

Employers should ensure that they pay the required hourly rates for nonexempt employees and the required minimum salaries for exempt employees. In addition, employers should adopt policies dealing with the appropriate exempt/nonexempt classification of employees, overtime pay, recognition and recording of work time, and other requirements based on a full examination of FLSA requirements.

The FLSA also requires employers to keep accurate records as to hours worked by "non-exempt" employees. Appropriate time-charging and record-keeping policies and practices should be implemented to satisfy these requirements.

Q 34.14.9 What notice requirements are imposed by wage/hour laws?

Employers must post notices prescribed by the U.S. Department of Labor to inform employees of the applicable minimum wage, overtime requirements, and other rights and employer obligations under the FLSA.

Q 34.14.10 What other requirements should be considered?

The FLSA severely limits jobs, tasks, days, and hours that legally can be worked by employees younger than eighteen years of age.

In addition, employers should note that many states and some localities have laws that require the payment of minimum and overtime wages higher than those specified by the FLSA. Employers must comply with those stricter laws; the FLSA establishes a floor, not a ceiling, on such wages.

Like most employment-related statutes, the FLSA prohibits employer retaliation against employees who oppose, complain about, or participate in investigations of suspected minimum wage, overtime, or other FLSA violations. Such activity is protected whether it is within the employer's operations or external (with the Department of Labor).

Benefits

ERISA

Q 34.15 What types of benefit programs are subject to federal regulation?

The Employee Retirement Income Security Act (ERISA)[11] regulates both pension plans and certain welfare benefit plans, such as group health and disability insurance plans. Any benefit plan that is funded by either payments to a trust fund or set-aside account, or to a third-party benefits provider/administrator, should be examined to determine if it is covered by ERISA.

Q 34.15.1 What does ERISA generally require?

ERISA requires employers to provide various disclosures and notices to employees, comply with their pension/benefit plans as announced to the employees, manage their plans in a responsible manner, and not discriminate with respect to pension plan eligibility and benefits.

ERISA also sets minimum standards to ensure that employee benefit plans are established and maintained in a fair and financially sound manner.

One of the most important requirements for employers is ERISA's imposition of fiduciary obligations on employer plan sponsors. This means that employers who manage and control plan funds must manage them for the exclusive benefit of the participants and beneficiaries, administer the plans in a prudent manner, and avoid conflicts of interest. It also requires employers to fund the plans and benefits in accordance with both the law and the plans' terms.

Q 34.15.2 What are the reporting requirements associated with employee benefit plans?

Employers with ERISA-covered plans must file a variety of reports with, and make various disclosures to, various federal agencies (primarily the IRS and the Department of Labor's Pension and Welfare Benefits Administration). Numerous reporting and disclosure requirements also apply with respect to participants and beneficiaries of ERISA plans.

HIPAA

Q 34.16 What are the HIPAA requirements?

The Health Insurance Portability and Accountability Act (HIPAA)[12] imposes a variety of requirements on employer-sponsored health insurance plans. HIPAA provides for improved portability of health insurance coverage when employees change employers, sets limits on "preexisting condition" exclusions from group medical coverage, and prohibits discrimination against employees in enrollment based on health-related factors or because they have made health insurance claims.

HIPAA also regulates the use and disclosure of "individually identifiable health information." Such medical information can only be disclosed and used in specific circumstances, and even then only as minimally necessary. HIPAA requires that most employers develop policies concerning the collection, handling, disclosure, use, and safeguarding of employee medical information and provide training to employees who will administer the policies.

Family/Medical Leave

The Family and Medical Leave Act

Q 34.17 What are an employer's obligations regarding family and medical leave?

The Family and Medical Leave Act (FMLA)[13] requires that, in various circumstances, an employer must provide up to twelve weeks of unpaid leave annually to certain qualifying employees. The employer must continue the employee's medical benefits during

FMLA leave and must reinstate the employee to his or her job (or a substantially equivalent one) upon completion of the leave. The FMLA also requires that various notices be posted, that various disclosures be given to employees, and that employers keep records of employee use of FMLA leave.

Eligibility

Q 34.17.1 Who qualifies for FMLA leave?

FMLA leave is available to individuals who have been employed for at least twelve months and worked at least 1,250 hours during the previous twelve months.

Q 34.17.2 When is FMLA leave available?

FMLA leave is available for any one or more of the following:

- an employee's serious medical condition that causes him or her to miss to work;
- a serious medical condition afflicting the employee's spouse, child, or parent;
- the birth or care of a new child;
- the placement with the employee of a child for adoption or foster care;
- certain "qualifying exigencies" related to military service of the employee or of a family member; or
- certain qualifying circumstances requiring care of a family member injured in military service or suffering from a condition aggravated by military service.

The FMLA regards a "spouse" as a legal or common law spouse and not a "domestic partner" or "significant other." A "parent" for FMLA purposes is a biological parent and anyone *in loco parentis* when the employee was a minor; "parent" does not include parents-in-law.

"Serious Medical Condition"

Q 34.17.3 What qualifies as a "serious medical condition" under the FMLA?

The FMLA defines a "serious medical condition" as one that:

- requires in-patient care at a medical facility; or
- continuing treatment by a healthcare provider (that is, incapacity for three or more consecutive calendar days, or subsequent treatment of the same condition that involves treatment two or more times by a healthcare provider, or continuing treatment by the healthcare provider that involves prescription medications or therapy with special equipment).

Q 34.17.4 Must a "serious medical condition" also qualify as a "disability" under the ADA?

A "serious medical condition" for FMLA purposes may or may not qualify as a "disability" under the Americans with Disabilities Act. For example, the medical condition may be a short-term condition from which the employee will fully recover. In such a case, FMLA leave may be required, while a "reasonable accommodation" is not required under the ADA.

Parental Leaves

Q 34.17.5 Is a leave for the birth or adoption of a child only permitted for the mother?

No. The FMLA requires that parental leave be given to both female *and* male employees who request it in connection with the birth or adoption of a child. Thus, a new father may take leave to care for a newborn baby even though his non-employee wife is also at home with the baby. If both parents are employed by the same employer, their total leave time for a birth or adoption is limited to twelve weeks. (For serious medical conditions, however, they each are entitled to twelve weeks.)

Notice/Application Requirements

Q 34.17.6 How does an employee request FMLA leave?

FMLA leave can be sought informally. The employee need not specifically mention the FMLA or provide a doctor's note when first asking for time off. The request can be made to a front-line supervisor; the FMLA does not require that the leave requests be made to a human resources department.

Q 34.17.7 Are there restrictions on how FMLA leave time may be taken?

An employee may use his or her twelve-week allotment of FMLA leave either in a single block or, in some instances, intermittently. If the leave is necessitated by a serious medical condition of the employee or a family member, the employee is entitled to take the leave intermittently, subject to the requirement that the employee schedule any planned treatments so as not to unduly disrupt the employer's operations. If the leave is sought in connection with the birth or adoption of a child, it may be taken intermittently only with the employer's consent.

An employee who is entitled to intermittent leave may use the leave in increments as small as one hour or may request a reduced leave schedule (such as working only half-days or working only three days per week). The total hours and days used are aggregated and counted against the twelve-week entitlement—for example, if an employee normally scheduled to work five days per week must take FMLA leave for two days every week to get treatment of a serious medical condition, the employee could continue on such intermittent FMLA leave for up to thirty weeks.

Q 34.17.8 What notice and medical documentation are required for FMLA leave?

An employee usually must give thirty days' notice of a planned FMLA leave. If such notice is not possible, the employee must give notice that is reasonable under the circumstances. Employers normally must respond to requests for FMLA leave within two business days and must designate the leave as "FMLA" if it is going to be counted against the employee's twelve-week annual entitlement.

An employer may require an employee requesting FMLA leave to provide medical certification supporting the need for leave for a serious medical condition of the employee or a family member. An employer may also require periodic recertifications and reports during the leave about the employee's status and intent to return to work.

Pay and Benefits During Leave

Q 34.17.9 What are the requirements pertaining to pay during FMLA leave?

FMLA leave is unpaid. There is no requirement to provide any wages or salary for the employee's time while on FMLA leave.

Employees may choose to use accrued paid leave during FMLA leave that is taken for a reason that qualifies under the employer's applicable paid leave program. In addition, and subject to certain exceptions, an employer may require that an employee who qualifies for FMLA leave use accrued paid leave during the FMLA period and count that paid leave time against the twelve-week FMLA leave allotment.

Q 34.17.10 What are the requirements pertaining to benefits during FMLA leave?

Group medical insurance coverage must be continued during an employee's FMLA leave period on the same terms and conditions as before the commencement of the leave. If the employer normally pays all premiums for the coverage, those premium payments must be made during the FMLA leave. If a portion of the premiums is normally deducted from the employee's pay, the employee can be required to pay that same amount during the leave.

Returning from Leave

Q 34.17.11 What are an employer's obligations to an employee returning from FMLA leave?

An employee returning from FMLA leave must be reinstated to the same job he or she held before the leave or to a substantially equivalent job. A job is "substantially equivalent" if it involves similar job duties and responsibilities on the same shift and has equivalent pay and benefits.

The reinstatement requirement does not apply if the employee would otherwise have been discharged for reasons unrelated to the FMLA leave—for example, a reduction in force that would have eliminated the employee's job. Certain individuals who qualify as a "key employee" as defined under the FMLA are not entitled to reinstatement if they are informed of their "key employee" status before their FMLA leave commences.

An employee's use of FMLA leave cannot result in the loss of any employment benefits that were earned before the leave, nor can FMLA leave be counted against an employee under a "no-fault" attendance program.

Military Caregiver Leave

Q 34.17.12 What leave rights does an employee caring for a sick or injured service member have?

Subject to certain other special rules that may apply, an employee caring for a family member injured in, or suffering from a condition aggravated by, military service may take up to twenty-six weeks of unpaid leave.

Compliance Programs

Q 34.18 What FMLA policies should employers adopt?

Employers should adopt written policies that set forth employee FMLA rights, the employer's procedures for implementing FMLA requirements, and related issues.

The FMLA also requires that employers display certain posters informing employees of their FMLA rights and how to file claims if they believe their FMLA rights have been denied or violated.

A compliance program should also ensure that employers do not treat employees differently because they have sought or used FMLA leave. Retaliation against employees who oppose or complain of suspected FMLA violations, or who participate in investigations of

FMLA violations, is prohibited, regardless of whether the complaint or participation is inside the employer's operations or external (with the Department of Labor).

Military Leave

Uniformed Services Employment and Reemployment Rights Act

Q 34.19   What statute governs military leave?

The Uniformed Services Employment and Reemployment Rights Act (USERRA)[14] requires an employer to give employees unpaid leave to serve in the Army, Navy, Marines, Air Force, Coast Guard, Public Health Service, Air or Army National Guard, or Reserves, and to reinstate employees to work upon return from such leave. These requirements apply regardless of whether the employee's military service is voluntary or compulsory. USERRA also prohibits employer discrimination against job applicants or employees based on their military service.

Employers must post notices informing employees of their rights under USERRA.

Notice Requirements

Q 34.19.1   What notice requirements does the USERRA impose?

Employees must give reasonable notice of their need for military leave. In addition, various notice periods are prescribed for employees to give notice to their employers that they are released from military service and ready to return; the length of the "return to work" notice depends on the length of the leave.

Pay and Benefits During Leave

Q 34.19.2   How must pay and benefits be handled for employees on military leave?

USERRA does not require that an employee be paid while on military leave, but it does require that the employee be given the same benefits (if any) as are provided to employees on other types of leaves. Employees on military leave are entitled to continuation of group medical insurance benefits (similar to COBRA, discussed below).

Returning from Leave

Q 34.19.3 What requirements apply to reinstatement of employees returning from military leave?

USERRA requires that an employee returning from military service be reinstated to the position that he or she would have held if the military duty had not occurred, for up to five years after the leave began. If the employee has been on leave for more than ninety days, the employer may return the employee to a different position for which he or she is qualified if the position has the same seniority, status, and pay as the position the employee would have held had there been no leave. An employer is relieved of the reinstatement obligation only in very limited circumstances—for example, if the employee would have been released in a reduction-in-force that occurred during the leave.

Reinstated employees may not be discharged except for "cause" for various periods of time after their return (depending on the length of the military service).

Medical Insurance Coverage

COBRA

Q 34.20 What statute governs employees' medical insurance?

The Consolidated Omnibus Budget Reconciliation Act (COBRA)[15] requires that an employer who sponsors a group health insurance plan provide covered employees and their dependents with the option of continuing their medical insurance (at the employee's own expense) after specified "qualifying events" that would otherwise cause a loss of coverage. A qualified employee or dependent may elect continuation coverage for up to eighteen months in most cases, but longer in some circumstances such as a loss of coverage due to disability or divorce.

Q 34.20.1 What are "qualifying events" under COBRA?

The COBRA right to continue health insurance coverage is triggered by the occurrence of any of the following "qualifying events":

- termination of the covered employee's employment (except for discharge for gross misconduct);
- reduction in the covered employee's work hours that results in a loss of medical insurance coverage;
- divorce or legal separation of the covered employee causing loss of coverage for a non-employee spouse or dependents; and
- death of the covered employee.

Q 34.20.2 What are the notice requirements under COBRA?

COBRA imposes a variety of disclosure and notice requirements on employers. The most important of these requirements is that, following the occurrence of a "qualifying event," the employer must issue to the affected employee and dependents a detailed written notice that describes COBRA's health insurance coverage continuation rights and the procedures and deadlines for exercising those rights.

Plant Shutdowns and Mass Layoffs

Worker Adjustment Retraining and Notification Act

Q 34.21 What are the notice requirements for plant closings and layoffs?

The Worker Adjustment Retraining and Notification Act (WARN)[16] requires that an employer give sixty days' written notice of a "plant closing" or "mass layoff" at a single site of employment.

Q 34.21.1 What events trigger WARN requirements?

Either a plant closing or a mass layoff triggers WARN's notice requirements. A "plant closing" is either the closure of the entire site of employment or the cessation of discrete operations resulting in a loss of employment for at least fifty employees. A "mass layoff" occurs if 500 employees are released from a single site or if one-third of the employees at the site—but at least fifty employees—are released.

Significantly, the fifty-employee minimum that triggers the notice requirement can be met by the aggregation of discrete employment losses over any ninety-day period for related reasons. Thus, an employer making phased reductions in force must, at the time of each employment loss action, look back ninety days and ahead ninety days to determine if the fifty-employee threshold has been or will be met. If the threshold is or will be satisfied, then the sixty-day notice must be given.

Q 34.21.2 What notices must be given if a WARN trigger event occurs?

The sixty-day notice must be given to affected employees, any union that represents the employees, and certain state and local government agencies ("dislocated worker units"). The notice must be in writing; its required content varies to some extent for each of the required recipients of the notice.

Q 34.21.3 When must the notices be given?

The notice must be given a minimum of sixty days prior to the employment loss for each employee. The sixty-day period is measured on an employee-by-employee basis, such that each individual employee must receive at least sixty days' notice of the date of his or her employment loss.

Polygraphs

Employee Polygraph Protection Act

Q 34.22 When may polygraphs be used for employment-related purposes?

The Employee Polygraph Protection Act (EPPA)[17] generally prohibits employer use of polygraphs (defined broadly to include a wide array of electro-mechanical devices used to detect lying) with job applicants and employees. Polygraphs may be used only in very limited circumstances, such as certain instances of suspected employee theft. As a practical matter, there is almost no use of polygraphs by private-sector employers due to the tight restrictions that EPPA imposes.

Q 34.22.1 What limitations apply to the use of polygraphs?

In those very limited situations when a polygraph may be used, EPPA requires that prior to the polygraph examination the employer provide extensive and specific disclosures to the person to be tested about the reasons for and nature and content of the examination. In addition, there are extensive qualification requirements for the polygraph examiner and detailed procedural prescriptions for the examination.

In addition, EPPA prohibits employers from threatening employees or applicants with the use of a polygraph, regardless of whether a polygraph examination is ever actually administered.

Unions

National Labor Relations Act

Q 34.23 What employee activity is protected under unionization?

The National Labor Relations Act (NLRA)[18] guarantees employee rights to organize and participate in a union, to engage in group activities for mutual aid and protection, to bargain collectively with the employer about terms and conditions of employment, and to strike. The broad term that encompasses this protected conduct is "concerted activity." Employees also have the right to refrain from engaging in concerted activity.

Subject to a variety of arcane and fact-specific limitations, the employer must generally permit employees to engage (or refrain from engaging) in such activity. The NLRA prohibits employer discrimination based on union (or anti-union) affiliations and activities, as well as interference with employees' exercise of their rights under the NLRA.

Q 34.23.1 What legal obligations apply when employees try to join or form a union?

The process by which employees may establish a union is highly regulated through a large body of both substantive and procedural legal regulation formulated and administered primarily by the National Labor Relations Board. While an employer has the right to communicate its views on unionization, that right is not unfettered and must be exercised with careful attention to the applicable legal requirements.

Q 34.23.2 What are the compliance implications of employees unionizing?

If employees form a union that is properly "certified" by the National Labor Relations Board, or in some instances properly recognized by the employer following a showing that a majority of the employees support the union, then the employer must deal with the union as the employees' exclusive representative. The employer must bargain with the union concerning all terms and conditions of employment affecting the employees. Direct dealing with individual employees on such terms and conditions is strictly limited.

Q 34.23.3 What are the compliance implications of a collective bargaining agreement?

Once a union is in place, a collective bargaining agreement is negotiated between the employer and the union to memorialize the terms and conditions of employment on which the parties have agreed for the employees represented by the union. Such agreements typically specify the wages, hours, and other working conditions of the employees in considerable detail. The employer must abide by the terms of the agreement for its duration, and failure to do so can result in arbitration of grievances and/or findings of "unfair labor practices" by the National Labor Relations Board.

Government Contracting

Q 34.24 What laws govern employment issues with government contractors?

Executive Order 11246 ("E.O. 11246"), the Rehabilitation Act of 1973,[19] the Vietnam Veterans Readjustment Assistance Act,[20] and a variety of other laws apply to employers who contract with the federal government, whether as a prime contractor or subcontractor. These laws prohibit discrimination against applicants or employees based on race, color, sex, national origin, religion, disability, and Vietnam-era or special disabled veteran status.

In addition, E.O. 11246 requires covered employers to engage in a self-analysis to identify any "under-utilization" of women or minorities in the workforce—that is, statistical workforce analysis to determine whether fewer women and minorities exist in a job group than would be reasonably expected in light of the availability of qualified workers in the job market.

Affirmative Action Plans

Q 34.24.1 How must employers comply with requirements regarding identifying under-utilization of women or minorities?

E.O. 11246 also requires each covered federal contractor to develop and implement a detailed affirmative action plan (AAP)—a set of specific and results-oriented procedures to remedy any under-utilization or to preserve the existing situation if there is no under-utilization. The AAP must include goals, timetables, and plans for ensuring the diversity of the workforce and must address the employer's efforts to hire, promote, and fairly compensate women, minorities, Vietnam-era veterans, and disabled persons. Employers must create and retain certain documents concerning implementation of the AAP and may periodically be audited by the Department of Labor's Office of Federal Contract Compliance Programs to assess their efforts.

There are numerous highly technical requirements that apply to AAPs and the related requirements. Employers doing business with the federal government should develop a good understanding of those requirements to ensure compliance.

Wages and Benefits

Q 34.24.2 What types of prevailing wage requirements might apply?

The Service Contract Act of 1965,[21] Davis-Bacon Act,[22] Walsh-Healey Public Contracts Act,[23] and a variety of other statutes require employers who contract with the federal government to pay certain specified "prevailing" wages and benefits to their employees. These requirements are usually referred to in the employer's contract with the government, but in some instances they may apply even if the contract fails to contain any such reference. Federal contractors should assess their contracts to determine if they implicate such prevailing wage requirements and should ensure that the various requirements are being satisfied.

Labor and Employment Law

Notes

1. The fact that only an overview is provided should not, however, be viewed as minimizing the importance of compliance in this area. There is probably no area of legal compliance that arises more frequently in the day-to-day operation of a business than labor and employment compliance, and for most businesses employment-related actions (and inaction) are one of their most frequent sources of legal claims. Whether these claims take the form of a lawsuit, an administrative charge, or a governmental investigation, they have high potential to create significant costs, sizeable liabilities, and bad publicity that can seriously damage an employer's public image. It is only because of the sheer breadth of labor/employment regulation that a fuller discussion is not possible here.

2. For example, many state statutes and local ordinances extend nondiscrimination laws to characteristics such as sexual orientation, marital status, or personal appearance that are not protected by federal statutes. Likewise, many state minimum wage statutes and local "living wage" or "prevailing wage" ordinances guarantee higher minimum wages or overtime pay requirements than federal law provides.

3. 29 U.S.C. § 1802 *et seq.*
4. 15 U.S.C. § 1681 *et seq.*
5. 42 U.S.C. § 2000e *et seq.*
6. 42 U.S.C. § 2000e(k) *et seq.*
7. 29 U.S.C. § 621 *et seq.*
8. 29 U.S.C. § 706 *et seq.*
9. 29 U.S.C. § 201 *et seq.*
10. *Id.*
11. 29 U.S.C. § 1001 *et seq.*
12. 42 U.S.C. § 201 *et seq.* See chapter 24 for more detailed coverage of HIPAA compliance issues.
13. 29 U.S.C. § 2601 *et seq.*
14. 38 U.S.C. § 4301 *et seq.*
15. 26 U.S.C. § 162 *et seq.*
16. 29 U.S.C. § 2101 *et seq.*
17. *Id.*
18. 29 U.S.C. § 151 *et seq.*
19. 29 U.S.C. § 791 *et seq.*
20. 38 U.S.C. § 4212 *et seq.*
21. 41 U.S.C. § 351 *et seq.*
22. 40 U.S.C. § 3141 *et seq.*
23. 41 U.S.C. § 35 *et seq.*

35

Consumer Product Safety Act

Charles E. Joern, Jr.

Compliance with consumer product safety laws is not optional. Consumer product safety regulations are both complex and wide-ranging. Failure to comply exposes businesses to significant civil penalties of up to $15 million for a related series of violations and, for certain violations, criminal penalties of up to five years' imprisonment. In addition to civil and criminal penalties, failure to comply with the Consumer Product Safety Act (CPSA) can result in nationwide recalls of non-compliant consumer products, which can be extremely expensive and potentially devastating to businesses.

Businesses must know and understand their products as well as the ongoing changes to the CPSA and its implementation. Companies should have a basic, enterprise-wide compliance structure that is flexible enough to accommodate change on an ongoing basis. Compliance with the CPSA requires continuous and diligent efforts by all regulated businesses as well as the assistance of knowledgeable counsel.

To that end, this chapter looks first at the regulatory framework and jurisdiction of consumer product regulation in the United States, before examining the requirements that manufacturers, importers, private labelers, distributors, and retailers of consumer products must comply with, including compliance related to testing and certification of products, reporting non-compliant, defective, and hazardous products, and recalls.

Regulatory Framework 1301
    Jurisdiction 1301
    Business Application 1302
    Statutes 1302
Consumer Product Safety Compliance 1302
    Consequences of Non-Compliance 1302
    Prohibited Acts 1303
    CPSA Requirements 1304
    Product Safety Standards 1305
    Unregulated Products 1307
    Voluntary Standards 1307
    Children's Products 1308
Testing and Certification 1309
    Reasonable Testing Program 1310
    Stay of Enforcement 1311
Reporting Requirements 1312
    Substantial Product Hazard 1313
Recalls 1315
    Mandatory and Voluntary Recalls 1315
    Fast-Track Recalls 1316
    Requirements for Recall Notices 1316
Publicly Available Consumer Product Safety Information
    Database 1317
Future Outlook 1318

Regulatory Framework

Jurisdiction

Q 35.1   How are consumer products regulated in the United States?

The Consumer Product Safety Commission ("Commission") enforces consumer protection laws involving over 15,000 different types of consumer products. The Commission is an independent federal regulatory agency created by Congress in 1972 and charged with protecting the public "against unreasonable risks of injury associated with consumer products."[1]

Q 35.2   What is a "consumer product" for regulatory purposes?

A consumer product is generally any article or component part that is produced or distributed for sale to a consumer for use in or around a household, residence, school, in recreation, or otherwise. Examples of consumer products include, among others:

toys	clothes	jewelry
household appliances	furniture	books
computers	sporting goods	cookware
household chemicals	power tools	children's products

The following items are not consumer products:

tobacco products	motor vehicles or motor vehicle equipment[2]
pesticides	firearms and ammunition
aircraft	boats
drugs	medical devices
cosmetics	food

In addition, consumer products do not include any article not customarily produced, distributed, used or consumed by consumers.[3]

Business Application

Q 35.3 What businesses are covered by consumer product safety laws?

Manufacturers, importers, private labelers, distributors, and retailers of consumer products are all regulated by consumer product safety laws. The Commission has jurisdiction over all such businesses regardless of their size or number of employees. Resellers of used products, such as thrift shops, are also covered.

Statutes

Q 35.4 What consumer product safety laws does the Commission enforce?

The primary governing statute is the Consumer Product Safety Act of 1972 (CPSA) as significantly revised by the Consumer Product Safety Improvement Act of 2008 (CPSIA).[4] In addition to the CPSA, the Commission enforces provisions of the following acts:

- Federal Hazardous Substances Act (FHSA)[5]
- Flammable Fabrics Act (FFA)[6]
- Poison Prevention Packaging Act (PPPA)[7]
- Refrigerator Safety Act (RSA)[8]
- Virginia Graeme Baker Pool and Spa Safety Act[9]
- Children's Gasoline Burn Prevention Act[10]

Consumer Product Safety Compliance

Consequences of Non-Compliance

Q 35.5 How important is consumer product safety law compliance?

Compliance with consumer product safety laws is not optional. Consumer product safety regulations are both complex and wide-ranging. Failure to comply exposes businesses to significant civil penalties of up to $15 million for a related series of violations.[11] Further, individual directors, officers, and agents of a corporation are subject to criminal penalties of up to five years' imprisonment for knowing and willful violations of the CPSA.[12]

The CPSA also mandates the destruction of non-compliant imports. Imported products that do not comply with the CPSA will be refused admission into the customs territory of the United States and shall be destroyed (unless the Secretary of the Treasury in response to a special application permits the export of the product in lieu of destruction).[13]

In addition to civil and criminal penalties, failure to comply with the CPSA can result in nationwide recalls of non-compliant consumer products. Such recalls can be extremely expensive and potentially devastating to businesses.

Prohibited Acts

Q 35.6 What constitutes a violation under the CPSA?

Businesses have varying obligations under the CPSA, but generally it is unlawful under the CPSA to

> sell, offer for sale, manufacture for sale, distribute in commerce, or import into the United States any consumer product . . . [that violates any] applicable consumer product safety rule under [the Consumer Product Safety Act], or any similar rule, regulation, standard, or ban under any other Act enforced by the Commission.[14]

Other "prohibited acts" include the sale, offer for sale, manufacture for sale, distribution in commerce, or import into the United States of any consumer product that has been recalled in consultation with the Commission, contains a "substantial product hazard" (see Q 35.16), or is a banned hazardous substance under the FHSA. The failure to report non-compliant products to the Commission, the failure to issue a required product certificate, and other acts and omissions enumerated in section 19 of the CPSA are all prohibited acts.[15]

CPSA Requirements

Q 35.7 What requirements must a business meet to comply with the CPSA?

The CPSA is a complex law. Its interpretation and enforcement are evolving and ongoing. The Commission has averaged twenty-six rule-making activities affecting the CPSA each year for 2009, 2010, and proposed for 2011. Application of the CPSA and related rules and regulations as they pertain to specific products requires individual analysis. Generally, however, a business must:

- comply;
- test and certify;
- report.

Q 35.7.1 What does it mean for a business to "comply"?

A company must ensure that the consumer product it manufactures, imports, distributes or sells is in conformity with all applicable consumer product safety rules under the CPSA and any similar rules, regulations, standards, or bans under any other act enforced by the Commission.[16]

Q 35.7.2 What are a business's specific testing and certification obligations?

In most circumstances businesses are obligated to certify, based on an appropriate testing program, that their product meets each applicable consumer product safety rule under the CPSA or similar rule, ban, standard, or regulation under any other act enforced by the Commission.[17] In February 2011, however, the Commission announced a revision of the terms of an existing stay of enforcement on certain testing and certification provisions until December 31, 2011.[18] (See Q 35.14, below, discussing the application of the revised stay.)

Q 35.7.3 What are a business's reporting obligations?

If a manufacturer, distributor, or retailer of a consumer product obtains information that reasonably supports the conclusion that a product:

(1) fails to comply with an applicable consumer product safety rule (or voluntary standard the Commission relied on to develop a rule);
(2) fails to comply with any other rule, regulation, standard, or ban under the CPSA or other act enforced by the Commission;
(3) contains a defect that could create a substantial product hazard; or
(4) creates an unreasonable risk of serious injury or death,

then the manufacturer, distributor, or retailer must "immediately" inform the Commission of such a problem pursuant to section 15(b) of the CPSA.[19]

Product Safety Standards

Q 35.8 Does the Commission certify that products comply with applicable product safety standards?

No. The Commission will not pre-approve products as compliant with the applicable standards or rules. The Commission does not have the authority to test or certify products for safety prior to products being sold to consumers. Compliance with applicable product safety laws is a business's own responsibility.

Q 35.9 How does a business know what product safety standards apply to its product?

A business should determine (1) if its production falls within the jurisdiction of the Commission and (2) if so, what specific standards apply.

Q 35.9.1 How do we determine if our product is a "consumer product" under the jurisdiction of the Commission?

Many products are statutorily excluded from regulation by the Commission. The CPSA specifically defines both the term "consumer product" and the products that are excluded from the definition of a consumer product.[20] If a product is not within the Commission's jurisdiction, the business does not have compliance obligations under the

CPSA—but it may have obligations under the other statutes referred to in this section of the CPSA.

In addition, the Commission's jurisdiction does not include false advertising, fraud, or poor product quality not related to safety. The Federal Trade Commission has the responsibility for handling false advertising, fraud, and product quality complaints.

Q 35.9.2 Once we determine that our product is a consumer product, how do we decide what specific standards apply?

Proper and complete identification of what standards apply to individual products is a difficult task that requires a complete understanding of both a company's product and the CPSA itself. In general, some consumer products are subject to specific regulations, while other consumer products are considered "unregulated." "Regulated" products must comply with specific regulations applicable to the CPSA or other acts enforced by the Commission (the FHSA, FFA, PPPA, etc.). Examples of regulated products include cigarette lighters, cribs, power lawn mowers, mattresses, toys, and wearing apparel.

Q 35.9.3 What sources of information can we use to determine what regulations apply to our product?

There are a number of regulations that apply to the CPSA and other acts enforced by the Commission. The Commission's website contains links to regulations for the CPSA and each of the other acts enforced by the Commission.[21] Determining exactly what regulations apply to a particular product requires a detailed analysis of the product and the law. The Commission is aware of the difficulties businesses face in trying to determine how to comply with a complex set of regulations. In addition to the general link to all applicable regulations, the Commission provides a "look-up" table linking specific types of regulated products for which the Commission has issued mandatory safety standards.[22] The table also provides links to miscellaneous documents relevant to regulatory provisions for the listed products.

In February 2011, the Commission issued an updated chart of CPSA requirements and stays of enforcement for testing and certification of both non-children's products and children's products. The chart lists specific rules, bans, and standards for a number of products regulated by the Commission.[23]

Ultimately businesses should consider retaining knowledgeable counsel to assist in determining the regulations applicable to their products under the current law.

Unregulated Products

Q 35.10   What is an "unregulated" product?

If the product is not covered by a specific regulation, but is a consumer product within the jurisdiction of the Commission, the product is nominally considered "unregulated." Unregulated consumer products are still subject to the general product safety obligations, including the obligation to report defective or dangerous products to the Commission (see Q 35.15).

Voluntary Standards

Q 35.11   What are voluntary standards?

Besides mandatory government standards, the CPSA also considers non-governmental "voluntary" standards. These include industry standards issued by private entities such as ANSI, ASTM, and Underwriters Laboratories. Although the Commission does not officially endorse these voluntary standards, failure to meet a voluntary standard could lead to a Commission determination that a particular product contains a "substantial product hazard" (see Q 35.16). Failure to report such a product to the Commission is a "prohibited act" under the CPSA.[24] The converse, however, is not true. Compliance with a voluntary standard does not exempt a firm from an obligation to report a product otherwise reasonably suspected to be defective and dangerous.

Voluntary standards also sometimes form the basis for Commission-adopted regulations and may provide useful compliance guidance. In addition, voluntary standards may assist a business in developing a reasonable testing program required for General Conformity Certification (see Q 35.13).

Children's Products

Q 35.12 Is the Commission's treatment of children's products different from its treatment of non-children's products?

Yes, very much so. The CPSIA was Congress's response to a wave of product recalls in 2007, the most highly publicized of which involved the recalls of imported Chinese-manufactured toys containing lead paint. As a result, many new provisions regulating children's products were added to the CPSA.

When trying to determine what standards apply to a product, it is extremely important to determine whether the product is a children's product or a non-children's product. The CPSA defines a children's product as "a consumer product designed or intended primarily for children 12 years of age or younger." The CPSA then lists four factors to consider in this regard.[25] The Commission recognized that the determination of whether a particular product should be classified as a "children's product" is often difficult. In October 2010, the Commission issued a Final Interpretive Rule designed to provide additional guidance on factors that are considered when evaluating what constitutes a "children's product" under the CPSA.[26] Despite the detailed guidelines, the determination of what is a "children's product" often depends on case-by-case facts unique to each product. A detailed evaluation of the particular product may therefore be necessary to comply with applicable regulations for children's products.

Of the many provisions that regulate children's products, the restrictions on lead content are particularly difficult to comply with. Acceptable total lead-content limits have been progressively lowered under the CPSA. On August 14, 2011, manufacturers, importers, retailers, and distributors of children's products must comply with the new 100-ppm limit for total lead content. The new limit, however, does not apply to inaccessible (internal) parts of children's products or certain component parts of children's electronic devices.[27] Further, newly passed legislation excepts off-highway vehicles (ATVs) as well as bicycles and related products from lead-content limits for children's products. Certain used children's products are also excluded from lead-content regulations. (See Q 35.24.)

Testing and Certification

Q 35.13 What testing and certification requirements apply to our product?

Once a company identifies the product safety rules applicable to its product, that company (if it is a domestic manufacturer or an importer) must certify that the product complies with all such safety rules. The certification must be based on an appropriate testing program and must specify each rule, ban, standard, or regulation applicable to the product.[28]

There are two different types of certifications required by the Commission depending on whether the product is a "children's product" or not:

1. General Conformity Certification (GCC), also called a "supplier's declaration of conformity," is required for all products (other than children's products) that are subject to consumer product safety rules. This type of certification must be based on a test of each product or a "reasonable testing program."[29]
2. A certification based on tests done by third-party laboratories that are recognized and approved by the Commission to perform such certification testing are required for children's products.[30]

Product-testing certifications must "accompany" each product shipment and be "furnished" to each distributor and retailer of the product. Electronic certificates satisfy these requirements if the certificate is uniquely identified and can be accessed via an Internet URL reference reasonably available to authorities and distributors and retailers.[31]

Q 35.13.1 Are all businesses required to issue certifications?

No. Except as otherwise provided in a specific standard, Commission regulations require that only importers and domestic manufacturers provide certification. Retailers and distributors are not required to issue certificates.[32]

Reasonable Testing Program

Q 35.13.2 What is a "reasonable testing program" as required for a General Conformity Certification?

In order to issue a valid GCC, manufacturers/importers must certify that a product, pursuant to a "reasonable testing program, complies with all applicable rules, bans, standards and regulations." As of July 2011, the Commission had not finalized what constitutes a "reasonable testing program." The proposed testing rule, issued in May 2010, contained five essential elements for a "reasonable testing program."[33]

1. *Product specifications.* The consumer product must be described in enough detail so that it can be sufficiently identified and distinguished from the other products made by the manufacturer. The relevant safety rules, standards, etc., must also be included with the product specifications.
2. *Certification testing.* Samples of the product that are identical to the finished product in all material respects must be tested and demonstrate that the product is able to pass the tests prescribed by the standards.
3. *Production testing plan.* A production testing plan must state what tests should be performed and at what frequency, in order to provide a high degree of assurance that products manufactured subsequent to certification will meet all applicable safety standards.
4. *Remedial action plan.* In the event that the testing of product samples yields results that fail to meet applicable standards, a company must have a sufficient plan in place to investigate and address such unacceptable results.
5. *Record keeping.* A reasonable testing program must maintain records of the GCC for each product; each product specification; each certification test (including required information on third-party testing, if applicable); compliance with production testing plan requirements; and details of all remedial actions taken.

Stay of Enforcement

Q 35.14 Currently, do all consumer products have to be tested and certified?

No. In February 2011, the Commission extended the stay of enforcement of certain testing and certification requirements pertaining to total lead content in children's products and certain related products. The stay extends through December 31, 2011.[34] Until that date, products covered by the stay will not require certification. The Commission similarly stayed the enforcement of the testing of youth all-terrain vehicles until November 27, 2011.[35] However, while the enforcement of certain testing and certification requirements has been stayed, it is important to remember that the actual products must still comply with all applicable product safety rules.

Q 35.14.1 The stay is applicable to what products?

Over the last two years, the Commission has several times stayed the enforcement of testing and certification for various products. These have been modified over time. As of July 2011, the following applies to the various stays of enforcement:

(1) A stay of enforcement on testing and certifications of total lead content in children's products is extended until December 31, 2011, at which time the stay will expire.[36]

(2) A stay of enforcement with regard to the lead content in certain parts of youth motorized vehicles that contain those parts is extended until December 31, 2011, at which time the stay will expire.[37]

(3) A stay of enforcement with regard to the lead content in certain parts of bicycles and related products is extended until December 31, 2011, at which time the stay will expire.[38]

(4) A stay of enforcement also remains in effect for children's products subject to safety rules for which third-party testing laboratories requirements have not yet been published.[39]

(5) The December 31, 2011 stay of enforcement is also in effect for compliance testing under mandatory toy safety standards (ASTM F-963) and banned phthalates in children's products.

(6) A stay of enforcement of the testing of youth all-terrain vehicles by third-party laboratories is in effect—subject to certain conditions—until November 27, 2011.[40]
(7) The stay of enforcement does not apply to testing and certification of metal components in children's metal jewelry.[41]
(8) The stay of enforcement also does not apply to testing and certification of lead in paint and surface coatings.[42]
(9) The stay of enforcement is no longer in effect for non-children's products subject to regulations pertaining to vinyl plastic film, carpets/rugs, and clothing textiles. The stay has been lifted as of January 26, 2011. Manufacturers/importers must issue a GCC for those products.[43]

As referenced above at Q 35.9.3, the Commission staff has created a comprehensive chart of CPSA requirements and stays of enforcement. The chart is a good reference source, current as of February 2011.[44]

Q 35.14.2 May a company rely on testing of component parts in order to fulfill compliance requirements?

Yes. The Commission adopted an interim policy in December 2009 that states the circumstances in which component testing is allowed. This policy applies, under stated conditions, to certification of children's products as meeting both lead-paint and lead-content limits.[45] In May 2010, the Commission submitted a notice of proposed rulemaking regarding the conditions and requirements for testing of component parts in consumer products to demonstrate compliance with applicable rules, bans, etc. Under the proposed rule, component-part testing may be sufficient to demonstrate that the finished product complies with applicable consumer product safety rules—if the strict testing requirements set forth in the proposed rule are met.[46]

Reporting Requirements

Q 35.15 What reporting requirements should a business be aware of?

Section 15(b) of the CPSA requires manufacturers, importers, distributors, and retailers to report to the Commission information that reasonably supports the conclusion that a product:

(1) does not comply with a safety rule issued under the CPSA (or voluntary standard that the Commission has relied on for a rulemaking);
(2) does not comply with any other rule, regulation, standard, or ban under the CPSA or any other act enforced by the Commission;
(3) contains a defect that could create a "substantial product hazard"; or
(4) presents an unreasonable risk of serious injury or death.[47]

Q 35.15.1 What type of information can trigger a report?

Any information that a company receives, including product returns, customer complaints, quality control data, lawsuits or other information that indicates a defect, safety rule violation, or unreasonable risk of injury or death can lead to a reporting obligation.

Substantial Product Hazard

Q 35.16 What is a "substantial product hazard"?

Deciding whether a product contains a "substantial product hazard" is a significant determination that may require both forensic engineering and legal analysis. The CPSA defines a "substantial product hazard" as:

(1) a failure to comply with an applicable consumer product safety rule under [the CPSA] or a similar rule, regulation, standard, or ban under any other Act enforced by the Commission that creates a substantial risk of injury to the public, or
(2) a product defect that (because of the pattern of defect, the number of defective products distributed in commerce, the severity of the risk, or otherwise) creates a substantial risk of injury to the public.[48]

The CPSC may also specify by rule that a particular product or class of products contains characteristics that constitute a substantial product hazard. In June and July 2011 the CPSA issued rules determining that two classes of products—hand-held hair dryers without circuit interrupters[49] and children's upper outerwear, in certain sizes, with drawstrings[50]—each contained substantial product hazards. These products are subject to CPSA reporting and recall provisions and shall be refused entry into the United States.[51]

Q 35.17 What should we do if we are uncertain if there is an actual product safety problem with a product?

It is the nearly universal Commission recommendation that companies err on the side of over-reporting. Failure to report can result in significant civil and, in extreme cases, criminal penalties. Businesses should also note that the filing of a report is not an admission of a defective and dangerous product.

Applicable regulations state:

> Subject firms should not delay reporting in order to determine to a certainty the existence of a reportable noncompliance, defect or unreasonable risk. The obligation to report arises upon receipt of information from which one could reasonably conclude the existence of a reportable noncompliance, defect which could create a substantial product hazard, or unreasonable risk of serious injury or death.... A subject firm in its report to the Commission need not admit, or may specifically deny, that the information it submits reasonably supports the conclusion that its consumer product is noncomplying, contains a defect which could create a substantial product hazard within the meaning of section 15(b) of the CPSA, or creates an unreasonable risk of serious injury or death.[52]

Q 35.18 How soon must a company report a problem?

The CPSA requires manufacturers and importers distributors and retailers to "immediately inform the Commission" of reportable problems.[53] While there is some reasonable interpretation to the term "immediately," it is imperative that a company move as rapidly as possible in this regard. The applicable regulations state that the Commission will, under ordinary circumstances, allow a maximum of five business days for information obtained by an official of a firm to reach the chief executive officer, official, or employee responsible for filing a 15(b) report to the Commission.[54] In addition, applicable regulations state that an investigation and evaluation should not take more than ten business days unless a company can demonstrate that a longer period is reasonable.[55]

Q 35.19 What should a firm do to ensure compliance with CPSA reporting obligations?

Businesses should institute a system that captures any information that reasonably suggests a product safety problem may exist. This system should channel such information to appropriate persons in the company for evaluation and reporting if appropriate.

Q 35.19.1 If a lawsuit is filed against my company, do I have to file a report with the Commission?

Section 37 of the CPSA requires that manufacturers report to the Commission any product that is the subject of at least three civil actions "filed in Federal or State court for death or grievous bodily injury [within a twenty-four-month period that] results in either a final settlement involving the manufacturer or a court judgment in favor of the plaintiff. . . ."[56] Depending on the circumstances, a single lawsuit combined with other information may give rise to a reporting obligation under section 15(b).

Q 35.19.2 If I report a suspected problem, will my business have to recall the product?

Not necessarily. Only about half of the section 15(b) reports result in a recall. (This excludes so-called Fast-Track agreed recalls.)

Recalls

Mandatory and Voluntary Recalls

Q 35.20 When does a company have to recall a product?

Recalls may be mandatory or voluntary. Mandatory recalls are ordered by the Commission. They are rare. The vast majority of recalls are voluntary recalls. Voluntary recalls are initiated by companies in conjunction with the Commission. In 2009, 100% of the recalls announced to consumers were voluntary.[57]

Q 35.20.1 Under what circumstances does the Commission decide that a recall is not necessary at all?

Once a company files a report with the Commission under section 15(b), the Commission staff investigates the report to determine if a "Corrective Action Plan" (which may include a recall) is appropriate. In many cases, no Corrective Action Plan is required because the Commission concludes that the reported product does not create a substantial product hazard.

Fast-Track Recalls

Q 35.21 What is a fast-track recall?

A fast-track recall is a Commission-created program in which the company filing a section 15(b) report agrees to voluntarily recall the product within twenty working days of the filing of the report. If the company's proposed Corrective Action Plan is acceptable to the Commission staff, the staff will not investigate the product or make a "preliminary determination" that the reported product is defective and creates a substantial product hazard.

Requirements for Recall Notices

Q 35.22 What information must be included in recall notices?

The Commission approved a rule setting forth the information that must be included in mandatory recall notices. The required information identifies the recalled product, identifies the hazard involved, and indicates what remedy is offered concerning the product. While the rule does not contain voluntary recall notice requirements, it does serve as a guide for drafting such notices.[58]

Publicly Available Consumer Product Safety Information Database

Q 35.23 Is there a database of consumer product safety complaints?

Yes. The Consumer Product Safety Improvement Act of 2008 (CPSIA) required the creation of a new Publicly Available Consumer Product Safety Information Database. The database is a collection of reports of harm relating to consumer products. The reports (or complaints) identify specific manufacturers, importers, or private labelers ("manufacturers") and their products. The database is accessible through the Commission website at www.saferproducts.gov.

The database contains reports of harm that include not only actual injury, but also reports concerning the risk of injury or death relating to the use of consumer products. The database also contains information the Commission obtains from recall notices and additional information the Commission determines is in the public interest.

Q 35.23.1 Does the database affect businesses?

Yes. The database is a source of self-verified complaints that contain claims about the safety of a company's product. Because the database is Internet-based, reports about a company's products are available to consumers and others worldwide. The reports may therefore have significant impact on the public's perception of a company and its products. In addition, reports submitted to the database could (under certain circumstances) give rise to a company self-reporting its own product to the Commission under section 15(b) requirements.

Q 35.23.2 Is a company notified of reports concerning its products?

Yes. If a company registers with the Commission through the specified business portal, the named company will receive prompt electronic notice of reports before they are published in the database.

Q 35.23.3 Can a company submit anything to the database?

Yes. Within strict designated time frames, companies may submit comments that will be published concurrently on the database with the publication of the complaint. Companies may also submit objections concerning material inaccuracies or confidential company information contained in reports, prior to the time the reports are published. In certain situations, the Commission will correct materially inaccurate or confidential reports prior to the report's publication in the database.[59]

Future Outlook

Q 35.24 What aspects of the CPSA are expected to change?

On July 11, 2011, President Obama issued an Executive Order directed to independent regulatory agencies, including the Consumer Product Safety Commission.[60] The Executive Order requires "Retrospective Analyses of Existing Rules" to modify, streamline, expand, or repeal existing regulations so as to make the commission's regulatory program more effective or less burdensome in achieving its regulatory objectives.[61] Whether this Executive Order will result in actual regulatory changes by the politically divided commission remains to be seen.

Several changes are taking place in the CPSA currently. On August 1, 2011, Congress passed H.R. 2715[62] (the Act), which modifies several provisions of the CPSA. On August 12, 2011, President Obama signed H.R. 2715 into law. The Act gives the Commission new authority and discretion in enforcing consumer product safety rules. Changes include the following:

(1) Limitations on lead in children's products:
- The 100 ppm lead-content limit that goes into effect will apply prospectively only to goods manufactured after August 14, 2011.
- Products, product classes, materials, and components may be excepted from lead-content limits if they qualify for a "functional purpose exception."
- Off-highway vehicles (ATVs), as well as bicycles and related products, receive exceptions from lead-content limits.

- Used children's products also receive lead-content exclusions with certain designated exceptions.

(2) Third-party testing requirements:
- The Commission must seek public comment on ways to reduce the cost of third-party testing. The Commission may then enact rules that reduce the testing burdens. If the Commission lacks the authority for such rules, it must notify Congress and seek the necessary authority.
- Small batch manufacturers (less than $1 million in gross revenues) may qualify for alternative testing requirements or even exemptions from third-party testing requirements.
- Ordinary books and printed material and metal components of bicycles are excluded from third-party testing requirements.

(3) Other changes:
- Future revisions to standards for "durable nursery products" (cribs, etc.) will apply only to manufacturers and importers of cribs unless the Commission determines otherwise for health or safety reasons.
- Phthalate limits are excluded for "inaccessible" component parts. Within a year, the Commission must issue a guidance rule on what is considered inaccessible.
- The Commission may exclude products or classes of products from tracking label requirements if the Commission determines it is not practicable to label such children's products.
- The rules for the new public database are modified. If the Commission receives a claim that a report or comment is materially inaccurate, the Commission will delay publication in the database for an additional five days. Other changes encourage—but do not require—the submission of product model or serial numbers of the product named in the database complaint.
- The Act also modifies the Commission's subpoena powers and separately sets a one-year deadline for the Commission to issue rules for ATVs.

The Act makes immediate and tangible changes for certain businesses and products. Beyond that, the Act also gives the Commission new discretionary powers to grant exceptions concerning other businesses and products. In the past, requests for exceptions were often denied because of the rigid provisions of the CPSA. The real and practical effect of this legislation on companies will only be understood when the Commission exercises its new authority.

In the meantime, it is unlikely there will be any other legislative changes to the CPSA in the near future. Regulated businesses must therefore monitor the evolving implementation and enforcement of the CPSA in order to effectively comply with the law.

Notes

1. 15 U.S.C. § 2051(a)(3).
2. For purposes of the Consumer Product Safety Act, the terms "motor vehicles or motor vehicle equipment" are limited to those products "as defined by Sections 102(3) and (4) of the National Traffic and Motor Vehicle Safety Act of 1966, sections 30102(a)(6) and (7) of Title 49." 15 U.S.C. § 2052(a)(5)(C).
3. 15 U.S.C. § 2052(a)(5).
4. 15 U.S.C. § 2051 et seq.
5. 15 U.S.C. § 1261 et seq.
6. 15 U.S.C. § 1191 et seq.
7. 15 U.S.C. § 1471 et seq. The CPSC does not regulate children's drugs. However, the CPSC regulates child-resistant packaging for both adult and children's drugs as required by the PPPA.
8. 15 U.S.C. § 1211 et seq.
9. 15 U.S.C. § 8001 et seq.
10. Children's Gasoline Burn Prevention Act, Pub. L. No. 110-278, 122 Stat. 2602 (2008).
11. 15 U.S.C. § 2069.
12. 15 U.S.C. § 2070.
13. 15 U.S.C. § 2066(e).
14. 15 U.S.C. § 2068(a).
15. *Id.*
16. 15 U.S.C. § 2068.
17. 15 U.S.C. § 2063.
18. Revision of terms of stay of enforcement, 76 Fed. Reg. 6765 (Feb. 8, 2011).
19. 15 U.S.C. § 2064(b).
20. 15 U.S.C. § 2052(a)(5).
21. *See* www.cpsc.gov/businfo/actreg.html.
22. *See* www.cpsc.gov/businfo/reg.html.
23. U.S. Consumer Product Safety Comm'n, Consumer Product Safety Consumer Act: February 2011 Update of CPSIA Requirements and Stays of Enforcement, www.cpsc.gov/ABOUT/Cpsia/reqstay.html.
24. 15 U.S.C. § 2068(a)(4).
25. 15 U.S.C. § 2052(a)(2).
26. Interpretation of "Children's Product," 75 Fed. Reg. 63,067 (Oct. 14, 2010).
27. Press Release No. 11-278, U.S. Consumer Product Safety Comm'n, CPSC Announces New, Lower Limit for Lead Content in Children's Products (July 15, 2011), *available at* www.cpsc.gov/cpscpub/prerel/prhtml11/11278.html.
28. 15 U.S.C. § 2063.

29. 15 U.S.C. § 2063(a)(1)(A).
30. 15 U.S.C. § 2063(a)(2).
31. 16 C.F.R. § 1110.13.
32. 16 C.F.R. § 1110.7.
33. Testing and Labeling Pertaining to Product Certification, 75 Fed. Reg. 28,362 (May 20, 2010).
34. Consumer Product Safety Act: Notice of Commission Action on the Stay of Enforcement of Testing and Certification Requirements, 76 Fed. Reg. 6765 (Feb. 8, 2011).
35. Notice of Stay of Enforcement of Testing and Certification Pertaining to Youth All-Terrain Vehicles, 76 Fed. Reg. 5565 (Feb. 1, 2011).
36. 76 Fed. Reg. 6765, *supra* note 34.
37. *Id.*
38. *Id.*
39. *Id.*
40. 76 Fed. Reg. 5565, *supra* note 35.
41. 76 Fed. Reg. 6765, *supra* note 34.
42. Press Release No. 11-116, U.S. Consumer Product Safety Comm'n, CPSC Extends Stay of Enforcement for Testing and Certification of Lead Content in Children's Products Until December 31, 2011 (Feb. 2, 2011), *available at* www.cpsc.gov/cpscpub/prerel/prhtml11/11116.html.
43. Consumer Product Safety Act: Notice of Commission Action Lifting Stay of Enforcement of Certification Requirements for Certain Non-Children's Products, 75 Fed. Reg. 81,236 (Dec. 27, 2010).
44. U.S. Consumer Product Safety Comm'n, Consumer Product Safety Consumer Act: February 2011 Update of CPSIA Requirements and Stays of Enforcement, www.cpsc.gov/ABOUT/Cpsia/reqstay.html.
45. Interim Enforcement Policy on Component Testing and Certification of Children's Products and Other Consumer Products to the August 14, 2009 Lead Limits, 74 Fed. Reg. 68,593 (Dec. 28, 2009).
46. Conditions and Requirements for Testing Component Parts of Consumer Products, 75 Fed. Reg. 28,208 (May 20, 2010).
47. 15 U.S.C. § 2064(b).
48. 15 U.S.C. § 2064(a).
49. Substantial Product Hazard List: Hand-Supported Hair Dryers, 76 Fed. Reg. 37,636 (June 28, 2011).
50. Substantial Product Hazard List: Children's Upper Outerwear, 76 Fed. Reg. 42,502 (July 19, 2011).
51. 16 C.F.R. § 1120.1–.3.
52. 16 C.F.R. § 1115.12.
53. 15 U.S.C. § 2064(b).
54. 16 C.F.R. § 1115.14(b).
55. 16 C.F.R. § 1115.14(d).
56. 15 U.S.C. § 2084.

57. Press Release No. 10-106, U.S. Consumer Product Safety Commission, CPSC Approves Final Rule on Guidelines for Mandatory Recall Notices, *available at* www.cpsc.gov/cpscpub/prerel/prhtml10/10106.html.

58. Guidelines and requirements for mandatory recall notices, 75 Fed. Reg. 3355 (Jan. 21, 2010).

59. 16 C.F.R. pt. 1102.

60. Improving Regulation and Regulatory Review, Exec. Order No. 13,563, 76 Fed. Reg. 3821 (Jan. 18, 2011).

61. *See* White House, Office of Press Secretary, Executive Order—Regulation and Independent Regulatory Agencies (July 11, 2011), *available at* www.whitehouse.gov/the-press-office/2011/07/11/executive-order-regulation-and-independent-regulatory-agencies.

62. H.R. 2715, 112th Cong. (2011).

Index

(References are to question numbers unless otherwise indicated.)

A

Accounting
    asset valuation methods, 28.38.3
    audit committee, relationship of auditor to, 28.13, 28.13.1
    auditing standards
        documentation of audit. *See* subhead: documentation of audit
        generally, 28.39
        internal audit reports, review of, 28.39.2
        PCAOB auditing standard, 28.41, 28.41.1
        procedures for testing internal controls, 28.39.1
    Committee of Sponsoring Organizations of the Treadway Commission (COSO)
        Enterprise Risk Management—Integrated Framework report (COSO II). *See* subhead: Enterprise Risk Management—Integrated Framework report (COSO II)
        generally, 29.2
        Internal Control—Integrated Framework report (COSO I), 29.2, 29.2.1
    company-auditor relationship, effect of Sarbanes-Oxley Act on, 28.12, 28.12.1
    compliance program, as risk area to address in, 2.5.1
    contingent liability valuations, 28.38.4
    continuing compliance requirements
        generally, 28.43
        optimization, methods of achieving, 28.43.2, 28.43.3
        risk assessment techniques, use of, 28.43.4, 28.43.5
        SEC expectations for, 28.43.1
        top-down approach, 28.43.2, 28.43.3
    documentation of audit
        generally, 28.41.1
        record retention, 28.42.1
        reviewability standard, 28.42
        standard for, 28.42
        subjects for which records should be retained, 28.42.1
    Enterprise Risk Management—Integrated Framework report (COSO II)

Accounting, Enterprise Risk Management—Integrated Framework report (COSO II) *(cont'd)*
    components of, 28.37.2, 29.2.5
    enterprise risk management, defined, 29.2.4
    generally, 29.2.2
    voluntary, COSO II as, 29.2.3
  equity and equity-based executive compensation, accounting for. *See* Executive compensation
  executive compensation, accounting for. *See* Executive compensation
  expense accounting, 28.38.2
  foreign auditors, regulation of
    generally, 28.16
    U.S. firms relying on foreign firms, requirements for, 28.16.1
  government contractors, cost accounting by. *See* Government contractors
  Internal Control—Integrated Framework report (COSO I), 29.2, 29.2.1
  internal control report, requirement for
    assessment of internal controls, 28.38.8
    asset valuation methods, 28.38.3
    auditing standards. *See* subhead: auditing standards
    auditors, advice from, 28.37.7
    contents of, 28.37
    contingent liability valuations, 28.38.4
    continuing compliance requirements. *See* subhead: continuing compliance requirements
    COSO framework for internal controls, components of, 28.37.2, 29.2.5
    customizing controls to individual businesses, 28.37.3
    documentation of internal controls, 28.38.6
    expectations for internal controls, 28.37.4, 28.37.5
    expense accounting, 28.38.2
    generally, 28.38, 28.38.7, 29.1.3
    manipulation of financial reports, areas of, 28.38–28.38.5
    parties responsible for designing and developing internal controls, 28.37.6
    problems with internal controls, disclosure of. *See* subhead: problems with internal controls, disclosure of
    processes for developing internal controls, 28.37.8
    reasonable assurance of reliability in financial statements, 28.37.4, 28.37.5
    revenue recognition, 28.38.1
    scope of internal controls over financial reporting, 28.37.1
    section 404 requirements, 28.38.7
    special purpose entities, issues related to, 28.38.5

Index

problems with internal controls, disclosure of
    categorizing problems, factors considered in, 28.40.4
    control deficiencies, 28.40.1
    generally, 28.40
    material weakness, 28.40.3, 28.40.6, 28.40.7
    significant deficiencies, 28.40.2, 28.40.5
procedures, 28.14
Public Company Accounting Oversight Board (PCAOB)
    auditing standard, 28.41, 28.41.1
    audits, effect of PCAOB rules on, 28.15.2
    disciplinary or remedial sanctions, imposition of, 28.15.1
    generally, 28.11
    powers of, 28.15
revenue recognition issues, 28.38.1
risk management, principles guiding, 29.2.6
Sarbanes-Oxley Act
    audit committee, relationship of auditor to, 28.13, 28.13.1
    company-auditor relationship, effect of act on, 28.12, 28.12.1
    Congress's passage, reasons for, 29.1.2
    cost of compliance with section 404, 29.3.1
    financial collapse of 2007–08, effect of, 29.4
    foreign auditors, regulation of, 28.16, 28.16.1
    generally, 28.11
    internal control report, requirement for. *See* subhead: internal control report, requirement for
    objectives of, 29.1
    procedures, 28.14
    Public Company Accounting Oversight Board (PCAOB). *See* subhead: Public Company Accounting Oversight Board (PCAOB)
    reactions to, 29.3, 29.3.1
    restructuring of accounting profession and its oversight by, 28.11, 29.1.1
    SEC guidance on section 404, 29.3.1
special purpose entities, issues related to, 28.38.5
Administration of compliance programs
    anti-money laundering compliance programs. *See* Anti-money laundering compliance programs
    audit committee, role of, 2.7.3
    auditing of compliance program. *See* Auditing and monitoring of compliance programs
    background checks of employees, 2.7.6
    bad actors, exclusion of, 2.7.6
    certification requirements, 2.7.3

Administration of compliance programs (*cont'd*)
    compliance officer or committee, designation and responsibilities of
        anti-money laundering compliance programs, 26.19.3, 26.19.13
        generally, 2.7.2
        managed care organization compliance programs, 22.6.2
        Medicare Part D compliance programs, 21.16.2
    "culture" of compliance, 2.7.4, 2.7.5
    enforcement of compliance program. *See* Enforcement of compliance programs
    Federal Sentencing Guidelines requirements, 2.7, 2.7.1, 2.7.3
    generally, 2.7
    monitoring of compliance program. *See* Auditing and monitoring of compliance programs
    Sarbanes-Oxley Act requirements, 2.7, 2.7.2, 2.7.3
    senior management, responsibilities of
        anti-money laundering compliance programs, role in, 26.19.14
        audit committee, role of, 2.7.3
        certification requirements, 2.7.3
        generally, 2.7.1
        role of senior management, 2.7.3
    training. *See* Training and education
Advertising. *See* Marketing
AECA. *See* Arms Export Control Act (AECA)
Age Discrimination in Employment Act (ADEA), 34.5
Agencies, federal. *See* Federal agencies
AIFP. *See* Automotive Industry Financing Program (AIFP)
AKS. *See* Anti-Kickback Statute (AKS)
American Investment and Recovery Act
    Buy American provisions, 15.17.2
Americans with Disabilities Act (ADA). *See* Employment discrimination, subhead: disability discrimination, prohibition of
Anticompetitive and unfair business practices
    compliance program, as risk area to address in, 2.5.1
    government contractors, 15.10.13
    international investigations. *See* International investigations
Antideficiency Act
    government contractors, compliance issues for, 15.18
Anti-Kickback Statute (AKS)
    government contractors, compliance issues for, 15.11.6
    healthcare organizations and providers, issues related to. *See* Healthcare organizations and providers
    Medicare Part D stakeholders, compliance issues for. *See* Medicare Part D

Index

patient assistance programs (PAPs)
    Medicare Part D risks. *See* Medicare Part D
    outside Medicare Part D, risks for PAPs that operate, 21.7
pharmaceutical and medical device makers, applicability to.
    See Pharmaceutical and medical device makers
Anti-money laundering compliance programs
    administration of program
        generally, 26.19.8
        ongoing administration, 26.19.12
        parties or departments who should administer program, 26.19.13
        senior management, role of, 26.19.14
    auditing and monitoring program, 26.19.5
    Bank Secrecy Act (BSA) requirements
        financial institutions required to have compliance program, 26.7
        generally, 26.7, 26.7.2, 26.19, 26.19.2
        risk-based anti-money laundering program, 26.7.3
    compliance officers, selection and responsibilities of, 26.19.3, 26.19.13
    creation of program, 26.19.8
    designing program, 26.19.11
    enforcement of program, 26.19.12
    exemption from compliance program requirements, tracking potential changes affecting, 26.19.1
    Federal Register as source for tracking regulatory changes, 26.19.1
    generally, 26.19
    independent audits, 26.19.5
    "Know Your Customer" procedures
        generally, 26.19.2, 26.19.6
        methods of verifying customer's identity, 26.19.6
        practical considerations, 26.19.7
    one-size-fits-all program, lack of, 26.19.10
    reasons for having compliance program, 26.19
    senior management, role of, 26.19.14
    Sentencing Guidelines programs, relationship to, 26.19.9
    standard program, lack of, 26.19.10
    training requirements, 26.19.4
Anti-money laundering statutes and regulations. *See* Money laundering
Antitrust. *See* Anticompetitive and unfair business practices
Arms Export Control Act (AECA)
    generally, 15.17.8
    licensing requirements, 15.17.9
    penalty provisions, 15.17.10

Asset Guarantee Program, 27.2.5
ASSP. *See* Auto Supplier Support Program (ASSP)
Attorney-client privilege
    crime-fraud exception
        generally, 6.14.3
        past wrongdoing, as inapplicable to disclosures of, 6.14.4
    elements in establishing, 6.14
    federal prosecutorial guidelines on waiver
        current policy, 6.17.5, 8.5.5
        Filip Memorandum, 6.17.4, 8.5.4
        generally, 6.17, 8.5
        Holder Memorandum, 6.17.1, 8.5.1
        McNulty Memorandum, 6.17.3, 8.5.3
        Thompson Memorandum, 6.17.2, 8.5.2
    Filip Memorandum, waiver of privilege under, 6.17.4, 8.5.4
    forensic experts, applicability to work of, 6.8.4
    former employees, applicability to communications with, 6.14.1
    generally, 6.7.1, 6.13.1, 6.14
    Holder Memorandum, waiver of privilege under, 6.17.1, 8.5.1
    international investigations, applicability to, 16.5
    interviews, applicability to
        generally, 6.11.10
        interviewee, applicability of privilege to, 6.11.11
        waiver of confidentiality for information disclosed during interview, 6.11.12
    McNulty Memorandum, waiver of privilege under, 6.17.3, 8.5.3
    past wrongdoing, disclosures of
        crime-fraud exception as inapplicable to, 6.14.4
        disclosing witness may not prevent company from waiving privilege, 6.14.5
    professional investigators, applicability to work of, 6.8.2
    scope of, 6.14.3, 6.15.1
    third parties, applicability to communications with, 6.14.2
    Thompson Memorandum, waiver of privilege under, 6.17.2, 8.5.2
    voluntary disclosures, effect of
        generally, 8.4
        reasons for voluntary disclosures, 6.16.1
        scope of voluntary disclosures, 6.16.2
        waiver of privilege, 6.16–6.16.3
    waiver
        disclosing witness may not prevent company from waiving privilege, 6.14.5
        federal prosecutorial guidelines on. *See* subhead: federal prosecutorial guidelines on waiver
        generally, 6.16
        inadvertent waiver, 6.16

Index

    intentional waiver, 6.16
    limited waivers, 6.16.3
    scope of, 6.16.3
    voluntary disclosures, 6.16–6.16.3
Attorneys
    American Bar Association (ABA) rules, relation of SEC rules to, 28.28
    attorney-client privilege. *See* Attorney-client privilege
    chief legal officers (CLOs), responsibilities of
        absence of appropriate response, actions upon, 28.26.4, 28.26.5
        appropriate response to finding of material violation, 28.26.2, 28.26.3
        documentation requirements, 28.26.1
        generally, 28.26
        inquiry into reported material violation, requirement for, 28.26
        reported material violations, steps CLO must take in response to, 28.26
        violations, attorneys' options for dealing with, 28.26.6
    credible evidence, reporting of, 28.22, 28.22.1
    foreign attorneys, requirements for, 28.27
    gatekeeper role of, 28.17.1
    general counsel, role of
        best interests of corporation, determining, 28.32.7
        CEO, relations with, 28.32.2
        changing role of general counsel, 28.32.3
        directors, relations with, 28.32.1
        generally, 28.32
        management, relations with, 28.32.1
        organization tools and steps to assist general counsel, 28.32.6
        privileged communications, effect of Sarbanes-Oxley Act requirements on, 28.32.5
        responsibilities mandated by Sarbanes-Oxley Act, 28.32.4
    insurance considerations, 28.31
    material violations, reporting of, 28.23
    penalties for violations of SEC rules, 28.21.2, 28.30, 28.30.1
    potential violations, reporting of, 28.24
    qualified legal compliance committees (QLQC)
        establishment of, 28.25.1
        generally, 28.25
        operation of, 28.25.2
    reporting requirements
        attorney-client relationship, effect on, 28.21.1
        credible evidence, reporting of, 28.22, 28.22.1

Attorneys, reporting requirements *(cont'd)*
    generally, 28.21
    material violations, reporting of, 28.23
    potential violations, reporting of, 28.24
    public disclosures, 28.21.1
    up-the-ladder reporting requirements. *See* subhead: up-the-ladder reporting requirements
responsibilities of, 28.17.1
Sarbanes-Oxley Act requirements
    applicability of, 28.17.2, 28.17.3
    chief legal officers (CLOs), responsibilities of. *See* subhead: chief legal officers (CLOs), responsibilities of
    foreign attorneys, requirements for, 28.27
    gatekeeper role of attorneys, 28.17.1
    general counsel, role of. *See* subhead: general counsel, role of
    generally, 28.17
    insurance, effect on, 28.31
    limitations on, 28.17.3
    penalties for violations of SEC rules, 28.21.2, 28.30, 28.30.1
    qualified legal compliance committees (QLQC). *See* subhead: qualified legal compliance committees (QLQC)
    reporting requirements. *See* subhead: reporting requirements
    responsibilities of attorneys, 28.17.1
    subordinate attorneys. *See* subhead: subordinate attorneys
    supervisory attorneys. *See* subhead: supervisory attorneys
    training programs, 28.29, 28.29.1
    up-the-ladder reporting requirements. *See* subhead: up-the-ladder reporting requirements
state rules, relation of SEC rules to
    differences between SEC and state rules, 28.28.1
    generally, 28.28.2
    preemption of conflicting state rules, 28.28
subordinate attorneys
    generally, 28.20, 28.20.1
    task, subordinate/supervisory status of attorneys dependent upon particular, 28.20.2
    up-the-ladder reporting requirements, applicability of, 28.18.1
supervisory attorneys
    generally, 28.19
    task, subordinate/supervisory status of attorneys dependent upon particular, 28.20.2
    up-the-ladder reporting requirements, applicability of, 28.18.1

Index

training programs, 28.29, 28.29.1
up-the-ladder reporting requirements
    futile, reporting requirements where reporting to chief legal counsel or CEO is, 28.18.2
    generally, 28.18
    outside counsel, applicability to, 28.18.3
    subordinate attorneys, applicability to, 28.18.1
    supervisory attorneys, applicability to, 28.18.1

Audit committee
    administration of compliance programs, 2.7.3
    auditor, relationship to, 28.13, 28.13.1
    compensation of, 28.6.1
    independence of committee members, 28.6.1
    independent financial expert, requirement for, 28.6.1, 28.6.2
    internal auditors, relation to, 2.9.5
    qualifications of, 28.6.1
    responsibilities of, 28.6.3
    Sarbanes-Oxley Act requirements
        auditor, relationship to, 28.13, 28.13.1
        compensation of committee members, 28.6.1
        generally, 28.6
        independence of committee members, 28.6.1
        independent financial expert, requirement for, 28.6.1, 28.6.2
        qualifications of committee members, 28.6.1
        responsibilities of audit committee, 28.6.3

Auditing and monitoring of compliance programs
    anti-money laundering compliance programs, 26.19.5
    audit committee, relation of internal auditors to, 2.9.5
    export compliance programs, 18.8.6
    external audits, 2.9
    generally, 2.9
    internal audits
        audit committee, relation of internal auditors to, 2.9.5
        defined, 2.9.2
        export compliance programs, 18.8.6
        generally, 2.9, 2.9.2
        reasons for conducting, 2.9.3
        role of, 2.9.4
    managed care organizations (MCOs) compliance programs, 22.6.5
    Medicare Part D compliance programs, 21.16.6
    questions auditors should ask in evaluating program, 2.9.1

Auto Supplier Support Program (ASSP), 27.2.10
Auto Warranty Commitment Program (AWCP), 27.2.11
Automotive Industry Financing Program (AIFP), 27.2.9
AWCP. *See* Auto Warranty Commitment Program (AWCP)

B

Backup systems. *See* Disaster recovery plans
Bank Secrecy Act (BSA)
    anti-money laundering compliance programs. *See* Anti-money laundering compliance programs
    bulk cash smuggling
        currency, defined, 26.13.3
        exceptions to reporting requirements, 26.13.4
        FinCEN Form 105, filing requirements for, 26.13.1
        generally, 26.13
        monetary instruments, defined, 26.13.3
        penalty provisions, 26.13.2
    currency transaction reports (CTRs), 26.11.1, 26.11.2
    customer identification programs (CIPs), 26.8
    financial institutions, applicability to
        defined, 26.6.2
        generally, 26.6.1, 26.7.1
    generally, 26.6, 26.7.1
    information sharing requirements
        generally, 26.10
        mandatory information sharing
            confidentiality of, 26.10.5
            financial institutions subject to, 26.10.2
            generally, 26.10.1
            positive reports, 26.10.3, 26.10.4
            response to section 314(a) mandatory information sharing requests, 26.10.3
            Suspicious Activity Reports (SAR), section 314(a) request as factor in filing of, 26.10.6
        voluntary information sharing
            civil liability, safe harbor from, 26.10.14
            confidentiality of, 26.10.12
            generally, 26.10.7
            participation in, procedures for, 26.10.10
            parties who may share information, 26.10.9
            parties with whom information may be shared, 26.10.11
            safe harbor from civil liability for, 26.10.14
            Suspicious Activity Reports (SAR), section 314(b) voluntary information sharing as factor in filing of, 26.10.13
            types of information that may be shared, 26.10.8
    IRS Form 8300
        currency, defined, 26.11.4
        generally, 26.11.1, 26.11.3
        multiple-payment transactions, handling of, 26.11.7

      related, transactions considered, 26.11.6
      reportable transactions, 26.11.5
   large cash transaction reporting requirements
      bulk cash smuggling. *See* subhead: bulk cash smuggling
      currency transaction reports (CTRs), 26.11.2
      generally, 26.11
      IRS Form 8300. *See* subhead: IRS Form 8300
      record-keeping requirements, 26.12
      structuring violations, 26.14, 26.14.1
   record-keeping requirements, 26.12
   structuring violations
      generally, 26.14
      penalty provisions, 26.14.1
   suspicious transactions, reporting requirements for
      disclosures allowed, 26.9.1
      filing requirements, 26.9.3
      financial institutions subject to, 26.9.1
      generally, 26.9
      safe harbor for reporting suspicious transactions, 26.9.2
      time for filing report, 26.9.3

Banking and financial institution compliance programs
   affiliates, compliance considerations applicable to transactions by and among, 25.5.1
   agencies regulating banking industry, 25.4.1
   anti-money laundering compliance programs. *See* Anti-money laundering compliance programs
   Banks Secrecy Act (BSA) provisions. *See* Bank Secrecy Act (BSA)
   compliance risk, defined, 25.2
   culture of organization supporting compliance, 25.6.5
   custom tailoring of program to specific institution, 25.3
   employees, motivating compliance by, 25.6.5
   ethics breaches, consequences of, 25.1.1
   independent testing of compliance programs
      frequency of, 25.6.1
      generally, 25.6
   maintaining compliance
      culture of organization supporting compliance, 25.6.5
      employees, motivating compliance by, 25.6.5
      legal, legislative and regulatory developments, keeping up-to-date on, 25.6.3, 25.6.4
      parties or departments responsible for tracking legal, legislative and regulatory developments, 25.6.4
      regulator's current emphasis on compliance with all regulatory requirements, 25.6.2

Banking and financial institution compliance programs, maintaining compliance *(cont'd)*
    sources for monitoring legislative or regulatory changes or amendments, 25.6.3
  money laundering
    anti-money laundering compliance programs. *See* Anti-money laundering compliance programs
    statutes and regulations. *See* Money laundering
  need for compliance program
    ethics breaches, consequences of, 25.1.1
    generally, 25.1
  nonbanking activities, compliance policies applicable to, 25.5
  noncompliance, penalties for. *See* subhead: penalties for noncompliance
  penalties for noncompliance
    compliance risk, defined, 25.2
    formal enforcement actions, 25.2.2
    generally, 25.2.1
    Groob v. Key Bank, 25.2
    informal enforcement actions, 25.2.2
  policies, 25.3.1
  regulatory framework
    agencies regulating banking industry, 25.4.1
    anti-money laundering statutes and regulations. *See* Money laundering
    Bank Secrecy Act (BSA) provisions. *See* Bank Secrecy Act (BSA)
    generally, 25.4
    single compliance policy covering related regulations, use of, 25.4.2
    state laws and regulations, 25.4.3
  senior management, role of, 25.3
  single compliance policy covering related regulations, use of, 25.4.2
  state laws and regulations, 25.4.3
  structure of, 25.3
  testing of compliance programs. *See* subhead: independent testing of compliance programs

Bayh-Doyle Act
  conflict of interest provisions. *See* Biomedical research/clinical trials

Berry Amendments
  government contractors, compliance issues for, 15.17.6

Biomedical research/clinical trials
  Bayh-Doyle Act provisions
    generally, 23.15

Index

heightened scrutiny, criteria for subjecting sponsored research projects to, 23.15.2
nonprofit grantees, considerations for, 23.15.1
objectives of, 23.15
charging for investigational drugs
    FDA approval, requirement for, 23.19
    generally, 23.19
    treatment IND, charging for drugs used pursuant to, 23.19.1, 23.19.2
Common Rule
    assurance of compliance with, 23.18.9
    exceptions to informed consent requirement, 23.18.3
    generally, 23.17.1
    Institutional Review Board (IRB), requirements for. *See* subhead: Institutional Review Board (IRB)
conflicts of interest, rules and regulations governing
    Bayh-Doyle Act provisions. *See* subhead: Bayh-Doyle Act provisions
    FDA financial disclosure requirements. *See* subhead: FDA financial disclosure requirements
    generally, 23.11
    industry guidance documents, 23.11
    National Institutes of Health (NIH) Guidelines, 23.14, 23.14.1
    National Science Foundation (NSF) requirements, 23.13, 23.13.1
    Public Health Service (PHS) Rules. *See* subhead: Public Health Service (PHS) Rules
FDA financial disclosure requirements
    bias to study, factors FDA considers in assessing risk of, 23.16.3
    compromised studies, actions FDA may take in event of, 23.16.4
    disclosable financial arrangements, categories of, 23.16.1
    generally, 23.16
    investigator, obligations of, 23.16.2
    studies/marketing applications to which applicable, 23.16
FDA regulations
    financial disclosure requirements. *See* subhead: FDA financial disclosure requirements
    protection of human subjects, rules and regulations governing
        exceptions to informed consent requirements, 23.18.2
        generally, 23.17.2
generally, 23.10
human-subject research, rules and regulations governing. *See* subhead: protection of human subjects, rules and regulations governing

Biomedical research/clinical trials (*cont'd*)
    informed consent requirements
        contents required in informed consent, 23.18
        exceptions to, 23.18.1–23.10.3
        generally, 23.18
    Institutional Review Board (IRB)
        expedited review procedures, 23.18.7
        membership requirements, 23.18.4
        minimal risk, defined, 23.18.8
        operational requirements, 23.18.5
        research approval by IRB, criteria for
            expedited review procedures, 23.18.7
            generally, 23.18.6
    investigational drugs, charging for. *See* subhead: charging for investigational drugs
    Medicare coverage
        complications arising from trials, coverage of, 23.20.4
        generally, 23.20
        qualifying clinical trials, 23.20.2, 23.20.3
        routine costs, coverage of, 23.20, 23.20.1
    National Institutes of Health (NIH) Guidelines, 23.14, 23.14.1
    National Science Foundation (NSF) requirements, 23.13, 23.13.1
    protection of human subjects, rules and regulations governing
        E6 guidance (ICH guidance), 23.17.4
        FDA regulations. *See* subhead: FDA regulations
        generally, 23.17
        HHS regulations, 23.17.3
        ICH guidelines, 23.17.4
        informed consent requirements. *See* subhead: informed consent requirements
        World Medical Association Declaration of Helsinki principles, 23.17.5
    Public Health Service (PHS) Rules
        conflict of interest, defined, 23.12.7
        conflict-of-interest policies, requirement for maintenance and enforcement of, 23.12.2
        designated officials, responsibilities of, 23.12.6
        generally, 23.12
        institutions to which applicable, 23.12.1
        investigators subject to significant financial interest disclosure requirements, 23.12.5
        management of conflicts of interest, 23.12.8
        penalties for failure to comply with, 23.12.19, 23.12.10
        significant financial interest
            defined, 23.12.3

Index

investigators subject to disclosure requirements, 23.12.5
remuneration not constituting, 23.12.4
Board of directors
    See also Directors; Senior management
    Sarbanes-Oxley Act requirements
        generally, 28.5.1
        independent directors, regulations regarding, 28.5
Bribery
    compliance program, as risk area to address in, 2.5.1
    Foreign Corrupt Practices Act (FCPA). *See* Foreign Corrupt Practices Act (FCPA)
    government contractors. *See* Government contractors
    international investigations. *See* International investigations
BSA. *See* Bank Secrecy Act (BSA)
Buy-American Act
    DOT grants for construction projects, applicability to, 15.17.3
    exemptions, 15.17.3
    generally, 15.17.2
    penalty provisions, 15.17.4

C

CAA. *See* Clean Air Act (CAA)
CAP. *See* Capital Assistance Program (CAP)
Capital Assistance Program (CAP), 27.2.2
Capital Purchase Program (CPP), 27.2.1
Cash transactions, reporting requirements for. *See* Bank Secrecy Act (BSA)
Centers for Medicare & Medicaid Services (CMS)
    Medicare Part D audits, 21.18
CERCLA. *See* Comprehensive Environmental Response, Compensation, and Liability Act (CERCLA)
Certification of financial statements. *See* Financial statements, certification requirements for
CFATS. *See* Chemical Facility Anti-Terrorism Standards (CFATS)
Chemical Facility Anti-Terrorism Standards (CFATS)
    covered facilities, requirements for, 33.14.1
    generally, 33.14
    penalty provisions, 33.14.2
Civil penalties
    government contractors. *See* Government contractors
Clean Air Act (CAA)
    air pollutants regulated by EPA, 33.7.1
    emission standards, 33.7.3

Clean Air Act (CAA) (cont'd)
    greenhouse gas emissions, regulation of, 33.7.4
    national ambient air quality standards (NAAQS), 33.7.2
    National Emission Standards for Hazardous Air Pollutants (NESHAP), 33.7.3
    New Source Performance Standards (NSPS), 33.7.3
    New Source Review (NSR) permits, 33.7.5
    ozone-depleting chemicals, restrictions on, 33.7.3
    penalty provisions, 33.7.7
    permitting requirements, 33.7.5
    purpose of, 33.7
    record-keeping requirements, 33.7.5
    risk management programs, 33.7.5
    state implementation plans (SIPs), 33.7.2
    sulfur dioxide emissions program, 33.7.3
    Title V operating permits, 33.7.5
    violations, actions constituting, 33.7.6
Clean Water Act (CWA)
    dredge and fill permits, 33.8.9
    effluent limitations, 33.8.2
    National Pollutant Discharge Elimination System (NPDES) permits
        applications for permits, data and testing companies must provide on, 33.8.6
        generally, 33.8.2, 33.8.5
        storm water discharges, for, 33.8.7
    nonpoint sources, regulation of, 33.8.4
    penalty provisions, 33.8.14
    point source discharges, regulation of, 33.8.3
    pollutants regulated by, 33.8.1
    publicly owned treatment works (POTWs), permit requirements for discharges to, 33.8.8
    purpose of, 33.8
    Spill Prevention Control and Countermeasures (SPCC) regulations
        components of SPCC plan, 33.8.12
        generally, 33.8.10, 33.8.13
        oil, defined, 33.8.11
        oil-handling personnel, training of, 33.8.13
        training requirements, 33.8.13
    storm water discharges, permit requirements for, 33.8.7
    wetlands regulations, 33.8.9
Climate change
    SEC reporting requirements, 33.16
Clinical trials. *See* Biomedical research/clinical trials
CMS. *See* Centers for Medicare & Medicaid Services (CMS)

Index

COBRA. *See* Consolidated Omnibus Budget Reconciliation Act (COBRA)
Code of ethical conduct
    elements of, 2.6.2
    Federal Sentencing Guidelines requirements, 2.6.1
    generally, 2.6
    government contractors, FAR requirements for, 15.3.2
    legal requirements, 2.6.1
    number of codes company should have, 2.6.3
    Sarbanes-Oxley requirements
        code of ethics, defined, 28.4
        filing of code of ethics with SEC, 28.4.1
        generally, 2.6.1, 2.6.3
        public posting of code of ethics, 28.4.1
Colleges. *See* Institutions of higher education
Community Development Capital Initiative, 27.2.8
Compliance and ethics programs
    administration of. *See* Administration of compliance programs
    anti-money laundering compliance programs. *See* Anti-money laundering compliance programs
    auditing of. *See* Auditing and monitoring of compliance programs
    banking institution compliance programs. *See* Banking and financial institution compliance programs
    benefits of
        corporate performance, link between corporate governance and, 1.8.1
        cost benefits, 1.7.2
        generally, 1.8
        mitigation of effects of misconduct, 1.4, 1.8.2
        sentencing, mitigating factor in, 1.8
        whistleblower complaints, protection against, 1.8
    Boeing Company case study, 1.8.2
    building program, 1.9.1
    business growth and, 1.9.2
    corporate culture, changing, 1.3.1
    corporate performance, link between corporate governance and, 1.8.1
    cost considerations
        benefits of compliance programs, 1.7.2
        case studies, 1.7
        generally, 1.6
        governmental investigations, costs of responding to, 1.7
        white-collar crime, costs of, 1.7.1

Compliance and ethics programs (cont'd)
    costs. See Costs
    criminal conduct, detection of, 1.1.2
    data privacy and security program, 13.7
    defined, 1.1
    designing and implementing. See Designing and implementing compliance programs
    due diligence in prevention and detection of offenses, 1.1.1
    effective programs, elements of
        Federal Sentencing Guidelines. See Federal Sentencing Guidelines
        generally, 1.2
    enforcement of. See Enforcement of compliance programs
    ethical corporate culture, assessing and managing. See Ethical corporate culture
    export compliance programs. See Export compliance programs
    False Claims Act actions and. See False Claims Act (FCA)
    federal agency requirements, 1.5.2
    Federal Sentencing Guidelines standards. See Federal Sentencing Guidelines
    federal statutory requirements, 1.5, 1.5.2
    financial institution compliance programs. See Banking and financial institution compliance programs
    focus of, 1.1.2
    government contractors. See Government contractors
    Health Insurance Portability and Accountability Act (HIPAA) compliance programs. See Health Insurance Portability and Accountability Act (HIPAA)
    healthcare organizations and providers. See Healthcare organizations and providers
    identifying existence of program, 1.9
    institutions of higher education compliance programs. See Institutions of higher education
    internal investigations, role of. See Internal investigations
    legal requirements
        court decisions, 1.5.3
        federal agency requirements, 1.5.2
        federal statutory requirements, 1.5, 1.5.2
        In re Caremark International, Inc. Derivative Litigation, 1.5.3
        state law requirements, 1.5.1
        United States v. Merck-Medco Managed Care LLC, 1.5, 1.5.3, 11.23
    managed care organizations (MCOs). See Managed Care Organizations (MCOs)
    Medicare Part D stakeholders. See Medicare Part D

Index

mitigation of costs and damages of regulatory violations, 1.4, 1.8.2
money laundering, compliance programs related to. *See* Anti-money laundering compliance programs
monitoring of. *See* Auditing and monitoring of compliance programs
prevention of ethical or illegal conduct, 1.3
protective reasons for, 1.8
reasons businesses need compliance programs
    Boeing Company case study, 1.8.2
    failure to implement program after learning of government investigation, 1.4.2
    generally, 1.4
    government investigations, programs begun after, 1.4.1
    mitigation of costs and damages of regulatory violations, 1.4, 1.8.2
records management program. *See* Records management program
role of
    corporate culture, changing, 1.3.1
    prevention of ethical or illegal conduct, 1.3
sentencing, as mitigating factor in, 1.8
state law requirements, 1.5.1
TARP programs, managing risk related to participation in, 27.5
training. *See* Training and education
visibility within organization of, 1.9
whistleblower complaints, as protection against, 1.8
Comprehensive Environmental Response, Compensation, and Liability Act (CERCLA)
    clean-up provisions, 33.4.2
    defenses to liability, 33.5.3
    generally, 33.4
    landowner liability protections, 33.5.3
    liability provisions
        defenses to, 33.5.3
        exemptions, 33.4.4
        generally, 33.4.3
        landowner liability protections, 33.5.3
    release reporting requirements, 33.4.1
    remedial actions, 33.4.2
    removal actions, 33.4.2
    Superfund Recycling Equity Act (SREA). *See* Superfund Recycling Equity Act (SREA)

Computing resources
    audit requirements, 14.7.2
    cloud-computing model
        compliance obligations, impact on. *See* subhead: compliance obligations, impact on
        generally, 14.2.3
        maintaining computing resources. *See* subhead: maintaining computing resources
    compliance obligations, impact on
        cross-border transactions, compliance risks related to, 14.8.2
        generally, 14.8
        multiple jurisdictions/regulatory regimes, compliance risks related to, 14.8.2
        service provider actions, liability for, 14.8.1
        third-party storage of data, compliance risks associated with
            data security protections, 14.9.1
            generally, 14.9
            security standards, compliance with, 14.9.1
    generally, 14.1
    in-house model, 14.2.1
    integration of new computing resources into existing systems
        generally, 14.6
        interfaces that allow new and existing systems to work together, rights to, 14.6.1
        legacy data, challenges posed by, 14.6.4
        open-source software, considerations related to, 14.6.2, 14.6.3
    intellectual property rights issues
        agile development model for software development, 14.5.2
        corporation's own IP rights, protection of
            agile development model for software development, 14.5.2
            generally, 14.5
            improvements, feedback and other licensee ideas, ownership of, 14.5
            systems access by vendors, 14.5.1
            traditional (waterfall) development model for software development, 14.5.2
        grants of IP rights, language for, 14.4
        improvements, feedback and other licensee ideas, ownership of, 14.5
        systems access by vendors, 14.5.1
        traditional (waterfall) development model for software development, 14.5.2

Index

maintaining computing resources
    audit requirements, 14.7.2
    employee policies, role of, 14.7.3
    generally, 14.7
    service level agreements (SLAs), 14.2.2, 14.7.1
    service level objectives (SLOs), 14.7.1
outsourcing model
    compliance obligations, impact on. *See* subhead: compliance obligations, impact on
    generally, 14.2.2
    maintaining computing resources. *See* subhead: maintaining computing resources
procurement models
    choosing appropriate model, 14.3
    cloud-computing model. *See* subhead: cloud-computing model
    comparison of models, considerations in, 14.3
    generally, 14.2
    in-house model, 14.2.1
    intellectual property rights issues. *See* subhead: intellectual property rights issues
service level agreements (SLAs), use of, 14.2.2, 14.7.1
service level objectives (SLOs), 14.7.1
types of, 14.1
vendor lock-in
    generally, 14.10
    reducing threat of, 14.11–14.11.3
    source code escrow agreements, 14.11.3
    transition assistance, negotiating for, 14.11.2
    unconditional access to data, 14.11.1
Confidential information, protection of
    compliance program, as risk area to address in, 2.5.1
    conflicts of interest, establishing policies related to, 12.5
Conflicts of interest
    biomedical research/clinical trials, conflicts of interest related to. *See* Biomedical research/clinical trials
    competitor companies, interests in
        generally, 12.3
        policies prohibiting working for competitors, establishing, 12.3.3
        thresholds for determining when conflict exists, establishing, 12.3.1
        working for competitor, conflicts arising from, 12.3.2, 12.3.3
    compliance program, as risk area to address in, 2.5.1
    concerns raised by, 12.1.1
    confidential information, establishing policies related to, 12.5

Conflicts of interest (cont'd)
    corporate opportunity doctrine, 2.5.1, 12.6
    customers, employee relationships with
        generally, 12.4
        policies for avoiding conflicts, establishing, 12.4.1
    defined, 12.1
    directors, conflicts involving, 12.2
    disclosure of conflict by interested person, 12.9
    employees/agents, conflicts involving
        competitor companies, interests in. *See* subhead: competitor companies, interests in
        confidential information, 12.5
        corporate opportunities, 2.5.1, 12.6
        customers, relationships with, 12.4, 12.4.1
        how conflicts arise, 12.2
        imputation of employee's conduct to company, 12.2.1
        trade secret information, 12.5
        vendors, relationships with, 12.4, 12.4.1
    ethical ramifications of, 12.1.1
    government, working with. *See* subhead: Government contractors
    highly regulated industries, financial arrangements considered conflicts for companies in, 12.7.3
    legal ramifications of, 12.1.1
    pharmaceutical and medical device industry, conflicts of interest related to biomedical research/clinical trials conducted by. *See* Biomedical research/clinical trials
    policy addressing
        annual certification that employee/director has read policy, 12.8.1
        contents of, 12.8.1
        entities required to have conflicts of interest policy, 12.8
        generally, 12.8
    trade secret information, establishing policies related to, 12.5
    vendors, employee relationships with
        generally, 12.4
        policies for avoiding conflicts, establishing, 12.4.1
Consolidated Omnibus Budget Reconciliation Act (COBRA)
    health insurance, continuation of
        generally, 34.20
        notice requirements, 34.20.2
        qualifying events, 34.20.1
Consumer Product Safety Act. *See* Consumer product safety laws
Consumer product safety laws
    businesses subject to, 35.3

Index

certification requirements
    businesses required to meet, 35.13.1
    generally, 35.7.2, 35.13
    stay of enforcement. *See* subhead: stay of enforcement on testing and certification requirements
    types of, 35.13
children's products, treatment of, 35.12
compliance with consumer product safety laws
    Consumer Product Safety Act (CPSA) requirements. *See* subhead: Consumer Product Safety Act (CPSA) requirements
    generally, 35.5
component parts testing, 35.14.2
Consumer Product Safety Act (CPSA) requirements
    certification obligations. *See* subhead: certification requirements
    compliance with, 35.5, 35.7–35.7.3
    generally, 35.7
    penalties for violations, 35.5
    potential for amendments or interpretive changes to, 35.24
    prohibited acts, 35.6
    recent developments, 35.24
    reporting obligations, 35.7.3
    standards. *See* subhead: product safety standards
    testing obligations. *See* subhead: testing program requirements
Consumer Product Safety Commission, enforcement by
    generally, 35.1
    statutes enforced, 35.4
Consumer Product Safety Improvement Act of 2008 (CPSIA), *See* subhead: Publicly Available Consumer Product Safety Information Database
Corrective Action Plans, 35.20.1
definition of consumer product, 35.2
fast-track recalls, 35.21
notice requirements for recalls, 35.22
product safety standards
    applicable standards, determining, 35.9–35.9.3
    children's products, treatment of, 35.12
    Commission does not pre-approve products as compliant, 35.8
    consumer product, determining status as, 35.9.1
    regulated products, 35.9.2
    sources of information on, 35.9.3
    unregulated products, 35.10
    voluntary standards, 35.11

Consumer product safety laws (cont'd)
  Publicly Available Consumer Product Safety Information Database
    businesses, effects on, 35.23.1
    generally, 35.23
    notifications, 35.23.2
    submissions, 35.23.3
  recalls
    Corrective Action Plans, 35.20.1
    fast-track recalls, 35.21
    generally, 35.20
    mandatory recalls, 35.20
    notice requirements, 35.22
    voluntary recalls, 35.20
  reporting requirements
    compliance with reporting requirements, ensuring, 35.19
    failure to report, penalties for, 35.17
    generally, 35.15
    immediate reporting, 35.18
    information that can trigger, 35.15.1
    lawsuit as giving rise to, 35.19.1
    recalls as not a necessary result of reporting suspected problems, 35.19.2
    substantial product hazard, products containing, 35.16
    time for reporting, 35.18
    uncertainty as to existence of safety hazard, reporting required where, 35.17
  stay of enforcement on testing and certification requirements
    component parts testing, 35.14.2
    generally, 35.14
    products to which stay is applicable, 35.14.1
  substantial product hazard, reporting requirements for products containing, 35.16
  testing program requirements
    generally, 35.13.2
    stay of enforcement. *See* subhead: stay of enforcement on testing and certification requirements
Contingent fee arrangements
  government contractors, 15.11.7, 15.11.8
Contract Work Hours and Safety Standards Act
  government contractors, compliance issues for, 15.13.5
Copeland Act
  government contractors, compliance issues for, 15.13.4
Copyrights
  creation of, 32.19.1
  generally, 32.19

institutions of higher education, issues related to. *See* Institutions of higher learning
rights of copyright holders, 32.19.2
Corporate opportunity doctrine
    generally, 2.5.1, 12.6
Costs
    compliance programs, costs of. *See* Compliance and ethics programs
    electronic discovery, costs of, 7.11
Counsel. *See* Attorneys
CPP. *See* Capital Purchase Program (CPP)
Criminal penalties
    government contractors. *See* Government contractors
"Culture" of compliance
    demonstrating, methods of, 2.7.5
    ethical culture, assessing and managing. *See* Ethical corporate culture
    generally, 2.7.4
Customer identification programs (CIPs), 26.8
CWA. *See* Clean Water Act (CWA)

D

Damages
    False Claims Act violations, damages for
        generally, 11.4
        qui tam actions, negotiating damages in, 11.17, 11.17.1
    qui tam actions, negotiating damages in, 11.17, 11.17.1
Data privacy and security. *See* Personal information, privacy and security of
Davis-Bacon Act
    government contractors, compliance issues for, 15.13.1
Defenses
    CERCLA liability, defenses to, 33.5.3
    False Claims Act actions, defenses to, 11.20
Deficit Reduction Act (DRA)
    employee education provisions, 11.24
    healthcare organizations and providers, applicability to. *See* Healthcare organizations and providers
Designing and implementing compliance programs
    export compliance programs. *See* Export compliance programs
    industry practices and standards, relevance of, 2.4
    risk areas, identification of
        common risk areas, examples of, 2.5.1

Designing and implementing compliance programs, risk areas, identification of (cont'd)
    generally, 2.5
    size of company, relevance of
        generally, 2.4.1
        small versus large companies, compliance programs for, 2.4.2
    small versus large companies, compliance programs for, 2.4.2

Directors
    See also Board of directors; Senior management
    compensation issues. See Executive compensation
    insurance. See Directors and officers (D&O) insurance
    penalty provisions
        cases involving, 28.8.2
        civil penalties, 28.8.1
        criminal penalties, 28.8.1
        generally, 28.8
        SEC powers to petition for judicial freeze of corporate assets, 28.8.1
    prohibited conduct, 28.7
    Sarbanes-Oxley Act requirements
        generally, 28.7
        insurance implications, 28.9
        penalty provisions. See subhead: penalty provisions
        prohibited conduct, 28.7
        underwriters, impact on, 28.9.1

Directors and officers (D&O) insurance
    Enforcement Manual, 30.8.1
    procedures
        Enforcement Manual, 30.8.1
        generally, 30.8
    Sarbanes-Oxley Act, effect of, 28.9
    SEC investigations, coverage of
        expenses potentially covered by D&O policy, 30.7.1
        generally, 30.7
        mitigation of risks of rescission, 30.7.3
        rescission of coverage, 30.7.2, 30.7.3
        timely notice to insurer, 30.7

Disaster recovery plans
    generally, 5.7
    records management program, relation to, 5.7.1

Disclosure
    environmental liability disclosure requirements
        climate change, disclosures related to, 33.16
        conditional asset retirement obligations disclosures, 33.15.5

Index

    contingent remediation liabilities, disclosure of, 33.15.1
    description of business disclosures, 33.15.3
    environmental legal proceedings, disclosure of, 33.15.2
    generally, 33.15
    management discussion and analysis (MD&A) disclosures, 33.15.4
executive compensation. *See* Executive compensation
financial disclosure requirements applicable to pharmaceutical and medical device makers conducting biomedical research/clinical trials. *See* Biomedical research/clinical trials, subhead: FDA financial disclosure requirements
government contractors, by
    FAR requirements for disclosure of violations. *See* Federal Acquisition Regulation (FAR) compliance program provisions
    lobbying disclosures, 15.11.19
Health Insurance Portability and Accountability Act (HIPAA). *See* Health Insurance Portability and Accountability Act (HIPAA)
internal investigations, disclosure to employees of. *See* Internal investigations
pharmaceutical and medical device makers conducting biomedical research/clinical trials, financial disclosure requirements applicable to. *See* Biomedical research/clinical trials, subhead: FDA financial disclosure requirements
political action committees (PACs), disclosure requirements for, 19.5.1
Sarbanes-Oxley Act disclosure controls. *See* Sarbanes-Oxley Act
SEC investigations, disclosure of, 30.1.5
voluntary disclosures. *See* Voluntary disclosures
Discovery
    document production. *See* Document production
    electronic discovery. *See* Electronic discovery
Discrimination. *See* Employment discrimination
Document production
    electronic discovery. *See* Electronic discovery
    qui tam actions, in. *See* Qui tam actions
    SEC investigations. *See* SEC investigations
Document retention policy. *See* Records management program
DRA. *See* Deficit Reduction Act (DRA)
Drug-Free Workplace Act
    government contractors, compliance issues for, 15.13.7
Due diligence in prevention and detection of offenses, 1.1.1

E

EAR. *See* Export Administration Regulations (EAR)
Economic sanctions programs
    administration of, 18.6.3
    barred persons or entities, lists of, 18.6.2
    exceptions to export prohibitions to embargoed countries, 18.6.1
    jurisdiction, 18.6.5
    lists of persons or entities barred, 18.6.2
    penalty provisions, 18.7.2–18.7.5
    prohibited activities, 18.6
    regulatory scheme, 18.6.3
    U.S. person, defined, 18.6.4
E-discovery. *See* Electronic discovery
Education. *See* Training and education
Effective compliance programs
    Federal Sentencing Guidelines. *See* Federal Sentencing Guidelines
    generally, 1.2
Electronic Communications Privacy Act (ECPA) provisions
    email, monitoring of, 13.3.2
    penalty provisions, 13.3.1
    purpose of, 13.3
Electronic discovery
    attorney review costs, 7.11
    backup tapes, collecting data from, 5.8.1, 7.8.3
    collection of documents
        backup tapes, collecting data from, 5.8.1, 7.8.3
        beginning to collect documents, 7.7.1
        generally, 7.2, 7.7
        imaging of data, 7.7.3
        keyword searching, 7.7.2
        pitfalls and hazards of, 7.9
        vendors, use of. *See* subhead: vendors, use of
    contexts giving rise to, 7.2.1
    cost of, 7.11
    defined, 7.2
    destruction due to routine operation of system, effect of, 7.9.1
    electronic data, significance of, 7.1
    good cause requirements for requests for "not reasonably accessible" ESI, 5.8
    keyword searching for collection of documents, 7.7.2
    litigation holds
        documents that litigation hold should cover, 7.5.3

    enforcement of, 7.5.4, 7.5.5
    events triggering duty to preserve, 7.5
    hazards to avoid, 7.6.2
    in-house counsel, enforcement of litigation hold by, 7.5.4
    key players, identifying and notifying, 7.5.1, 7.5.2
    lifting of, 7.6.4
    outside counsel, enforcement of litigation hold by, 7.5.5
    parties who should receive litigation hold notice, 7.5.1, 7.5.2
    senior management, enforcement of litigation hold by, 7.5.4
    spoliation for failure to preserve evidence. *See* subhead: spoliation of evidence
    systems that litigation hold should cover, 7.5.3
preservation of data
    alteration of data, avoiding, 7.4.2
    copying of potentially relevant data, 7.4.1
    deletion of data, avoiding, 7.4.2
    generally, 5.8.2, 7.2
    litigation holds. *See* subhead: litigation holds
    methods of preservation, 7.4.1
    relevant data, preservation of, 7.4
    SEC investigations. *See* SEC investigations
    spoliation for failure to preserve evidence. *See* subhead: spoliation of evidence
processing and production
    formats for producing data, 7.10, 7.10.1
    generally, 7.2
records management program
    generally, 7.3
    good cause requirements for requests for "not reasonably accessible" ESI, 5.8
    litigation holds. *See* subhead: litigation holds
    "not reasonably accessible" ESI, requests for, 5.8
    preparation for responding to requests for ESI, 5.8.1
SEC investigations. *See* SEC investigations
spoliation of evidence
    case studies, 7.6.3
    defined, 7.6.1
    generally, 7.6
    sanctions for, 7.6, 7.6.3
vendors, use of
    concerns related to, 7.8.2
    cost of, 7.11
    generally, 7.8, 7.8.1, 30.12
    quality control issues, 7.8.2

Embargo regulations. *See* Economic sanctions programs
Emergency Medical Treatment and Active Labor Act (EMTALA)
    enforcement of, 20.11.2
    generally, 20.11, 20.11.1
    penalty provisions, 20.11.2
    purpose of, 20.11
    screening mandated by, 20.11.1
    treatment mandated by, 20.11.1
Emergency Planning and Community Right-to-Know Act (EPCRA)
    generally, 33.6
    hazardous chemicals regulations, 33.6.1
    penalty provisions, 33.6.2
Employee Polygraph Protection Act (EPPA), 34.22, 34.22.1
Employee Retirement Income Security Act (ERISA)
    benefit plans subject to, 34.15
    generally, 34.15.1
    reporting requirements, 34.15.2
Employer/employee issues. *See* Labor and employment law
Employment discrimination
    age discrimination, prohibition of, 34.5
    Americans with Disabilities Act (ADA) provisions. *See* subhead: disability discrimination, prohibition of
    association discrimination, prohibition of, 34.4.2
    compliance issues
        harassment, prohibition of. *See* subhead: harassment, prohibition of
        notice requirements imposed by discrimination laws, 34.11
        prohibited actions, 34.8
        reasonable accommodation, requirements regarding, 34.9
        retaliation against employees asserting rights, prohibition of, 34.12
        written statements and policies to assure nondiscrimination compliance, 34.10
    disability discrimination, prohibition of
        compliance issues related to hiring process, 34.6.6
        confidentiality requirements, 34.6.7
        disability, defined, 34.6.1
        employee's family, protections extended to, 34.6.3
        generally, 34.6
        qualified individuals, 34.6.2
        reasonable accommodation requirements, 34.6.4
        standards employers may maintain for disabled individuals, 34.6.5
    disparate impact discrimination, prohibition of, 34.4.1
    "English only" speaking requirements, regulations regarding, 34.4.6

Index

Equal Pay Act (EPA) provisions. *See* subhead: gender-based pay discrimination, prohibition of
gender-based pay discrimination, prohibition of
    generally, 34.7
    permissible pay differences, 34.7.1
harassment, prohibition of
    compliance considerations, 34.13.4
    conduct constituting harassment, 34.13.1
    generally, 34.13
    hostile environment harassment, 34.13
    policies addressing harassment, adoption of, 34.13.2
    quid pro quo harassment, 34.13
    racial harassment, 34.13
    religious harassment, 34.13
    retaliation, prohibition of, 34.13.4
    sexual harassment, 34.13
    training requirements, 34.13.3
national origin discrimination, prohibition of, 34.4.5
pregnancy discrimination, prohibition of, 34.4.4
religious beliefs, accommodation of, 34.4.3
religious discrimination, prohibition of, 34.4.3
statutory framework, 34.2
Title VII provisions
    association discrimination, prohibition of, 34.4.2
    disparate impact discrimination, prohibition of, 34.4.1
    "English only" speaking requirements, regulations regarding, 34.4.6
    generally, 34.4
    national origin discrimination, prohibition of, 34.4.5
    pregnancy discrimination, prohibition of, 34.4.4
    religious beliefs, accommodation of, 34.4.3
    religious discrimination, prohibition of, 34.4.3
types of discrimination prohibited, 34.3
Employment eligibility and verification
    background checks, use of credit reports for
        Fair Credit Reporting Act (FCRA), applicability of, 34.1.3, 34.1.4
        generally, 34.1.3, 34.1.4
    E-Verify system. *See* E-Verify system
    Form I-9 filing requirements
        failure to file I-9 forms, consequences of, 34.1.2
        generally, 34.1.1
    government contractors
        E-verify system. *See* E-verify system
        generally, 15.14

Enforcement of compliance programs
    anti-money laundering compliance programs, 26.19.12
    disciplinary actions, 2.11
    generally, 2.7, 2.11
    Medicare Part D compliance programs, 21.16.5
    positive reinforcement, 2.11
    self-disclosure to regulatory authorities, 2.11.1
    unethical conduct, dealing with, 2.11.1
Environmental law
    Chemical Facility Anti-Terrorism Standards (CFATS). *See* Chemical Facility Anti-Terrorism Standards (CFATS)
    Clean Air Act (CAA). *See* Clean Air Act (CAA)
    Clean Water Act (CWA). *See* Clean Water Act (CWA)
    compliance program, as risk area to address in, 2.5.1
    Comprehensive Environmental Response, Compensation, and Liability Act (CERCLA). *See* Comprehensive Environmental Response, Compensation, and Liability Act (CERCLA)
    disclosure of environmental liabilities. *See* Disclosure
    Emergency Planning and Community Right-to-Know Act (EPCRA). *See* Emergency Planning and Community Right-to-Know Act (EPCRA)
    Environmental Protection Agency (EPA), role of, 33.1
    generally, 33.1, 33.2
    implementation of federal law, 33.1
    Resource Conservation and Recovery Act (RCRA). *See* Resource Conservation and Recovery Act (RCRA)
    Toxic Substances Control Act (TSCA). *See* Toxic Substances Control Act (TSCA)
Environmental Protection Agency (EPA)
    generally, 33.1
EPA. *See* Environmental Protection Agency (EPA)
EPCRA. *See* Emergency Planning and Community Right-to-Know Act (EPCRA)
Equal Employment Opportunity clause
    government contractors, compliance issues for, 15.13.6
Equal Pay Act, 34.7, 34.7.1
ERISA. *See* Employee Retirement Income Security Act (ERISA)
Ethical corporate culture
    aligning goals, behaviors and values
        behaviors and values, aligning, 3.8.3
        generally, 3.8
        goals and behaviors, aligning, 3.8.2
        goals and values, aligning, 3.8.1
    barriers to ethical culture
        generally, 3.9

Index

risk factors, identifying and addressing. *See* subhead: risk factors
behavior. *See* subhead: organizational tone
characteristics of, 3.4
compliance, linkage of culture and
    culture, relevance of focusing on, 3.2
    Federal Sentencing Guidelines elements, implementation of. *See* subhead: Federal Sentencing Guidelines elements, implementation of
    misconduct within organizations, reasons for occurrence of, 3.1
creating an ethical culture
    actions addressing root cause problems, development of, 3.11.4
    ethics issues, identification of, 3.11.1
    first step in addressing cultural issues, 3.12
    generally, 3.11
    linking cultural factors to ethics risks, 3.11.5
    risk factors related to company's ethics issues, identification of, 3.11.2
    root causes allowing risk factors to flourish
        actions addressing root cause problems, development of, 3.11.4
        generally, 3.11.3
culture, relevance of focusing on, 3.2
Federal Sentencing Guidelines elements, implementation of
    generally, 3.3
    organization's evaluation of, 3.3.2
    prosecutors/regulators, factors indicative of ethical culture to, 3.3.1
    sufficiency of program, evaluating, 3.3
framework of ethical culture, elements of
    behavior. *See* subhead: organizational tone
    generally, 3.4
    goal. *See* subhead: goals of individuals and organization
    values. *See* subhead: values
goals of individuals and organization
    aligning goals, behaviors and values. *See* subhead: aligning goals, behaviors and values
    challenges to business goals, raising, 3.5.3
    compensation of employees, role of, 3.5.1
    ethics and business goals, link between, 3.5.2
    generally, 3.4, 3.5
    misconduct, employee reporting of, 3.5.3
misconduct within organizations, reasons for occurrence of, 3.1

Ethical corporate culture *(cont'd)*
   organizational tone
      aligning goals, behaviors and values. *See* subhead: aligning goals, behaviors and values
      behavior supporting, 3.6
      employees, role of, 3.6.3
      generally, 3.4, 3.6
      leaders in organization, role of, 3.6.1
      middle management, role of, 3.6.2
      peer pressure, role of, 3.6.4
      top management, role of, 3.6.1
   reducing risks to ethical culture. *See* subhead: creating an ethical culture
   risk factors
      assessing risks
         culture risk assessments, 3.10.1–3.10.3
         employee satisfaction surveys, use of, 3.10.1
         generally, 3.9, 3.10
      culture risk assessments
         generally, 3.10.1
         goals of, 3.10.2
         information, gathering, 3.10.3
      identifying risk factors
         corporate pride values, risks associated with, 3.9.1
         generally, 3.9, 3.9.1
         internal cohesion values, risks associated with, 3.9.1
         relationship values, risks associated with, 3.9.1
         survival values, risks associated with, 3.9.1
         transformation values, risks associated with, 3.9.1
      reducing risks. *See* subhead: creating an ethical culture
   values
      aligning goals, behaviors and values. *See* subhead: aligning goals, behaviors and values
      Barrett values model, 3.7.1, 3.9, 3.9.1
      categorization of, 3.7.1
      collective/shared values, role of, 3.7.1
      generally, 3.4, 3.7
      unstated values, 3.7
Ethics
   code of. *See* Code of ethical conduct
   ethical corporate culture, assessing and managing. *See* Ethical corporate culture
   witness preparation, 9.1.1
E-Verify system
   exemptions, 15.15.1
   existing workforce, verification of, 15.15.2
   generally, 15.14, 15.15

Index

time for enrolling in and using, 15.15.3
Executive compensation
    accounting
        phantom stock payments, for, 31.15.1
        stock appreciation rights (SARs), for, 31.15.1
        stock options, for, 31.15
    blackout period trading prohibition
        exemptions, 31.18.17
        generally, 31.18.16
        notice requirement, 31.18.18
        remedies for violations of, 31.18.19
    change-in-control plan or agreement
        generally, 31.2.4
        golden parachute payments. *See* subhead: golden parachute payments
    deferred compensation
        generally, 31.5
        non-qualified deferred compensation plans. *See* subhead: non-qualified deferred compensation (NQDC) plans
        taxation. *See* subhead: taxation
    disclosure requirements
        certification of CCR and CDA, requirements regarding, 31.16.19
        Compensation Committee Report (CCR), disclosure of, 31.16.18, 31.16.19
        Form 8-K disclosures, 31.16.17
        generally, 31.16.15
        NQDC or employee stock plans, securities law requirements for, 31.18.2–31.18.5
        processes and procedures related to determining executive compensation, disclosure of, 31.16.17
        Proxy Disclosure Rules. *See* subhead: Proxy Disclosure Rules
        related-party transactions, 31.16.16
    employment agreements, elements of compensation pursuant to
        change-in-control plan or agreement, 31.2.4
        generally, 31.2
        non-plan compensation arrangements, 31.2.2
        severance pay provisions, 31.2.3
        tax-qualified plans and trusts, 31.2.1
    equity and equity-based compensation
        accounting. *See* subhead: accounting
        advantages of, 31.14
        backdating of stock options, 31.14.10
        incentive stock options (ISOs), grants of, 31.14.3, 31.14.4

Executive compensation, equity and equity-based compensation (cont'd)
  non-qualified stock options, grants of, 31.14.3, 31.14.5
  phantom stock payments, 31.14.8, 31.15.1
  plan, equity awards pursuant to, 31.14.2
  reissuance of stock options if price goes down, permissibility of, 31.14.9
  restricted stock, grants of, 31.14.6
  stock appreciation rights (SARs), awards of, 31.14.7, 31.15.1
  types of equity compensation plans, 31.14.1
 generally, 31.1
 golden parachute payments
  base amount, defined, 31.13.4
  contingent on a change in ownership or control, payments constituting, 31.13.7
  disqualified individuals, 31.13.5
  excess parachute payments, 31.13.3, 31.13.8, 31.13.9
  exempt payments, 31.13.2
  generally, 31.13
  payments in the nature of compensation, payments constituting, 31.13.6
  taxation of excess parachute payments, 31.13.9
  types of payments considered to be parachute payments, 31.13.1
 non-plan compensation arrangements, 31.2.2
 non-qualified deferred compensation (NQDC) plans
  attributes of, 31.6
  excess plans, 31.6.1, 31.6.2
  funded plans, 31.6.5
  generally, 31.5
  offshore nonqualified deferred compensation plans
   exceptions to section 457A provisions, 31.12.5
   generally, 31.12
   nonqualified deferred compensation plan, defined, 31.12.1
   nonqualified entities, 31.12.2
   section 457A provisions, 31.12, 31.12.1 *et seq.*
   substantial risk of forfeiture, 31.12.3
  registration of sales of stock in connection with employee stock plans. *See* subhead: registration of sales of stock in connection with employee stock plans
  securities, treatment as
   disclosure and reporting requirements, 31.18.2–31.18.5
   generally, 31.17, 31.17.1
   investment contract, treatment of NQDC qualifying as, 31.17.2

Index

registration of sales of stock in connection with employee stock plans. *See* subhead: registration of sales of stock in connection with employee stock plans
select group of management and highly compensated employees, 31.6.4
split-dollar insurance, 31.6.6, 31.6.7
supplemental executive retirement plans (SERPs), 31.6.1, 31.6.3
taxation of. *See* subhead: taxation of non-qualified deferred compensation
unfunded plans, 31.6.5

profit recovery rules
exempt transactions, 31.18.12
filing requirements, 31.18.11
generally, 31.18.8
insiders, defined, 31.18.9
transactions occurring within six months of becoming an insider, treatment of, 31.18.10

Proxy Disclosure Rules
Compensation Discussion and Analysis (CDA), disclosures required in, 31.16.4, 31.16.5
confidential information, treatment of, 31.16.8
differences in compensation policies for different executives, identification of, 31.16.7
director compensation, disclosures required for, 31.16.14
executives to which applicable, 31.16.6
foreign issuers, rules applicable to, 31.16.3
generally, 31.16.1
named executive officers, applicability to, 31.16.6
narrative disclosures supplementing tabular disclosures, requirements regarding, 31.16.10
perquisites, 31.16.11, 31.16.12
personal benefits, 31.16.11, 31.16.12
registered investment companies, rules applicable to, 31.16.3
small business issuers, exemption for, 31.16.2
stock appreciation rights, disclosures related to grants of, 31.16.13
stock option grants, disclosures related to, 31.16.13
tabular disclosures, requirements regarding, 31.16.9, 31.16.10

registration of sales of stock in connection with employee stock plans
disclosure and reporting requirements, 31.18.2–31.18.5
exemptions, 31.18

Executive compensation, registration of sales of stock in connection with employee stock plans (cont'd)
    Form S-8, filing of, 31.18.1
    Securities Act of 1933 requirements, 31.17.3
    Securities Exchange Act of 1934 requirements, 31.17.4
  related-party transactions, disclosure requirements regarding, 31.16.16
  resales of stock, limits on
    affiliate, defined, 31.18.14
    generally, 31.18.13
    registered stock, resales of, 31.18.13
    Rule 144 conditions, 31.18.15
    unregistered stock, resales of, 31.18.13
  Sarbanes-Oxley Act provisions
    blackout period trading prohibition. *See* subhead: blackout period trading prohibition
    generally, 31.18.20
  securities laws requirements
    blackout period trading prohibition. *See* subhead: blackout period trading prohibition
    disclosure requirements. *See* subhead: disclosure requirements
    non-qualified deferred compensation plans. *See* subhead: non-qualified deferred compensation (NQDC) plans
    profit recovery rules. *See* subhead: profit recovery rules
    Proxy Disclosure Rules, disclosures required by. *See* subhead: Proxy Disclosure Rules
    registration of sales of stock in connection with employee stock plans. *See* subhead: registration of sales of stock in connection with employee stock plans
    resales of stock, limits on. *See* subhead: resales of stock, limits on
    shareholder approval of plans providing equity securities, 31.18.6, 31.18.7
  severance pay provisions, 31.2.3
  shareholder approval of plans providing equity securities
    exempt plans, 31.18.7
    generally, 31.18.6
  taxation
    alternative minimum tax (AMT), 31.3.3, 31.3.4
    cash accounting method of accounting, implications of, 31.3
    constructive receipt doctrine, 31.3
    deferred compensation, rules for
      generally, 31.3

Index

    non-qualified deferred compensation. *See* subhead: taxation of non-qualified deferred compensation
  economic benefit doctrine, 31.3
  excess parachute payments, taxation of, 31.13.9
  generally, 31.3
  gross-up covenants, 31.3.1
  incentive stock options (ISOs), rules applicable to, 31.3.2, 31.4.3
  split-dollar insurance, taxation of, 31.6.7
taxation of non-qualified deferred compensation
  generally, 31.4
  immediate taxation, avoidance of, 31.8.13
  incentive stock options (ISOs), treatment of, 31.4.3
  mispriced stock options, effect of, 31.4.5
  non-qualified stock options, treatment of, 31.4.4
  penalties for failure to comply with section 409A provisions, 31.11
  permitted distributable events under section 409A
    change in control, activities constituting, 31.9.4
    disabled, service recipient becomes, 31.9.2
    fixed-schedule payments, requirements for, 31.9.3
    generally, 31.9
    separation from service, 31.9.1
    specified time payments, requirements for, 31.9.3
    unforeseeable emergency, defined, 31.9.5
  rabbi trusts, effect of, 31.4.1, 31.10.8
  reporting requirements, 31.11.1
  section 409A exemptions
    accrual method of accounting used by both service provider and service recipient, 31.8.10
    employee stock purchase plans, 31.8.2
    fair market value of stock, relevance and determination of, 31.8.12
    foreign plans, 31.8.8
    generally, 31.8
    non-statutory stock options, 31.8.3
    qualified employer plans, 31.8.6
    restricted property and stock plans covered by section 83, 31.8.5
    service provider's actively engaged in trade or business, 31.8.11
    severance plans, 31.8.9
    short-term deferrals, 31.8.1
    statutory stock options, 31.8.2
    stock appreciation rights, 31.8.4
    substantial risk of forfeiture, 31.8.14, 31.8.15
    welfare benefit plans and arrangements, 31.8.7

Executive compensation, taxation of non-qualified deferred
   compensation (cont'd)
      section 409A provisions
         deferral of compensation, occurrence of, 31.7.2
         effective date, 31.11.2
         examples of plans subject to section 409A, 31.7.5
         exemptions, 31.8–31.8.15
         form of payments, effect on, 31.8.16
         generally, 31.3, 31.4, 31.7, 31.7.1
         immediate taxation, avoidance of, 31.8.13
         material modification of plan, 31.11.3
         penalties for failure to comply with, 31.11
         permitted distributable events, 31.9–31.9.5
         reporting requirements, 31.11.1
         service provider, 31.7.3
         service recipient, 31.7.4
         time of payments, effect on, 31.8.16, 31.10–31.10.8
         Voluntary Compliance Program, 31.11.4
      time of payments
         acceleration of payments, 31.10.2
         delay of payments to key employees, 31.10.1, 31.10.3
         generally, 31.8.16, 31.10
         initial deferral elections, rules affecting, 31.10.4–31.10.6
         rabbi trusts, effect on, 31.10.8
         subsequent deferral elections, rules affecting, 31.10.4, 31.10.7
      transfers of property as compensation, treatment of, 31.4.2
      Voluntary Compliance Program, 31.11.4
   tax-qualified plans and trusts, 31.2.1
Export Administration Regulations (EAR)
   Commerce Control List (CCL), 18.5.2, 18.5.3
   deemed exports, 18.5.4
   export, defined, 18.5.4
   items requiring export license, 18.5.2
   penalty provisions, 18.7.1, 18.7.3–18.7.5
   re-exports, restrictions on, 18.5.4
   scope of, 18.5.1
   technology requiring export license, 18.5.2
Export compliance programs
   compliance personnel, roles of, 18.8.2
   designing compliance program
      generally, 18.9
      initial steps in drafting program, 18.9
      one-size-fits-all program, lack of, 18.9.1
      pitfalls to avoid in drafting program, 18.9.2
      risk areas, identifying, 2.5.1, 18.9.3
   disciplinary procedures, 18.8.8

Index

export compliance program manuals, importance of, 18.8.3
industry best practices
    compliance personnel, roles of, 18.8.2
    disciplinary procedures, 18.8.8
    export compliance program manuals, importance of, 18.8.3
    generally, 18.8
    internal audits, 18.8.6
    management commitment, 18.8.1
    record-keeping obligations, 18.8.5
    training, 18.8.4
    violations, mechanism for reporting, 18.8.7
internal audits, 18.8.6
management commitment, 18.8.1
record-keeping obligations, 18.8.5
risk areas, identifying, 2.5.1, 18.9.3
training, 18.8.4
violations, mechanism for reporting, 18.8.7
Export controls
    agencies regulating exports, 18.1.2
    commercial dual-use goods and technology, exports of
        Export Administration Regulations (EAR). *See* Export Administration Regulations (EAR)
        licensing requirements, 18.5.5, 18.5.6
        penalties for violations of, 18.7.1, 18.7.3–18.7.5
        regulatory scheme, 18.5
    compliance programs. *See* Export compliance programs
    defense articles and services, exports of
        International Traffic in Arms Regulations. *See* International Traffic in Arms Regulations (ITAR)
        licensing, 18.4.2, 18.4.3
        penalties for violations of, 18.7, 18.7.3–18.7.5
        registration requirements, 18.4.2
        regulatory scheme, 18.2
    economic sanctions programs. *See* Economic sanctions programs
    generally, 2.5.1, 18.1.1
    goals of, 18.1
    institutions of higher education, issues related to. *See* Export controls applicable to institutions of higher education
    international investigations
        generally, 16.8.8, 16.8.10
        technology industry, compliance and risk management in, 16.8.9
    International Traffic in Arms Regulations. *See* International Traffic in Arms Regulations (ITAR)

Export controls (cont'd)
  licensing requirements
    commercial dual-use goods and technology, exports of, 18.5.5, 18.5.6
    defense articles and services, exports of, 18.4.2, 18.4.3
  penalty provisions
    BAE Systems plc case study, 18.7
    Balli Aviation case study, 18.7.1
    calculation of penalties, 18.7.4
    case studies, 18.7, 18.7.1, 18.7.5
    commercial dual-use goods and technology export violations, 18.7.1, 18.7.3–18.7.5
    defense articles and services export violations, 18.7, 18.7.3–18.7.5
    economic sanctions programs violations, 18.7.2–18.7.5
    factors considered in assessing penalties, 18.7.5
    ITT Corporation case study, 18.7.5
    parties subject to, 18.7.3
Export controls applicable to institutions of higher education
  compliance procedures, setting up, 32.30
  deemed exports, 32.24.1
  educational information, treatment of, 32.26.2
  export, defined, 32.24.1
  federally sponsored research, requirements related to
    accounting and reporting requirements
      cost sharing arrangements, 32.31.4
      cost transfers, accounting for, 32.31.3
      human-subject research, standards applicable to, 32.31.5
      patentable inventions, 32.31.7
      stimulus funds, requirements related to research funded by, 32.31.6
      summer salaries, accounting for, 32.31.2
      time and effort reporting, 32.31.1
    Bayh-Dole Act requirements, 32.31.7
    generally, 32.31
    OMB circulars, 32.31
    patentable inventions, requirements related to, 32.31.7
    statutory and regulatory requirements, 32.31
  foreign campus, setting up, 32.29
  foreign students and researchers, applicability to
    citizenship status, permissibility of asking for, 32.24.4
    generally, 32.24.2
    parties considered to be "foreign student," 32.24.3
  fundamental research exception, 32.26.2, 32.27.1
  generally, 32.24
  institution activities that may be subject to, 32.25

publicly available information not subject to, 32.26.1
research, regulation of
    federally sponsored research, requirements related to. *See* subhead: federally sponsored research, requirements related to
    fundamental research exception, 32.26.2, 32.27.1
    generally, 32.27
    grants or funding, tips for avoiding pitfalls in negotiating, 32.27.3
    limitations on public dissemination of research results, 32.27.2
teaching, regulation of
    educational information, treatment of, 32.26.2
    generally, 32.26
    publicly available information not subject to export controls, 32.26.1
teaching abroad, 32.28

F

Fair Credit Reporting Act (FCRA)
    background checks, use of credit reports for, 34.1.3, 34.1.4
Fair Labor Standards Act (FLSA). *See* Wage-and-hour regulations
False Claims Act (FCA)
    case studies; conduct giving rise to liability, 11.5
    claims
        defined, 11.2.1
        false claims. *See* subhead: false claims
    compliance programs
        Deficit Reduction Act of 2005, employee education provisions of, 11.24
        generally, 11.22
        lack of compliance program, effect of, 11.23
    conduct that may give rise to liability, 11.2, 11.5
    damage provisions
        generally, 11.4
        qui tam actions, negotiating damages in, 11.17, 11.17.1
    defenses to FCA claims, 11.20
    Deficit Reduction Act of 2005, employee education provisions of, 11.24
    deliberate ignorance standard, 11.3
    false claims
        deliberate ignorance standard, 11.3
        generally, 11.2.2

False Claims Act (FCA), false claims (cont'd)
    "knowing" submission of, 11.3
        reckless disregard standard, 11.3
        simple "falsity," distinguished, 11.2.2
    government contractors, violations by. See Government contractors
    healthcare organizations and providers, applicability to. See Healthcare organizations and providers
    Healthcare Reform Act, effects of, 11.5, 11.7, 11.24
    institutions of higher education, issues related to. See Institutions of higher education
    "knowing" submission of false claims, 11.3
    managed care organizations (MCOs), applicability to. See Managed Care Organizations (MCOs)
    penalties for false claims, 11.4
    prohibited activities, 11.2, 11.5
    qui tam actions. See Qui tam actions
    reckless disregard standard, 11.3
    state false claim statutes, 11.25
    statute of limitations, 11.21
    TARP-related programs, provisions applicable to, 27.4
    types of actions brought under, 11.1
    United States v. Merck-Medco Managed Care LLC, 1.5, 1.5.3, 11.23
    whistleblower actions. See Qui tam actions
False Claims Act provisions
    pharmaceutical and medical device makers, sales and marketing of drugs and devices by, 23.8, 23.8.1
Family and Medical Leave Act (FMLA)
    benefits during leave, requirements regarding, 34.17.10
    circumstances for which leave is available, 34.17.2
    compliance programs, 34.18
    generally, 34.17
    medical documentation for leave, requirements regarding, 34.17.8
    notice requirements, 34.17.8
    parental leave applicable to mother and father, 34.17.5
    persons qualifying for FMLA leave, 34.17.1
    reinstatement requirements, 34.17.11
    requests for leave, procedures for, 34.17.6
    restrictions on how leave may be taken, 34.17.7
    return from leave, obligations to employee upon, 34.17.11
    serious medical condition
        defined, 34.17.3
        disability under ADA, as, 34.17.4
    service member who is sick or injured, leave rights of employee caring for, 34.17.12

Index

unpaid, FMLA leave as, 34.17.9
Family Education and Privacy Act (FERPA). *See* Institutions of higher education, subhead: student education records/information, FERPA protections for
FAR. *See* Federal Acquisition Regulation (FAR) compliance program provisions
FARA. *See* Foreign Agents Registration Act (FARA)
FCA. *See* False Claims Act (FCA)
FCPA. *See* Foreign Corrupt Practices Act (FCPA)
FCRA. *See* Fair Credit Reporting Act (FCRA)
Federal Acquisition Regulation (FAR) compliance program provisions
    See also Government contractors
    code of business ethics and conduct, 15.3.1, 15.3.2
    cost accounting
        applicability, 15.10.11
        Cost Accounting Standards, 15.10.11
        cost principles, 15.10.10
    debarment provisions. *See* subhead: suspension and debarment provisions
    disclosure of violations
        generally, 15.3.6
        incentives, 15.3.7
        knowing failure to disclose. *See* subhead: knowing failure to disclose violation
        mandatory disclosure requirements, 15.3.6
        parties to whom disclosure must be made, 15.3.9
        timely reporting of violation, requirement for, 15.3.7
        types of violations that must be disclosed, 15.3.10
        written disclosure, requirement for, 15.3.8
    full cooperation with government, requirement for, 15.3.12
    generally, 15.3
    hotline or helpline for internal reporting, 15.3.5
    internal controls system, 15.3.3
    internal reporting system, 15.3.5
    knowing failure to disclose violation
        generally, 15.3.11
        suspension and debarment provisions, 15.3.13, 15.6
    parties subject to, 15.3.1
    performance evaluations, compliance program as consideration in, 15.5
    significant overpayments, failure to report, 15.3.13, 15.3.14
    subcontractors, flow-down of compliance clauses to, 15.4
    suspension and debarment provisions
        debarment, implications of, 15.8.2
        generally, 15.6, 15.6.1, 15.8.3

Federal Acquisition Regulation (FAR) compliance program
   provisions, suspension and debarment provisions (*cont'd*)
      knowing failure to disclose violations, 15.3.13
      suspension, implications of, 15.8.1
   training program, 15.3.3
Federal agencies
   banking and financial institutions, regulation of, 25.4.1
   export controls, agencies regulating, 18.1.2
   mandatory compliance procedures, agencies requiring, 1.5.2
Federal Sentencing Guidelines
   administration of compliance programs. *See* Administration of compliance programs
   auditing of compliance program. *See* Auditing and monitoring of compliance programs
   code of ethical conduct, 2.6.1
   compliance program
      administration of compliance programs. *See* Administration of compliance programs
      auditing of compliance program. *See* Auditing and monitoring of compliance programs
      defined, 1.1
      designing and implementing compliance programs. *See* Designing and implementing compliance programs
      effective compliance programs. *See* subhead: effective compliance programs
      enforcement of. *See* Enforcement of compliance programs
      reporting systems, 2.10, 2.10.1
      risk assessments. *See* Risk assessments
      training. *See* Training and education
   designing and implementing compliance programs. *See* Designing and implementing compliance programs
   effective compliance programs
      components of, 2.3, 2.3.1 *et seq.*
      duty of management to ensure business has, 2.2.1
      ethical corporate culture, fostering. *See* Ethical corporate culture
      policies and procedures addressing risk areas, 2.3
      relation of Sentencing Guidelines to, 2.2, 2.2.1
      standard compliance programs, lack of, 2.3.3
      steps companies must take to create, 2.3.2
      2010 proposed amendments to, 2.3.2
   enforcement of compliance program. *See* Enforcement of compliance programs
   ethical corporate culture, fostering. *See* Ethical corporate culture

Index

gap analyses
    performance of, 4.5.1
    purpose of, 4.5
generally, 2.1
monitoring of compliance program. *See* Auditing and monitoring of compliance programs
reporting systems
    generally, 2.10
    non-retaliation policy, 2.10.1
risk assessments. *See* Risk assessments
training. *See* Training and education

Filip Memorandum
    privilege waivers, 6.17.4, 8.5.4

Financial institution compliance programs. *See* Banking and financial institution compliance programs

Financial statements, certification requirements for
    disclosure controls, 28.44.1, 28.44.2
    enforcement actions by SEC, 28.36
    federal tax returns, signing, 28.34.5
    generally, 28.34
    liability for false certifications, 28.34.2
    non-GAAP reporting, 28.35, 28.35.1
    precertification actions, 28.34.6
    section 302 requirements, 28.34.3, 28.34.4
    section 906 certificate, 28.34.1

Fly American Act
    government contractors, compliance issues for, 15.17.7

FMLA. *See* Family and Medical Leave Act (FMLA)

FMS. *See* Foreign Military Sales (FMS) Program

Foreign Agents Registration Act (FARA), 19.17.6

Foreign Assistance Act
    government contractors, civil penalties for violations by, 15.7.17

Foreign Corrupt Practices Act (FCPA)
    "anything of value," meaning of, 17.5
    business purpose test, 17.10
    "corruptly" requirement, 17.3
    "foreign official," scope of, 17.4
    generally, 2.5.1
    influencing or inducing act or decision of foreign official requirement, 17.9
    international investigations
        generally, 16.8.5
        parties subject to FCPA, 16.8.6
    jurisdiction
        domestic concerns subject to FCPA, 17.2.2

Foreign Corrupt Practices Act (FCPA), jurisdiction (*cont'd*)
    generally, 17.2
        interstate commerce requirement, 17.2.3
        issuers subject to FCPA, 17.2.1
        nationality principle of jurisdiction, 17.2.3
    penalty provisions, 15.11.11
    permissible payments, 15.11.10
    prohibited activities, 15.11.9, 17.1
    third parties, liability for payments through
        authorization of illicit payments by third parties, standard for, 17.8
        generally, 17.6
        knowledge standard, 17.7
Foreign Military Sales (FMS) Program
    government contractors, compliance issues for, 15.17.11
Foreign payments
    Foreign Corrupt Practices Act (FCPA) provisions. *See* Foreign Corrupt Practices Act (FCPA)
    government contractors, compliance issues for. *See* Government contractors
Forfeiture of Claim statute
    government contractors, civil penalties for violations by, 15.7.18
Fraud
    government contractors, by. *See* Government contractors
Fraud Enforcement and Recovery Act (FERA)
    TARP-related programs, provisions applicable to, 27.4
Freedom of Information Act (FOIA)
    government contractors, compliance issues for, 15.21

G

Gap analyses
    performance of, 4.5.1
    purpose of, 4.5
Gift and travels rules of House and Senate
    generally, 19.21, 19.21.1, 19.21.2, 19.22
    gift rules
        acceptable gifts, 19.23.2
        commemorative item exception, 19.23.8
        charitable event exception, 19.23.7
        exceptions to, 19.23.3, 19.23.5–19.23.9
        food or drink of nominal value exception, 19.23.9
        generally, 19.23

Index

    gift, defined, 19.23.1
    lobbyists, gifts from, 19.23.4
    pay-to-play laws
        compliance programs, 19.29
        disclosure, 19.28
        entities (investment funds and quasi-governmental), 19.27.3
        federal, 19.27.1
        generally, 19.27
        localities, 19.27.3
        states, 19.27.2
    personal friendship exception, 19.23.5
    widely attended event exception, 19.23.6
  information and guidance on rules, obtaining, 19.21.3
  parties subject to, 19.21
  penalties for violations, 19.21
  travel rules
    aircraft travel, rules for, 19.25
    generally, 19.24
    "necessary expenses," defined, 19.24.2
    "officially connected" travel, payment of expenses of, 19.24.1
    "one-day fact-finding trips," rules for, 19.24.4
    parties who may pay for "officially connected" travel, 19.24.3

Government contractors
  administrative penalties
    Antideficiency Act violations, 15.18
    FAR suspension and debarment provisions. *See* Federal Acquisition Regulation (FAR) compliance program provisions
    kickbacks, 15.11.6
    Program Fraud Civil Remedies Act, 15.8.4
  anticompetitive behavior, prohibition of, 15.10.13
  bidding on contracts
    certification requirements, 15.10.1
    eligibility to bid on contracts, 15.10.2
    Excluded Parties List System, 15.10.3
    generally, 15.10
    "responsible" contractors, 15.10.3
  bribes/illegal gratuities
    acceptable gifts, 15.11.4
    distinction between bribes and gratuities, 15.11.3
    foreign officials, of, 15.11.9, 15.11.11
    generally, 15.11.2
    penalties for, 15.11.5

Government contractors (*cont'd*)
    civil penalties
        anticompetitive behavior, 15.10.13
        Arms Export Control Act (AECA) violations, 15.17.10
        Buy American Act violations, 15.17.4
        criminal versus civil, factors influencing whether case is, 15.7.1
        Foreign Assistance Act violations, 15.7.17
        foreign officials, payments to, 15.11.11
        Forfeiture of Claim statute violations, 15.7.18
        kickbacks, 15.11.6
        lobbying-related violations, 15.11.18, 15.11.19
        Program Fraud Civil Remedies Act, 15.7.16
        Truth in Negotiations Act violations, 15.7.15
    compliance programs
        benefits of, 15.1
        components of, 15.2
        FAR provisions requiring. *See* Federal Acquisition Regulation (FAR) compliance program provisions
        generally, 15.1
        goals of, 15.2
        risk areas, identifying, 2.5.1
    conflicts of interest
        generally, 12.7
        gift-giving, establishing policies related to, 12.7.1
        highly regulated industries, financial arrangements considered conflicts for companies in, 12.7.3
        organizational conflicts of interest. *See* subhead: organizational conflicts of interest (OCIs)
        personal conflicts of interest. *See* subhead: personal conflicts of interest
    conspiracy to defraud, 15.7.8
    contingent fee arrangements, 15.11.7, 15.11.8
    contract performance, compliance issues arising during
        bribes/illegal gratuities. *See* subhead: bribes/illegal gratuities
        conflicts of interest. *See* subhead: conflicts of interest
        contingent fee arrangements, 15.11.7, 15.11.8
        domestic and foreign preference requirements. *See* subhead: domestic and foreign preference requirements, compliance with
        expenditures, tracking, 15.18
        foreign officials, payments to. *See* subhead: foreign officials, payments to
        generally, 15.11
        intellectual property. *See* subhead: intellectual property compliance issues

Index

kickbacks, 15.11.6
lobbying activities. *See* subhead: lobbying activities
procurement information and documents, compliance with statutes and regulations related to, 15.11.1
subcontractor sales, unreasonable restrictions on, 15.12
wage-and-hour statutes and regulations. *See* subhead: wage-and-hour statutes and regulations, compliance with

cost accounting
applicability, 15.10.11
anticompetitive behavior, prohibition of, 15.10.13
FAR's Cost Accounting Standards, compliance with, 15.10.11
FAR's cost principles, compliance with, 15.10.10
generally, 15.10.9

country of origin procurement requirements. *See* subhead: domestic and foreign preference requirements, compliance with

criminal penalties
amount of fines, 15.7.2
anticompetitive behavior, 15.10.13
Antideficiency Act violations, 15.18
Arms Export Control Act (AECA) violations, 15.17.10
bribes/illegal gratuities, 15.11.5
Buy American Act violations, 15.17.4
civil versus criminal, factors influencing whether case is, 15.7.1
conspiracy to defraud, 15.7.8
false statement violations, 15.7.4
foreign officials, payments to, 15.11.11
generally, 15.7
kickbacks, 15.11.6
mail fraud, 15.7.5
major fraud, 15.7.7
obstruction of justice, 15.7.10
RICO violations, 15.7.9
wire fraud, 15.7.6

defective cost or pricing data, price reduction for, 15.9

disclosure requirements
FAR requirements for disclosure of violations. *See* Federal Acquisition Regulation (FAR) compliance program provisions
lobbying activities, 15.11.19

domestic and foreign preference requirements, compliance with
American Investment and Recovery Act provisions, 15.17.2

Government contractors, domestic and foreign preference
  requirements, compliance with (*cont'd*)
    Arms Export Control Act requirements. *See* Arms Export
      Control Act (AECA)
    Berry Amendments requirements, 15.17.6
    Buy-American Act requirements. *See* Buy-American Act
      certification requirements
    Foreign Military Sales (FMS) Program requirements,
      15.17.11
    generally, 15.17, 15.17.1
    Trade Agreements Act requirements, 15.17.5
  employees, liability for acts of, 15.6.1
  employment verification requirements
    E-Verify system. *See* E-Verify system
    generally, 15.14
  E-Verify system. *See* E-Verify system
  expenditures, tracking, 15.18
  False Claims Act violations
    criminal penalties, 15.7.4
    false statement violations, offenses constituting, 15.7.4
    generally, 15.7.3
  FAR provisions. *See* Federal Acquisition Regulation (FAR)
    compliance program provisions
  Foreign Assistance Act violations, civil penalties for, 15.7.17
  foreign officials, payments to
    bribes, prohibition of, 15.11.9
    penalties for violations, 15.11.11
    permissible payments, 15.11.10
  Forfeiture of Claim statute violations, civil penalties for, 15.7.18
  fraud
    Forfeiture of Claim statute violations, 15.7.18
    mail fraud, 15.7.5
    major fraud, 15.7.7
    Program Fraud Civil Remedies Act, 15.7.16, 15.8.4
    wire fraud, 15.7.6
  Freedom of Information Act (FOIA), compliance issues arising
    under, 15.21
  GSA contracts, issues arising under, 15.19, 15.19.2
  illegal gratuities. *See* subhead: bribes/illegal gratuities
  intellectual property compliance issues
    copyright protections, 15.16.2
    generally, 15.16
    limited rights, grants of, 15.16.1
    patented inventions, rights in, 15.16.3
    restricted rights, grants of, 15.16.1
    technical data and computer software rights, 15.16.1

Index

kickbacks, 15.11.6
labor and employment law
    affirmative action plans, 34.24.1
    generally, 34.24
    wage-and-hour statutes and regulations, compliance with. *See* subhead: wage-and-hour statutes and regulations, compliance with
liability
    administrative penalties. *See* subhead: administrative penalties
    civil penalties. *See* subhead: civil penalties
    criminal penalties. *See* subhead: criminal penalties
    employees, liability for acts of, 15.6.1
    FAR suspension and debarment provisions, 15.3.13, 15.6, 15.6.1
    generally, 15.3.6, 15.6
    principal, defined, 15.3
    types of, 15.6.2
    unallowable costs, penalties for, 15.9
lobbying activities
    disclosure requirements, 15.11.19
    generally, 15.11.18
    penalty provisions, 15.11.18, 15.11.19
mail fraud, 15.7.5
major fraud, 15.7.7
obstruction of justice, 15.7.10
obtaining government contracts
    bidding on contracts. *See* subhead: bidding on contracts
    conflicts of interest. *See* subhead: conflicts of interest
    cost accounting. *See* subhead: cost accounting
organizational conflicts of interest (OCIs)
    biased ground rules OCIs, 15.10.5
    contract procurement, conflicts arising after, 15.11.17
    defined, 15.10.4
    developments and changes in the field, 15.10.8
    Federal Awardee Performance and Integrity Information System (FAPIIS) database, 15.10.8
    generally, 12.7.2, 15.10.4
    identification of, 15.10.6
    impaired objectivity OCIs, 15.10.5
    mitigating effects of, 15.10.7
    types of, 15.10.5
    unequal access to information OCIs, 15.10.5
penalties and sanctions applicable to violations by. *See* subhead: liability

Government contractors (cont'd)
  personal conflicts of interest
    current government employees seeking employment with contractors, restrictions on, 15.11.13
    ethics opinions, obtaining, 15.11.16
    former government employees currently working for contractors, restrictions on, 15.11.14
    generally, 15.11.12
    government employees who previously worked for contractors, restrictions on, 15.11.15
  principal, defined, 15.3
  procurement information and documents, compliance with statutes and regulations related to, 15.11.1
  Program Fraud Civil Remedies Act
    administrative penalties, 15.8.4
    civil penalties, 15.7.16
  RICO violations, 15.7.9
  Sarbanes-Oxley Act requirements
    advantages contractors have in dealing with, 15.20.1
    certification requirements, 15.20.2
    generally, 15.20
    in-house lawyers, obligations of, 15.20.4
    officers, obligations of, 15.20.2
    product line executives, obligations of, 15.20.3
    program managers, obligations of, 15.20.3
  small business contracts, issues arising under, 15.19, 15.19.1
  subcontractor sales, unreasonable restrictions on, 15.12
  Truth in Negotiations Act (TINA) provisions. *See* Truth in Negotiations Act (TINA) provisions
  wage-and-hour statutes and regulations, compliance with
    Contract Work Hours and Safety Standards Act requirements, 15.13.5
    Copeland Act requirements, 15.13.4
    Davis-Bacon Act requirements, 15.13.1
    Drug-Free Workplace Act requirements, 15.13.7
    Equal Employment Opportunity requirements, 15.13.6
    generally, 15.13, 34.24.2
    Service Contract Act provisions, 15.13.2
    Walsh-Healey Public Contracts Act requirements, 15.13.3
  wire fraud, 15.7.6

Index

H

Healthcare organizations and providers
    Anti-Kickback Statute provisions
        Bryan v. United States, 20.8.2
        exceptions to, 20.8.5
        False Claims Act, violations of Anti-Kickback Statute also violating, 20.8.4
        generally, 20.8
        "knowingly and willfully," defined, 20.8.2
        OIG advisory opinions, 20.8.8
        "one purpose" standard, applicability of, 20.8.3
        penalty provisions, 20.8.4
        remuneration, defined, 20.8.1
        safe harbor regulations, 20.8.6, 20.8.7
        United States v. Gerber, 20.8.3
    Certification of Compliance Agreement (CCA), 20.3.3
    compliance and ethics programs
        components of effective programs, 20.3, 20.3.1
        creating effective programs, OIG guidance on. *See* subhead: Office of Inspector General (OIG) compliance guidance
        effective compliance programs, components of, 20.3, 20.3.1
        enforcement actions, anticipating, 20.1.3
        financial benefits of, 20.1.1
        generally, 20.1, 20.1.2
        OIG compliance guidance. *See* subhead: Office of Inspector General (OIG) compliance guidance
        In re Columbia/HCA Healthcare Corp., 20.1.2
    Corporate Integrity Agreements (CIAs), 20.3.3
    Deficit Reduction Act provisions
        employee education about false claims laws, requirement for, 20.12.3
        employee handbooks, requirements regarding, 20.12.5
        generally, 20.12
        healthcare entities subject to, 20.12.1, 20.12.2
        penalty provisions, 20.12.6
        policies required by, 20.12.3
        written or electronic format, requirement policies be available in, 20.12.4
    Emergency Medical Treatment and Active Labor Act (EMTALA) provisions. *See* Emergency Medical Treatment and Active Labor Act (EMTALA)
    employee benefit programs, 20.5.3
    enforcement initiatives, 20.3.4, 20.3.5

Healthcare organizations and providers (cont'd)
   False Claims Act (FCA) provisions
      Anti-Kickback Statute violations also triggering violations of, 20.8.4
      generally, 20.7
      "knowingly" committing fraud as violation of, 20.7.1
      penalty provisions, 20.8.4
      risk areas, 20.7.2
   HCREA. *See* subhead: Healthcare Education Reconciliation Act (HCERA)
   Health Information Technology for Economic and Clinical Health Act (HITECH). *See* Health Information Technology for Economic and Clinical Health Act (HITECH)
   Health Insurance Portability and Accountability Act provisions. *See* Health Insurance Portability and Accountability Act (HIPAA)
   Healthcare Education Reconciliation Act (HCERA), effects of, 20.3.5
   Healthcare Reform Law, effects of 20.3.5
   investigations
      Office of Inspector General (OIG), role of, 20.3.2
      settlements. *See* subhead: settlements
   managed care organizations (MCOs). *See* Managed Care Organizations (MCOs)
   Medicaid, 20.5.2
   Medicare
      generally, 20.5.1
      Part D. *See* Medicare Part D
   Office of Inspector General (OIG), enforcement by, 20.3.2, 20.3.3
      compliance program guidance of. *See* subhead: Office of Inspector General (OIG) compliance guidance
      investigations, role in, 20.3.2
   Office of Inspector General (OIG) compliance guidance
      annual work plans, 20.2.2
      compliance program elements, 20.3.1
      generally, 20.2
      industries covered by, 20.2.1
      publications providing, 20.2.2
      voluntary, OIG guidance as, 20.2.3
   Patient Protection and Affordable Care Act (PPCA)
      enforcement, 20.3.5, 20.6
      reimbursement framework
         employee benefit programs, 20.5.3
         generally, 20.5
         Medicaid, 20.5.2
         Medicare
            generally, 20.5.1

Index

Part D. *See* Medicare Part D
risk areas, 20.4
settlements
    Certification of Compliance Agreement (CCA), 20.3.3
    Corporate Integrity Agreements (CIAs), 20.3.3
    generally, 20.3.2
state False Claims Act (FCA) statutes, 20.7
statutory and regulatory scheme
    Anti-Kickback Statute provisions. *See* subhead: Anti-Kickback Statute provisions
    Deficit Reduction Act provisions. *See* subhead: Deficit Reduction Act provisions
    Emergency Medical Treatment and Active Labor Act (EMTALA) provisions. *See* Emergency Medical Treatment and Active Labor Act (EMTALA)
    False Claims Act (FCA) provisions. *See* subhead: False Claims Act (FCA) provisions
    generally, 20.6
    Health Information Technology for Economic and Clinical Health Act (HITECH). *See* Health Information Technology for Economic and Clinical Health Act (HITECH)
    Health Insurance Portability and Accountability Act provisions. *See* Health Insurance Portability and Accountability Act (HIPAA)
    Physician Self-Referral Act (Stark law) disclosures, 20.9.1
    provisions, 20.9
Health Information Technology for Economic and Clinical Health Act (HITECH)
    generally, 20.13
    goals of, 20.13
    rules implementing, 20.13.1
Health insurance coverage
    Consolidated Omnibus Budget Reconciliation Act (COBRA) provisions. *See* Consolidated Omnibus Budget Reconciliation Act (COBRA)
    Health Insurance Portability and Accountability Act (HIPAA) requirements. *See* Health Insurance Portability and Accountability Act (HIPAA)
Health Insurance Portability and Accountability Act (HIPAA)
    business associates
        defined, 24.1.3
        generally, 24.1.4
    compliance programs
        business associate agreements, 24.5

Health Insurance Portability and Accountability Act (HIPAA), compliance programs (cont'd)
    generally, 24.4, 34.16
    key documents, 24.5
    notice of privacy practices, 24.5
    ongoing compliance, requirement for, 24.6
    privacy officials, designation and functions of, 24.4.2
    risk analysis, conducting, 24.4.1
    security officials, designation and functions of, 24.4.2
    written policies and procedures, 24.5
  covered entities
    business associates, 24.1.4
    employers, 24.1.2
    generally, 24.1
    health plan, defined, 24.1.1
    state law requirements, 24.7
  employers, applicability to, 24.1.2
  generally, 20.10, 34.16
  improper disclosure, action subsequent to, 24.9
  notice requirements for improper disclosure, 24.9
  parties who must comply with Act. *See* subhead: covered entities
  pre-existing conditions exclusions, limits on, 34.16
  privacy rule
    generally, 24.2, 34.16
    key requirements, listing of, Table 24-1
    protected health information, defined, 24.2.1
    use and disclosure of protected health information, restrictions on, 24.2.2
  protected health information (PHI), defined, 24.2.1
  security rule
    electronic PHI, applicability to, 24.3.1
    generally, 24.3, 24.3.2
    key requirements, listing of, Table 24-1
  state law requirements for covered entities, 24.7
  student health/medical records, protection of. *See* Institutions of higher education, subhead: student health/medical records, HIPAA protections for
  subpoenas, disclosure of PHI pursuant to, 24.8
HIPAA. *See* Health Insurance Portability and Accountability Act (HIPAA)
HITECH. *See* Health Information Technology for Economic and Clinical Health Act (HITECH)
Holder Memorandum
  generally, 11.22
  privilege waivers, 6.17.1, 8.5.1

Index

Hotlines
    generally, 2.10
    government contractor compliance programs, 15.3.5
    Medicare Part D compliance programs, 21.16.4
House gift and travels rules. *See* Gift and travel rules of House and Senate

I

Identity theft
    business-to-business (B2B) identity theft, 13.4.1
    entities not covered by Red Flag Rules, requirements for, 13.4.3
    generally, 13.4
    prevention program, 13.4.2
    Red Flag Rules, 13.4.1
Implementing compliance programs. *See* Designing and implementing compliance programs
Information technology (IT) resources, procuring. *See* Computing resources
Insider trading
    compliance program, as risk area to address in, 2.5.1
Institutions of higher education
    admissions decisions
        gender-based. *See* subhead: gender-based admissions decisions
        race-based. *See* subhead: race-based admissions decisions
    campus safety and security
        annual security reports, requirement for, 32.9.1
        best practices for prevention and responding to violence, 32.9.3
        Clery Act requirements
            annual security reports, requirement for, 32.9.1
            failure to comply, consequences of, 32.9.2
            generally, 32.9.1
        duty of care between institution and injured party, 32.9
        emergency response and notification systems, 32.9.3
        failure to comply with Clery Act, consequences of, 32.9.2
        legal counsel's role in improving security, 32.9.4
        prevention and responding to violence, best practices for, 32.9.3
        threat assessment teams (TAT), 32.9.3
        violence on campus, liability for, 32.9

Institutions of higher education (*cont'd*)
    compliance programs
        admissions decisions
            gender-based. *See* subhead: gender-based admissions decisions
            race-based. *See* subhead: race-based admissions decisions
        components of, 32.1.1
        export controls, compliance with, 32.30
        False Claims Act (FCA) liability, limiting exposure to, 32.33
        generally, 32.1
        parties who should be involved in, 32.1.2
        risk assessment, 32.2
    copyright issues
        copyright policy, implementation of, 32.22
        faculty members use of copyrighted work without permission of copyright owner
            face-to-face teaching exemption, 32.20.2
            fair-use doctrine, 32.21
            generally, 32.20.2
            TEACH Act provisions, 32.20.2
        faculty-produced work, ownership of copyright in
            generally, 32.20
            specially ordered or commissioned work, copyright in, 32.20
            work-for-hire doctrine, 32.20, 32.21
        infringement, liability for
            contributory infringement, 32.23.1
            Digital Millennium Copyright Act safe harbor provisions, 32.23.2, 32.23.3
            generally, 32.23
            indirect liability of institution, 32.23.1
            ISP, Digital Millennium Copyright Act safe harbor provisions for institutions acting as, 32.23.2, 32.23.3
            joint and several liability, 32.23.1
            penalties for infringement, 32.23
            students or faculty, liability for acts of, 32.23.1
            vicarious liability, 32.23.1
        work-for-hire doctrine
            academic exception, 32.20.1
            generally, 32.20
    disabled persons, obligations regarding
        Americans with Disabilities Act (ADA) and amendments, applicability of, 32.5, 32.5.1
        generally, 32.5
        psychiatric disabilities, challenges posed by persons with, 32.5.1

Index

    Rehabilitation Act provisions, 32.5
education records/information, FERPA protections for. *See* subhead: student education records/information, FERPA protections for
export controls. *See* Export controls applicable to institutions of higher education
False Claims Act (FCA) provisions
    certifications made in connection with receipt of government funding, liability related to, 32.32.2
    compliance program, setting up, 32.33
    federally sponsored research, liability related to, 32.32.3
    generally, 32.32
    improper medical billing, liability related to, 32.32.1
    penalty provisions, 32.32
    public institutions, applicability to, 32.32.4
Family Education and Privacy Act (FERPA) requirements. *See* subhead: student education records/information, FERPA protections for
federal student aid (FSA) programs, participation in
    code of conduct for financial aid personnel, 32.8.4
    eligibility requirements
        institutional eligibility, 32.6
        program eligibility, 32.7
    financial counseling for students, 32.8.6
    institutional eligibility, 32.6
    penalties for violations, 32.8.8
    preferred lender lists, requirements regarding, 32.8.3
    private lenders, requirements for, 32.8.7
    program eligibility, 32.7
    Program Participation Agreement (PPA) requirement, 32.8
    statutory requirements, 32.8
    student loan information notification and disclosure requirements, 32.8.5
    student recruiters, compensation of
        generally, 32.8.1
        incentive compensation prohibition, 32.8.1
        penalties for violations, 32.8.8
        permissible compensation plans under Title IV, 32.8.2
gender-based admissions decisions
    constitutionality of, 32.3.3
    generally, 32.3
    justifications for, 32.3.3
    noncompliant admissions policies, consequences of, 32.3.4
    standard for, 32.3

Institutions of higher education (cont'd)
   Health Insurance Portability and Accountability Act of 1996, protection of health/medical records under. See subhead: student health/medical records, HIPAA protections for
   privacy requirements
      student education records/information, privacy of. See subhead: student education records/information, FERPA protections for
      student health/medical records, HIPAA protections for. See subhead: student health/medical records, HIPAA protections for
   race-based admissions decisions
      compelling interest to consider race, 32.3.1
      generally, 32.3
      justifications for, 32.3.1
      narrowly-tailored programs, 32.3.2
      noncompliant admissions policies, consequences of, 32.3.4
      strict scrutiny standard for, 32.3
   risk assessment, 32.2
   student education records/information, FERPA protections for
      disclosures not requiring student consent
         college officials, disclosure of records to, 32.14.5
         court order, disclosure pursuant to, 32.14.6
         directory information, disclosure of, 32.14.1
         former high school's release of records to post-secondary institutions, 32.14.3
         generally, 32.14
         health or safety emergency exception, 32.14.8, 32.14.9
         legal action between student and educational institution, effect of, 32.14.7
         outside institutions that may access student records, 32.14.4
         parents claiming student as dependent, disclosures to, 32.14.2
         subpoena, disclosure pursuant to, 32.14.6
      education records
         defined, 32.12
         exclusions, 32.12.1
         personally identifiable information, protection of, 32.12
      enforcement of FERPA, 32.10.2
      enforcement within institution, 32.16
      Family Policy Compliance Office (FPCO), enforcement by, 32.10.2
      generally, 32.10
      investigations, 32.10.4
      no private cause of action against institutions, 32.10.3

notice of FERPA rights, 32.17.1
outsourcing of information in student records
    direct control requirement, 32.15.1
    generally, 32.15
    types of information that may be outsourced, 32.15
personally identifiable information, protection of, 32.12
privacy rights under FERPA, 32.10.1
reasonable methods to protect records, requirement for, 32.16
record-keeping requirements
    documenting disclosures, 32.17
    generally, 32.17
    notice of FERPA rights, 32.17.1
records to which FERPA is applicable, 32.10
schools to which FERPA is applicable, 32.10
student access to records
    amendment of inaccurate or misleading information, right of student to request, 32.13.2
    generally, 32.13
    limitation on student's right to access records, 32.13.1
violations, consequences of, 32.11
student health/medical records, HIPAA protections for
    FERPA provisions, interaction of HIPAA provisions and, 32.18.1
    generally, 32.18
    situations where records become subject to, 32.18.2

Insurance
    attorneys insurance policies, effect of Sarbanes-Oxley Act on, 28.31
    directors and officers (D&O) insurance. *See* Directors and officers (D&O) insurance
    Sarbanes-Oxley Act requirements, impact of
        attorneys insurance policies, 28.31
        directors and officers insurance policies, 28.9

Intellectual property
    computing resources, intellectual property rights issues in procuring. *See* Computing resources
    government contractors, compliance issues for. *See* Government contractors
    international investigations
        industries vulnerable to IP rights infringement, 16.8.13
        remedies for infringement, 16.8.14

Internal controls system
    auditing of compliance programs. *See* Auditing and monitoring of compliance programs
    government contractor compliance programs, 15.3.3

Internal controls system (cont'd)
   monitoring of compliance programs. See Auditing and monitoring of compliance programs

Internal investigations
   allegations of wrongdoing triggering investigation
      assessment of seriousness of allegation, 6.1.2
      external allegations, 6.1
      generally, 6.1
      internal allegations, 6.1
      low-risk allegations, 6.1.1
      serious/high-risk allegations, 6.1.1
      seriousness of allegation, assessment of, 6.1.2
   attorney-client privilege. See Attorney-client privilege
   collection of relevant data
      generally, 6.10.6
      litigation holds, 6.10.7, 6.10.8
      records custodian, responsibilities of, 6.10.9
   counsel for company employee witnesses
      criminal investigation, counsel for employees who are targets of, 6.12.9
      generally, 6.11.8, 6.12.7, 9.3
      importance of, 9.3
      in-house counsel, use of
         disadvantages of, 9.4
         generally, 9.4
         Upjohn warnings. See Upjohn warnings
      joint defense agreements, use of, 6.12.8
      outside counsel, procedures for obtaining, 9.5
      Upjohn warnings. See Upjohn warnings
   decision to initiate investigation
      factors affecting, 6.2
      full-scale investigation, deciding whether to initiate, 6.2.1
      high-risk allegations, evaluating, 6.2.1
      low-risk allegations, evaluating, 6.2.1
      parties responsible for, 6.2.1
   disclosure of investigation to employees
      circulation of notice, methods of, 6.12.2
      contents of notice, 6.12.4, 6.12.5, 6.12.10
      counsel for employee witnesses. See subhead: counsel for company employee witnesses
      criminal investigation, contents of notice where company under, 6.12.5
      criminal investigation, treatment of employees who are targets of, 6.12.9
      employee's rights if approached by law enforcement, 6.12.6
      generally, 6.12

Index

    investigated employees, identification of, 6.12.1
    statements in defense of company, 6.12.3
  document and data preservation
    collection of relevant data. *See* subhead: collection of relevant data
    document destruction policies, suspension of, 6.10.1, 6.10.2
    e-data, preservation of, 6.10.2, 6.10.3
    generally, 6.10
    offsite e-data, identification and preservation of, 6.10.3
    relevant documents and data, identification of
      collection of relevant data. *See* subhead: collection of relevant data
      generally, 6.10.4
      guidance in identifying relevant data, 6.10.5
  facts, gathering, 6.9
  government allegations, investigations in response to
    civil investigative demand (CID), ramifications of, 6.3.6
    generally, 6.3.3
    government agent or attorney, obtaining information from, 6.3.7
    grand jury subpoenas, ramifications of, 6.3.6
    scope of government's inquiry, determining, 6.3.4–6.3.7
    search warrants as source of information, 6.3.5
  initiating investigation
    decision to initiate investigation. *See* subhead: decision to initiate investigation
    document and data preservation. *See* subhead: document and data preservation
    facts, gathering, 6.9
    interviews. *See* subhead: interviews
    leadership. *See* subhead: leadership
    purpose of investigation, defining. *See* subhead: purpose of investigation, defining
    scope of investigation. *See* subhead: scope of investigation
    staffing. *See* subhead: staffing
    timing of investigation, 6.5, 6.5.1
    type of investigation, determining. *See* subhead: type of investigation, determining
  interviews
    attorney-client privilege, applicability of, 6.11.10–6.11.12
    interviewers as representatives of company, 6.11.3
    parties who should be interviewed, 6.11
    parties who should conduct interviews, 6.11.2
    qui tam actions, witness interviews in, 11.13
    refusal of witness to cooperate, 6.11.9
    separate counsel for witness. *See* subhead: counsel for company employee witnesses

Internal investigations, interviews (*cont'd*)
    Upjohn warnings. *See* Upjohn warnings
    when interviews should be conducted, 6.11.1
    work-product doctrine, applicability of, 6.11.10–6.11.12
  leadership
    confidentiality of investigation, maintaining, 6.7.1
    in-house counsel, selection of, 6.7.2
    legal counsel, use of, 6.7–6.7.2
    outside counsel, selection of, 6.7.2
  pre-investigation considerations
    allegations of wrongdoing triggering investigation. *See* subhead: allegations of wrongdoing triggering investigation
    decision to initiate investigation. *See* subhead: decision to initiate investigation
  privileges
    attorney-client privilege. *See* Attorney-client privilege
    generally, 6.13
    work-product doctrine. *See* Work-product doctrine
  purpose of investigation, defining
    generally, 6.4
    logistical needs of investigation, 6.4.1
    methods of investigation, 6.4.1
  qui tam actions, in response to. *See* Qui tam actions
  scope of investigation
    factors considered in determining, 6.6.1
    generally, 6.4.1, 6.6
    initial decision as to, 6.6.2
  SEC scrutiny of attorney actions in conducting, 28.33.1
  staffing
    forensic experts, use of, 6.8.3, 6.8.4
    generally, 6.4.1, 6.8
    professional investigators, use of, 6.8.1, 6.8.2
  timing of investigation, 6.5, 6.5.1
  type of investigation, determining
    external non-government sources, effect of allegations from, 6.3.8
    government authorities, effect of allegations from. *See* subhead: government allegations, investigations in response to
    high-risk allegations, investigation of, 6.3.1
    internal allegations, effect of, 6.3.2
    low-risk allegations, investigation of, 6.3
  Upjohn warnings. *See* Upjohn warnings
  voluntary disclosures, subsequent to
    areas investigation should cover, 8.3.1

Index

    discovery of and response to problem, reporting information related to, 8.3.3
    financial impact of disclosed activities, calculating, 8.3.4
    generally, 8.3
    internal investigation reports, 8.3.2, 8.3.3
    scope of activity, reporting information related to, 8.3.2
    self-assessment reports, 8.3.4
    verification investigation by government, 8.3.5
  witnesses
    counsel for company employees. *See* subhead: counsel for company employee witnesses
    interviews. *See* subhead: interviews
  work-product doctrine. *See* Work-product doctrine

International business practices
  compliance program, as risk area to address in, 2.5.1
  export controls. *See* Export controls
  Foreign Corrupt Practices Act (FCPA) regulations. *See* Foreign Corrupt Practices Act (FCPA)

International investigations
  anticompetitive and unfair business practices
    cartel practices. *See* subhead: cartel anticompetitive and unfair business practices
    noncartel practices, 16.8.4 *et seq.*
  attorney-client privilege, applicability of, 16.5
  bribery
    foreign anti-bribery statutes, 16.8.7
    Foreign Corrupt Practices Act (FCPA) provisions, 16.8.5, 16.8.6
    parties subject to FCPA, 16.8.6
  cartel anticompetitive and unfair business practices
    Corporate Leniency Program, 16.8.3
    frequency and significance of government investigations, 16.8.1
    generally, 16.8.1
    problems in investigating and prosecuting cartels, 16.8.2
    success of government investigations, reasons for, 16.8.3
  client, knowledge of, 16.9
  conducting investigation
    parties who should conduct investigation, 16.9.1
    preliminary considerations, 16.9
  corporate governance investigations
    external triggers for, 16.8.12
    internal triggers for, 16.8.11
  document collection and review, 16.3
  export controls
    generally, 16.8.8, 16.8.10

International investigations, export controls (cont'd)
    technology industry, compliance and risk management in, 16.8.9
  generally, 16.1
  intellectual property investigations
    industries vulnerable to IP rights infringement, 16.8.13
    remedies for infringement, 16.8.14
  investigative plan, establishing, 16.9
  issue spotting, 16.9
  issues raised by
    attorney-client privilege, applicability of, 16.5
    document collection and review, 16.3
    generally, 16.2
    jurisdiction. *See* subhead: jurisdiction
    travel considerations, 16.7
    witness interviews. *See* subhead: witness interviews
  jurisdiction
    conduct outside United States, laws applicable to, 16.6.1
    U.S. courts, jurisdiction of, 16.6
  objectives and priorities of investigation, establishing, 16.9
  parties who should conduct investigation, 16.9.1
  practice areas where international investigations occur, 16.8, 16.8.1 *et seq.*
  preliminary considerations, 16.9
  travel considerations, 16.7
  witness interviews
    generally, 16.4
    on-site visits and interviews, 16.4.1
    telephone interviews, 16.4.1
    video conference, interviews by, 16.4.1
International Traffic in Arms Regulations (ITAR)
  broker, defined, 18.4.4
  brokering, defined, 18.4.5
  Commodity Jurisdiction (CJ) requests, 18.3.6
  deemed exports, 18.4
  defense article, defined, 18.3.1
  defense services, defined, 18.3.3
  determining whether an article or service is ITAR-controlled, 18.3.6
  exports, defined, 18.4
  licensing
    applications for, 18.4.2
    exemptions, 18.4.3
  look through treatment, 18.3.4
  penalty provisions, 18.7, 18.7.3–18.7.5
  re-exports, authorization requirements for, 18.4.1

Index

retransfers, authorization requirements for, 18.4.1
scope of, 18.3
technical data, defined, 18.3.2
United States Munitions List (USML), 18.3.5
Interviews
    internal investigations, in. *See* Internal investigations
    SEC investigations, in. *See* SEC investigations, subhead: witness testimony
Investigations
    healthcare organizations and providers, of. *See* Healthcare organizations and providers
    internal investigations. *See* Internal investigations
    international investigations. *See* International investigations
    SEC investigations. *See* SEC investigations
ITAR. *See* International Traffic in Arms Regulations (ITAR)

J

Jurisdiction
    economic sanctions programs, 18.6.5
    Foreign Corrupt Practices Act (FCPA). *See* Foreign Corrupt Practices Act (FCPA)
    international investigations
        conduct outside United States, laws applicable to, 16.6.1
        U.S. courts, jurisdiction of, 16.6

K

Kickbacks
    See also Anti-Kickback Statute (AKS)
    compliance program, as risk area to address in, 2.5.1
    government contractors, 15.11.6

L

Labor and employment law
    benefit programs
        Employee Retirement Income Security Act (ERISA) provisions. *See* Employee Retirement Income Security Act (ERISA)

Labor and employment law, benefit programs *(cont'd)*
    Health Insurance Portability and Accountability Act
        (HIPAA) requirements. *See* Health Insurance Portability
        and Accountability Act (HIPAA)
    compliance programs and issues
        discrimination issues. *See* Employment discrimination
        employee relations as risk area to address in, 2.5.1
        Family and Medical Leave Act (FMLA) policies, 34.18
        wage-and-hour issues. *See* Wage-and-hour regulations
    Consolidated Omnibus Budget Reconciliation Act (COBRA). *See*
        Consolidated Omnibus Budget Reconciliation Act (COBRA)
    discrimination. *See* Employment discrimination
    email, monitoring of
        generally, 13.3.2
        written email policy, 13.3.3
    employee privacy
        Electronic Communications Privacy Act (ECPA) provisions,
        applicability of, 13.3, 13.3.1, 13.3.2
        email, monitoring of. *See* subhead: email, monitoring of
    employment eligibility and verification. *See* Employment
        eligibility and verification
    family and medical leave. *See* Family and Medical Leave Act
        (FMLA)
    government contractors, statutes and regulations applicable to.
        See Government contractors
    health insurance coverage
        Consolidated Omnibus Budget Reconciliation Act (COBRA)
            provisions. *See* Consolidated Omnibus Budget
            Reconciliation Act (COBRA)
        Health Insurance Portability and Accountability Act
            (HIPAA) requirements. *See* Health Insurance Portability
            and Accountability Act (HIPAA)
    layoffs. *See* Worker Adjustment Retraining and Notification Act
        (WARN)
    military leave. *See* Uniformed Services Employment and
        Reemployment Rights Act (USERRA)
    National Labor Relations Act (NLRA) provisions. *See* National
        Labor Relations Act (NLRA)
    plant closings. *See* Worker Adjustment Retraining and
        Notification Act (WARN)
    polygraphs, regulation of, 34.22, 34.22.1
    Uniformed Services Employment and Reemployment Rights Act
        (USERRA). *See* Uniformed Services Employment and
        Reemployment Rights Act (USERRA)
    wage-and-hour regulations. *See* Wage-and-hour regulations

Index

Layoffs, WARN provisions applicable to. *See* Worker Adjustment Retraining and Notification Act (WARN)
LDA. *See* Lobbying Disclosure Act (LDA) of 1995
Litigation holds
    duration of, 5.9.2
    electronically stored information (ESI) and. *See* Electronic discovery
    generally, 5.9
    internal investigations, 6.10.7, 6.10.8
    notice to employees, 5.9.1
Lobbying activities
    bundled contributions, reporting requirements for, 19.13.1
    government contractors, by. *See* Government contractors
    Lobbying Disclosure Act of 1995 provisions. *See* Lobbying Disclosure Act of 1995
Lobbying Disclosure Act (LDA) of 1995
    certification requirements, 19.17.3
    covered official, defined, 19.16.7
    compliance programs, 19.20
    executive branch lobbying, registrations and filings for, 19.17.5
    filing schedule, 19.17.4
    foreign corporations, requirements for in-house lobbyist for, 19.17.6
    generally, 19.16
    Government Accountability Office (GAO), oversight, 19.19
    lobbying activities, defined, 19.16.5
    lobbying contact
        defined, 19.16.3
        exceptions to, 19.16.4
    lobbyist, defined, 19.16.6
    penalty provisions, 19.16.2
    prosecutions under, 19.18
    quarterly reports, contents of, 19.17.2
    registration requirements
        contents of registration, 19.17.1
        de minimis exception, 19.17
        parties who must register, 19.16.1
        procedures for registration, 19.17
    reports
        audits, 19.19
        quarterly reports, contents of, 19.17.2
        semi-annual reports, contents of, 19.17.3
    semi-annual reports, contents of, 19.17.3

M

Making Home Affordable Program (MHAP), 27.2.12
Managed Care Organizations (MCOs)
    compliance programs
        auditing and monitoring of, 22.6.5
        CMS requirements, 22.6, 22.6.1 *et seq.*
        communication, developing effective lines of, 22.6.4
        compliance committee, functions of, 22.6.2
        compliance officer, functions of, 22.6.2
        corrective action, procedures for, 22.6.7
        disciplinary guidelines, 22.6.6
        failure to comply, penalties for, 22.7
        FFS compliance programs, differentiated, 22.5
        generally, 22.4
        MA-PD plan compliance program requirements, 22.6.8
        penalties for failure to comply, 22.7
        training requirements, 22.6.3
        written policies and procedures, contents of and requirements for, 22.6.1
    denial or unavailability of care
        failure to provide care, consequences of, 22.14.1
        fraud and abuse determinations, factors considered in, 22.14
    False Claims Act (FCA) provisions
        elements required for liability, 22.9.1
        generally, 22.8
        Medicare Advantage (MA) MCOs, risk areas for, 22.11
        parties subject to liability under, 22.9
        penalty provisions, 22.9.2
    federal monitoring and enforcement, 22.1, 22.2
    fraud and abuse
        federal monitoring and enforcement, 22.1, 22.2
        state monitoring and enforcement, 22.3
    marketing practices of Medicare MCOs, regulation of, 22.15
    Medicare MCOs, regulation of marketing practices of, 22.15
    physician incentive plans (PIPs), liability issues related to, 22.12
    prompt payment requirements
        clean claims, defined, 22.13.1
        failure to make prompt payments, consequences of, 22.13.2
        generally, 22.13
    state monitoring and enforcement, 22.3
    statutory scheme
        False Claims Act (FCA) provisions. *See* subhead: False Claims Act provisions

Index

generally, 22.10
Marketing
    Medicare MCOs, regulation of marketing practices of, 22.15
    Medicare Part D stakeholders, guidelines for
        co-branding, standards for, 21.11
        patient steering, risks posed by, 21.12
    pharmaceutical and medical device makers. *See* Pharmaceutical and medical device makers
McNulty Memorandum
    pre-existing compliance programs, relevance of, 1.4.1
    privilege waivers, 6.17.3, 8.5.3
MCOs. *See* Managed Care Organizations (MCOs)
Medicaid, 20.5.2
Medical device manufacturers. *See* Pharmaceutical and medical device makers
Medicare
    clinical trials, Medicare coverage in. *See* Biomedical research/clinical trials
    generally, 20.5.1
    Part D. *See* Medicare Part D
Medicare Improvements for Patients and Providers Act (MIPPA), 21.3
Medicare Part D
    Anti-Kickback Statute provisions
        coinsurance waivers, 21.8
        deductible amounts, waivers of, 21.8
        electronic health records safe harbor, 21.14
        electronic prescribing safe harbor, 21.13
        financially needy individuals, exception for waivers for, 21.15
        free or discounted drugs, pharmacies offering, 21.9
        generally, 21.5
        manufacturer rebates/price concessions, 21.10
        marketing guidelines. *See* subhead: marketing guidelines
        patient assistance programs (PAPs), risks associated with. *See* subhead: patient assistance programs (PAPs), Anti-Kickback Statute risks associated with
        price concessions, negotiation and disclosure of, 21.10
        rebates, pharmacy's handling of, 21.10
        reduction of cost-sharing exception, 21.15
        safe harbor provisions, 21.13, 21.14
    benefits provided by, 21.1.2
    CMS audits, 21.18
    co-branding, standards for, 21.11
    coinsurance waivers, 21.8

Medicare Part D (cont'd)
  compliance programs
    auditing and monitoring of, 21.16.6
    communication, developing effective lines of, 21.16.4
    compliance committee, requirement for, 21.16.2
    compliance officer, requirement for, 21.16.2
    components of, 21.16
    enforcement of, 21.16.5
    fraud and abuse plans, 21.16.7
    generally, 21.2
    hotline, use of, 21.16.4
    self-reporting as voluntary, 21.16.8
    training and education requirements, 21.16.3
    written policies and procedures, contents of and requirements for, 21.16.1
  deductible amounts, waivers of, 21.8
  delegation of compliance duties, 21.17
  detection of fraud. *See* subhead: prevention/detection of fraud
  electronic health records safe harbor to Anti-Kickback Statute, 21.14
  electronic prescribing safe harbor to Anti-Kickback Statute, 21.13
  free or discounted drugs, pharmacies offering, 21.9
  generally, 21.1
  marketing guidelines
    co-branding, standards for, 21.11
    patient steering, risks posed by, 21.12
  Medicare Improvements for Patients and Providers Act (MIPPA) provisions, 21.3
  OIG audits, 21.19
  patient assistance programs (PAPs), Anti-Kickback Statute risks associated with
    independent charities, risks for PAPs associated with, 21.6.3
    manufacturer-affiliated PAPs, risks for, 21.6.1, 21.6.2
    True Out-of-Pocket Cost (TROOP) requirement, subsidies helping beneficiaries meet, 21.6.1, 21.6.2
    uninsured patients, risks for PAPs providing benefits to, 21.7.1
  patient steering, risks posed by, 21.12
  prevention/detection of fraud
    CMS audits, 21.18
    OIG audits, 21.19
  price concessions, negotiation and disclosure of, 21.10
  rebates, pharmacy's handling of, 21.10

Index

risk areas
    Anti-Kickback Statute provisions. *See* subhead: Anti-Kickback Statute provisions
    generally, 21.4
voluntary program, as, 21.1.1
MHAP. *See* Making Home Affordable Program (MHAP)
Military leave. *See* Uniformed Services Employment and Reemployment Rights Act (USERRA)
MIPPA. *See* Medicare Improvements for Patients and Providers Act (MIPPA)
MLCA. *See* Money Laundering Control Act (MLCA)
Money laundering
    anti-money laundering compliance programs. *See* Anti-money laundering compliance programs
    Bank Secrecy Act (BSA) provisions. *See* Bank Secrecy Act (BSA)
    compliance programs related to. *See* Anti-money laundering compliance programs
    defined, 26.1
    generally, 26.1
    goals of, 26.1
    methods for laundering money
        forms that money and property can take, 26.1.5
        generally, 26.1.1
        integration stage, 26.1.4
        layering process, 26.1.3
        placement stage, 26.1.2
    Money Laundering Control Act (MLCA) provisions. *See* Money Laundering Control Act (MLCA)
    money services businesses (MSBs)
    rules applicable to, 26.17
    foreign requirements, 26.18
    specially designated persons, prohibited transactions with
        generally, 26.15
        OFAC list, 2.5.1, 26.15
        penalty provisions, 26.16.1
        types of transactions prohibited, 26.16
        United States person, defined, 26.15.1
    statutory and regulatory framework
        Bank Secrecy Act (BSA) provisions. *See* Bank Secrecy Act (BSA)
        corporate liability principle, applicability of, 26.2.1
        generally, 26.2
        Money Laundering Control Act (MLCA) provisions. *See* Money Laundering Control Act (MLCA)
        money services businesses (MSBs), rules applicable to, 26.17, 26.18

Money laundering, statutory and regulatory framework (cont'd)
    parties subject to anti-money laundering laws, 26.2.1
    specially designated persons, prohibited transactions with.
        See subhead: specially designated persons, prohibited transactions with

Money Laundering Control Act (MLCA)
    definitions
        criminally derived property, 26.5.2
        deliberate indifference, 26.3.2
        financial institutions, 26.3.6
        financial transactions, 26.3.4
        knowledge, 26.3.2
        monetary instruments, 26.3.5
        monetary transactions, 26.5.1
        some form of unlawful activity, 26.3.1
        specified unlawful activity, 26.3.3
        willful blindness, 26.3.2
    engaging in monetary transactions in property derived from specified unlawful activity; section 1957
        criminally derived property, defined, 26.5.2
        extraterritorial jurisdiction, 26.5.3
        generally, 26.5
        monetary transaction, defined, 26.5.1
        penalty provisions, 26.5.4
    generally, 26.3
    jurisdiction
        engaging in monetary transactions in property derived from specified unlawful activity; section 1957, 26.5.3
        laundering of monetary instruments; section 1956, 26.4.5
    laundering of monetary instruments; section 1956
        extraterritorial jurisdiction, 26.4.5
        generally, 26.4
        penalty provisions, 26.4.4
        sting operations, prohibitions related to, 26.4.3
        transaction money laundering, prohibition of, 26.4.1
        transportation money laundering, prohibition of, 26.4.2
    parties subject to, 26.3
    penalty provisions, 26.3
        engaging in monetary transactions in property derived from specified unlawful activity; section 1957, 26.5.4
        laundering of monetary instruments; Section 1956, 26.4.4

Monitoring of compliance programs. *See* Auditing and monitoring of compliance programs

Motions
    qui tam actions, in, 11.16

N

National Labor Relations Act (NLRA)
    collective bargaining agreements, 34.23.3
    negotiations with union, 34.23.2
    unionization activities
        employer obligations with regards to, 34.23.1
        protected activities, 34.23
NLRA. *See* National Labor Relations Act (NLRA)
Non-retaliation policy, 2.10.1

O

Obstruction of justice
    government contractors, violations by, 15.7.10
OFAC. *See* Office of Foreign Assets Control (OFAC)
Office of Foreign Assets Control (OFAC)
    list of suspected terrorists, 2.5.1, 26.15
Office of Inspector General (OIG)
    healthcare organizations and providers, monitoring of. *See* Healthcare organizations and providers
    Medicare Part D plans, audits of, 21.19
Officers
    compensation issues. *See* Executive compensation
    compliance officers. *See* Administration of compliance programs
    insurance. *See* Directors and officers (D&O) insurance
    penalty provisions
        cases involving, 28.8.2
        civil penalties, 28.8.1
        criminal penalties, 28.8.1
        generally, 28.8
        SEC powers to petition for judicial freeze of corporate assets, 28.8.1
    prohibited conduct, 28.7
    Sarbanes-Oxley Act requirements
        generally, 28.7
        insurance implications, 28.9
        penalty provisions. *See* subhead: penalty provisions
        prohibited conduct, 28.7
        underwriters, impact on, 28.9.1
OIG. *See* Office of Inspector General (OIG)

P

PACs. *See* Political action committees (PACs)
PAPs. *See* Patient assistance programs (PAPs)
Patient assistance programs (PAPs)
    Anti-Kickback Statute, risks associated with
        Medicare Part D risks. *See* Medicare Part D
        outside Medicare Part D, risks for PAPs that operate, 21.7
    generally, 21.6
    Medicare Part D compliance. *See* Medicare Part D
PATRIOT Act. *See* USA PATRIOT Act
Penalties and sanctions
    See also specific statutes
    banking and financial institutions, actions against. *See* Banking and financial institution compliance programs
    export control violations, penalties for. *See* Export controls
    false claims, penalties for, 11.4
    government contractors, liability of. *See* Government contractors
    misbranding, penalties for, 23.2.5
    records management program, sanctions for noncompliance with, 5.6.2
    SEC investigations, remedies sought pursuant to. *See* Wells Process, subhead: remedies SEC may seek
    spoliation of evidence, sanctions for, 7.6, 7.6.3
Personal information, privacy and security of
    compliance programs, 13.7
    data privacy laws
        compliance with, 13.1.2
        concerns addressed by, 13.1
        personal information, defined, 13.1.1
    employee privacy. *See* Employer-employee
    identity theft. *See* Identity theft
    privacy policy
        administration of policy, 13.2.4
        choices available to data subjects, 13.2.3
        fair information practices, principles of, 13.2.2
        generally, 13.2
        links to privacy policy, use of, 13.2.1
        modification of policy, 13.2.5
        placement of policy, 13.2.1
        principles of, 13.2.2
        third-party seals of approval or certifications of, 13.2.6
    security protections, 13.6
    third-party security audits, 13.6

Index

Pharmaceutical and medical device makers
  advertising
    brief summary of side effects, contraindications and effectiveness, requirement for, 23.4.2, 23.4.3
    broadcast requirements, 23.4.3
    contents of advertisements, requirements for, 23.4.1
    defined, 23.4
    exceptions to advertising requirements, 23.4.5
    filing of advertisement with FDA, 23.4.8
    generally, 23.3
    misbranding, 23.4.9, 23.4.10
    post-marketing approval reports, 23.4.8
    pre-approval by FDA, 23.4.6, 23.4.7
    true, balanced and not-misleading advertising, requirement for, 23.4.4, Table 23-1, Table 23-2
  Anti-Kickback Statute (AKS) provisions
    benefits to purchases, considerations related to providing, 23.7.6
    consultant training, education and sales, considerations related to, 23.7.8
    consulting arrangements, considerations related to, 23.7.11
    discounts, considerations related to, 23.7.2
    donations to charitable organizations, considerations related to, 23.7.5
    educational grants, considerations related to, 23.7.4
    generally, 23.7
    gifts, considerations related to, 23.7.9
    price reporting, considerations related to, 23.7.7
    product support services, considerations related to, 23.7.3
    remuneration, defined, 23.18
    research funding, considerations related to, 23.7.5
    risk areas, 23.7.1
    switching arrangements, considerations related to, 23.7.10
  biomedical research/clinical trials. *See* Biomedical research/clinical trials
  False Claims Act provisions, 23.8, 23.8.1
  labeling
    communications constituting, 23.2
    contents of label, requirements regarding, 23.2.1
    exemptions from labeling requirements, 23.15.2
    generally, 23.3, 23.2
    medical devices, 23.2.3
    misbranding, 23.2.4, 23.2.5
    over-the-counter drugs, 23.2.2
  Medicare Part D. *See* Medicare Part D

1403

Pharmaceutical and medical device makers (*cont'd*)
    misbranding
        advertising violations, 23.4.9, 23.4.10
        labeling violations, 23.2.4, 23.2.5
        off-label promotion, 23.16.3
        penalties for, 23.4.10, 23.2.5
    off-label uses
        advertising or promotion of off-label use, prohibition of, 23.5.2
        generally, 23.5
        intended use, 23.5.5
        misbranding, off-label promotion constituting, 23.16.3
        prescribing drug for off-label use, legality of, 23.5.1
        unapproved new drug, off-label promotion constituting introduction of, 23.5.4
    penalties for misbranding, 23.4.10, 23.2.5
    Prescription Drug Marketing Act provisions
        free samples, permissibility of providing, 23.9.1
        generally, 23.9
    risk areas
        advertising. *See* subhead: advertising
        biomedical research/clinical trials. *See* Biomedical research/clinical trials
        generally, 23.1
        labeling. *See* subhead: labeling
        sales and marketing. *See* subhead: sales and marketing
    risk areas for, 23.1
    sales and marketing regulations
        Anti-Kickback Statute provisions. *See* subhead: Anti-Kickback Statute (AKS) provisions
        False Claims Act provisions, 23.8, 23.8.1
        generally, 23.6
        Prescription Drug Marketing Act provisions, 23.9, 23.9.1
        state laws and regulations, 23.6.1
Physician incentive plans (PIPs)
    managed care organizations (MCOs), liability issues for, 22.12
Physician Self-Referral Act
    healthcare organizations and providers, applicability to, 20.9, 20.9.1
PIPs. *See* Physician incentive plans (PIPs)
Plant closings, WARN provisions applicable to. *See* Worker Adjustment Retraining and Notification Act (WARN)
Political action committees (PACs)
    bundled contributions, reporting requirements for, 19.13.1
    compliance, ensuring, 19.5.3
    contribution limits, 19.5.2

Index

defined, 19.4
EIN. *See* subhead Employer Identification Number (EIN)
disclosure requirements, 19.5.1
Employer Identification Number (EIN), 19.5
expenditures corporation may make, 19.4.2
formation of PACs, 19.5
generally, 19.4
multi-candidate PACs
    contribution limits, 19.5.2
    notice of multi-candidate status, filing of, 19.5.1
participation in PACs, restrictions on, 19.4.1
separate segregated funds (SSFs). *See* Separate segregated funds (SSFs)
treasurer, role of, 19.5.3
Political activities
    coordination
        corporations, permissibility of coordination by, 19.11.5
        defined, 19.10
    corporate activities
        aircraft, permissibility of allowing candidate to fly on, 19.15.2
        coordination, 19.10
        corporate communications regarding federal candidates. *See* subhead: corporate communications regarding federal candidates
        corporate resources or facilities, permissibility of use of, 19.15
        electioneering communication, defined, 19.8
        expenditures of corporate resources that are permissible, 19.3
        express advocacy, 19.6
        impermissible activities, 19.1
        independent expenditures, 19.9
        inviting candidate to corporate facility, permissibility of, 19.15.1
        issue advocacy, 19.7
        lobbying. *See* Lobbying activities
        permissible federal corporate political activities, 19.2, 19.3
        political action committees (PACs). *See* Political action committees (PACs)
        prohibited activities, 19.1
    corporate communications regarding federal candidates
        Citizens United v. Federal Elections Commission, 19.11.1
        coordination, permissibility of, 19.11.5
        disclosure requirements, 19.11.6
        electioneering communications, regulation of, 19.11.4

Political activities, corporate communications regarding federal candidates (*cont'd*)
    employees outside restricted class, permissible communications to, 19.11.1
    express advocacy, regulation of, 19.11.2
    issue advocacy, regulation of, 19.11.3
    public, permissible communications to, 19.11.1
    restricted class, permissible communications to, 19.11
  electioneering communications
    corporate communications, regulation of, 19.11.4
    defined, 19.8
  employee activities
    bundling of contributions, prohibition of, 19.13, 19.13.1
    contributions limits, 19.12
    corporate reimbursement of contributions, prohibition of, 19.12.1
    foreign nationals, prohibition of contributions from, 19.12.1
    work hours, political activity conducted during, 19.14
  express advocacy
    corporate communications regarding federal candidates, regulation of, 19.11.2
    defined, 19.6
  gift and travels rules of House and Senate. *See* Gift and travel rules of House and Senate
  independent expenditures, defined, 19.9
  issue advocacy
    corporate communications regarding federal candidates, regulation of, 19.11.3
    defined, 19.7
  lobbying. *See* Lobbying activities
  local laws and regulations, 19.26
  political action committees (PACs). *See* Political action committees (PACs)
  state laws and regulations, 19.26
PPIP. *See* Public-Private Investment Program (PPIP)
Prescription Drug Marketing Act (PDMA)
  free samples, permissibility of providing, 23.9.1
  generally, 23.9
Privacy
  employee privacy. *See* Employer-employee
  personal information, privacy and security of. *See* Personal information, privacy and security of
  student education and medical records, privacy of. *See* Institutions of higher education
Privileges
  attorney-client privilege. *See* Attorney-client privilege

Index

work-product doctrine. *See* Work-product doctrine
Product safety
    compliance program, as risk area to address in, 2.5.1
Program Fraud Civil Remedies Act
    government contractors, violations by
        administrative penalties, 15.8.4
        civil penalties, 15.7.16
Public-Private Investment Program (PPIP), 27.2.7

Q

Qui tam actions
    See also False Claims Act (FCA)
    complaints
        filing of, 11.9
        seal, length of time complaint remains under, 11.9.1
        service of, 11.9
    damages, negotiation of, 11.17, 11.17.1
    defendant's learning that action is pending, 11.9.3
    document production
        generally, 11.11
        government use of produced documents, 11.11.3
        negotiation as to scope, timing and methodology of, 11.11
        protective orders, seeking, 11.11.1
        responding to, 11.11.2
    internal investigation, conducting
        disciplinary actions, 11.13.1
        disclosing findings to government, 11.12.1
        generally, 11.12
        witnesses, interviews of, 11.13
    intervention by government, 11.9.2
    lifecycle of case
        damages, negotiation of, 11.17, 11.17.1
        document production. *See* subhead: document production
        generally, 11.10
        information from government, obtaining, 11.14
        internal investigation, conducting. *See* subhead: internal investigation, conducting
        motions practice, 11.16
        pre-intervention presentations, 11.15
        retaliation against whistleblower, prohibition of
            contracting partners, whistleblower working for or associated with, 11.19.1
            current employee as whistleblower, 11.19
        settlement, negotiation of, 11.18

Qui tam actions *(cont'd)*
    motions practice, 11.16
    pre-intervention presentations, 11.15
    procedures
        complaints. *See* subhead: complaints
        defendant's learning that action is pending, 11.9.3
        intervention by government, 11.9.2
    retaliation against whistleblower, prohibition of
        contracting partners, whistleblower working for or associated with, 11.19.1
        current employee as whistleblower, 11.19
    service of complaint, 11.9
    settlement, negotiation of, 11.18
    whistleblower/relator
        amount of recovery that may be awarded to, 11.8
        generally, 11.6
        limitations on, 11.7
        parties who can be, 11.7

R

Racketeer Influenced and Corrupt Organizations Act (RICO)
    government contractors, violations by, 15.7.9
RCRA. *See* Resource Conservation and Recovery Act (RCRA)
Records management program
    applicable law, retention periods set by, 5.5
    backup systems, relation to, 5.7.1
    benefits of, 5.1
    business rules, 5.1.1
    components of, 5.1.1
    designing program, 5.1.3
    disaster recovery plans, relation to, 5.7.1
    discovery. *See* Electronic discovery
    drafts of important documents, treatment of, 5.3.4
    duplicate records, treatment of, 5.3.4
    electronically stored information (ESI)
        discovery. *See* Electronic discovery
        European Commission standards, 5.3.2
        generally, 5.3
        metadata, 5.3.1, 5.5.2
        modernizing records management programs, 5.3.2
        National Archives and Records Administration (NARA) standards, 5.3.2

Index

    standards applicable to records management programs, 5.3.2
European Commission standards, 5.3.2
generally, 7.3
implementing program
    mistakes in, effect of, 5.6
    sanctions for noncompliance, 5.6.2
    training program, 5.6.1, 7.3
lifecycle of relevant records, 5.3.3, 5.3.4
litigation holds. *See* Litigation holds
litigation issues
    discovery. *See* Electronic discovery
    generally, 5.8.2
    preservation of relevant materials, 5.8.2
    spoliation of evidence, 5.8.3
metadata
    generally, 5.3.1
    retention of, 5.5.2
modernizing records management programs, 5.3.2
National Archives and Records Administration (NARA) standards, 5.3.2
records
    defined, 5.2
    information, distinguished, 5.2
    relevant records. *See* subhead: relevant records
records "destruction" or "retention" programs as, 5.1.2
records management policy
    creating policy, 5.4, 5.4.1
    generally, 5.1.1
    goals of, 5.4.1
relevant records
    identification of, 5.2.1
    lifecycle of, 5.3.3, 5.3.4
retention schedule
    applicable law, retention periods set by, 5.5
    destruction of records upon expiration of retention period, 5.5.4
    generally, 5.1.1, 5.5
    metadata, retention of, 5.5.2
    retention periods, determining, 5.5.1
    rule of reasonableness, 5.5.1
    sample retention schedule, 5.5
    statutes of limitation, role of, 5.5.3
rule of reasonableness, 5.5.1
sanctions for noncompliance, 5.6.2
senior management, role of, 5.1.4

Records management program (cont'd)
  spoliation of evidence, 5.8.3
  standards applicable to, 5.3.2
  statutes of limitation, role in setting retention periods of, 5.5.3
  training program, 5.6.1, 7.3
Reporting systems
  generally, 2.10
  government contractor compliance programs, 15.3.5
  hotlines. *See* Hotlines
  non-retaliation policy, 2.10.1
Resource Conservation and Recovery Act (RCRA)
  Corrective Action requirements for releases, 33.3.6
  generally, 33.3
  generators, management and disposal of waste by
    generally, 33.3.2
    reporting requirements, 33.3.3
    storage and accumulation of waste, requirements regarding, 33.3.4
  hazardous waste, defined, 33.3.1
  lead-based paint regulations, 33.3.8
  penalties for RCRA violations, 33.3.9
  releases or suspected releases, reporting of, 33.3.6
  underground storage tanks (USTs), regulation of, 33.3.5
  used oil, regulations applicable to, 33.3.7
RICO. *See* Racketeer Influenced and Corrupt Organizations Act (RICO)
Risk
  assessment of. *See* Risk assessment
  designing compliance program, identification of risk in
    common risk areas, examples of, 2.5.1
    generally, 2.5
    Health Insurance Portability and Accountability Act (HIPAA) compliance programs, 24.4.1
Risk assessment
  business risks, identifying, 4.2
  compliance matrix, 4.4.1
  compliance program, implementation/modification of, 4.4.4
  counsel, performance by, 4.1.3
  data gathering
    amount of data to gather, 4.3.2
    document reviews, 4.3.1
    methods of, 4.3
    processing data. *See* subhead: processing data
  goals of, 4.1
  identifying risks
    business risks, 4.2

Index

likelihood of conduct in each risk area, assessment of, 4.2.1
types of risk that should be assessed, 4.2
persons who should perform assessment, 4.1.3
prioritizing responses to risk areas, 4.4.3
processing data
   compliance matrix, 4.4.1
   compliance program, implementation/modification of, 4.4.4
   generally, 4.4, 4.4.2
   prioritizing responses to risk areas, 4.4.3
reasons for conducting, 4.1.1
senior management, role of, 4.1.2
types of risk that should be assessed, 4.2

S

Sanctions. *See* Penalties and sanctions
SARA Title III. *See* Emergency Planning and Community Right-to-Know Act (EPCRA)
Sarbanes-Oxley Act (SOX)
   accounting. *See* Accounting
   administration of compliance programs, 2.7, 2.7.2, 2.7.3
   almost-public companies, provisions applicable to, 28.50, 28.50.1
   attorneys. *See* Attorneys
   audit committee. *See* Audit committee
   board of directors
      generally, 28.5.1
      independent directors, regulations regarding, 28.5
   certification requirements. *See* Financial statements, certification requirements for
   code of ethical conduct. *See* Code of ethical conduct
   colleges, provisions applicable to, 28.55
      convergence of EU and SEC standards, 28.53.3
   directors. *See* Directors
   disclosure controls
      certification requirements related to, 28.44.1, 28.44.2
      components of, 28.44.7
      contents of disclosure, 28.44.5
      continuing compliance, 28.44.8
      disclosure committee, role of, 28.44.6
      generally, 28.44
      procedures for, 28.44.4
      purpose of, 28.44.3

Sarbanes-Oxley Act (SOX) *(cont'd)*
    executive compensation, provisions impacting. *See* Executive compensation
    financial statements, certification of. *See* Financial statements, certification requirements for
    generally, 28.3
    government contractors, requirements for. *See* Government contractors
    international companies
        Eighth Company Law Directive, EU, 28.53.1, 28.53.3
        EU negotiations for exemptions, 28.53.2
        EU response to SOX, 28.53.1
        generally, 28.53
        reporting standards, 28.53.3
        Statutory Audit Directive, 28.53.3
    issuers, applicability to
        generally, 28.1
        parties qualifying as issuers, 28.2
    non-profit governmental organizations, provisions applicable to, 28.54
    non-public banks, provisions applicable to, 28.51
    non-public insurance companies, provisions applicable to, 28.52
    officers. *See* Officers
    parties subject to
        almost-public companies, 28.50, 28.50.1
        colleges and universities, 28.55
        international companies. *See* subhead: international companies
        issuers, 28.1
        non-profit governmental organizations, 28.54
        non-public banks, 28.51
        non-public insurance companies, 28.52
        privately held companies. *See* subhead: privately held companies, provisions applicable to
    privately held companies, provisions applicable to
        ERISA violations, increase in penalties for, 28.49
        generally, 28.1, 28.47
        record retention requirements, 28.48
    private rights of action
        attorneys for issuers, actions against, 28.46.3
        generally, 28.46
        private 10b-5 litigation, effect of SOX on, 28.46.2
        statute of limitations applicable to securities litigation, enhancement of, 28.46.1
    SEC investigations. *See* SEC investigations

Index

Securities and Exchange Commission (SEC), powers and role of. *See* Securities and Exchange Commission (SEC)
universities, provisions applicable to, 28.55
whistleblower actions. *See* Whistleblower actions
SEC. *See* Securities and Exchange Commission (SEC) investigations
    cooperation, SEC guidance on
        benefits of cooperation, 30.4
        generally, 28.33, 30.3
        individuals, cooperation by. *See* subhead: individuals, cooperation by
        internal investigations, conduct of attorneys in handling, 28.33.1
        obstacles to cooperation, 28.33.2
        In re Lucent Technologies, Inc., 28.33.1
        role of cooperation, 30.3
        Seaboard Report, 30.3, 30.4
        SEC defense counsel, company's obligations to, 30.2
    counsel representing both company and employees
        advantages of, 30.20.1
        generally, 30.20
        limitations to, 30.20.2
    directors and officers (D&O) insurance. *See* Directors and officers (D&O) insurance
    disclosure of investigation in SEC filings, 30.1.5
    document requests and production
        generally, 30.8, 30.10
        negotiation with SEC as to scope, timing and sequence of, 30.11
        outside e-discovery vendor, use of, 30.12
        preservation of documents. *See* subhead: preservation of documents
        selective disclosure. *See* subhead: selective disclosure of privileged information
    Enforcement Division, role of, 30.1.2
    Enforcement Manual, 30.5, 30.8.1
    formal investigations, 30.1.4
    Formal Order of Investigation, 30.1.4
    generally, 30.1
    individuals, cooperation by
        Apple, Inc. case study, 30.5.5
        cooperation agreements, 30.5.2
        deferred prosecution agreements, 30.5.3
        Enforcement Manual, 30.5
        generally, 30.5
        Homestore, Inc. case study, 30.5.5

SEC. *See* Securities and Exchange Commission (SEC) investigations, individuals, cooperation by (*cont'd*)
    immunity requests, 30.5.5
    non-prosecution agreements, 30.5.4
    proffer agreements, 30.5.1
    Putnam Fiduciary Trust Co. case study, 30.5.5
    SEC policy statement on, 30.5
  informal advocacy during investigation, 30.22
  internal investigations, conduct of attorneys in handling, 28.33.1
  joint defense agreements, 30.21
  parallel civil and criminal investigations
    disclosure of, 30.6.2
    generally, 30.6.1
    latitude of government in conducting, 30.6.2
    simultaneous proceedings, 30.6.3
  persons subject to investigation, 30.1.1
  preliminary investigations, 30.1.4
  preservation of documents
    AIG case study, 30.9.4
    Banc of America Securities, LLC case study, 30.9.4
    electronic documents, preservation of, 30.9.1
    generally, 30.9, 30.9.3
    Lucent Technologies, Inc. case study, 30.9.4
    penalties for inadequate document preservations, 30.9.2
    scope of document preservation, 30.9.4
  procedures
    document requests. *See* subhead: document requests and production
    settlement negotiations, 30.8, 30.28
    Wells Process. *See* Wells Process
    witness testimony. *See* subhead: witness testimony
  related investigations
    civil authorities, coordination with, 30.6
    coordination with other law enforcement agencies, 30.6
    parallel investigations. *See* subhead: parallel civil and criminal investigations
  remedies SEC may seek. *See* Wells Process
  same counsel for company and employees, use of. *See* subhead: counsel representing both company and employees
  selective disclosure of privileged information
    confidentiality agreements, effect of, 30.14
    courts rejecting, 30.14
    determining whether to disclose privileged information, 30.14.2
    generally, 30.13, 30.14

Index

outlook for, 30.14.1
United States v. Reyes, 30.14
settlement negotiations. *See* Settlements
triggers for, 30.1.3
types of violations investigated by SEC, 30.1
Wells Process. *See* Wells Process
witness testimony
    conduct of examination by SEC enforcement staff, 30.17
    counsel for witness, permissible activities during examination by, 30.18.3
    Fifth Amendment privilege against self-incrimination, invoking, 30.18.1
    generally, 30.8, 30.15
    informal advocacy during investigation, 30.22
    informal discussions with SEC enforcement staff, 30.15.1
    joint defense agreements, 30.21
    lay opinion, avoiding, 30.19
    parties from whom testimony may be requested, 30.15
    preparing witness for testimony, 30.16
    refusal of witness to testify, 30.18.1, 30.18.2
    rights of witnesses, 30.18–30.18.3
    same counsel for company and employees, use of. *See* subhead: counsel representing both company and employees
    speculation, avoiding, 30.19
Securities and Exchange Commission (SEC)
    enforcement, effect of increased SEC budget on, 28.45.2
    expansion of SEC into new areas, 28.45.3
    growth of SEC, 28.45.1
    investigations by. *See* SEC investigations
    powers granted SEC under Sarbanes-Oxley Act, 28.45
    Sarbanes-Oxley Act
        enforcement, effect of increased SEC budget on, 28.45.2
        expansion of SEC into new areas, 28.45.3
        growth of SEC under, 28.45.1
        powers granted SEC under, 28.45
Senate gift and travels rules. *See* Gift and travel rules of House and Senate
Senior management
    See also Board of directors
    administration of compliance program, role in. *See* Administration of compliance programs
    anti-money laundering compliance programs, role in, 26.19.14
    banking and financial institution compliance programs, role in, 25.3
    litigation holds, enforcement of, 7.5.4

Senior management (*cont'd*)
    records management program, role in, 5.1.4
    risk assessment, role in, 4.1.2
Separate segregated funds (SSFs)
    corporate support of SSFs, limits and restrictions on, 19.4.2
    generally, 19.4
    participation in SSFs, restrictions on, 19.4.1
    restricted class, 19.4.3, 19.4.4
    solicitation of contributions, restrictions on, 19.4.3
    voluntary, requirement contributions be, 19.4.3
Service Contract Act
    government contractors, compliance issues for, 15.13.2
Service level agreements (SLAs), 14.2.2, 14.7.1
Service level objectives (SLOs), 14.7.1
Service of process
    qui tam actions, in, 11.9
Settlements
    administrative compliance agreements
        contractor responsibility program (CRP), establishment of, 10.4.7
        duration of, 10.4.7
        elements of, 10.4.7
        generally, 10.4.6
        reporting requirements, 10.4.7
    administrative settlement agreements
        administrative compliance agreements. *See* subhead: administrative compliance agreements
        certificate of compliance agreements (CCAs), 10.4.5
        compliance-related provisions in, 10.4.1
        corporate integrity agreements (CIAs). *See* subhead: corporate integrity agreements (CIAs)
        generally, 10.4
        SEC settlements. *See* subhead: SEC settlements
        types of, 10.4.2
    certificate of compliance agreements (CCAs), 10.4.5
    civil settlement agreements
        administrative agencies as parties to, 10.6.1
        administrative agency declining to participate in, 10.6.2
        compliance-related provisions in, 10.6
        reporting requirements, 10.6
    compliance, role of
        administrative settlement agreements, compliance-related provisions in, 10.4.1
        civil settlement agreements, compliance-related provisions in, 10.6

corporate integrity agreements, compliance-related provisions in, 10.4.4
ongoing compliance monitoring, settlement agreements imposing. *See* subhead: ongoing compliance monitoring as condition of settlement
prior compliance efforts, role of, 10.1
corporate integrity agreements (CIAs)
compliance-related provisions in, 10.4.4
duration of, 10.4.3
generally, 8.7, 10.4.3
criminal plea agreements
deferred prosecution agreements. *See* subhead: deferred prosecution agreements
generally, 10.7
deferred prosecution agreements
advantages of, 10.7.2
disadvantages of, 10.7.3
generally, 10.7.1
global settlements, 10.3.1
healthcare organizations and providers, actions against. *See* Healthcare organizations and providers
ongoing compliance monitoring as condition of settlement
compensation of monitor, 10.2.2
generally, 10.2
independent compliance monitor or review organization, monitoring by, 10.2.1
selection of monitor, 10.2.2
parallel proceedings, effect of
generally, 10.3
global settlements, 10.3.1
qui tam actions, negotiating settlement in, 11.18
SEC settlements
generally, 10.5, 30.8
mechanisms for settling with SEC, 10.5.1, 30.28
penalties SEC may impose, 10.5.2
voluntary disclosures, resolution of, 8.7
SLAs. *See* Service level agreements (SLAs)
SLOs. *See* Service level objectives (SLOs)
Society of Corporate Compliance and Ethics
compliance program, defined, 1.1
Software resources, procuring. *See* Computing resources
SOX. *See* Sarbanes-Oxley Act (SOX)
Spoliation of evidence
defined, 7.6.1
preserve evidence, failure to. *See* Electronic discovery

Spoliation of evidence (*cont'd*)
    records management policy, destruction of records in accordance with, 5.8.3
SREA. *See* Superfund Recycling Equity Act (SREA)
SSFs. *See* Separate segregated funds (SSFs)
Stark law. *See* Physician Self-Referral Act
State law
    false-claims statutes, 11.25
    mandatory compliance procedures, 1.5.1
Statutes of limitation
    False Claims Act violations, for, 11.21
    records management program, role in setting retention periods in, 5.5.3
Subcontractors
    Federal Acquisition Regulation (FAR) compliance program provisions, applicability of, 15.4
Superfund. *See* Comprehensive Environmental Response, Compensation, and Liability Act (CERCLA)
Superfund Recycling Equity Act (SREA)
    purpose of, 33.5
    recyclable material, defined, 33.5.1
    recycling arrangements, criteria for qualifying as, 33.5.2
Systematically Significant Failing Institutions Program/AIG Investment Program, 27.2.3

T

TALF. *See* Term Asset-Backed Securities Loan Facility (TALF)
Targeted Investment Program, 27.2.4
TARP. *See* Troubled Asset Relief Program (TARP)
Term Asset-Backed Securities Loan Facility (TALF), 27.2.6
Terrorism
    OFAC list of suspected terrorists, 2.5.1
Thompson Memorandum
    privilege waivers, 6.17.2, 8.5.2
Toxic Substances Control Act (TSCA)
    asbestos, regulation of, 33.10
    chemicals regulated by, 33.9.1
    inventory of existing chemicals, 33.9.1, 33.9.2
    lead-based paint, regulation of, 33.11
    new chemicals, review of, 33.9.1
    penalty provisions, 33.13
    polychlorinated biphenyls (PCBs), regulation of
        disposal requirements, 33.12.2
        generally, 33.12

Index

  marking requirements for materials containing PCBs, 33.12.2
  permissible uses of PCBs, 33.12.1
  record-keeping requirements, 33.12.2
  storage requirements, 33.12.2
  waste manifests, 33.12.2
 pre-manufacture notice (PMN) requirements, 33.9.2
 purpose of, 33.9
 reporting requirements, 33.9.3
Trade Agreements Act
 government contractors, compliance issues for, 15.17.5
Trade secrets, protection of
 compliance program, as risk area to address in, 2.5.1
 conflicts of interest, establishing policies related to, 12.5
Training and education
 anti-money laundering compliance programs, 26.19.4
 attorney training related to SEC Rule 205 and Sarbanes-Oxley Act requirements, 28.29, 28.29.1
 employees requiring, 2.8.1, 2.8.2
 export compliance programs, 18.8.4
 generally, 2.8
 government contractor compliance programs
  generally, 15.3.3
  parties who should participate in training, 15.3.4
 managed care organizations (MCOs) compliance programs, 22.6.3
 Medicare Part D compliance programs, 21.16.3
 periodic training and communication, requirement for, 2.8.3
 records management program, 5.6.1, 7.3
Travel rules of House and Senate. *See* Gift and travel rules of House and Senate
Troubled Asset Relief Program (TARP)
 Asset Guarantee Program, 27.2.5
 Automotive Industry Financing Program (AIFP), 27.2.9
 Auto Supplier Support Program (ASSP), 27.2.10
 Auto Warranty Commitment Program (AWCP), 27.2.11
 Capital Assistance Program (CAP), 27.2.2
 Capital Purchase Program (CPP), 27.2.1
 Community Development Capital Initiative, 27.2.8
 compliance risks
  False Claims Act provisions, 27.4
  Fraud Enforcement and Recovery Act (FERA) provisions, 27.4
  generally, 27.4
  managing TARP risks, 27.5

Troubled Asset Relief Program (TARP) *(cont'd)*
    Congressional Oversight Panel (COP), oversight responsibilities of, 27.3.3
    Financial Stability and Oversight Board (FSOB), responsibilities of, 27.3.1
    generally, 27.1
    Government Accountability Office (GAO), oversight responsibilities of, 27.3.4
    Making Home Affordable Program (MHAP), 27.2.12
    Office of the Special Investigator General TARP (SIGTARP), role of, 27.3.2
    oversight and enforcement, 27.3–27.3.4
    programs constituting, 27.2–27.2.12
    Public-Private Investment Program (PPIP), 27.2.7
    Systematically Significant Failing Institutions Program/AIG Investment Program, 27.2.3
    Targeted Investment Program, 27.2.4
    Term Asset-Backed Securities Loan Facility (TALF), 27.2.6
Truth in Negotiations Act (TINA) provisions
    civil penalties, 15.7.15
    "cost or pricing data"
        generally, 15.7.12, 15.10.12
        submission of, 15.7.13
    defective pricing claims
        civil penalties, 15.7.15
        generally, 15.7.14
        price reduction, 15.9
    generally, 15.7.11
    price reduction for defective cost or pricing data, 15.9
TSCA. *See* Toxic Substances Control Act (TSCA)

U

Underwriters
    Sarbanes-Oxley Act requirements, impact of, 28.9.1
Unfair business practices. *See* Anticompetitive and unfair business practices
Uniformed Services Employment and Reemployment Rights Act (USERRA)
    benefits during leave, requirements regarding, 34.19.2
    generally, 34.19
    notice requirements, 34.19.1
    pay during leave, requirements regarding, 34.19.2
    reinstatement requirement, 34.19.3

Index

return from leave, obligations to employee upon, 34.19.3
Unionization activities. *See* National Labor Relations Act (NLRA)
Universities. *See* Institutions of higher education
Unlocking Credit for Small Business Program, 27.2.8
Upjohn warnings
    generally, 6.11.4, 9.4.1
    information that should be conveyed to witness, 6.11.6
    oral warnings, 6.11.5
    standard form for, 6.11.7
    written statement of warning, use of, 6.11.5
USA PATRIOT Act, 2.5.2
USERRA. *See* Uniformed Services Employment and Reemployment Rights Act (USERRA)

V

Vocational institutions. *See* Institutions of higher education
Voluntary disclosures
    attorney-client privilege, effect on. *See* Attorney-client privilege
    benefits of, 8.1.1
    contents of disclosure
        elements of, 8.2
        initial disclosure, information required in, 8.2.1
    cooperation following, 8.6
    criminal prosecution not precluded by, 8.1.2
    federal agency voluntary disclosure programs and policies, 1.8, 8.1.1
    generally, 8.1
    internal investigation subsequent to. *See* Internal investigations
    resolving investigation, 8.6
    settlements. *See* Settlements
    verification investigation by government, 8.3.5
    work-product privilege, effect on. *See* Work-product doctrine

W

Wage-and-hour regulations
    compensatory time in lieu of overtime payment, permissibility of, 34.14.6
    compliance policies
        generally, 34.14.8, 34.14.10
        notice requirements, 34.14.9
    computer-related professionals exemption, 34.14.5

Wage-and-hour regulations (cont'd)
    employees/employers subject to FLSA, 34.14.1
    exemptions
        computer-related professionals exemption, 34.14.5
        generally, 34.14.2
        white collar exemptions, rules applicable to. *See* subhead: white collar exemptions, rules applicable to
    Fair Labor Standards Act provisions, 34.14–34.14.10
    generally, 34.14
    government contractors, wage-and-hour statutes and regulations applicable to. *See* Government contractors
    hours of work, determining, 34.14.7
    minimum wage requirements, 34.14
    overtime pay requirements, 34.14
    white collar exemptions, rules applicable to
        duties of employee, requirements regarding, 34.14.3
        generally, 34.14.3
        "salary basis" requirement, 34.14.3, 34.14.4
Waiver
    attorney-client privilege, waiver of. *See* Attorney-client privilege
    work-product doctrine, waiver of. *See* Work-product doctrine
Walsh-Healey Public Contracts Act
    government contractors, compliance issues for, 15.13.3
Wells Process
    charges SEC may bring, 30.25
    companies, remedies SEC can obtain against
        administrative remedies, 30.26
        amount of penalties, 30.26.1
        civil penalties, 30.26, 30.26.1, 30.26.2
        factors considered in determining whether to assess penalties, 30.26.2
        generally, 30.26
        other remedies SEC may seek, 30.26.3
    directors and officers, remedies SEC can obtain against
        amount of penalties, 30.27.1
        generally, 30.27
        other remedies SEC may seek, 30.27.2
    generally, 30.8
    remedies SEC may seek
        companies, remedies SEC can obtain against. *See* subhead: companies, remedies SEC can obtain against
        directors and officers, remedies SEC can obtain against. *See* subhead: directors and officers, remedies SEC can obtain against
    Wells Notice, 30.8, 30.23

Index

Wells Submission
    discoverable in civil litigation, as, 30.24.1
    generally, 30.8, 30.24
    SEC's use of submissions in enforcement proceedings, 30.24.1
Whistleblower actions
    burden of proof, 28.10.1
    company actions
        internal policies and procedures, 28.10.2
        investigation of complaint, 28.10.3
    compliance program as protection against, 1.8
    False Claims Act, actions brought under. *See* Qui tam actions
    prevailing party, whistleblower as
        employee, damages recoverable by, 28.10.4
        penalty provisions, 28.10.5
    Sarbanes-Oxley Act protections
        burden of proof of whistleblower, 28.10.1
        generally, 28.10
        prevailing party, whistleblower as. *See* subhead: prevailing party, whistleblower as
    state law protections, 28.10.6
Witnesses
    internal investigations, witness interviews in. *See* Internal investigations, subhead: interviews
    international investigations, witness interviews in. *See* International investigations
    preparation of witness
        advance planning by corporation, 9.2
        control, right and responsibility of witness to take, 9.7.1
        cost of, 9.1.2
        ethical considerations, 9.1.1
        importance of, 9.1
        "leveling the playing field" as means of, 9.7.1
        rules for witnesses, 9.8
        steps in, 9.7
        telling the truth, emphasizing, 9.6
        witness coaching, distinguished, 9.6
    SEC investigations, witness interviews in. *See* SEC investigations
Worker Adjustment Retraining and Notification Act (WARN)
    events triggering WARN requirements, 34.21.1
    notice requirements
        generally, 34.21, 34.21.2
        timing of notice, 34.21.3
Workplace safety
    compliance program, as risk area to address in, 2.5.1

Work-product doctrine
    crime-fraud exception, 6.15.2
    federal prosecutorial guidelines on waiver
        current policy, 6.17.5, 8.5.5
        Filip Memorandum, 6.17.4, 8.5.4
        generally, 6.17, 8.5
        Holder Memorandum, 6.17.1, 8.5.1
        McNulty Memorandum, 6.17.3, 8.5.3
        Thompson Memorandum, 6.17.2, 8.5.2
    Filip Memorandum, waiver of privilege under, 6.17.4, 8.5.4
    forensic experts, applicability to work of, 6.8.4
    generally, 6.7.1, 6.13.1
    Holder Memorandum, waiver of privilege under, 6.17.1, 8.5.1
    interviews, applicability to
        generally, 6.11.10
        interviewee, applicability of privilege to, 6.11.11
        waiver of confidentiality for information disclosed during interview, 6.11.12
    McNulty Memorandum, waiver of privilege under, 6.17.3, 8.5.3
    professional investigators, applicability to work of, 6.8.2
    protected materials, 6.15
    scope of, 6.15.1
    substantial need, disclosures required pursuant to showing of, 6.15.2
    Thompson Memorandum, waiver of privilege under, 6.17.2, 8.5.2
    undue hardship, disclosures required pursuant to showing of, 6.15.2
    voluntary disclosures, effect of
        generally, 8.4
        reasons for voluntary disclosures, 6.16.1
        scope of voluntary disclosures, 6.16.2
        waiver of privilege, 6.16–6.16.3
    waiver
        federal prosecutorial guidelines on. *See* subhead: federal prosecutorial guidelines on waiver
        generally, 6.16
        inadvertent waiver, 6.16
        intentional waiver, 6.16
        limited waivers, 6.16.3
        scope of, 6.16.3
        voluntary disclosures, 6.16–6.16.3